D1565496

INFORMATION AND SECRECY

Vannevar Bush, Ultra, and the Other Memex

by
COLIN BURKE

with a foreword by
MICHAEL BUCKLAND

The Scarecrow Press, Inc.
Lanham, Md., & London

Frontispiece:
Vannevar Bush & Stanford C. Hooper with the Differential Analyser, the Comparator, the Bombes, and the Rapid Selector (U. S. Navy, MIT Museum, Hagley Museum, NSA)

British Library Cataloguing-in-Publication data available

Library of Congress Cataloging-in-Publication Data
Burke, Colin B., 1936
Information and secrecy : Vannevar Bush, Ultra, and the other Memex / Colin Burke ; with a foreword by Michael Buckland.
p. cm.
Includes bibliographical references and index.
ISBN 0-8108-2783-2 (alk. paper)
1. Cryptography equipment industry--History. 2. Electronic analog computers--History. 3. World War, 1939-1945--Cryptography.
4. Bush, Vannevar, 1890-1974. 5. Information scientists--United States--Biography. 6. Information science--History. I. Title.
HD9696.C772B87 1994
338.4'70058'0973--dc20 93-39656

Manufactured in the United States of America
Printed on acid-free paper

I wrote this a decade ago. I mean it more than ever:

To my wife Rose, who gave me my son, Andy, my very special gift in life.

Table of Contents

Illustrations

Vannevar Bush with the Product Integraph
(MIT Museum)

Preface and Acknowledgements

The research for this book began almost a decade ago when my interest in the history of computers led me to the archives at the Hagley Museum and Library. My attention turned to some rather mysterious activity at the Massachusetts Institute of Technology. The 1930s MIT work seemed to be connected to even more guarded navy activities in Washington, D.C., Dayton, Ohio and St. Paul, Minnesota during the 1940s. I began to think those veiled projects were "the" holes in the history of the development of the modern computer. It was difficult to see if my early hunch was correct because the projects were wrapped in "Most Secret" classifications such as Ultra. I soon realized that the American navy wanted to keep its role in automating cryptanalysis and reading Germany's most important messages away from public view.

Being stubborn, I decided I would find out how close the American navy's cryptanalytic machine group in Dayton (OP-20-G / NCML) came to matching the achievements of their British counterparts and to see if Vannevar Bush's 1930s work for the navy was truly a prelude to the modern electronic computer. Then, I discovered that Bush was also attempting to build revolutionary machines for the library at MIT. I wanted to know if that work led to his proposal for a now widely admired computer-like machine, the Memex. None of those questions turned out to be easy to answer.

Finding enough data was very difficult, even for the unclassified projects. Unlike the Hollerith tabulating machine, which was controlled under one of the most fundamental patents in American history, Bush's machines, the Selector for the library and the Comparator for codebreaking, were patent orphans and thus difficult to trace. The tabulating machine was the child of one company, IBM. In contrast, the

Selector was tossed from sponsor to sponsor and place to place with no one having responsibility for maintaining its historical records. Following the history of the Comparator was even more difficult.

The demands by the American and British governments that the Comparator and its children be kept well-guarded secrets made the task of uncovering the history of the first modern machines for secrecy very frustrating. But, slowly, I convinced the powers-that-be that I already knew enough so that their archives should be made to produce once top secret documents. As those papers began to be released, more was written about Ultra and Magic by other scholars. By the late 1980s, a great deal had been revealed and an American Ultra machine, the Bombe, was put on public display at the Smithsonian Institution. But all that did not make my job an easy one. Much about the other cryptanalytic machines remained classified and relevant public documents were scattered over many different collections and archives.

During my ongoing search for evidence about the machines for the codebreakers, I began to realize that it would be impossible to separate the histories of the new technologies for cryptanalysis from those for the library and information processing. The careers of Bush's two quite similar machines, the Rapid Selector and the Comparator, linked cryptanalysis and the emergence of the information industry together in the most immediate ways. Moreover, as the once secret documents began to satisfy my curiosity about the technical details of the navy's machines, I began to see that the important story was not one of technical computer history or even of institutions, it was one of policy. I saw that the careers of the machines for information and for secrecy had depended upon decisions about American science policy, military research and the role of American academics. Detailing the connections among people and institutions took more years of digging in archives and libraries. Tracing those who had been so important to the development of the technologies was also time-consuming.

The delicate nature of the subjects, the continued protection surrounding many of the navy's projects, and the potential to draw inaccurate conclusions from incomplete evidence called for caution and patience and led to much frustration. That was made tolerable because during the years of searching for facts and ideas I had many pleasant experiences. I met very gracious and devoted people, so many that I cannot name them all and certainly cannot repay the scholarly and personal debts I owe them.

County clerks in several small Midwestern and Southern towns deserve thanks for guiding me through court and civil records of long-dead participants in the race to create an American Ultra machine. Corporate archivists gave me very precious time and information and the groups at the military and legal branches of the National Archives proved that the many salutes to John Taylor and his professional colleagues are well deserved. Tours through the impressive stacks at the National Archives's Suitland facility always led to some unexpected documents. The staff at the Smithsonian Institution's archives and computer history offices frequently went beyond the call of duty as did the staff at the Naval Historical Center. The Library of Congress's manuscript room staff, though overburdened and strangled by security regulations, gave much more than prompt and courteous service over a number of years. The archivists at the University of Pennsylvania, the Rockefeller Center, the Massachusetts Institute of Technology and Dartmouth College not only helped me through seas of documents but sent me to the safe and pleasant hotels in their areas. Several times, the staff of the Charles Babbage Institute proved that photocopying does not have to take weeks and that electronic mail can find its way through a maze of university computers. Even the days at the Patent Office's frantic search rooms, with their screeching microfilm machines, proved rewarding.

Many figures in the history of computing, cryptology, and the library answered my letters and responded to my phone calls. The codebreakers always found ways to balance the need for secrecy with their desire to help me. Joe Eachus and Waldron MacDonald and his lovely wife did more than anyone should expect. Jeff Wenger gave me much time. Many very patient government attorneys at the Office of Naval Research, the Office of Naval Intelligence, the Justice Department, the Federal Bureau of Investigation, and the Naval Research Laboratory turned themselves into archivists to answer my persistent requests for information that "I knew" was there. Professionalism and a desire to serve are the words needed to describe the staff at my interlibrary loan division. For years, they have traced often times vague and difficult references without complaint. They also put up with many questions about the history of the library and librarianship.

There are three institutions and groups of people who deserve special thanks. The historians and archivists at the Naval Security Group Command, though very overworked, always responded as gentlemen and scholars. The historians and archivists at the National Security Agency, whose charge to protect secrets and at the same time inform the public makes their professional lives very frustrating, gave me unexpected and much appreciated help. My admiration for them and for the incredible generation of men and women who forged America's Ultra capability grew as my contacts increased. This nation has been very lucky to have an institution that is committed to secrecy filled with people devoted to democracy.

Over the years, one institution became a favorite. As I read through all the computer-related papers at Wilmington, Delaware's Hagley Museum and Library I became accustomed to the best of all possible academic worlds. A group of devoted professionals, who became valued friends, and a physical setting of beauty and peace frequently led me to find excuses to return for more data on the history of computers, information, and secrecy. The Hagley is what a librarian might have dreamt of creating as a final salute to the profession.

During my research I encountered some insurmountable roadblocks. Technical people are rarely historically minded, at least in their younger years. So, many projects remain undocumented. Worse, it seems that growing legal problems have led many corporations to either seal or eliminate their archives. America has lost a very valuable part of its history because of lawsuits or the threat of them. An institution critical to the history of the Selector, the Comparator, and postwar information technology decided to protect itself by destroying many of its archive holdings. A great deal could have been learned if more of the history of Eastman-Kodak had been preserved.

Colin Burke
Columbia, Md., 1993

Vannevar Bush and the Differential Analyser
(MIT Museum)

Foreword

This book tells the complex tale of a man, Vannevar Bush, and of some little-known but historically significant machines--the "Rapid Selectors" and the "Comparators." These were the first machines to use electronics to conquer new and important problems in libraries and in codebreaking, *before* digital computers. The careers of these machines were intertwined with the generation-long struggles to develop two new fields: Mathematical Cryptanalysis and Information Science. Further, the tale of their development illuminates a kaleidoscope of important developments affecting universities, industry, research and development, the military, and, especially, changes in the relationships between them.

Vannevar Bush made major contributions in engineering, in the use of science in the conduct of the Second World War, in proposing the National Science Foundation, and in re-shaping the institutions of research and development in America. Yet it is in Information Science that Bush has become a mythic hero. He has even been hailed as a "Father" of Information Science, the beginning of which is often (and misleadingly) taken to be 1945 when Bush's think-piece "As We May Think," with its fantasy of a desk-top personal information machine called the Memex, was published in the *Atlantic Monthly*.

There is no doubt that Bush's forceful paper, "As We May Think," has had a highly inspirational impact. It is common practice to use a reference to it as a point of departure in articles in Information Science. Linda C. Smith's analyses of references to this particular paper have documented the importance of Bush to thinking in Information Science.[1]

One can argue that Bush's writings reveal little real understanding of information retrieval and, it seems, little respect for those who were

[1] Linda Smith, "Memex as an Image of Potentiality Revisited," in James M. Nyce, and Paul Kahn (ed), *From Memex to Hypertext: Vannevar Bush and the Mind's Machine* (Boston: Academic Press, 1991).

expert. Burke shows that Bush caused large sums to be spent on the development of information retrieval machines that generally did not work. So Bush makes a curious folk hero for Information Science. G. P. Zachary has suggested that Bush is rightly famous, but perhaps for the wrong reasons.[2] The explanation, I think, is that Bush has been viewed uncritically, unhistorically, and primarily in terms of this one speculative paper. His ideas have indeed been inspiring, but they have rarely been subjected to critical scrutiny. His actual achievements in information retrieval are little known and scant attention has been paid to the context and antecedents of his work. The achievements of others, even of such important predecessors as Emanuel Goldberg in Germany, who had built earlier machines like Bush's, and Paul Otlet in Belgium, who had operated hypertext-like information services early in the century, have remained overlooked until recently. In fact, the features of the electronic library of the twenty-first century--compact storage, ease of reproduction, hypertext, the use of telecommunications and CRT screens for remote access to texts, and equipment capable of sophisticated searching in complex indexing systems--were being foreseen, at least in outline, by 1935 by pioneering bibliographers and librarians, such as Paul Otlet, Fritz Donker Duyvis, and Walter Schürmeyer in Europe and Watson Davis in the U.S.A. Burke provides a detailed and realistic reconstruction of Bush's work rather than a mythic or hagiographic view and the field is better for it.

In the early 1930s a brilliant new kind of machine emerged: A photoelectric cell with associated digital circuitry could be used to search long spools of microfilm for any specified pattern. Once found, the circuitry could instigate a copy of the desired record in library applications or count the frequency of occurrence of the code for cryptanalysts.

Microfilm had captured the imagination. It was a reproducible, transportable, and an immensely compact storage medium. During the 1920s and 1930s there were widespread attempts, in Europe and in America, to develop applications of microfilm technology. In 1925 Emanuel Goldberg had demonstrated resolution equivalent to having

---

[2] G. Pascal Zachary, "Vannevar Bush Backs the Bomb," *Bulletin of the Atomic Scientists* 48(1992): 24.

fifty times the entire text of the Bible on one square inch of film. But how was one to search among such microscopic records?

To use the speed of light itself to search a highly compact storage medium was a heady prospect in the days of punched cards, before digital electronic computers had been developed. And the same technology could also be used both for codebreaking and to construct mechanized, miniaturized libraries. Fortunes might be made mechanizing the records of businesses and government agencies! Vannevar Bush was far from being alone in trying to harness microfilm for information retrieval or for cryptanalysis, but his efforts were so intimately tied to major forces in America during World War II and the Cold War that his projects deserve special attention.

This book is, among several other things, the most detailed account of this early optical technology and of the obstacles Bush and others faced in trying to make it *the* technology to rescue the codebreakers from the threat of new machines such as the Enigma, scientists from librarians' inability to cope with the "explosion" of technical publications, and bureaucracies from their rising flood of paper records. Professor Burke, after years of painstaking research, has achieved a remarkable reconstruction of a little-known episode of great significance in the history of information technology.

Exciting though this technological tale is for connoisseurs of mid-twentieth-century inventing, the significance of Colin Burke's research is much broader because, as a serious historian, he has provided a slice of life which is revealing in several different ways, not least in adding to our understanding of the changed relationships between government, industry, universities, and the funding of research.

Burke's account of the struggles of American intelligence agencies to modernize and of Bush's role in the effort to develop suitable machines brings forward the close affinity of information retrieval with cryptanalysis in both task and history. The similarity has not been widely appreciated. Both fields have the same objective: Finding instances of some desired pattern of code. Searching is substantially the same task in both applications. The difference is in the prior stage, in the opposing objectives of indexing and of encryption: The former is intended to make subsequent searching as successful as possible; the latter designed to make it as difficult as possible. No wonder that similar searching machines could be used in the two fields and that the same individuals who were trying to build a library machine should also be designing machinery for the forerunners of the National Security Agency.

A difference between the two fields, however, was in their relationships to national priorities. During and after World War II, the cryptanalysts were given all they desired while information scientists continued their technological quests on budgets of the 1930s rather than those of the affluent 1950s. It was not until the American government recognized that the Cold War had made *both* information *and* secrecy vital to national defense that funding flowed generously for both.

Relating the biographies of Vannevar Bush's machines to broader trends in American life is also a sign of good historical work: A well-rounded account of anything will be relevant to many topics. It is good for us to have our interests presented in new and, especially, unexpected contexts. Readers will find much of interest in what follows: the strategies of corporations such as National Cash Register; the history of the Ultra secret; and the story of the policy battles behind the American effort to establish its own cryptanalytic capabilities to fight the Axis powers and, then, the Cold War. There is much, too, about the redefinition of the roles of universities and of science as the United States played its role as a world power. Underlying the story of the machines is one of differences of opinion concerning the relationships between government, universities, corporations, and the military and concerning the funding and administration of research and development. Burke shows how the reshaping of American science is vital to an understanding of the modern library, the information industry, and the secrecy establishment.

A well-connected history has another advantage: It may serve to alert us to possible mistakes in the future. As we enter the era of the "virtual" library and of electronic highways, the history of the early years of electronic information machinery should make us aware that, as one disappointed information science pioneer of the 1950s pointed out when the fabled Bush Rapid Selector proved unworkable, good theory, much more than hardware, is needed to make a system valuable.

Finally, it is very fitting that this valuable book is published by the Scarecrow Press, the press founded by Ralph Shaw, a man made internationally famous by his role in the story that follows.

Michael Buckland
School of Library &
Information Studies
University of California,
Berkeley

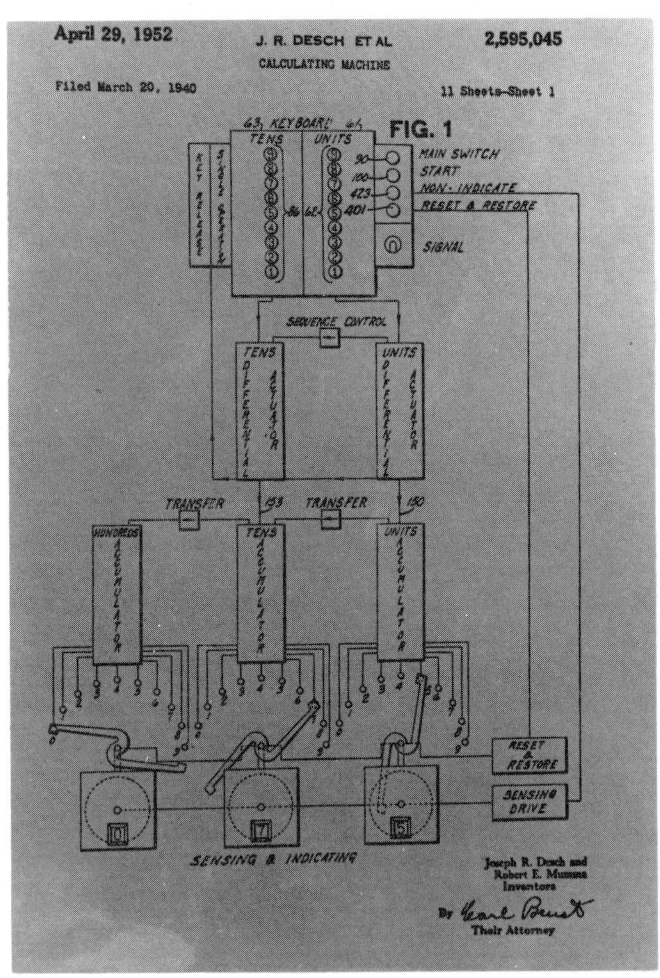

Desch / NCR Electronic Calculator Patent, 1940

Terms and Abbreviations

Abel	U. S. Navy production Bombe prototype
Abner	U. S. Army post WWII electronic computer
Adam	U. S. Navy Bombe prototype
Atlas	U. S. Navy post WWII electronic computer
Bomba	Poland's version of Bombe
Bombe	Electromechanical machines built by Britain and the U. S. to attack the Enigma
BuShips	U. S. Navy Bureau of Ships
Cain	U. S. Navy production Bombe prototype
Center of Analysis	Bush-MIT machine development and computation center
CIA	U. S. Central Intelligence Agency
Cinema Integraph	MIT film optical-electrical analog scientific measuring device, 1930s
CNO	U. S. Navy, Chief of Naval Operations
Colossus	Britain's special purpose electronic computer to attack German Fish system
Comparator	Bush's tape based-electronic cryptanalytic machines
Copperhead	OP-20-G WWII advanced versions of tape based electronic cryptanalytic machines
CSAW	U.S. Navy, Communications Supplementary Activity, Washington

Differential Analyser	Bush's electromechanical analog computer of the early 1930s
DNC	U. S. Navy, Director of Naval Communications
"E"	Enigma machine
ECM	U. S. Navy advanced encryption machine
Enigma	German encrypting device
ERA	Engineering Research Associates
Eve	U. S. Navy Bombe Prototype
"F"	Machine development branch in U. S. Army's SIS
Fish	German teletype-like automatic encryption system and devices
FOSDIC	Census Bureau microfilm processing system of the 1960s and 1970s
Freak	U. S. electromechanical cryptanalytic machine, WWII
Fruit	Special electrical-mechanical adding machine built for OP-20-G by NCR, WWII
"G"	OP-20-G
GC&CS	Britain's Government Code and Cypher School, Bletchley Park
Goldberg	OP-20-G postwar advanced version of Comparator
Hypo	Analog optical cryptanalytic machine built by Eastman-Kodak, WWII
IBM	International Business Machine Corporation
ICKY	OP-20-G special microfilm machine
IC Machine	Film plate machines MIT-Eastman made for OP-20-G, WWII

INTREX	1960s library and information science project at MIT
JN	Japanese naval codes
Letterwriter	Special data entry machines IBM built for OP-20-G, WWII
Locators	OP-20-G and SIS electronic cryptanalytic machines of WWII that only identified the location of a code item, they did not count or tally
"M"	Machine development division, OP-20-G
Madame X	SIS relay-based machine to attack German Enigma
Magic	Name for U. S. attack on Japanese code systems, 1930s
Mathew	OP-20-G electromechanical cryptanalytic machine, WWII
Memex	Bush's proposed information machine
M4	Four wheel version of Enigma used by Atlantic U-boats
Mike	U. S. electromechanical cryptanalytic machine, WWII
Minicard	Advanced microform retrieval machines built by Eastman-Kodak, post WWII
MIT	Massachusetts Institute of Technology
NARA	U. S. National Archives and Records Administration
NAS	National Academy of Sciences
NBS	National Bureau of Standards
NCML	Naval Computing Machine Laboratory
NCR	National Cash Register Company
NDRC	National Defense Research Committee

NRC	National Research Council
NRL	Naval Research Laboratory
NSA	National Security Agency
NSF	National Science Foundation
ONI	U. S. Navy, Office of Naval Intelligence
ONR	U. S. Navy, Office of Naval Research
OP-20-G	U. S. Navy, cryptanalytic branch
ORI	Office of Research and Inventions, precursor to ONR
OSRD	Successor to NDRC
OSS	Office of Strategic Services
OTS	Office of Technical Services, U. S. Dept. of Commerce
Purple	SIS OP-20-G analog machine built for the attack on the Japanese diplomatic ciphers
Python	OP-20-G electrical analog of Japanese enciphering machine, WWII
RAM	U. S. Navy Rapid Analytical Machine Program
Rapid Arithmetical Machine	Bush's planned electronic digital computer of the 1930s, it was never built
Rapid Selector	(Selector) Bush's and ERA's automatic microfilm and electronic bibliographic machine
Rattler	U. S. Navy electronic machine to attack Japanese automatic encryption systems
Reference Selector	Proposed name for Bush's Rapid Selector

Robinson	Britain's tape-based electronic machines, similar to the Comparator
Rockefeller Analyser	Bush-MIT updated version of Differential Analyser financed by Rockefeller Foundation, completed in the late 1930s
Rockefeller Computer Project	Postwar MIT project to build an electronic computer, project abandoned
Rossi Circuits	Electronic circuits for "and-or" condition testing
SAL	Scientific Aids to Learning Project
Shark	German U-boat special Enigma system
SIS	U. S. Army cryptanalytic agency
T/A	Traffic Analysis, a method using only call signs and transmission patterns of radio traffic to gain information on enemy strength and intentions
Tabulator	Electrical-mechanical card processing machines, built by the Remington-Rand and IBM corporations
Tessie	Optical cryptanalytic machine built by Eastman-Kodak in WWII, the tetragraph tester
Viper	OP-20-G electrical analog of Japanese enciphering machine, WWII
Walnut	Advanced microform retrieval

	machines built by IBM, post WWII
Wavelength Analyser	MIT optical-electric analog scientific measuring device, 1930s
Whirlwind	Postwar electronic digital computer built at MIT by group outside of Bush's circle
Yellow Problem	SIS's early name for Enigma work
003	Madame X

Chapter I
Introduction and Overview: The Age of Information and Secrecy

The Data Problem

Many of the predictions of the imminent arrival of the Age of Information were the fluff of 1960s and 1970s advertising campaigns. But some were based on serious study and a few came close to the historical mark. An information industry did appear as the electronics revolution of the era allowed a surge in the volume of data, if not knowledge. More importantly, by the 1970s the digital computer made the production and distribution of bytes an important part of the economies of the western world. The technological changes made it appear to some that a true knowledge revolution had suddenly occurred. But others thought that computerization had compounded the problem of an overwhelming flood of meaningless data. The information revolution and the data problem were highlighted in the popular press during the 1970s but perception of an information crisis and the search for methods to turn data into useful information began well before the electronic computer became a common feature of American life.[1]

The mechanical, chemical and transportation revolutions of the nineteenth century laid the foundation for a service and information economy because they made it less and less expensive to print, to calculate, and to communicate over long distances. However, the wave of improvements in communications and data technology created what many perceived as an unwieldy deluge of books, scientific papers, business records and memoranda. A few thought the first information revolution had turned on itself: There was so much data that no one had the time or power to change it into useful knowledge. The problem of managing the mountains of paper began to be addressed in the mid-nineteenth century when business record-management firms arose and when the library began to be rationalized by men such as Poole, Dewey and Cutter. But until the era of World War I, the emphasis remained on the production of data rather than its management.[2]

In the mid-1920s attention began to shift as increasing numbers of observers in America and Europe agreed that serious problems were developing. The problems, they said, were too many books and articles and too great an economic burden to preserve a degree of democratic access to it all. Even scientists and engineers, who were so proud of the knowledge revolution they were creating, began to complain. They demanded new ways of organizing and accessing library materials. They wished to avoid replicating previous work and wanted to be able to identify important links among discoveries in their constantly changing fields.

Some did more than complain. One result was the transformation of the methods and institutions of data management. Businessmen and scientists began to create their special versions of the library and library science. On their own, they began to address the problem of too much data and to form organizations. Knowing they were unlikely to stem the flood of paper, they focused on systematizing it. Business machine companies and government bureaucracies concentrated on the office.[3] Others began more challenging quests.

Science and the Information Problem

While established companies such as IBM, Eastman-Kodak and Remington-Rand provided solutions for the information problems of business, a rather unique cluster of people advocated new approaches to the organization and distribution of scientific and academic materials. Their efforts and their associations defined the information problem from the early 1930s through World War II. For them, the problem was the management and distribution of the most advanced scientific papers and reports. Their goal was to create systems tailored to the special needs of the elite scientists and engineers in the universities, corporate laboratories and the emerging government applied science agencies. They explored new methods and technologies, ones that were radically different from library catalogs, the inherited indexes to technical literature and even the book. Some of the reformers had greater ambitions and argued for a radical transformation of the traditional library. Assuming their special needs were the same as those of the general public, they criticized the likes of Dewey and Cutter and sought ways to turn the library into an efficient tool of science.

The crusade was not confined to the United States. By the mid-1930s, European and American reformers had complaints, ideas and technical visions that were quite similar. They met together at international congresses to discuss the goals and methods for the library of the future. The Europeans had much to say and in many ways were far ahead of the American reformers. Although the United States was famous for its creation of the efficient office through the application of technology, the Europeans had more experience with the logic of organizing research materials.[4] The Americans had not begun to build research and scientific libraries until the late nineteenth century and they continued to look to Europe for advances in formal science. But the onset of the conflicts that led to World War II meant that it was the United States that had the time and resources to attempt to change ideas into systems. In the 1930s, the brash and energetic Americans took the initiative and began a search for the technology needed to solve what they tagged as the information problem.[5]

Typically, the Americans were not of one voice or centrally organized. During the 1930s, several individuals and groups with incompatible definitions of the information problem became active in the United States. In some ways, they are best described by what they were not. Significantly, public librarians and the men who were building machines for the office were not central to the new movement. Public librarians had other priorities, and, while the business machine and supply companies may have been aware of the bibliographic difficulties, they had to attend to the needs of those who could afford their products. Also, those who made their living organizing historical archives were not prominent founders of American Documentalism or the later Information Science. Surprisingly, among the missing were most university librarians. They had neither the pressing need nor the resources to provide expensive services to what they felt was a small minority of their patrons. The science information problem was, by default, left to others.

During the 1930s those others were a varied lot who shared a common interest in the future of American science and a near religious faith in technology, especially microfilm. They all had radical ideas and they all decided it was necessary to work outside of existing organizations such as the American Library Association. A significant number of the reformers were connected to established libraries, but unusual ones. They were from the largest government science libraries, institutions that had special mandates. The government librarians had ties to another group of reformers, a small cluster of men who came from the top of the fledgling bureaucracy of American science. Their interest in the information problem was part of their drive to enhance the status of science in America. In addition, in the 1930s, at least one very important player came from the world of academic engineering. But that man, Vannevar Bush, stayed at arms length from the others and he continued to define himself as an electrical engineer rather than as a Documentalist.

Like him, the other reformers did not begin their crusade because of a desire for riches or even to earn a livelihood. None foresaw the dramatic changes that would be brought about by the explosive appearance of military related science. No one thought that information management would become a profession and the basis for an industry. What emerged as a big business and a new professional field a generation later remained amorphous and disorganized throughout the 1930s and 1940s.

Although the majority of reformers viewed microfilm as a near magic solution to the problem of the distribution of information and although all looked to automation to solve the retrieval problem, there was not a full consensus concerning ends or means. There was not even agreement on what the information problem was. Yet, there was a center to the 1930's reform movement. Those who called themselves the American Documentalists were the ones who began to set boundaries. A combination of professional science advocates and government librarians, they founded the American Documentation Institute in early 1937 after several years of informal cooperation. That organization did not hold the allegiance of all who were interested in reform, however. Many of the scientists and engineers who became important to the evolution of information management technology stood outside of the ADI, and, quite frequently, viewed its members as competitors for scarce resources. The disagreements and the organizational separation among the groups continued during the 1940s and the 1950s. As important, the movement remained small and weak until the computer era.[6]

Science and Information Become National Priorities

As late as the 1950s, the older reformers behaved more like academic mendicants than members of a powerful professional group. There was good reason for that because there was little basis for a profession. During the first decades of their crusade there were no generous sponsors, there was almost no market for Documentalists and there were no special information machines that could serve as the foundation for an industry. But the emergence of big government science during World War II created an urgent need for a solution to the information problem. America's new role in the world order had a profound impact on the nature of the library reform movement.

The national priorities during World War II and the Cold War, combined with the incredible wealth of the United States, led to the emergence of what many of the 1930s reformers had desired so intensely: Big Science.[7] Scientific and engineering projects of undreamed of magnitude became common, universities and academics became research entrepreneurs and the military services developed bureaucracies that demanded instant retrieval of information from seas of data. As a consequence, the information problem finally became a government priority, and, an opportunity. Documentalism was no longer a crusade to improve the life of isolated scientific researchers or to reform the library. It was turned into a business charged with solving immediate and critical military problems. As a result, as they were being made full members of the grantsmanship club, a new generation of Documentalists redefined the mission of their organization. With the explosion of demand in the 1950s, a glimmer of professional definition emerged. The Cold War changed what had begun as a search by a few frustrated academics for subsidies for a hard-pressed civilian science into an occupation. By the mid-1950s, Documentalists were turning into Information Scientists.[8]

Before the Technology Was Ready

As the Cold War became institutionalized, the new generation began to offer a wide range of information management solutions and to change what had begun as almost a moral crusade into a search for technological redemption. In doing so they altered the tone if not direction of the earlier cause. The vocabulary of those who were creating the 1950s special library, report distribution systems and the first blushes of information science seems very odd today--much more foreign than the language of the founders of the 1930s. It is difficult to understand why they talked in bewildering private languages and why they paid so much attention to what now seem arcane and insignificant technical points. And, one wonders why so much energy was spent on arguments about very minor aspects of indexing, coding and sorting. The historical imagination is also challenged trying to understand why so many intelligent people continued to pursue what now seem to be dead-end ideas and technologies. But, there was reason behind the semantic madness, the methodological nitpicking and the odd techniques and machines of the 1940s and 1950s. There were also reasons why the new information specialists remained distant from the mainstream librarians.

The emerging information specialists of the 1940s and 1950s attempted to create a new library and new automated information retrieval and distribution systems before the underlying technology was ready. Until the appearance of the powerful electronic computer, one armed with vast and inexpensive memory, every attempt to solve the information problem had to be limited, arbitrary, and overlaid with bewildering concepts that puzzled traditional librarians and even the clients of the information managers. Creaky technology also meant partial solutions and the need to rely upon intellectual cleverness to make the retrieval systems seem worthy.

The Documentalists of the 1930s realized the limits imposed by the absence of a viable technology and they desperately tried to overcome them. While they were relentlessly seeking replacements for the hated categories inherited from traditional librarians and indexers, they searched for new machines to allow the automation of the information retrieval and distribution. They were not very successful in the 1930s and 1940s but they kept trying. During the first decade of the Cold War, that search became much more intense and millions of dollars were spent trying to devise a unique technology for the special new library for Big Science.

Technology Saves the Dream

In the 1990s, the goals of the early Documentalists seem to have been attained and they appear to have built their perfect machine. In America, institutions such as the National Technical Information Service provide academic and industrial researchers with instant bibliographies of specialized reports. Everyone, not just scientists, receives some degree of satisfaction from the new computerized information systems. A professional can sit at an inexpensive personal computer, dial into large libraries and commercial data bases and then ask questions in specialized terms to create up-to-date bibliographies of books, articles and reports. Copies of the desired documents may be sent over the same communications lines that serve the Internet. A non-professional can go to a library and use its computers to instantly search its holdings by general subjects. A librarian can use the same computer systems to manage a library or archive and to order a book from a repository a continent away.

However, the 1990's solution to the information problem is not the result of some great breakthrough in the organization of human knowledge by the Documentalists and their offspring, the information scientists. They were unable to develop a grand scheme for the organization of knowledge. There was no great intellectual revolution, no astounding theoretical discovery in information and library science. And, the Documentalists and their allies were not successful in their search for a special technology. The 1990's solution was not a result of the quest for an information engine between 1930 and 1960.

The solution was the result of improved technology, but that technology was not a direct descendant of the amazing efforts during the 1930s, 1940s and 1950s to create specialized information machines, ones usually based upon microfilm. There are ties to the past, but there is also a great discontinuity in the history of the emergence of information science and information technology. The Cold War and the rise of the electronic computer created a new environment that made many of the goals and techniques of the information crusaders of the pre and postwar eras quite outdated. The unprecedented expenditures on science, technology and intelligence gathering during the 1950s and 1960s brought the modern universal electronic computer to the point where it could be an information machine as well as a calculator. By the 1960s, the computer was becoming the platform for information systems for scientists and engineers. But, it took another generation to lower costs enough to make the computer a commonplace in the library and to transfer the systems built for the bureaucracies of science to the university and the school. The computer was what allowed a new information age. By the 1980s it even helped to begin reuniting librarians and information scientists.

Despite the revolutionary impact of the powerful computers of the 1970s and 1980s, there are some historical continuities that link the information crusades of the prewar years to the modern era. The information managers of today stand on the shoulders of the Documentalists and engineers of the 1930s and 1940s. They also stand on the shoulders of another prewar group, the American codebreakers.

Information and Secrecy

The relationships between the birth of information science and the development of the technology and institutions of secrecy in America were not apparent. Librarians and information specialists did not realize that the technological revolution that was causing the information problem was also creating the age of secrecy. Few understood that because the logic of secrecy was the mirror-image of the logic of information many methods in one realm were transferable to the other. Only a very select few knew that much of information technology of the Cold War years was sponsored and developed by the cryptologic and intelligence agencies.

The birth of information science was tied to the emergence of the American security state in many ways. The same technologies that created the overflow of information allowed the widespread use of codes and ciphers. That built a demand for another type of information science--mathematical cryptanalysis. By the 1920s, the new automatic encryption machines, such as Germany's Enigma, led to a search for revolutionary cryptanalytic tools and methods. At the same time that the Documentalists were forging their ideas and organizations, a group of reformers in the American military was attempting to create a new technology for cryptanalysis. That search created a very direct, though secret, connection to the crusade for the modern library, a relationship that continued through World War II and into the postwar era.

Vannevar Bush

In the 1930s, the American army's and navy's codebreakers were not aware of the rise of Documentalism, but they became entangled with a man whose work was central to the history of information technology for more then two decades. Through the urging of one of the navy's most progressive officers, Stanford Caldwell Hooper, the navy's cryptanalysts tied their long-term program to Vannevar Bush's proposed information machine, the Rapid Selector. It is the career of that grand machine and its cryptologic cousin, the Comparator, as well as the lives of Hooper and Bush, that provide the direct historical link between the birth of the information age and the age of secrecy in the United States.

Although Bush worked independently of the Documentalists in the 1930s, his dreams arose in response to the same trends that led to American Documentalism. And, his machines became central to the efforts to develop a new information technology in the immediate postwar years. His projects became interlaced with those of the library crusaders through their contacts with the major institutions of American science. Bush was also important to the following generations of Documentalists, especially those who entered the field as the modern computer was emerging. His Memex idea is now held as the inspiration for the latest cutting edge information systems. As important, his achievements in structuring postwar American research set the stage for much of modern information science.[9]

The Other Memex

Vannevar Bush of the Massachusetts Institute of Technology was one of the outstanding academic engineers of his time. He was also one of the greatest scientist-politicians in American history and a mover and shaker in the rise of Big Science during and after World War II. His decades long attempt to build an information machine, the Rapid Selector, was linked to his crusade for American science. Because of Bush's ties to science policy, the Rapid Selector touched the lives of all those who were laying the foundations of information science and mathematical cryptanalysis. Bush's attempts to combine new technologies to create a machine for the library, and one for the codebreakers, were also related to his idea for a machine to go far beyond contemporary information science. He called his greatest dream, the Memex.

Bush's Memex idea was stirring in the early 1930s and by the end of World War II he published an influential article about a desk size bibliographic machine for personalized indexing and retrieval. Memex was to allow the use of the revolutionary logic of association and was to free a researcher from the physical and logical walls of the library. The Memex would, Bush claimed, liberate the scholar from the artificial categories of traditional librarians and indexers and would make every desk a library in itself. Memex later became an influential ideal and by the 1980s it was hailed as the inspiration for hypertext and other new ways to organize and retrieve information. But, a Memex was never built. Bush never even tried to build one! The long history of his other Memex, the Rapid Selector, shows why Memex remained as only a fantasy until the recent revolution in micro-electronics.

Science and the Navy

The career of Bush's other Selector, his cryptanalytic machine, the Comparator, was also marked by the frustrations caused by the inability to achieve expected technological goals. Admiral Stanford Caldwell Hooper suffered professionally and personally because of those failures. His dream, as tended by his protege, Joseph Wenger, was only partially realized. Hooper wanted to bring the most advanced science and technology to the navy, especially its communications division. He fought for the creation of a link between the navy and university scientists and he struggled for a program to institutionalize innovation in cryptanalysis. He almost lost both battles.

The navy cryptanalysts eventually received a Comparator to attack cipher systems; they did construct a series of fantastic machines to penetrate the most advanced encryption devices of the Germans and Japanese in World War II (including the Bombe for the Ultra secret); they went on to become one of the most important sponsors of postwar information machines; and, the navy did create a research bureau. But Hooper and Wenger had to wage a constant battle, from the early 1930s through the 1950s, to gain the support they needed to bring innovation to naval communications. They had to rescue the Comparator from neglect; they struggled to save their World War II machine project from imminent defeat; and, they had to put their professional reputations on the line to preserve what they had built during World War II. The battles took their toll, especially on Hooper. Near the end of his life he received not a thank-you, but a depressing slap on the wrist from the navy.

Vannevar Bush ended his career a happier man but his drive for the automated library was not a success. His bibliographic robot, the Rapid Selector, which was based on microfilm and digital electronics, had a not quite respectable history. Hundreds of thousands of dollars were spent developing it over more than twenty years but it went through round after round of grand expectations, then failure. Sadly, just as a working Selector was finally brought to life, the modern computer began to turn it into a technological dinosaur.

Technology and Policy

The histories of Bush's and Hooper's dreams for the Rapid Selector and the Comparator are more than just sad but fascinating stories of struggles to turn ideas into hardware. They are stories of the transfer of technology to and from the private and military sectors and they are windows into the American struggle to establish and control applied science. The lives of the two machines were tied to all the major institutions of the nation. To describe and explain their travails means calling in the history of American science, national educational policies, the contracting system of the military and the relationship of research to the success of the American corporation.

Understanding Bush's and Hooper's contributions and the relationships between information and secrecy also calls for a broad view of the history of technology. Fundamental is the realization that technology is a social creature. It depends upon people and institutions and, in turn, it shapes them. Bush's and Hooper's projects were not exceptions. Their machines and their successes and failures were the result of much more than the limited technological options of Bush's generation. In immediate and practical terms, this means we will bounce back and forth between many topics, including thirty years of the history of philanthropic foundations, universities, the military and business machine companies.

Circling Through American Institutions

The next three chapters focus on the history of the institutions needed to put Hooper, Bush, and the Documentalists in context. The initial chapter is a biography of Bush and his home-base, the Massachusetts Institute of Technology. It provides key pieces to the puzzle of the emergence of Bush's information and secrecy machines. It also helps to understand the where and why of his concept of an ideal intellectual engine, the Memex. In the following chapter, the career and goals of one of the most underrated men in American history, Stanford Caldwell Hooper are explored. Admiral Hooper's life as a leader in naval communications, as a crusader for bringing science to the military and as an advocate of professional control of the navy are essential to an understanding of the cryptanalytic problem and to the fate of Bush's information machines. The next chapter does not focus on a single individual but follows the development of several of America's high-tech corporations in the 1930s and their involvement in preparing America for World War II. Those companies and their connections with the military were significant to the postwar technology of the library as well as to Bush's dreams for American science.

Tracing the career of Bush's machines, and thus much of the history of both American Documentalism and America's cryptanalytic capability, is a more complex task. The histories span more than three decades and weave in and out of institutions and projects. Although chapter five deals with the rise of discontent with the traditional library and its methods, chapters four through fourteen are essentially organized around machines rather than people or institutions. Of necessity, there is an almost bewildering trail from the first Selector to America's version of the anti-Enigma machine, the Bombe, and, finally, to the birth pangs of a useful general purpose electronic computer in the 1960s.

The story is not always a happy one. Repeatedly, Bush asked too much of technology and people. In fact, the history of the centerpiece machine, the Bush Rapid Selector, is one of failure. Worse, its potential as a useful solution to the information problem was misconceived if not misstated. The first Selector project, begun in 1938, fell victim to a blind faith in raw computing power, the subtle influence of commercial enticements and the failure to explore the logic of information retrieval.

The history of the other projects, whether the ones run by the military to break the Axis (and, later, Russian) codes and ciphers, or IBM's electromechanical contributions to postwar information retrieval, are somewhat less depressing. At first, the Bush Comparator of the 1930s proved an embarrassment to Admiral Hooper and led to friction between the branches of the navy. The Comparator almost killed the far seeing project to make the American navy the most technically advanced communications intelligence agency in the world. However, after a disastrous beginning the crash programs of World War II led to the creation of some of the era's most complex electronic information processing machines.

Unfortunately, the progress during the war was not great enough to provide ready-made technological solutions to the information problem. The wartime work honed some of the technology Bush counted on for machines for the library and for scientific creativity (microfilm and electronics) but neither he nor the Documentalists were able to organize and finance a successful postwar project. Despite the clamor of the Documentalists, few were willing to pay for the creation of a machine for the new library during the immediate postwar years. Existing institutions, such as the National Bureau of Standards, though willing to participate in the information and computer revolutions, were not allowed the necessary funds or power.

For example, the second Rapid Selector project, which began in 1947, was burdened with a clutter of contractual mishaps and financial desperation. The pressures led to another failure to examine the logic of information retrieval. As bad, that project almost ended the hopes of Hooper and his protege, Joseph Wenger, to maintain the navy's technical prowess through the creation of a new private company. The Selector became mired in the difficulties faced by Engineering Research Associates as it tried to be a secret firm competing in the commercial market. Its men, though Bush's ex-students, found it impossible to continue to build the new machines for secrecy and at the same time to devote the energies needed to make Bush's information dreams a reality. To the disappointment of the intelligence and Documentalist communities, several other attempts to rescue what was left of the Selector were unsuccessful during the 1950s.

The drive to automate the library might have ended with little more than frustration if it had not been for the Cold War. Its related science and intelligence projects finally led rich and willing sponsors to subsidize attempts to create information machines in the 1950s and early 1960s. But the appearance of new types of sponsors meant a change in the nature of information technology. With near unlimited research and development funds available, the locus of innovation shifted away from academics to the major corporations. At the same time, the user changed from the librarian and scientist to data managers in engineering, military and intelligence information centers. As IBM and Eastman-Kodak and spinoff companies turned to the task of building information machines, Documentalism itself underwent a subtle but important change. It was no longer for scientific creativity in the library but for military-scientific bureaucracies. As an indication of the change, there is no record of Bush's or any other of the special microfilm and electronic information machines of the era being used in a traditional library.[10]

Historical Consistencies

The trip through the biographies of the machines, the projects and institutions is complex, but keeping track of it all is made easier by some important historical constants. Several themes run throughout the three decades of the history of the Selector, the Comparator, and their relatives.

Underlying all of the early information projects was the technological bet. At the beginning of every innovative project a commitment to a technology's future has to be made. Risks have to be taken if there is to be progress, but costly failures can result from an initial commitment to a fundamental technology that is not ready. Faith has to be placed in what has yet to be and engineers have to believe that core problems are just about to be overcome; but too much optimism can turn projects into costly dead-ends.

Bush, Hooper and the early Documentalists were technological optimists and they began their crusades with visions of finding next day solutions rather than becoming involved in a generation long battle. Their particular bets were on microfilm and digital electronics. Neither were finished and sure technologies in the 1930s. Bush's energy and salesmanship to the contrary, no one was or could be certain they could be nudged into usefulness. Digital electronics eventually proved to be the most trustworthy despite its poor reputation in the prewar era. From the 1930s through to at least the early 1950s, microfilm appeared to be a very reasonable choice for high-speed and large-scale memory. To everyone's surprise, it always remained just on the verge of technological maturity.

The history of the information and secrecy machines was also shaped by the state of American science and the struggle to determine the nature of the institutions of what became known as Big Science. From at least the mid-1920s, Bush, Hooper and their followers were almost consumed by the drive to turn science policy to their needs. Bush sought to have the control over the new sciences in the hands of a civilian scientific elite, even during times of national crisis. At first, he fought to have the private foundations of the 1930s make ever increasing grants for research on the basis of scientist defined priorities. Then, his wartime National Defense Research Committee was premised upon civilian control of military research. Such civilian control meant power and funds to the best scientists at the largest institutions. Bush's postwar plans for the National Science Foundation followed the same principles, although his worry in the late 1940s was not the military bureaucracy; rather, it was Congress.

Those policies were entwined with his visions for the American university. Bush and his allies had always wanted to make American higher education the equal of Europe's. To accomplish that meant vastly increasing the income of universities and shifting their priorities from teaching to research. That was one reason for his drive for national funding of elite science and one of the major reasons for his attention to the modernization of the library. Unfortunately, the search for funds and the drive to create the research oriented university led to some unexpected and undesirable complications. Linking the welfare of the university to defense contracts brought problems as well as needed dollars. Bush was one of the first to encounter such disappointments. The Cold War universities only appeared to have achieved what Bush and his like had fought so hard for since the 1920s, financial independence. Their financial sparkle was the result of a new dependency. The Cold War system gave the illusion of self-determination; in truth, university men did not have the important final say in the determination of projects.

One of the other constants that runs through the history of the Selector and the Comparator is the difficulty of transferring technology to and from the military. From the first ideas for the Comparator in the mid-1930s, Bush was frustrated by incompatibilities between university research goals and military procedures and needs. In fact, at one point his grand design for the National Defense Research Committee was endangered by the inability of his MIT group to complete a promised machine for the navy's codebreakers. The careers of others were shaped by the similar difficulties.

Admiral Hooper's great plans for the navy centered about joining the military to the university and his drive to establish professional control of the navy was an attempt to overcome the technological conservatism of the naval establishment. He almost lost the battle in the late 1930s, but the American military did create a permanent link with academic science after World War II. Because of that, it began to influence the Documentalist movement. By the late 1940s, the influence was very direct although the relationship was not always smooth. The military became the Documentalists' best customer and the only one willing to subsidize major research and development projects. The reason for the military's influence is simple, it had the money. America's new universities and private foundations could not finance development on their own. A few independent scientific institutions, such as the American Chemical Society, made contributions and the National Science Foundation supported some work, but it was the military and its contractors that financed the major information technology projects. Unfortunately, Hooper's particular vision of the proper relationship between science and the military was never realized and he died a very disappointed man.

Another thread runs through the thirty-year history of information and secrecy. Traditional librarians and their organizations, such as the American Library Association, had almost no contact with the many early information machines and their sponsors. The financial status of libraries and library associations improved after the war, but even so, they had little chance to be innovative. The reasons for the separation from the Documentalists run deeper than money. In part, the split is explained by what the Documentalists emphasized over and over again: The problems they were addressing were new and the solutions had to be found and controlled by them. The librarians, trained to serve a general user, were not consulted because the methods and problems of the general library seemed irrelevant. The Documentalists' emphasis upon information systems for scientists does not explain everything, however. All the reasons for the separation and the consequences of the division between librarians and information scientists remain to be identified.

Another influence that runs silently through the thirty-year history of the Selector and its mates is the absence of a major information project. Although the military's technical groups were well financed throughout World War II and the Cold War, the United States never had an information initiative to compare with the development and utilization of atomic energy or the greatest Big Science breakthrough, the space program.[11] Even the postwar information machine projects were relatively short term and had to answer to several masters. More fundamental, none of the projects was intended to create the information machine. Each was targeted towards a particular application. Successful innovation and implementation were difficult if not impossible under such conditions.

There is one more constant: simultaneous invention. As in other technical realms, it is almost impossible to determine who first thought of a method or who was the first to construct a particular type of machine. The idea of using microfilm for document storage; the concept of associations so tied to Memex and today's hypertext; and, the use of subject codes to automatically retrieve information, came from many sources in Europe and America at almost the same time.

Although the judgments of patent examiners may determine who controls a technology and who makes a fortune, this book pays little attention to the task of identifying the inventor of any of the information technologies. One reason is that the history of the patenting of information and secrecy technologies is so cluttered with mistakes and oversights that the role of patents in determining the history of information retrieval was very limited. In fact, patents played a somewhat negative role. Because of the difficulty of establishing patent protection in the field, few commercial companies wished to invest major resources in developing a special technology of information management. Even the patent-wise Vannevar Bush could not turn his Selector and Comparator into a source of income for MIT or his corporate sponsors.

Painless Technical History

This is a story about scientific and technological policy but it is also a technical history. I have tried to make it as nontechnical and painless as possible, however. I address the wonderful but mythical average reader and I mention technical details only when they are critical. Then, I describe them, as far as possible, in everyday language. There are only a few technical terms that need prior explanation.

One of them is analog. It is used in two ways in this book. The first is to indicate that electricity was being used as a continuous flow in computing machines. Such machines measured how much rather than counting how many. The other way is to indicate that calculating and information machines were direct and limited physical models of whatever it was that was being calculated or searched. Such machines were special purpose because they were electrical or mechanical copies of a particular process or machine. As we will see, many of the machines built by the navy's cryptanalysts were electrical models of code and cipher systems rather than universal machines that could imitate any system. In contrast is the modern digital programmable electronic computer.

A digital computer is one that depends upon sharp pulses of electricity, pulses that are counted. A digital machine answers the how many question. Such electronic counting was a great and difficult achievement but a universal machine was an even greater one. A general purpose digital computer, in contrast to a specialized analog computer, is one that is built with the potential to model any machine or process through a quickly changeable program. Most of the machines we will discuss were not perfect representations of the universal computer. They were not run by easily changed programs nor were they based on pure binary logic or hardware. But, they were very significant steps towards electronic general purpose digital computing.

Two other terms, electromechanical and relay, are related. Before the electronic radio tube was changed into an on-off switch with no moving parts, the fastest building-blocks available to computer builders were devices that used electrical pulses or flows to change the state or position of a mechanical component. IBM's tabulating machines used pulses of electricity to move counting devices and to control small gates in sorting machines. The usual electromechanical component of early computing machines were relay switches. In a relay, a charge of electricity moves a metallic part to open or close an electrical pathway. Automatic telephone systems came to rely upon such switches during the 1930s and, then, more complex variants called stepping switches. While faster than purely mechanical devices, relays were much, much slower than electronic components.

A Babble of Tongues and a Sea of Hyphens

I have also tried to avoid the use of special terms from the worlds of cryptanalysts, Documentalists, information scientists and bureaucrats. Uniterms, Coordinates, random superimposed code, inverted matrix, and the like will rarely be found. When such frightening words as superencryption and serial processing did creep into the text, I did my best to define them in common terms. To the possible horror of some, I have also put readability ahead of historical purity in the use of a few words and concepts. The term "punched card" was pushed aside in favor of "punch card" and I have emphasized the rather unique nature of those associated with the American Documentation Institute by using an upper case "D" and adding an "ism" here and there. Although the historical actors may not have seen themselves in a movement with an ideology, terms such as Documentalism do underscore their devotion to reform.

I made another dangerous stylistic commitment. I decided to try to avoid using hyphenated words and I did my best to avoid creating new words through joining old ones. That caused some worry on the part of my copy editors. But, frustrated by the many conflicting style manuals and mandates of the 1980s and fearful of the increase in the use of hyphenated words, I usually trusted my fate to a standard dictionary--at least when I had the opportunity to decide whether or not to hyphenate or join words. As with the formats for citations I tried to let common usage and common sense rule. I was able to avoid pages full of hyphens although "high-speed" will be found throughout the book. Proudly, I included only a few inventions that have become commonplace in the more specialized literature, such as "codebreakers" and "codebooks."

Perhaps the most dangerous part of my attempt to talk to the average reader was the commitment to avoid bureaucratic hair splitting. I have not made fine distinctions among divisions, offices and department and I have not followed name changes through the years. I have attempted to maintain continuity by using one name per organization. OP-20-G is used for all the navy cryptanalytic departments and the Bureau of Engineering (later, the Bureau of Ships) is used for all its subdivisions. I employ as few names as possible for the army's cryptanalytic branches and I tried to use only one name, National Defense Research Committee, for Bush's World War II science organization.

Alphabet Soup

Although I tried to limit the number of special names and abbreviations many quite forbidding ones found their way into the text. The list of abbreviations and acronyms in the front matter should help a reader keep track of the dozens of agencies and machines that were so important to the technology of information and secrecy.

A Complex Story

Because the history of information and secrecy was the product of so many different forces, institutions and people, the story remains a complex one. Even the career of Vannevar Bush and his academic home, the Massachusetts Institute of Technology, demand a discussion of much of America's educational and technological history.

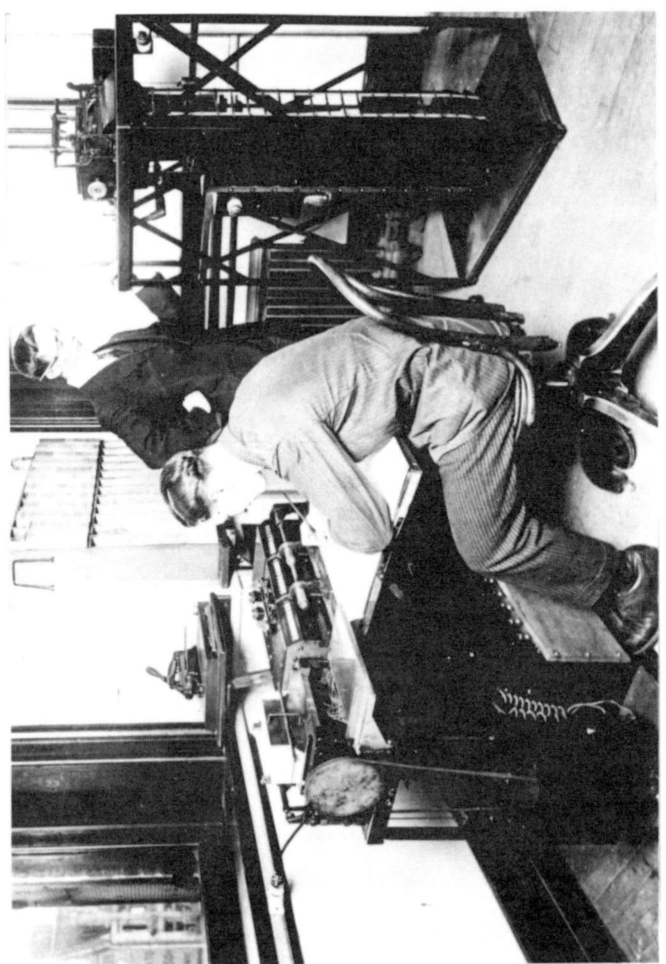

Tabulating Equipment, 1920s
(*IBM Archives*)

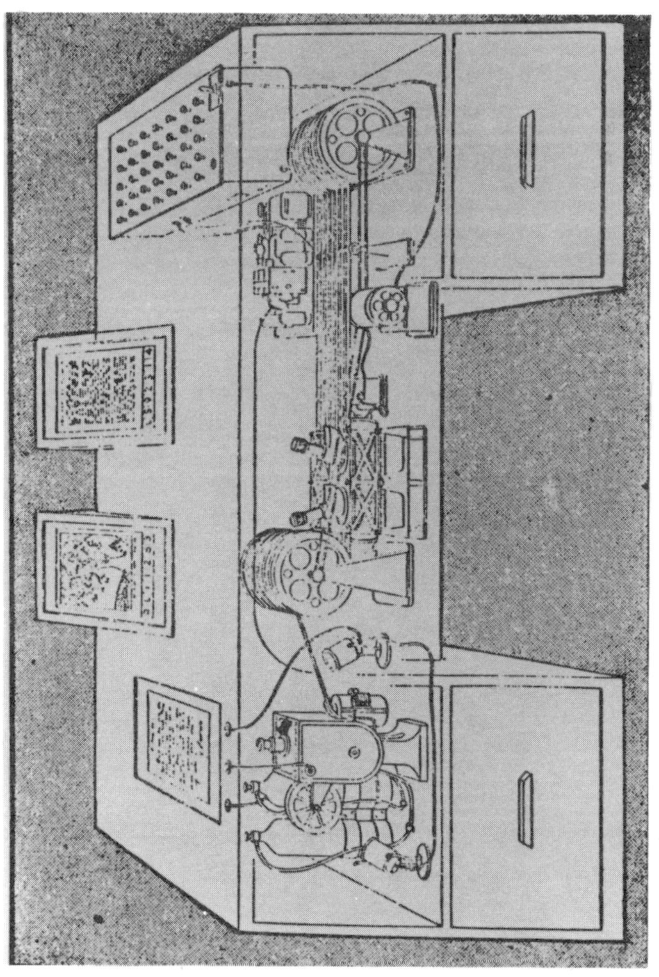

Memex
(Hagley Museum & Library)

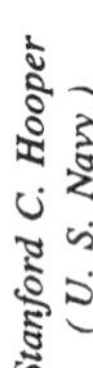

Stanford C. Hooper
(U. S. Navy)

Chapter II
An Institution and a Man for American Technology

Since its birth on the eve of the Civil War, the Massachusetts Institute of Technology had been devoted to applying science to practical affairs. Its founders rejected much of the curricula of the traditional American liberal arts college as well as the simple vocational program of the trade school. They made MIT an example of how practical men who worked in cooperation with the new institutions of science and industry could turn a university into a force for positive change. Its founders, such as William Barton Rogers, wanted to create men of vision, men who would bring the benefits of technology to a backward America. Technology, wisely applied through the creation of "industrial intelligence," thought Rogers, would bring about a world of plenty and peace. Rogers and his colleagues were not just philosophers and educators. They were the builders of some of the most important instruments of the American industrial revolution. Their famous Comparator, for example, allowed the exact replication of mass produced parts.[1]

Rogers initiated MIT's long-term policy of conducting research for business and government agencies and of having its faculty actively engaged in technological and business efforts. His men were to be of the world, not just commentators on the state of society. The policy of engagement was of benefit to the young Institute in several ways. Aiding industry and the local economy created friends who could help the school to overcome its financial problems and instructors who were involved in other enterprises would bring valuable and practical knowledge into the classroom. In addition, with faculty members earning outside income, they would be unlikely to leave the Institute because of the always inadequate academic salaries. Anticipating the utilitarian strategies of the state university presidents of the next generation, Rogers also thought that a faculty active in technology and science would be a political asset.

Despite those policies, friends in elite circles and financial help from the state, the Institute was not a guaranteed success. It was badly hit by the recession of the 1870s and its future remained unsure until the watershed years of American life in the 1890s. Then, with a more secure financial condition and a growing body of alumni and friends who had benefitted from the work of its faculty, the Institute expanded its curricula, acquired modern equipment and established itself as a force in American academic and industrial life. The Institute gained a solid reputation in civil and mechanical engineering, architecture, naval construction, chemistry, and electrical engineering. MIT's entry into the field of high power electricity was important to its future. The dynamic head of its new and innovative electrical engineering program, Dugald C. Jackson, spent almost thirty years producing students who became the nation's leaders in electrical research and technical education. He established close relationships with the large corporations, sharing students and expertise with such giants as General Electric. He also created a niche for the Institute's faculty in the research programs of the high power electrical industry. But Jackson did not let his men rest. He pushed his department into new technologies and by the 1920s the sparkling electrical engineering department added a focus on the new fields of electronics and communications.

Stratton and Scientific Measurement

The inauguration of Samuel W. Stratton as MIT's president in 1923 accelerated the shift to electronics and reinvigorated the school's attempts to create measurement devices for industry and science. Stratton's background was consistent with MIT's history and its new goals. While a young man in the Middle West he established one of the first electrical engineering programs in America. That gained him national attention and he was asked to move to America's newest and very rich research university, the University of Chicago. He assisted and then become a colleague of the nation's great modern physicist, Albert A. Michelson. Michelson, educated at the Naval Academy, then at the graduate schools of Europe, founded the physics program at Chicago in the 1890s and soon received a Nobel prize for his fundamental contributions. His forte lay in the art of scientific measurement. His measurement of the velocity of light contributed to Einstein's grand theory. Stratton assisted Michelson in building the most illustrious scientific measuring machine of the era, the famous analog Harmonic Analyser. Sponsored by the National Academy of Sciences, it provided the first means to quickly solve the most difficult mathematical equations. It could handle Fourier series of as many as eighty terms. That mechanical analog analyser of 1898 became a resource for the nation's scientists and remained so despite the improvements in the first electric digital machine, the Hollerith tabulator.

Stratton's and Michelson's Analyser was at the cutting edge in the 1890s and it anchored Stratton's reputation. He was soon asked to take on a greater challenge, to pull the federal government's research capabilities into the modern era. Only in his early forties, he was asked for a plan to change an old and rather moribund bureau for weights and measures into an engine for the modernization of American industry. He was given an opportunity to create America's version of the great national laboratories of Europe. In 1901, he began his attempt to make the National Bureau of Standards the center for applied scientific research. Stratton planned to have the Bureau do much more than advise other government agencies, it was to provide information and services to all of American industry.

Although an adept politician and a member of the nation's scientific elite, Stratton was unable to realize his dreams for the Bureau. But, he was able to turn what was a small government office into a significant institution. Stratton made sure that Standards was well connected to the nation's largest corporations and the scientific community. In fact, the Bureau was near to becoming the largest research organization in America. For a time, Stratton thought he could overcome the remaining forces of scientific conservatism that blocked his other ambitions.

Measurement was central to the Bureau's mandate to help government agencies and industry. Among Stratton's hopes was that Standards would become the national center for scientific calculation. He realized that American industry could not advance unless it was provided with a stream of up-to-date tables, ones allowing engineers to apply advanced mathematics to manufacturing problems. Mathematical table construction and large-scale calculation were the kind of efforts that small businesses could not afford. So, an NBS calculation center would be a force for democracy and economic opportunity. Significant to Stratton's plans was his belief that the Bureau's calculation activities would not interfere with the ambitions of academics or entrepreneurs. He saw no indication that America's weak and poorly funded formal scientific establishment would be able to go far beyond what had been done at Chicago or that commercial firms would enter the field of large-scale scientific calculation.[2]

Stratton was able to take steps to make Standards a center for measurement and calculation, but much of his program remained uncoordinated and burdened with immediate and practical aspects of measurement. Necessarily, most of the techniques his men employed were analog, but the Bureau became involved in an unfortunate foray into the new field of automatic digital counting. To its political embarrassment, the Bureau became entangled in the bizarre fight between the Census Bureau and the man whose company would soon become the foundation for IBM, Herman Hollerith.

Herman Hollerith's tabulator, which had been built for census work in the late 1880s, faced a long-term battle to enter the market for scientific calculation because the analog Harmonic Analyser and its cousins were more efficient mathematical machines. The same forces that put an end to Charles Babbage's grand dreams of a universal digital machine continued to place the tabulator and the new mechanical desk calculators at a disadvantage. The nature of the scientific problems of the era, combined with the enormous cost and speed advantages of analog over digital calculation, made the slide rule, the planimeter and machines such as the Analyser the calculation tools of choice for most engineers and scientists until well after World War II.[3]

Although there was an increasing demand for Hollerith's digital calculation machines, he remained sensitive to any threats. He was primed for trouble when the Census Bureau, reacting to what it thought were Hollerith's excessive demands for the rental of his tabulating devices, asked Standards to develop an alternative digital technology. The Bureau did so by creating a research branch, hiring some of Hollerith's most important employees and by placing development in charge of a rather mysterious engineer, James Powers. Using the government's funds, Powers devised a successful mechanical digital technology and, for a time, he avoided many of Hollerith's strongest electromechanical patent claims. Government machines began to replace Hollerith's at the Census Bureau.

By the time Powers completed the first machines for the Census, the intense legal and political battles between Hollerith and the government were threatening Standards's hopes of being seen as a non-political institution guided by the objectivity of science. The politics of measurement worsened when Powers decided to found his own company. By taking the census machine patent rights with him, he put Standards in the untenable position of having paid for the development of the patents then allowing them to be used to create a private company. In the eyes of many, Standards and the Census Bureau had interfered in the private market. The government, in fact, had sponsored the only contender to what became IBM.

Powers's company was not a great success and it was saved only by its purchase by the Remington-Rand conglomerate in the mid-1920s. However, the Powers episode continued to be a part of the arsenal of those who objected to the government being in the business of science. It was used by politicians who worried about Stratton's drive to build a huge federal institution, one that had the potential to regulate as well as serve private business. Similar objections would reappear a generation later when Henry Wallace and his allies again tried to make Standards a center for the application of technology to information processing.[4]

After Powers's difficulties, the Bureau of Standards continued to explore other digital technologies. One of its missions in the 1920s was to make the office as well as the factory efficient, but that was made difficult by its need to avoid the kind of situation that had led Hollerith to cry "socialism."[5] Thus, while he was able to maintain his stature in the American scientific and industrial community, Stratton became more and more frustrated by the politics of governmental science. When MIT gave him a nod, he found the offer of the presidency of a major private university irresistible.

Stratton's background and interests blended with those of MIT. In the early 1920s the Institute needed someone like Stratton to sustain its drive to keep research and theoretical science a part of its program. His work at Standards had paralleled many of the efforts at the Institute and his national and international connections were needed for MIT's effort to make sure, despite its commitment to hands-on engineering education, that it did not gain a reputation as a trade school. Stratton had another type of connection that proved important to the history of the Institute and its later role in the information and secrecy revolutions. He was an active member of the Naval Reserve and he created new ties to the navy that shaped the Institute's future.

There was more that made Stratton's 1923 appointment a natural. His interests and goals fit with those of the Institute's faculty, especially some of the younger men who sought administrative approval of their visions for MIT. All at the Institute seemed to agree that more support should be given to research and most hoped that the school would become a center for the application of formal mathematics to engineering problems. In addition, the faculty of the 1920s wanted to reinvigorate the Institute's role in industrial consulting. Some of those younger men may have argued that the decline of the National Bureau of Standards was an opportunity for MIT. The Institute could become a private version of what Stratton had wanted the Bureau to be, the national center for measurement. One of the junior faculty with such a hope was Vannevar Bush. The harmony between Bush and Stratton's views had much to do with the younger man's success. Bush received critical support from Stratton, allowing him to become one of the most important men in the history of American science and technology.

A Man for All Technologies

A generation later, at the end of World War II, Vannevar Bush was one of the most powerful scientists the world had ever known and a man familiar to most Americans. The heritage of his policies continues to shape the organization of academic research in America. Although his plan for a federal role in science was not completely fulfilled, the National Science Foundation is testimony to his influence.

Bush was a persuasive and popular spokesman for science. His many articles and books made an impact on the general public as well as on policy makers. His World War II role as the head of the greatest organization of scientific talent in the nation's history gave his words unchallenged credibility. His involvement with the most important defense matters, combined with his amazing ability to make science and technology understandable and exciting, led to the widespread acceptance of his ideas. His views on atomic energy, science policy, the relation of technology to democracy and even the future of the library received widespread attention. Articles about his ideas even appeared in *Time* and in *Life*.[6] Bush was important because of his influence in such matters as the beginnings of the atomic bomb project and the establishment of the NDRC and the National Science

Foundation. His stature was so great that he could publish a popular autobiography when he was eighty years old. But soon after that, Bush was neglected, if not forgotten. Despite his enormous contributions while at MIT; despite his influence within the inner circles during World War II and the Cold War; and despite his role in shaping the nature of Big Science, and thus the modern American university, little was written about him until very recently.[7]

The new interest has taken a rather unexpected turn. Instead of focusing on his policy contributions, the spotlight has been on Bush's role in the emergence of computers and information processing. The research on his contributions to computers arose as the new field of computer history was born in the 1980s. The seemingly more intense interest in his role in the birth of information science was generated by the rediscovery of Bush's work on automatic data retrieval. His ideas for a mind machine, Memex, are now treated as the origin of hypertext and similar knowledge systems.[8]

The parallels between Bush's concepts of a bibliographic machine for individual scientists, described in his 1940s Memex articles, and the present tools such as hypertext, sparked the rebirth of Bush as a popular hero of American technology. The influence of Bush's writings on the young engineers who developed the advanced software for the first modern computer workstations has sustained the interest in Bush. However, the fascination with Memex has not spilled over into popular interest in Bush's machine for the library, the Rapid Selector.[9] The existing view of the Selector, like the new view of Bush, is more than a bit one dimensional. The Selector has been treated as just the physical embodiment of the grand ideas for Memex. But the Selector had its own history, one as important as Memex's. Its role in the history of information science can only be established by tracing Bush's life and by placing his contributions in the context of the traumas of prewar American science and, then, the merger of technology and national defense.

More Than an Ingenious Yankee

Vannevar Bush was born at the right time and in the right place. Eighteen-ninety was a turning point in the history of American life and New England was the center of its technical progress. Bush grew up seeing the miraculous and profound changes in daily living brought about by the spread of new technologies. His formative years were those when electricity began to alter the world. Being the son of a Universalist minister was also the right thing. The young Vannevar got much from his father. Vannevar inherited a great deal of intelligence and a personality marked by energy and perseverance. Those traits were evident throughout Bush's long career and were important to his success. But more than natural talent shaped his life. He was taught much by his parents. He learned about handling people, was taught responsibility, was given a firm sense of right and wrong and was shown that technology should be directed to the fulfillment of morally worthy goals. Chelsea, Massachusetts' schools reinforced his family's values and encouraged his scientific interests. Those interests were not abstract. Even as a youngster, Bush merged science with tinkering, if not technology. He was an inventor and a natural at putting technology together in different combinations to fulfill a need. His efforts were always goal oriented because he realized that inventions required a market to be successful. Bush paid attention to the commercial aspects of technology and built a enviable list of patents on devices ranging from thermostats and typewriters to electronics.[10]

Bush's family decided to send him to Tufts, perhaps because tuition was free to the son of a minister alumnus. Tufts was not as devoted to technology as was MIT, but it had more than respectable science and engineering departments whose faculty made students aware of the future of technology. The telephone and radio made some of their first American appearances in Tuft's laboratories. Of course, Bush's bachelors and masters degrees in engineering came with a strong dose of the moral teachings of a traditional American liberal arts college. After graduation, Bush gained some shop floor experience while working for the giant General Electric corporation. As a junior electrical engineer he found the going a bit difficult and decided to explore the possibilities of an academic career. Short of funds, he pushed himself to complete a joint Harvard-MIT doctoral program in electrical engineering. He suffered through a great deal of tedious calculation for his thesis. Naturally, he searched for shortcuts to complete his mathematical analysis of complex electrical circuits and applied some of the many tricks mathematicians used before the advent of the modern computer. The work was oppressive but worthwhile. The doctoral degree and the favorable impression Bush made on Dugald Jackson of MIT soon proved of great value.[11]

Bush's new academic title and Jackson's influence gained the twenty-six year old entry into the inner realm of America's elite science. Immediately, he became involved with a project that was a model for conducting applied research. Just out of school, Bush became associated with World War I's New London research laboratory where the famous Robert Millikan brought the nation's best men to focus science on the critical U-boat threat. An illustrious group of scientists and farseeing military men were involved with the detection project and they formed bonds that lasted throughout their lives.[12] Bush contributed to the research with a significant detection system, joined the Naval Reserve and became at least a junior member of the national military-scientific establishment. Bush never forgot that first experience and he used it during World War II when he set up the academic scientist's dream, the National Defense Research Committee.

The navy's failure to accept much of the advice of the New London scientific group reinforced Bush's dislike of bureaucracies, at least those he did not control. Bush always wanted freedom for scientists to pursue long-term plans on their own and to take research gambles. His experience with the navy in World War I convinced him that only when scientists were in charge of selecting and funding research would there be valuable discoveries. In particular, Bush thought that, with a few great exceptions, military bureaucracies would always be against scientists, if not science.

Despite encountering much technological conservatism, the war years were valuable for Bush. His submarine work led to other important contacts and he was soon able to participate in a radio effort supported by the Morgan banking interests. A complex path eventually led to Bush being one of the creators of Raytheon, a company that was able to challenge RCA's patent monopoly over radio. Raytheon became one of the many important companies tied to MIT and its students.[13] Bush's postwar entrepreneurial ventures war did not end his academic ambitions, however. He made a very important decision. He accepted a position as an assistant professor in MIT's Electrical Engineering Department. It was understood that he would concentrate on the problems of high power transmission, a focus that was sure to attract support from the private power companies which were beginning to construct large regional networks. Those networks had problems that called for the type of research an academic institution could pursue.

Bush soon began to prove his technical, managerial and academic abilities. Although married and having young children, he excelled at the Institute while establishing himself as a private consultant. A string of articles on power problems and the mathematical techniques useful for their solution advanced his academic standing. At the same time, he was a forceful teacher who could motivate and guide the work of a large number of bright students. He was co-authoring what became the standard text in electrical engineering at the same time that he took an increasing part in administering his department and the university. The Institute experience did not turn him into an abstract academician nor force him into such specialization that his interests narrowed, however. The driving characteristics of his youth remained in play and, in fact, intensified.

Bush's ambition was to put science and technology to work. His New England heritage, his family's history of facing and dealing with a rough and tumble world and his education made him, in a sense, one of America's greatest professional tinkerers. All technology was in his domain and his mission was to put it together in new combinations to fulfill some social or economic goal. Once Bush sensed a need that could perhaps be met with the technologies he commanded, he never let go. His only fault was that he sometimes became too enthusiastic about a technology and overlooked its limitations.

The Politics of Mathematics and Engineering

Although Bush was a practical man, he was also a missionary for the application of mathematics to engineering and science. He realized he had limited formal mathematical skills but he compensated by supporting the work of men like the renowned Norbert Wiener. Wiener was brought to MIT to integrate advanced mathematics with teaching and engineering research. Bush also encouraged his students to expand the frontiers of mathematical engineering, with some great results. Claude Shannon, a father of mathematical information theory, was one of the many young men influenced by Bush and Wiener.

Bush was adept at gaining the loyalty of such young men. He had a cadre of supporters who carried out his projects and who acted as his advocates. Very important, many of MIT's faculty of the 1930s and 1940s began as Bush's students. They continued to look to Bush for leadership and they became a resource for him, allowing him to pursue many activities and projects at the same time. Building and maintaining such support was not easy, however. Two of Bush's major concerns were how to attract the best young men to his electrical engineering program and, then, how to ensure their successful careers. The former was the least difficult because of MIT's academic reputation. Providing the right education for the young men and starting them in their careers was more difficult. Bush spent much time raising the money needed to support graduate students and a great deal of his time went into arranging the right kind of projects at the Institute, ones that would give his men a chance to establish the first companies to exploit a new technology. Despite many difficulties, Bush was successful in keeping the loyalty of a large group of students and alumni.[14]

During his first years on the Institute's faculty, Bush showed that he was a good manager and an astute academic politician. He was given more and more administrative responsibilities and he fulfilled them without alienating too many people. His personal skills were also reflected by his climb within the national scientific establishment. Within a decade after his MIT appointment, Bush was a member of the most important scientific organizations. Although the United States did not have truly powerful scientific institutions, ones with the financial resources to shape the course of research, such bodies as the National Academy of Sciences, the National Research Council and the National Advisory Committee for Aeronautics could influence what science policy there was and did provide invaluable contacts for their members. By his late forties, Bush had become more than a member of such groups. He was a statesman of American science.

Bush also developed into one of the best grantsmen in the nation. His choice for the title of his autobiography, *Pieces of the Action*, was on the mark. He was always looking for opportunities for himself, his "boys," and MIT. By the 1930s, his ability to sense what funding agencies desired and to combine the hot ideas of the time had become finely honed professional skills. Bush was also unsurpassed in using one grant as the basis for more funding. He knew how to make small changes in his projects to allow them to fit with the plans of other agencies. But his many hat in hand trips to seek funding reinforced his dislike of bureaucrats as well as his desire to find a means of allowing the best scientists to determine the nation's research policies.[15] Bush also built a network of contacts with the executives of the county's leading companies, providing resources for his projects and employment for his students.

The Manager of Science

After a long stint as dean and then as vice president of MIT, Bush became a true national force. In 1938 he became the head of the Carnegie Institution, one of the most important scientific research agencies in the world. That led to his assuming the leadership of World War II's very powerful National Defense Research Committee. The NDRC filtered hundreds of millions of dollars of government funds to privately directed research for the war effort.[16] The NDRC was an improved and vastly expanded version of the World War I submarine project and was the fulfillment of some of Bush's long held dreams about research in America. The NDRC allowed academics something close to the best of all worlds: they received government funding free of most bureaucratic direction. It also fit with Bush's belief that the military would only change in response to outside pressures. Bush's success in establishing such conditions for scientists gave him even greater influence in the scientific community. By the end of the war, Bush was the most powerful man in American science and was a force the military had to recognize.[17]

Bush and Stratton's Dream

But Vannevar Bush did not begin his MIT career at the top and it took more than a decade for him to gain his national reputation. Bush began his work at MIT with research on electrical systems (usually in coordination with corporate giants such as General Electric) and through that moved into a field that put him in harmony with MIT's new president, Samuel W. Stratton. In the early 1920s, Bush directed his students to expand the reach of analog computing. They began with rather simple combinations of rods and gears to create machines for the automatic calculation of differential equations. But those first integraphs were more than extensions of the old wire and cone contraption that had made Stratton's reputation. The young men edged towards solving the major mechanical problems that had prevented the engineer's friend, the planimeter, from becoming a truly powerful tool. By the late 1920s, Bush and his men were convinced they had overcome the critical problem of torque. They persuaded Stratton and the other influentials at MIT that a new and startling version of Lord Kelvin's machines could be constructed and put to productive use in a few years. They declared they could make MIT a national calculation center.

MIT committed major resources to Bush's project. Some twenty-five thousand dollars of university funds (a sum equal to a year's wages of twenty school teachers) were put in his hands. He was allowed to assign the best graduate students to the creation of the Differential Analyser. It was a big and expensive project and Bush's standing at the Institute and in the nation were at stake. But he came through. In 1931, he announced to the scientific community that the world's largest and most powerful calculating machine stood ready at MIT to advance science and engineering.

The Differential Analyser was a room full of gears and rods and shafts and motors that took mechanical analog computing to the limits. It brought international fame to Bush and MIT. The popular press called the Analyser a "giant brain." Bush came in for his share of publicity as the scientific community rushed to use and to copy the machine. International visitors came to the Institute and clones were built in Europe and America. Aberdeen Proving Grounds and the University of Pennsylvania built versions and General Electric found it so useful it invested in a copy for itself.

The Analyser overshadowed other projects at the Institute, ones that were more revolutionary. They had greater potential for the future of calculation because they were based on electricity, electronics and photoelectricity.[18] That was one reason why Bush was not content with his electromechanical giant. Another frustration was more practical. Unfortunately, despite all the world-wide publicity the Analyser did not bring the hoped for torrent of money to MIT. To support his students and to continue research at the Institute, Bush began a search for ways to raise funds, That became a frustrating six year long exercise in ingenuity and perseverance.

Bush Confronts Little Science

Bush began his fund-raising trek at the worst of times. The world and the nation were entering the Great Depression, MIT was having internal difficulties, corporations had little to donate and the handful of foundations that supported research in America were besieged by every scientist and university. Yet, Bush sought to do much more than get money for his own students. Beyond financing his projects, Bush felt that he should contribute to the general well-being of the Institute. MIT did need help. Just as Bush's Analyser was given so much by the Institute in the late 1920s, the school lost its state subsidy. Worse,

Stratton's hopes that America's largest corporations would donate a constant stream of funds to MIT proved unrealistic. Many expedients were tried in order to raise the funds needed to maintain the school's quality. The institute began offering special courses in advanced marine engineering for naval officers and it expanded its services to the aviation industry. But, MIT found it more and more difficult to finance research with its own resources and its leaders feared that it might be forced to retreat to the vocational model of technical education. The faculty, including Vannevar Bush, was on its own and all had to struggle for the means to continue research and to finance their graduate students. Unlike what had happened during previous moments of crisis for the Institute, no Mr. Smith (George Eastman) appeared with millions in sorely needed gifts. When MIT's administration changed hands, the pressures on Bush and his colleagues intensified.

The Institute's new president of 1930, Karl T. Compton, was as much a part of elite science as Stratton, but he was more academic in orientation. A famous physicist, Compton arrived with a mandate to turn the Institute back towards a true scientific curricula and to integrate the latest science with both teaching and research. He also arrived with some questions about the results of the Institute's long held policy of encouraging faculty entrepreneurship. Although he continued many of Stratton's policies and placed great trust in Bush, Compton laid down new guidelines concerning faculty research. Wishing to reduce the growing ethical and educational problems stemming from the staff's business activities, and hoping to secure the funds needed to allow internal financing of research, Compton let it be known that he desired more effort for the Institute and less for faculty pocketbooks and corporate sponsors.[19] But, he realized that banning faculty consulting and research for outsiders during the Great Depression might spell the end of MIT. With Bush's help some compromises were made. Informally, faculty were asked to conduct research of general, not particular, import. Formally, consulting fees were to be shared with the Institute and patents were to become the property of the school if the work had been internally funded. To control the increasingly complex patent problems and to avoid the dangers inherent in a university holding patents, MIT decided to turn to the Research Corporation of New York City. It was to handle all patent matters, including determination of patentability, allocation of shares to MIT, sponsors and faculty, and, to deal with all related legal questions.

The Research Corporation was another of the many patches on America's ailing scientific establishment. It was founded by one of America's most farsighted and generous scientists, Frederick Cottrell. The creator of devices critically important to science and industry, such as the air cleaning precipitator, Cottrell had begun to address the problems of research in America early in his career. One of those he examined was access to information and he was one of the first to suggest the use of microfilm for scientific publications. But most of his thoughts went to the question of financing academic research in the age of America's Little Science. He devised an unusual and very worthy solution.[20] Signing over his own work to begin the process, his plan was to place patents from sponsored research in the name of a foundation; license patent use at a fair price; and, turn the profits around to sponsor further research. In addition, the foundation's staff of experienced administrators and attorneys was to help academics through the unfamiliar territory of patent applications and negotiations with private corporations. By the mid-1930s the Research Corporation and MIT became quite close, with ex-MIT men serving as important executives. The new connection and Compton's policy did not solve Bush or MIT's financial problems, however. Faculty members continued to have to raise funds for their projects, their students and the institution. And, times were more than hard!

Even the great Vannevar Bush found it difficult to raise funds and the less famous fared badly. An outstanding junior faculty member at the Institute, Harold Edgerton, struggled for any means to support his work. His important and innovative projects limped along with pittances from the Institute because outside sponsors were so difficult to find. To keep his high-speed flash camera work alive, the Institute had to turn its eyes away from his use of its facilities for his consulting work and the unpaid research associate status of the two other members of what became the world famous EG&G corporation. Luckily for Edgerton, his work matured before the Institute began to insist upon sharing patent rights.[21]

Bush did not do much better than the rest of the faculty until the second half of the 1930s. He spent years knocking on foundation, corporate and bureaucratic doors with saleable plans, but with no results.[22] Meanwhile, he continued his remarkable work on a variety of devices, gaining some dozen patents between just 1932 and 1937.[23] The patents, assigned to firms with which he was associated, such as

Raytheon, may have brought some money to the Institute. They certainly encouraged actions such as Raytheon's donation of tube manufacturing machines to MIT. But that type of gift was not enough to support a department. So, Bush launched upon an almost frantic search for combinations of technologies that might attract sponsors.

Bush looked like a man willing to combine a set of chosen technologies in any combination that would satisfy a donor's predispositions. Among other attempts of the 1930s, he toyed with a machine to identify fingerprints; he tried to devise a high-speed pneumatic printer; he played with the use of high-speed metal tape and wire systems to send secret messages; and, he tried to find ways to automate libraries. He was able to help John Wilbur obtain minimal amounts from the Singer interests for a mechanical equation solver and he kept as many of his students as busy as he could running the old Differential Analyser. But he suffered through many years without the kind of financial support that Stratton's earlier policies had promised and, most telling, he could not find the financing needed for what emerged as his grand plan for the Institute.

Bush's Great Plan

After testing reactions at the Rockefeller and Carnegie foundations, and after considering his possible role in Compton's drive to make MIT scientifically respectable, Bush put together a grand plan. It was one he thought would attract a wide range of donors, would be applauded by the scientific community and would lead to a permanent source of support for the Institute. As well, it would call upon the experience and talents of faculty from several of MIT's departments.

Bush decided to make MIT the national center for calculation and for the development of pathbreaking scientific calculation devices. If Bush had his way, MIT, not the NBS, would realize Stratton's dream.

Bush knew that his Analyser had taken mechanical technology to its extreme, so his plan for the Center of Analysis included much more than proposals to extend mechanical analog calculation. Electronics, photoelectricity and new memory media were to be developed and combined to produce revolutionary computers. Bush also wanted the center to explore the new markets for what would later be called "data processing." His plans included digital calculation and machines to solve the escalating problem of file management in science and bureaucracy.[24] He announced that he would create machines that would outdistance all competitors, especially the IBM tabulator.[25] His efforts began at a very difficult time, but he persevered. Supported by a group of gifted junior faculty and a cadre of adoring graduate students, he joined together all of the existing measurement and calculating projects at the Institute and began to weave new ideas for future devices.[26]

Bush had a far reaching strategy for his center. To attract funding, he planned to make it innovative and unique, yet politic. Of great importance, it had to avoid making enemies of those it might call upon for financial support. The center would not last long if it competed with private data processing companies or infringed on the patents and markets of calculator manufacturers. Bush's search for alternatives to the tabulator and its standard data card and his lack of contact with IBM are partially accounted for by such concerns. Bush also had to deal with competition from within academia but he wanted to avoid the appearance of a head-on challenge. In England, at Iowa State College and at Columbia University in New York City scientific calculation centers were emerging using advanced methods on modified tabulators. Even Harvard's faculty was thinking of mechanized calculation and was soon to begin a project with IBM and Howard Aiken to build the worlds largest, fastest and most complex combination of tabulator and relay technology. IBM, the only significant American manufacturer of such equipment, also gave direct and significant support to its Columbia University center by providing free machines.[27]

There were other factors shaping Bush's plans during the early 1930s. As part of a university, the proposed MIT center could not be allowed to finance itself through the manufacture and sale of devices. Patents on new inventions might provide some income if they were carefully managed, but an academic institution could not maintain its credibility if it became the appendage of a particular company. So, licenses from discoveries had to be offered to all. The problem with such a policy was that it made it difficult to attract corporate sponsors whose self-interest demanded a monopoly over important technological innovations. Later, Bush had to overlook some of those rules to meet the demands of corporate sponsors.

Unless one of those rare donors such as George Eastman appeared with a huge endowment, the center had to be financed from support for particular projects and on-going income from contract calculation work. Unlike the NDRC years of World War II, when scientists determined the nature of their own projects and the results flowed into the public domain, Bush had to bend his 1930s proposals to match the existing programs of the few research foundations in the country and he had to try to balance the self-interest of private companies with the need to keep the Institute free from outside control. In addition to the necessity of matching projects to the desires of possible sponsors and the need to avoid making enemies among those in the calculation business, Bush's strategy for the proposed center was shaped by the state of technology and the talents of the men at MIT.

Beyond Analog Mechanical Machines

Mechanical analog devices were approaching their limits of precision and speed in the 1930s. Although there were no commercial competitors for such huge devices as the Differential Analyser,[28] Bush saw little worth in cloning it in slightly improved form. If support was to be found, he had to make a major technological leap in analog computing. But, there was a more fundamental challenge and opportunity for the center: the growing demand for digital calculation, something MIT's machine builders had not yet explored. The rise of the social sciences was creating a market for digital calculators and even engineers and physical scientists, who had been so well served by analog devices for more than a century, were tackling problems that called for digital methods. Bush also knew of the increasing need for high-speed digital calculation in the bureaucratic and business worlds. He realized his center would be incomplete unless it served those whose work demanded counting rather than measurement and he sensed opportunity because there had not been a major innovation in large-scale digital machinery since Hollerith patented his tabulator.

The call for digital processing merged with another growing need, information retrieval. Business and governmental files had grown to unmanageable proportions. The hand, mechanical, and electromechanical methods of data retrieval were not satisfying bureaucratic demands.[29] In addition, scientific publications were suffering the same fate as "lost" bureaucratic records. Influential researchers in many sciences found it increasingly difficult to keep up with their areas of interest because of the deluge of articles. Some worried that the difficulty of retrieving and disseminating findings was slowing the development of science. Bush and many others predicted that traditional librarians would never offer solutions and they lobbied for projects that would allow scientists and engineers to take the lead in the new field of Documentation.[30]

Bush and his colleagues spent much of their time in the 1930s putting together a small number of technologies in different configurations to fulfill such unmet needs and, hopefully, to attract sponsors. They surveyed all the computing technologies, ranging from the traditional tabulator card to the very esoteric realm of magnetic recording, and arrived at a set of relatively new combinations. Bush had begun thinking of possible technological configurations and applications as soon as the Differential Analyser was in its final construction stages. In the early 1930s, pondering how to best use the expertise of his colleagues at the Institute, Bush decided to concentrate on the exploitation of three technologies: photoelectricity, digital electronics and film.

Although new, they were much closer to being ready for application than the still delicate magnetic recording. By 1930, informed engineers and scientists in the western world knew of the evolution of these technologies and many were thinking of the range of possible applications. The motion picture industry had spurred the development of reliable film and allied mechanical components. Business needs had led to the use of microfilm for bureaucratic files by the mid-1920s. At the same time, photoelectric cells, which first emerged in the early 1900s, were improved and were becoming off the shelf items. They were being used in many measuring and automatic control devices, such as MIT's light-based analyzers for scientific measurement. The electronic components necessary to amplify and measure, if not count, the signals from the cells were also becoming available.[31] In addition, the use of electronic tubes as on-off digital devices was spreading. Since the end of World War I, physicists had linked them in series to count radiations and, by the mid-1930s, men such as Wynn-Williams of England were building quite sophisticated digital electronic measuring instruments. Textbooks on digital circuits and their applications were being published showing applications in both industry and science.[32]

By focusing on the application of these technologies to scientific calculation problems, Bush hoped to be innovative and to avoid conflict with commercial firms. His surveys of the scientific literature and patents had led him to believe (incorrectly, as we shall see) that he would be among the very first to try to use them for calculation and file management.[33] Most important, he thought their use would attract the sponsorship of the prestigious funding organizations. Such foundations had interests and goals matching those of academic institutions.

Some of Bush's proposed machines were simple extensions of the 1920s work on light-based analog calculation at the Institute.[34] Others moved MIT towards digital calculation. Inspired by Norbert Wiener, Gordon S. Brown, who was also working with Bush on robotics, conceived and built the analog Cinema Integraph. It used amounts of light passing through moving films and stationary masks to perform integrations. Another important device was developed by George Harrison. His unique Wavelength Analyser extended his previous use of photoelectricity, photographic plates and high-speed photography. He put them in a special combination in the Wavelength machine to turn analog measurements into digital output. Photoelectricity was also used as the basis for an automatic curve following device that was later attached to a version of the Differential Analyser. It became one of the foundations of the Institute's pre-robotic, servomechanism programs.[35] MIT's film and photographic expertise was being deepened through the work of yet another of its many talented men, Harold Edgerton. He and his assistants turned his ultra high-speed photographic system of the early 1930s from a crude prototype into a device useful for industrial and scientific analyses. By the mid-1930s, his stroboscopic inventions provided new opportunities for the application of film technology to library problems.[36]

Meanwhile, Bush was defining his own leap for analog computing. Responding to positive reactions by the Rockefeller Foundation, Bush sketched a radical new design for an Analyser and, by mid-1936, succeeded in raising the funds he needed to build the next generation of his great analog machine. The Rockefeller Differential Analyser was to be much faster and much easier to program than the mechanical version. Although it remained an analog device, it incorporated electronics, digital circuits, some photoelectric parts and program tapes. These allowed Bush to eliminate most of the cumbersome mechanical components of the first model.

The very impressive one hundred thousand dollars he received from the Foundation was not, as we will see, a pure blessing. The new Analyser soon became a very demanding over budget and behind schedule drain on the resources of the Institute and a burden to its students and faculty. The long delayed appearance of the Rockefeller

Analyser also became a threat to the credibility of Bush and the electrical engineering department.[37] However, Bush was planning even greater technological adventures. Based on the new developments in electronics, photoelectricity and film he was moving into digital calculation and what we now call information retrieval. By the mid-1930s, Bush had rough plans for a electronic "programmed" computer and refined ideas about information machines.[38]

Beyond Calculation, Information Machines

Bush had been tussling with one idea since the early 1930s. It was eventually turned into the Rapid Selector. No one will be able to establish the exact chronology of development, but as early as 1930 or 1931[39] Bush had begun sketching the outlines of devices to seek and reproduce microfilmed documents. One of his goals was to solve the growing problem of compiling scientific bibliographies, another was a more fantastic reach for what was a precursor of the 1980s workstation. He called that fantasy machine, the Memex. It was to be a model of the human mind and was to fill the need for an automatic creativity dynamo.

But Bush's first practical move towards his document retriever, the Rapid Selector, was caused by a mundane need, money. Bush seems to have adapted his retrieval ideas to fit the desires of a potential sponsor, the FBI. In fact, Bush told several colleagues that it was an FBI project rather than a library related idea that was the start of the Selector.[40] Sometime in 1935 or early 1936, Bush and the FBI came together to attempt to speed the process of criminal identification. Bush began the design of a system and a machine that would be fast enough to run through the millions of fingerprint and allied records in the FBI's ever growing files. The goal was to match a suspect's prints, in the form of codes, with those in the FBI files and immediately provide officials with biographical information. Bush turned to the basic technologies of microfilm, optics and flash photography and recommended a device that looked much like the library Selector that would emerge in 1940.[41] However, Bush found it difficult to work with the FBI and the project was deferred if not abandoned.[42] But, he was not one to let an investment in engineering design and a patent search go to waste. He began to think of ways to modify the proposed FBI machine to fit the needs of other sponsors. Then, luck and history came together to reshape the work at MIT.

Two Men For Technology

At the same time that Bush was revising the FBI design and was presenting his great outline for automated computing, "Instrumental Analysis," to an audience of the nation's most important scientists, he received a visit from an old acquaintance.[43] The arrival of Admiral Stanford C. Hooper and his young assistant, Joseph Wenger, would lead to one the most bizarre episodes in American academic history, would complicate Bush's task of establishing his center, and would link MIT's foray into information machines with the world of secrecy.

A project that had the potential to define the role of the academic scientist in the development and evaluation of military technology turned into an exercise in bureaucratic bickering. More than half a decade was spent dealing with organizational problems rather than with those that were holding back the realization of the potentials of electronic technology. Despite all the efforts of Stanford C. Hooper, Joseph Wenger, and Vannevar Bush, the United States lost an opportunity to complete the first electronic data processing machines and to make them operational before the attack on Pearl Harbor.

Chapter III
A Man for Technology and the Navy

Stanford C. Hooper prided himself on being an innovator and he devoted his career to introducing new technology to a usually reluctant United States Navy. Graduating from Annapolis in the early 1900s and assigned to the Pacific fleet, he immediately began to create the navy's first radio system. Transferred to Washington, he stole hours to study at Samuel W. Stratton's new National Bureau of Standards. Mastering the latest radio science, Hooper then lobbied for the establishment of the navy's own radio research division.

Hooper's knowledge and advocacy of electronic communications soon thrust him into military and civilian policy making. Although still a young man and a junior officer, he was instrumental in creating the Radio Corporation of America, the giant electronics corporation formed at government request at the close of World War I. Begun as an exception to America's anti-trust laws, and with control over all the major electronic patents of the era, RCA merged the old American radio companies and what was left of the German and British holdings. Hooper hoped that it would use its special advantages for a mission greater than profit; he hoped that it would make the United States a world leader in electronics and provide the military with the technological advances necessary for the maintenance of American sea power. Very early in his career, Hooper realized that the new command and control potentials of radio could turn the American navy into an international force, but during World War I he had seen the dire consequences of not attending to the latest technological advances.

Because of its need for world-wide command and control, the navy had a special stake in the success of RCA. RCA inherited a net of radio stations the navy found invaluable, and, as or more important, the Corporation seemed large enough to finance research, something a budget starved post World War I navy found very difficult.[1] Hooper also hoped that RCA's special position would make it confident enough to overcome the fear that government work would threaten its patents. Such anxieties made large corporations reluctant to help the military.[2] The hopes of RCA serving as a research branch of the navy were not completely fulfilled, but Hooper continued to use its men and facilities while he searched for help from others.

Hooper's contributions to the navy's modernization and his administrative skills soon led to his appointment to a series of civilian and military commissions concerned with communications. Although he remained an active naval officer, he was so well regarded as a scientist and an administrator that he became a presidential advisor on radio policy. As well, the United States government relied upon him for representation abroad and his frequent trips to Europe for radio conferences kept him aware of both technological advances and foreign intentions. Hooper always tried to turn such civilian work and contacts to the navy's benefit. By the early 1930s, Hooper was advancing through the navy's ranks, was a much honored figure in electronics and an acquaintance, if not friend, of the leading scientists and inventors of the nation. He became a member of the close-knit alumni association for those who had tried to apply science to the U-boat problem of World War I. He used such contacts and his expertise to devise and forward plans for a fully integrated and modern information system for the navy, one which was to include every advanced technology. He had an even greater vision, to permanently wed science and the navy.[3]

Although he could have become a successful business executive or bureaucrat, Hooper remained a navy man and throughout the interwar years fought to join science, technology and the military. To achieve that goal he had to make sure that the navy's bureaucratic structure did not insulate the service from innovations arising in the private sector. He was determined to prevent the navy from being as unprepared as it was for World War I. As a result, he became allied with other officers who fought for professional control of naval policies and operations. Hooper became tied to those in favor of centralized administration and increased power for the Chief of Naval Operations. Structure was only a means for Hooper, however.

Hooper's World War I experiences reinforced his belief that technology had become essential to military power but he knew that America's retreat from international involvements after the war meant that little research could be done within the armed forces. He had also come to believe that the era of the lone inventor had passed. Technology had grown so complex that it was foolish to base America's defensive capabilities on unknown geniuses who might suddenly provide needed technological miracles. Hooper's struggles over radio development and the tussles with RCA also taught him that few opportunities existed to create private companies that were willing or able to devote themselves to long-term military needs. The services could find and support only a few Elmer Sperrys and Hannibal Fords.[4]

Putting those pieces together with what he correctly predicted would be very slim naval budgets in the 1920s and 1930s, Hooper began to develop a strategy, one somewhat different from the plans of other of the navy's new Progressive reformers. He thought it was imperative that the navy establish permanent relationships with private institutions that could, in a sense, subsidize military readiness. He was willing to depend on outsiders. Although he helped give birth to the Naval Research Laboratory and was able to create special research sections, such as the Code and Signal desk in the Bureau of Engineering, he believed the navy would have to rely on the new research centers that were emerging in the largest corporations and universities.

There were several reasons for his disenchantment with in-house research and his turn toward civilians. Time after time he had found himself at odds with the navy's scientists, including those at the Naval Research Laboratory and the Bureau of Engineering. He became skeptical of their ability to manage research or to encourage industrial cooperation.[5] In addition, unlike other naval officers, his World War I experience with outsiders had been cordial and rewarding and he continued to have faith in such elite organizations as the National Academy of Sciences and the National Research Council. He was willing to associate with the abstract, impractical and, at times, condescending new scientists and corporate leaders. In fact, he counted many of them as friends.[6]

A Little Military Meets Little Science

Ending his stay as head of the Bureau of Engineering's radio section, where he fought for a radio modernization program, Hooper moved from technical to more general policy concerns. His appointment as Director of Naval Communications in 1928 gave him an opportunity to aggressively pursue his vision. And, when he assumed the newly created position of special scientific advisor for the navy in the mid-1930s and chaired its Technical Research Liaison Committee, he had the chance to expand his reach well beyond the traditional boundaries of communications. All science related fields, ranging from ballistics through medicine and atomic energy, became part of his domain.[7]

He and his most trusted proteges toured the nation seeking ideas and establishing contacts with scientists. The brightest names in corporate and academic research were visited. Jewett, Maxim, and Bowman were just a few who became even closer to Hooper during the early 1930s. As part of his plan, he laid the bases for permanent cooperation with laboratories and executives at Eastman, AT&T, General Electric, and a host of other corporations. To create a similar link with the universities, he found a way to award special military commissions to academics so they could remain in the universities yet be a part of the navy's modernization effort.[8] In addition, he collaborated with the National Research Council; aiding it by finding projects and having it help the navy by identifying qualified investigators.

Hooper's attempt to cement relations with one of the leading private foundations was less successful. When he visited the offices of Warren Weaver, then head of the natural science division of the important Rockefeller Foundation, a rather embarrassing scene developed. Weaver had not checked into Hooper's background and did not know of his ties to men like Vannevar Bush. During the interview, he hastily concluded that Hooper and his ideas were foolish and treated Hooper rather badly. Weaver left some comments about the meeting in his diary that he must have kept closely guarded once he learned of Hooper's connections.[9]

Hooper Confronts the Bureaucracy

Despite such incidents Hooper continued his search for able men. But the identification of willing scientists and new technologies were only parts of his task. A crucial and politically sensitive step was to convince the various divisions of the navy to accept the civilian men and ideas. The way Hooper handled that had a great deal of influence on the long-term history of the automation of American cryptanalysis and wedded the history of such machines as Bush's Comparator and Selector to the broader struggle for professional control within the navy.

Hooper pushed, sometimes too hard, to bring innovations to the bureaucracies. His admiration for the country's top men led him to attempt to force ideas upon unwilling navy bureaucrats and skeptical technicians. And, because he saw science as relevant to every aspect of military life, he thought he had the right to advise all the departments of the navy.[10] As a result, he alienated many powerful men; partially accounting for how long he waited to become a Rear Admiral and helping to explain the resistance to his plans for cryptanalytic machines. By 1937, serious complaints reached the naval hierarchy about what was seen as interference in the affairs of the various bureaus. Hooper had to defend himself to the Chief of Naval Operations:

> The Chiefs of Bureaus seem to feel that this desk is endeavoring to invade on their cognizance. That has been exactly what I have tried not to do...
> All I have tried to do is learn, and pass to the Bureaus and Officers of operations what I learned. I have had to have a list of the problems, and to become somewhat familiar with them, in order to provide me with the background so that when I visited Industrial concerns and Universities I would be able to intelligently ask questions. Also, I have to visit those concerns in order to get the background needed.
>
> The National Research Council recommended we embark on this task, and the Bureaus recommended that it be done. I get no help from most of the Bureaus unless I drag it out of them, and I feel this is due to the apprehension of Chiefs of Bureaus about cognizance. Most of the desk officers and members of the Research Committee are cooperative, but hardly any one outside of Operations initiates any effort to get any help from me.[11]

After the confrontations and the complaints to the CNO, Hooper softened his approach, but he continued to advocate the types of technological innovations that did not fit with the service's existing bureaucratic structure. He went ahead with his effort to modernize and professionalize the navy but the political battles of 1936 and 1937 took their toll on him.

His appointment as the coordinator of radio research for the navy in the late 1930s plunged him into such critical scientific affairs as radar, advanced radio scanning and sonar. The new office had less scope and power than the earlier scientific advisory position but he continued to fight for his policies and he formalized his plan for a truly effective and integrated communications system. Even when ill health and perhaps some political complications arising from his worries about America's military readiness[12] led to a reduction of his efforts in the 1940s, he remained an important advisor on technical and scientific matters and a member of such high science and big budget organizations as the National Advisory Committee for Aeronautics. And, he had a number of admiring young officers to carry on his work. By the time he formally retired in 1943 he had, along with a few other senior officers, laid the intellectual if not organizational foundations for the Office of Naval Research. The ONR became the organization the navy successfully used to bring academic science into the military after World War II. The ONR became one of the major sponsors of applied mathematics and computers in the United States.[13]

Hooper's influence did not end in 1943. Although retired, he continued as a consultant to major corporations and became deeply involved with a company founded by some of his admiring young men. The fascinating postwar Engineering Research Associates was planned as a showcase for some of Hooper's dreams. It was to be what RCA never became. Staffed by the very brightest and best from the navy and the scientific community, it was to be a private company serving the advanced scientific needs of the military. As we will see, ERA's history brings together the postwar lives of the secrecy and information machines because it became the torchbearer of the navy's advanced cryptanalytic computers and the most famous of the automatic machines for the library, Bush's and Ralph Shaw's Rapid Selector.

Another Plan for Science and the Navy

Hooper was unable to create an ERA in the 1930s, but he continued his struggle to link the corporations and the universities to the navy. However, Hooper's model for research, which centered about cooperation with the private sector, was not the only one put forward by navy reformers. During the 1930s, one of the navy's Progressives who played an important role in the history of the Selector, the Comparator and the organization of military research in the postwar era was much less trusting of outsiders. Harold Bowen, one of the fathers of the Office of Naval Research, put his energies to strengthening the navy's own science and development capabilities.

Harold G. Bowen was a career engineering officer who had, like Hooper, taken up the cause of modernizing the navy. Keeping in touch with the latest technical advances through contacts with industry and academia, including taking post graduate courses at MIT, he made high temperature steam power his cause. Throughout the 1920s and 1930s, he fought an uphill battle against the Bureaus and their contractors. That fight intensified and became political during his tenure as the Chief of the Bureau of Engineering from mid-1935 to 1939.[14] While Chief, he came in conflict with the Bureau of Construction and its allies the private shipbuilders over the design of the navy's new destroyers. Bowen was the political loser and he remained convinced that the Secretary of the Navy's order to merge Engineering and Construction into one new agency, the Bureau of Ships, was a victory for the technical and political "mossbacks."[15]

Like Hooper, Bowen made many enemies because of his fight to keep the navy up-to-date by bringing in new ideas from industry and academia. But Bowen had a somewhat different picture of how research should be conducted and was less willing than Hooper to share power with civilians. He wanted more research within the navy and had faith in a revitalized Naval Research Laboratory. He even supported the NRL work on atomic power in the 1930s. And, he wanted central control over any outside research. One of his last acts as Chief of the Bureau of Engineering was to create its Office of Research and Inventions. It would later play a significant role in the history of Bush's Comparator and Selector. Staffed by the experienced Lybrand Smith and some very enthusiastic young officers, the ORI began to do what Hooper had been advocating for years: integrate Engineering with the most talented men in private industrial research laboratories and universities. The Office of Research and Inventions became the navy's organization to coordinate with Bush's NDRC. That led Lybrand Smith and Vannevar Bush to become quite close despite the growing frictions between Bush and Bowen over research policies. Smith also became an important player in the history of the Comparator.

By the end of World War II, Smith and Bowen had convinced the navy to create something Hooper had always wanted, the Office of Naval Research. But Bowen's version had significant variations that did not match the plans of either Hooper or Bush. Bowen made sure the ONR had the money, power, and contracting laws to control the relationships it established. The ONR would use academia and industry to bring science to the navy, but it was given enough power to allow the navy, not civilians, to direct research. Bowen hoped that it also had enough power to withstand the protests of the old bureaucrats and politicians.[16]

Bush Loses a Friend

Bowen had always been more fearful of civilian power over the navy than Hooper and that fear increased after what, in effect, was his dismissal from Engineering in 1939. As in the case of Hooper, his politics led him to be pushed to the periphery as war approached. He was made a technical aide to the Secretary of the Navy, probably being warned about Hooper's past political mistakes. Then, when the Naval Research Laboratory was taken from Engineering and put directly under the Secretary of the Navy, Bowen was made its head. But that was not a powerful position. The NRL's budgets remained low, partly because of the policies of Bush and his NDRC.

Bowen, once an ally, became alienated from Vannevar Bush when the NDRC started to take the development of significant technologies away from the Laboratory. Despite its early work, leading to fundamental breakthroughs in several scientific-military fields, Bush felt no obligation to the NRL and wished to create independent, civilian controlled agencies to exploit the discoveries. Especially galling to Bowen was Bush's claim on radar and atomic energy. Although Bowen was the navy's representative on the NDRC's board, he was unable to block Bush's ambitions. When Bush did his best to exclude the navy from what became the Manhattan Project, Bowen must have begun to think of ways, such as the ONR, to bring control back to the navy. One of Bowen's motives for establishing the ONR was to allow the navy to develop its own program for atomic energy which, he hoped, would lead to an atomic powered ship program.

Hooper Confronts the Bureaucracy, Again

While Bowen was trying to convince the navy to adopt his ideas for steam propulsion during the 1920s and early 1930s, Hooper was concentrating on radio development. Hooper viewed science, research and innovation as significant to every naval activity but he maintained a special interest and role in naval communications. He was instrumental in the establishment of a radio division within the Bureau of Engineering shortly after World War I and, although he was not a codebreaker, his plans for advancing radio communications led him to become involved with the navy's cryptanalytic branch, OP-20-G.

The relationship was a natural one because the advent of military radio and modern command and control meant that an enemy's most valuable messages could be intercepted in a new way. No longer did men have to be captured or headquarters raided. The radios of all nations could pick up the signals of all others if the right equipment was available. Knowing this, every nation began to use more and more sophisticated codes and ciphers to protect their increasing volumes of radio traffic.[17] This, of course, called for the development of counter measures and Hooper became a crusader for the expansion and modernization of American interception, codebreaking and all other signals intelligence capabilities. It was that involvement that eventually led Hooper to MIT in late 1935.

Hooper was one of the few men who did not undervalue radio intelligence and as early as World War I he began thinking of ways to improve it. As with his electronics work, Hooper's plans for cryptanalysis came to center around institutionalized scientific research. At the same time, he supported the expansion of the navy's cryptanalytic operating division, OP-20-G. But whether the goal was initiating research or hiring more codebreakers, Hooper faced decades of frustration. Perhaps the major hurdle for all his plans was the nature of the navy's bureaucracy. To understand why Hooper and Bowen fought so long for an organization such as the ONR, and why Bush's Comparator project had such a bizarre history, calls for a look at the bureaucratic structure in which Naval Communications and OP-20-G were embedded.

For historical reasons, Communications (OP-20) rather than the Office of Naval Intelligence, housed the super secret cryptologic department that became known as OP-20-G.[18] And for other bewildering reasons, OP-20-G depended upon the Bureau of Engineering for the design, purchasing and manufacturing of its equipment. Another naval branch handled contractual details. To further complicate the bureaucratic tangle, OP-20-G's Research Section (Y) was the small group charged with communications security, and, significantly, the exploitation of the lack of security of the communications of other nations. On top of that, and despite OP-20-G-Y's mandate, yet another research group was set up within Engineering to explore related technological questions. Adding to the confusion over power and domain was the Naval Research Laboratory.

All this led to inefficiency and the inability to develop a truly self-directed signals intelligence capability.[19] Of special importance to the history of the Comparator and Selector, was the Bureau of Engineering. It was a bureaucratic maze caught in a larger tangle. In addition to the organizational clutter were political factors that put debilitating cross pressures on all decision makers.

The navy's bureaucratic structure had grown layer upon uncoordinated layer since the Civil War. Engineering had turf battles with the Bureau of Construction and both constantly fought with a separate organization that drew up contracts and kept an auditor's eye on manufacturers. In addition, all the bureaus worked under an onerous contracting system that had not been overhauled since 1861. Detailed specifications had to be drawn, advertisements placed for bids, then bids evaluated, then the apparent low-cost alternative selected. An oppressive overlay of Congressional regulations was built up over the years making the entire process beyond cumbersome for anything but the procurement of standard items. The system precluded contracting for research, development, or secret projects and only an oversight in Congress during World War I had allowed the navy's Progressive's to introduce vital technologies during the war. That loophole was soon closed and it was not until a few months before Pearl Harbor that the constant protests led to liberalized contracting laws which better fit the needs of research and development.[20]

The Bureau of Engineering was also under extreme political pressure during the 1930s. Like all the other bureaus, it was a political creature as dependent on the White House and the Secretary of the Navy as on the Chief of Naval Operations. Although naval officers, the Bureau Chiefs were politically appointed, something which became more and more irritating to the naval professionals as they prepared for World War II. Worse, Engineering had to contend with Congressional demands, such as those forcing the contracting system to serve as a means of maintaining particular local economies. Because of their tendency to become the servants of outside interests, the Bureaus were a thorn in the side of the office of the Chief of Naval Operations, especially in 1930s when the drive for professionalism and centralization came up against determined efforts to maintain the independence of the Bureaus.[21] Battles were fought on almost every issue including, sadly, who was to approve, conduct and integrate research. The fights were more than irritating power struggles; they had significance for budget allocations for important institutions such as the Naval Research Laboratory and programs like the navy's exploration of atomic power. Most importantly, the byzantine inner workings of the Bureaus seemed ill suited to encouraging rapid technological innovation.

OP-20-G and Communications did not escape the bureaucratic troubles. In addition to being dependent on the bureaus they had their own organizational problems and some bewildering divisions of responsibility. Although their core functions were under the direct command of the CNO in the critical years of the 1930s, communications and cryptanalysis had a tough go of it in the navy.

A Few Men and Women for Secrecy

The navy's very small cryptologic group, OP-20-G, began its life during World War I but was not active until the mid-1920s.[22] One reason for its inaction was that just as it was founded the incredible Herbert Yardley was lobbying for the creation of what became the famous American Black Chamber. His group was to serve the cryptanalytic needs of the army and the State Department. Stealing resources away from the private cryptanalytic group that had been developing at the estate of the flamboyant millionaire, Colonel Fabyan, Yardley achieved some amazing victories. He broke the codes and ciphers of the major powers which allowed the United States to predict the bargaining positions of the important players in the naval arms limitation negotiations of the 1920s. Yardley's work made him some good friends but also some enemies. A few rash decisions on his part also led to the closing of his Chamber in 1929 and the transfer of its files to the army's old code organization under William Friedman. Yardley then decided to take one of the most fateful steps in the history of American cryptanalysis. He published a book that told the when, what, and why of American cryptanalytic success. One horrible consequence was that the Japanese began to change all their code and cipher systems. That made the task of the navy's OP-20-G much, much more difficult.[23]

OP-20-G remained small but it had managed to survive the attempts by men like Secretary of State Stimson to dismantle all of the nation's unsavory and ungentlemanly spying bureaus. But OP-20-G did not receive much official navy support. Until the mid-1920s, when it came under the command of a young and bright officer, Laurance F. Safford, it was almost a shadow organization. Safford arrived just in time to take advantage of the "acquisition" of a copy of part of Japan's secret naval code. The code proved invaluable and OP-20-G began providing critical information to the navy. But that did not mean recognition or adequate funding. OP-20-G limped along on thin budgets, at times saved only by a super secret fund set up at the end of World War I. The situation was so bad that several times in the 1920s and 1930s, the charity of the Bureau of Engineering had to be called upon for OP-20-G's survival.[24]

OP-20-G's relationships with other groups in the navy were not always harmonious. Its interactions with the Office of Naval Intelligence were, at times, ones of strain as well as frustrating dependency. ONI did much of the needed dirty work to obtain code books and information about cipher machines and it had the responsibility for interpreting the intentions of America's enemies. But, the ONI and OP-20-G were bureaucratically separate and at key times there was mistrust. For example, in the early 1930s, the Chief of Naval Operations ordered OP-20-G to prevent ONI from learning that Japan's new code had been penetrated.[25]

Despite severe handicaps, the tiny and largely self-taught OP-20-G research group broke into the codes of many countries.[26] Its most famous achievement was the reading of the highest level systems of the Japanese navy. At first, that cryptanalytic job was relatively simple. Safford's team was provided with a copy of the code book in the early 1920s, probably by Naval Intelligence.[27] Although they had to solve the encipherments of the code words and translate the some one hundred thousand entries in what was called the Red Book, the cryptanalysts found it not too difficult to tap Japan's most important messages. But other codes and ciphers were much more frustrating and the team knew that all the major powers were moving to the use of sophisticated mechanical systems.[28] Stanford Hooper especially feared the new enciphering machines. Hooper realized radio intelligence and cryptanalysis faced technical challenges. In 1928, immediately after he became the head of Naval Communications, he expanded the network of intercept stations used to pick up enemy broadcasts and he helped set up the on-the-roof gang, an ever expanding group of noncommissioned navy men who staffed the new stations. And, he fought for new technologies. He incessantly lobbied for the best direction finding equipment; he helped OP-20-G obtain the funds for special Japanese language typewriters; and, he explored sophisticated new systems to identify individual transmitters. Then, he began to search for ways to apply science and technology to OP-20-G's most challenging work, decoding and decryption.

The Search for Pure Cryptanalysis

Through his academic and corporate contacts Hooper learned of the potentials of mechanized automatic control and of the increasingly mathematical nature of science and cryptanalysis. His awareness of the expanding reach of statistical techniques, the potentials of high-speed calculators and the use of light-sensitive devices in astronomy were perhaps sharpened by visits and discussions with Vannevar Bush.[29] Whatever the particular source of his knowledge, Hooper believed that the new electric and mechanical ciphering devices introduced by the major powers, including the United States, would force cryptanalysts to become statisticians. They would have to perform seemingly impossible feats of calculation to penetrate the ciphers produced by such complex machines as the Kryha and the Enigma.[30] Hooper and OP-20-G predicted that Japan, America's number one threat, would soon turn to such devices. By early 1930 that prediction was fulfilled when Japan introduced its Red machine on its diplomatic networks and soon followed that with a version for higher level naval use. Some worried that the Japanese Navy would begin to use such machines for much more than attache traffic, perhaps for all of its operational systems.[31]

As soon as he assumed command over Communications, OP-20-G informed Hooper of its progress against the cipher machines. The cryptanalysts showed him their paper and pencil methods and perhaps told him of some of the tricks they used to break into the various systems. The cryptanalysts were quite proud of their secret and clever techniques, ones they thought were essential because of the impracticality of a pure mathematical approach.[32] Although they employed statistical techniques, they had effective short cuts such as finding a copy of a secret message sent in a known code; locating often repeated phrases (cribs); or, uncovering the pattern of the way an enemy announced the wheel settings for a cipher machine network. They were also quite proud of their craftsmen's tools for attacking ciphers such as paper wheels, long strips of wood with alphabets painted on them and overlay sheets with punched holes.

But Hooper and his new right-hand man, Joseph Wenger, were not impressed by the tricks and they thought that OP-20-G's technology, if not methods, were woefully behind the times. In late 1930, Hooper, worried about the increasing use of cipher devices, suggested to OP-20-G and the Bureau of Engineering that they begin to develop automated cryptanalytic machines and, by implication, to formalize their approach to analysis.[33]

Hooper wanted machines that would free OP-20-G from tricks and dependencies and that would allow the use of advanced mathematics. Those machines would have to be very innovative because the new cipher devices presented cryptanalysts with problems far different from those of code systems. Codes were secret lists of words (or combinations of numbers) that stood for other words. In contrast, cipher machines dynamically changed letters into different ones with no predictable relationship between the original and the cipher letters. The goal of the creators of the new cipher machines was to create a purely random relationship between a letter that was entered and the one that exited the machine.

Code systems, however, had underlying meaningful relationships and each system had a limited number of code word substitutions for any natural language word. The limited vocabulary of a code meant that acquiring a copy of a codebook was an effective solution, unlike the situation with sophisticated cipher machines in which having a copy of the enemy's machine was only a small step toward reading messages. A limited vocabulary and the nonrandom relationship between code words and meaning also dictated what techniques could be used against code systems. The key method an analyst used to solve a code was to identify the relationships between a particular code word and other words. Correlation analysis and the use of a decoded word to predict the meaning of another were viable methods. The new cipher systems demanded less obvious approaches. The cipher system designers' goal during the 1920s and 1930s was to avoid the meaning embedded in any code system. The American Hebern cipher machine and its European cousins, such as Enigma, took the old principle of random substitution of one letter for another to a new level. They went far beyond the centuries old cipher tables and handy substitution algorithms.

All of the new machines relied upon sets of wired rotors (or relay analogs of them) whose internal electrical connections produced a unique substitution cycle of such complexity and length that it could be penetrated only through time consuming analysis of forbidding amounts of data. Unless the operators of the encryption machines made a mistake, or the cipher breakers had a constant source of information on the settings of the cipher wheels, incredible amounts of calculation were needed for pure cryptanalysis. Germany's very adept cryptanalysts and mathematicians had determined that its enemies would need so much time to apply statistical analyses that any penetrations of the German Enigma messages would provide only outdated information. Their own pure analysis had led them to believe they had built a system so secure that even the capture of their cipher wheels would not endanger their communications. On the other hand, Hooper was sure that the growing use of the new cipher machines and the shortage of experienced cryptanalysts meant an end to the power of informal methods. He saw no alternative but to develop formal techniques and advanced machines.

More than an abstract faith in scientific cryptanalysis led to Hooper's drive for new machines. There were very practical reasons. "G" had to be made independent and ready for an emergency. Older methods, for either codes or ciphers, demanded too many experienced codebreakers who had spent years working on particular systems and on information supplied to OP-20-G by others such as Naval Intelligence. But, in 1930, the navy had only one skilled professional cryptanalyst.[34] And, even if new formal methods were developed, Hooper knew that few trained mathematical cryptanalysts would be available. OP-20-G could not even expect to have enough people ready to compile, let alone apply, the required statistics by old methods.[35]

Automation and formal procedures would have to substitute for professional skill and experience as well as the old codebreaker's standby, intuition.

But, in 1930, the navy's bureaucracy and even the crew at OP-20-G were less than accepting of formal analysis and machinery. They may have thought that Hooper, who had no practical cryptanalytic experience, was quite naive.[36] The codebreakers at OP-20-G were aware of the emergence of the new ciphering devices and, in fact, were building their own versions as well as tackling the systems of other nations. They had been intimately involved with the flamboyant inventor, Edward H. Hebern of California. His development of a series of increasingly complex enciphering machines received encouragement and financial help from the American navy. OP-20-G had investigated all aspects of the Californian's pathbreaking machines and its leading civilian cryptanalyst had spent a year working for him before his company went bankrupt.[37] That, and experience with earlier cipher systems, gave OP-20-G a cipher breaking capability, one that did not call for the use of automatic machines. OP-20-G had invented methods, ones admittedly labor intensive and dependent upon operator's mistakes, for cracking the Hebern and similar devices.[38] When exploring the first cipher machines, OP-20-G's group may have come to the conclusion that pure cryptanalysis was a great dream that was impossible to put into practice.

Because of their direct experience with automatic enciphering devices, Hooper's September 1930 "suggestion" about methods and automation was not too well received. OP-20-G's principal civilian cryptanalyst, Agnes Meyer Driscoll, who had worked with Hebern, did not like the idea at all. Additionally, the cryptanalysts felt insulted because Hooper's request contained an implicit criticism of their work and skills. They thought that formal methods, while helpful, would never replace an experienced codebreaker. And their years of work had taught them that decryption was usually dependent upon some type of informal initial entry into a system, whether it be a psychological insight, a theft of materials, or the transmission of a message in both clear and enciphered form.[39]

In addition to the codebreakers' distrust of those who proposed unrealistic methods and machines, the small OP-20-G staff was too busy analyzing Japanese code systems to deal with methodological speculations.[40] More importantly, they were in the midst of handling the torrent of communications coming from the great Japanese fleet maneuvers. They had to provide the navy with the information that was so vital to understanding Japan's already ominous intentions. And, the type of machines Hooper hinted at seemed to be of little use against codes, the form then used for almost all Japanese naval messages.[41] The result was a polite but noncommittal reply that put off any action on Hooper's request.

Despite the rejection, Hooper decided to make another try. Although he may have wanted to place cryptologic machine development within OP-20-G, the less than enthusiastic response from its staff forced him to another tack. He thought he would eventually tempt OP-20-G into applying formal methods by presenting it with a demonstration device. Hooper soon arranged to have the Bureau of Engineering create a new section for advanced code and signal research[42] and then made sure that someone who would pursue his goals filled the post. A young officer who had been one of the first students in OP-20-G, who had experience as a sea-going communications officer and who was already a protege of Hooper, was selected. Joseph Wenger, a thirty year old Annapolis graduate, followed Hooper's cues and began a search for new technologies for all aspects of communications with, of course, an eye open for new devices for ciphering and deciphering messages. With some interruptions caused by shifting naval assignments, Wenger continued that search through the 1930s and 1940s and became the driving force behind what became the most technically advanced cryptanalytic agency in the world by the late 1940s.[43]

From Electronics to Electromechanics

In the early 1930s, although Hooper and Wenger knew of the electromechanical tabulating machines built by companies such as IBM and Powers, Hooper's academic contacts turned him towards something much more innovative. Scientific friends, including the fast rising Vannevar Bush, had told him about some of the potentials of the new and very esoteric optical-electronic calculation. Its emerging use in scientific research in astronomy and physics hinted at its value in cryptanalysis. Wenger followed-up those hints and spent some time studying the subject. Supported by Wenger's findings, Hooper felt secure enough to successfully prod the Chief of Naval Operations into sending a very specific and strong directive to the Bureau of Engineering in late 1931.[44] It ordered the Bureau to devote resources to study the new optical sorters and special devices for blind reading and came close to demanding that such technologies be used to build a deciphering device.[45] Hooper and Wenger may not have realized how great a technological adventure they were urging the Bureau to begin.

The CNO's mandate included more than cryptanalytic investigations, it was a signal to Hooper to intensify his efforts to link science to the navy. Under pressure from Hooper, the Bureau provided Wenger with the money needed to make a grand tour of America's research laboratories. From late 1931 to well into 1932 Wenger visited major corporations and universities seeking ideas and allies. Hooper's connections helped the young man gain access to the great men of American science and industry, such as Alexanderson of General Electric, and to hear the ideas of the less famous but still important. Hooper's old friend, Walter S. Lemmon, for example, was intent upon developing the radio-telegraph for communications and cryptology and became a significant resource for the navy.[46] During his visits, Wenger encountered some fantastic new technologies that had at least long-term promise for solving the difficult cryptanalytic problems. But most, such as the use of photoelectricity for sorting machines, and the new automatic radio spectrum scanning devices, seemed to demand a protracted and expensive development period.[47] Wenger was especially disappointed when he realized that optics and electronics were not quite ready to produce a cryptanalytic machine. If such a machine was to be built, the navy would have to invest in a lengthy development program.

Perhaps because of that and because of a sudden realization by OP-20-G that it would need some type of mechanical aids, Wenger turned his attention to a more established technology. The Hollerith and Powers electromechanical tabulating and sorting machines were evolving into quite sophisticated devices by the late 1920s. In addition, they were machines that were immediately available for use. Unlike the optical devices that might have to be designed, tested and built by the navy, they were commercially produced. Wenger examined the Remington-Powers and IBM tabulators and did enough research to allow Hooper to again, but more authoritatively, suggest that OP-20-G investigate them. It was difficult for the officer in charge of OP-20-G, Laurance Safford, to ignore Hooper's urging any longer.[48] But, Hooper's grand dream suffered a temporary yet important setback.

Just as Wenger was exploring the various technical possibilities, it was discovered that the Japanese had replaced their Red Code with a completely revised set that could not be penetrated. Perhaps because of Yardley's indiscretions, seven years of work on the previous code had become valueless! OP-20-G's codebreakers knew they would be unlikely to obtain a copy of the Blue and the three other new systems[49] and decided to take on the formidable task of breaking the code through pure methods. Safford discouraged the idea of stealing a copy of the new code because he wished to build OP-20-G's independent capabilities before the outbreak of the anticipated war with Japan. Safford's decision was a momentous and demanding one. The Japanese continued to use the old type of superencipherment system, the modular addition of random numbers to the code groups, so it was a relatively easy target. But the code itself, he knew, would demand years of work. Over one hundred thousand words had to be decoded. Such an effort called for either vastly increased manpower or mechanical aides.[50] Everyone knew that "G" was unlikely to be allocated more men.

People were too expensive, so, in early 1932, OP-20-G's cryptanalysts studied Wenger's tabulator survey and decided to select the type centered upon electrical rather than mechanical reading of cards. Seeing Remington-Rand's system as inflexible, they hurried to rent the electromechanical IBM tabulating devices. Projecting a five thousand dollar a year expenditure when all the desired equipment was in place, they negotiated with the company and were promised the very first of IBM's newest machines, ones built to handle alphabetic characters as well as numbers. The punch card era seemed to have begun at OP-20-G.

Then, one of the many institutional problems that would plague the history of the attempt to automate American cryptanalysis dampened all hopes. Someone, perhaps Hooper, had been a bit naive. He had placed too much faith in the bureaucracy. The navy hierarchy declared that it was unwilling to fund the experiment! Despite the argument that for what was the salary of two low level cryptanalysts, the navy would get the equivalent of the work of a dozen clerks, Safford's machine request was denied. The five thousand dollars was impossible to raise; certainly, OP-20-G could not squeeze enough from its own stingy allotments.

Safford and Wenger did not give up. But, in continuing their crusade to fund the IBM machines, they led OP-20-G into some political as well as financial tangles. The search for financing may also have been the beginning of serious bureaucratic frictions. OP-20-G pressured the Bureau of Engineering to scrape some funds from its already slim budget,[51] but the Bureau was able to raise only a few hundred dollars, not several thousand, to start the project. It continued to piece together small amounts during the 1930s to support the tabulators. But it always felt that OP-20-G did not fully appreciate its efforts.[52]

Not Quite Hooper's Dream

The first blushes of technical advance at OP-20-G began in chaos and as something of a whimper. Only a machine or two arrived at the OP-20-G rooms in the old building on Washington's mall. And their experimental use, which soon turned into a necessity in the eyes of many at OP-20-G, survived only as a near underground activity. Several times during the 1930s OP-20-G almost had to relinquish its tabulating machines because of the lack of a few hundred dollars. It even prepared for the embarrassment of taking its secret work to the IBM factory in Georgetown, D.C. to be processed on machines rented by the hour.[53]

Despite the hand-to-mouth funding of its few machines, the OP-20-G tabulator crew continued with its work and made major contributions to the penetration of the new Japanese codes. In doing so the navy men developed methods similar to those used by the library reformers of the 1950s.[54] To correlate code words, sorting routines and display formats that predated the much vaunted KWIC indexing were devised. As time progressed, the navy added devices to the tabulators that anticipated the Documentalists' use of machines that could sort on many data columns simultaneously. The navy also explored new ways to store data on IBM cards and during the war it helped develop special tabulating machines whose descriptions fit those of the devices made famous by a later major figure in mechanized information retrieval, H. P. Luhn.[55]

Ironically, OP-20-G's early 1930s tabulator related achievements had a negative influence. Although the search for cryptanalytic technology and methods had been motivated by Hooper's deep fears concerning the new automatic ciphering machines, including Britain's,[56] the crisis caused by the change in Japan's older code system shifted attention to more immediate problems and forced a commitment to available devices. The more sophisticated machine options were dropped in favor of the tabulators. The tabulators were well suited to many decoding procedures, especially those calling for sorting and, later, collating operations, but they were not the mathematical or truly high-speed statistical devices needed to break into the new cipher machines. Despite the development of special attachments, such as those that would emerge from the IBM sponsored scientific center at Columbia University, tabulators were not built for rapid mathematical chores.[57]

Furthermore, the relatively sudden commitment to the off-the-shelf tabulating technology was made without the type of understanding that Hooper wanted from industry. He desired agreements made at the highest levels in business and government that benefitted the navy by bending corporate research policies to military needs. The leasing of a few tabulators did not link IBM to any long-term commitments to OP-20-G or Engineering. Although IBM played a significant role in certain extensions of electromechanical technology before and during World War II, it did little truly far ranging research for the cryptanalysts during the 1930s. The company may not even have felt obligated to supply the navy with copies of devices it created for scientific researchers. For example, there is no indication that IBM hurried to provide OP-20-G with special machines such as the difference tabulator created for the Columbia University group in 1929 or the sequence-program device the company developed for them in the 1930s. There is also no indication that IBM let OP-20-G know of its many 1930s optical-electronic related patents and experiments.[58]

Not Too Much of a Backwards Step

Despite the abandonment of Hooper's optical-electronic dreams, the use of tabulators was a great step in the history of cryptanalysis. OP-20-G was one of the first codebreaking agencies in the world to employ tabulating equipment and the IBM machines did prove to be very productive.[59] But the commitment to tabulators took away much of the incentive to make the great technological leap Hooper had desired. The very hard-pressed staff at OP-20-G had more than enough to do to learn how to exploit the IBM equipment. As important, the regulars at the Bureau of Engineering thought such devices used the most advanced yet practical hardware and that technological limits had been reached.

Then, when older cryptanalytic methods triumphed over Japan's new cipher machine, the Red, there was little excuse for an emergency development program. The analysis of Red was so complete that the young naval officer in charge of OP-20-G during Safford's absence, Jack Holtwick, was able to create an inexpensive analog copy of it. The

Bureau's technicians who turned Holtwick's ideas into hardware were quite proud and thought they had carved out a very special role for themselves in all future developments.[60] They became familiar with relay and electromechanical technology and they became experts in electromechanical construction when they helped OP-20-G build the navy's enciphering devices and the analogs of Japan's automatic enciphering machines. But the Bureau did not have the time, the inclination or the manpower to go beyond immediately feasible technologies.[61] The success against Red undermined arguments that an advanced in-house developmental group should be established within the Bureau.

A Young Man for the Future

Something else helped to turn the navy away from Hooper's plans for truly advanced automated cryptanalysis. Joseph Wenger, who was Hooper's man in the Bureau of Engineering, and who had become an ardent believer in the value of science and technology, was returned to sea duty in mid-1932. Traditions demanded rotation of posts and assignments and all young officers who had any desire for promotion had to obey what many called the "Manchu" regulations. Although Wenger used the new assignment to visit the major European nations to survey cryptological developments (for example, he visited the Enigma factory in Germany) and then became the communications officer for the Asiatic fleet,[62] Hooper lost an advocate and a coordinator for several critical years.

Although he was not a leading cryptanalyst, Joseph Wenger was invaluable. He could handle people and administer scientific projects. In the early 1930s he had been able to do the near impossible, to keep the Bureau of Engineering, OP-20-G, and Hooper in agreement. He had been skillful enough to introduce new technology without creating insecurities or engendering bureaucratic turf wars. And, Wenger was a thinker. Because of his interest and skills he became the long-term planner for prewar cryptanalysis. He supplied Hooper's grand outline for communications with the details needed for OP-20-G's technical and organizational future.[63] As significant, while on sea duty, he refined and codified the important method later known as traffic analysis. Hedging all bets, Wenger sought a method for using radio intercepts when enemy codes and ciphers could not be read. He thought that when war did begin, the Japanese would alter their codes and ciphers so frequently that even the best cryptanalytic group might not be able to keep up with the changes. Thus, he combined direction finding, call-signs, and traffic flows into a highly effective tool.[64] To prove the worth of the approach, he reconstructed the Japanese naval maneuvers without being able to read the contents of the radio signals.[65] His "T/A" became a major factor in the American victory in World War II.

The Dream Postponed, Again

Wenger's transfer to sea duty in 1932 allowed him to help unravel Japan's naval tactics and to refine America's eavesdropping capability in the Pacific, but it was near devastating to the cause of automating code and cipher breaking. Almost as bad for Hooper's cause was Laurance Safford's assignment to sea for four years. His absence until 1936 stretched the resources of OP-20-G to the breaking point and left Hooper without an in-house advocate. When Safford returned to Washington the growing crisis in the Pacific, including the sudden change of a major Japanese code in 1936, left him with no time for experimentation. He and his few men could not keep up with their operational work. In addition, with Wenger's departure, OP-20-G, the Bureau of Engineering and Hooper began to drift apart, each pursuing somewhat separate objectives. Despite OP-20-G's dependency on the bureau for hardware development, the engineering branch was left without a spokesman for advanced cryptographic technology. What men Engineering could spare became involved in the difficulties of inventing and manufacturing electromechanical encryption devices. The bureau, along with the Naval Research Laboratory, also faced increasing demands and few thanks for radio and radar development.[66]

At the same time, OP-20-G became deluged with new and more difficult code and cipher problems as Japan carved out its Asian Empire. The tiny crew had little time for technological or mathematical speculation. Spare moments were used to improve the methods for the tab machines, but the necessary emphasis in "G" was on finding time-saving tricks. Additionally, instructed to focus upon the threat in the Far East, Safford and his group had little time for the cipher systems of the Germans, Italians and Spanish. At the same time, Hooper became burdened with more and more administrative duties. He relinquished the directorship of Naval Communications and became head of the new technical division of the navy. He had little time to pursue his dream of automated cryptanalysis. He was able to squeeze some moments to polish his grand plan for integrated naval communications, but he did not have the men or resources to implement it.[67]

The Dream Reborn, for a Moment

Because of the failure of the 1930 attempt to bring automation to OP-20-G, some five years of development time were lost and there seemed little hope of a rebirth of the project. It was only Wenger's return in mid-1935, and the Roosevelt-Vinson decisions to expand the navy, that allowed Hooper to again pursue his cryptanalytic goals. Wenger had the experience, the energy, and the desire to restart the program, and naval expansion hinted at the possibility of funding.[68]

The changes at OP-20-G in 1935 extended to more than the renewed hopes for new machinery. Probably through Hooper's intervention, OP-20-G was thoroughly reorganized. Of extreme importance was the creation of a new post, one intended to allow OP-20-G some freedom from the Bureaus. Wenger was made the head of OP-20-G's new research desk. The new "Y" section was to be devoted to the application of science to cryptanalysis and to the type of long-term planning for development that the CNO was encouraging in all parts of the service.[69] Then, when Safford came back to Washington in 1936, Hooper gained still another ally. Hooper perhaps thought the reappearance of the two young officers would mean clear sailing for his renewed effort to create sophisticated decryption devices.

As Hooper scoured the country seeking advice on the broader aspects of his communications dream, including the potentials of direction finders, fax, radar, and voice scramblers, Wenger began another round of visits to the centers of American science and technology. Hooper joined with him in the first phases but he had to delegate details to Wenger, returning to help only with final negotiations.[70] Among those Hooper visited in 1935 then recommended to Wenger was a man he had known for years, perhaps from the days of World War I when they both worked on the problem of submarine detection, Vannevar Bush.[71]

Bush, Wenger, and Hooper joined forces at a time when their interests seemed to be in perfect harmony and when they thought they had the resources and power to initiate and complete a major program. Bush's grand ambitions for his Center of Analysis were forming just as

Hooper began to define his plans for a powerful communications system. Hooper thought he had the support of the navy and Bush thought the Institute could devote itself to Hooper's need for revolutionary cryptanalytic machines. The interests appeared to merge. Bush needed money to begin the first steps in a series of innovations for his Center, each building on the other. Hooper wanted someone who was a highly trustworthy American, who was at the edge of technology, and who possessed impeccable scientific credentials. And Wenger wanted someone who could, if necessary, convince naval higher-ups that bureaucratic boundaries should be erased. What he and Hooper had in mind called for the prestige of one of America's elite scientists. Bush's scientific status was perhaps the major reason why Hooper looked to MIT rather than to the large corporations such as NCR or IBM or RCA or to the National Bureau of Standards for help in automating American cryptanalysis.

The initial formal meetings with Bush in late 1935 must have left Hooper and Wenger with great expectations. Knowing he could be trusted, they described the latest cryptanalytic methods and problems, hoping that Bush would provide the needed technical solutions.[72] Bush already knew of the limitations of electromechanical tabulating and he had begun to think of alternatives for digital processing. On a gentlemen's agreement, Bush began to draft a plan for the navy and Wenger returned to Washington filled with enthusiasm. He was convinced that the ten thousand dollar consulting fee Bush expected was a great bargain. Bush dashed off his report and submitted it in the first weeks of 1936. He was able to respond so quickly because of the optics-film-electronics work he and his colleagues at MIT had been doing for several years. Of great importance, he had begun thinking of and lobbying for the development of electronic cryptanalysis well before 1935.[73]

Bush's initial proposition was not for the production of specific equipment. Rather, it defined his role as that of a consultant to the navy. He sketched the general outlines for a long-term project centered about the creation of high-speed optical-electronic devices which would be hundreds of times more powerful than the tabulators. He recommended that the navy design and develop what became known in the intelligence community as Rapid Analytical Machines (RAM). Bush's proposal excited Wenger and Hooper. Everything finally seemed to be falling into place for them and Bush in early 1936.

Little Science Meets the Little Navy, Again

Hooper thought he was having Bush subsidize his great plan for the navy. Bush thought the navy would subsidize the beginnings of MIT's calculation center and its entry into digital processing. Wenger thought he had a set of ideas that would launch the navy on a full scale development project. None of them realized there were built-in conflicts. Hooper probably did not know of the financial pressures on Bush and MIT during the 1930s; ones which led Bush to seek so many different sources of support for so many different projects and to promise so much to so many. In turn, Bush did not suspect that Hooper and Wenger had not convinced the navy of the worth of their approach to introducing innovations.[74]

Hooper was not trying to deceive Bush. He thought he had gained the CNO's approval for the venture with Bush and much more. Just as Bush submitted his proposal, which contained hints about the nature of the first Rapid Analytical Machine, the Comparator,[75] Hooper was presenting his plea for a total communications intelligence system to a sympathetic, highly secret and influential navy board.[76] Hooper and Wenger must have believed the navy was ready for a new relationship with innovators from the outside. They thought the navy would accept Bush's demand for freedom from supervision and would finally allow the navy to pay for what was the true stock and trade of scientists, ideas. Then, just as the prospects for Bush's Center rapidly brightened and as Hooper was receiving signals that his comprehensive plan for all communications activities would be approved, the navy made an unexpected, critical and disappointing decision. This time Wenger was unable to work any of the bureaucratic magic that had smoothed the way for the introduction of the tabulators in 1932. For a second time the attempt to revolutionize cryptanalysis seemed to have been defeated by the tangled navy bureaucracy and the men Bowen called "mossbacks"!

Before Bush's navy project truly got underway he and his naval allies became involved in an organizational nightmare. The problems were partly a result of his rules of the game for the relationship of academic researchers to military investigations. Bush thought freedom from interference was essential if academia and the military were to join together and he believed that no absolute time tables and guarantees could be given for truly innovative work. Hooper and Wenger agreed that heavy handed bureaucratic oversight would doom any creative effort. Wenger hoped that Bush's status and persuasive powers would be able break the navy bureaus' resistance to outsiders. But the naval bureaucracy had a different opinion.

The Bureau of Engineering's men very bluntly told Hooper and Wenger that they wanted nothing to do with a "college professor," his demand for an outrageous fee or his wild ideas. They declared his first plans unrealistic and his demands outrageous. They refused to cooperate. They were soon joined by the contracting arm of the navy which declared many parts of Hooper's model for academic-military cooperation ill-advised if not illegal. They would not give the needed approval and the project that could have led to the creation of the first electronic digital data processing device seemed dead in early 1936.

Although Hooper promised a fight to the finish, Bush concluded that the navy would not bend and he turned his attention to his many other projects. He immediately began another effort to raise funds for his Center of Analysis. With great vigor, he started to court another type of donor, the corporations. Again, history and chance came together. The return of the influential Colonel Deeds as the operating head of the National Cash Register Company would help turn the fortunes of MIT, would allow the first Selector to emerge and would eventually have an impact on the nature and organization of the nation's intelligence services.

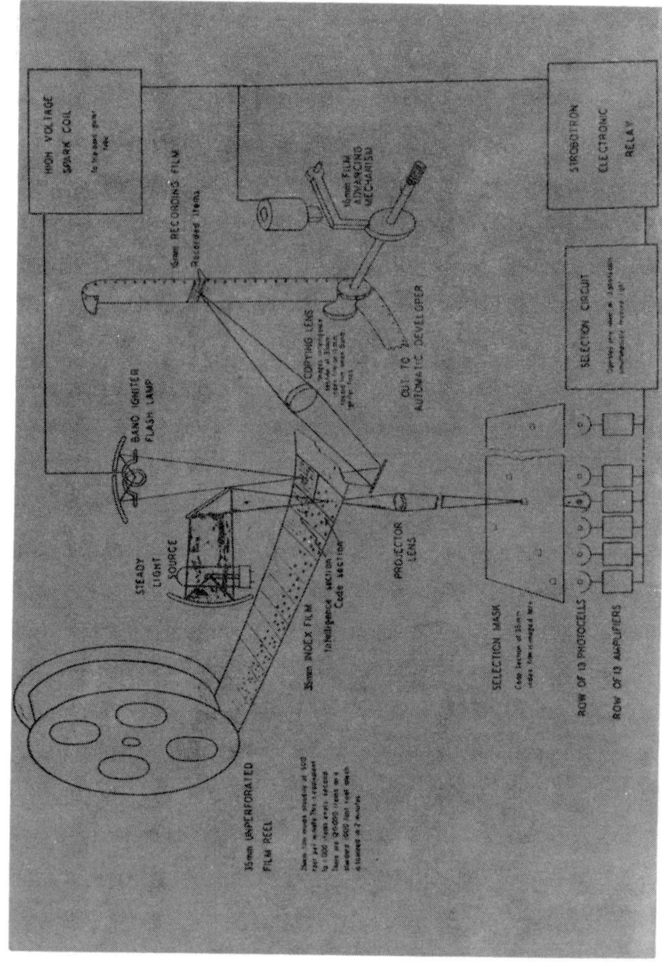

Rapid Selector Schematic
(Hagley Museum & Library)

Chapter IV
Little Science, Big Corporations and the Calculation Problem

Another set of institutions shaped the lives of the first electronic machines for information and secrecy. The struggle to finance scientific research in America brought MIT, the navy, and America's largest foundations and corporations together in sometimes conflicting relationships. Hooper and Wenger took their crusade to MIT in 1935 because it was part of the infrastructure of American science, but the technical schools and universities were not the center of research in the nation. In early twentieth century America, corporations and private foundations were more important than government or higher education. As a result, corporate research policies and decisions by the leaders of the philanthropic foundations played a determining part in the history of Bush's and Hooper's crusades. Decisions by Eastman-Kodak, AT&T, IBM, and especially the National Cash Register Company were critical to the emergence of the Selector and the Comparator.

Before the Age of Government Science

Before World War II, the federal government had little influence over the amount and nature of scientific research. Earlier wars had led to outbursts of government activity and to the creation of national scientific institutions, such as the National Academy of Sciences and the National Research Council. But the end of the conflicts saw the dismantling of projects and the national agencies reduced to rather toothless review and recommending bodies. Efforts to have the government adequately fund science agencies were never successful and the nation was left without a true center for science.

American politics was unsuited to centralized and elite science. Congress thought the nation's industries had done quite well on their own and that borrowing technology from Europe was a wise and frugal policy. When the politicians did grant funds to research, the monies were invariably directed to limited and applied projects. A few federal agencies thought they were to have permanent research divisions but none fulfilled the hopes of their creators. Stratton's Bureau of Standards fell on such hard times during the Great Depression that it turned to private philanthropy for budgetary supplements. The Weather Bureau and the Geodetic Survey were unable to drive the revolutions in physics and astronomy and the Bureau of Mines had to concentrate on rather mundane problems. The federal support of engineering research was too little to make a significant impact and medical research remained a stepchild of the military. The National Advisory Committee for Aeronautics, aided by the private charity of the Guggenheims, was able to channel some funds to university researchers but most federal agencies were unable to become world leaders in science or to subsidize research in the colleges and universities.

There was one partial exception. American politics led to an anomaly. The largest federal research program was not for industry or science but agriculture. The Morrill Act of the Civil War era, the continuing political power of the farm interest and a sincere belief that science could rescue American farmers meant that as late as the eve of World War II, the U. S. Department of Agriculture spent more than twice as much on research as all other government civilian agencies combined. Its size was so great that it spent three million dollars more on research in the 1930s than the military.[1]

The impact of agricultural experimentation was less than indicated by such comparisons. Almost all of the funding went to a limited set of research stations established under the Land Grant Act. As significant, most went for applied activities. There were exceptions, however. Agricultural funds did help build one of the most advanced centers for applied statistics in the United States and "Ag" research led to some breakthroughs in chemistry. Also, congress gave the Department of Agriculture enough to allow it to maintain one of the largest central scientific libraries in the country. Its obligation was to serve everyone engaged in agricultural science. However, the library, the statistics department at Henry Wallace's Iowa State College, and the discovery of new vitamins were the type of fundamental activities that were rare within Agriculture's program.[2] Like other government agencies, it was mandated to handle immediate, not long-term problems and it did not have the power to raise American science to world-class standing.

American scientists, especially those who were engaged in abstract research, found there was no "Federal Angel." As late as the 1930s, the scientists' lobbying efforts to make pure science one of the targets of federal support were failures. They were rebuffed by congress as well as by the usually openhanded Franklin D. Roosevelt. As a result, there was no pure science program in the nation. Scientists hobbled along during the 1930s with the scraps from emergency employment programs and funds targeted to reclaiming American youth. The nation's most important mathematical table building project of the mid-1930s used unemployment funds and the young physicist who later built the pathbreaking ENIAC computer used National Youth Administration grants to hire part time human calculators.[3] The American states provided even less than the federal government. The best they could or would do was to try to maintain general support for their state universities and colleges.

The Private World of Science

Corporations had become interested in research but that had not led to significant support for universities or independent investigators. A few corporations, such as General Electric, had minor cooperative agreements with schools like MIT, but the major corporations focused their resources on their own research centers and products. Private foundations and voluntary professional groups were left with much of the responsibility for academic science. The professional organizations had no financial resources, so, during the first forty years of the twentieth century, the nation's scientists looked to two sets of foundations, those created by Andrew Carnegie and John D. Rockefeller. Their fortunes, generated by the technological revolution of the nineteenth century, became the fuel for American academic science.

The importance of the two foundations was due to more than their huge endowments. Their decision in the 1920s to finance research within the elite American universities was critical to the history of American science. As important, they created the first bureaucracies designed to manage long-term, very expensive scientific programs. Those programs accounted for perhaps as much as ninety percent of such activity during the 1920s and 1930s and their managers became key players in the shaping of scientific institutions during and after World War II.[4] Although the foundations' contributions were dwarfed by the wartime federal science budgets, their influence continued. The men who had led the foundations ran the wartime science programs. The administrators of the 1930s private foundations, including Vannevar Bush, became the overlords of 1940s science and then became the leaders of the early Cold War scientific and high-tech agencies.

The importance of the Carnegie and Rockefeller foundations to the universities was not foreordained, however. Despite what seemed an obvious need to aid academic scientists at the beginning of the twentieth century, it took more than a generation for the foundations to agree that universities were a proper place for scientific research and to begin to fund individual projects and professors. The help was desperately needed.

At the turn of the century, America's first professional academics found it difficult just to keep up with their fields and near impossible to meet university administrators' demands for constant research productivity.[5] The tensions increased as world-class research became essential to academic careers. But it was becoming too expensive for individual professors or their institutions. The expedient of subsidizing research through the university teaching budget was no longer viable[6] and the system was in a crisis by World War I. Few universities could afford to create enormously expensive laboratories or to finance the near constant replacement of the always outdated scientific equipment. Fewer still could maintain the libraries needed by a research faculty.[7] The policies of the nation's only institution of pure academic research in the 1930s reflected the difficulties. The Institute for Advanced Study at Princeton decided to confine itself to the low overhead work of abstract mathematicians and theoretical physicists because they used their minds as their laboratories. John von Neumann and Albert Einstein tagged the IAS for high salaries, but their work did not depend on the huge sums needed by such applied physicists as MIT's Robert Van de Graff.[8]

Where Should Science Be

In the early 1900s, when leaders of American science, such as John Shaw Billings, considered how the latest Carnegie donations should be spent, they did not turn to academic science. Although Billings knew of the growing problems in the schools, he was not sure that funds should be diverted from social problems to the support of either high or applied science. It took some time to shift priorities and programs.[9] Carnegie and Rockefeller had a long history of donations made directly to universities for teaching and Carnegie's support of the American library system was a reflection of the value he placed on popular education. However, neither had given much thought to the sciences or to academic research. It was not until World War I, when a new group of leaders took charge of the foundations, that policies began to change. The young men ordered a turn to research, but, at first, not to university-based science.

For a time, there was a reluctance to be involved with any research within the colleges and universities. The Carnegie and Rockefeller foundations created separate institutes with their own staffs and buildings. Although the institutes did some abstract work, immediate medical and social problems were the target. Only gradually did the foundations begin to support science in general. It took longer for them to decide to fund research within the academic community and, then, to allow professors to determine the nature of their work. As outside research became more attractive, the foundations turned to the old national science institutions for help. The National Academy of Sciences and the National Research Council were energized with foundation monies and began to act as scientific go-betweens. The NRC managed many projects for Carnegie, advised other foundations about national needs and recommended worthy scientists and projects.[10] After those first steps, the foundations began to help some individual academic researchers--just as MIT's new president launched his faculty, including Vannevar Bush, on a sweep for research funds.

While Karl Compton, like other university presidents of the time, was trying to rebuild endowments so MIT could support research, his faculty explored the new opportunities at the major foundations. Although MIT had not received much from Carnegie or Rockefeller in the past, Bush and his peers looked to New York and Washington for critical help. The earlier connections Bush made with the National Research Council while he was an administrator at the Institute proved essential to his success at the foundations. Very important to Bush were the decisions by one of the new young administrators at the Rockefeller foundation, Warren Weaver. Weaver had much to do with the history of the Selector, the Comparator, Bush's grand plan for a Center of Analysis and the eventual emergence of information science.[11]

A Man for Applied Mathematics and Information

Warren Weaver was one of those new bright scientific men brought to the foundations to reformulate policy. His ex-teacher and mentor, Max Mason, plucked Weaver from his teaching post at the University of Wisconsin and placed him in charge of the Rockefeller's natural science division.[12] Mason's selection of Warren Weaver in 1932 was not influenced by Vannevar Bush, but Weaver turned out to be the perfect man for Bush and the Center of Analysis. Warren Weaver came from the same type of respectable but non-elite background as Bush. He began his academic life with a degree in civil engineering but his education at Wisconsin was not a shop floor apprenticeship. He came into contact with a new breed of academic, the applied mathematician. That changed Weaver's life and he became committed to expanding the reach of mathematics. His faith in the importance of numbering to all the sciences was reinforced when he spent part of World War I at the National Bureau of Standards as an air force researcher. After being discharged from the Army Air Corps he began a career as a mathematician, appropriately enough at the fast-rising California Institute of Technology. He moved to the Middle West, but his dozen years in the more traditional mathematics department at Wisconsin did not lead him to abandon his belief in the value of mathematics.

Central to Weaver's plan for the revamped natural science division of the Rockefeller foundation was the creation of instruments to encourage the use of mathematics in every field. One of his first surveys of American science was a tour of all the computers in the nation. Weaver gauged the abilities of the men at the University of Pennsylvania's Moore School of Engineering; he learned of the possibility of turning Hannibal Ford's fantastic gun control devices into calculating engines; and, he made a visit to the world famous Bush Differential Analyser at MIT.[13] Bush took advantage of that. He soon became a frequent visitor to Weaver's office and by the mid-1930s convinced him that the world of science was ready for new generations of Analysers. Then, Weaver successfully lobbied his superiors for a ten thousand dollar study grant for Bush's proposed partially electronic machine. Just a year later, he secured an astounding eighty-five thousand dollars for the Rockefeller Analyser project at MIT.[14] Weaver grew to be an even better friend of Bush and the Institute. He shared Bush's thoughts about a new machine for the library,[15] explored Bush's suggestions about the value of microfilm to a solution to the scientific information problem and kept the secret of Bush's "machine for the government," the Comparator.[16] Weaver's faith in Bush and MIT could not be shaken. As the Rockefeller Analyser project fell more and more behind schedule and climbed over its already generous budget, rather than complain, Weaver promised more aid. At the same time, he turned down the pleas of Howard Aiken and John Atanasoff for funds for their Harvard and Iowa State computer projects. Half a dozen years later, Weaver again showed his faith in MIT when he funded another huge computer project at the Institute; one for an electronic digital programmed computer.[17]

Weaver was also very supportive of Bush's ideas for automating information processing. Although he was unable to find money for Bush's information machine, the Rapid Selector, in the mid-1930s, Weaver was inspired by Bush's concept of the library of the future. Weaver began to explore all possibilities. In addition to conducting a survey of the promising breakthrough in information technology, microfilm, he began to see information through the lenses of modern mathematics.[18] Weaver did not have a chance to make his own contribution to information science until the end of World War II, but when it finally appeared, it was a grand one. Weaver collaborated with one of MIT's brightest students of the 1930s, Claude Shannon, to write what was for many years the theoretical justification for mathematical information science. Shannon's early encounters with Norbert Wiener's cybernetic ideas and his wartime exploration of the mathematics of secret communication led him to write a major but intellectually difficult statistical work on the transmission of information. Weaver became interested and saw an opportunity to create a new field of study. He turned Shannon's manuscript into a persuasive essay justifying another expansion of the domain of numeracy.[19] The combination of Weaver and Claude Shannon led to the highly influential, *The Mathematical Theory of Communication*.

The Aids to Learning Project and Information

A decade before his book made its appearance, Weaver and the other foundation administrators were making a rather different impact on the futures of computers and information machines. To understand that influence calls for a detour to a history of Bush's relations with the Carnegie interests and his plans for the role of science in World War II.

The Carnegie foundations had tied their programs much closer to the older scientific community than had the Rockefellers. Soon after World War I, Carnegie's men granted what were then vast amounts to provide the National Academy of Sciences a permanent home and staff. They also helped the National Research Council. Although the Carnegie group did not provide the Council with the ability to independently finance research, it gave it purpose through the administration of a significant program of advanced fellowships in the natural sciences.[20] The NRC also filled the role of overseer for many other Carnegie sponsored programs and its panels conducted surveys and studies that identified major needs in the sciences. Meanwhile, the several Carnegie foundations continued to select and fund projects on their own. Some of those projects were related to information and the struggles of America's scientific institutions.

Since the nineteenth century, when Andrew Carnegie began to encourage American towns to build libraries, his foundations remained interested in education in the broadest sense. Because of that continuing interest it had not taken too many suggestions from the NRC to convince them to fund what was seen as the first coordinated attempt to bring technology to the rescue of learning in America. In 1937, under NRC supervision, the Scientific Aids to Learning project was begun. Directed by a scholar-lawyer-diplomat and member of the Federal Communications Commission, the project was broad in scope, perhaps too broad.[21] Although Irvin Stewart was an experienced manager, he was not able to make it clear whether the program was one to improve learning in the lower schools, to develop information technology in general, or to help scientific research. Perhaps he and his committee thought that all those goals were compatible.

Relying upon the NRC's connections, Stewart brought in experts from fields with potentials to alter the standing orders of the library and learning. A wide variety of technologies were surveyed, ranging from sound recording through the promised alternative to the book, microfilm. Among those who participated in the Aids project were Vannevar Bush and one of the men who became vital to Documentation, Vernon Tate. Tate was another man whose career became tangled with that of Vannevar Bush's Rapid Selector. Although he was not aware of it in the mid-1930s, his work would bridge information and secrecy.

A recent Berkeley history Ph.D., Tate worked at the Library of Congress where he learned of the vast project under Samuel Bemis to microfilm the great documents of Western Civilization.[22] He then became head of the pathbreaking division of photographic reproduction at the recently established National Archives.[23] The Archives was involved in a massive microfilming effort to preserve and distribute historic documents. With the help of the experts at the National Bureau of Standards, Tate became one of the world's leading experts on and advocates for microfilm. He was a crusader for new library methods and he represented the nation's librarians at the 1930s international meetings of the European Documentalists. He agreed with them that the library was due for modernization.

Because of his previous work, Tate did not need long to fulfill his assignment for the Scientific Aids to Learning Project, a survey of all aspects of microfilm. He reported on its technical problems and its uses in libraries and schools. He paid much attention to the market for microfilm readers. He even reported on the possibilities of automatic retrieval of information from microfilmed documents. He mentioned such devices as the microfilm selector under patent application by Merle E. Gould and the suggestions for the use of large microfilm plates put forward by the MIT physicist, Ralph Bennett.[24] Tate shared his reports with Bush and others associated with the Learning project. Partly as a result of Tate's survey, his American Documentalist friends were able to parlay the NRC connection into some small grants from the Rockefeller and Carnegie foundations.[25]

Bush's hopes that the NRC-Carnegie Learning project would contribute money to his information machine, the Rapid Selector, were not fulfilled, however. For years, Bush had lobbied the Rockefeller and Carnegie interests for funding for his version of a machine to select information from microfilmed records. His pleas were rejected. Perhaps they thought his proposal a bit too speculative.[26] But, Bush was able to work his grantsman's wonders for his Center of Analysis. Although the mandate for the Learning project may not have included sponsorship of research facilities, Bush put the MIT man in charge of the new Analyser to estimating the needs for computation in the United States. Not surprisingly, Sam Caldwell found an enormous unfulfilled demand for advanced calculation. He also concluded that MIT's proposed center could meet all the nation's requirements. Bush quickly found justifications for financing a computation center as part of the Learning program.[27] The National Research Council's board gave its approval, perhaps not realizing how busy Caldwell's group was and perhaps being unaware of the existence of other such centers. Immediately, the Carnegie foundation gave MIT a generous forty-five thousand dollars for the general support of Bush's updated version of Stratton's dream, the Center of Analysis.[28]

American Science and the War, the NDRC

The Scientific Aids to Learning project had an unexpected influence on Bush's career. His participation deepened his Washington contacts and heightened his reputation as an academic statesman. The result: By early 1938 he was negotiating with the fabled Carnegie Institution of Washington. In mid-year, he was chosen as its president and was about to become a major power in American science.[29] The Learning project also had profound consequences for American science. Continuing their meetings after Bush moved to Washington, the inner core of the Learning group became advocates for American intervention in the emerging European conflicts. They began to consider ways to mobilize American research and what they decided to do altered the history of America's universities and brought men such as Warren Weaver back into the story of Bush's information and secrecy machines.

The growing European problems had not led to a major change in the American military's research policies or to the reorganization of American science. Even Japan's rampage in China and the invasion of Poland were not catalysts for the mustering of America's technical resources. No one seemed interested in and capable of initiating and sustaining long-term projects. Military leaders like Bowen and Hooper reached out to industry through the expanded Research and Invention bureau and orders for military equipment increased, but the armed forces had little time and no money to explore speculative technological options. With a few exceptions, military budgets had to be used to acquire proven equipment. America's institutions of science could not fill the research void.

The National Academy and the Research Council followed the nation's formal neutrality policy and did not begin programs to bring science to the service of the nation. Even in 1939, there was no great surge to change the NRC back into the kind of organization that had led the scientific effort against the U-boats in World War I and that had sent young mathematicians such as Norbert Wiener to the Aberdeen proving grounds to explore the mathematics of anti-aircraft fire. America certainly did not have and apparently did not want its equivalent of Britain's scientific "Wizards" of war, men who had begun to mobilize British science as early as 1935.[30]

Only a few in America realized that Germany was inventing a new type of high technology warfare and that fundamental science might be needed to combat the horrors of atomic weapons and long range bombers. Vannevar Bush and his close scientific friends were among those few. They recognized the Nazi threat and feared the consequences of the dangerous assumptions about the length of time America had to prepare for a European war. They were especially worried that a conservative military would never come to terms with the new type of conflict. As bad was the possibility that when the nation finally dealt with the need to link science to the military it would create an organization run by military bureaucrats. Bush and his friends did not want scientists to become mere employees of the generals.

Never a man to sit by and let the world determine his fate, Bush sought ways to ensure a flow of contributions to the war effort. [31] Because reigning powers at the National Academy did not seem to be moving toward any solutions, Bush energized the Learning group. They decided to take action on their own. To bolster the Learning cadre's political influence, Bush brought in the heads of America's largest corporate research centers and some of the more progressive military men. After much discussion and planning, an organizational framework was agreed upon. Then, other scientists were recruited to the cause. They helped muster political support.

In the process, Learning's men changed themselves into one of America's first modern science interest groups and began to lobby the government to support a wide range of new programs. Bush took the proposals to the top and won a major victory. He convinced President Roosevelt to create the powerful and well funded National Defense Research Committee in June 1940. Within a year, its scope and its powers to initiate and control projects were vastly expanded. The new Office of Scientific Research and Development was a dream come true for Bush. It was almost the perfect science foundation for elite American academics.

The NDRC was responsible to the president, not the military or congress, and its scientists could determine what projects to begin or end. Bush's plan allowed his men to be free of the intrusions that could lead to the cancellation of a promising investigation or to the embarrassment of having to take a device from the test-bench before it was ready for the field. Under the rules, the NDRC's administrators controlled a project until it was ready for manufacture. In addition, they were free of the political pressures that had sidetracked the work of the science agencies of World War I. The NDRC did not have to waste time attending to the ideas and demands of mere inventors, their congressional friends or the administrators of second rank universities. The NDRC could devote itself to maximizing the talents of the best scientists. Hundreds of millions of dollars came under the control of the NDRC. Scientific wish lists were examined and worthy projects that seemed related to military needs received generous funding.

The NDRC was subsidizing science as well as potential weapons. Its policies and structure fit with Bush's long-term purposes and he made sure that men who shared his view of the relation of science to the society filled the slots under him. That meant that the administrators of foundation science, who were friends of the universities, were selected to head the major branches of the NDRC. The old Carnegie-Rockefeller circle, which included the leading men from the leading universities, moved from private to military philanthropy during the war and, along with Bush, were able to circumvent the "mossbacks" in the military and the older organizations of science.

As they began their work, Bush and Weaver realized that a substantial bonus might await them. A job well done by the NDRC in the universities might become the critical argument for federal support for peacetime academic science. The NDRC could be the historic breakthrough needed to give American academics the best of all possible worlds after the war: massive federal funding controlled by top scientists. Predictably, Bush pushed the NDRC to fund research and development at a select group of universities and corporate research centers. He placed projects at the best places and with the best men.

Well before the NDRC's formal beginning, Bush and his associates began to comb the country looking for men and ideas. After surveys in early 1940, Bush concluded that a number of very promising technologies were receiving too little attention from the military and its contractors.[32] At the head of the list were radar, atomic energy and the proximity fuse. The NDRC feared that Germany was developing atomic weapons and wanted America to be first with a bomb. As well, the success of Germany's dive-bombers and worries about guided missiles made radar early warning systems and the deadly smart fuse necessities.[33] In the fall of 1940, the NDRC began its work on those three major challenges. At the same time, it began to explore other defense technologies, ones that were too speculative for the military or its older industrial allies. Of great importance was the computer effort headed by Warren Weaver.

Because of Weaver's mathematical background and his prewar experience evaluating computing proposals, Bush made him head of the mathematical and scientific instrument section of the NDRC. One of his first chores was to develop a program to solve technical problems created by the advance of German military technology. There was a vital need for automatic control of anti-aircraft weapons, high-speed counters for ballistic tests and scientific instruments to monitor atomic processes.[34] In each case, Weaver turned to electronic solutions. He called upon all those known to have worked in electronic counting and launched a program for the development of special purpose devices. He soon had the computer builders George Stibitz and Sam Caldwell to help him supervise the work. As important, he was able to pursue another opportunity. He created a center for applied mathematics. It would permanently change academic mathematics in America.

Weaver's achievements, however significant, were just a small part of the NDRC's part in changing the American campus and the lives of American scientists. The war made America's leading universities into engines for research. Radar soon became the basis for MIT's vast expansion and the proximity fuse led Johns Hopkins to create what became the Applied Physics Laboratory. Although the NDRC turned the atomic program over to the army's Manhattan project, the initial explorations at Columbia and the University of Chicago developed into a permanent relationship between academic physicists, universities and the federal atomic energy programs.

The NDRC was a blessing to Bush and his academic friends, but to others it was a politicized and unnecessary organization that threatened the military research agencies such as the Naval Research Laboratory.[35] To Admiral Bowen, Bush was leading a group bent on playing favorites among the military services and the universities. He soon concluded that the NDRC worked to the disadvantage of the navy.

To some in the academic community, the NDRC seemed to be working for an inner university circle.[36] To Admiral Hooper, however, Bush and the NDRC appeared, at least at the beginning, to be the only way the intelligence community could acquire the advanced machines it needed. But, as will be described, computers were far down on the NDRC list and cryptanalysis entered their world only because of the long chain of associations between Bush, the navy, and the corporations and universities that were at the center of the NDRC.

Corporate Charity and the Selector

MIT had always had good relations with America's leading corporations, especially those with an interest in the application of science to technology. Well before the 1920s, MIT's administrators and faculty were very familiar with the names DuPont, Thomson, Bell, and Eastman. The Institute received funds directly from them and developed cooperative programs in their shops. General Electric and the other large firms sponsored research projects at the Institute and used its faculty as consultants.[37] Bell Laboratories was a frequent destination for the Institute's brightest alumni. The corporations had not always done all that was expected of them, however. Stratton's program to put corporate giving on a regular basis had not lived up to his hopes during the 1920s. But, it was natural for Vannevar Bush to look to the major corporations when he began his search for support for his calculation center in the early 1930s. He beat on many of corporate doors, but among them, two became especially important.[38] Both are somewhat of a surprise because other more likely candidates backed away from the proposed center and pursued their own computing programs.

General Electric had a research branch that was a leader in applied mathematics. It had used the Institute's staff for several chores, but it decided to keep most of its work in-house rather than make any large investments in Bush's center. Paralleling General Electric's reaction, Western Electric and Bell Laboratories were willing to supply critical parts for the Rockefeller Analyser and to give advice on the type of tools and services mathematicians desired. But, they did not offer major financial support to Bush's 1930s projects. One reason was that Bell Laboratories, well on its way to becoming the premier private research institution in the world, had a group of mathematicians who were already busy constructing mathematical machines.[39] Thorton C. Fry, the Lab's head mathematician, was an expert on analog computing and was the sponsor of the development of at least two major computers. He built a mechanical analog harmonic analyser in the mid-1930s and then gave young George Stibitz the green light on his proposal for a relay digital calculator.[40]

George Stibitz was an applied mathematician at Bell Laboratories who became involved with the many challenges of the expanding long distance telephone network. His work called for the calculation of what are termed complex numbers, calculations that were extremely expensive and error prone. Beginning with rough ideas in 1938, he and the talented engineer from Western Electric, S. B. Williams, completed a keyboard-based digital binary relay computer by the first days of 1940. Neither he nor Williams nor their fellow scientists seem to have known of the massive relay totalizator computer put into operation a decade before by Harry Straus. Straus and his engineers built the modern "tote" for racetracks in their small Baltimore shop, went on to become millionaires and, after World War II, sponsors of the first commercial electronic computer company.[41]

Stibitz's machine performed much more complex calculations than the totalizator, however, and it became renowned as a first by the scientific community. The Complex Number Calculator was the star of the American Mathematical Society's 1940 convention and was immediately hailed as a breakthrough for digital calculation. Of importance, Stibitz was soon drafted into the computer program of the NDRC where he not only supervised the work of others but was instrumental in the creation of a long series of huge Bell-Western Electric relay calculators for the military. Also, in 1942 he designed the fabled Madame X for the army codebreakers.[42] Then, while Stibitz minded his NDRC administrative duties, Sam Williams moved on to the use of more advanced technologies. He had the plans for a machine that used spinning commutators by early 1942 and then detailed an electronic fixed purpose computer for the Weaver-NDRC antiaircraft project.[43]

Unfortunately for Bush, Western Electric decided not to take part in the establishment of the MIT analysis center. Other high-tech companies may have not been allowed the chance to reject Bush's 1930's proposals. Among those was IBM. Many of the reasons for Bush's negative attitude toward IBM will never be revealed, but he frequently voiced his dislike of Tom Watson's research and patent policies. Patents and their relationship to technological progress were always of concern to Bush. Like Admiral Hooper, he had a love-hate relationship with the American patent system. He was torn between the idea that patent protection was needed to bring technology to the market and the fear of the potential of patents to halt technological advance. Any company, Bush usually said, would need the guarantees of profit secured through patents. But in his more dark moments he worried that companies such as IBM gained patents in new technologies to protect their existing products. Patents could serve as a block to progress through suits to stop the introduction of new machines. In addition, Bush feared that the search for patents might lead research organizations to focus on the mundane and immediate.[44]

Good Corporate Neighbors

In comparison to his attitude toward IBM, Bush heartily approved of the policies of another firm that was entering into the information business, Eastman-Kodak. George Eastman's ideas of how to take photography out of the hands of professionals and make it a popular hobby turned his company into an international business by World War I.[45] Eastman soon entered into data processing. The company became a world leader in microfilm for use in business and the library; it had plans for its own microfilm selector; and, it invested in fundamental research. By the 1930s, Eastman had one of the largest and most advanced research departments in the world and it was well integrated into the international scientific community.[46] The skills of its men included optics, chemistry, physics and mathematics. Part of its staff specialized in mechanics and they were frequently called upon to help its instrument makers construct new devices to aid experimentation. In World War II, those men became computer builders for Weaver's NDRC.[47]

The Eastman corporation of the 1930s was not as generous with MIT as its founder had been, but it remained a very good friend of the Institute. When Bush needed advice on topics ranging from chemistry to film drives he could always turn to the men in Rochester. He became a close friend of its great experts such as C. E. K. Mees who was also an advocate for science in industry.[48] In turn, Eastman's men respected Bush. The company was so supportive they agreed to finance the development of Bush's machine for the library in the late 1930s although they had their own similar project and knew of selector work in Europe. That commitment to Bush led Eastman to become important to the navy and the future of Hooper's program for codebreaking.[49] Of even greater importance to the nation was Bush's relationship with a corporation that did not have a reputation for research. Why Bush became so close to a company that made cash registers is explained by Bush's friendship with the famous team of Colonel Edward A. Deeds and Charles Boss Kettering. That friendship linked National Cash Register, MIT, the NDRC, and the Ultra secret.[50]

Cash Registers in the Service of Science

Deeds and Kettering were more than members of the inner circle of America's industrial leaders, they were revered deans. Deeds was one of the most influential financiers and organizers in the nation. Kettering was the director of research for General Motors and had replaced Edison and Ford as the guru of American technology.[51] Deeds began his career as a construction engineer for the National Cash Register Company in Dayton, Ohio. Kettering's first triumph was the electrification of the cash register for the same firm, saving it from onslaughts by its predatory competitors in the early 1900s. The two young men then joined forces and invented the self-starter for the automobile, founded Delco, and later became rich from the growth of General Motors. Additionally, Deeds and Kettering headed the Liberty Engine project in World War I. Deeds went on to be a major force in the creation of the American airline and machine tool industries. From there, he became a power in the world of American corporate finance and a builder of combinations. Meanwhile, Kettering kept searching for significant problems that could be solved through technology. He proceeded to invent ethyl gasoline and a superior diesel engine to prevent, he thought, depletion of natural resources. And, he continued his involvement with the development of the airplane and early versions of guided missiles. He shaped the research program at General Motors and he became a bridge between the military and inventors during World War II.

Bush first came in contact with Deeds and Kettering through the institutions of American science. Bush and Deeds served on important advisory committees that steered aeronautical research in the United States, such as the precursor to NASA, the National Advisory Committee for Aeronautics. Although not formally appointed to head the NACA until 1938, Bush was involved with it and the airline industry throughout the 1930s.[52] Bush shared a great deal more than an interest in aeronautics with Deeds. He shared beliefs and ideas. Deeds's and Kettering's faith in the use of science and technology to solve America's problems, even those of the Great Depression, surpassed Bush's. And, like Hooper, all three were committed to modernizing America.

Deeds had direct ties to MIT. Bush's exploitation of them began when Deeds chose to set aside some of his grand plans for the nation and to concentrate on helping his old employer, National Cash Register. In 1931, Deeds consented to serve as Chairman of the Board of National Cash Register. He was needed because National had become somewhat inflexible and faced a profitability crisis. The management problems that had begun after the death of the company's dynamic founder were intensified by the Great Depression. The company almost fell into the hands of its New York financiers in the 1930s.

The strong-willed and autocratic founder of National, John Patterson, had created a philosophy of management, salesmanship, and service in the 1890s that was later transferred to IBM by the ex-National executive, Tom Watson. That philosophy made National a world leader. Under Patterson's direction, NCR controlled almost ninety percent of the market for cash registers.[53] But his family seemed unable to follow his maxims, even with the help of men like Deeds and Kettering. Although one of the founders of modern management theory, the elder Patterson had made NCR his business, creating a difficult situation for his successors. There had been little innovation in the company's products since Kettering's days. By the late 1920s, sales and earnings at NCR were threatened as competition from other register manufacturers increased. National had to find new products and markets.

Partly because of IBM's control of the one technology that matched the 1930s needs for large-scale data handling, National was excluded from the expanding market for record processing. And the company was late in offering banking and payroll machines. Corporations such as Burroughs had gone far beyond their desk calculators and had a significant head start on the amazing new posting/bookkeeping machines. And, a new competitor, Remington-Rand, had surged ahead of NCR to become the largest business supply company in the world.

For someone trying to rebuild NCR, the best opportunities were those that demanded a technology not found in the corporation's offerings of the 1920s. NCR needed new machines to move deeper into information processing. Inventory, retail sales and personnel management, for example, had demands met only by devices that had some sort of large scale memory. But, a halt in technological development had left the old-fashioned punch card of the 1880s as the best mass memory. Although punch cards were old, they and IBM remained difficult to beat for file management. That company controlled the card market because of its manufacturing skills, excellent service and patents.[54] It also had a corner on electrical tabulating and allied devices, resulting in an extraordinary profit level and insulation from the impact of the Great Depression. Despite intense research, Remington-Rand and other data processing companies found it impossible to produce a competitive machine, at least within the framework of electromechanical technology.[55]

There had been some rumblings at NCR about entering into IBM's markets after World War I. But the purchase of such patents as Justin Compton's for an electronic device in 1923[56] did not lead the company to introduce any startlingly new products. The failure to create offerings to compete with IBM was one reason for the demand for a thorough shake-up at National Cash Register in 1936. Just as Vannevar Bush was arguing with the Bureau of Engineering over the optical-electronic machines for Hooper, Deeds accepted the NCR presidency with a mandate to reinvigorate the company. He goal was to make NCR aggressive and profitable. By 1940, when he stepped back to board membership and gave operational responsibilities to Stanley C. Allyn, the company was more than on the road to recovery.

One of the reasons for Deeds's success was the value he placed on research. Throughout his career Deeds maintained his contacts with Kettering and his friends who were advocates of science and technological solutions. Such friendships aided Deeds in achieving one of his goals for National: to develop a research capability in innovative technologies. Kettering shared Deeds's interest in reviving the old cash register company through research in fields ranging from chemistry to electronics. Their devotion to National was heightened because both had strong ties to Dayton, Ohio. They were involved in the Wright companies which, with NCR, were vital to the town's prosperity.[57]

While Deeds slashed expenditures in many parts of the company, he increased allocations for research. He pushed the efforts to move NCR into the electrified bank-posting and billing machine business and he looked forward to finding a technology to challenge IBM's grip on automated file management. Previously, Deeds had applauded NCR's very quiet acquisition of the rights to a fantastic machine for the era, the Hofgaard relay computer.[58]

Rolph Hofgaard was a very innovative and prolific Norwegian inventor[59] whose work had the potential to yield a memory based machine for inventory and similar data heavy chores. Hofgaard's 1920s experimental devices were very advanced for the time and predated the use of relays for large-scale calculation by men such as Stibitz and the now famous Konrad Zuse of Germany.[60] The original Hofgaard patents described posting-billing machines with remote input and output through modified typewriters and control keyboards. After acquiring the rights to his ideas, NCR's men took the design much farther and created a room-sized machine at Dayton to test their improvements.

Both the 1930 and 1938 NCR relay computer patent applications cited a machine with an architecture quite like that of the modern serial computer. It had a central processing unit and addressed storage. The machines operator would enter, for example, the quantity of an item ordered on the input keyboard, press a key to send it to a register, then enter the code number of the item. The price of the item, stored in another register, would be sent, along with the quantity to the arithmetic processor. The processor would, if desired, multiply the two quantities, then store the result as the same time that it was printed on the appropriate line of the card in the machine's output typewriter.[61] The computer could also search for discounts for items and include them in the calculations. It performed at least three of the four basic arithmetic functions and had the ability to calculate, store, and print totals and subtotals for many different items. NCR's men knew that if the machine's memory could be expanded and its input-output made more rapid, the Hofgaard calculator held the potential to be an instant inventory or a truly automatic accounting device. An expanded group under Mr. Coe was put to work on the Hofgaard machine in the mid-1930s. Its men began thinking of ways to speed up data input and explored the idea of replacing its relays with electronic tubes.[62]

Although Hofgaard's machine was quite promising, Deeds ordered NCR's research director Harry N. Williams to drop the project and investigate other technological options. Deeds was probably advised to do so by Vannevar Bush who was aware of the Hofgaard patents and who had just completed his survey of computing technologies.[63] Bush advised a jump into electronics. The men at NCR learned much about the progress of electronics and film-optical combinations in scientific measurement from Bush. And, they studied publications such as Keith Henny's, *Electron Tubes in Industry*.[64] They also became aware of IBM's explorations of electronics.[65]

NCR Takes Up the Cause

Bush did more than serve as an unofficial advisor to Deeds, he established a long-term relationship between NCR and the Institute. By early 1937, while the navy was still debating the Bush-Hooper proposal, Bush convinced Deeds to donate a token but regular amount to the Institute and to send a team of NCR engineers to see its work on electronics and film.[66] On their visit to MIT, the lead NCR engineers, Green and Sullivan, were probably shown all the electronic analog devices, Edgerton's stroboscopic work, and the amazing and impressive 1930 Differential Analyser. More importantly, they received an introduction to the progress on the Rockefeller Analyser, the already designed Rapid Selector,[67] the first ideas for the electronic calculator, and, perhaps, some of the designs of Bush's counting and logic circuits for the navy's machine.[68] Being old hands in the data processing business, the NCR men realized that electronics and microfilm held significant patent opportunities. They could be the way to surpass IBM and Burroughs. Bush's faith in microfilm's potential as a memory for calculating machines and for file processing must have impressed them. They were certainly interested in the MIT work on smaller and more reliable tubes because even mechanical engineers could see the value of low power and fast miniature tubes for machine design.[69] Their positive reaction to the operation at MIT resulted in a endorsement of Bush's suggestion to use the Institute as a resource for NCR. And, it reinforced the pressures Deeds and Kettering had put on National to invest in long-term research in electronics.

Within three months, National Cash Register made Sam Caldwell, the professor in charge of the Rockefeller project, a consultant, and agreed to pay him a fee of ten thousand dollars a year. He was to report on progress at MIT, coordinate research for the company at the Institute, and help to apply MIT's discoveries to NCR products. Ten thousand dollars a year was a great sum at that time; a relatively senior engineer at NCR was paid twenty-five hundred dollars in the late 1930s. And, Deeds probably knew that hiring Sam Caldwell would only be the first in a long series of arrangements with the electrical engineering group at the Institute.[70]

The Navy Comes in Second

After all the disappointing appeals to the foundations and the troubled negotiations with the navy, Bush finally gained a pliable and generous sponsor. NCR had the potential of being as important to Bush's center as Warren Weaver and it was certainly easier to work with than the navy. NCR did what the Bureau of Engineering refused to do a year before, use the university and its professors as intellectual resources. Deeds's approval of Caldwell's consulting fee, the same amount Bush had first asked of the Bureau of Engineering, made the Bureau's attitude seem even more backwards to Bush. It made him less willing to devote his time to the navy's project.[71]

The work for NCR went slowly, but the failure of Bush, Caldwell and the "boys" at the Institute to provide anything of immediate value did not make Deeds lose faith. In fact, he expanded the relationship with the Institute just a few months after engaging Caldwell. When Bush asked Deeds for help in developing his information machine, the Rapid Selector, he received a positive response although Deeds was encouraging similar developments at NCR. Deeds was very generous. Bush was willing to yield patent and licensing rights to NCR but Deeds, with an attitude few corporate executives could take, gave strong hints he would subsidize the work with just a promise that NCR could have a license to use the inventions.[72] He also welcomed Eastman-Kodak to the project.

Bush knew a good thing. Within a few months, he and Caldwell returned to Deeds requesting money for Harold Edgerton's work and for the proposed universal electronic computer, the revolutionary Rapid Arithmetical Machine. Explaining that it was still on paper, but underscoring that other work had already led to the building of successful electronic circuits, Bush was able to get Deeds's attention.[73] The first discussions about the electronic computer may have started with hints that MIT could immediately build an electronic calculator for NCR. But the beleaguered Rockefeller project led Caldwell and Bush to scale down their ambitions. In late 1938, Caldwell asked that NCR's Dayton facility take over the task of constructing the Rapid Arithmetical Machine.[74] Caldwell asked that MIT be allowed to confine itself to the investigation of underlying technologies, the preparation of patents and the planning of an electronic machine more advanced than the one he asked NCR to build.[75] He continued to rely on NCR's generosity, however. In addition to the increased subsidies, NCR promised to help the Center of Analysis by providing it with a second copy of the proposed Dayton electronic computer.[76] Although the budget for the Rapid Arithmetical machine project at MIT was not large, some four thousand dollars a year,[77] it and the allied agreement with NCR about fundamental patents for magnetic recording were important to MIT's future.

Bush, already very busy, had a limited role in the Rapid Arithmetical project. He restricted himself to writing overviews of its architecture. Caldwell had the hands-on responsibility although he had so many other duties. He tried to get the work moving but found that he was very short of student help. He assigned one or two young men to the project. First, it was W. H. Radford. Then, an alumnus, Wilcox Overbeck, conducted the investigations. They concentrated on the creation of new multifunction tubes and circuits and on what was so vital to NCR's search for memory, magnetic recording. They sent frequent reports to NCR and promised to follow the agreement that any innovative tube designs would be shared with National.[78]

The Institute Suffers from Success

Like the other projects at the Institute, the Rapid Arithmetical Machine fell behind schedule. In late 1939, the situation was so grave that Caldwell had to promise to halt other work and to concentrate on MIT's obligations to NCR. The pace of work was increased and NCR was willing to sign another set of agreements. They included a greater NCR subsidy for magnetic recording research and promises of an intensified MIT investigation of the use of film as input to computers.[79] The magnetic work was of such special importance to NCR that Deeds's usual generosity was put aside; NCR demanded that all patents rights go directly to it. Caldwell agreed to that policy.[80] Responding to the pressure from NCR, Caldwell began to think of ways to shift more men to the company's work. He demonstrated his willingness to live up to the promises Bush had made by submitting a plan for a business machine with fast magnetic memory.[81] Then, he asked NCR if it would like to participate in the construction of a race track totalizator to be financed by a private association.[82]

Deeds Finds a Practical Man

Despite his patience and Caldwell's promises, Deeds could not leave the future of his company in the hands of an academic institution. Following Bush's suggestion, NCR established its own electronics research laboratory in the spring of 1938.[83] It was small and it worked closely with the MIT group, but it pursued independent research and development. In many ways it was more successful than the activity in Cambridge. One reason was the Dayton activity's different orientation; it was product directed. And at its head was a man who was a unique combination of practicality and vision.

Colonel Deeds had asked Bush for help establishing and staffing the laboratory, but for unknown reasons, Bush did not send any of his men to Dayton.[84] NCR's research director, trying to balance the abstract MIT influence, then decided to begin his electronics branch with experienced, practical men. He soon found what he wanted, an engineer whose contributions to American history remain unknown to the public although he was awarded the highest civilian honors by the military. The man Williams selected to lead the Dayton lab, Joseph Desch, was not of the elite engineering circles. A graduate of a local college and a shop trained man, Desch was especially good at turning ideas into products and at quality control. He had worked on various engineering challenges, including many that dealt with radio and electronics. His stay at General Motors' radio research division and his work at Frigidaire were unique blends of exploration and application. His experience included work on a radio-teletype system that linked electric typewriters, one that later became of great interest to the navy and to IBM.[85] He was a natural for the job at NCR's new lab because of his willingness to teach himself and to work in new fields.

He continued to explore when he went to NCR. Establishing his laboratory in April 1938 he and his few assistants taught themselves about the latest electronic developments.[86] Soon, they became as skilled as the university trained men at MIT. Frequently, it was Desch, rather than Caldwell's men, who was first to arrive at new discoveries and to build working machines. In fact, Desch beat MIT to the creation of an electronic digital calculator, partly because Bush's men were too busy with their other projects.[87] He completed a calculator by 1940 and explored the application of electronics to many types of business machines.[88] Independent of MIT's related work, Desch's staff explored the use of microfilm, high-speed printers, miniature tubes, and magnetic digital recording. Very important, Desch soon gained a reputation as a designer of innovative electronic tubes.[89]

Then, just as Desch's work was leading to the construction of hardware, the crisis in Europe and Deeds's patriotism ended his commercial projects. His expertise in electronics and, as importantly, his unique manufacturing abilities, attracted the attention of the men in Weaver's group at the National Defense Research Committee. Before the end of 1940, Desch became part of the rise of Big Science. Within another year, he became central to the history of the Bush's Comparator and to OP-20-G's future. Of course, he had to stop all the work he was doing on microfilm data machines, ones that were quite like what Bush had been proposing as a means of conquering the information problem.

Rapid Selector Data Entry Device, 1940
(Hagley Museum & Library)

Chapter V
Little Libraries and Little Science: The Information Problem

While Vannevar Bush was coping with the frustrations of scientific calculation and as Stanford Hooper was confronting the challenges created by automated ciphers, another science related problem was demanding attention. The failure of American libraries to satisfy the demands of important scientists was underscoring the inadequacies of the institutional support for research in America. To complicate matters, more than one library problem had developed. That seemed to make it impossible to find solutions that could balance the interests of those demanding the creation of a system for elite researchers with the needs of those responsible for improving America's public library system.

The Many and Varied Library Problems

Just as technology led to a secrecy crisis, improvements in printing, communications and transportation created a bundle of opportunities and frustrations that, by the end of World War I, began to be called the "library problem." That problem was less obvious and objective than the one created by the new code and cipher machines and there was a much wider range of proposed solutions. Librarians and their patrons could not agree on a diagnosis of the supposed information malady. About all they agreed on was that the situation had reached critical proportions by the onset of World War II.

For some literary populists, and for most librarians, the problem was unequal access to books. Others emphasized the growing cost of library materials and predicted a devastating financial implosion. Patrons complained of the difficulty of using what was already held in the libraries while managers of research collections warned they were running out of space. Some influential users declared the truly important problem to be the inability of the traditional library to serve its most important client, the scientific researcher. As a result of the multiple complaints, many groups, including important ones outside the traditional bounds of librarianship, began to vie for the scarce resources needed to reform the library.

The awareness of what later became known as the information problem was not confined to the United States. In fact, some believed that Europeans were taking the lead in meeting the majority of the complaints. During the first decades of the twentieth century, there were hints that Europe might leap-frog the United States in providing democratic access to reading materials. All agreed that Europeans had the best archive methods and the best research libraries. Their Documentalists had outdistanced all others in exploring advanced methods of indexing, cataloging and retrieving new types of materials.[1] Informed Americans looked to Paul Otlet and his colleagues who had created ways that seemed better suited to the needs of scientists and bureaucrats than those used in America.[2] Such European ideas had some impact on the American library movement, but it was internal influences that shaped the definitions of the library problems and that created the link to the machines for cryptanalysis.

Reform by Outsiders

In particular, it was two of the many American library reform urges that bridged the worlds of information and intelligence. Both were involved in the rise of applied science and both were outside the library mainstream. Academic engineers, such as Vannevar Bush, and a group from the emerging federal infrastructure of the physical and biological sciences, the American Documentalists, took the point. They argued for their very special interpretation of the 1930s information problem and went on to win control over the information technology of the postwar era. They shared a faith in advanced technology and both prescribed microfilm and electronic machines.

The two clusters of reformers put forward unique solutions, ones that did not mesh with the needs and views of the traditional librarians nor the typical library user. Of great importance for the history of the library, both were advocates of systems for scientific specialists and they called for a much larger role for scientists in setting information methods and policies. As a result, they quite innocently demanded solutions that had more than a touch of elitism. They were not united in the 1930s, but they shared four things; they searched for the means to subsidize increasingly expensive library services for a tiny minority of users; they proposed methods and techniques that became useful to the government during the 1940s; they became linked to forces that changed their quest from one to aid science to one to establish what later became known as the information industry; and, from the beginning, they bypassed established library and data management organizations.

In the 1930s and early 1940s, the lines between the two reform groups and the business machine industry were clear, but the relationships with the organizations that represented the traditional librarians, the American Library Association and its spinoffs, such as the associations for industrial and academic research libraries, were more complex. The engineer, Bush, saw professional data managers as irrelevant, unless they were willing to subsidize his work, and he looked on librarians in much the same way. Bush did not go to librarians for advice and he ignored the work of the European Documentalists. He certainly did not include any of them in his networks of influence and support, ones which were confined to engineers and the foundations that financed applied science.

During the first years of American Documentalism, its leaders approached business machine companies asking them to subsidize their work, but they were sent away. They received a somewhat warmer response from a segment of the traditional library community, those representing the largest research universities and what were then called "special" libraries. The initial relationship was not close, however, and soon after World War II its tenuous nature became evident as the American Documentalists cut their ties to library organizations. At the same time, they began to link with business machine manufacturers and to assume the international role of those who had been their mentors in the 1930s, the European Documentalists.[3]

The separation from traditional librarians came very early but even in the 1930s few understood why those who ran the typical library showed such little interest in reform. When Bush and the Documentalists offered their plans for intellectual and technical revolutions they were puzzled by what they interpreted as insensitivity to modern information needs. But, there were some very good reasons why the mainstream librarians appeared to shun Bush and the

Documentalists. The absence of librarians from among those who turned to advanced technology during the 1930s, 1940s and 1950s is explained by the very early history of the American library system, by the nature of the nation's research institutions and universities and by the economic dependency of America's struggling pre-World War II science.

Libraries and Librarians for the People

In the antebellum period, generations before institutionalized science became a major force in the nation, the lowered costs of paper and printing, the expansion of a literate and wealthy population and the first blushes of the specialization of knowledge led to a publications revolution. Private publishers and booksellers were the center of the growing production and distribution systems, but the old small libraries in America changed in response to the new opportunities. College libraries began to expand, older voluntary libraries sought public funds to create a system for the general population, and the few large elite libraries in the nation searched for the means to manage larger collections and please increasing numbers of demanding patrons.[4] By 1900, the American library system was essentially public, but, like the nation's school system, it was decentralized. It was locally oriented, financed, and governed. The United States was dotted with more than three thousand small libraries, ones tied to each other only through the very fragile links of a few cooperative programs among the larger libraries, private library service organizations and a growing but weak library profession. In the era of the Civil War, there were only a handful of men and women who called themselves librarians. In 1900, over three thousand Americans, mostly women, identified themselves as professionals and their numbers began to double every decade. Such explosive growth was not the result of professional imperialism, for the librarians had shrunk rather than expanded their domain.

An umbrella organization for professionals and interested citizens, the American Library Association, was formed in the third quarter of the nineteenth century.[5] Its founders took a broad view of the emerging profession. They advocated and, in some cases, invented new methods and technologies for the organization of all types of information. However, the Association quickly lost its connection with innovation and advanced technology. It also lost its drive to establish librarians as information managers and educators whose skills could be used in all settings. Librarians failed to establish themselves in academia as "professors of books," and data processors displaced them in the business world.[6] As a result, librarians were trained in a narrow range of skills and faced a limited market for their services. There were so few great research libraries that only a handful of librarians became specialists in acquisitions and preservation; fewer still were employed by indexing and abstracting organizations; and, the corporate and industrial librarian-archivist was more than rare.[7] As the librarians withdrew to the confines of the small public library, they became less able to control their own destinies and less willing to support technological innovations.[8] Given that librarians invariably were employees in nonprofit organizations, there was little chance for the emergence of the type of professional power that was developing in the American individual practice legal and medical professions of the early twentieth century.[9]

Thus, the information market was the determining force, not the profession. Despite the obvious role of politics and philanthropy in the public library system, and although librarians were trained to see themselves as public servants, what was supplied to the libraries, what was read and the nature of librarianship was demand-driven. Of course, there were limits to the role of the market, ones set by general moral and political standards. But, the commercial book market determined what was available to the libraries and the demands of readers determined what libraries housed and the services they could offer. The size and clientele of the library also determined the librarian's orientations and responsibilities. Only those employed in the few large national, city and university libraries escaped the impact of the market forces. It took massive infusions of dedicated funds to give librarians the professional freedom needed to determine library holdings or to be able to channel resources to professionals and intellectuals. Very few institutions had the funds or the mandate needed to support the early vision of the librarian as a powerful and highly paid information professional. The vast majority of librarians were employed in budget starved general purpose libraries whose mission was to serve patrons who presented the most general and unsophisticated requests.

A System Without a Center for Science

The American library system led to more than low budgets, low salaries, and lack of professional power. The United States developed a unique infrastructure for its libraries. Again, it was the market that determined such things as what and how library materials were indexed and abstracted. Unlike the more affluent European nations, the United States did not have a great central national library or the type of government needed for top-down solutions to any of the library problems. Especially important was the limited role of the federal government.

American federalism precluded the establishment of a widespread system of national libraries and subsidized services. The limited federal presence had a negative impact on the development of library methods and the profession. Of significance to the history of Documentalism and Bush's library machine, the government could not compensate for the absence of market support for the information needs of scientists and technicians. The Library of Congress and the Smithsonian Institution were the closest America came to having a general national library, but both were weak and struggling institutions until well into the twentieth century. They could not, for example, serve as effective centers for indexing and cataloging the flood of new technical articles from around the world. They certainly could not aspire to what Paul Otlet and his associates were building in Europe, a world bibliography. The Library of Congress did make some efforts to act like a true central library, but its projects were usually defeated by slim budgets. It began to develop a research-oriented classification system in the early 1900s, to act as a central cataloging agency and to compile what amounted to a national catalog of books and periodicals. But its slow moving programs depended upon the cooperative efforts of the nation's already hard-pressed libraries.[10]

The federal bureaucracy's role in the organization and distribution of information also remained very limited and disorganized until the mid-twentieth century. There were no national technical and professional libraries of scope and merit. For example, for many years the indexing and cataloging of medical literature was done by army physicians during their off-duty hours, and the whims of a fickle congress and the largesse of private donors determined the fate of national medical publications.[11] Not surprisingly, there was even less federal influence in organizing the literature in other scientific fields. Another weakness was that each government bureaucracy had its own separate and usually small and poorly funded publications branch. By the 1930s, when the

New Deal led to the expansion of the federal bureaucracy, the situation reached a state of chaos.[12]

The fledgling voluntary scientific and professional groups of the country did make attempts at organizing information in their fields, but most remained too poor to compensate for the absence of true national scientific and technical libraries. Voluntary organizations founded journals, published indexes to relevant literature, and compiled bibliographies. Local professional groups continued to support technical libraries in their cities and they attempted to link themselves through such things as "special library" associations. But, no profession, whether it was physicians, engineers or historians, could build a national library or satisfy all the very expensive information demands of its members.[13] Even the American Chemical Society's income from the German patents seized in World War I was not enough to allow it to fill the needs of its industry.[14]

The libraries of the American higher educational system could not fill the void and the emerging corporate research departments would not. Despite their growing and increasingly costly collections, the American universities and professional schools were unable to take on the burden of solving the scientific or any other library problem. The American universities were not organized in a way that allowed them to effectively subsidize truly national or international scholarship. The rich private universities had to focus on serving their own faculties and students and state institutions were mandated to serve local, not national, needs. In all cases, a university's library was a means of increasing its competitive advantage in the academic marketplace. That usually meant devoting its resources to the faculties in the humanities, being watchful of the impact of such tentative moves toward innovation as interlibrary loan systems and forming special associations that further removed the university from the public libraries.[15]

Furthermore, the university libraries had established their traditions before the rise of applied science. It was not until the twentieth century that specialized science played a great role in American universities, as reflected in the purchasing and service policies of their major libraries. Even institutions devoted to technology gave little attention to scientific publications. The nation's technical schools quite naturally used their scarce funds for equipment rather than books. In addition, the literature in scientific fields presented special problems for any library. It was concentrated in journals and no school had the financial ability to purchase, let alone catalog and cross reference, all the articles in all the scientific periodicals. The prewar situation was not as grave as in the 1950s when it was estimated there were fifty thousand scientific journals with over a million useful articles, only half of which were indexed. But it seemed clear that a crisis was at hand, one that private universities could not overcome.[16]

Unfortunately for librarians and scientists, there was little chance that the market would ever compensate for the nature of the university system. By default, much of what there was of an infrastructure for the library system became part of the private for-profit sector. The names Bowker, Poole, and Wilson, among many, became familiar to librarians who needed indexes to general periodicals and books as well as abstracts.[17] But what those companies could index and abstract was determined by the financial support of their subscribers. Since few libraries had users who needed intensely indexed technical materials, the private firms could not devote resources to the professions.

The First Library Problem

The lack of attention to the needs of special groups, such as scientists, was a result of the evolution of the American library system. From a long-term perspective, it is easy to understand why the first library professionals considered the library problems to be the very practical ones of devising the methods and supplying the workforce for the populistic general purpose American library. Given the resources available to them, those problems were more than enough to handle.[18] After the Civil War, the more vocal of the library reformers, such as Melvil Dewey, were strong advocates of the democratization of knowledge through the creation of what became the public library.[19] Although they desired the creation of state agencies to cap the systems and looked forward to majestic research libraries, they had to accept the American system of local support and control. A continued demand for centralized systems or a focus on the needs of special groups, such as scientists or scholars, would have been politically dangerous. As the membership of the American Library Association reflected the growth of the local libraries, the needs of the majority of its members had to become the focus of that always threadbare organization. These small libraries and isolated librarians needed practical and inexpensive solutions to their problems.[20] There were no funds and little demand for esoteric approaches.

There was no chance for a top-down revolution.[21] Even the best friends of the American library were populistic. The emphasis on creating a widespread net of local libraries was enshrined in the policies of the wealthy Carnegie philanthropies. Although Carnegie and the Rockefellers gave millions to establish major research libraries, millions more to supply them with copies of rare materials from Europe and sponsored research into library organization, their policies in the formative years favored simple solutions to the problem of the distribution of general knowledge. That commitment had consequences for library training and methods.[22]

The rush to establish local libraries increased the need for low paid library workers. Starting with a handful of institutions in the Civil War era, the nation created several thousand libraries in a single generation. The holdings of the libraries also grew, leading to the need for full-time attendants. In 1875, the federal government's statisticians thought a collection of three hundred books was worthy of being called a library. Thirty years later, five thousand books was used as the cutting point to qualify for the name.[23] Such libraries could no longer use intuitive methods for cataloging, storing and managing their collections. But, few of them could afford to pay grand salaries or to support the high cost services and staff of large research institutions. Thus, for early leaders like Melvil Dewey, the library problems were the considerable ones of recruiting several thousand workers to a yet-to-be profession, convincing them to be committed to public service, and training them to be efficient managers of the emerging general purpose library. The solutions Dewey and his colleagues devised fit with the time and place.[24] But, they left a few users dissatisfied with the American library. By the 1920s, scientists were especially anxious to undo much of what the founders established as a library culture.[25]

In building a library profession, the initial leaders had faced many constraints. Most were financial, making economy and efficiency necessities. The leaders had to attract and train a skilled workforce, but one that a decentralized and egalitarian library system could afford. Library methods had to be efficient and equipment could not demand high capital investments. Cataloging and indexing rules had to be simple and as much of the library work as possible had to be put on the shoulders of unsophisticated patrons. Such early technical innovations as the card catalog satisfied the need for "library economy" by allowing the user to be his own reference librarian.[26]

Few libraries could afford salaries much greater than those paid to the low status teachers in the common schools. Thus, recruitment from among those destined for the established professions or the business world was impractical, as were the cries demanding that librarians have a college education. The hope that librarians would be trained as experts in various subject matters so they could have a status equal to the professionals they might serve was also unrealistic.[27] Professional control and rigorous standards were also impossible to achieve. The number of professional librarians was not large, library groups were not wealthy and they were not politically powerful. There were three thousand ill-paid librarians in the United States a generation after the first library association was founded and less than a third of them belonged to a professional organization.[28]

Melvil Dewey's recruitment of females into his 1880s training program, the practical curricula of the early library schools and their short terms were a result of institutional and economic constraints. Women had few options for high paying jobs and even those with college educations saw librarianship as one of the few ways to channel their general education into their careers.[29] The use of on the job training during the nineteenth and early twentieth century was quite rational for both men and women who could expect a very low rate of economic return from their investment in professional education. Thus, it was very difficult to establish librarianship as a legitimate academic subject. Although the major foundations changed their orientation from encouraging library construction to the upgrading of services, librarians remained without the academic prestige needed to impose standards from above.

The attempt by the Carnegie interests to create a modern library science by founding a doctoral program at the University of Chicago in the mid-1920s, and the associated movement to reform all library education, did not lead to changes in the profession or the death of the essentially vocational approach to training. The faculty at the new school at Chicago was filled with respected experts from a range of traditional humanistic and social science fields. They were highly motivated outsiders who wished to change all aspects of the American library and to make it fit with their perception of the needs of the emerging scholarly community. But, their influence was very limited, perhaps because of their overly academic orientation. They were as much or more concerned with the creation of a new field which treated the library as a subject of scholarly inquiry as with reshaping the profession. They and those who followed them, such as the more pragmatic Louis Round Wilson, who turned the Chicago school toward professional training, found it difficult to define library science and to turn it into a course of study.[30] It was impossible for them to overcome the underlying economics and politics of the American library system.[31] Given the financial condition of the nation, they saw little chance for the introduction of revolutionary technologies. Simplified library methods and the emphasis on the most basic of library tools remained in place because of the market forces.[32]

Methods and Tools for the Public

The librarians of the nineteenth century had to develop labor-saving methods and inexpensive equipment. Melvil Dewey's and Charles Cutter's widely accepted subject oriented cataloging-shelving systems and their various modifications were simple, fit with the intellectual training of the era and were very convenient for librarians who had to provide reference services for a wide range of nonspecialized patrons.[33] When given a choice between Dewey's very simple approach and the later and much more detailed and complex Library of Congress classification system, the vast majority of American libraries stood by Dewey.[34] Such sparse systems as his allowed the librarian to deal with a limited and logically arranged set of terms and thus to fill at least minimal needs of all types of patrons. Although the method meant that professionals had to be paid to catalog a book, using a short class number for a volume saved enormous sums of money. Importantly, professional control avoided intellectual and semantic chaos. The run away use of new terms was something feared even by those who indexed and cataloged for the professional societies. The Dewey number also served a vital managerial function. It could be extended in a rational way to become a unique physical identifier. That eased the shelving problem and made the loan process much more efficient. A single identifier also minimized the cost of maintaining library catalogs and allowed a display of materials that turned a user into his own browsing reference librarian. But, such savings came at a cost and Dewey's system came under fire as soon as it was born in the mid-nineteenth century.

Librarians in the larger and specialized libraries found it simplistic. They and the academic and scientific professionals complained that its intellectual structure and vocabulary were dated, that it did not truly allow unique identification of books, and that it was unsuited to the newer mode of intellectual communications, the specialized periodical. Especially irksome to the rising academic professionals was the established practice of indexing by one or a few hierarchial librarian-specified categories, rather than by multiple terms and those used by current practitioners. The librarian imposed category systems and limited use of index terms were not well suited to the needs of experts. Certainly, they could not indicate the wide range of subjects covered in a book or journal. Furthermore, they usually imposed an intellectual order and vocabulary that was strange to those in the rarified and rapidly changing fields in science and technology. Even laymen were puzzled when they found that works on light bulbs had to be found through categories such as: incandescent-light--electric.

The librarians close to the new scientists yearned for classification and indexing systems such as the one the European Documentalists developed at the close of the nineteenth century, the Universal Decimal Classification system. It was a highly sophisticated refinement of Dewey's system, its terms and categories fit with the new scientific concepts and it was oriented to scientists' ways of using of books and articles. The Library of Congress's complex and pragmatic classification system was a response to such demands, but many scientists wanted something more radical. They looked to the time when they, not professional librarians or indexers, would determine the terms and categories used to index and catalog publications. Such control, they thought, would allow scientists to share the latest research through indexing by multiple and contemporary specialized terms. By the end of World War I, scientists were voicing their frustrations and sought ways to establish what the market would not support: an information system for science.

The Other Library

At times, humanists and professional librarians joined with the scientific reformers, but men like Vannevar Bush and the American Documentalists usually stood alone when they went beyond advocating the most basic technological solutions. The separation between them and the traditional librarians continued well into the computer era and shaped the nature of applied information science in America.[35] The primary reason for the distance between the groups was that the scientific problems and many of the proposed cures had little relevance for the general purpose library or the vast majority of library users--including traditional scholars in the humanities. Another reason was that the proposed solutions demanded a reallocation of scarce resources; scientific information systems called for massive subsidies.

The American library began a full generation before research was more than an interest of educated gentlemen, but even in the 1870s there were indications of how expensive a science information system would be. When the famous John Shaw Billings, then of the Army Medical Service, thought of advancing American medicine by compiling an up to date international bibliography on medicine and related sciences, he found that the printing and distribution of his planned eight volume series would cost the equivalent of a week's wages of three thousand respectable American workers. If he had factored in the costs of acquiring, indexing,and abstracting all the books and journals covered in his bibliography, the American Congress would have been even more horrified at the prospect of supporting the birth of an indexing service for American science.[36] Congress did allow the army to allocate some funds for Billings's projects, but then it was unwilling to fully support his or any other scientific information project. There was no institution to fill the vacuum.

From Advocacy to Industry

Many were frustrated, but few knew what to do. Besides men like Vannevar Bush, it was a small group of men outside both the traditional libraries and the American university system that began to change discontent into the outlines of solutions and institutions. Until the mid-1930s, they did not have a name for themselves, but they eventually adopted one borrowed from the special European librarians they so admired, Documentalists. The American Documentalists achieved few of their goals, but the organization they formed, the American Documentation Institute, became the bridge between their starved idealism of the 1930s and the huge information industry of the Cold War.[37] The Documentalists began alone, but during World War II they started to forge alliances that would lead them to become important to the institutions that came to define the nature of America's military-academic Big Science. The Documentalists' World War II experiences shaped the future of the information industry and, a generation later, the library.

The efforts by the American Documentalists during the 1930s gave them a technical and political advantage over traditional librarians during World War II. Many of the Documentalists were called upon to fill emergency needs for information on America's enemies. The NDRC, the OSS, the Censorship Office and the intelligence agencies all sponsored massive information projects. And, applied science activities such as the Manhattan Project and the Radiation Laboratory demanded new types of information services. The achievements in handling tons of documents during the war allowed the first Documentalists to seize the new opportunities of the Cold War and to gain the funding they had begged for during the 1930s. But the successes of the 1950s drew the reformers further away from the librarians. Their attempts to fill the information needs of government sponsored science led them to expensive solutions, ones ill suited to the typical American library.

The dependency on Cold War science altered the orientation of the early reformers and attracted new players. What began as an altruistic search in the 1930s for subsidies to rescue a struggling American science became an enormous profit oriented industry tuned to the needs of government science and the intelligence programs of the 1960s. From there, those who developed the methods and machines for government science took a leading part in the computerization and commercialization of the American library. At the same time, Documentalism was turned into information science. The information science movement of the 1950s and 1960s tended to bring the engineers, the inheritors of the business machine industry and the old Documentalists together. But, librarians continued to remain on the outside and, as in the prewar years, to be regarded as conservatives who resisted technological and intellectual change.

The First Documentalists

At first glance, those who founded the American Documentalist movement seem rather odd people whose deep commitment to a technological revolution in the library made them unable to work with mainstream librarians or with data managers in the business and bureaucratic worlds. But, the early Documentalists were not just technology advocates fixated on microfilm and automation. They were deeply involved with building new institutions for a threatened American science; they had special information problems that separated them from others; and, they were frequently rejected by those in business and academia. The Documentalists had good reasons for creating their own organization.[38]

Their story dates from well before World War I, when there was a drive to force American higher education, including professional schools, to conform to the elite university model. One of those who became involved was Edward E. Slosson, a scientist turned publicist. He investigated the nation's universities and then became a spokesman for the concentration of academic resources. He emerged as a valued advisor to the major educational foundations. Among his many writings in behalf of modern science his, *Great American Universities*, of 1910, helped to shift the attention of the philanthropic organizations to the needs of the research universities.[39] Slosson was not alone in his pre-World War I efforts. Men directly connected to the Carnegie and Rockefeller foundations, such as Abraham Flexner, toured the medical and law schools of the nation and argued for policies to turn them into creators of knowledge.

Such frankly elitist views did much to shape the policies of educational accrediting agencies and the major foundations. But Slosson and his colleagues knew that more had to be done to gain the massive funding needed to allow American scientists into the circle of world-class research. They had to gain public favor for science. As a result, Slosson wrote dozens of popular articles and books that were aimed at convincing the American people and their legislators to subsidize research. Other science advocates joined Slosson and, like him, become entangled with the library problem. Unlike Vannevar Bush, they were not committed solely to academic science or to the university system. The majority of them looked toward a larger federal role and an expanded government scientific bureaucracy.[40]

The search for support for research became desperate. For example, Frederick Cottrell, an academic biochemist, became so worried about the state of American science by World War I that he devoted the appreciable royalties from his discoveries to financing the work of others. He used his fortune to launch what he foresaw as a self-financing, nonprofit corporation to rescue the American scientist. He hoped that his Research Corporation would become a major force in American science through funding investigations then using the income from any resulting patents to sponsor other worthy proposals. His plans were not implemented until the end of World War I, but his early work for the cause brought him into contact with the other leaders of American science.[41] One of those was also an applied chemist, Atherton Siedell. Siedell worked in the major scientific bureaus in Washington, including the Department of Agriculture and the small but important federal medical agencies. He became an internationally recognized figure because of his research and because of his definitive reference works in applied chemistry. His scientific and bibliographic achievements made him very sensitive to the failures of the nation's libraries and he turned his attention to finding ways to allow the United States to access the world's scientific literature.[42]

Meanwhile, Slosson had been busy organizing to bolster science. In 1921, he agreed to head the Science Service of Washington, D.C., a publications agency created by the struggling national institutions, such as the National Academy of Sciences.[43] The job of the Service was to popularize science and lobby for private and governmental support. Slosson was soon joined by a younger man who had also migrated from a scientific career to writing in behalf of research, Watson Davis.[44] Working under Slosson for a decade, Davis took over the Science Service in 1933 and quickly became an influential science advocate. He continued Slosson's policies but added some embellishments. One of those was to put more effort into solving the scientific information problem.

Davis Tries to Rescue Science

Much of what Davis put forward was very idealistic and, at times, grandiose. He shared many dreams with the crusading European Documentalists and their allies such as H. G. Wells.[45] Davis hoped to create a constantly updated world bibliography of science. A key part of his plan was to have abstracting and indexing done by authors.[46] He also foresaw a new type of interlibrary loan service for scientific publications and he had an ambitious idea for a new type of publications center. It was to house a master copy of technical papers and reports that had not been formally published. Under Davis's plan, abstracts in scientific journals would inform scientists of the existence of a report and those who were interested could order a copy from his centralized nonprofit service. Like some of the European Documentalists, he and his colleagues even thought of miraculous machines that would sort through and reproduce specialized bibliographies at unheard-of speeds. Such machines would make another dream possible, a service that would automatically provide researchers with selections from all the world's journals based upon their known professional interests.[47]

Many of Davis's ideas emerged in the 1920s, but he was unable to turn them into programs until the mid-1930s. The long delay was due to several factors. Especially important was his inability to convince traditional librarians to integrate their work with his. As a result, Davis concluded that he would have to form his own library group rather than just encourage established institutions, such as the Library of Congress, to provide the desired services. That created organizational and financial problems. Another of the reasons for the long delay was that all of Davis's plans had to await a solution to the difficulties with what he saw as the technology that would sweep away most of the library troubles--microfilm.[48]

The Great Hope, Microfilm

Davis and his allies were not alone in seeing microfilm as the basis for a data and information revolution. Pundits foresaw miracles of data storage. In the 1920s, there were hopes of being able to attain a reduction ratio of two hundred to one and there was talk of putting an entire Bible on a frame of microfilm. In Europe, the microfiche was hailed as the replacement for the book. But, microfilm was seen as much more than a storage medium or as just a solution to the memory problem. It was predicted to be the way to overcome the high cost of data entry and reproduction. In America, business machine companies knew filming had the potential to beat typewriters or keypunch machines. One camera shot could record an entire document in a few seconds. There was even more that made microfilm so attractive: It was lightweight and compact; it cost little to mail; and, it could be automatically copied.

It was no wonder that Watson Davis argued that microfilm could be the means of allowing what Europeans such as Paul Otlet called for as early as 1906, an "edition of one" to allow specialized research reports to be circulated. Microfilm was also touted as the solution to the problems of library storage. The Documentalists were joined by some Americans, usually those in charge of larger research libraries, who looked to it for a cure for their particular difficulties. Mandated to build huge collections and prodded to permanently keep all materials that entered the library, they had fears their buildings would soon run out of space.[49] They thought microfilm was about ready to solve the problem. Microfilming also seemed to be the ready answer to the high cost of acquiring and preserving rare research materials. In addition, administrators at the largest libraries shared Davis's faith in microfilm as the basis for an interlibrary loan system.[50] Unfortunately, neither microfilm nor the equipment needed to make it useful were close to being ready before the mid-1930s. Davis and the others had to wait for major and expensive improvements in film, cameras, and the means of searching and reading microforms.[51]

Miniature photography was born almost as soon as photography itself, but, despite famous episodes such as sending secret messages out of Paris during the siege of 1870, the frontiers of microphotography had not been reached by the 1920s. Germany's Emanuel Goldberg had made tremendous advances in all the technologies of microfilm, including the invention of a rapid search machine, but even his genius could not turn it into the foundation of a cost-effective data and information processing technology.[52] It was the rise of the movie industry, then developments in the business world that financed the creation of the first microfilm revolution.[53] When Eastman-Kodak took over the ideas and crude equipment of the banker-inventor George L. McCarthy in 1926, it found there was a huge demand for an inexpensive way to create and store commercial archive records.[54] Eastman invested in film and camera systems and, beginning in the mid-1930s, it and a few of its competitors began to develop special microfilm devices for America's bureaucracies.[55]

Such achievements came too late to suit Watson Davis. When he began his microfilm crusade in the 1920s, he toured the country trying to convince corporations to spend the money for the development and production of film, camera and readers. But he found it impossible to gather support for the creation of the special devices. He was politely dismissed by foundations and corporations that saw little future in what was sure to be a costly development program. Of course, they knew that scientists and librarians could never provide a significant market. Even Vannevar Bush offered little encouragement. As a result, Davis decided he could no longer wait. Without adequate financing, he launched his own microfilm programs including one for the creation of special cameras and readers.[56]

Unfortunately, he made his move just as commercial and bureaucratic demands were leading Eastman and other companies to develop the equipment that soon made the use of microfilm relatively common in American research libraries.[57] Within a few years of Davis's first commissioning of special equipment, many libraries were independently using microfilm to provide copies of their materials and microfilm was employed in massive projects to bring rare documents to America.[58] Because microfilming had become so common, Davis's 1934 attempt at creating an interlibrary loan program, the Bibliofilm Service at the National Agricultural Library, and his 1936 "edition of one," Auxiliary Publication Service in Washington, D.C., might seem to deserve little historical attention. But, along with the founding of the American Documentation Institute in 1937, there was a very special feature of Davis's projects that made them important to the history of the library problem. Unlike the other microfilm projects, Davis's efforts were directly tied to and run by those involved with the libraries of federal scientific agencies.

Davis's microfilm interlibrary loan system was located at what was then one of the few libraries that had a national system responsibility, the Library of the Department of Agriculture. Besides housing the premier collection of materials on agricultural science, it had to supply the dozens of agricultural research stations with copies of scientific reports from around the world. And, through Atherton Siedell, Davis tied his loan service to another of the few national scientific libraries, the one at the National Institute of Health. Those connections, along with the influences of World War II and the Cold War, saved Davis's American Documentation Institute from experiencing the quiet death of his microfilm projects.

The First ADI Meets Big Science

Davis had never intended to form an organization divorced from traditional librarians or one that would represent an industry. His intentions when creating the American Documentation Institute in 1937 were to focus attention on the information needs of science, to create nonprofit institutions to provide scientific information services and to extend the reach of a new type of librarianship. The Institute was begun as a voluntary organization whose members were to represent the most important research libraries and scientific organizations. Its purpose was stated as the encouragement of the development of Documentalism which was broadly defined as, "the assembling, classification and distribution of documents of all sorts in all fields of human activity."[59]

Davis told the founding members, a group that included high level representatives from the American Library Association and the humanities oriented, American Council of Learned Societies, that Documentalism was "not specifically limited to the fields of the physical and natural sciences... it includes all phases of the issuance, use and interchange of recorded information."[60]

Sadly, the Institute did not accomplish much in its first decade. It was unable to prevent Davis's two pet projects from languishing and it could not find a way to start other nonprofit services for science. The Institute might have withered away if a new generation of men, with new connections and interests, had not begun to replace the founders. Men such as Ralph Shaw, Vernon Tate, Eugene Miller, and Mortimer Taube brought new energy to the organization and forged a more intensely scientific definition of the library problem.[61] Many of those postwar leaders began their careers as scientists rather than librarians and those who had been trained as librarians had very special responsibilities. They were in charge of huge data bases and mandated to supply reports to demanding expert patrons spread across the country. They implemented the older dreams of multiple subject indexing, user defined vocabularies and intense abstracting. And, they were able to go far beyond microfilm in their search for technology for the science library. In the early 1950s, the Institute was changed to represent a new breed of Documentalist, those who were forging the methods and machines for the emerging federal scientific establishment of the Cold War. Within another few years, the separation from the librarians became more obvious and by the late 1960s the organization changed its name to the American Society for Information Science. By that time, it represented a new high status occupation and a for-profit industry, one that depended upon methods and equipment, especially computers, that very few American libraries could afford or effectively employ.[62]

Beyond the Library Problem: Memex

Many of the new information scientists of the 1960s came from an engineering background or had begun their professional careers in the computer industry. It was natural for them to trace their intellectual ancestry to the ideas of the engineer and the computer builder, Vannevar Bush, rather than to Watson Davis. During his career, Bush made many different recommendations about the library problem but his 1930s vision of a microfilm-based machine he called the Memex came to be seen as the grandfather of the most advanced methods and machines of information science.[63] The ideas behind Memex went far beyond the usual definitions of the library problem and the common faith in microfilm.[64] They pointed to an era when the librarian and his methods would be replaced by scientists using a creative automaton. It is no wonder that 1980s hypertext, information networks, associational memory systems and computer workstations have been traced to Bush's inspirational article, "As We May Think."[65]

Although Bush did not publish his ideas about Memex until the end of World War II, he had begun thinking about it and the library problem in the early 1930s. He shared Davis's concern about the state of American libraries, but his solutions were more radical, he was more removed from traditional librarians than were the Documentalists and he was more committed to high cost technological solutions than other library reformers. Bush wanted a fundamental reform of the library to make it conform to the concepts of the new scientist and engineers. He looked forward to the time when machines would allow practicing scientists to take charge of, if not just be able to bypass, the library.

For Bush, the great and dark enemy was the librarians' outdated hierarchial indexing schemes. It is unlikely that Bush ever examined existing or proposed systems, such as those of the European Documentalists or of the Library of Congress, but it is clear that he thought librarian defined systems would always be outdated and confining. Control had to be taken from the librarians and put into the hands of experts in the sciences. At minimum, Bush thought, scientists should be able to specify subject terms for indexes and catalogs. Without such control, Bush argued, new findings would continue to be lost in the growing mountains of scientific publications. But Bush had much more in mind and hinted that technology was ready to support a major revolution in information retrieval.[66] With the help of electronics and microfilm, Bush asserted, retrieval systems could be based upon the human dynamics of creativity and association, not the static categorical systems of the old librarians. Scientists would be able to leave trails of their inspired connections among articles and the ideas they contained. They would not be restricted by fixed systems, ideas, or even words.[67]

His Memex was to work like the human mind. Association among ideas rather than categories was to be its intellectual foundation. The machine was to be capable of performing typical searches based on unlimited numbers of mnemonic subject codes, but the trail of associations was to be its heart. The associational feature would be automatic. A scientist would specify which ideas were to be joined then pointers linking records would be instantly recorded on the microfilms in the machine. Memex might even be able to automatically create the links. Once established, the trail could be followed by a researcher or one of his colleagues. The ability to share the creative trails by shipping films from one location to another was a key element of Bush's view of the future of scientific information. Scholars in every field were to communicate with each other, free from the interference of artificial cataloging systems.

Bush realized that his vision of the Memex's hardware was one for the future, but, he claimed, a not too distant future. He described a desk size machine coordinating as many as seven reels of microfilm at one time. All or any of the reels could be replaced. Driven by instructions entered through keyboards and screens, the machine's photocells and electronics would automatically search all items at ultra high speeds (a thousand a second) and, when needed, record the associative trails or display or reproduce desired records and graphics through instant dry photography.[68] The machine had the potential to be a scientist's personal library because the films could contain hundreds of thousands of articles, most of which would be supplied on prepared tapes. Bush never explained how the original tapes would be created because he assumed that and many other institutional and logical problems would be solved by the physical scientists he urged to take charge of the coming information revolution.

Bush never built a Memex but he maintained a life long interest in the library problem. After World War II, he continued his attempts to put engineers and scientists in charge of the new library and to find sponsors whose subsidies could overcome the market forces that blocked the emergence of scientific information systems. To a significant degree, he was successful in attracting technologists to the cause of the library. MIT and its new computer scientists, among others, took leading roles in many military and civilian information projects, even ones initiated by those originally concerned with the traditional library. For example, the Ford Foundation's amply funded

Council on Library Resources placed much of the responsibility for new solutions in the hands of MIT's technological experts during the 1960s.[69] Like Bush, they recommended expensive technological systems that fit the needs of the emerging scientific institutions. At the same time, they attempted to shift the control over information from the librarian to the new information scientist, a man who was to deal with all information in all settings, not just in the old-fashioned public or university library.

Despite the similarity of their goals and those of Vannevar Bush, few of the new men realized how entangled their profession was with Bush's 1930s attempts to build his machines for secrecy and information, the Rapid Selector, and the Comparator.

Rapid Selector Electronics, 1940
(Hagley Museum & Library)

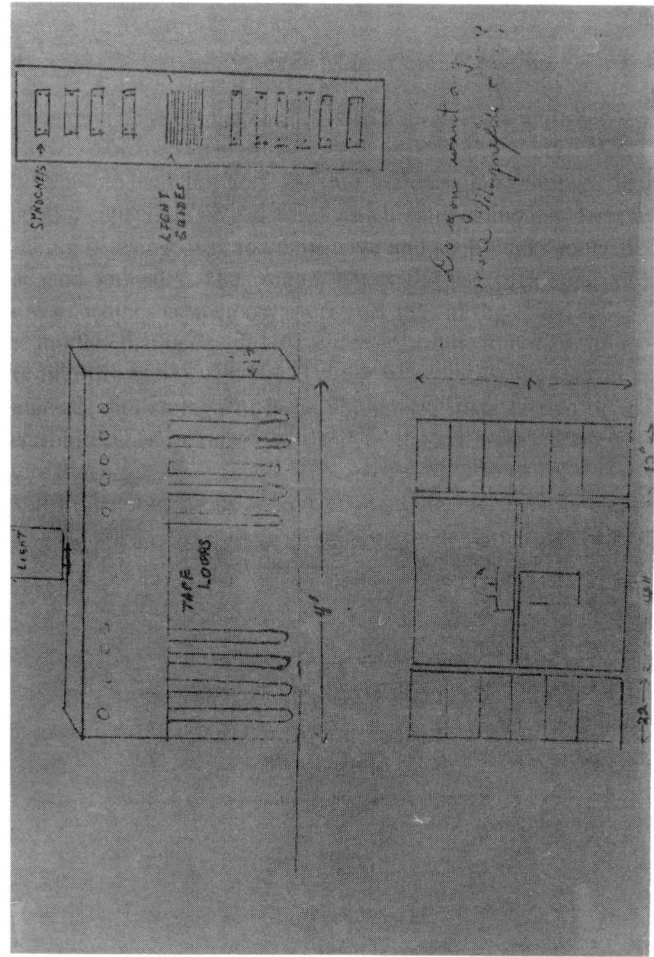

The Comparator, circa 1938
(W. S. MacDonald)

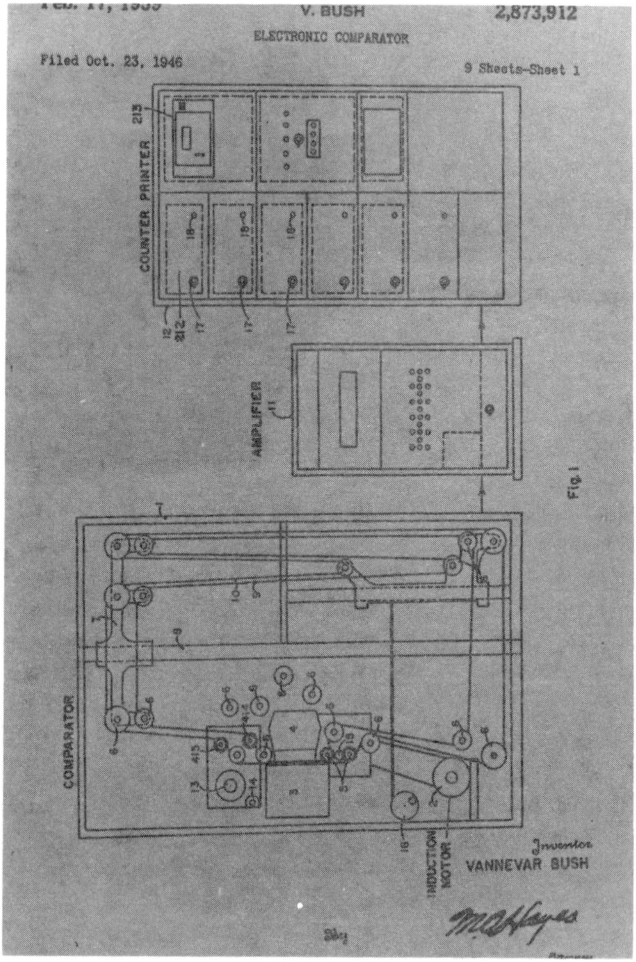

Feb. 17, 1959 V. BUSH 2,873,912
ELECTRONIC COMPARATOR
Filed Oct. 23, 1946 9 Sheets-Sheet 1

Inventor
VANNEVAR BUSH

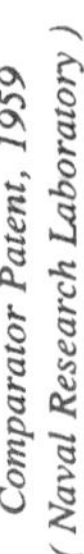

Comparator Patent, 1959
(Naval Research Laboratory)

Chapter VI
Machines for Secrecy: Perhaps

Remembering Hooper's Plans and the Bureau's Reaction

The technological changes that caused the library problems were creating greater challenges for 1930s codebreakers. The development of new cipher machines and the maturation of radio led to a critical byte problem for America's cryptanalysts. There was more and more data and it was overwhelming those who were charged with turning it into useful information for policy makers. The failure to predict the attack on Pearl Harbor, for example, was the result of too many bytes. The thousands of intercepted Japanese naval messages could not be analyzed with the men and equipment available to Laurance Safford's OP-20-G.[1]

The challenges to librarians and codebreakers were very similar. Vannevar Bush realized the similarity and knew the two groups could share technology and methods. Captain Stanford C. Hooper might not have been aware of the trends in scientific literature, but he was certainly frightened by the secrecy problem. It was what led him and his protege, Joseph Wenger, to Bush in late 1935.[2] After the initial meeting, Wenger became the liaison with Bush and the driving force behind the fight to overcome the Bureau of Engineering's technological conservatism.

Hooper's and Wenger's trip to Cambridge in late 1935 led to more than the first round of the Rapid Analytical Machine battles. Their contact with Bush locked the fates of the Selector and the Comparator together for more than twenty years. The library Selector and the cipher breaking Comparator shared more than technology and people.

They had similar and rather tortured life histories. Unfortunately, both suffered through years of naive expectations that were shattered by stubborn technologies, debilitating military and academic politics and mismanaged programs. The machine for secrecy was the first to confront those adversaries and it did not do very well during the 1930s. Despite Hooper's vision and Wenger's efforts, OP-20-G began World War II without any operating high-speed devices. The Rapid Analytical Machine project had to begin over again in 1942 and in conditions ill suited to long-term development. More than six years of opportunity had been wasted.

The reasons for the failure of Hooper's 1930s plans for the application of scientific-mathematical methods to codebreaking are complex. Bureaucratic tangles, bad luck, personality clashes, Bush's stubbornness, international crises, and the intransigence of technology partially account for the lost opportunity. But the major factor was institutional. Above all else, the military had not yet placed great faith in the kind of information cryptanalysis or other signals intelligence could provide.[3]

The Institutional Context

By the mid-1930s, Hooper and his admiring young officers feared that America would be dragged into a war with Naval Communications unprepared for a face-off with any power. Hooper's 1930s strategy, to collaborate with universities and corporate centers, was an attempt to compensate for the lack of money needed to prepare for a modern war. The Chief of Naval Operations supported his plans but the CNO's approval did not mean smooth sailing for Hooper and his men. Despite congress's and Roosevelt's decision to expand the fleet in the mid-1930s, OP-20-G's coffers did not overflow nor did those of the Bureau of Engineering. In some ways, naval expansion made the relationship between Communications, Hooper's science office, and Engineering more difficult.

Although Engineering's allocations were increased, the expansion of ship construction meant more, not less, pressure on its staff. By the end of the decade, technical and bureaucratic disputes over ship design ate up much of the Bureau's energies. Thus, even if it had been willing, Engineering had only a few men such as Lybrand Smith and a few moments to devote to abstract science or to speculative research.[4] To

Hooper's regret, OP-20-G continued to have to depend on Engineering because navy law and "G's" pauper budgets allowed little else. More independence and money might have come to OP-20-G if there had been widespread faith in signals intelligence. But, despite the contributions of Herbert Yardley's Black Chamber during the 1920s, then OP-20-G's penetration of Japanese naval codes, and, then, the cracking of her diplomatic messages, codebreaking remained a step-child of the American military.[5] Ironically, the reading of the Japanese naval and diplomatic code and cipher systems during the 1920s and 1930s masked the need for the long-term programs required for the development of advanced methods and machines. Even the navy's operating cryptanalysts did not lobby for such a program.[6] Only two men, Hooper and Wenger, saw the need and were willing to suffer the possible career penalties imposed on those who became advocates for unpopular causes. They were the ones brave enough to gamble on Vannevar Bush and the ones who had to overcome the Bureau's objections to "college professors" in 1936.[7]

Hooper and Wenger Are Enthralled

Hooper and Wenger had never abandoned their 1930 hopes for machines that would be much more advanced than the tabulators.[8] As discussed in Chapter Three, that led to their trip to Cambridge in late 1935.[9] At their first meeting, Bush was receptive and thought the navy's inquiry might lead to some income for his starved department. In turn, Bush and MIT impressed the navy men so much they decided that as soon as possible a return visit should be made to be sure Bush would not abandon them. Wenger sped back to Cambridge in late January and discussed OP-20-G's hopes and problems in more detail. Bush presented Wenger with a handwritten eight page outline of his plan for automating OP-20-G's cryptanalytic section and Wenger rushed to Washington to describe the exciting ideas to his superiors.[10]

Within a week, Wenger had retyped Bush's memorandum, discussed it with the men at the Bureau of Engineering and secured the new Director of Naval Communications's approval of the proposed relationship with Bush. All the necessary papers were forwarded to the Bureau of Engineering just as Hooper gained the endorsement of his great plan for all aspects of naval communications.[11] Wenger was ecstatic and looked forward to the realization of what he and Hooper had worked for since 1930. Wenger thought the agreement with Bush came just in time because it was evident that the world was rushing into a bloody conflict. The troubles in China and Germany's rearmament pointed in one direction, war, and signals intelligence was a critical resource.[12]

The First Defeat, Bush is Rejected

Just as Wenger proudly submitted his own visionary outline for the reorganization of OP-20-G, he received a slap in the face. The Bureau of Engineering refused to approve the agreement with Vannevar Bush![13] Wenger tried to work the bureaucratic magic that had smoothed the way for the introduction of the tabulators in 1932, but his informal efforts were ineffective. The situation developed into more than a standoff. Within six months after he had carried Bush's proposal to Washington, the conflict with the Bureau turned into a formal battle. Heated memos revealed an organizational nightmare and a contest between very different perspectives on the proper relationship of science and the navy.

Wenger was surprised by the Bureau's rejections and its long delay in explaining its reactions to Bush's ideas. He was especially upset because he thought he had arranged a firm agreement with the Bureau that ten thousand dollars would be allocated for the MIT research.[14] He also had thought that Bush's status would overawe any bureaucrat who might argue over details. He was wrong. When the Bureau finally responded it was with objections of every nature. Wenger felt betrayed. He was not alone in becoming emotional. An outburst came from Engineering's top officers. They became incensed when they realized that Wenger and Hooper had gone to Bush without consulting them about either technical or contractual questions. Apparently, Hooper had made at least a gentlemen's agreement with Bush before consulting Engineering.[15]

As bureaucrats, the engineers were upset because they were legally responsible for contracts, the supervision of manufacturing and the operational performance of machines. As friends who had sliced their own budgets to support the tabulators at OP-20-G, they may well have been angered at Hooper's seeming ingratitude. As technicians, the Radio men felt slighted because they had given OP-20-G so much help in designing the new naval enciphering machines, revising the IBM tabulators, and constructing Holtwick's novel analogs. They had also been very responsive to requests for advice on many other electrical and electronic matters. Thus, when they examined the details of Bush's contractual and technical proposals their alienation deepened. They became quite stubborn and would not yield to pleas from Wenger and his allies to pay deference to the great Vannevar Bush and to approve Hooper's plan for the relationship between scientists and the military.

Bush and Science and the Military

There was reason for the Bureau's alienation. What Bush demanded and Hooper and Wenger agreed to was startling. In 1936, Bush demanded of the navy what he would achieve only with the founding of the NDRC: having the government pay the bill while he remained free of supervision. He wanted the relationship with the navy to match the ideal relationship between university researchers and major private foundations. The researcher would submit a general proposal, then be funded without any interference from the grantor. Because the role of the university was discovery, even time schedules, Bush declared, could be unproductive. Following on his beliefs, Bush had refused to sign a typical navy contract or to make any promises about the results of his work. He tried to create a new role in the military, the highly paid private consultant. He did not wish to be supervised, especially by the Bureau of Engineering, and he probably asked that any patent rights go to MIT, not the government.[16] In addition, the original understanding did not include a promise to construct any machinery. The navy was to regard his thoughts on the subject of cryptanalytic machines as a product.[17] Bush and Wenger had also agreed to ignore the regulations demanding competitive bidding on naval contracts. Both thought it was irrational to subject such creative and secret work to public processes even if it could be broken down into small tasks. Bush obtained another understanding from Wenger that did not conform to bureaucratic rules: He was to be paid before the work began. Although academics were accustomed to such arrangements, the Bureau's men must have trembled at the thought of a congressman learning of an irresponsible commitment of government funds.[18]

More than deviation from naval contract law was involved. Bush requested what was an enormous amount of money in the era, at least for the navy. His ten thousand dollar consulting fee might have been common to the MIT faculty, but it was not what the Bureau was used to paying. Its men thought that ten thousand dollars just to outline his machines was outrageous. His later demand for an additional eight thousand dollars to finance more specific designs created even more intense reactions. The engineers may have pointed out that the amount Bush demanded could have been used to hire as many as six well paid civilian cryptanalysts, the same number of Bureau engineers, or, to triple the number of OP-20-G's tabulating machines. To hire Bush meant taking precious resources from the Bureau and from OP-20-G.

A Machine Too Soon

There were also serious technical objections. Although only the barest sketch, Bush's early 1936 proposal showed that he wanted the navy to use optical-scanning, high-speed data tapes, electronic computing and microfilm in a series of increasingly complex cryptanalytic machines. Such technologies, Bush emphasized, would allow processing speeds from ten to one hundred times faster than the tabulators. While Wenger and Hooper were thrilled by Bush's willingness to explore new technologies, Engineering thought that his recommendations were speculative and liable to very costly failures. Engineering's staff had good reason to be worried about the technical ideas. The core technologies Bush recommended were, to significant degrees, still experimental. Optical scanning of tapes was new and optical reading of microfilm codes was yet to prove itself in day-to-day operations. Electronic digital counting was confined to rather esoteric and error prone devices used by atomic scientists. There were also valid concerns about the mechanical parts cited in Bush's sketches.

Although the telegraph and moving pictures provided some experience in tape transport, few engineers had ever attempted to construct reliable devices for the speeds Bush's machines demanded. As telling, there were no established manufacturers of the contrivances Bush recommended and Engineering rightly feared that it might have to assume burdens of construction as well as maintenance. They thought they might be saddled with unworkable designs. They feared they would be blamed for any failures while Bush remained untouched in his role of respected technological pundit. The worries caused by the technical issues were overshadowed by disagreements over exactly what had been asked and accepted.[19] Wenger and the Director of Naval Communications claimed that a firm promise of support had been made by Engineering. Its men, however, could not imagine that anyone would have agreed to such an arrangement.

Bush's demands compounded the growing friction caused by Captain Hooper's tendency to push too hard to bring the most advanced science and technology to the navy.[20] In his search for the nation's best men and best science, he had become somewhat insensitive to the situation the navy's bureaucrats faced and may have left the impression that he had little respect for the navy's engineers. In addition, the Bureau's engineers claimed they had their own solution to the problem of automatic cipher machines. They were reluctant to give Wenger even a hint of their approach, however.[21] Perhaps they were in the midst of revising the Holtwick electromechanical analogs of the Japanese cipher machines. They may have been thinking of making modifications to the tabulating machines, ones that would allow the performance of statistical functions at increased speeds. Or, they may have had ideas about modifying the emerging electrical typewriting systems.[22]

Whatever its secret alternative to Bush's proposals, Engineering had accepted the tabulator. It was an off the shelf technology that had a stable manufacturer. IBM knew the ropes of government contracting and was investing in ongoing development with its own funds. As important, the Navy Yard's group was beginning to acquire a deep knowledge of tabulators and was building a relationship with IBM that would lead to more complex technical refinements during the war. Many of Engineering's men were already creating significant and clever modifications to IBM's machines, making them more effective cryptanalytic tools. They gladly helped Holtwick, OP-20-G's officer in charge of the tabs, with a rewiring that reduced by almost one-half the sorting time needed to analyze some Japanese systems. They began to go far beyond that simple modification. The Yard was using components that allowed the machines to select various "classes" of items, and its men were probably advising OP-20-G on how to add relay banks to turn the tabulators into machines that could aid in the identification and subtraction of the random numbers added to Japanese codes.[23]

The engineers may have tried to explain their technical position to Wenger but the description turned into an argument. The situation grew heated and went far beyond disagreements over engineering matters. Feelings got involved. By mid-year, the Bureau's radio men refused to allow a "college professor" who, they thought, was impractical and naive, if not egotistical, to have anything to do with their activities. Worse, the conflict became entangled with the battle over the distribution of power in the navy and, thus, with the question of the role of civilians, the bureaus, and the Chief of Naval Operations in setting research agendas.[24]

In addition, the views of OP-20-G's cryptanalysts were not in complete harmony with Wenger's. The operational staff had little idea as to what they would get from MIT and even less idea of how to put it to effective use. The operational cryptanalysts wondered who could steal the time to devise the new procedures necessary to make such strange technology useful. By the mid-1930s, Laurance Safford and Jack Holtwick became more allies than enemies of Hooper's long-term plans, but the remainder of the staff were willing to join with Engineering in seriously questioning the value of Bush's machines.[25] All the objections and emotions meant that by mid-1936 the attempt to bring electronics to American cryptanalysis was deadlocked, if not defeated. But Stanford Hooper, Vannevar Bush and Joseph Wenger were determined men. They decided not to let the program die. They collected the needed political support, drew up a new plan and outflanked the Bureau and the conservative cryptanalysts.

Hooper and Wenger Try Again

The first recruit to the new Wenger-Bush team was Admiral Bowen. He had been appointed head of the Bureau of Engineering in the spring of 1935, but had not been aware of the standoff between Hooper and the Radio Division. Hooper called on Bowen for help in mid-year. Safford and Wenger then gained the support of the new leader of Naval Intelligence, Captain Puleston. They found another ally in the Director of Naval Communications, Leigh Noyes. And, they may even have had Bush travel to Washington to persuade the navy's most powerful officers.[26]

While allies were being recruited, Hooper and Wenger determined a new strategy to surmount any remaining objections. To placate the engineers, Hooper agreed to ask Bush to submit a more detailed and specific proposal. Bush was contacted and he replied that he was willing to draft a new description of his work and to cooperate with Hooper and Wenger in finding ways around the Bureau's objections.[27] Bush, without pay, spent some significant amount of time in 1936 preparing an outline of the revised project. Hooper then made an end run and gained a partial victory. The new Bush proposal was submitted to a special research group in the navy rather than to Engineering. In

September 1936, within a week after he received the new plan, Hooper reported to Bush that the prestigious research board had approved his project. That made it impossible for the Bureau to continue to resist Bush's ideas on technical grounds.[28] Wenger and Bush developed compromise positions on the bureaucratic and legal objections then presented the new proposal to Engineering. The Bureau gave in, but it took almost all of October and November 1936 to draft an acceptable contract. Even then, additional conflicts between Wenger and the head of the Radio Division blocked its approval. The DNC had to call the two men to his office and order them to end their bickering.[29]

A Compromise a Year Too Late

On what was close to being the anniversary of Wenger's first meeting with Bush, a contract was finally signed. Reflecting the temporary balance of power, the navy came to Bush, not he to the navy. The signing was in the exclusive St. Botolph's Club in Boston in early January 1937. That was a fitting setting for an elite scientist to display what he thought was his victory over the bureaucracy.[30] The contract was not a final solution to the question of the proper relationships between academics and the military, however.

Aided by Hooper's influence and Wenger's hard work, Bush had won many of his demands. But, several of the new conditions were framed to repair egos at the Bureau of Engineering. Under 1937's formal contract, Bush agreed to focus on the details of a particular device so that Engineering could have something concrete. He was to submit four reports, each detailing a major component of the proposed machine. The commitment to details and the year and one-half time limit for delivery of all the reports helped to satisfy the Bureau's demand for a scheduled product.[31] Bush also compromised on the question of payments. Someone found an old World War I law that allowed payment when segments of a contract were completed. Bush agreed to the receipt of one-fourth of the contract price as each of his reports was submitted.

In return, Bush received a great deal. First, came an additional eight thousand dollars. That made the amount Bush was to receive the equivalent of the salaries of several electrical engineers. That must have been a difficult amount for the Bureau's underpaid technicians to accept.[32] Bush's greatest triumphs were procedural ones, however. Following the customs of the private foundations, he was to be left free from interference, supervision, or evaluation. His only contacts with the navy about technical matters were to be with cryptanalysts who would explain their methods. As significant, his naval liaison was to be his new friend, Joseph Wenger, not some bureaucrat or junior technician from Engineering. Most galling for the Bureau, it was forced to accept Bush's reports without any review or criticism. He could submit anything he wanted to and receive payment. The question of patent rights was not really settled; both sides assumed there would be no conflict.[33]

Hooper's role in all this was one of the causes of those severe complaints about his interference in the affairs of the navy bureaus. It may have led to the termination of his role as scientific advisor to the CNO. Bowen may also have harmed his career. He created some enemies within his own bureau because of his pro-Bush stance.

The Decision to Build a Machine

Bush had become attached to Wenger and Hooper and their pleas convinced him to make a gentleman's promise that he soon regretted. He told them he would try to build a machine and if he succeeded he would give it to the navy at no additional cost--except for shipping charges for the finished machine.[34] Hooper and Wenger interpreted Bush's statements as a commitment that would be broken only under the most severe pressures. They looked forward to having a operating machine in Washington by the summer of 1938.[35] It had become very important to Wenger to have a device. To ensure that his project would not die when Bush's contract ended, Wenger needed a machine to prove that photoelectronics was practical. A working device would make it impossible for the engineers and the cryptanalysts to resist change or to reject Bush's reports as just more fantasies.

Once Bush agreed to try to construct a machine, he had several reasons to have it built at MIT rather than at the Navy Yard or a commercial firm. First, he could control the men on the project and thus safeguard his reputation. Unlike navy technicians or outside contractors, his students were unlikely to just throw up their hands and proclaim his ideas unworkable. They would carry on until the navy machine worked. A more positive reason was that Bush could transfer the experience gained while building the machine to his other related projects, such as the machine for the library. The navy's machine could serve as a test bed for many of its components. Apparently, it did. By the time the navy's project was producing its first hardware, Bush was preparing patent applications for many features of the yet to be built Selector.[36] Another reason for attempting to build a device at the Institute was that a successful navy project might lead to a business opportunity for one or more of Bush's students. Someone with the expertise gained from the first project might well receive handsome contracts for other secret machines and their technological cousins, the library selectors. Bush could fulfill his obligations to his graduate students through such projects.[37] On the other hand, the Bureau of Engineering's men were pleased when they heard that a machine might be delivered. An MIT effort meant they would not have to take the responsibility for constructing Bush's fantasy.[38]

Bush Is Too Busy

Bush was not sure that he could build a machine in time, but in early 1937 he was absolutely sure of one thing: MIT's work for OP-20-G would be cut off by mid-1938 when the contract with the Bureau terminated. He found it difficult to tell his friends, Wenger and Hooper, but Bush wanted to sever his ties to the navy. The haggling over his contract had alienated him. But more than what he considered shabby treatment by the Bureau was involved in the change in his attitude toward the navy project.[39] In 1936, while waiting for the navy to resolve its internal conflicts, Bush and the electrical engineering department at MIT began to suffer from success. During the year of bickering with the navy, Bush and MIT's fortunes changed. He became involved in an increasing number of projects that were critical to the Institute's planned analysis center and his career. One consequence was that the navy's project became more of a burden than an opportunity.

After years of badgering Warren Weaver of the Rockefeller Foundation (and Weaver putting Bush through intense interrogations[40]) Bush received the developmental grant for the new Differential Analyser in mid-1935.[41] It took Bush and some of his best young faculty such as Sam Caldwell several months to create the outline for the proposed partially electronic Rockefeller machine. Then, in early 1936, just after Wenger's initial visits to Bush, the astounding sum of eighty-five thousand dollars was awarded for building the new Rockefeller Analyser.[42] The grant was a wonderful prize, but a great deal was promised to attain it, including an unrealistic 1939 delivery date. The Analyser, with many parts still inoperable, did not emerge until late 1942.[43] But in 1935 and 1936 Bush and the staff at MIT were sure a machine could be finished before the end of the decade.

The new Analyser was to use electronics and to have punch tape programs so that it could be easily changed from problem to problem. Its mechanical integrators were to be more precise and the project was to include the creation of a component to convert digital to analog signals. That converter was a very new idea and it had not been implemented at the time of the award.[44] It was something that held great promise for automatic control in industry. The proposed feature led Hannibal Ford, National Cash Register, and Pratt and Whitney to invest in the Analyser.[45]

The Analyser was a burdensome commitment and very soon MIT's men were hard-pressed to meet any of its deadlines. The Rockefeller administrators were willing to put up with delays and to contribute even more to the project but the successful completion of the Analyser, which eventually filled several rooms, was critical to the reputations of Bush and the faculty at MIT.[46] It was a highly touted project in international scientific circles and Bush's grand plans for his Center of Analysis hinged on the new electronic device. He felt he would have little chance to sell his ambitious ideas for automated calculation if the Rockefeller machine was less than a brilliant innovation and an example of the efficiency of the Institute.[47]

Some fifteen to twenty young engineers were always assigned to work under Sam Caldwell. Other projects had to take second-best and some of MIT's closest friends, such as NCR, had to be given less than adequate attention in order to save the Analyser.[48] Despite the priority, Caldwell soon became overwhelmed and embarrassed by the faltering Rockefeller project.[49] Bush and Caldwell did not stop with the Analyser, however. Bush spent much time on the initial designs for an astounding general purpose electronic digital computer. He sent his students and colleagues the first of several outlines of the proposed digital device, soon to be called the Rapid Arithmetical Machine, in January 1937.[50] Other projects followed. Of great importance, by mid-1937 Bush was promised at least minimal funding for his library machine, the Rapid Selector.[51]

In the three years after the first contacts with the navy, Bush and his men had put all the years of struggle behind them. Bush had raised more than two-hundred thousand dollars in grants and had his "boys" immersed in three highly innovative digital projects: the electronic

Rockefeller Analyser; the electronic, programmable Rapid Arithmetic Machine; and, the Rapid Selector. Other faculty at the Institute were completing the Cinema Integraph and the amazing Wavelength measurement machine.

But success carried problems. Bush was taking on too much. His new responsibilities were not limited to MIT. He became entangled with time consuming memberships on national scientific boards and by early 1937 he was negotiating for the more than full-time position as head of the very important Carnegie Institution. At the end of the year, he was in Washington and well on the road to becoming America's most powerful scientist.

It is not known if Bush informed his navy friends that he and his "boys" were accepting so many tasks in 1937 and 1938. The naval officers who had taken the politically touchy step of dictating to the Bureau of Engineering might have reconsidered their decision if they thought Bush was not going to give his all to the service. They and the cause of automated cryptanalysis needed results that would clearly show the investments in "professor" research were well spent. Wenger certainly needed best efforts and he needed them on a long-term basis. During the first stages of negotiations over the navy job, and before the other Center of Analysis projects materialized, Bush had indicated that he would commit to an ongoing effort for Wenger. But Bush changed his mind. In 1937 he told one trusted colleague that he sought an end the relationship with the navy. It had become too burdensome in time and emotion.[52]

Bush and Wenger Select a Problem

Bush had misgivings about the navy's ways but he was a hardworking and honest man of the old school. He was determined to try to fulfill his immediate responsibilities to Wenger and Hooper. As soon as the conflict with the Bureau seemed to be resolved, Bush began to outline the 1937 project. The first step was the selection of the cryptanalytic problem to be tackled. Then, he had to decide whether or not to carry through with his promise to build the machine at the Institute.

Bush consulted with Joseph Wenger and opted for a device to help OP-20-G apply the latest statistical techniques to the cipher problems.[53] But more than the hopes for the application of formal statistics went into the determination of the exact nature of the Comparator. Bush had to take into account that he had less than eighteen months to complete the design, if not the machine itself. He also knew that if a machine was built it had to be one that was reliable enough to convince the Bureau to fund a long-term RAM project. In addition, Wenger urged him to meet a very demanding criteria. The machine could not mechanize an ad hoc or brute force method that would be useful for attacking only one or a few systems. Spending so much money on a machine that might be discarded when the enemy changed a system would be a political disaster. Furthermore, Bush knew that any machine he created would have to outperform OP-20-G's tabulators and the special mechanical devices[54] that had become so dear to many of its staff. His machine had to be much faster than the electromechanical devices.[55]

There were many advanced cryptanalytic methods for Bush to select from. By 1930, mathematicians and the men and women in the bureaus of the various nations had created a range of new formal techniques.[56] A host of statistical tests had been borrowed from biology and the use of more esoteric methods such as group theory was approaching.[57] There had been attempts to mechanize several of the techniques. Some nations employed overlay sheets and constructed photoelectric machines to search for prime numbers.[58] The German codebreakers may have been thinking of ways to develop tape and optical systems quite like those Bush first suggested to Hooper.[59] And, perhaps unknown to Bush or Wenger, the United States Army's cryptanalyst, William F. Friedman, was toying with ideas about the use of optical scanning. In April 1937, just as Bush was filling in the design of his machine, Friedman filed a patent for a system. The application did not mention cryptanalysis and its examples of possible use were related to analog business applications, such as the sorting of packages, but Friedman must have realized that optical scanning had great potential for cryptology.[60] Despite such projects, Bush was facing the great challenge of creating what was the world's first high-speed cryptanalytic machine. Balancing all the factors, including his almost unshakable commitment to the three technologies of film, optics and electronic counting, Bush decided to automate one of the most central new statistical methods, the Index of Coincidence.

The Index

The method Bush and Wenger selected for the machine, the Index of Coincidence, was the most ubiquitous of the new theoretically justified statistical procedures. It was a formal and universal method that could not be made worthless by a slight change in a cipher system. It was based on the laws of probability, not the kind of brute force logic the Poles and British would engineer into the Enigma Bombes of 1938-1940.[61] The Index was rugged and independent because it needed only intercepted cipher text and because it could attack any type of cipher system.[62] It also had a wide range of powers. The Index allowed an analyst to identify messages, or portions of messages, that were produced by the same settings of an encryption device. That was a first step to determining the wiring and settings of the encrypting components of the machines. The Index of Coincidence could then be put to work to identify a cipher key or the order of the cipher wheels in a machine.

Such new methods were essential to an independent attack on the cipher devices. The wired wheel and stepping switch machines, such as the Japanese Purple and the German Enigma, were designed to be unbeatable. They had cascades of transposing rotors which changed one letter to another. Although each rotor was simple, together, they produced a long sequence of letter substitutions without repetition or pattern. The first A in a message might be changed to an X but the next changed to a C and so on with no apparent relationship of either X or C to A. Such machines as Red, Purple, and the Enigma, because of their erratically moving bank of cipher wheels, came close to creating a random sequence, but not quite. They appeared to be random because of the length of the cycle of unique substitutions created by the three or four rotating enciphering wheels or switches. But, after 26 x 26 x 26 or more rotations, the wheels returned to their initial positions and the machine began to repeat its letter substitutions. That made them technically nonrandom and allowed many nations to use Index methods against the simple Enigmas of the Spanish Civil War.[63] However, every nation was improving its cipher machines. Additional wheels with unique transpositions, varied latches that turned a neighboring wheel erratically and plugboards to further disguise a machine's input-output relationships were added to many devices. The combinations of wheels, wheel settings and plugboard links meant that trillions of possibilities had to be explored.

In response, cryptanalysts countered with various forms of automation. But most, like Poland, bet on limited methods and machines, ones to exploit the quirks of particular cipher machines or the procedural errors of the enemy. There was good reason for such a turn away from science. The German specialists in charge of the Enigma, who were aware of the laws of probability and also of the speed of film and optical machines, were confident that it would take any formal attack too long to be of use to an enemy. Given the special defenses built into the Enigma they calculated that it would take any machine so long to perform a statistical analysis that by the time a setting was identified its messages would be of no military value.[64]

Many other cryptanalysts agreed that the new statistical methods were appealing but impractical. They kept faith in their more traditional techniques. The Poles, for example, found the Germans to be using a method of indicating initial settings that allowed a decryption with relatively little mathematical work. OP-20-G and the American army's cryptanalysts may have found a similar way to exploit Japan's indicators. Although England's codebreakers used their own hand versions of formal methods, they depended upon shortcuts to vastly reduce the amount of statistical work. The British came to rely upon known plain text words in a message as well as the bad habits of the Enigma operators.[65] Of course, Wenger did not approve of such approaches because they made cryptanalysis too dependent on chance and intuition. When he sat with Vannevar Bush in 1937 to decide exactly what type of machine to design, his goal was the creation of a device so rapid that pure statistical analysis would be practical. After balancing the needs of OP-20-G and the technological possibilities, he and Bush decided to automate the heart of the IC method, coincidence counting.

A coincidence was the appearance of the same letter in the same relative position in two or more messages or in an offset of two copies of the same message. The method could be extended to the identification and counting of more than single letter matches, but the essence of the Index was the counting of single matches. If the number of matches exceeded the number expected from a random distribution of letters, then both messages were probably a product of the same wheels, wheel settings, and portion of the encryption machine's cycle. The method was demanding. It asked for more than the number of appearances of particular letters. It required the number of instances in which the same letters appeared in the same relative positions in the texts. That called for different and more error prone methods than simple counting of the frequency of particular letters in a message.

Furthermore, in Index analysis, one message had to be shifted one step relative to the other until all positions of the first message were compared to the second. As the enciphering machines became more complex, the Index developed an almost insatiable demand for data. Longer and longer messages were needed and thus more and more simple but time consuming and mind deadening tallying was required.

The Index had been calculated by hand. American cryptanalysts had used the Index since the 1920s to analyze various ciphers, including those produced by their own automatic machines. One technique was to write the messages on long strips of paper then have the analyst slide, letter by letter, one strip over the other. At each offset, the number of matching letters at each position was tallied. Another method used overlay sheets with holes punched to indicate letters. Coincidences revealed themselves by showing the color of the table under the stack of sheets. The Index could also be computed with electromechanical machines, such as a counting-sorter or a tabulator with additional relay circuits. But even with the IBM machines, the process was very slow and labor intensive; a long message could take days to analyze. One of the reasons the Index was selected as the method for Bush to automate was that it was so difficult to perform on electromechanical equipment.

There was another and very practical reason for selecting the Index. There were more sophisticated analytical methods, but their use would have been impossible given the budget and the schedule of the MIT project. By 1935, cryptanalysts had devised, for example, the more refined Chi test. Unfortunately, Chi called for the recognition of particular letters and needed repeated multiplications and additions--not just the simple tallying of coincidences. The Index asked only for the appearance of the same two letters, not their identity. If Hooper and Wenger wanted to prove to the navy that electronics could be successful, they could not ask Bush to take on Chi because it demanded a machine that could identify particular letters and that could perform a complex sequence of the four mathematical functions. The Chi test would have demanded a very large and sophisticated device and the development of truly revolutionary components.

Bush Outlines the Machine and Sets Difficult Goals

After the navy contract was signed in January 1937, Bush took time away from his other duties to work on the architecture of his Index machine, the Comparator. But it was June before he had the funds and men to begin detail design. While he awaited the first navy payments, he readied workshops and outlined the general requirements for each component. He decided to divide the project into four major parts, corresponding to functional units of the proposed machine. Then, he chose what hardware was to be used in each. Last, came an equally challenging step, finding the four men he needed to fill out his sketches and, perhaps, build a machine.

By the time Bush's outlines were ready, MIT's Electrical Engineering department was a busy place and it was difficult for him to hire a staff. He had to step very carefully because he did not want to endanger the Rockefeller Analyser or cause any frictions within the department. The scarcity of men forced Bush to make a fateful decision about the project: It would be a summer effort. Each man would work on his part, submit it, then be released back to Sam Caldwell and the Analyser as soon as possible--perhaps as quickly as two months. Only the project manager, if he could find one, was to be a full-time, full-term employee.

Bush had a frustrating time finding qualified men. Faculty members were too busy with other projects to be considered. Bush could not ask any of them to supervise the effort. Current or ex-students seemed his only option because he did not want to hire outsiders. Bush treated all his projects as ones to support and train students and he had no wish to change the Institute into a pseudo factory filled with troublesome employees. The only exceptions to his staffing rules were alumni whose current situation and talents fit with the needs of the Institute or technical employees whose skills, such as machine tooling, were unique. The need for secrecy made it even more difficult for Bush to locate men and still maintain good relations with the faculty. Wenger and Hooper had to impose the highest possible classification on the project because if other nations learned of the device they might find means to protect their encryption systems. So, Bush could not tell Sam Caldwell, who so badly needed almost all of the department's students for the Analyser, what was going on. Only three people at MIT, really two, knew what the work was for. Bush and the project manager knew details, but MIT's president learned only that secret work was in progress. The men who were to build the components and their regular faculty supervisors were not told of the navy connection. Once employed, they were instructed to be confidential about their work but not told why. They would never be informed as to what their components were for.[66]

The secrecy requirements also caused problems after Bush chose his students. When Sam Caldwell learned that some of his men might be taken from him without any explanation, he became irritated. Bush could offer few calming arguments and other faculty members soon joined Caldwell in protesting what seemed to be an indefensible power play by Bush. Later, others at the Institute were put-off by the evasiveness of those Bush selected to work on the Comparator. When certain sections of the department were declared out of bounds, even to faculty, there was increased dissatisfaction. That added to the tensions at the Institute; American academics were not yet accustomed to having secret work on campus.[67]

A Very Few Good Men

There were more difficulties. Bush found only three qualified students and they were already committed to the Rockefeller project. They had little time to spend on the navy's work. The Analyser's needs meant that Bush had to demand they submit their detailed designs to local machine shops at the close of summer 1937. And, although they were able men and became engineering luminaries, some did not have refined skills in optics or electronics. Two graduate students received the initial assignments. Jerry Jaeger, who had a background in machine tools and automatic controls, was given the first task, to build the critical input mechanism. Richard Taylor, who was already important to the Rockefeller project's electronics and who would soon take charge of the Center of Analysis, was chosen to be responsible for the electronic circuits. The third man, who was asked to develop the component to read the data tapes, was in a somewhat different position at the Institute than Jaeger or Taylor. Herbert E. Grier was a graduate of 1933 who, like Kenneth Germeshausen, remained at the Institute as an unpaid research associate of Harold Edgerton. Grier had developed a high-speed camera for Harold Edgerton's stroboscopic device and he and Germeshausen survived through the profits of the strobe partnership, consulting, and work within the Institute. Then, with the outbreak of war, the engineering firm of EG&G began its climb to fame.[68]

Bush was unable to find the needed fourth man among the student body. One reason was Bush's uncertainty about the nature of the machine's memory. When he made his decision, he found that few young men at the Institute were skilled in the required craft of high tolerance machine tooling. He turned to one of the Institute's machinists, Walter Kershner, to design and construct what seemed to be the least challenging part of the Comparator, its data input device. Kershner probably had been working on a similar automatic tape punch for the Rockefeller Analyser.

Finding a manager for the project was a greater challenge. It was not until early summer that Bush thought he had a lead on a qualified engineer. A unique man was needed to supervise the work, to refine all the components and, if possible, finish the navy's machine. Almost by chance, Bush found a man with a professional background that was an ideal match to the needs of the Comparator.

An Idealistic Man for a Practical Job

By late spring 1937 Bush was very busy with his MIT duties and he suspected he might soon leave for his new job in Washington. He needed someone with experience in all of the Comparator's technologies to supervise the navy project. Besides having technical and managerial abilities, that person had to be trustworthy enough to keep the secret of the device. Another requirement was as demanding: The supervisor would have to work full-time and for as long as a year. That eliminated the faculty and students in the department. Then, as Bush worried about fulfilling the gentleman's agreement with Hooper, chance played a part, as it would so many times in the histories of the Comparator and the Selector.

Bush had let his professional friends know that he was in search of a talented and trustworthy man to supervise an important project. After he realized that he probably would not find a student to take the position, he also let it be known that he was willing to pay a professional salary. Even with that enticement, his informal network did not find a man. So, Bush listed the opening with the Institute's alumni employment bureau.[69] It took some time, until summer 1937, but someone finally appeared with the appropriate background and skills. Another of the many young men who remained loyal to Bush long after they severed connections with the Institute returned to the campus. Waldron Shapleigh MacDonald was one of the most unusual and fascinating of MIT's students and he remains an unrecognized figure in the birth of the modern computer.

MacDonald first appeared at MIT in the early 1930s when he enrolled as a special undergraduate student. His initial year in Cambridge was spent trying to prove to the electrical engineering faculty that his lack of formal preparation was not a barrier to academic success. Although he performed well in his classes, he was unable to surmount bureaucratic hurdles, illness, and the depletion of his savings. He had to leave MIT without a degree. But, he quickly found very well-paying work as an engineer and began a lifelong career as an innovator in computers and automatic controls.

MacDonald's early life accounts for his unusual academic and professional career. He was the son of a well-to-do MIT alumnus who died when Waldron was fourteen. More than the death of his engineer father altered MacDonald's future. Because of a recurring illness, he had to leave Montclair, New Jersey high school just before graduation. After a year recovering, instead of returning to school for his degree, he was taken under wing by a family friend who headed one of America's high-tech corporations of the 1920s. Just barely eighteen years old, MacDonald was given employment as a junior engineer at the American Machine and Foundry company. After a successful stay learning about the latest machines for the automated factory, he found another mentor and moved to Western Electric. Like AMF, Western Electric, the manufacturing arm of the Bell System, was one of the most advanced companies in the world.

Because of an amazing knack for mechanical and electrical engineering, the teenager was asked to participate in exciting work that exposed him to the latest techniques in high tolerance mechanics, automatic control, optics, and electronics. One of his first assignments at AMF, for example, was to help with a machine that automatically sorted cigars into sixty categories of color and shape. That gave him hands-on experience with optical systems. At Western Electric he learned about relay circuits and the logic of switching. Other assignments taught him about gears and servomechanisms. His learning was real and direct, the kind of sensual engineering that appealed to men of Bush's generation.[70]

But MacDonald decided that a young man who wanted a fulfilling career should have a formal education, not just one on the shop floor. After he calculated that he had saved enough to support himself, he searched for a reputable college that would accept someone without a high school diploma. At the onset of the Great Depression, he was admitted as a conditional student at the University of Virginia where he took a general education course. For various reasons, including his relative maturity, he left Virginia after a few semesters and petitioned MIT for entry into its electrical engineering department as a special student. MacDonald spent a year proving that his unusual educational background was not a true handicap. He did well as a regular undergraduate but, just before graduation in 1933, he faced a combination of bureaucratic oversights, another illness, and an empty savings account. He recovered his health but that did not solve his financial problems. The department, despite the valiant attempts of the faculty to fund projects to support students, did not have enough scholarships or work for all its undergraduates, even ones as needy as MacDonald. Typical of the Institute, he was not simply abandoned, however. The faculty helped find him a position with the electronic company so closely associated with Vannevar Bush and MIT, Raytheon. Unfortunately, there were some work related conflicts and MacDonald began to search for another job. In 1934, after a year at Raytheon, he moved to another of the nation's most innovative companies, Foxboro, which had offered him a much better paying position.

Foxboro was a leading manufacturer of automatic control devices, with a specialty in equipment for the oil industry. As important for MacDonald's future, it was in the first stages of exploring the use of electronics for industrial applications. For example, by the outbreak of World War II, it developed a electronic analog computer for measurement and control. MacDonald learned much in his three years at Foxboro but he became upset over internal politics and in mid-1937 sought advice from his old mentors at MIT. He contacted the head of its employment bureau, but with little result. Then, to his surprise, he received an unexpected and very important letter from the illustrious Vannevar Bush. Bush had been impressed with MacDonald's resume despite his "unusual" academic record and the problems at Raytheon. Bush had his friends make some discreet inquiries and may have asked Wenger to have Naval Intelligence explore MacDonald's loyalty to the nation. Then, Bush wrote the young engineer asking for a face-to-face meeting.

After a time, Bush offered MacDonald a professional salary and help in obtaining a Master's degree in electrical communications at the Institute. In return, MacDonald was asked for a firm commitment to come to MIT to see the navy's project through to completion. Few young men could think of refusing an offer from Bush and, of course, it was accepted. But MacDonald needed time to fulfill his responsibilities to Foxboro and he did not arrive at MIT until September 1937, leaving only some ten months to become oriented, to check and revise the Comparator's parts, prepare reports and assemble and test the historic machine.[71] The assignment was a difficult one, but MacDonald had the right qualifications for the job. His education and career balanced practical experience with the more abstract orientation of university engineering education. And, his previous work had touched on all aspects of Comparator-like components. In addition, Bush reasoned that MacDonald's age made it likely that the younger men on the project would cooperate with him despite his lack of academic credentials. Bush also felt that MacDonald was a man who could make a project go with little supervision.

MacDonald's skills and his determination are reflected by his post Comparator career. During World War II he worked at the Naval Ordnance Laboratory where he contributed several important improvements to acoustic and magnetic mines.[72] After the war, rather than follow the pattern of engineers of the era and work for the government or a large corporation, he returned to the Boston area and attempted to become an independent engineer-entrepreneur. At first working for the famous Baird Associates, which was sponsored by the renowned American Research and Development Corporation, MacDonald soon launched out on his own. In the late 1940s he built and marketed one of the first electronic computers for the commercial market, the Magnefile.[73]

He constructed that innovative machine for inventory management with some help from Baird and with much engineering gumption. A tribute to practical ingenuity, he created one of the first and most efficient magnetic drums in his own small workshop. But, he was unable to raise the capital needed to build programmed computers and could not meet the competition from the large firms such as IBM. In the 1950s, he turned back to the machine tool industry and began to make computers into machine controllers. While manufacturing some unique electronic components, he patented several important products for the automatic control of machine tools in the 1950s and 1960s.[74]

MacDonald's ingenuity and his hands-on engineering ability were needed on the navy's 1930s project, but his role was not a truly creative one. Well before he arrived in late 1937 the design of the machine and the schedule for the project had been determined. His job was to make what Bush had specified come to life, and, to do it before the end of the navy contract. Unfortunately for MacDonald, he inherited a fixed design, components which were hastily made by others, Bush's order to "get the job done on time" and full responsibility. By September 1937 Bush was already too busy with his other work to attend to the now rather inconsequential navy project. Among other things, Bush was readying himself to assume the leadership of the powerful Carnegie Institution.

Comparator Scanner, circa 1945
(National Security Agency)

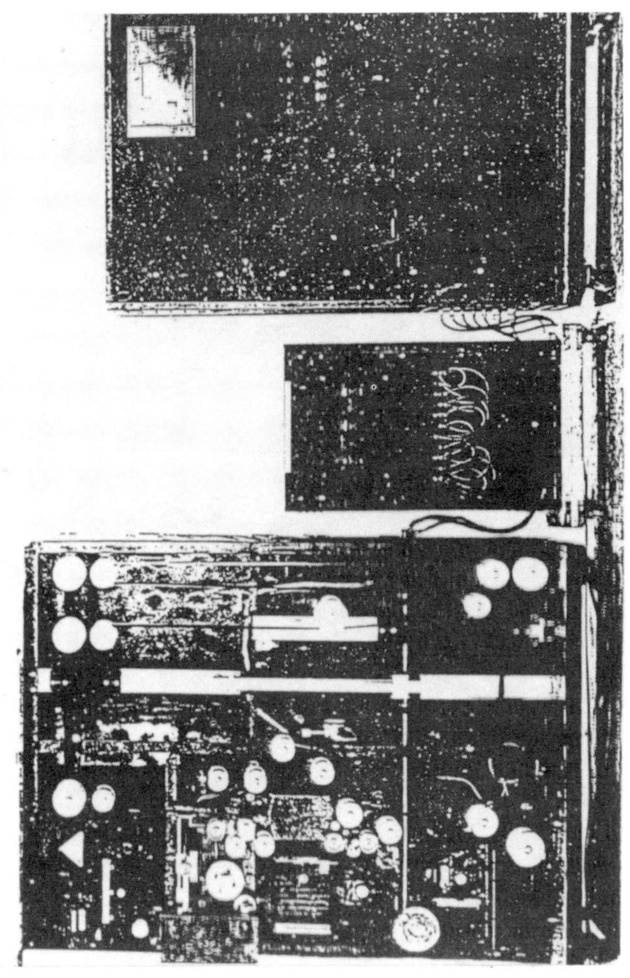

The Comparator, circa 1944
(National Security Agency)

Chapter VII
The Machine That Wouldn't: The Comparator

As we have seen, in 1936, as Bush's role was changing from that of a general consultant to a designer, he and Joseph Wenger picked a target for the navy's work. The decision to concentrate on what later became known as the Comparator was the result of balancing political, technological and cryptanalytic possibilities. The machine was a compromise between Wenger's early hopes, the constraints imposed by the settlement with the Bureau and the resources and time that remained available to Bush and MIT.

Bush and Wenger were very wise in setting the limited goal of a machine for the Index of Coincidence. Electronic computation was having its birth pangs and no one had a way to create a machine whose hardware could be made to imitate any process. There were grand ideas about, and, just as Bush and the navy made their agreement, there was an outburst of attempts to create computers. However, they were all experimental and, despite the size of some of them, none approached being an all-purpose machine. A major reason why all the 1930s computers were limited in function was the absence of a viable memory technology.[1] A universal data computer, one that worked on large volumes of input and that had high-speed memory, did not appear until the 1950s. Then, machines such as the UNIVAC depended upon very demanding, slow and expensive magnetic tape memory systems.[2]

Bush's first sketches of his Comparator reflected the limitations of the memory and electronic technologies. To minimize cost and maximize reliability, he drew a sparse design with as few components as possible. The functional and architectural simplicity did not mean the Comparator's construction would be a simple engineering task, however. Each of the Comparator's four major components had its own very significant practical challenges. Even if Bush had more time and money and had organized the work differently, the project would have been a difficult and trying one. The state of the technology did not allow elegant solutions to the problems of high-speed input, sensing, counting and recording. That led to the Comparator's components being ungainly and Rube-Goldberg like. But, in the context of the 1930s, Bush made very reasonable decisions. Most of his choices were sensible, but the combination of difficult technical hurdles, a hurried pace, and just bad luck led to some unfortunate results. The most important consequence was the navy's decision not to exploit its great opportunity. Because of the conduct of the 1930's Comparator project and the nature of OP-20-G's early wartime efforts, it was not until late 1943 that America had more than the patched up Bush Comparator to represent its near fifteen years of attempts to build sophisticated electronic codebreaking devices.

A Machine in Time

Of course, Bush had not intended such a future for the Rapid Analytical Machine program. In mid-1937 he thought he had a design that would be of enormous value to the navy. Although construction was delayed until summer 1937, and although the project's new manager announced that he would be unable to begin work until the fall, Bush and Wenger were very confident.

Bush fixed the general nature of the machine's components by June and set his men to work. Some sort of tape was to be the memory and optical sensing and electronics would be used for counting. Bush warned his young men that he would not tolerate deviations or any blue sky engineering. He gave each man orders to spend only two months or so working on detailed specifications. Then, if needed, they were to find a contractor to build their part of the machine. At that stage, they were to submit their reports and return to the more important project, the Rockefeller Analyser.[3] The young engineers were on their own during the summer. MacDonald refused to leave Foxboro before he had completed his obligations and Bush was too busy to oversee details. Among other projects, Bush was seeking patents and financing for his microfilm library Selector.[4] So, each man worked independently and was coordinated only through Bush's original architectural and functional specifications.

Too Much to Ask of Mere Machines

Bush had thought of using microfilm for the input and memory of the navy's devices, but his faith in it was temporarily shaken when he learned that too many "bugs" existed to make it the basis of the 1937 Comparator project. He knew that the problems of precisely registering data and of aligning and reading microfilm were too great to be solved by June 1938. Abandoning microfilm did not make the students' jobs easy, however. Bush continued to demand an ultra high-speed machine, but one based on low speed memory. Becoming responsible for making traditional mechanical components match electronic speeds made the students' assignments more difficult.[5]

In order to impress the Bureau, Bush had promised very high-speed performance. Wenger thought his pledge would be fulfilled if he constructed a device that had the raw power of fifty tabulators.[6] Bush thought he could do much better and hinted at a machine one hundred fifty times as rapid as Tom Watson's products.[7] That translated into twenty thousand comparisons a minute.[8] Bush had much more ambitious long-term goals, however. He hoped for machines that did at least fifty thousand comparisons a minute and as many as two hundred thousand.[9] He wanted such speeds because the Comparator was intended to make the Index practical.

The Index was a demanding cryptanalytic method. To tally all the possible single letter coincidences in two messages calls for (n*(n-1)) comparisons.[10] If two four-letter messages are examined for coincidences, twelve comparisons must be made; five-hundred-letter messages demanded almost two hundred and fifty thousand tests; a two thousand letter message called for almost four million. Complete analyses of long messages could take days or weeks by hand and tabulator methods. Compounding the challenge of raw speed was Wenger's demand that the Comparator be able to handle the longest of messages. There was good reason for that because the more characters in a message the more likely that something of value would emerge from an analysis. Fortunately, cryptologists around the world knew that messages with too many words posed a danger to their systems and instructed that messages be limited to as few words possible. The very upper limit was two thousand characters. Messages of two hundred characters were typical, but the need to analyze longer ones in a timely way made speed and a large memory important goals.[11]

Combined with Bush's desire for a minimal number of electronic components, the call for speed created unexpected challenges for the students at MIT. One of them was printing. The proposed processing rate of the 1937 machine was too great to allow the printing of results between each pass of the tapes. No existing printer could spew the needed line of six four-digit numbers between comparison runs. But to maintain speed, printing had to be done while the tape was running. Bush did not want to burden the Comparator with the thousands of tubes or relays needed to store all the tallies for later printing. The solution he and his men devised was sensible but crude and it led to a need for an even faster mechanical tape drive. Printing was to take place while a blank portion of tape was running. In practice, this meant that approximately one-half of each tape was blank, thus halving the number of possible comparisons during a run of the tape. Because of that, Bush's men had to double the originally planned speed of the drive to achieve the processing goals.[12]

Even without the tape handicap, Bush had to outdo much existing technology to achieve his minimum Comparator speed.[13] Bush wanted the machine to deliver data to the reading station at over thirty times the rate of standard telegraph equipment and sixty times faster than a movie projector. If it was to reach the goal of twenty thousand comparisons a minute[14] the Comparator had to sense and route data at rates forty times greater than an IBM sorter and one hundred and sixty times faster than a tabulator. No wonder the men at the Radio division of the Bureau had raised some questions about the "college professor."[15]

Wenger thought that he might overcome the Bureau's protests if Bush could add parallel features to his essentially serial machine. He asked him to include a way to make isomorphic and three and four letter (polymorphic) coincidence tests. Bush convinced Wenger that he could present the navy with a convincing display of the power of technology if the machine was made to do even more, to make several tests simultaneously. With those capabilities, Wenger could argue that if the simple comparison rate was reduced to only five thousand a minute, the Comparator would still be more powerful than a building full of tabulators. Bush thought he would be able to make the Comparator perform four or five tests at a time, ones that were impossible to do by hand.[16]

As important to Wenger as processing power were reliability and price. The Bureau's men knew that creating a machine for the day-to-day Index work was a major engineering challenge and they were skeptical of Bush's promises to present them with an operational machine. Because Bush was recommending the use of yet to be proven technological combinations, the Bureau had justified qualms about feasibility and reliability. Wenger had to prove that Rapid machines could be put into production and that they would demand little maintenance. In addition, the cost of the machine and its allied processes had to be reasonable. If Bush could build a machine for under twenty thousand dollars, Wenger could claim the Comparator would save the navy tens of thousands of dollars a year because tabulators and related equipment were expensive. Exclusive of labor and punch cards, renting a combination of a tabulator, a key punch, and a sorter cost OP-20-G five thousand dollars a year. Even a slow five thousand comparison a minute device could replace dozens of the tabulators and their operators.[17]

No Thanks for the Memories

Because the Comparator was a data dependent machine, the greatest problem facing Bush's students was how to store and retrieve information. The Comparator needed a large-scale and very high-speed memory, but such memories did not exist in the 1930s[18] What was on the technological horizon was not encouraging. Storage in massive banks of capacitors or resistors, which some computer designers were thinking of using, was too expensive and such banks took too long to load and unload.[19] The rumors about the use of special versions of television tubes as memory were just that in the mid-1930s. And, no one thought that delay lines would ever be able to hold more than a few bits of information. In 1937, work was just beginning on magnetic memories and storage of large amounts of data in two or multi-state electronic tubes or relays was out of the question.[20] There were few alternatives.

Unfortunately for Bush and Wenger, there had been few advances in tape technology since the introduction of modern automatic telegraph readers in the early twentieth century. Standard teletype technology had not evolved into a competitor to the punch card.[21] In early 1937, the only option seemed to be microfilm.

Bush thought that microfilm had the potential to meet all the needs of a cryptanalytic machine's memory. Data could be recorded instantly through photography. More important, microfilm could present data at a rate to match that of electronic processing. It would also allow the repeated use of a data set, a significant requirement because messages had to be analyzed several times. Microfilm's greatest advantage was that it could hold so much information in a tiny space. Its density could compensate for the limitations of serial processing and the low speeds of mechanical tape drives. While teletype tape held eight or ten characters an inch, microfilm had the potential to hold hundreds. At a density of one hundred characters per inch and with a drive speed of four hundred feet per minute, Bush's long-term goals of fifty or two hundred thousand comparisons seemed possible. Neither the required data density nor the transport speed seemed too far fetched.[22] Whether such densely packed information could be read and tallied was another question, however.[23]

Bush thought his men would overcome the difficulties caused by film shrinkage and distortion when the film was sped past a reading station.[24] Unfortunately, microfilm proved too difficult for a machine that could meet the mid-1938 deadline for the delivery of the Comparator. As a result, in mid-1937 Bush sent his students on a hurried search for another medium and a way to move it at incredible speeds. He told them to find a technological combination that would allow an acceptable balance between data packing and speed of transport. That was a tough assignment.[25]

Bush's men examined all the available media and mechanisms.[26] The use of microfilm sheets or plates was immediately ruled out.[27] Teletype tape was eliminated because it could not stand the strain of a high-speed drive, because it could not hold enough information and because light penetrated through it. The only other alternative materials were punched photographic film or special papers. The MIT men soon rejected film and chose a unique 70mm wide paper tape that Eastman-Kodak used for packaging its movie film. It was strong, wide enough to accommodate Bush's coding scheme and, very important, it blocked light because of its acetate coating and its alternate red-black layers.[28] Also, early tests indicated the tape would maintain its structural integrity after being punched. All those features justified the high cost of the Eastman product although it was soon learned that its data capacity would not be much more than that of telegraph tape.[29]

The disappointingly low density meant that much effort had to be put into the development of a high-speed tape drive, one burdened with some very special demands. In addition to the need for ultra high-speeds, the tape transport had to pass two tapes in perfect alignment over the reading station, then step one tape one character relative to the other until all possible comparisons had been run.[30] That complexity was required because of the nature of the Index and because of Bush's early decision to build the machine around the smallest possible number of electronic components. His design dictated that only one set of photoelectric readers would be used. That, and the limits of tape memory, put heavy demands on the mechanical components of the Comparator.

The Limits of Mechanics

The first man on the summer crew was given the responsibility of creating the mechanical combination needed to compensate for the low data carrying power of the Eastman tape. His immediate goal was to drive the tapes at speeds close to three miles and hour but he hoped to double that to allow at least fifty thousand comparisons a minute. His problem was compounded by the need to run the two tapes over each other in exact alignment and to accurately step one of the tapes after each pass by the reader. Tolerances of less than one-thousandth of an inch were demanded if coincidences were to be correctly tallied. For an analysis of a one thousand letter message, that meant a million passes by the reading head in perfect alignment and perhaps one thousand steppings of one of the tapes. Some of Bush's designs made the drive problem a bit easier. The decision to have one-half the length of the tapes blank saved the young designer months of work because, along with the nature of the Index method, it allowed him to avoid the use of a complex reel mechanism. Instead, he used two loops of tape. Loops of six, twelve, twenty-four and forty-eight feet, the size depending upon the number of characters in the message, would make rewinding unnecessary after each pass, would avoid the cracks and tears caused by winding on reels and would eliminate the need for sophisticated motors for the reels.[31]

Already familiar with the drives in the machines used in the cloth and newspaper industries, the young engineer decided to center his component around a four foot long frame to hold the tapes. Pulleys were to maintain the required tension on the loops of tape. They could be adjusted for the length of the tapes and be used to compensate for such practical difficulties as stretching caused by changes in humidity. Driven by a fast electric motor and a system of shafts and gears, the tape was guided by both rollers and sprockets.[32] Static guides were also used. As the tapes flew over the reading station they were brought closely together so that light from a hole on the upper tape would reach the sensors only when there was a true coincidence with a hole in the lower tape. A set of stepping switches and relays regulated the shifting of one tape relative to the other. The entire transport was mounted on tall legs and stood some four feet off the ground to ease the chore of changing tapes.[33]

The tape transport was well designed and was delivered on schedule, but it did not reach the speeds Bush desired. At its best moments it ran at less than two and a half miles an hour, not the five or more needed for a truly rapid machine. When running correctly, the drive allowed for sixteen thousand comparisons a minute. However, that pace could not be maintained and when the Comparator was finally used on operational runs, the drive ran at less than two miles per hour.[34] The significance of the drive's limitations was not realized until much later. In mid-1937 all the men on the project were pleased that its design had been fixed because the next steps depended on knowing its specifications. The tape was the machine's timer and set many of the requirements for the other major components. Once its features were known, work on the reading station and electronic counters could be completed. Armed with Bush's previous instructions and the specifications for the tape drive, the next man tackled the problems of photoelectric sensing.

Let There Be Light, But Not Too Much

One of Bush's first technical commitments was to the sensing of the presence of light rather than its absence. Following on that, he ordered his men to code each letter of a message by punching a hole in a column of the seventy millimeter wide tape. There was to be only one hole to a column of twenty-six fields. An additional field in each column served as a timer. If a column held data, this extra field was punched. When two active columns overlapped, light was directed to a timing cell which then readied the sensing photocells to examine many data columns simultaneously.

There were to be at least ten data columns, thus letters, packed into a linear inch of tape. Each letter was signified by a minute hole punched in one position of a column. The hole was smaller than a period on this page and the spaces between columns were no greater. To accommodate Wenger's need for counting more than single coincidences, ten letters were to be read at one time. This called for ten photocells for message characters, one to each column.

In Bush's design, if the same character fields in the overlapped tapes had holes a "hit" would be registered. Because a coincidence was recorded if light penetrated through both tapes, the reader was very prone to mistakes. Even if the transport brought the tapes over the sensors in perfect alignment, light could easily spill from column to column or dust or flakes of paper might block or scatter the light. All this meant very difficult problems in channelling and sensing light and in regulating the photocells and their electronic amplifiers.

The student engineer was left on his own to solve those difficult light problems. He had to make some important decisions very early in his work. An initial one was based on the old engineering rule of keeping mechanisms as simple as possible. To avoid the complexity of an on-off light system, such as the one developed by Edgerton, the student decided to use a steadily burning high intensity lamp positioned above the two tapes. Other of his design choices were more difficult. Much had to be done to turn Bush's sketch of the reader into a reliable component. The engineer had to create a mask to ensure that light that shone through the first tape did not drift before it fell on the lower one. He also had to find a lens that would direct the light beams from overlapping holes, one for each column, onto the correct sensing photocell. An allied problem was more challenging; he had to keep light from a coincident column from spilling over into the area of another column's photocell.

The state of photocell technology did not allow easy solutions to any of the reader's problems. Photocells had emerged from the laboratory in the early part of the century but they remained rather unpredictable until improvements in the mid-1920s led them to become parts of new automatic machines and scientific instruments.[35] By the 1930s, photocells were stock items for manufacturers such as RCA and General Electric, but they continued to have serious limitations. Among other problems, they remained fairly large. As a result, the young MIT engineer could not put ten of them directly under the columns of the

Comparator's tapes. They had to be placed far under the reader and were arranged in a "U" pattern. That meant that the straight, parallel light from the coincident columns had to be accurately deflected. Moreover, complete electronic packages for the photocells were not supplied by manufacturers. The MIT engineer had to tune each photocell and build the amplification circuits to turn the signals from the photocells into the discrete pulses needed by the third major component of the Comparator, the electronic counters.

The Most Difficult Problem of All, But It Wasn't

With the knowledge of the tape and photocell systems, the third young man began his work on the final details of what everyone thought would be the most difficult part of the project, its electronic counting system.

Precise digital counting with electronics was in its early years and all attempts at creating tube-based calculating circuits were risky. Electronic tubes were designed for analog work and it was only empirical tweaking that allowed them to be on-off switches. The physicists who made the first digital counters after World War I accepted such imperfections because the systems they built to measure radiation did not have to be fully accurate. The physicists' goal had been to slow the radiation pulses by passing them through a number of tubes until their frequency was reduced enough to be registered on mechanical counters. That was not as demanding as the counting chores assigned to the Comparator.

The electronic technology of the 1930s was also limited in terms of speed, reliability and circuit design. Although the maturation of the radio industry led to many improvements, electronic tubes remained slow, bulky and temperamental monsters that generated too much heat. As late as 1940, the best experimental electronic counters worked at twenty thousand decimal counts a second during their cooperative periods. In fact, in 1939, MIT's explorations for its digital electronic computer produced estimates of reliable operation at only half that speed and its men continued to worry about the designs of the most fundamental circuits.[36] Thus, it was natural for Bush to fret over the electronic components of the Comparator, even though he had restricted their functions to two rather simple tasks: tallying counts and providing the switching needed for the parallel sensing. While Bush was not asking his machine to add or to subtract, to multiply or divide, or to have the infinite flexibility of the modern computer, he was correct in thinking electronics was a challenge. Despite the functional simplicity, the third young MIT engineer took on a very difficult job. Although he already had experience in electronics and was the circuit designer for Caldwell's Rockefeller project, he had to teach himself a great deal to complete the counter-printer portion of the Comparator.[37]

One of his greatest challenges was the circuitry for the Comparator's parallel processing feature. It was needed to allow the machine to perform the simultaneous multiple letter tests that were so valuable to the cryptanalysts. Without parallel processing, the machine's power would be reduced by a factor of four. The student engineer had to construct five independent electronic counters which were to tap the data from the reading station at the same time. Four of the counters were to hold a maximum count of nine hundred ninety nine. The other was to increment up to ten thousand. The five counters called for the use of hundreds of tubes, none of which could miss a beat during runs of several minutes. With the goal of twenty thousand comparisons a minute, Bush's engineer was asked to build counters that were quite fast.[38] Although the young man wanted such a rapid machine, he took the safe technological route. Instead of using the very high-speed but delicate vacuum tubes, he chose to stay with the more predictable and familiar gas filled Thyratrons. Ironing out the problems with vacuum tubes for digital work would have been a project in itself and their use would have endangered the Comparator's schedule.[39]

The choice of architecture for the counters was also driven by the need to send the navy at least a feasible design, if not a machine, by mid-1938. Like the other electronic computer builders of the era, the young MIT engineer decided to imitate mechanical calculating machines.[40] His counters were decimal, not binary. Although such a design limited the range of the application of a computer, it was known to work and was simpler to construct than binary circuits. Each of the decimal counters was to consist of three or more rings of ten tubes with the needed electronics for arithmetic carrying, power and control. Despite the wise choices to stay with the older tubes and the more familiar architecture, the Comparator was a breakthrough and a gamble. In 1937, just maintaining a machine with over one hundred tubes was regarded as an engineering feat.

Providing the option of performing several different analyses at one time meant additional challenges. Bush had designed the machine to allow the analysts to select the particular tests for each run. He wanted them to be able to seek, for example, matches in the first, second and fourth columns and the fifth and seventh and the ninth and tenth. In addition, they were to be able to select several of those combinations on each run. To permit this, the young engineer incorporated a set of "and" circuits that could be set to test for the desired combinations. The Comparator's Rossi "and" circuit was the key to the machine's flexibility and parallelism. It was the creation of a physicist who had extended the usefulness of electronic counting. He invented complex circuits that allowed counters to be incremented only if a set of conditions were fulfilled. His circuit designs were published in scientific journals and were well known. In the Comparator, a plugboard was used to allow the operator to connect the Rossi circuits in the desired combinations.[41]

In addition to the counters and the "and" circuits, the third engineer was handed another tough job. He was given the responsibility for creating the banks of electrical relays needed to stand between the high-speed tube counters and the much, much slower printer. At the end of each pass, the counters had to be polled for their contents and numbers sent to the relays. The relays worked as a short term memory sending pulses to the magnets that controlled the print bars.[42]

The Easiest Becomes the Most Difficult

There was a fourth man. He was in charge of the crucial data entry system. At the beginning of the project a data entry device was seen as the least challenging of the components and it received little attention. But, from late 1937 and for a decade to follow, the punch for the data tapes proved to be the achilles heel of the Comparator. The problem was a perhaps inescapable result of the use of paper tape, as was Bush's inefficient one-of-twenty six coding scheme.

The technology of the 1930s led him to reject a method of coding that could have increased densities on the tapes by at least a factor of five and that would have led the Comparator's codes to fit with the navy's modern communication system. The use of a five field character code, the Baudot code, would have allowed at least five letters to be placed on a line (column) of the 70mm tape. But the size and sensitivity of holes and photocells, the problems of aligning tapes and the desire to limit the electronics of the machine precluded the use of that coding pattern.[43]

To compensate for his one character per column format, Bush ordered his men to find a way to pack as many columns in a linear inch of tape as possible. At the first stages of the project, the young men thought they could punch twenty characters in an inch of tape. That was twice as many as on telegraph tapes. But they soon confronted physical limitations: The holes would be too small for reliable punching heads. Disappointed, the MIT group compromised on a density not much greater than in the commercial telegraph system, ten per inch. But that did not mean they could turn to a commercially manufactured punch. Bush's special coding scheme demanded a custom made and very complex mechanism. However, in 1937, no one seemed to realize how sophisticated and rugged that punch would have to be. Continuing to think that mechanical parts would be the least troublesome, the assignment of someone to the construction of a useful punch was deferred. And, because few of MIT's students had experience with high tolerance toolmaking, the responsibility eventually went to an Institute employee who had many other duties.

The MIT machinist was instructed to make a keyboard operated device to simultaneously punch two exact copies of a message. It had to keep the two tapes in perfect synchronization and to make precisely spaced tiny holes in each column and row. The punch had to advance the tapes with absolute precision. Most challenging, it had to maintain the integrity of its tiny and sharp needle-like punching arms despite the impact as the arms struck the Eastman tape. The machinist was given even more to do. He was asked to devise tape cutters and the means to ensure that the spliced ends of the tapes would not pull apart during the runs.

Unfortunately, the punch was the last component of the Comparator to be turned over to the project manager and then it was "not satisfactory."[44] The punch's inadequacies can not be blamed on the machinist; the responsibility has to be placed on the original design for the Comparator. Bush had not foreseen it, but the most intransigent problems with the Comparator and all of its technological cousins were not electronic, they were mechanical. Between 1938 and 1945 several teams of engineers tried to produce a viable data entry system for the paper tapes; none was able to build a rugged and reliable punch. Although not evident in the fall of 1937, there were many more problems with the Comparator.[45] As bad, the Comparator's schedule unravelled.

Beyond Murphy's Law

Bush had not anticipated serious difficulties as the fall 1937 term began at MIT. He believed his young men had made great progress during the summer and he thought his machine would prove that universities should participate in military research. Bush had been so confident that he turned away from the Comparator before his graduate students began their summer work. He concentrated on his preparations to take over the Carnegie Institution and on the last minute details of his many other projects. He thought that any of the Comparator's loose ends would be handled by the experienced and skilled man coming to the Institute to take charge of the project.[46]

When Waldron MacDonald arrived in September, Bush gave him an office, a secretary, a workroom and full responsibility. Bush was so pressed for time that he visited him no more than once a month. Despite the great burden, MacDonald was also positive and optimistic. He looked forward to completing an exciting machine, to obtaining a Master's degree, and, perhaps, to establishing himself as one of the first experts and businessmen in the rapid machine field. His faith seemed justified during the autumn of 1937. Everything fell into place. The three student engineers had sent their work to local machine shops and Bush trusted their judgement so much that, without examining the parts, he put MacDonald to writing the descriptive reports for the navy. MacDonald had the honor of being Bush's technical ghost writer. He took Bush's first schemes for each component, added what the students had done, and sent the reports to the navy for payment.[47] The reports, including the final one submitted in the spring of 1938, were upbeat and gave the specifications for what everyone thought would be the first operating electronic data processing machine.[48]

Although the reports contained a bright picture, the Comparator project had fallen victim to a host of problems. The early battles with the Bureau, Bush's success as an academic statesman, the demands of other projects at MIT and even chance worked against the Comparator. The navy's policy of rotating its officers from shore to sea duty also played a part. But, the main reason for the problems in 1937 and 1938 was the technologies Bush so admired. They were not ready to be turned into useful machinery--at least in the context of a short term development project. Bush had asked too much of his men.

However, the troubles were not apparent in the early weeks of fall 1937. Wenger wrote his colleagues in OP-20-G about the progress at MIT in enthusiastic terms. His need to see a successful project may have led him to interpret what he heard about the work in ways that contributed to later disappointments. Wenger wrote:

> Construction is already nearly completed. It will do all we asked for and a lot more. In one operation, for example, it makes comparisons at the rate of over four hundred million per minute! They recently told us that they had figured out a way to multiply the speed by twenty, but unfortunately couldn't incorporate the change in this model because construction was too far along.[49]

Why anyone would have made a claim of four hundred million comparisons a minute and why Wenger accepted such an estimate defies explanation. His belief that the machine was nearly complete is as baffling. In November 1937 the Comparator was very, very far from the end of its construction cycle. By the end of the year, it was in serious trouble, and, just after Wenger wrote his letter, the problems started to become evident, at least to MacDonald. Wenger, however, retained his near blind faith in Bush and the Comparator throughout the coming months. He did not realize what was happening to his dream. He was unaware that as the students submitted their reports to MacDonald in early fall and returned to Caldwell's project, Bush declared that his role in the navy work was effectively over although he planned to provide OP-20-G with a machine on schedule.[50] Unfortunately, the results Bush and his young men expected on the basis of their early bench tests did not carry through to the parts they gave to MacDonald. The Comparator was far from ready for assembly. And, only MacDonald was left to rescue it! MacDonald had much, much more to do than simply link the components together. Almost every component had to be reworked.

He put much thought and energy into reshaping the electronic components and he more than fine-tuned the tape transport. The first engineer had done a good job on the design of the tape drive and the reputable Harvard Square machine shop had done professional work constructing it. But, MacDonald had to make several adjustments to it.

More basic work had to be done on the reader. The optical system needed a complete overhaul and it took much of MacDonald's attention. To bring the correct amount of light to each of the ten cells, he devised a 1930's version of fiber-optics. Very thin shafts of clear lucite were shaped to act as light guides. They were as wide as the data area of the tapes, but very thin. MacDonald had to precisely shape and bend them to bring the light to the appropriate cells without leakage. He also had to construct a frame that kept the shafts at exact positions under the reader.

Thus, MacDonald's assignment turned into something much more demanding than either he or Bush had imagined in mid-1937. MacDonald was not sure that he could solve all the problems of the transport, counters and optical sensors. Worse, he had no assurance that the critical punch difficulties could be overcome.[51] The printer also remained in the realm of hope.[52] However, Bush did not seek men to help rebuild the major components. MacDonald was left alone. The burden was perhaps too much to ask of any single engineer, even for a man Bush considered the most able research assistant he had ever had.[53]

MacDonald's past experience might have allowed him to overcome the hurdles, but chance compounded an already difficult situation. In the fall, MacDonald decided to take a break from his work and play a game of touch-football. It was a friendly game, but he was knocked out by an unlucky "poke on the jaw," a very serious poke. MacDonald remained unconscious and confined to bed for several weeks. His energy was seriously drained for months afterwards.[54] Despite the injury, Bush chose not to replace MacDonald. Bush hoped that MacDonald's expertise would compensate for the problems with the original components and the time lost because of the accident. MacDonald returned to his duties as soon as he could. But his illness meant the end of his dream of finishing a Master's degree.[55] And, more than touch football worked against the Comparator.

What Hooper had complained about for so many years, the lack of appreciation of science in the navy, again struck the Comparator. The navy held that young officers were to be rotated among jobs and from sea to shore duty every few years. A career officer had to follow what some called "Manchu" demands if he had any desire to progress through the ranks. The rotation policy included those men who were involved in very specialized duties, even cryptanalysis. In 1938, that meant that all the experienced officers at OP-20-G, with only one exception, Laurance Safford, were to be transferred to other duties and away from their highly technical work.[56]

The Comparator was about to lose its strongest advocates. The earlier episode was being repeated: Joseph Wenger received transfer orders. Wenger rushed to Bush and asked for his help. Bush quickly agreed and used all his influence to prevent Wenger from being taken away from what some were calling the Rapid Machine project. Bush thought Wenger was essential to the first Rapid Machine, the Comparator, so he pulled as many political strings as possible. He drafted a plea to the Chief of Naval Operations in December 1937:

> We have been making reasonable progress I believe, and while my own attention to the matter is nearly complete as far as the particular piece of work which I undertook is concerned, nevertheless I feel that in order for the result to be of greatest benefit to the Navy, the result should be taken over by the Navy with the attention of a man who is thoroughly familiar with the matter and its entire range of aspects.[57]

Bush's pleas were ineffective and Wenger, the strongest voice for a revolution in the technologies of signals intelligence and cryptanalysis, readied himself to leave for sea duty in mid-1938. Wenger had to spend the five months before he was rotated putting the finishing touches on the detailed reports for Hooper's grand proposal for a modern communications system. His studies, which ranged from fax systems to direction finding, prevented him from taking a direct hand in the work at MIT.[58] Wenger left the country just a month before MacDonald shipped the troubled Comparator to Washington.

There was an ironic twist to Wenger's years of sea duty in the late 1930s. He was away from OP-20-G when it became involved in the severe political ramifications of the failure to predict the attack on Pearl Harbor. His absence allowed him to return to OP-20-G in 1942 untarnished by the intelligence failure and free from the many related intense political and personal conflicts. He was able to begin a third crusade for the Rapid Machines.[59] But, in 1937 there was no reason to think Wenger's transfer would have a positive role in the history of the Comparator.

During the last months of 1937, when Wenger was desperately trying to avoid reassignment, the bad news about the Comparator project had still not reached Washington. Its navy friends continued to praise it. At the end of 1937, Laurance Safford, then head of OP-20-G, submitted a report on the Bush project that was as upbeat as Wenger's evaluation of a month earlier:

> As matters have turned out it appears that we have struck a remarkably good bargain. For $18,000 we are getting not only the reports and plans called for in the contract but actual usable machinery which promises to exceed in performance our fondest hopes.[60]

Meanwhile, after recuperating, MacDonald returned to his work and was able to write all the reports Bush needed to fulfill the Bureau's requirements. MacDonald did experience frustrations, however. He had to put an unexpected amount of additional effort into reworking the components and into making them compatible with each other. But, in spring 1938, he began test runs on the rebuilt parts.[61] MacDonald also had the chore of instructing the engineer the navy sent to learn about the machine. Wenger had arranged for a Bureau technician to spend some time at MIT. During the spring, Frederick Dulong, one of the many ex-navy men who stayed on in Washington as civilian employees, was sent to MIT. Although classified as a Radio Man, he had done much of the mechanical work on the tabulators and had helped the Navy Yard's Don Seiler to build America's own ciphering machines. Dulong left Cambridge to return to the Yard in April, just as MacDonald was submitting the final report and as Bush was predicting the Comparator would arrive in Washington in June 1938. What Dulong told his colleagues at the Bureau is unknown, but he may have quietly let them know that what he had seen in Cambridge was a very strange and unreliable machine. MacDonald later admitted that in June 1938 the Comparator remained a "semi-finished" device.[62]

But Wenger continued to have a very different view of the machine and the situation. After an April meeting with Bush he was still full of admiration. He considered Bush very generous for having constructed a machine and approved Bush's suggestion that MacDonald be hired by the navy to fine-tune the Comparator once it was in Washington. Wenger interviewed MacDonald, then persuasively argued that since eighteen thousand dollars had already been spent, a few hundred more for MacDonald to come to Washington was a wise investment.[63] The Bureau agreed and requested MacDonald to travel to Washington with the Comparator and to stay for three months. He was to adjust the machine and to instruct both technicians and cryptanalysts in its use. Safford, now in charge of the Comparator, was pleased that the Bureau promised to give him some additional, if not permanent, help. He looked forward to having an operating and productive machine within a few weeks. He thought Hooper's and Wenger's dreams of a permanent Rapid Machine program were about to be fulfilled.

Grand Plans Face the Limits of Technology and Time

As soon as Bush signaled that a machine would be sent to Washington, Wenger began expensive preparations. He requested the money for tapes and lights and extra tubes and he readied an area for the Comparator within OP-20-G's secret rooms. The cost of the supplies, one thousand dollars, indicated how much faith was placed in Bush. That amount was equal to one-fifth of the money spent for the rental of all OP-20-G's IBM equipment. In a few weeks, additional funds were requested for the hardware necessary to prepare the tapes for the Comparator.[64] Wenger went much further. Describing a new era in cryptanalysis, he convinced the navy brass to give serious consideration to funding more devices.[65] By the end of 1938, OP-20-G's budget request included more than twenty thousand dollars for additional Bush devices and special additions to the first machine.[66] In addition, "G's" new war plans contained a request for a Comparator for the proposed major cryptanalytic station at Pearl Harbor.[67]

Bush and MacDonald were not as excited as Wenger. In April 1938 Bush informed Wenger that he wished to withdraw from any more work for the navy. He desired at least one free year. During that time, he said, OP-20-G could gain experience with the Comparator and MIT's men could work on a new project that might lead to the promised twenty-fold improvement in the performance of electronic cryptanalytic machines. Bush did not state it directly, but he had microfilm in mind. Bush also advised Wenger that as soon as the new MIT development was completed and its technology transferred to cryptanalytic work, the navy should launch into a major project to build many other electronic devices. Bush may have been seeing the next round of OP-20-G work as an opportunity for some of his young men to found their own companies. As he later told MacDonald, the project eventually had to move out to a private manufacturer.[68] MacDonald may have had some hope that he would found such a company, but in mid-1938 he had more important matters in mind. He wanted to be married.[69]

Spring is a Time for Love, Not Machinery

In response to Bush's suggestion to bring MacDonald to Washington, Wenger began another loyalty check then requested the funds to pay him. Once he had the navy's approval, Wenger asked MacDonald to accompany the Comparator on its trip from Cambridge. MacDonald's reply startled the navy! Without telling the navy's men the reason (he wished to travel to England to convince his sweetheart to marry him) he informed them that he did not want to start any new work until August, some two months after the Comparator was scheduled to arrive in Washington. That may have puzzled the Bureau, but MacDonald's next demand alienated its officers. MacDonald stated he wanted at least twenty dollars per diem, a very high rate, especially in comparison to the wages paid at the Yard. On a yearly basis, the salary he demanded was three times that of a Chief Petty Officer and twice that of some of the top civilian cryptanalysts.[70]

Safford overcame the protests about MacDonald's late arrival and his salary. But, he was unable to prevent the men at the Yard from recognizing something very important: When the Comparator arrived in Washington in late June, a month late, it would not start.[71] As bad, two of its most important parts had not been shipped. Safford, although still an advocate for the Rapid Machines, must have been worried when he found he was unable to contact MacDonald or to find anyone at the Institute who knew where he, the punch, or printer were.[72]

The Comparator's career was not going well. About a month behind schedule and still only "semi-finished," it found a new and well-intentioned guardian. But Fred Dulong could not give full attention to the machine. By mid-July, Dulong was able to run the counting circuits[73] but any more work was stalled because of the missing punch and printer. Unknown to anyone, they had been placed in a Cambridge safe-deposit box by MacDonald--to await his return to the country in

August.[74] If Dulong could have restarted the entire machine he would have found that it did not perform up to the goals set by Bush and Wenger in 1936. An informed guess is that the limitations of the tape drive and the electronic counters held the machine to less than one-fourth of the goal of twenty thousand comparisons per minute.[75] With an incomplete and inoperable machine on their hands, the already sensitive technicians at the Bureau of Engineering must have wondered if they had agreed to take over the responsibility for an ill-fated and embarrassing project. If Stanford Hooper learned about the condition of the machine he must have worried that his hopes of uniting academia and the military would never be realized.[76] If the contract officers at the Bureau knew of the situation, they must have protested against relying upon nonspecific contracts. Engineering must have asked how much more of its precious time would have to go into the limping machine.

The cryptanalysts certainly did not have the time to wet nurse the Comparator. While the Bureau's men bewailed the results of becoming entangled with an impractical professor, the cryptanalysts in charge of the day-to-day work were coming under incredible pressures to penetrate all of the sophisticated Japanese code and cipher systems. They had no time for a grand experiment. Japan's invasion of China in 1937 had made it clear that war was imminent[77] and by 1938 OP-20-G was facing crisis conditions. The sinking of the Panay in December led to a scramble to protect American codes. In addition, there were hints that Japan was about to make another sweeping change in its codes and to introduce its famous Purple cipher machine.[78] Unfortunately, Roosevelt's reinvigoration of the American navy did not lead to a significant expansion of the workforce at OP-20-G. What energies it had were necessarily devoted to developing techniques and machines that gave immediate results. Its faith was, quite naturally, placed in the direct analogs of Japan's enciphering machines and its men wanted resources devoted to modernizing the tabulators.

Thus, Waldron MacDonald did not arrive in Washington at the right time for any experimentation at "G" or the Bureau. Driving from Cambridge with his bride in August 1938, he had the Comparator's punch and printer in the back of his station wagon. Settling in a small apartment to begin a working honeymoon, he soon found that his expectations about the navy's long-term intentions would not be met. He became depressed. In addition to Washington's near unbearable summer heat and its lazy Southern way of life, he found the Comparator in what he considered a state of neglect.[79] He also sensed a very negative attitude at OP-20-G. But he got to work, determined to fulfill his professional obligations. Working in OP-20-G's downtown offices, MacDonald attempted to save his and Bush's reputation.

He hurried the Yard's efforts to build tape duplicators and splicers and soon convinced the Bureau to build a new punch. The one from MIT could not be coaxed into working. Don Seiler, who had done so much to help Safford over the years, took on that challenge.[80] Then, MacDonald began working on the other components. Dulong may have helped and been given more instructions about the Comparator's maintenance and use. Although no major changes were made to the Comparator, it took an unexpected fourth month of work to announce a finished machine in November. The navy had spent perhaps an additional two thousand dollars on salaries.[81] The total cost of the Comparator and its supplies had climbed to more than twenty-five thousand dollars.

The Comparator Just Fades Away

During MacDonald's months in Washington, Laurance Safford was kind to him and his new wife. He took them to Annapolis to see its beautiful grounds and to a football game. Perhaps Stanford Hooper was the Admiral who dropped by the secret workrooms to view MacDonald's progress.[82] The cryptanalysts at OP-20-G, however, had little time to socialize, to study the Comparator or to devise the methods that would make it useful against the Japanese systems.[83] But, as MacDonald worked, he and Bush discussed the possibility that the navy might renew its efforts to develop the other Rapid Machines. They thought such a project would provide a wonderful career opportunity for MacDonald.[84] The navy did offer him a job, but as a low paid employee. And, by the time of the offer, he had become alienated by the navy's ways.[85] He was put off by what the navy was willing to offer as a salary, "one-tenth" of what his wartime job would pay, and by technological indifference at OP-20-G. MacDonald decided to leave both the project and Washington at the end of 1938. No one at OP-20-G seemed able or willing to take the responsibility for what he thought was a chance to build the world's most advanced electronic machines.

Although he may not have known it, Wenger's absence at sea was important to MacDonald's decision. Wenger was vitally needed because no one in Washington remained as a strong advocate for the Comparator. Hooper was too busy with higher level matters and perhaps too taken up with the fallout from his earlier attempts to reshape the Bureaus. Budget problems were also taking their toll. Even the program for the acquisition of electromechanical equipment slowed. The order for the new and very useful IBM collator was cancelled[86] and no new tabulators were brought into "G" during 1938 and 1939.[87]

Safford was disappointed that MacDonald did not stay on but he was satisfied with his work and with the Comparator. In late 1938, OP-20-G's leader congratulated Bush and informed him the cryptanalysts and the Bureau's men planned to spend the next year experimenting with the wonderful and reliable machine. And, he said, they awaited Bush's return to their work in early 1940. Possibly because they now realized how much a well schooled optical-electronics engineer would cost, OP-20-G did not make an effort to hire a replacement for the MIT engineer or, as planned earlier in the year, to construct at least one more Comparator.[88] With Wenger gone, no one pressed for immediate extension of the program.[89] Bush, in turn, quickly fended off another attempt by the navy to link him to "G's" projects. He found a plausible excuse for not accepting a special naval officer's commission for high level scientists.[90] Of greater significance, Bush and the navy did not get together within a year and the plans to start building new devices during the 1940 fiscal year were put aside.[91]

The consequences of the failure to continue on with the Comparator project in 1938 were severe. Soon after MacDonald left Washington the Comparator again became inoperable. It was so temperamental that the only attention it received was from Dulong whose many other duties allowed just part-time work.[92] It was listed on OP-20-G's equipment roster in 1939, but it was never used, not even on the type of important project for which it had been designed, the breaking of the Japanese Purple cipher machine.[93] Its technical problems became so great that it was removed from the cryptanalysts' quarters and sent to the Navy Yard where it could be tinkered with. The Bureau's attitude, if Safford is believed, did not help matters. It made no great attempt to rescue the Comparator or the Rapid Machine project. It may well have killed Safford's mid-1939 request for an additional ten thousand dollars to "finish" the MIT machine.[94]

Although overworked because of the Japanese code and cipher crises, Safford had asked for a report on the Comparator and received some very disheartening news. Dulong responded that nothing but the electronic counters proved reliable and the machine had not been functional long enough to allow in-depth development of procedures. The Navy Yard's men did not think there was any possible quick-fix for the device. Most ominous was the failure of the data entry component, the punch. Even the second version of that purely mechanical and supposedly simple mechanism could not be made to produce precise tapes. There was little hope of basing an entire system of analytical machines around the original Bush design if there was not an efficient and reliable data entry device.[95]

In 1940, Safford, who two years before declared the Comparator a reliable and useful invention, had to admit the machine never worked and that the entire project had not progressed as planned. He threw a few stones at the Bureau about dragging its feet, especially in 1938 and 1939, but also blamed himself and his friend Wenger for some inappropriate decisions at the first stages of the project. Safford felt that he had failed Stanford Hooper and his dreams of modernizing OP-20-G.[96]

The Comparator was more than in trouble. The failure to match the perhaps inflated claims for the Comparator led to the tabling of the plans for other high-speed analytical devices. Such machines were not mentioned in "G's" 1940 war plans although it was thought the navy would finance some two-hundred thousand dollars a year in tabulator rentals.[97] When Bush finally reestablished contact with OP-20-G in the summer of 1940, he concluded there was little hope the navy would resume any serious work on his grand outline, either inside or outside of the Bureau. He wrote MacDonald that while the project had not been cancelled there had been little progress. His tone suggests that he thought that Hooper's dreams had died a very ungracious death at a pivotal moment in the history of American cryptanalysis.[98]

The Copperhead Scanner, circa 1945
(National Security Agency)

The IC Machine, circa 1943
(National Security Agency)

Chapter VIII
The Next Machine That Wouldn't: The Other Memex

As the Comparator's future was being threatened by the squabbles of 1936, Vannevar Bush was busy with another use for his favored technologies. He wished to put film, optics and electronics together to create an information engine. His definition of such a machine was never stable and his concept of who and what the device was for changed repeatedly during the 1930s. What became known as the Rapid Selector took on many different faces as possible sponsors appeared then retreated.

The Selector was the closest Bush ever came to building a Memex, but it has attracted much less attention than his proposed association machine. There are some good reasons for its anonymity. The most fundamental was that it was not a success. Although its decades long history provides the direct link between the pre and postwar years of American information technology, and, although its builders were central to the struggle to bring science to American cryptanalysis, the Selector, like the Comparator, had a less than happy life.

The Same Technology for Information and Calculation

Vannevar Bush's involvement in information technology traveled in and out of many institutions and causes from the 1920s to the end of the 1950s. His initial motive was his desire to extend the Institute's 1920s work on light-based analog calculation. Beginning in the early 1920s, his colleagues constructed a series of scientific measuring instruments for engineering and physics that made Bush think of the possibilities of using the same technology for digital calculation and information processing.[1] The expansion of MIT's uses of "radiation" for measurement was driven by the ideas of MIT's resident mathematician, Norbert Wiener. He suggested relatively simple devices to accomplish what Bush was doing with his huge Differential Analyser.[2] Wiener's urgings were first embodied in an infrared integrating instrument developed by one of the MIT graduate students of the 1920s, King Gould. During the 1930s, similar contrivances moved to the use of normal light and photoelectricity. Soon, there were borrowings from the hardware of the moving picture industry. Reels of film were used in some devices while others incorporated the new advances in high resolution plate photography. George Harrison's amazing Wavelength Analyser extended astronomers' previous use of photoelectricity, photographic plates and high-speed photography in a special combination to turn analog measurements into digital output. Photoelectricity was also the basis for an automatic curve follower that was later attached to the Differential Analyser. That automatic input device became the foundation for the Institute's servomechanism program.[3] But the machine that pointed Bush to the Selector was Gordon Brown's Cinema Integraph.[4]

Gordon S. Brown was another of MIT's graduates who became a valued faculty member. He became essential to the Institute's projects on robotics and feedback mechanisms. Brown and his students, including "Junior" Howard, worked on the Cinema Integraph from the mid to the late 1930s, revising it whenever a new idea or mechanism became available. The Cinema Integraph measured the amount of light passing through moving films with clear and opaque areas that represented the functions to be integrated. The device was significant for reasons beyond the use of film in a scientific measuring instrument. Its development led to sophisticated optical-electronic components, including advanced photocells and electronic amplifiers. The machine also used improved film drives. It had a complex relay circuit to step the films and its engineers developed an automatic printer.

A Competitor to the Card?

Inspired by the Integraph and primed by hints of markets, Bush took the next step. He put the advances in servomechanisms and high-speed photography together with microfilm.[5] Bush's focus was on the library and scientific information, but he had many other motives for pursuing his version of the light machines in the mid-1930s. Central to them was that he was convinced that microfilm was going to break the hold of the punch card and provide the foundation for the first competition to IBM. Although the ideas were not precise or well examined, Bush, and others, thought microfilm would become the mass memory of the 1940s. He was sure that optical scanners could be developed to read the minute dots on the films and that electronic circuits would emerge to replace the mechanical counters and relays of the tabulators.[6] Bush knew of the rapidly expanding use of microfilm in the business world. He was also aware of the rush by the business machine companies to gain important and fundamental patents in the field, ones which included devices to quickly locate items on microfilmed records.[7] He correctly sensed that MIT could gain support from those who wished to get a jump on IBM. But, the first stirring of his interest in the practical application of light machines to microfilm were related to science and the library.

An immediate stimulus was his meeting with that dynamic advocate of the use of microfilm for the scientific library, Watson Davis. In 1932, they discussed Davis's microfilming projects[8], and, perhaps, his ideas for a device to locate documents placed on rolls of microfilm.[9] Bush was courteous and he tried to help Davis. He recommended the use of large sheets of film for the dissemination of scientific literature. But that was about all.[10] Little came of the meeting because Davis was looking for financial help, something Bush was unable, as well as unwilling, to give during MIT's lean years. Those associated with Davis were seeking and, at times, receiving funds from the foundations[11] and Bush may have viewed them as competitors rather than allies.[12] That became evident when, in mid-decade, Davis and his colleagues developed outlines for devices to locate records on microfilms.[13]

Bush turned to more prestigious groups than the Documentalists for aid. Many in the sciences were aware of the inadequacies of indexing and accessing systems for scientific materials and by the mid-1930s there were even rumblings from those associated with the Carnegie and Rockefeller foundations of subsidies to modernize the library. Like the scientists, their leaders were displeased with the typical categorization systems and hoped to find ways to allow practitioners to take charge of indexing.[14] Bush sensed a need and an opportunity for a machine for the scientific bibliographic problem.

The First Selector

However, the first chance to turn his Memex-like ideas into hardware did not come from the world of high science or even the business community. The first plan for a Rapid Selector system had an unlikely sponsor, the Federal Bureau of Investigation.[15] Unfortunately, after all the work he put in on its project, Bush decided to back away because he found the Bureau too difficult to work with. After the failure of the FBI project, Bush dropped the Selector and devoted himself to other challenges, including the first phases of the navy's work. He did not abandon the Selector, however. By early 1937 he had revised the original FBI design and had a well developed sketch of an information processor he thought could be used for library applications.[16] Somehow, he was able to have his young men do enough work on Selector-like components to be able to join the growing ranks of inventors filing fundamental patents on automatic microfilm location devices.[17] After contacting the Research Corporation, Bush filed a sweeping claim for a high-speed machine to examine coded microfilmed records and to instantly reproduce those that were selected. Much of what he claimed in October 1937 could have been used in the Comparator.

When he submitted the patent application, Bush knew of some competitors, such as International Filmbook of Connecticut, but he thought he had beaten everyone to the essentials of an information machine. He was wrong. What turned out to be a flawed patent search had long-term consequences for the history of his machine.[18] But, in 1937, with the general idea in hand and patents on the way, Bush felt confident enough to resume the search for financing for his Selector.

The Second Selector

In early 1937, Bush targeted the private foundations. He focused his presentations on a machine for the indexing and retrieval of comments on scientific and technical articles. He said he had a design for an engine that could remedy one of the most serious problems of science, the isolation of researchers. One reason for his emphasis on the problems of the scientific community was his awareness of the interests of the Scientific Aids to Learning Project. He knew of the survey of microfilm resources by one of the leading Documentalists, Vernon Tate.[19] Bush hoped he would gain support from the foundations before Tate and his associates asked the foundations to underwrite their microfilm plans.[20] Bush polished his ideas and developed what he thought was a unique and sure-fire plan for a new system, one the large foundations could not resist. He began making the rounds in the spring of 1937. As usual, he stopped at Warren Weaver's office and, as usual, got a receptive hearing for his plan for the "Reference Selector."[21]

The Reference Selector was a variation on the ideas that became the basis for the Rapid Selector. The 1937 Reference Selector, although to be built of the same components, was different. It was a machine that would create a new stage in the "fellowship of learning."[22] His system, he told Weaver, would fill a gap created by the nature of the existing classification, bibliographic and indexing services. It would be a critically needed supplement, if not replacement, for the card catalog and tools such as *Engineering Index* and *Chemical Abstracts*.

Under Bush's plan, experts would read articles in their fields, tag each for its subject, then write a small critical note. The note, about one hundred words, was the unique and significant part. It was what made the system valuable and, Bush said, was what would allow the expert scientists a role in the library. The note would let them provide their peers and students with a qualitative evaluation of each article, something the traditional indexes did not and could not do. With the Reference Selector, he claimed, future researchers would not have to spend time sorting through materials of little value.

At first glance, Bush's system appeared practical and faultless. After a week or so of note taking, a researcher would send a pile of entries to his library where they would be typed and a machine-readable code entered next to the comment. Then, the pages would be microfilmed and added to the reels of criticisms on file in the library. All that would be useless, of course, without the machine, the Selector. It was, Bush said, the technological key that would let researchers spin through and locate what others had contributed to a vast pool of materials. Without the revolutionary high-tech device, the "multiple intelligence of the reviewers whose judgments are stored for the use of others," would be lost.[23]

Unfortunately, Bush never fully explored nor solved the inherent conflict between his ideas of private association and the needs of a system for a large and heterogeneous group of scholars. He did not show exactly how his system would be more effective than the give-and-take among scientists through peer reviews and comments in professional journals. And, he did not explain how the criticisms could be widely distributed or integrated with the work of the existing indexing and abstracting services.[24] Perhaps it was for those reasons that the foundations decided not to fund Bush's Reference Selector in 1937. The failure to secure a sponsor within the high-science community had a great impact on the history of his information engine. Bush would find sponsors, but not ones whose aim was to produce a machine to liberate scientists from librarians and indexers.[25]

The Third Selector

While the foundations were drafting their rejection letters, Bush reworked some of his ideas and devised justifications for yet another version of a Selector. Then, he contacted many of MIT's old friends. Quite soon, he made a successful connection, one that would lead to a long series of involvements linking the Selector, the Comparator and the Ultra Secret. The connection was with the new head of the National Cash Register Company, Colonel Deeds. The NCR involvement meant that Bush's Reference project took on a new character.[26]

After Bush contacted him in mid-1937, Deeds came to appreciate the potentials of Bush's ideas for NCR as well as for American science. He and his advisors knew that electronic calculation was in the offing and they knew their competitors were beginning to establish a patent position in optics, film and electronics. The success of firms such as Recordak in applying microfilm in banks and the chance that film-based machines might lead to the first viable competitors to the IBM tabulator[27] dictated that NCR explore the new technologies and establish a foothold before IBM locked others out of the market.[28] Deeds decided to support the MIT microfilm and electronics work and to use Bush's men as advisors. He was especially interested in Edgerton's flash systems.[29]

Bush rushed to Deeds to arrange an agreement for a Selector. He informed Deeds of work already in progress at Eastman-Kodak but assured him that the patent situation was such that NCR would benefit from MIT's explorations. Deeds, with an attitude few corporate executives could take, gave strong hints he would subsidize the work with just a promise that NCR could have a license to use the inventions.[30] Then, Bush began courting Eastman-Kodak, asking it to join NCR in a three-way development project. Bush was perhaps unaware of how much Eastman had already learned about microfilm retrieval and foreign patents in the field.[31]

Eastman, although a good friend of the Institute, was less accepting than NCR. It took Bush much longer to gain a gentleman's agreement. However, because he was willing to yield licensing rights, Eastman finally gave its word.[32] Bush then turned all the legal details over to the organization that MIT had chosen to handle its relations with the commercial world, The Research Corporation.[33] The Research Corporation conducted the negotiations with Deeds and Eastman and searched for other support, including the possibility of having the Sears-Roebuck interests and the Carnegie Foundation participate in a joint development effort.[34] There were some tense moments when a new patent search indicated that Bush had been too confident. The Corporation found several companies that held patents related to a Selector and discovered challenges to Harold Edgerton's flash photography system which was so vital to the Selector.[35] The search revealed ongoing work at IBM and in the shops of a number of independent inventors.[36] Much to Deeds's credit, he did not let the patent report deter him. Soon, Eastman followed along. With the promises of twenty-five thousand dollars from the two companies, Bush restarted the Selector project in March 1938.[37] But, he did not put his student engineers to work until June--just as the Comparator was leaving the Institute.[38]

Bush was given a free hand by NCR and Eastman but he subtly bent the project toward business needs. He focused on the creation of a Selector for documents, not just "references." However, he continued to tell his foundation friends that he was creating a machine to revolutionize the library. Meanwhile, NCR and Eastman went ahead with their own research into microfilm systems. Deeds established NCR's electronics laboratory under Joe Desch in March 1938 and launched Desch on microfilm as well as electronic calculation projects.[39] Desch, in touch with the men at MIT, had a design and a breadboard model of a business version of a Selector by mid-summer. His first work on a utilities billing machine used two 35mm tapes with punched holes and had photocells and a selection circuit.[40] At the same time, in Cambridge, Bush firmed-up his plans. He decided to concentrate on technology. The logic of selection was to be investigated later, after hardware had been developed.

If he had been funded by Carnegie or a library association Bush might have begun with an exploration of the logic of data retrieval. But the commercial ties, the need to secure patents before the competition could monopolize the technology, and his near blind faith in personal coding led to the concentration on hardware.[41] At the end of the spring 1938 semester, Bush brought together a new team of graduate students to build the Selector. Their goals and schedule were set by Bush at the beginning. The construction of a machine was the first priority. Second, was the preparation of patent reports. After the completion of the prototype, to take some two years, the men were to find an application for the Selector and, if needed, revise it.

The Fourth Selector

By then, Bush was no longer thinking of the machine as a version of Memex or as a Reference Selector for the library. The machine was acquiring a new name, the Rapid Selector, and Bush was compiling a new list of possible applications. He now saw the machine as useful in areas ranging from the business to the medical world. He also took a much expanded view of the relationship of his machine to the library and scientific information. By fall 1938 he was telling confidants that the device could be the basis for a total revolution in the library. It had the potential to be a bibliographic engine that could replace the card catalog. But he did not dictate a particular use for the machine to his men. They were to build it, protect it with patents, and then find an application that would allow the system to be tested and used as a springboard for additional funding.

Even Bush did not realize how much the Selector project was changing. The hardware design was the same as a year before, but the direction and focus of the work had shifted. Although the men at the Institute were not fully conscious of it, the Selector was becoming more of a business than a library machine. In fact, Bush seems to have suggested to his student assistant in the fall of 1938 that the Selector eventually be turned into a statistical machine.[42] In addition, the project lost some direction because Bush was busy preparing to move to Washington to head the Carnegie Institution.

It might have been more efficient to wait and bring MacDonald to the Selector project, but Bush could not wait for the conclusion of the navy's work. He had to take advantage of the summer when MIT's students were free to work on projects full-time. Of course, Bush did not want to take men from the behind schedule Rockefeller project. So, he decided to use the students who had been closely associated with the Cinema Integraph. At the same time, Bush made another important decision. He kept the project isolated from those outside the MIT, Kodak, and NCR circles. Although he continued to tell some influential colleagues that he was building a machine for the library of the future, and described the Selector to others as a statistical tool for a new calculation center for genetic research, he severed whatever ties he had established with librarians, Documentalists and outside statisticians.[43] Predictably, Bush made no attempt to link his 1938 Selector to the projects of Watson Davis and the Documentalists[44] nor did he contact the established abstracting organizations or the mainstream librarians represented by the American Library Association.

Staying Isolated

Of importance, all the men on the MIT project were engineers, and when Bush sought any outside suggestions, "outside" meant the faculty of MIT's engineering departments.[45] The isolation extended to more than professional contacts. Bush was so confident of his own circle's advantage that he did not launch another major patent search in 1938; something that turned out to be a serious and complicating oversight. Despite warnings by the patent examiners, Bush's men did not attend to the threat of the 1931 patent of the German, Emanuel Goldberg, and several other inventors of Selector-like devices.[46]

One reason for the patent difficulties was that Bush gave the project over to his students before he had completed all the administrative work. But, he thought the Research Corporation and the young men could deal with any complications. Bush had chosen his men from a very talented group of young engineers. The Selector's team included the man who was later held to be the father of information science, Claude Shannon. And, Russell C. Coile, who proposed his own version of the machine in the 1950s,[47] joined the project thinking its purpose was the retrieval of business records.[48] But the three young MIT students who became central to the long history of the Rapid Selector, the Comparator, and OP-20-G's decryption devices were John Howard, Lawrence Steinhardt, and John Coombs. They would spend more than a decade with the Selector and its technology and with the problems of America's emerging Big Science.

The three young men were especially suited to the 1938 project. Howard and Coombs had worked on the Cinema Integraph and Steinhardt had special qualifications. He had studied under MIT's professor Parry Moon and was becoming an expert in the technologies of light and color. Steinhardt came back to MIT after having spent a year as an advisor to the Walt Disney studios. His expertise in optics had been put to good use in Disney's pathbreaking technicolor feature-length cartoon.[49]

At MIT, under the direction of John Howard, Steinhardt and Coombs had a sense of purpose and believed that a successful machine would be completed on time. They and Bush had reason for optimism because, in concept, the Rapid Selector was simple and its engineering direct. Further, much of the technical work had already been explored and solved during the Cinema Integraph and Comparator projects.[50] Bush explained that the previous experience using photocells and film in the Cinema Integraph ensured that the mechanism for selecting documents would work as planned. Unfortunately, because it was a national secret, Howard was not informed of the difficulties of the Comparator. He was not told of its great weaknesses, data input and mechanics.

A Machine for Science, for a Time

John Howard was given a clear outline of the machine and definite instruction to stay with Bush's 1937 ideas. Changes were to be made only when hands-on experience ruled the original ideas unworkable. After gaining advice from Eastman-Kodak, Howard drew more detailed specifications and set the functional goals for what he thought was to be a machine for scientific documents. Howard decided that the new thirty-five millimeter stock microfilm would be used to record abstracts of documents in one-half of a frame. The abstract portion was to have six lines, for a total of some one hundred words. The other half of a frame would be for codes which would be recognized by a photoelectric system. Each document was to be identified by clear dots in the code portions of the frame. Each of the six code areas were to hold two sets of twenty-six fields. As many as twelve code letters could be used. The code dots were to be less than a third of a millimeter in size.

With a microfilm reduction factor of over twenty-five, some sixteen short documents and their codes could be packed in an inch of microfilm. Once selected, they were to be brought back to their original size by an automatic reproduction system. A reduction factor of twenty-five was standard in the microfilm industry but other aspects of the new Selector were beyond the current technology. Howard was told to make the Selector check more than sixty thousand documents a minute and reproduce a selected item within less than a second. That goal called for a film system that had to present perfectly stable images and a comparator assembly that kept the film perfectly aligned over the photocell sensors while the film drive worked at close to five miles an hour.[51] Howard was also charged with overcoming what had proven to be the stumbling block for the navy's Comparator, a reliable and speedy data entry system.

Despite the problems with the Comparator, Bush did not foresee insurmountable data entry problems. The document (still intended to be a scientific abstract) was to be recorded by a custom-made typewriter that had a wide paper roll and the precise stepping mechanisms to allow the typing of both text and codes. Although there was mention of entering the codes by punching holes in the appropriate portion of a page, it was decided to build the special typewriter with two different printing carriages. One would be for the text, the other for the code dots. The codes would be precisely aligned and made uniform in color and density by custom built components. Once the codes and text were typed, the roll of abstracts was to be microphotographed. Enormous numbers of abstracts could be stored on just one reel because of the twenty-five to one reduction ratio. The planned two thousand foot reel was to hold as many as four hundred thousand documents. High density on the microfilm was essential to Bush's plans for the Selector because, as with the Comparator, Bush was promising a speed revolution: He predicted the examination of one thousand documents a second.

Technology Before Logic

Limiting the document to six lines plus the single twelve letter code was the result of more than Bush's 1937 Reference idea and its call for only a short note from a scientist. The limit was dictated by Bush's goal of ultra high-speed searching. That emphasis on speed led to the rejection of some reasonable design alternatives. For example, Bush could have used a record format that placed much less of a burden on the photocell system. A record could have been composed of two frames. The first would have contained a set of codes, each with large dots. The machine, sensing a match between one of those codes and the selection mask, would have had time to ready itself to reproduce the following record. Or, Bush could have told Howard to develop logic components and a printing system so that an unlimited number of text records could follow the code frame. However, Bush demanded a rapid machine. The short, densely packed format of the 1937-38 Selector tapes allowed Bush to describe his promised machine in compelling terms. He announced that one hundred thousand items could be searched in one hundred seconds. But the density needed for such speeds challenged the architecture and hardware of the Selector. Packing code dots so densely called for unattainable precision.

The coded sections on the film were to pass over a mask which indicated what category or subject was to be selected from the roll. The mask would be punched, for example, to choose documents related to stress in metals by a code such as METALSTRESSX. When the codes on the frame exactly matched the mask, enough light would flow from the high intensity lamp in back of the film to the set of photocells and their amplifiers. They would trigger a reproduction system[52] which was based on Harold Edgerton's high-speed light device. Edgerton's flashlamps, Bush thought, would allow the selected documents to be reproduced without slowing the data tape. The selected image would be brought back to original scale by the special lens system built into the high-speed document printer. The printing system had to be very sophisticated. After a page was filled, a new sheet of paper would automatically be loaded without slowing the Selector. At the end of a search, the photosheets were to be taken to a developing area then returned to the patron in a matter of some three minutes. [53]

Bush was sure of his design.[54] He expected the young men to produce a machine that was, at very minimum, one hundred and fifty times more powerful than the IBM electromechanical devices and hundreds of times faster than teletype equipment. Promising such power, Bush easily convinced his sponsors that an information revolution was about to take place.[55] However, the required data packing demanded a great deal from the 1930s optical-electronic technology and the young students. The heart of the Selector, its scanning station, was the great challenge although it was not as complex as the one in the Comparator.

In the Comparator, the medium containing the items to be matched was a moving tape, in the Selector, it was to be a stationary card. A high power lamp, always illuminated, was placed over the Selector's scanning station. The card, which contained holes representing the code of the items to be selected, was placed between the light and the film. In the Comparator, a match triggered a set of counters while a complete coincidence in the Selector was to activate an Edgerton flash and camera system. Extremely important, the allied circuitry in the Selector was less complex than the Comparator's.

In the Selector, the set of photocells for the codes, plus one for checking the alignment of a frame, were to be linked to gas filled tubes acting as switches. If all the holes in the mask and the transparent dots on the microfilm were coincident, each cell would receive an adequate amount of light. The cells were tied together in a series. Only if all were turned on would the selection-reproduction systems be activated. Although the Selector had one photocell per code field, the series wiring provided for fewer choices than the Comparator. Only when all the cells sensed light and thus all of the tubes were triggered, would a copy of the abstract be reproduced on the special photographic paper.

A Simple Machine for a Complex Task

Like the Comparator, the Selector sensed light rather than its absence. That could have served as the basis for a device allowing as many selection choices as the Comparator. However, in the two decades of the history of the Bush Selector, that potential to test for many codes simultaneously was not exploited. The Selector's circuits remained primitive. Although Bush did suggest that some means be incorporated to short circuit the tubes for code areas that were blank, thus avoiding the need to have all the cells activated during a search, attention was always turned to raw speed. And, even with the short circuit feature, Bush's proposed selection circuit would not have been as flexible as that in the Comparator.

Neither Bush nor his students attempted to put in Rossi "and" circuits during the 1930s or 1940s. The Selector remained based upon all-or-none rather than the more sophisticated partial "and" logic of the Comparator. Of course, there is no hint that Bush planned to revise the scanner to accommodate "or" logic. However, because speed was essential, Bush did suggest that the film be able to run backwards as well as forwards. He also recommended that the circuitry necessary for an automatic cut-off be incorporated in the device. It could be set to prevent more than a specified number of items to be selected per search.[56]

Bush's exploration of the logic of the Selector was very limited. He and the others associated with the project were so enchanted by the speed of microfilm tape scanning that little attention was paid to file organization, coding schemes or logistics. Apparently, Bush did not realize all the negative consequences of tape (serial) processing, or of a coding scheme without hierarchy and without code position significance. And his drive to quickly produce a machine led his team away from the electronics, such as multiple scanners, that could have made the Selector a viable bibliographic tool.

Bush's ideas about coding were very primitive. He was so oriented to a system for experts in particular fields that he thought he could ignore all the complexities that tormented professional catalogers and indexers. In his Selector scheme, a researcher would place, in any of the twelve code fields, a letter indicating a subject contained in an abstracted article or book. Although he sometimes urged the use of as few code letters as possible, his important examples usually filled all twelve fields. The examples and discussions of them did not indicate that Bush had an appreciation of the value of hierarchial and position significant coding schemes. Without such features, generic and general subject searching was difficult if not impossible.[57]

Even with the recommended short circuiting of the code scanning tubes, Bush's scheme would have made a general subject search very tedious. For example, if a code system was using "L" to indicate the abstracted document was relevant to the study of languages a search for all "L" abstracts on a roll of film would have to use a unique selection mask for each of the twelve possible positions of the "L" and to short circuit all but the target cell during the separate runs. When a search was concerned with, say, two matches such as the conjunction of "L" and "S," the number of required runs would escalate to perhaps as many as one hundred thirty two.

Bush never pointed out such problems to his sponsors or to his development team. Nor did he examine the practical ramifications of his tendency to confuse the Selector and the Memex. That led to some significant weaknesses in the Selector system when he attempted to change it from a machine for an expert's notes to a machine for the library or the office. For example, Bush did not determine how specialists in various fields would arrive at common code meanings. As important, he never explained how a librarian was to manage the many special vocabularies generated by the experts.

His coding schemes were certainly not user or librarian friendly. Bush wanted the encoders to use up to twelve letters to represent the contents of an article, leading to such complex and difficult to remember keys as DMUHCORMENVS.[58] He did not show how a searcher was to arrive at such lengthy and impossible to remember keys. And, his few references to code books were asides rather than answers to the logistics and economics of indexing. Bush made some allusions to standard abbreviations in each specialized field, but he did not take human perception and memory into account.

Staying with the Design

Unaware of such limitations and ordered to concentrate on hardware, the young men on the Selector project began to refine Bush's ideas. By February 1939 their design seemed so feasible and the team was so committed to avoiding anything that might delay the project that a very important decision was made. With the approval of the new faculty supervisor, Harold Hazen, and under Bush's advice, a significant option for the Selector was rejected. In early 1939, Eastman-Kodak's A. F. Sulzer notified Bush of a great invention by a man at its Rochester center. Like NCR, Eastman had a group working on microfilm reading and recovery. Its R. S. Morse had just completed a sophisticated selection system that Eastman thought avoided the reading problems caused by film shrinkage, distortion and specs of dust.[59] The system, centered around multiple frequency tracks for codes, allowed a much more flexible use of codes than the Bush coincident dot arrangement. The Morse frequency-based design allowed generic and hierarchial searches, testing for what statisticians call cross classifications and the use of weighted inquiries such as the selection of an item if four out of five categories matched a request.

Bush, now in Washington, consulted with Hazen then quickly advised Eastman he thought Morse's idea unsuited to the MIT project.[60] He informed Rochester that Morse's device would not, as claimed, simplify the equipment needed for a Selector. He told Sulzer that the problems with the MIT machine, such as how to ensure that code dots were exactly registered on the film, were corrected. Bush admitted, however, that Morse's approach might be valuable at a later stage of the Selector project when attention would perhaps be turned to "multiple sorting." The lead student in the MIT group, John Howard, agreed with Bush. His men had progressed far enough that changing the system seemed unwarranted.

Although he consulted with Kodak's experts and with Joe Desch, Howard sought his own solutions and obeyed Bush's rule about completing projects on time.[61] In the spring of 1939 he told the Eastman group that the major problems with the Selector were mechanical, not electronic or optical. He emphasized, however, that all the mechanisms, including the very precise film drive and alignment aides, were progressing satisfactorily.[62] By mid-1939, Howard and his team had built at least breadboard versions of all the major components of the machine. The only changes to the original plans that Howard had allowed were those dictated by engineering needs. The team remained committed to using only one scanner and Howard's men resisted more suggestions from those supporting Morse's ideas. But, Howard did have to make some significant changes. Most were made within the first year of the project when many of Bush's technological goals quickly proved unrealistic.

The ambitious printing system was the first to be abandoned. Moving the copy paper at a speed fast enough to prevent having to slow the data film proved impossible. So, instead of filming a selected item onto paper, a roll of 16mm film became the output of the machine. Howard was sure the new film could be advanced in synchronization with the master film.[63] More fundamental, the master tape system had to be changed. Because of torque and other problems, the maximum length of a reel was reduced to one thousand feet, thus halving the data capacity of the system. The next major changes were to the size of the data record and the code indicators. Serious difficulties with photocell sensing led to a twelve line text area and separate lines for each of the twelve code fields. This allowed a larger area for the codes; from the minute 7/1000 inch dot to a .005 by .01 inch rectangle. The change also reduced the difficulties involved in trying to crowd thirteen photocells underneath the scanner. But, the change in the record size challenged Bush's promise of sixty thousand tests a minute. To compensate for almost halving the data density, Howard tried to increase the speed of the tape drive to five hundred feet a minute.

Howard, Coombs, Steinhardt, and the Institute's machinist spent the rest of 1939 working out the details of the Selector. In addition, much time was devoted to preparing patent applications for the Research Corporation. The team also began to think of how to apply their information machine. The young men completed the promised Selector on schedule and with some ten thousand dollars remaining in their budget. But, all was not well.[64]

The Not-Memex

The machine that emerged in 1940 was certainly not the desk size and affordable apparatus that Bush envisioned in the early 1930s. Its heart was a typical seven foot high relay rack which housed the film drives, scanner, and reproduction apparatus. Electronics took another cabinet. The modified electric typewriter for preparing the abstracts, which used long rolls of paper advanced by a special stepping mechanism, was itself the size of a desk. Significantly, it could not be coaxed to meet Bush's early hopes of solving the input problem.

The MIT team was unable to build the special typewriter Bush had pictured, one to enter both the abstracts and the tiny code dots. They could not create a double carriage that was precise enough to meet the tolerances needed for the dots. The result was another large component. For the codes, they substituted a set of sliders that were attached to the side of the now separate filming desk. The operator of the camera, who recorded the abstracts from the rolls of paper produced on the special typewriter, had to read the codes written at the beginning of an abstract then set twelve sliding metal tabs so that holes in the sliders corresponded to the intended code letters. A simple mechanical problem dictated another unexpected and very significant change. Because of the time needed to project a selected abstract onto the 16mm film for reproduction, the code entries for an abstract had to be staggered four frames from their allied text. In addition, the selection mask, once planned to be a card, was changed to a drum with sliding bands. That change made off-line preparation and storage of retrieval orders impossible.

More ominous was the inability to fulfill the promises concerning the use of 16mm film for copying the selected abstracts. The mechanism designed to shift that film without slowing the master film proved unsatisfactory. Even with the four frame lag for the codes, if selected items were too close together on a reel, they would be by-passed. The only solution the MIT team could devise was a very unhandy one. To avoid contention and the skipping of a selected item, all abstracts had to be checked to make sure that ones with identical codes (or, by implication, ones with the same generic codes) were spaced at least ten frames apart. That, Howard realized, was a serious handicap even if searches were restricted to infrequently occurring twelve code items.[65] In his reports to Eastman and NCR, Howard made only passing mention of that and other limitations of the 1940 system. Although critical to the effective application of the Selector, he never did more than assert that generic searches could be made.[66]

Again, Logic Is Too Costly

There were more than technical problems. Bush and Howard had not explored the economics of information retrieval. Howard did not report how long it took for a reviewer to compose an abstract or the cost of typing it. But he gave enough information to allow a skeptical observer to note that just the filming step might be financially prohibitive. It took an average of thirty seconds to set the code tabs and film an already typed abstract. Thus, the filming of one roll of microfilm would alone call for 1,000 hours of work. Even in the 1940s, that was expensive. It meant almost one-half year of full-time wages. And, unless several filming and coding stations and several workers were used, the preparation of one roll of film would take six months--much too long. Howard and Bush may have hoped to solve this problem through the creation of automatic data entry, coding, and filming devices, but other emerging Selector problems seemed insurmountable.[67]

A serious disappointment was the patent situation. Bush had filed patent claims in late 1937. By 1939, the MIT group received so much bad news they began to fear they would produce a machine that infringed on established rights. In late October 1939, only one of some twenty claims had been allowed and the growing list of relevant patents held by others was starting to crowd the Research Corporation's application file.[68] And the list of new filings included ones from the crew at IBM's research division. IBM's chief inventor, James Bryce, was intent on staking an IBM claim on the use of microfilm in business machines. The applications of the mysterious census-linked inventor Townsend, whose devices paralleled the Memex and Selector, and that of the man who had developed the Index of Coincidence, William F. Friedman, also pointed to difficulties.[69]

The situation was so tangled that the Research Corporation's lawyers abandoned the 1937 application. But the ever positive Bush convinced them to file a new and more inclusive set on the same day in November 1940. Howard had spent much of his time carefully preparing those forty new claims during 1939 and 1940 but he was soon confronted by another critical patent examiner. Worse, during World War II, Howard and Bush had little time to wage a time consuming battle against the patent office.[70]

The Next Selector

Despite the early enthusiasm, by the summer of 1940 Howard and his men were very worried about the Selector's future. Much more than the patent and mechanical problems caused their depression. Logical and logistic deficiencies caught up with the machine. As a result, Bush and Howard were ready to take a step that meant abandoning the Rapid Selector, at least as an information machine.[71]

During the first half of 1940 Howard had spent much time exploring the possible applications for the 1940 device. His immediate focus was on finding a model application in order to test and advertise the system. The 1938 Selector had begun as a library machine, but Howard was now more interested in the long-term commercial possibilities. Given the new sponsors of the project, Eastman and NCR, it was not surprising that Howard and Bush spent little time seeking a library or bibliographic use. The view of the machine's future had changed since Bush's first sketches in the mid-1930s.[72] One of the reasons why Howard turned away from library applications was that some of the most influential pundits at MIT rejected the idea of using mechanical aides to compile scientific bibliographies. Norbert Wiener condemned the Selector and its underlying premises. Despite Bush's attachment to association and indexing, Wiener lashed out against mechanized bibliographic machines because they used fixed categories and allowed for, he thought, only one association per record. Harold Hazen, the new project supervisor, and others at MIT did not reject Wiener's rather odd comments.[73]

Under much prompting from Bush and Hazen, who were concerned about their obligations to NCR and Eastman, Howard focused on applications in the bureaucratic and commercial markets. He tried to reinvigorate the old efforts at the FBI and the Patent Office. He thought about using the Selector at the Mayo Clinic's x-ray center.[74] Ironically, at least twice he tried to convince a straight faced Bush that the Selector would find another sponsor it if were used in cryptanalytic work. Bush, unable to tell Howard of the Comparator project, simply denied the Selector's worth in such efforts.[75]

Howard persisted in his search for a use for the document retrieval machine, without success. At the deadline for finding an application, he reported the results of his survey of business and bureaucratic applications. Using Social Security files as an example, he gave his supervisors negative and shocking news![76] Howard's report indicates that Bush's failure to consult with those most familiar with file management and retrieval techniques before fixing the design of the Selector had been a serious mistake. The report also reflects the lack of integration of digital logic into the MIT's culture during the 1930s.[77]

In his April 1, 1940 report to Carroll Wilson of the Research Corporation, Howard described three data retrieval situations. Unfortunately, he did not use clear terms and he described file structures in words that seem quite inadequate today. His conclusion was obvious, however: There was no application for the Selector, older techniques and methods were more efficient!

Howard's first scenario was one in which the search was for what he termed a "single item"; the logic of each test being binary, yes or no. The example was concerned with locating records for individuals by name and date of birth, a complete match being required. In his example, the Selector's file was not ordered (sorted) by the identifiers of interest. (It is of importance to note that Howard never outlined a way to sort the items on a reel.) He compared the time a Selector search would take to the time needed by the alphabetically arranged Social Security's paper filing system. With fifty-two million records, the Selector would take fourteen hours, the Social Security system one minute. Depressing and perhaps embarrassing news! Just as was the finding that for telephone number look-ups, the old-fashioned telephone books were much more effective. Worse, he had to admit that library card files were much better in cases in which classification was hierarchial.[78] Later, he had to report that Eastman-Kodak had found that Selector-like devices were ineffective means of locating records in business microfilm archives.[79]

The next situation Howard described was one in which the search was more general; one looking for any of those items or people that fit into two categories. The target files were not arranged according to the search (category) keys. His description of the situation was not well put but his conclusion was. Old-fashioned files, even when not arranged for any version of what we might now call random or direct access, were more efficient! Unless such searches were frequently done, he said, the use of a Selector was unjustified. If there were many such searches, the most efficient approach would be to duplicate records as did the Patent Office. The third scenario was one with more than two search keys.

Again, Howard had to conclude that the Selector ran a very far second to traditional files arranged according to the search keys.[80]

Howard had investigated more than the Social Security system. Applications to patent and fingerprint work were also ruled out as well as the Selector's use in the new long-distance telephone system. Howard gave bibliographic work on the Selector a nod at the end of his report but his subtle evaluation of such use was negative.[81] He then made a startling assertion in his conclusion about the Selector. What had to come first, Howard said, was a categorization-coding scheme. After that had been developed machines to fit the scheme might be constructed. That was a courageous statement for a young man who had been directed to think of hardware first. Luckily, it did not alienate Bush.

Howard took a much more positive tone at the end of his final report and he recommended something that had direct consequences for the Selector, the Comparator, and the history of America's war against its enemies' secret communications. Howard, following some hints from Bush, recommended the Selector be turned into a statistical machine and applied to census work. He wanted it to be changed from selecting and reproducing documents to incrementing counters when desired cross classifications of census material were encountered. Hazen, then Bush, concurred.[82]

The Selector Becomes a Civilian Comparator

Everyone at MIT had given up and the proposed revolutionary machine for the library died without much of a struggle. None of the men involved suggested any of the possible quick fixes to the Selector that might have kept it to its original mission. There is no hint that adding additional scanners to facilitate multiple classification searches was considered. And, no one seems to have thought of the expedient of fooling the single category, serial search machine into behaving like a more sophisticated device by using a stepped film with many search codes instead of the code drum. The MIT group had sidelined if not abandoned the Selector as a document retriever. Bush also gave in. After finding a rather subtle excuse for the failure of his design, he advised the new MIT supervisor of Howard's team, Harold Hazen, to concentrate on converting the Selector to a counting device:

> I think the matter of adding ring counters will be of particular interest in commercial applications. Howard and I talked about adding it into the present development, but we felt that we ought to get the main job in hand before taking on something which is essentially auxiliary. There is no doubt in my mind that the machine with this addition would be of use in various statistical studies.
>
> ...
>
> I have no doubt whatever that general library indexing of a multidimensional type would be exceedingly useful, and that use of the rapid selector in connection with it would be powerful. This I tried to bring out in earlier memoranda, but of course did not present the actual system that could be used. To develop such a system would be quite an undertaking in itself.[83]

Despite his last minute revival of the idea of a library application, Bush did not turn the Selector back to its original purpose. It was to be changed into a statistical machine. Howard and Hazen did not know it, but they were about to attempt to change the Selector into an improved version of the Comparator. The Selector was dead and a civilian version of the failed navy machine was about to be born.

During the summer and early fall of 1940, John Howard and the Selector team rushed to prepare patent applications and began thinking of how to revise the Selector to make it a statistical machine. They worked full-time, almost unaware of the tragedy overtaking the world. The defeat of France, Japan's switch to a new naval code and the threat of an invasion of England were of little importance to the young engineers.[84] Howard and his colleagues surveyed the results of the work of their fellow students on the proposed Bush electronic computer and learned of the MIT advances in high-speed vacuum tube circuits. They also reviewed the Institute's earlier work on glass plate microphotography and magnetic recording. They learned enough to begin construction of the new counting circuits during the summer.[85] A great deal of thought also went into revising the data and code entry systems, including thinking of a way to copy data on tabulator cards onto microfilm tapes.

An Heroic Death, Perhaps

Then, the work was suddenly cut off. The Comparator's earlier failure caught up with Bush and his men. The Selector was drafted for the war effort. The navy was willing to accept a new Comparator--if someone else was willing to pay for it. Bush agreed to sacrifice the library machine for a cryptanalytic one. He quickly gained money from the NDRC and then found a way to turn at least part of MIT into a secret workshop.

At first, it seemed that OP-20-G's revived project would become the basis for a major initiative within MIT and a showpiece for the NDRC. It had the chance to become a model for all the future work of the Committee. The new Comparator project had a greater potential than others to prove that civilian scientists and academic institutions could run critical military programs and could deliver on grand technological promises.

Bush had full control of the new work. The project was staffed by an experienced and loyal group. And, for the first time, he had adequate funding. Bush and navy had the chance to make up for the years that had been lost after the first Comparator had been pushed into a back room at the Navy Yard.

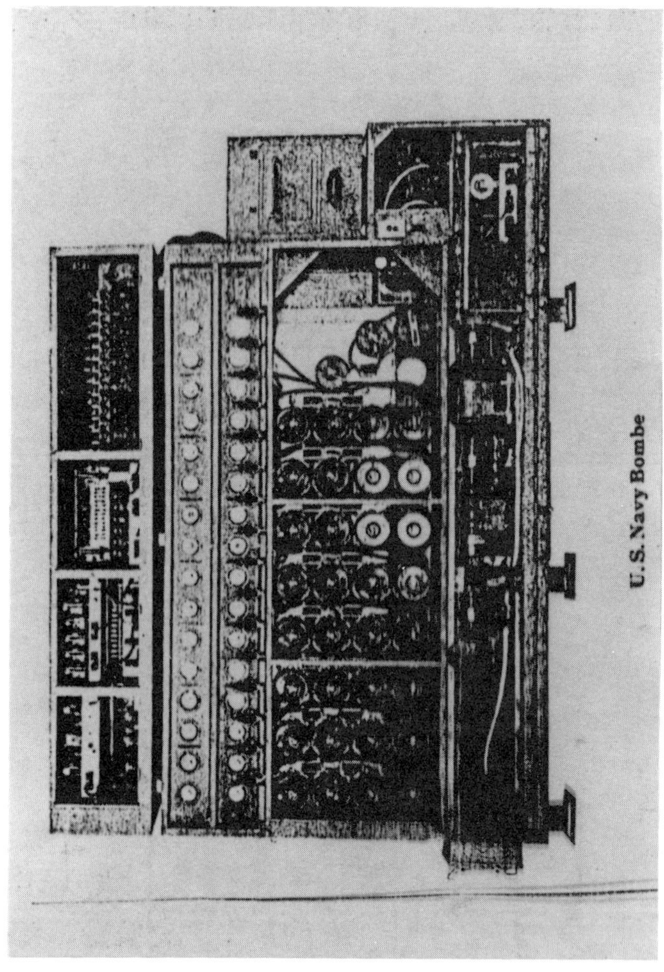

The American Bombe, circa 1944
(National Security Agency)

Chapter IX
Disorganizing for War:
The Comparator Fails, Again

Revisiting the Statistical Selector

When John Howard and his team were trying to save the microfilm Selector by turning it into an electronic tallying machine, Vannevar Bush was organizing the National Defense Research Committee. In Washington during the summer of 1940, he could not supervise Howard's rushed attempt to design what was an upgraded civilian version of a microfilm Comparator. Without knowledge of MacDonald's OP-20-G machine, Howard's men started to build a comparator with the speed Bush had promised the navy when he backed away from "G" in 1938. Howard's mid-1940 proposed statistical machine did not have a name, but it was to have the microfilm of the Selector and be twenty times faster and more flexible than the navy's defunct Comparator. It was to be able to identify and tally cross classified statistical data as its tapes flew by the photoelectronic sensors at speeds that would make it more powerful than hundreds of tabulators.

Bush asked John Howard to produce at least a prototype by year's end, so Howard and his team worked full time and spent much of the original Selector's remaining ten thousand dollars by the end of the summer.[1] They also put additional touches on the first Selector, having some hope that a sponsor for a document retrieval machine might appear.[2] But they focused on the problems of the new counting machine.

The similarity between the architecture and hardware of the old 1938 Comparator and what Howard chose for the 1940 device was a natural outcome of the technological context at the Institute. Because Bush had directed Howard to create a device that tallied, not one that could truly add or that could perform the other mathematical functions, Howard's team envisioned a machine like the Comparator, one that incremented counters when data classifications matched a set of criteria. But, unlike the Comparator, it was to run a microfilm data tape against a selection mask, not two punched paper tapes against each other.

Howard's men surveyed the latest work on the proposed Bush electronic computer and learned of MIT advances in high-speed vacuum tube circuits. They considered the tape reading components and the electronics of the unfinished Rockefeller Analyser; they had more conferences with the experts at Eastman about microfilm; and, they explored some of the Institute's work on alternative memory media. Plate microphotography and magnetic recording seemed to have potential, but the young men placed them in the same category as the Eastman-Morse frequency track microfilm system: things to be kept in mind for the future. Of importance, they never questioned using the familiar system of dots for the code system.

Some development work was begun on the new counting circuits, but another component took center stage.[3] The data input problem had to be solved. The shift away from a machine for document retrieval made a solution more important and much more difficult. Bush had committed to microfilm because of its ability to hold huge amounts of information in analog form, but he had no means of preparing statistical information for microfilming. His old idea of a special keyboard typewriter to rapidly prepare codes was a failure. Its replacement, the slider-photographic system Howard built for the Selector, was too crude and it was not at all suited to statistical work. Its forte was the reduction of graphic materials, not the insertion of statistical codes in machine readable form. A new data entry system had to be invented if the microfilm counting machine could hope to be successful. No company or bureaucracy would switch from their existing systems to a counting selector unless the cost of entering data onto microfilm was radically lowered. Of special importance was a way to allow an economic transfer of punch card files.[4] Howard searched for a method that would tempt those with a backlog of cards to use a statistical selector. He sought advice from all his colleagues and the men at Eastman-Kodak. He began to explore possibilities, but just as he was making progress, the project to revise the Selector was ended. In the fall of 1940, the old Selector went into limbo and the work on the version for statistical analysis was suspended.

Technological Steps Backwards to Help the Navy

The navy's secret Comparator was about to be reborn. Just as the funds from the old Selector project were running out, Bush gained another chance to prove the power of optical-electronic machines and the ability of academics to create the technologies of defense.[5] He arranged for Howard and his men to rescue the first paper tape Comparator and to design the long promised microfilm version. This second MIT OP-20-G project of late 1940 is of extreme historical importance because it became the foundation for the United States Navy's incredible Rapid Machines Program of World War II. That little known adventure rivalled Britain's famous work on the Ultra Bombes and the Colossus.

Tragically, that program is also important because of its failures. Although it began with expectations of producing electronic digital machines to attack the feared cipher devices of the Axis powers, it turned to older technology and logic. To be able to provide anything of value to OP-20-G, Howard's men had to step back from electronics, digital techniques and microfilm. Although the navy's cryptanalysts began World War II with promises that electronics could be made to work, they had to wait for almost two years after Pearl Harbor before any machines appeared that affirmed that Bush's ideas had potential.

The story of John Howard's navy project has to begin with the crises in Europe and Asia, policy decisions in the White House and London and the organization of American science in World War II. As seen earlier, the stories also travel through the history of computer technology in prewar America, the policies of the nation's largest corporations and the decisions of Bush's elite science National Defense Research Committee.

Big Science Begins to Emerge

Bush's high science friends were active in more than the cause of research. They were among the nation's earliest supporters of a positive response to the German threat. Like Bush, several were involved with the Scientific Aids to Learning Project and they used it as an opportunity to discuss the means of preparing American science and industry for the European conflict. Well before Roosevelt and Churchill agreed that the defeat of Hitler was the first priority, Bush's colleagues planned a technological counteroffensive against Germany. They learned of the mobilization of British science under Sir Henry Tizard and rushed to invent an American version of his amazing organization. They lobbied for the creation of the National Defense Research Committee and gained Franklin Roosevelt's approval just as France was overrun in June 1940. The NDRC was the realization of Bush's ideal way to link academia and the military. But it was not quite what Hooper or Bowen had in mind and certainly not what the Bureau of Ships saw as the proper relation between the military and its contractors. Bush made the NDRC independent and powerful. The NDRC became worrisome to the navy when it used its influence to pull several projects away from the navy's own researchers. The loss of control over radar and atomic energy, for example, were especially galling to men like Bowen.

In Bush's eyes, such decisions were victories for science. Given almost complete power by Roosevelt to shape the NDRC, Bush laid down ground rules that gave power to academics to begin research projects and to be free of military control. What was funded and how a project was evaluated were to be determined by groups of scientific luminaries in cooperation with the military. Innovations could not be blocked by the "mossbacks" in the services and ideas were declared a valued product. Having its own funds and being a presidential creature, the NDRC and its more powerful extension, the Office of Scientific Research and Development, could initiate blue-sky programs and carry them through to development.

One of those programs interlaced the NDRC with American cryptanalysis, but only after it had dealt with a long list of projects of much higher priority. Before Roosevelt funded the NDRC and before Tizard brought his boxes of scientific marvels to America, Bush's academic friends had compiled schedules of people and projects. Atomic power and radar were the leading problems and the scientists at the most prestigious universities and corporate research centers received the first calls from the NDRC's leaders.

The executives at the NDRC realized that atomic research and the development of the potentials of radar called for advanced computation, but, alone, those problems would have led to a minimal NDRC involvement in computers. It was a lower priority challenge that plunged the NDRC into computer research and established who would participate in the navy's future Rapid Machine effort. Atomic scientists were calling for electronic control devices, but most important for the history of OP-20-G was the hope that radar could be used to automatically control antiaircraft weapons. That led to the NDRC's involvement in the development of electronic fire control computers in the early 1940s.[6] The exploration of such electronic digital machines was the perfect type of work for the NDRC because it centered about unproven and experimental technologies. And, scientists had already staked out a claim over electronic calculation. Previous work on computers had been done in universities and corporate research laboratories. Academic physicists had created the high-speed counters[7] and the one prewar electronic gun control program was an RCA laboratory effort.

Although RCA had not remained as close to the American military as Hooper wished, the emergence of electronic controls in industry had led the army's Leslie Simon to convince Jan Rachman of RCA Laboratories to design an electronic gun director in 1939.[8] At first, Rachman explored an analog system. Soon, he turned to binary digital methods. However, by the time he had outlined a sophisticated binary system, the army lost interest. The navy then financed the project but, like the army, withdrew when it seemed that development would take much too long.[9] Then, both services decided that a technological step back would be wise. In 1940, the navy turned to its old friend the Arma corporation to design an electrical analog device and the army asked Bell labs to explore that technology for its new antiaircraft guns. To the disappointment of advocates of digital techniques, an analog system invented by an independent team at AT&T, the M-9, became the high-tech solution during the war for both services.[10]

However, the NDRC's scientists continued to think that digital electronics had potential and they rekindled the fire control projects. Hundreds of thousands of dollars were poured into fire control computer and atomic counter work in the first two years of NDRC's life. The amount invested was so great that it makes the money the NDRC spent on OP-20-G's problems seem an afterthought. Norbert Wiener, for example, received a grant for twice what the NDRC would spend on cryptanalytic machines just to study the mathematics of fire control prediction.[11] The importance of the gun control and counter work is also reflected by the NDRC's rush to forge agreements during its first weeks of life. NDRC's leaders, such as George Harrison, Warren Weaver and Sam Caldwell, had been involved with computers and electronics for a decade and were aware of the developments in Europe and America. As a result, before June 1940, all the nation's electronic centers were contacted about helping to develop the electronic technology for Fermi's Metallurgical Laboratory at the University of Chicago and the computers needed to link radar and artillery.

Joe Desch to the Rescue

NDRC's men selected old friends of Vannevar Bush's electronic efforts. The monies for the incredibly high-speed counters for the atomic bomb project were directed toward NCR and to an MIT man who had been working on Bush's digital electronic computer. At NCR, Joe Desch, the practical engineer, suddenly became a national resource because of the reputation he built while working with the MIT group. The young man at the Institute, Bill Overbeck, received his nod because he had studied with one of the nation's leading cosmic scientists at the University of Denver[12] and had spent the previous year devising high-speed vacuum tube circuits for Bush's most ambitious project, the Rapid Arithmetical Machine.

The atomic counter work was demanding. The atomic piles needed counting systems that operated at hundreds of thousands of beats per second, not the ten thousand or so that was typical in 1940.[13] Desch met the challenge.[14] Using the tubes and circuits he had designed for NCR's electronic calculator as a base, and with suggestions from Dr. Moon at the University of Chicago, Desch made history. Less than a year after taking his assignment he had a one million per second counting system. That astounding accomplishment led Desch to be seen as a technical and managerial miracle worker.

Others rushed to him with requests for electronic solutions and he took on more NDRC and military projects. Colonel Deeds, who put the needs of national defense above huge NCR profits, gave Desch the backing he needed. By 1941, in addition to his fire control work, Desch was building photoelectric counters to measure shell velocities for Aberdeen Proving Grounds and he created an electronic IFF flash-signal radio system.[15] He invented electronic remote controls for mine fields and ultra fast secret communications devices. During the same period, Desch and his men were refining their powerful miniature and multi-function tubes; ones which would be manufactured by the thousands by other electronic companies during the war. Some of Desch's electronics's work may have became a vital part of the very hush-hush proximity fuse project.[16]

While Desch was at work on his many devices, the young man at MIT's Arithmetic machine project was also busy with NDRC work. Overbeck was inventing new high-speed tubes and circuits. They were so well regarded that in 1942 he was ordered to Chicago to work directly under Fermi. That assignment led him into a lifetime in military and commercial applications of atomic energy.[17]

Fire Control

The NDRC began the first stages of its fire control project in June 1940. Bush's old friend Warren Weaver of the Rockefeller Foundation assumed command. The research at RCA, which had led to the design of the fastest binary circuits in the nation, if not the world, was picked up by the NDRC. Then, Weaver coordinated the work at RCA with wide ranging explorations at Eastman, MIT, Bell and, to some extent, NCR. Of significance for the history of OP-20-G's machines, IBM was again left out of the NDRC circle although its centers of electronic research were working on quite advanced components and systems.[18] Because of the NDRC's stimulus, by the time of America's formal entry into the war, RCA, Eastman, Bell and MIT had several proposals for digital-based fire control systems, ones the NDRC evaluators thought had great promise. In the spring of 1942, meetings were called and all participants, including Desch and Overbeck, shared their knowledge and designs.[19] The reports of the fire control projects were made available to the American technical community, which now included John Howard. He was made aware of the designs for the most advanced computer components.

Many of the fire control developments would find their way into cryptanalytic machines and into such pathbreaking computers as the ENIAC. In some of the NDRC projects, glass disks and cylinders with opaque and reflecting spots were to be read by photocells while calculations were made by electronic counters. In a proposed RCA system, films and optical sensing were to be used for analog integrations which would then be converted to digital signals.[20] Eastman-Kodak developed a significant two film optical comparator system to be linked with digital electronics.[21] Bell proposed a device which was to include commutator drums read by metal brushes. Electronic tubes were to handle the calculation and storage functions. Later, Bell's men designed a fully electronic machine.[22] Much more, including new memory options, came out of the NDRC projects. Banks of condensers and cathode ray tubes were proposed for high-speed memory and calculation. Some engineers suggested magnetic tape for secondary storage. Several versions of multi-function tubes, for both storage and computing, were put forward including the startling RCA Computron that held the promise of replacing hundreds of tubes.[23]

By mid-1942, there were great hopes for the development of at least a prototype electronic gun controller. But, when Warren Weaver and his assistants reviewed the progress in early summer 1942, they had to make a difficult decision. Digital electronics, they concluded, was too good. It was too fast and too precise for the guns used by the military. Electronics would work but would be a costly technological overkill. In July 1942, the fire control program was dropped--but with three important exceptions. The development projects for the Eastman film-based analog to digital signal convertor and RCA's fabulous multi-function Computron tube were to be continued as was NCR's counting circuit research. Although they were viewed as long-term projects, the three efforts were financed for only a few more months because the press of other work forced the NDRC to abandon them.[24]

The Second Comparator

Meanwhile, just weeks after the work on high-speed electronic counters and fire control computers had begun, Bush and OP-20-G came together. A visit with Bush in early summer 1940 indicated a reawakening of interest in the original Comparator which had sat unused at the Navy Yard for almost two years. But, it was not until October 1940, just as the original grant for the Selector was running out, that anything was done about its future. Discussions began concerning the possibility of MIT's Selector group helping to repair the old Comparator. More importantly, there was a mention of the Yard building a new upgraded version. Bush suggested that the new version should incorporate the innovations developed for the Selector and the mid-1940 proposed MIT statistical machine.[25] In response, the navy gave indications that it would accept advice from the Institute. A limited and secondary role for MIT was unacceptable to Bush, however. He sensed another opportunity to create an independent project. He returned to his old demand for freedom from bureaucratic control, and, within a few weeks, he was able to reshape the first murmuring about a new Comparator into a project that satisfied his ambitions.

Bush wanted the next Comparator-Selector project to include much more than a repair of the old machine and a consideration of microfilm; he wanted at least a prototype of a microfilm Comparator. While the first Comparator would continue to be a paper tape machine, the second generation Comparator was to be centered about microfilm. It would allow the some twenty fold increase in effectiveness Bush had promised in 1938. As important, Bush wanted full control of the project. He was determined to have independence from the military bureaucracy in order to prove that his treasured technological combination could work.

Bush achieved at least his organizational goal. He soothed Laurance Safford's anxieties about optical and electronic machines and told him that the new microfilm version of the Comparator would be delivered in time to be of use in the coming war. He assured him there would be no repeat of the problems of 1938. He then asked the very hard-pressed leader of OP-20-G to lobby in his behalf. He wanted the navy to allow the project to be financed and supervised by the NDRC. Safford pushed Bush's demands through the navy bureaucracy. After that, Safford regained all of his old enthusiasm about the Comparator and he wrote his mentor Stanford C. Hooper that his years of work had not been wasted. Understating the problems of the 1938 machine project, Safford wrote, "Our only trouble was we tried to take the machinery out of the laboratory a little prematurely," and informed him that the Comparator was about to be reborn.[26]

In late 1940, Safford encountered little resistance to the idea of transferring the project to MIT. The navy's cryptanalysts were too busy battling the Japanese naval codes and too worried about taking on the German systems to care about the loss of control over unusable machinery. In June 1940, they had been locked out of their main source of information about Japan's navy, its fleet code. Their agonizing work against the JN systems did not begin to yield any results until the end of the year. The first tiny crack in the new system came in fall 1940, but the navy remained unable to read the most important Japanese naval systems.[27] Ironically, the great triumph by the army's group, the penetration of the Japanese diplomatic Purple machine, led to even more work for the small staff of OP-20-G. It was required to help monitor Japanese diplomatic messages. OP-20-G was also taking on another burden, one for which it did not have the necessary skills or resources.

OP-20-G and Ultra

As early as mid-1940, the most important Americans were informed of some of Britain's promising though still limited powers over a few German cryptologic systems. But OP-20-G was not told how to break the Enigma or other important ciphers. America remained blind. Despite the British promise to share the information from Ultra, the Americans feared a British monopoly over Enigma. In addition, in early summer 1940 there were fears that Britain would collapse. OP-20-G's cryptanalysts worried they would have to assume responsibility for Enigma, something for which they were totally unprepared.[28] Yet, the need for power over "E" was becoming critical. America's growing involvement in the Atlantic was leading to demands for better information than the British were providing about the location and intentions of the U-boat fleet. The U-boat threat had already led to British pleas that OP-20-G and Naval Intelligence shift their scarce resources to direction finding and traffic analysis to compensate for their inability to read any significant German naval systems.[29] The cryptanalysts in Washington thus had little time to waste on what some of them regarded as Bush's technological fantasies. The navy's engineers, already overworked creating analogs of encryption machines, building advanced radio equipment and helping to revise OP-20-G's tabulators, were happy to be rid of the "college professor's" folly. They were too busy to demand control over the new project.

The navy's bureaucrats were less happy about yielding control even though they were not paying for the work. They agreed to most of Bush's conditions although they did want a contract and to have the MIT work coordinated through the navy's Office of Research and Inventions. The BuShips's (Bureau of Ships) demands in late 1940 were much less severe than in 1935, but it took some additional political maneuvering to put the Rapid Machine project back into the hands of the MIT students. In the last months of 1940, the navy gave in to Bush's last demands, but a few navy men wondered if a serious procedural mistake had been made.[30] They began asking that someone keep a close watch over the Cambridge work. Some in the navy hierarchy were worried that Bush's "boys" would again waste valuable time and money and produce machines that would not work.[31]

The NDRC, of course, had no reservations about helping to solve what Bush told them was a special problem. They promised over fifty thousand dollars for the two year project at MIT[32] and granted Bush another twenty thousand dollars to finance his own related work.[33] In addition, there was no resistance from the sponsors of the old Selector. Bush quickly won the approval of the Research Corporation, NCR and Eastman to suspend what was left of the project.[34] NCR was especially cooperative. It continued support for MIT's Sam Caldwell and the Institute's magnetic recording research although it realized little could be done given MIT's shift to defense matters.[35] The remaining funds for the Selector were put into a special account, and the machine was covered over with a tarpaulin. Soon, it was decided to stop holding the Selector ready to show someone who might sponsor an application. The document retriever was abandoned. It was crated and sent to a Boston warehouse.[36]

Putting Scientists to the Test

Under the 1940 agreement with the Bureau of Ships, Bush had full control of the new Comparator project. And, his men were to work at MIT, not at the Navy Yard. That ensured they would not be regarded as mere employees. The navy's role was limited to after-the-fact approvals of components and designs and the Bureau agreed to cease working on Comparator-like devices. The navy also agreed to wait for the results of the new MIT work before considering the construction of any more Rapid machines; whether with or without an MIT involvement. Bush made sure the liaison officer was MIT's old friend and future MIT professor of naval architecture, Lybrand Smith. The navy's only burden was to pay for the transport of all the machines to and from MIT.[37]

The navy was not asked to halt its development of tabulators or other electromechanical device. OP-20-G may not have told Bush, but it was not relying solely upon his ideas for machine processing; it had to protect itself through the use of older and proven technologies. The experienced cryptanalysts had insisted on a tabulator program, one that was to remain under their direct control. MIT's men were to have no say about the new tab projects. In early 1941, IBM was contacted about making major changes in its machines to allow its equipment to perform new tests. For example, relays were added to the machines to strip superencipherments from the Japanese codes and to flag repetitions of code groups. By mid-year, IBM was asked to do much more and to give OP-20-G very special attention.[38]

Whatever Bush knew or felt about OP-20-G's relationship with IBM, the 1940 agreement with OP-20-G was his victory. He was finally able to circumvent the bureaucracy and go his own way. He may have had ambitions to create a full Rapid Machine center at the Institute, one free of all military interference.[39] Final arrangements for the new project were made in November 1940. The old Comparator was to be shipped to MIT for repair and a new one was to be designed and constructed in Cambridge. Bush expected the 1938 machine to be revived and returned to OP-20-G in a short time and he wanted at least a prototype of the new microfilm version within two years. Bush had agreed to correct the problems with the failed tape punch from the first Comparator, but, at the last minute, the navy decided to construct the new version at the Yard--once MIT provided a detailed design.[40]

Pushed by the need to return to his other NDRC duties, Bush got the work going immediately, before any formal contracts were signed. But, he did not recruit additional men. Waldron MacDonald, the engineer on the first Comparator was in contact with Bush, but did not join the new project. Since leaving Washington he had taken an engineering position with a New Jersey company. After two years there, he contacted Bush about help finding a more exciting job. Bush pointed him to the Naval Ordnance Laboratory.[41] Meanwhile, Bush arranged security clearances for the three MIT graduate students from the Selector project and put them to work. Then, the navy's Frederick Dulong was called to MIT to examine the Rapid Selector and to evaluate the first ideas about a microfilm Comparator.[42] After that, Howard rushed to OP-20-G and the Bureau of Engineering's Radio laboratory and learned of the old Comparator's problems and the types of new machines the cryptanalysts desired. While there, he stroked as many egos as possible.[43] On his return to MIT, he informed Coombs and Steinhardt of their new assignments and, after consulting with Bush, brought in one of the Institute's machinists, Mr. Barnaby.[44]

Howard quickly became the man in charge. Once the 1940 negotiations with the Bureau were completed, Bush stepped far into the background. He was too busy with the NDRC projects, such as the development of an atomic bomb, to become mired in details.[45] Howard handled everything. Before the end of 1940 he began constructing secret rooms at the Institute. They had opaque windows and bars across their doors. He then ordered the high priority machine tools he needed.[46] With so many at MIT now involved in military or

NDRC contracts, this new round of secrecy did not lead to protests from the faculty. Most of MIT's electrical engineers, faculty or student, were too busy trying to finish the Rockefeller machine and to make some progress on the long delayed electronic computer to complain about what obviously was a high priority project. Howard put his three men to work as soon as possible--although the two-year deadline did not seem to demand that anyone rush. It took several weeks to finish the rooms and to have the old machine sent by truck from Washington, but the project was in full swing by early 1941.[47] Although the future of Bush's ideas rested upon the new microfilm Comparator the old paper tape machine and its punch became the focus of attention. The punch was a critical problem because its two previous versions were failures. The old paper tape Comparator would have to be abandoned if the new punch was ineffective. That would be a telling blow to Bush's reputation.[48]

Understandably, Howard urged his men to use caution as well as creativity, but the slow tempo of his project soon generated concern within the Bureau of Ships. During the first months of 1941, as time passed without results, the navy found it more and more difficult to accommodate to having its project run by a civilian agency. The slow work at the Institute might have fit with good engineering practice, but the Germans and Japanese had a different time-table. The Japanese had become very aggressive and the American military knew it would soon have a confrontation in the Pacific. At the same time, Britain's troubles and Roosevelt's policies led America to act as if it had a two ocean navy. Without the needed resources, the navy had to protect Atlantic convoys and to guard the Pacific. As a result, OP-20-G had enormous responsibilities placed upon it. Worse, although its men visited England in early 1941 to learn of British techniques and machines for reading the Axis code and cipher systems, OP-20-G remained without the power to break into the Enigmas or to read the main Japanese naval code.[49] In response, Lybrand Smith of Research and Inventions was ordered to pay increased attention to the MIT project.

So Long for So Little

In mid-1941, Frederick Dulong made another visit to Cambridge to review and consult.[50] What he saw may have given him some reason to agree with the navy's conservatives who were becoming very worried. The first cause for concern was the status of the old

Comparator, the only Rapid Machine. Although Bush had intimated that the first Comparator would be fixed and returned very soon, it could not be quickly repaired. Despite prodding from the navy, it took almost a full year for Howard's men to redo the old Comparator and it arrived in Washington three weeks after the Japanese struck at Pearl Harbor.[51] Then, it did not receive a triumphant welcome to room 1662 of the OP-20-G facility on Constitution Avenue. It had to remain in its crates until floor space was available and until one of the newly drafted navy engineers could pay some attention to it. Perhaps an embarrassment for Bush, the engineer was a man from IBM who had worked on Tom Watson's commercially motivated explorations of electronics.[52]

Howard's men may have taken longer than expected to deliver the old Comparator because of adding one new feature to Bush's 1938 design. The "locator" performed a function the navy had thought of adding in the late 1930s. It allowed the use of a transverse tape to find more complex pattern matches than was possible with the original system. With the locator, the codebreakers could quickly identify which messages held important code or cipher groups.[53] But, no other major changes were made to the Comparator, perhaps because the MIT group had written off a paper tape machine as far behind the times.[54]

Once in action in mid-1942, the old Comparator did help crack the Japanese naval attache cipher machine, but the Comparator's newest punch also malfunctioned.[55] As well, when on its best behavior, the revamped Comparator could not perform up to Bush's old minimum standard of twenty thousand comparisons a minute. Its tape ran at less than two miles per hour. The new punch and improvements to the optical scanner may have allowed greater data density on the 70mm paper tapes, but the machine took days to do tasks that Bush once thought could be done in hours.[56] And, the machine's bad temper called for a visit by one of the MIT men, Larry Steinhardt, who had to simplify the device to achieve reliability.[57]

The Search for the Second Comparator

While struggling with the old Comparator, the young men at MIT paid attention to its new microfilm version. As they worked, Bush became determined to see that their design led to the production of machines, even if the navy rejected MIT and the microfilm Comparator. Stretching the NDRC-OSRD mandate, Bush decided to lay the foundations for an extensive new microfilm Comparator program.

He began the construction of what was more than just a prototype. In early November 1941, the MIT-NDRC group was so positive about the future of a microfilm Comparator that Bush obtained another significant grant from the NDRC.[58] Then, although the NDRC was not supposed to be involved in production, Howard awarded a twenty-five thousand dollar contract to National Cash Register's electronics laboratory. Joe Desch agreed to build as many as thirty copies of the sets of new high-speed counters and fast printers needed for the future microfilm Comparators.[59]

At the same time, Howard and his men travelled to Washington to meet with OP-20-G's cryptanalysts and the Bureau's representatives. Bush was not present, but his status was reflected by OP-20-G's people calling John Howard "Professor." In the November 1941 meeting, Howard and his men sung the praises of the next Comparator and they declared they were ready to begin construction. They explained that the new Comparator would have ten times the power of the upgraded old machine. It would be able to make, at minimum, thirty thousand simple comparisons a minute and would perform all the other polymorphic and locator tests. That was not the twenty fold increase in raw processing speed promised in 1938 when Bush first told the navy of the possibilities of microfilm, but the combination of the dense packing of code dots on the 35mm film, the improved tape drives and the high-speed circuits offered a significant improvement over the first paper tape machine.

The day long meeting continued with more reports by the MIT group. Howard stated that he was especially pleased with experiments on a new method of microfilm data entry. But, he had to admit that his group had found it impossible to build a reliable punch for the paper tapes. In the strongest terms, he advised OP-20-G to abandon any hope of future paper tape machines. Then, he proudly announced that his men had at last found a solution to the microfilm data entry problem. It was a method that had first been explored for the MIT electronic computer and the aborted statistical Selector. It seemed to answer all the data entry problems for the navy and, although Howard did not mention it, for the future commercial versions of the Selector-Comparator.

The MIT group must have consulted with Eastman's scientists concerning automatic photographic techniques before arriving at the solution.[60] Under Howard's clever data entry proposal, Eastman and

IBM equipment would be joined in new combinations to allow very fast and precise photographic registration of data on microfilm. Data from punch cards, tapes, and, perhaps, typewriters, would be sent through fast, automatic mechanical readers which would translate their various codes into a uniform one. The new codes would then set patterns in a bank of tiny lights contained in a sealed box. Those light pattern images of the coded message would be microphotographed onto 35mm film. The photographic system, Howard said, would allow very dense recording of data, much more than the punch hole method, and would avoid all the problems that came with mechanical data registration.[61] Howard proposed that all data for the new microfilm version of the Comparator be entered with the lights. He did not discuss it during the navy meeting, but in a revised Selector, text could be directly photographed while the codes were entered with the light bank. Howard assumed that problems such as handling and developing the film would be insignificant.

In response to the good news, Safford's people saluted the experts but they cautioned the MIT men about trying to make the microfilm Comparator perform too many little used functions. Then, expecting to see the newest Comparator in a few months, and viewing the MIT group as a long-term resource, the OP-20-G analysts outlined needs for other devices. One of those outlines had a hidden significance. It would connect the MIT men to the Ultra Secret although they did not even know of Britain's ability to crack the Enigma or the critical negotiations between OP-20-G and Britain over sharing intelligence secrets.

Not Equal Partners in Ultra

Agreements were made at the very highest levels in 1940 and 1941 for Britain and America to share cryptanalytic methods and the military information that came from signals intelligence. In early 1941, an American delegation went to England with the valuable machines the United States used to attack Purple and other Japanese systems. The Americans returned with at least general knowledge of Britain's methods of penetrating some of the Enigma networks. Unfortunately, at the time, Britain had power over only a few German systems. But, soon after the men from the army, navy, and Federal Bureau of Investigation cryptanalytic units returned to America, Britain gained some control over the German naval systems. But the entries were not the result of pure cryptanalysis. The breaks came from captures of

Enigma wheels and instruction books and the British remained tied to such captures and to knowledge of the clear text of intercepted messages. Even Alan Turing's magnificent Bombes depended on cribs and captures. Thus, the British solution remained fragile. England's wizards had not found a mathematical solution to the Enigma! Without good guesses as to key words in messages and knowledge of the inner workings of the Enigma radio networks, Britain could, and would, become blind.[62]

Perhaps it was the fragility of the solutions that made the British somewhat less willing to share their secrets with the Americans after their early 1941 visit. Whatever the reason, the American's began to think it was necessary to have their own anti-Enigma capability. The British thought otherwise. Although Britain had pledged full cooperation with the United States in summer 1940, it also suggested that the Americans concentrate on the Japanese threat, leaving German cipher systems alone. But, OP-20-G was under too much pressure to go along with the demand to confine itself to Atlantic traffic analysis and direction finding. In late 1940, Safford shifted his one professional cryptanalyst, who had just made the first entries into the Japanese fleet code, to the German problems. The venerable Agnes Meyer Driscoll and three young navy officers began an attack on the frustrating German naval Enigma. However, they made little progress toward what the Americans needed, a purely mathematical cryptanalytic solution.

Although she had helped break into similar devices, was informed of some of the British methods and labored for almost a year, Driscoll could not find the ways and means for an American Enigma solution. Fortunately, she was willing to ask for help. During the November 1941 meeting between Howard and OP-20-G, she described her needs and Howard was asked to think of ways to automate her "problem." She was determined to develop a method more permanent than the ones Britain had chosen. Apparently, that called for a machine somewhat different from the Comparator. Howard accepted the responsibility and Driscoll was happy with the promises by the young men from MIT.[63]

Another Machine That Wouldn't

The cordial meeting with Howard in early November 1941 impressed OP-20-G's people. They assumed they could depend on the graduate student engineers for all types of technical solutions. But, OP-20-G and the Bureau of Ships became very worried and skeptical about university work when, just a few days after the Washington conference,[64] Howard wrote the navy that experiments were showing the new Comparator's microfilm to be deforming when used in test assemblies. Such warping and shrinkage were making it impossible to accurately locate coincidences on two or more tapes, he said. The needed tolerances of less than one-thousandth of an inch could not be achieved. A microfilm Comparator, he announced, would not work!

Howard was sincere when he stated that until late 1941 everyone at the Institute thought microfilm could be made to behave. He thought his team had overcome all the shortcomings of film that had cropped up since the early work on the Cinema Integraph. Howard may have explained his failure by describing the difference between the Selector and proposed microfilm Comparator. In the Selector, only one film moved, making the alignment problem less critical. The success of the Selector's drive and scanner made it easy to believe that a microfilm Comparator would work. But, in the Comparator, the need to precisely align two moving tapes and to shift them after each pass by the scanner presented too great of a challenge. Misaligned rows of tiny dots were creating havoc in the photoelectric scanner with light seeping into the wrong light guides.

The navy must have wondered how it could have taken the MIT group so many years to discover its primary technological assumption was untenable. The Bureau's representatives uttered some more "I told you so's" about "college professors." They may also have asked how OP-20-G's need for revolutionary cryptanalytic devices could be fulfilled if the responsibility continued to be left in the hands of the inexperienced NDRC and the young MIT students--people who failed to test underlying assumptions before wasting a critical year's work?

Trying to Save Bush's Reputation

Howard did the best he could to save Bush's dream. He advised the Bureau that photographic plates could be substituted for microfilm.[65] He suggested their use until some way could be found to prevent deformation of the microfilm tapes. He did not elaborate, but it was clear that machines based upon such plates would have little resemblance to the statistical Selector-Comparator. It was very unlikely they could perform like the machines Bush had proposed since the early 1930s.[66] Although very pessimistic, Howard did not give up on the Comparator entirely. He did not cancel the NCR contract for the counter-printers. But, as in the case of the Selector, the new Comparator project seemed to be another very embarrassing disaster. The Bureau certainly was unhappy and the navy's cryptanalysts thought they might be left out of the electronics revolution. Howard and his men must have felt quite inadequate.

Bush realized his plans for electronic cryptanalysis were in trouble. There was almost nothing to show for a decade's work. It was more than ten years since he first thought of Rapid machines and it had been more than five years since construction had begun. The funds for what amounted to some thirty engineering man-years had been invested in Comparators and their close relation, the Selector. But, the United States was entering World War II with one old paper tape Rapid Machine in crates awaiting shipment back to Washington, a Selector without a purpose and the fear that none of Bush's designs could be made to work. That was hardly a good technological or managerial track record![67]

And, John Howard's bad news could not have come at a worse time for the navy. He made his confession just as the American intelligence agencies were frantically searching for the final clues to where Japan would attack. In a few weeks OP-20-G had to face the consequences of the failure to predict Pearl Harbor. Given the trauma of December 7, and the failures of Bush's young men, it would have been natural for the navy to turn away from MIT and allow the Comparator project to fade away as did the fire control project. But a combination of factors gave Bush's men yet another chance. The ability of Howard to continue on independently (because he had a year's NDRC funding remaining) was important, but a more significant reason was the combination of the return of Joseph Wenger and the political influence of Vannevar Bush.

Yet Another Chance

Wenger returned from sea duty in the summer of 1941 and although assigned to OP-20's war plans section,[68] he contacted the cryptanalysts and Bush about the outcome of the year of NDRC work. After hearing of the situation, and despite Howard's bad news, Wenger talked with his contacts at OP-20-G and pleaded for a continuation of the relationship with MIT's men.[69] His urging and the dread of alienating the head of the NDRC, Vannevar Bush, allowed Safford to begin a program that would be vastly expanded when Wenger was sent back to OP-20-G in early 1942.

Wenger became critical to the survival of the Rapid Analytical Machine program. In part, his influence was due to historical contingencies. He was not involved in OP-20-G's intelligence work when the surprise attack on Pearl Harbor led men such as Laurance Safford to become mired in demeaning hunts for scapegoats.[70] Wenger came back to OP-20-G cloaked with innocence. In addition, Wenger had managed to avoid being tainted by his past association with Hooper. Hooper and some other officers had protested against Roosevelt's interventionist policies because they thought the American military was unprepared for war. Hooper feared that lives would be unnecessarily lost because the American armed forces were not ready to confront the technically advanced Axis powers. Because of that, his earlier confrontations with the Bureaus and his advanced age, he was pushed into the background during World War II.[71]

However, Wenger's influence at OP-20-G was due to much more than his innocence and Hooper's semi-retirement. It was the result of his long involvement in modernizing naval communications. He had a reputation as an expert in all communications fields. For over a decade he had advocated much more than the Rapid Machines. In fact, he was America's leading advocate of a high-tech alternative to cryptanalysis. In the 1930s, Wenger predicted that unless massive breakthroughs were made in cryptanalysis, such as the construction of a full range of Rapid Machines, it would be foolish to rely upon direct signals intelligence such as codebreaking. Until America built a truly innovative mathematical cryptanalytic capability, he argued, other signals intelligence resources had to be exploited.

The Other Alternative

Wenger argued that codes and ciphers were becoming too complex to crack with available techniques and, as important, an enemy's frequent changes of systems would always create blackouts at the most critical moments.[72] His prediction was based upon practical experience, not just theory. He had seen Japan suddenly change its code systems and then watched as it took years to fully reconstruct the new code books. He was also privy to the knowledge of the blackouts that came when the Japanese introduced new enciphering machines.[73]

Wenger had become America's advocate for what became known as "traffic analysis." He had spent years studying and developing T/A. In traffic analysis, the concern was not with the content of messages but with the easily identified call-signs of senders and receivers, the timing and numbers of messages in a network and the shifts in patterns of transmissions.[74] Traffic analysis was not a low-tech activity. It called for more esoteric and expensive hardware than traditional codebreaking. The method depended upon sophisticated direction finders to locate enemy stations and on other expensive equipment.[75] It was also very demanding in terms of personnel.

Wenger had urged the navy to establish a string of new intercept and direction finding stations during the 1930s, each with increasingly sophisticated and costly electronic equipment. He had made tours of the leading radio and electronics companies to identify sources of advanced equipment and he convinced the navy to begin an expensive program to acquire new devices. Revolutionary automatic scanners searched for active channels, oscilloscopes helped identify stations and operators and very sensitive receivers plotted transmissions.[76] The hardware was not the end of it, however. Optimal radio interception and plotting called for advice from physicists and the exploitation of the intercepts needed advanced analytical techniques. The intercepts and location estimates had to be correlated and subjected to time consuming analysis. The tabulators were frequently called upon to compile the necessary interaction matrices. And the expense and manpower seemed worthwhile, as shown by Wenger's reconstruction of Japanese naval maneuvers from T/A analysis.

By 1940, OP-20-G's intercept crews were logging thousands of messages a month from the Pacific and the Atlantic and the method was considered essential. With America and Britain unable to read the most important German systems, T/A was the only hope in the West.[77] But, tactical analysis became a vital tool in both oceans and remained so throughout the war. When the Japanese suddenly changed their codes, as in the period just before the Mariannas campaign, T/A was the only thing preventing a total blackout.[78] It had its limits, however. It could not reveal long-term plans; it gave just a picture of immediate intentions. It had other imperfections, as well. The most important was a dependency on very frequent communications. If a station did not broadcast, it could not be identified and located. Tragically, in 1942, T/A was unable to deal with the German submarine onslaught because the submarines off the American coast followed a routine of radio silence. Of course, it had also failed to prevent Pearl Harbor.

Wenger to the Rescue

Joseph Wenger's influence at OP-20-G was not diminished by the failure of T/A to live up to its promise. In 1942, he was granted the power he needed to implement his plan for a centralized organization of naval communications intelligence. Such an organization was favored by the new leaders of OP-20. They had been appointed to replace the old officers who had been disgraced by Pearl Harbor. The new leaders desired a tightly controlled agency, as did Wenger. In fact, he had drafted a detailed plan for the centralization of cryptanalytic activities and power in the 1930s. He wanted Washington, not local or regional naval commanders, in charge of signals intelligence and he was in favor of a large-scale center for analysis in Washington. Several small units, he argued, would lead to chaos. Unification, he said, would allow the efficient use of the required expensive equipment and skilled personnel. Only with central processing of all information would there be coordinated and thus effective analysis.

Wenger's ideas were quickly accepted.[79] Along with the approval of his plan came his appointment as the operating head of "G". In February 1942 he began to reorganize "G" and to revive Hooper's dream of bringing science and cryptanalysis together. Although Wenger had a great degree of freedom and undreamed of funds, he did not have an easy time achieving his goals. His first handicap was the years OP-20-G had wasted as a budget starved and little appreciated operation. Wenger had much to do to make up for the failure to develop and purchase critical equipment during the 1930s. Wenger also had to find and train a skilled workforce. "G" had been undermanned since its birth and previous attempts to create a cryptologic reserve had produced only a handful of men and women.[80] The new cryptologic correspondence courses and the classes established at some of the leading universities in 1941 had not been in operation long enough to recruit the hundreds of men he needed. The following table gives some idea of the challenging expansion of "G".[81]

Year	Staff at OP-20-G
1925	7
1939	41
1940	70
1941	107
1942	240
1943	1000
1944	3682
1945	5000

Wenger's task was more difficult because of changes in American policy. Following the nation's standard war plans, OP-20-G had focused upon the wrong cryptological system of the wrong enemy during the late 1930s. Japan's navy had been OP-20-G's target since the end of World War I. Then, in the late 1930s, "G" had been directed to divert much of its manpower to the Japanese diplomatic systems. Following that, in 1940, it was suddenly told that the Atlantic convoy problem was the first priority. OP-20-G had no German cryptanalytic capability. Yet it was ordered to crack the most secure communications net in the world, the U-boat system!

Worse for Wenger, just as he took over "G" the Atlantic challenge turned into a nightmare and the future of OP-20-G was at stake. In early 1942, the U-boats began to slaughter dozens of freighters in sight of the American coast. Within a few weeks, the Germans did more damage than the Japanese had done at Pearl Harbor. The U-boat threat to the Atlantic convoys was also growing so fast that a continuation of the sinkings threatened Britain's survival. Britain was unable to penetrate the new naval four wheel Enigma and OP-20-G remained without any power over German systems. Unfortunately for Wenger and OP-20-G, British and American T/A was unable to compensate for the closing-off of the U-boat Enigma.[82]

Mathematics to Meet the Great Challenge

The Atlantic crisis had a strange impact on OP-20-G's future. It both helped and hindered Wenger's crusade for the Rapid Machines. In its first phases, the crisis aided him. As part of his outline for the expansion of OP-20-G, Wenger had planned for the creation of a special research group. Its mission was to apply formal mathematics to cryptanalysis. OP-20-G had never before had a professionally trained mathematical team although Hooper, Wenger and Safford had done all they could to attract such men in the 1930s. They had scoured the university ROTCs and attracted a few mathematicians to the reserve force during the 1930s; they had arranged for faculty scouts in mathematics departments at leading colleges; and, they had convinced as many college men as possible to take their cryptologic course by mail.[83] But the number of recruits was disappointing. The programs had attracted a few "good men," however, and they became the core of the new "M" section established in Washington in 1942. Then, in February 1942, Wenger brought together the few professional mathematicians who had already been called to service. Of significance for World War II, and the history of the Rapid Machines, they were handed more than mathematical responsibilities. They were ordered to take on some technical radio problems. In addition, they were given some of the responsibility for the critical German systems. Next, the "M" section was handed Wenger's pet, the Rapid Machines project. Luckily, Wenger found the right man, Howard Engstrom, to direct the third major attempt to make optics and electronics into cryptanalytic tools.

Howard Engstrom had perfect credentials for leading the "M" group. He received his first academic degree in Chemical Engineering in 1922 when he was only twenty years old. He spent a few years acquiring a practical background in communications by working for Western Union. After that, he taught at New England colleges while earning a Ph.D. in mathematics. He obtained his degree from Yale in 1929. That feat was followed by a shower of academic honors. He became one of the renowned National Research Council fellows at Cal Tech and, then, was admitted to the most prestigious mathematical center in the world, Gottingen. The great figures of twentieth century mathematics and physics gathered there. The European visit helped Engstrom's career and he soon became a mathematics professor at Yale and, like Stratton and Bush, became a faithful member of the Naval Reserve. He was one of the very few men to complete the full range of cryptologic courses during the 1930s. He was also one of the few to devote his summers to the navy.[84]

When first called for the war crisis, Engstrom was asked to give advanced technical advice to OP-20-G's radio intercept and direction finding group.[85] That T/A assignment was a very important and demanding post. But heading "M" turned out to be much more of a challenge. The new job called for political as well as technical skills. By spring 1942, the Rapid Machines had again become political creatures. The apparent failure of Howard's 1941 microfilm Comparator had not ended his work or the interest of OP-20 in cryptanalytic machinery. But it did reopen the old battles over control of innovation in the navy.

Bureaucracy v Science, Again

Pearl Harbor, despite the blame hurled at the army and navy intelligence agencies, led to the release of funds and energies for cryptanalysis. For the first time in its history, OP-20-G had enough money to pursue technological dreams. In response, in early 1942 Safford, still the head of OP-20-G, initiated a survey of needs and wrote out a wish list that included Rapid Machines. There was enough money to explore all options. The first choice of the operating cryptanalysts was IBM electromechanical machinery. They asked for more standard equipment and for the development of a host of special attachments. Safford, without an "M" section and very short of personnel, turned to the Bureau of Ships for technical and administrative help. He found it easy to convince the Bureau to deal with the trustworthy IBM. Very soon, the Bureau of Ships established what it saw as a harmonious three-way relationship between IBM, the old hands at "G" and itself.

Safford also reawakened interest in the Bush-Howard ideas for photoelectronic machines, but the already skeptical Bureau did not wish a return to what it saw as the chaos of the previous Bush projects. While agreeing to work with Howard's MIT group, the Bureau wanted to bring all the machine projects under its direct control. It especially wanted the work put in the hands of experienced and responsible contractors. In the first weeks of 1942, the Bureau decided to allow OP-20-G to invest navy funds in an exploration of Rapid Machines but it demanded a heavy price, one which included a radical change in the relationship between MIT's men and the navy. The Bureau wanted Howard, Steinhardt and Coombs to became, at most, consultants, not project directors. In addition, the Bureau's men, not those from OP-20-G, were to run the technical and financial parts of the program. Above all, the Bureau wanted the projects out of the halls of MIT. Its officers demand that any work be done by established corporations that followed the navy's standard procedures. Safford had little time or energy to argue and he followed the Bureau's rules. He began contacting Eastman-Kodak, RCA, and Bell Labs about taking on the Rapid Machines and other electronics challenges. The Bureau trusted such companies and their way of managing projects. It assumed the corporations would need little supervision or technical assistance from the navy once traditional contracts were signed.

The Bureau did not establish a new special group for the cryptanalytic machines but, in early 1942, it began to take charge of the NDRC project, giving, it thought, badly needed managerial direction. To ensure some results from the NDRC and navy investments, they told Howard to restart work on a paper tape and punch version of the Comparator. At the same time, they instructed him to continue to consult with Eastman on film and plate possibilities.[86] Meanwhile, the Bureau explored ways to decrease its dependency on Bush's group. Then, the Bureau decided to show its power. It took the Comparator away from Bush and MIT.

In March 1942, Bush's structure for linking the military and academia, at least for cryptanalytic machines, began to be dismantled. Bush became increasingly upset as he saw his ideas and project slip into the hands of others. He exploded when the navy ordered the NDRC contract with NCR for the electronic counters to be changed to a regular navy one. Bush feared that other NDRC work would suffer the same fate. But he could not stop the Bureau. Nor could Colonel Deeds. Within another two months, Joe Desch's operation at NCR became a captive of the navy as he was instructed to drop his other NDRC work and to concentrate on helping the Bureau.[87]

At the same time, Howard, Coombs, and Steinhardt were reduced to advisors and aides to the navy. Coombs and Howard were made civilian employees of the navy and were stationed at Eastman and NCR. Steinhardt, who had been in the Naval Reserve since 1938, was brought directly to Washington. (It took Howard a year of intense lobbying to gain a commission.)[88] The work at MIT, perhaps with the exception of the designing of a punch, was ended and the secret workshop was shut down!

Despite the seeming progress, Wenger was frightened by the Bureau's actions. He wanted control over the Rapid Machines and he and Engstrom began a search for a way to break free of the Bureau, its methods and its contractors.[89]

A Seeming Victory for Science

As soon as Wenger returned to "G" and learned of the Bureau's actions he became angry. Wenger feared that even if they did not wither from the Bureau's disinterest, the corporate projects would produce machines the cryptanalysts could not use. Distraught, Wenger began an attempt to shift power back to OP-20-G. He asked Engstrom and his team for help and began to search for experienced engineers to augment the "M" group. Howard, Coombs and Steinhardt became the first of the engineering adjuncts. The search continued and by the end of 1942, OP-20-G had some of the leading men in computer electronics in the nation working under Engstrom's direction. Through formal and informal means, the name "M" came to mean machinery as well as mathematics.[90] The marriage of Engstrom's statistical-mathematics responsibilities with oversight of the machines was logical. New methods demanded new hardware and the mathematicians could best define the functions of the Rapid Machines.

Wenger would win more battles. He convinced the Bureau to give OP-20-G's Rapid Machine program near autonomy as well as its own facility and workforce. But it took a major intelligence crisis to achieve that. Wenger would not have been so successful and there would not have been a Naval Computing Machine Laboratory at the NCR factory in Dayton, Ohio if the British had been able to conquer the German submarine Enigma system or if the White House had insisted that OP-20-G remain dependent on Britain's Ultra.

The establishment of the Naval Computing Machine Laboratory and the increased power of Engstrom's Rapid Machine group did help OP-20-G to build a series of innovative cryptanalytic machines, including the American version of the Bombe. By the end of the war the American navy had some of the world's most advanced electronic machines. But, achievements never fulfilled expectations, especially those centered on Bush's early promises. The Rapid Machine project began too late and under crisis conditions. The consequences for the original ideas for optical-electronic machines and America's cryptanalytic capabilities were significant. Besides the cranky refurbished 1938 Comparator, there were no Bush type machines in operation before the last months of 1943. The only new photoelectric machine in use in 1942 was a technological retrogression based on an emergency use of the photoplates Howard had suggested. And, after that, the few microfilm and paper tape machines that appeared were much less powerful than those Bush had been promising since the early 1930s. OP-20-G and its new machine group could not overcome the stubborn problems of microfilm and electronics.[91]

Copperhead Punch, circa 1945
(National Security Agency)

Tabulator Repair, Op-20-G, Hawaii, circa 1944
(Naval Security Group Command)

Chapter X
Microfilm Not at War

A Look Ahead to 1945

America's entry into the war led to the release of torrents of money for codebreaking. A surprisingly large allocation was given to the Bureau for cryptanalytic machine development. Unfortunately, "G" and the Bureau were not prepared and they were unable to immediately establish a well coordinated project that could compensate for the years of lost opportunities. The funds came too late to found a long-term development program and "G's" resources had to be devoted to cryptanalytic fire fighting. Until very late in the war, OP-20-G's computer activities were driven by emergencies. Recurring intelligence crises and stubborn technological problems led to "G's" turning back to older analog and electromechanical solutions. Its brilliant mathematicians and engineers had little choice but to follow such a path. Until late 1943, they did not even have the time to think of machines that went beyond Bush's mid-1930s ideas or to plan their move from analog to electronic digital technologies.

After they made their great electromechanical contribution to the Ultra problem, the Bombe, they had more time. They built some digital electronic machines and they began to lay plans for a long-term computer program. However, by the end of the war they had not been able to turn Bush's faith in microfilm into advanced and reliable machines. Although the navy's computer group had a great deal of freedom and employed the best electronics men in the country, many of its solutions, especially during 1942 and 1943, were technological retrogressions. One reason for the backward steps was that Bush had promised too much for his three technologies. Film, optics and electronics proved a very difficult combination. The nation's top engineers had to back away from Bush's great dream of a universal microfilm Comparator. A Selector was too much of a luxury to deserve a share of precious resources.

One important consequence of the absence of the ultra fast digital machines was that Hooper's dream of relying upon pure statistical and mathematical cryptanalytical techniques had to be deferred. Like England, the United States had to rely upon the most expedient logical as well as technological solutions. During 1942 and 1943 OP-20-G's "M" group was unable to become a think-tank for pure methods and the engineers at "G" and the Bureau had to chose the easiest hardware solutions. The machines that emerged were not as fast or flexible as those outlined by Bush in the mid-1930s. In fact, until the end of 1943, the only proof of the practicality of the Wenger-Bush ideas was the stodgy first Comparator and a hurriedly lashed together recombination of the Selector. A series of increasingly advanced devices began to arrive in early 1944. But it was not until 1945 that OP-20-G's young engineers could begin to think of creating a multi-purpose Rapid Machine and when "M" could begin the exploration of the frontiers of mathematical cryptology. There were more than technical reasons for the gap between what Wenger and Hooper wanted and what was achieved during the war. OP-20-G's World War II machine effort began in crisis and continued to be driven by rapidly shifting demands.

The first crisis was the declaration of war. It led to a frantic search for solutions and it overwhelmed administrators at the Bureau of Ships. They attempted to bring some order to the situation in early 1942 but they took on too much and expected too much of themselves and the technicians they hired.

January 1942, Too Much Too Late

Soon after Pearl Harbor the Bureau gained the funds to support all the ideas that had been put forward by the various groups in OP-20-G and at the Yard. It created several uncoordinated and poorly supervised projects. Sure-fire technologies were the first hope. Contracts were let to IBM for more tabulator equipment and for the creation of a host of new special attachments. Those at the Bureau and OP-20-G who favored electromechanical equipment received recognition when IBM was also awarded a very large contract to develop a set of new machines to automate the processing of incoming data. At the same time, a group of navy engineers in Washington was allowed to build some electromechanical analysis machines of their own design. There was money to go further. The Bureau had enough resources to prevent Bush's Comparator from being locked away to die in the secret workroom at MIT. But, all film and microform work was taken out of the hands of the Institute's men. The Bureau quickly made an arrangement with Eastman-Kodak. Its experts, including those who had begun fire control projects, agreed to work on all the microfilm and plate ideas. This meant that Howard and his group were to be helpers, not supervisors.

Into the Hands of the Bureaucrats

The Bureau's decision to turn to Eastman threatened Bush's goal of autonomy and it worried him. More difficult for him to accept was the Bureau's decision to take a step back from microfilm and to breath new life into paper tape Comparators. It ordered Howard to help draw up new specifications. Then, it let a contract to Western Union's old research company, Gray Electric, to develop the heart of the machine, the tape delivery system. Soon, and much to Bush's anger, the old NDRC work at National Cash Register on the electronic counters was made a Bureau activity. Worse for Bush and Howard, because of the potential for embarrassing failure, the MIT men were asked to build yet another version of the punch for the newest paper tape version of the Comparator.[1]

All this took place under chaotic conditions, especially within OP-20-G. Laurance Safford had little time to supervise and coordinate the projects during the first months of 1942. He had to let the Bureau handle technical matters and to solve the delicate political and personal problems. When Joseph Wenger returned and established the "M" group under Howard Engstrom, he tried to regain control over his pets, the automatic machines. But it took some time to organize "M." In fact, if it had not been for the crisis in the Atlantic and the attitude of the man the Bureau had assigned to supervise the machine contracts, Wenger would not have been able to reassert OP-20-G's power over machine development. If the British had maintained control over the U-boat Enigma and if the Bureau had assigned someone besides Ralph Meader to oversee the crypto-machine projects, Wenger would not have been allowed to create his own computer program.[2]

Wenger Finds an Ally

Although more than forty, Ralph Meader was not of the Bureau's old guard. A reservist, he had spent more than two decades in the engineering divisions of America's largest electrical corporations. He earned a reputation as both a solid engineer and an even tempered executive. He learned how to work with, as well as to direct, creative people. When he was called up in 1940 and assigned to rather routine duties in the Bureau his talents were not fully utilized. But,when he was handed the remnants of Howard's NDRC project at NCR and the new contracts with Gray, Eastman and IBM, he sensed that he was involved in a challenging adventure. In the first months of 1942, he ran a free wheeling one man operation for the Bureau. Despite his freedom he began to experience the frustrations that had led Hooper and Bush to try to throw off the heavy hands of the navy's bureaucracy in the 1930s.

Meader became disenchanted with the relationships between the navy and the commercial contractors and concluded that formal procedures could not answer the needs of secret projects. He was frustrated just trying to gain the high level security clearances the corporate engineers needed. It was not until mid-year, for example, that any of Eastman's large team received the needed blessing from the Office of Naval Intelligence. Their work was delayed for months. Even with the help of Coombs and Howard and the contributions of Eastman's A. W. Tyler, Meader could not prevent the work at all the corporations from slowing to a crawl.[3] He came to feel that the companies were unresponsive and he compiled a list of complaints.

As he learned more about the nation's cryptanalytic crisis, Meader came to understand why Engstrom and Wenger were so distraught. He knew the Allies needed immediate results, but the established firms seemed unable or unwilling to produce them. For example, Eastman-Kodak, which had honed its electronics skills during the fire control projects, and which had the nation's leading experts in optics and film, was unable to deliver a sophisticated machine until the last months of 1943. However, the delays were not all due to Eastman's attitude toward OP-20-G. Many of Bush's ideas and Howard's first designs for machines proved impractical. They were not ready for production. The problems with microfilm meant that Eastman had to start from fundamentals, delaying the production of useful machines. And, the one microform machine it was able to send to OP-20-G before late 1943 was an example of the backward steps the engineers had to take to develop machines under crisis conditions. In addition, Eastman's more sophisticated devices of late 1943 also had to be based upon techniques very different from Bush's original ideas.

A Giant Step Backwards

When the Bureau went to Eastman in early 1942 no one had expected frightening delays or a need for radical redefinitions of "G's" machines. Eastman seemed the best choice in terms of continuity because the relationship between Eastman and MIT's machine work dated from the beginning of the Selector project. Also, Eastman's technical and managerial reputation from its NDRC projects pointed to a speedy solution to the problems that had halted the work at the Institute. Thus, it was natural for the Bureau to turn to it when Howard seemed to admit that he could not solve the problems of the proposed microfilm Comparator. But, Eastman would not meet the Bureau's expectations.

With help from John Howard's men, Eastman was able to ship the first version of what became known as the Index of Coincidence Machine before 1943.[4] But, it bore little resemblance to the functionally sophisticated engine Bush had originally promised the navy. The IC Machine was a relatively simple plate-based device that looked more like the early 1930s astronomers' instruments than Bush's Comparator.[5] The IC Machine did its job, but it was not automatic and it was certainly not one that was leading, as were the Bush designs, to the use of more complex digital circuits.

The desk top IC Machine followed some of the ideas of Bush's earlier plans: It was optical; it was based on microphotography; it was designed to help analysts compile the counts of coincidences needed for Index analysis; and, it helped to locate multiple-letter patterns. It used what Howard had mentioned in the November 1941 meeting with OP-20-G, the matrix of lights for the registration of data. But, it was neither a counting nor a tallying device. Designed for quick production, it was analog, not digital. It was a practical response designed to "get the job done" while OP-20-G fretted that Eastman might never solve the growing list of problems with the film machines.

In the IC Machine, two one by four inch messages plates were placed over a photocell. Each character on a plate was represented by a single dot in a column. To test for coincidences one plate was pushed by hand across and over the other. The machine had slide mechanisms to allow precise overlapping of the plates and allowed an analyst to identify their location in terms of offsets from the beginning of the text. Eastman was unable to fulfill Howard's promise of one thousand characters and could pack only six hundred characters worth of the tiny transparent micro-dots in each plate.[6]

The machine was electrical, not electronic. Eastman's team realized that a pulse-based system, even with the plates, would be too complex. Thus, an electric measuring system was built into the IC machine. As an analyst slid the plates over each other and if a significant number of the tiny dots were coincident the machine's photocell received enough light to trigger a signal. There was no counting, just a recognition that enough light had penetrated to the photocell. The analyst, who was able to specify the level of light required to trigger the coincidence warning, would then tally the overlapped dots or find their locations in a message.[7]

Eastman did attempt to go further. In early 1942 it took on the challenge of creating a microfilm comparator, but it soon turned away from trying to conquer the problem of combining microfilm and counting. Its Tessie machine was another pragmatic compromise driven by the immediate cryptanalytic needs of the first years of the war. In order to deliver something of value in what was hoped was a reasonable time, Tessie was designed as a special purpose device. Its job was to locate specific four character code groups (tetragraphs), not to count them.[8] Tessie's logic and architecture were more like those of a very simplified Selector than a Comparator. It used two 35 millimeter films. One sped past an optical reading station while the other remained stationary and acted as an identification mask. After the fast film made a complete revolution, the mask film was stepped one frame. If a desired tetragaph was located a signal was emitted. There was no ability to reproduce the tagged item as in Bush's Selector and there was no ability to tally as in the Comparator. Those features asked too much--even of Eastman's experts.

Tessie was different from the Comparator in a more fundamental way. Eastman feared that Bush's dot system would not work because of many weaknesses, including the deformation of films.[9] One of the reasons it took almost two years to deliver Tessie was the search for an alternative. Tessie's codes were implanted by passing the film in front of a bank of lights which produced, for each code letter, a unique degree of opaqueness. Each teletype baudot combination yielded a different "gray scale" rather than a transparent dot. When the two films were placed in the machine and were passed over each other, the optical readers looked for the amount of light released, not just coincident dots. That called for a very sophisticated reading system. Tessie was useful but it remained an analog retrogression.[10] And, despite the turn to the simpler architecture, Tessie was temperamental. It had to be sent back to Eastman for a major overhaul, then, after its return, the Washington crew had to rebuild it yet again.[11]

A Machine for Mrs. Driscoll's Special Problem

Eastman designed and built another of the very few (probably three and no more than four) types of microfilm machines used by OP-20-G during the war. The Hypo assignment came in a rush, but like Tessie, it took almost two years to complete. The name Hypo came from the "Hypothetical Machine" proposal drawn up in response to the requests of Mrs. Driscoll's Enigma group.[12] Hypo's task was to help Driscoll's small team make a traditional attack on the German device. Hypo was the first machine designed especially for the American's work on the "E" machine. In early 1942, the United States had hopes of cracking the Enigma in the same way it had broken earlier Japanese cipher machines, through methods that included statistical analysis and the use of overlay sheets which revealed the combinations and settings of enciphering wheels.[13]

Like Tessie, many of Hypo's technical details have been forgotten[14] and its exact cryptanalytic functions remain classified, but a few things are known. It was a microfilm machine and it was based on the dot system of coding and the light bank data entry system.[15] Hypo used two 35 millimeter microfilm tapes that had been prepared by passing them in front of a bank of three hundred and twenty-five tiny lights. Data cards or tapes signalled which one of the lights in each column would be lit. The men working on Hypo also conquered some of the problems of the stepping mechanisms. Once the data films were placed on the machine, one acted as a master with the other flashing by it. As in Tessie, when the second film completed a revolution, the first was stepped one increment. The desired coincidence was simply identified by enough light reaching a photocell. As important, as in Tessie, Hypo's photocells monitored a zone rather than an individual column.

Hypo was an analog machine designed to locate. It was not coaxed to tally until the end of the war. Even then, it remained a very simple device. Despite that, Hypo proved as or more useful than Tessie though neither machine solved any systems by themselves. Copies of Hypo were supplied to the army's cryptanalysts and a second and more complex version was constructed for OP-20-G later in the war. By early 1945, Hypo was also being used against Japanese systems after it had undergone some significant modifications.[16] But the first Hypo was not in operation until the end of 1943.

The delay made Meader and Wenger fear that Eastman would be unable to produce any device except the crude analog plate IC Machine. In those critical months of 1942 and 1943 they also feared that IBM would not deliver its promised data conversion machines. In addition, there were signs that the next model of the Bush Comparator was in serious trouble.

A Paper War, Perhaps

At the beginning of the war, OP-20-G was hedging all its technological bets. Although Howard had advised against a paper tape machine, the navy ordered him to drop his exploration of microfilm and draw up the essentials of an upgraded paper tape Bush Comparator. Howard helped draft a sketch of a slightly revised version of the old Comparator and sent it to the Bureau's contractors, NCR and Gray Electric.[17] NCR and Gray set out with a great deal of enthusiasm and the navy looked forward to a third version of the Comparator in a few months. Using the older 70 millimeter paper tape but with room for thirty-two rather than twenty-six characters, the new Comparator tallied and it employed parallelism. It was able to handle up to five pattern tests at once. Its circuits and plugboards were more complex than the earlier model and it was given an important new capability. It could locate. One tape could be held stationary while the other sped past it. The stationary tape then moved one increment for another pass of the second tape, stopping when a match was sensed.[18] As many as twenty of the new paper tape Comparators may have been constructed between 1943 and 1945.[19] Some were even made for the army. Of importance for the postwar history of the Rapid Selector, they became the basis for the navy's patent claims over optical-electronic devices.[20]

The World War II paper tape Comparator proved an essential tool for the jobs that needed tallying but, unfortunately, the new machines could not be convinced to run appreciably faster than the 1938 Comparator. Although they were more elegant and much more reliable because of their relatively slow speed they could not be used for all the cryptanalytic tasks Bush had planned for his original machine. As disappointing, like the other machines under the Bureau's early 1942 contracts, they had a very rocky development history. Howard and Meader found it difficult to coordinate the work of the two contractors. As a result, each component had its special problems, especially Bush's old nemesis, the punch. MIT had agreed to design a new technically bold one, but few men were left at the Institute to ensure its completion. Other technical and organizational problems stalled the work on the NCR and Gray components and, by late 1942, the Comparator seemed destined to fail again. There was too much for Meader and Howard to keep under control.

The Comparator Dies, Again?

John Howard spent the first months of 1942 travelling from place to place with Ralph Meader trying to force progress on the Eastman and NCR-Gray machines. John Coombs worked in Rochester with the Eastman engineers then moved on to NCR. Finding that the role of a coordinator was taking all of his time, Howard dismantled his secret MIT workshop in early summer and permanently left the Institute to work at the contractor's plants. Apparently, the responsibility for completing the punch was left to MIT's machinist.[21]

Meader and Wenger sensed that something was wrong with the Gray-NCR-MIT effort as early as mid-1942. They were proven correct as the project dragged on into late summer 1943. Then, to their embarrassment, when all the components were finally delivered to Washington, they did not fit together. The navy engineers had to spend a great deal of valuable time reworking the comparing and counter-printer units. That further delayed putting the machines into use. The new Comparator did not go into operation until September 1943.[22] The organization of the work had much to do with the problems, but underlying all of the difficulties were stubborn technologies. They made it impossible for the nation's best engineers to fulfill Bush's promises.

Even when "G" was given an independent group that had more time to work on the optical-electronic machines, its men had to pull back from Bush's overly ambitious designs. The machines built between late 1943 and the end of the war had to be retreats from Bush's visions for microfilm Selectors and Comparators. ICKY and the Copperheads, for example, had to be compromises between an engineer's pride and cryptanalytic needs.

You Can Use Some of the Technology Some of the Time, But

In operation by late 1943, ICKY had a strange birth. As OP-20-G waited for results from the contractors some of its engineers in Washington decided to give Bush's microfilm system another chance. ICKY began as a simple machine to test whether Bush's high density dot coded scheme could be coaxed into working. Then, it evolved into a multi-purpose machine useful against the Japanese navy's codes. As its name implies, it was related to the photoplate IC machine, but it was an attempt to return to the use of microfilm to automate locating groups. Like Eastman's machines, it simply located, it did not reproduce or count. It had no cameras and it had no counter-printer. When enough light was registered, the machine lit a signal lamp and its operator used a hand crank to turn the films back to the identified coincidence. At that point, another lamp was lit and the operator used a screen to read the location marks printed on the margins of the films.

From its beginnings as a bench model, ICKY evolved into a chest high box as wide as a refrigerator. On its top was a screen to view the located messages. Next to the screen were the reels and rollers for two 35mm microfilms. Underneath were the mechanisms that sped one of the films past the other and the ratchets that stepped the index film after each pass of the fast tape. ICKY's optical sensing gate was designed to allow the location of message patterns of up to thirty columns of data. Typically, a bright light was pointed through masks and lenses that segregated the light into thirty parallel columns. If light penetrated the two films, it was directed to thirty small mirrors which then sent the light beam to its photocell. The light management portion of the machine was complex and demanded perfect alignments. It was the demands of the photocell system that led to ICKY's having only forty columns of data per inch of film, a density far less than Bush had promised the navy.

ICKY was not a digital machine. Like OP-20-G's other World War II microfilm devices, it wandered back to the use of analog circuits. But, in some important ways, ICKY did go beyond Bush's 1938 Selector. It had a plugboard and resistor matrix system that allowed the selection of different combinations. Polygraphs of long lengths, or patterns of identical subgroups, or single letter coincidences could be identified.

ICKY had another feature that went beyond the original Selector. Its coding system could be changed and its circuits switched so that it responded to the absence of light rather than its presence.[23] The navy's men found the blackout method much more efficient when the job was to search for coincident areas (such as code groups) rather than single columns of data. With its use, they could pack more than one letter in a column. They could register a five letter or number message group. In the blackout system the two tapes were reciprocally coded so that a matched column would admit no light. A two of five character code allowed the use of that reciprocal scheme, but ICKY's scanner could also accommodate to Bush's older one of twenty-six pattern.[24]

Almost Another Digital Machine

The other major attempt by the navy's team to fulfill Bush's promises was the Copperhead series.[25] The Copperhead's were designed and built under Lawrence Steinhardt's direction at National Cash Register and at "M's" Washington engineering laboratory. Unfortunately, many of the more ambitious plans for the Copperheads had to be put aside because of technical problems and cryptologic emergencies.

In 1943, the Atlantic crisis eased somewhat giving "M" a bit of time to turn to Japanese problems. Lawrence Steinhardt was assigned the job of designing Rapid machines to attack additive systems. Additive systems were codes with random numbers added or subtracted from the underlying numeric codes. Among many others, the major Japanese naval codes used additives.

Discovering the additives was a tedious process calling on many different methods of attack. IBM equipment had been modified to speed their identification but the process remained very slow and seemed in need of Rapid Machines. Still excited about optical-electronics, Steinhardt prepared the outlines for at least five different devices for the Copperhead problems. Each design was more complex than the previous one as he varied his basic ideas in order to make the Copperheads handle increasingly difficult procedures. By the time he was through, he had sketched a third and very advanced generation of Bush punch tape Comparators. In his plans, the more complex models were to be able to add and subtract and to test statistical weights at electronic speeds.

Steinhardt was aware of the problems at Eastman and at the outset of his project he decided that the older punch tape approach would be best. But, he needed to improve the punch systems. Greater data density and higher speed were essential. Steinhardt's men had enough lead time to search for alternatives to the temperamental Eastman 70mm film-backing paper tape. They also had some time to explore the design of a new punch. More than a year was spent searching for a new tape and designing a revolutionary punch. After testing many materials, including aluminum foil, a 70mm opaque polystyrene tape was selected. It had the stability needed for very high-speed transport past the scanning station and did not distort because of changes in humidity. Of great importance, it could accommodate a data density about twice that of the Comparator's paper tapes.

The Copperhead punch was a major engineering feat. Its main cabinet was over six feet tall and was wider than a phone booth. It was packed with delicate mechanical and electronic parts that perfectly aligned two tapes and then punched a reciprocal code. Each column on the tape had room for twenty-five tiny dots for message characters and several others for identification of the message. The punch was designed around the blackout system. Learning from earlier microfilm explorations that the absence of light was easier to monitor than its presence, one tape was punched to be the complement of the two of five code on the other. The designers were so pleased with the Copperhead's punch they built modified versions of it for the older Gray-NCR Comparators.

The scanner on the Copperhead was also an advance on the original Comparator. But the improvements came at the price of complexity and size. The Copperhead's scanner-transport frame was as large as the 1990's rental trailers used for weekend furniture moving and it had many, many complex components. However, the tape transport was a major achievement. Its fast tape raced at almost ten miles an hour. That speed was achieved by abandoning Bush's old loop design in which two endless tapes were driven in a circle. Copperhead I used two sets of sophisticated motor driven reels. It had a sensor system to manage the end of tape condition and the mechanical components to automatically rewind and step the tapes.

Also, the machine was a landmark in optical sensing. It was built to scan one hundred message columns at a time! Steinhardt's men were able to link one hundred lucite light guides to one hundred photocells and amplifiers to sense coincidences. Some of the Copperhead designs included complex electronic circuits. Even Copperhead I's electronics were very sophisticated. Although the Copperheads were designed to use the blackout system, Steinhardt hoped to incorporate advanced forms of digital circuits to test and/or conditions and to perform calculations. However, his electronic dreams could not be achieved.

As with ICKY, the Copperhead team had to take some significant backwards steps to produce a machine to meet the war crises. The existing documents indicate that only one version of the Copperheads was built and it was unable to count. It, too, simply located message groups. As many as five of the Copperhead I machines were constructed and in operation by the opening of 1945. But they were very limited punch tape versions of the IC Machine and ICKY. Some work was done on Copperheads II and V but they were abandoned because it proved too difficult to incorporate the additional electronics needed for calculation.[26]

Like other of "G's" locators, in Copperhead I, one tape acted as a mask. The other sped by it while the scanner sought two adjacent columns that were identical. The mask tape was "indexed" after the loop tape completed a pass. The one hundred phototubes were wired with Rossi circuits to signal a match when any two adjacent tubes sensed a blackout. That signal stopped the machine. The operator then rewound the fast tape with a crank until the signal light announced the match. Looking through a periscope, he read the identification numbers of the message and the match's position. He could then glance at a row of one hundred lights at the top of the machine and identify which two of the one hundred columns in the scanning gate were coincident. When it worked properly, the machine was fast. The twenty column per inch memory and high tape speeds did yield more than two hundred thousand tests a minute. But the potentials of the machine were not realized. It just looked and stopped, that was all. Digital electronics was an overkill and it asked too much of the engineers. Mechanical parts also got even with OP-20-G for waiting too long to begin the Rapid Machines program.

The Punch, Again

Like Bush in the 1930s, Steinhardt made a poor technological bet: that mechanics would be the least of his problems. The very expensive and complex Copperhead punches proved slow and unreliable. At best, they could punch only forty average length messages an hour. That meant several hours to complete a tape. Worse, they had to be reworked several times before being sent to Washington. Then, they broke down so frequently that they had to be returned to NCR for a complete overhaul.

The Old Technologies Are the Best Technologies, for a Time

In the spring of 1942, the Copperheads were not yet well-formed ideas and all other Rapid Machines were in trouble. Wenger must have feared that his goal of automating cryptanalysis would be defeated by the combination of more than stubborn technological problems and the impossibility of forcing the Bureau's contractors to pay enough attention to OP-20-G's projects. Even the refurbished 1938 Comparator, the only working Rapid machine, was not proving its worth. Lawrence Steinhardt had to strip it of many of its original functions to make it reliable enough for use in mid-1942. The Selector also had to endure some insults because of the absence of other Rapid Machines.

The critical need for machines and the necessity of showing some evidence that the Rapid program would work led to the death of Bush's Selector. In August 1942, it was taken out of its Cambridge warehouse and shipped to Washington. Steinhardt pulled off many of its components and turned it into an emergency version of a locator for code and cipher patterns. Its camera system was probably disengaged and it was asked only to stop when a pattern on its moving film matched that of the selection mask. Worse for the Selector's self-respect, once the crisis was over, the remnants of the Selector were put into storage in Washington and seen only when parts were taken off to rescue other devices.[27]

The failure of the Bureau's contractors to produce machines had a broader impact. Wenger and Meader became disenchanted with the relationships with NCR, Gray, and Eastman by mid-1942 and sought some alternative to the Bureau's way of conducting highly secret work. But there seemed no possibility of breaking free of the Bureau. As frustrating, while Wenger worried about the absence of functioning

Rapid Machines, those who had advocated the development of older technologies seemed to be vindicated. The old timers, not Engstrom's group, were in charge of tabulator development and in 1942 they were the ones delivering cryptanalytic results.

IBM sent all the tabulators and sorters and collators OP-20-G could make room for and the company began to create a host of very powerful additions for its machines. After "G" moved to its new quarters at an elegant girl's school on Nebraska Avenue and had adequate space, OP-20-G became one of the world's largest users of IBM equipment. "G's" IBM machines were counted in the hundreds and they used millions of punch cards a week.[28]

Acquiring standard IBM machines was relatively easy. They were stock items and OP-20-G already had high priority status. But gaining IBM's commitment to customize its machines (or to allow OP-20-G to do so) proved more difficult. Joseph Wenger had to make a personal visit to Tom Watson to convince him to give OP-20-G's requests the special attention they needed. The visit was effective although it took some time for "G" and IBM to devise the ways to allow secret development work to be done at the IBM plants. However, by the end of the war, IBM and the armed service's engineers, many who were drafted from IBM, had created modifications that allowed the electromechanical machines to perform all the cryptanalytic functions. Because of those modifications, IBM's equipment remained the foundation of OP-20-G's operations throughout the war.

But it was not easy for OP-20-G to become an advanced IBM center. Although it had been one of the first cryptologic agencies to employ tabulator equipment, it had been too financially starved during the 1930s to continue to be at the cutting edge of electromechanical technology. It may even lagged somewhat behind the German codebreakers.[29] At the onset of the war, "G" did not have any of the IBM multiplying units which might have encouraged the use of more sophisticated mathematical analysis. Because of budget problems, "G" even had to wait several years to rent one of the machines IBM had developed for the Social Security System, the collator. The collator was a high-speed electromechanical machine that automatically merged two decks of cards, thus eliminating hours of dreadful sorting on the older devices. Along with other IBM machines, it could be used to produce the message offset cards needed for one of the most labor intensive code and cipher breaking methods, the Index. The Index was the central tabulator method for IC analysis because it avoided the near impossible counting demanded by regular IC analysis.[30]

The Index was used to identify messages sent with the same encryption machine setups or the same hand algorithm. It was then used to discover the particular settings. With the messages punched onto a series of cards, each one representing one letter of a message and containing an offset string of text, the cards were sorted on four or five letters to place the them in alphabetical order. The ordered decks were then run through the tabulators. As each major and minor letter of the significant portion of the code groups changed, the Class Selector ordered the printing of the number of previous repetitions of two or more letters. In addition to the running subtotals, the totals for each major letter group were printed.[31]

With the printed Index before him, an analyst would observe the number of repetitions of identical letter groups (polygraphs) and evaluate whether the number of repetitions suggested the messages were all produced by the same system and settings. He would then analyze the spacing between repetitions for factors. They gave an insight into the length of the encrypting cycle. With knowledge of those periods, additional card runs and statistical analysis might lead to the identification of the encryption system's internal workings and the settings for the group of analyzed messages.

Fortunately, during the 1930s, the cryptanalysts had been able to rent some enhancements that made the tabs and sorters better Index machines. Class Selectors sensed the end of a series in a sorted deck of cards and ordered the printing of subtotals. This reduced the time needed for tabulator-based Index analysis. There were several other helpful devices on the IBM machines at the beginning of the war. One suppressed arithmetic carrys and allowed the use of modular arithmetic. That was vital to the analysis of additive code systems. The task of identifying the numbers added or subtracted to code groups remained heroic, however. Hundreds of messages from the same systems had to be sorted on their starting point indicators. Then, all the letters in the message had to be offset. After the time consuming sorting and realignments thousands of subtractions (or additions) were needed to reduce the code groups to their original numbers.[32]

Other attachments were put on the tabulators during the late 1930s. Additions to the keypunches and card reproducers were used to identify a change in a number series on the punch cards. Attachments selected desired cards in a deck and allowed particular code groups to be located. Similar mechanical additions altered the machines so they selected only specific cards or columns for additions and subtractions. Highly useful were the multi-column sorting attachments.[33]

Those special attachments did not mean that OP-20-G had the most advanced IBM equipment during the 1930s or that it could afford all that it desired. Its attachments were standard IBM parts or ones slightly modified by the engineers at the Navy Yard. In late 1941, "G's" total IBM annual machine budget was less than one-third of what it had cost the navy for Bush's failed Comparator. It was not until the attack on Pearl Harbor that Safford thought that his previous requests for a vast expansion of the tabulator program would be funded and that the navy could buy machines as sophisticated as those Tom Watson had given to the Columbia University calculating center.[34]

With the outbreak of war, the tabulator group at "G" was able to expand and to convince IBM to produce specialized equipment. The old disagreements with the company were put aside and IBM and the navy began a cooperative effort that lasted throughout the war.[35] A flood of IBM men went to Washington and a host of new attachments were developed. Some provided more efficient additive stripping. New devices allowed more effective multiple key sorting and the offset and comparison of messages for IC analysis. The location of code words was made faster by other additions to the tabulators, sorters and punches.

Although IBM played an important role in OP-20-G's war it was not asked to take a significant part in the Rapid Machine program.[36] IBM, rather than the Howard-NDRC group, might well have provided the RAM leadership and expertise. But the separation of the tab and RAM programs during the 1930s and Wenger's ties to MIT led to IBM's exclusion--although it had more electronics researchers than NCR. OP-20-G decided that IBM's role in electronics would be confined to having some of its leading men, such as Ralph Palmer, Robert Blakely, and John Skinner, work with Engstrom's "M" group.[37]

One reason for not calling on IBM was that OP-20-G was already asking a great deal of the company. In 1942, the requests by the tab group at "G" for electromechanical and relay devices were enough to keep the company's best men busy. The OP-20-G-Yard crew did not demand the creation of an all-purpose tabulator or a general purpose relay computer, but they asked for some challenging engineering advances. The requests indicate the old timers had long had their own alternatives to Bush's mid-1930s Rapid Machine proposals. Among the more ambitious early proposals for IBM equipment were the NC machines. Unfortunately, much of the documentation for the devices seems to have been lost. But what remains suggests that OP-20-G helped IBM on the road to building its larger wartime relay computers for such agencies as the Aberdeen Proving Grounds.

In addition to the special electromechanical attachments for OP-20-G's tabulators, IBM created ambitious relay additions. They allowed OP-20-G's tabulators to perform more of the functions Bush had tried to build into his machines. The new IBM devices were better able to identify and tally particular code groups and to search for repetitions of character patterns. It is known that the army, beginning in 1942, helped to create a series of modified tabulators that extended the idea of testing a "dictionary" of code words against messages and to flag the location of matches. The navy probably had its own versions of those Slide-Run machines. Their banks of relays, which were used to store high frequency code words, served the same purpose as the mask tapes on the RAM locator machines.[38]

By 1945, the electromechanical advances made "G's" tabulator equipment look much like what IBM announced as breakthroughs for general information processing in the 1950s. There is no proof that the famous early information scientist H. P. Luhn worked on "G's" problems, but the parallels between the World War II machines and his modifications of the tabulators and sorters are striking. OP-20-G used tabulators and sorters with multiple reading heads, a feature that made Luhn's machines attractive to the information scientists of the 1950s. Like Luhn and other early information scientists, the cryptanalysts had blackout coding systems, they read cards edgewise and they used banks of relays to identify particular words. Although optical readers were not employed in OP-20-G's tabulators and sorters, other of its devices used hardware made famous in Luhn's special scanner. His methods also paralleled those of the cryptanalysts. OP-20-G's men, for example, used versions of what Luhn later called KWIC indexing.[39]

IBM's Most Special Contribution

During 1941 and early 1942, before Engstrom's group gained real power over machine development, and as the Eastman and Gray-NCR projects were faltering, IBM and the tabulator men at "G" developed another innovative system, the Letterwriters. Those devices brought OP-20-G's data handling into the modern era because they linked teletype, tape, card, and film media together. From unpretentious beginnings as data input equipment, the IBM Letterwriters blossomed into a number of increasingly complex machines that were used for a wide range of analytical tasks. The Letterwriter system tied special electric typewriters to automatic tape and card punches and eventually to film processing machines. Such automation of data processing was badly needed at OP-20-G. Without automation, it would have been unable to receive and process its wartime load of a million words a day. In 1941, its system was unable to handle a few thousand words.

Before the war the radio intercept personnel wrote out the messages on forms then forwarded them by mail or keyed them as telegrams. Because OP-20-G had just begun to develop teletype and radio networks, it took weeks to send all but the most vital messages from the Pacific.[40] There were more bottlenecks than long distance mail. Intercepted messages had to be recoded then decoded before analysis could be performed. And the navy's 1930s feeble modernization created an unforeseen problem. As the navy automated its communications systems, more and more information was sent by automatic non-morse radioteletype or automatic encryption machines. The increasing sophistication of the teletype and radio systems would have been wasted if there were not similar advances in data processing. In 1940, for example, OP-20-G was receiving several hundred Japanese intercepts a month, but the incoming messages were not in a useful card, worksheet or even standard teletype format. There was no sign "G" would be given the manpower needed to turn those intercepts into data ready for automated analysis.[41] New machinery was the only answer.

The timing is not entirely clear, but sometime in late 1940 the Bureau of Engineering put the suggestions from the tabulator crew and the Yard's men together and approached IBM. Within a year or so the first Letterwriter devices were delivered to the cryptanalysts. The timely appearance of the first machines was a result of IBM's earlier commercial efforts[42] at its Electromatic division. What IBM and the Bureau developed was not as technically radical as some of the NC devices but the Letterwriters were extremely important.[43]

The system centered about a special electric typewriter, a tape punch, and a tape reader. The typewriter was a modified version of IBM's expensive Electromatic machine. The tape punch and tape reader were bread box size metal frames filled with relays and sensing pins. The relays controlled reading and punching and were used to convert the teletype code to the signals needed by OP-20-G's other machines. Linked together, the punch, reader, and typewriter covered the top of a large desk. It was hoped they would eventually allow the creation of machine-ready data directly from "G's" new international telegraph system.

The Letterwriters were not intended to be analysis machines but, to fill the gap left by the delayed RAM program, the engineers in Washington turned the Writers into much more than data entry devices. By adding simple plugboards they were made to produce worksheets for the cryptanalysts and to change one code into another.[44] Vital were the components that changed the Letterwriter tapes to the formats needed by the tabulators and, later, the optical machines developed by Eastman and Steinhardt. More importantly, by 1942 the Letterwriters were evolving into machines for analysis. First, the typewriters were modified to allow the printing of even more sophisticated worksheets. The next steps were more ambitious. Plugboxes were added which allowed complex substitutions of one character for another. This helped determine the settings of the letter-changing plugboards on encryption machines. In addition to being useful for the analysis of steckering, the modified Letterwriters helped to strip cipher wheel patterns from messages.

Simple changes made the Letterwriter equipment useful for another very important but time consuming task, the analysis of wheel settings. When an analyst thought he had found the correct combinations on an enemy system he would set a copy of the encryption machine's wheels, lugs and plugboards and type in parts of the encrypted message. He then examined the output to see if it was sensible. By coupling a Letterwriter tape reader to one of the American copies of a foreign cipher machine, an analyst would not have to repeatedly enter a message through the machine's keyboard. The use of the Writer's tape saved hours of effort and frustration because the analyst could adjust the machine settings then just signal a rerun of the message tape.

Despite their usefulness and reliability, there was a drawback to the Letterwriters. They were not rapid machines. Because of the limits set by the mechanical nature of the typewriters and the punches, the system ran at eight characters per second or only 480 characters per minute. That was far, far slower than the Bush machines or the tabs. In addition, the Letterwriters did not come into full operation until 1943. And, there were recurring production difficulties. At one time they seemed so grave that Wenger and Engstrom claimed IBM was dragging its feet. They were angered by the company's refusal to set up a separate and top secret production line. But, compared to the progress on the Eastman and Gray-NCR Rapid machines, IBM's work on the Letterwriters now seems a miracle of wartime production.[45]

In the Absence of Rapid Machines

The delays in the delivery of the Rapid Machines led to another use for the Letterwriters. The Yard's men decided to build more far reaching extensions of them. The first of their 1942 creations was a frequency counter. Aptly titled, The Simple Frequency Counter, it was among the first of the new machines to be delivered to OP-20-G. It was running in May 1942 and it became a logical model for a series of similar machines manufactured during and after World War II. For example, the late 1940s Alcatraz was a room-sized version of the original desk top Counter.[46]

The 1942 Counter was an example of the value of technological retrogression. It was a machine that could have been built by any competent engineer during the 1920s and one wonders why the Yard did not make one for OP-20-G before the war. The Counter's architecture was lean. However, the Simple Counter and its descendants had a power Bush's machines did not possess: They were able to recognize and record individual letters. They could tell an A from a B. The recognition, counting and recording of particular letters and polygraphs demand too many complex electronic circuits and parts for computer technology of the early 1940s.

The mechanical Simple Counter was primitive but effective and reliable. It combined the stock Letterwriter tape punch and readers with two banks of commercially produced mechanical counters. The counters had displays quite like that of an automobile milage meter. Their purpose was to tally the frequency of up to thirty-two different letters or numbers. As the tape reader scanned the message tape it incremented the counter for the total number of characters and each particular character. At the end of the run, the operator viewed the set of counters (each was marked with its letter), wrote each result on a prepared form, then cleared the counters by turning a hand crank. Later, to save time, the bank of counters was photographed.

The Counter saved preparing IBM card decks and the many steps involved in repeated sorting. It was such an effective design that in 1943 a grand extension of the Counter was constructed at NCR. The NCR machine, Mike, tallied digraphs. Mike was a huge electro-mechanical contraption. Its bank of counters filled a wall but it took less space and power than an electronic version would have required. Mike was of great value in the struggle against the Axis codes, but it had its limitations. It was slow, at least in comparison to the possibilities of electronics.[47]

Despite the low speed of such devices as Mike, the inability to deliver any Rapid Machines led the Yard's men to create yet another type of relay-electromechanical analyser. In 1942, trying to fill the void caused by the delays in the Bush, Eastman and IBM projects, they designed a machine to perform additive stripping. That task took hours on the standard tabulating equipment. The first versions of Mathew were probably under construction by mid-1942. Like the Counter, the Mathews proved reliable and were used throughout the war. Mathew was so rugged that it was applied to more than traditional stripping.[48] It was used on such jobs as removing the influence of a cipher wheel from an encrypted message. If one considers the letters on rotors or stepping switches as numbers, the rules and methods for arithmetic may be used for an attack on cipher systems. The desk size Mathews automated the tiresome but valuable use of false addition and subtraction to pull out the influence of a wheel.

Its two Letterwriter tape readers were run in synchronization. One reader's tape contained a message while the other held the additive list. In the early version of Mathew, the readers were connected through relays to a permanently wired plugboard. The plugboard combined the two incoming numbers to the create the falsely added result. When the machine was in addition mode, if a two and a one, for example, were sensed by the contact pins, the plugboard sent out a three. If the subtraction switch was thrown, a two and one would yield a one. The results of the transit of the signals through the plugboard were sent to a Letterwriter punch and typewriter. The output tape aided further analyses and the printout was used as a worksheet.

The engineers made the Mathews more powerful. A twenty-six by twenty-six plugboard was added; the offsetting of message and additive tapes was made fully automatic; and, adjustments to the machine made it easy to produce special worksheets. Most importantly, near the end of the war, the fixed plugboards were replaced with a relay bank that allowed an analyst to quickly change the patterns of the false additions and subtractions. A one and a three could be made to produce a nine if desired. Over the years, the many Mathews (at least four were constructed) proved useful against a majority of the encryption systems attacked by OP-20-G. Mathew was not a general purpose machine, however, and its technology dated from the 1920s. Its processing power was limited by the speed of its tape readers and its typewriter. But, it was able to perform faster than the tabulators and to fulfill functions too complex for the electronic Rapid Machines of the era.

OP-20-G took another very effective but even greater backward technological step to deal with additive problems. It was probably recommended by the Yard engineers. A very complex special superencipherment "additive" desk calculator was manufactured for the navy by NCR. The Fruit machines seemed to have been planned very early, perhaps in late 1941. They were quite innovative but they were based on 1920s electric machine technology and they could only add and subtract. At their top was a row of some twenty windows, each holding a code group. Fruit's keyboard had five columns of numbers, each with keys for 1 through 9; buttons to reference the code group windows; and, special control keys. When the additives were entered in the keyboard and the window pointers and action keys were pressed, the additive was falsely added or subtracted from the target code group. The windows displayed the results. Some of the old timers did not think much of the machines, but later in the war they proved quite valuable and many copies were sent to the British forces.[49]

The engineers at the Navy Yard were making other contributions by recombining old technologies. During 1942 and 1943 they were building more copies of enemy encryption machines, such as Purple and Enigma. Constructed of cipher wheels or relay systems, the copies proved invaluable to the operating cryptanalysts. They allowed a rapid testing of probable machine settings and quick translations of messages once the keys for a day were identified. The Yard's men contributed even more. They supervised the companies building America's own advanced ciphering machine, the ECM, and they had the responsibility for wiring the super secret cipher wheels for the navy's older machines.[50]

The Rapid Machines Are Saved by the U-boats

The success of the machines based on the older technologies and the lack of results from the Rapid Machine efforts might have led Wenger to abandon his cause. But, at a critical moment it was saved by the greatest cryptological emergency of World War II. If the Atlantic situation had not become so grave, Wenger would have had to accept the Bureau's mode of organizing research and production; the "M" section would have been confined to mathematical and scientific work; and, the contractors would have continued to find reasons why Rapid Machines could not be constructed. But the onset of Operation Drumbeat and Britain's cryptanalytic priorities forced the Americans to search for solutions to the Enigma problem, solutions that seemed to call for technological leaps greater than Bush had imagined.

To understand the history of Wenger's drive to establish an independent research and development group and its failure to achieve all that it might have, the traumas of the Ultra Secret in Britain and America have to be traced.

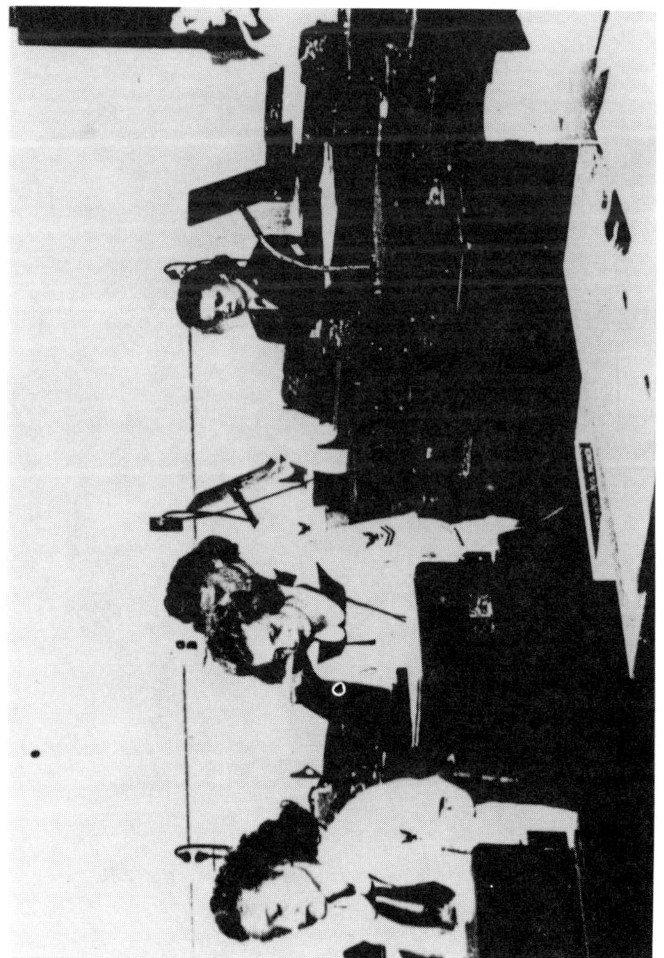

WAVES with Letterwriter Data Entry Equipment, circa 1944
(Naval Security Group Command)

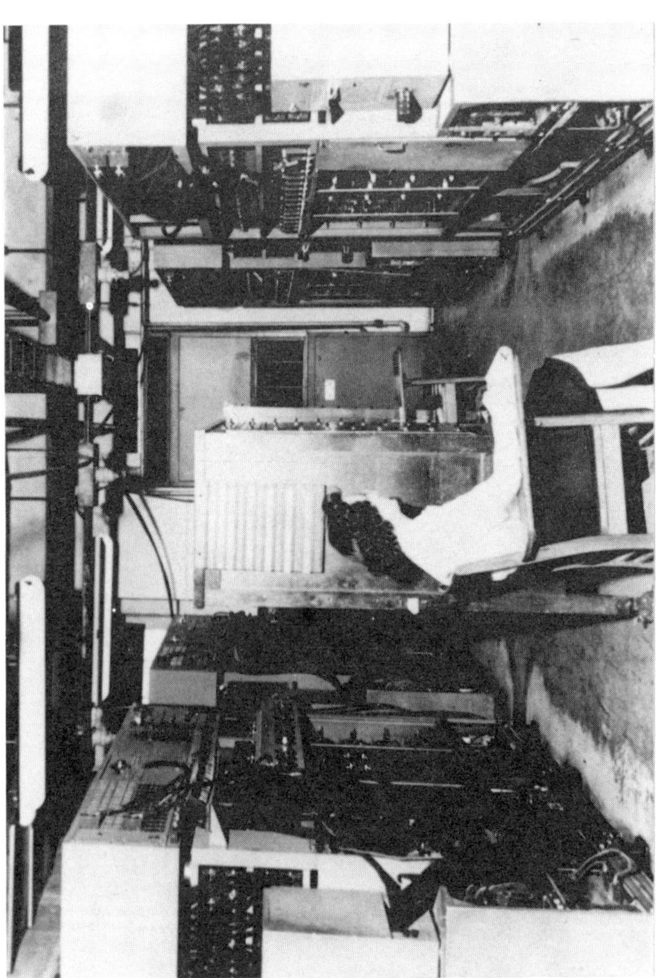

WAVE Tending Row of Bombes, circa 1944
(Naval Security Group Command)

Chapter XI
Back to Electromechanics: Ultra and the Bombe

Looking Ahead, Again: Ultra Saves RAM and OP-20-G Creates a Science Company

The history of Bush's machines would have been very different if Britain had the power to read the German U-boat messages during 1942. On the chance that its men could beat the British to a reentry into the U-boat Enigma, OP-20-G was granted its long sought Rapid Machine program and its own factory and workforce. But the establishment of what became known as the Naval Computing Machine Laboratory came at a price. Because the American navy had not attended to the Enigma and because Hooper and Wenger's pleas for machine development in the 1930s were not fully heeded, OP-20-G had to defer its attempts to create advanced electronic computers for pure cryptanalysis. To solve the "E" problem, the machine group spent most of its first year and one-half, and much of the next two years, coaxing electromechanical components into doing things never before expected of them. The conglomerations of electrical, mechanical and electronic parts called Bombes turned Engstrom's men away from solving the fundamental problems associated with Bush's designs and away from an exploration of the possibilities of a general purpose electronic machine.[1] At the same time, they had little chance to develop and apply mathematical methods. It was too easy to solve "E" through cribs and thefts and old timers' tricks. Until the very end of the war "M," which had evolved into the Technical Section, had to concentrate on practical methods and machines.

"M" held so much potential that Joseph Wenger could not let it die at the end of the war. He gave it a new life, as a private company. That new firm, Engineering Research Associates, became the navy's means to compensate for the failure of the Bush 1930's Comparator project, the hurried construction of the limited Rapid Machines of World War II and America's return to the prewar levels of funding for science and technology. ERA was expected to accomplish what had proven too difficult to do during the war, build working models of high-speed Selectors and full-fledged Comparators. Because the company was founded by the young MIT men who built the first Selector, Vannevar Bush became involved and used it as the means to give new life to his pet project. Bush chose ERA to save his idea for a machine to radically change the American library.

Engineering Research Associates was not exactly what navy reformers had sought for so long, a permanent link to the most advanced academic scientists and engineers. ERA was a twist on Hooper's and Bowen's early dreams because it was a small private business. Wenger thought that was necessary because of the special needs of OP-20-G. He rejected the idea of relying upon another new navy science organization, the Office of Naval Research, although it was a closer match to Hooper's old visions. It was an updated version of the navy office of scientific coordination and the World War II Office of Research and Inventions. It was staffed by navy scientists who were committed to research and its mandate was to continue the type of cooperation between the navy and academia that had been established under the NDRC/OSRD. Its attitude toward academics was one of respect and its job was to encourage research within the established universities and corporate centers. Because of that, even Vannevar Bush, who was fighting for a permanent peacetime version of the NDRC, could tolerate the ONR.

Wenger and Hooper approved of the ONR, but when they began to think of how to save the NCML they realized the ONR could not fulfill the needs of the highly secret OP-20-G. They wanted a select and experienced group that could design and manufacture classified equipment. The ONR was not meant for such work, and, at the end of the war, the established private contractors were severing their OP-20-G connections. Thus, Wenger and Hooper helped Engstrom's group of bright young men to establish themselves as a for-profit company. Wenger had a long list of projects for them because "G's" Rapid Machine group had been unable to achieve many of his goals during the war. Despite the millions of dollars put into development and all the technical progress between 1942 and 1945, OP-20-G remained without a machine suited to modern mathematical cryptanalysis. But, it did have more than a hundred of one of the most amazing machines every constructed, the American Bombe.

The "E" Machine

The Bombe was the example of the need for a technological retreat to deal with a cryptologic emergency. The reasons for the most significant American technical reversion dates to the early 1930s when Germany was rearming and when its closest neighbors feared it would soon take revenge on them. Unfortunately for America, it was one of the smallest of the European nations that attended to Germany's new secret communications system. Little Poland decided to take advantage of its ability to hear German military transmissions. When it did, it took on a formidable challenge. Despite Germany's destruction during World War I, and the crippling burdens imposed on it under the peace, it built a strong codemaking capability during the 1920s and 1930s. At the center was the Enigma encryption machine, the workhorse of its military communications networks. The Germans had done well when they selected the Enigma.[2] Although a more sophisticated machine based system, Fish, was used for the most important communications, and, while codes were used by many German organizations, the "E" machine was Germany's cryptologic treasure.[3] The Enigma was a typewriter size device that could be used in the field as well as in an office. It was electromechanical and used batteries to provide the electric current which passed through a series of shifting transposition rotors (commutators) to yield an extremely long encryption cycle. Physically, Enigma consisted of a keyboard to enter letters, a cascade of moving wheels that scrambled their inputs, a reversing wheel that sent the electrical impulses back through the wheels, a plugboard that further mixed the letters and a series of lamps which showed the final result of the encryption.

The reversing wheel was a very important feature of the Enigma. It received the pulse from the enciphering wheels, changed the letter again, then sent the current back through the first set of wheels on a new path. The use of the reversing wheel meant that no letter could be ciphered as itself and that encipherments were reciprocal; if an A had been changed to a Z, a Z would become an A. The reciprocal feature meant that one could easily decode an Enigma message if the receiving machine used the same wheels and settings as the sender's. If an A had been transposed into a Z, then entering a Z on the receiving device led to an A appearing on the bank of lights in the Enigma.[4] The reversing Uncle Walter wheel was not a pure blessing, however. It was one of the few Enigma weaknesses that codebreakers could exploit.

Despite the window provided by the reversing wheel, Enigma systems were tough. Because it was easy to alter the wheel orders and plugboard settings, each Enigma message could have a unique setup. There could not be a single solution to the Enigma and penetrating "E" was an ongoing battle. Each of the Enigma's transposing wheels had different wiring and some stepped in unique rhythms as letters were entered into the machine. The wheels could be placed in different slots in the Enigma; they could be set to begin their work at any of their twenty-six positions; and, they could have their outer rings moved to further hide the encryption cycle. The models in use during World War II had the additional feature of a plugboard between the wheel output and the lights. With that stecker, letters were transposed yet another time. For example, with the use of a double-ended wire, a B coming back out of the wheels would be changed by the plugboard to an E.

The Germans felt safe because they calculated that even if the wiring of the code wheels was known, it would take impossibly long for an enemy to identify the particular "key" settings of a message. In its early configuration, with just three of five available code wheels being used and no plugboard, Enigma had over one million possible settings.[5] When the plugboard was added to the military versions, the Germans felt even more confident. The possible combinations jumped into the range of two hundred million million million!

The Germans constantly changed the "E" to make it stronger. During Hitler's years, they enhanced the system by increasing the number of wheels to choose from. Each new wheel multiplied the possible combinations by several more millions. By the end of the war German codemen could choose from as many as nine main scrambling wheels when selecting a setup for their machines. More of a challenge was created in 1942. The Atlantic U-boat system added a fourth wheel inside its machines. That led some experts to estimate that hand methods of analysis would take some nine hundred million years to find one setting.[6] Later in the war, the Germans made the machine more robust when they changed the plugboard and attached the Uhr box. The Uhr added another level of complexity by eliminating some of the cryptologic weaknesses of the plugboards.

The Germans not only had good machines, they had sound operational procedures. Cipher machines have to be used by people and the best machines can be made useless by poor operational rules. The Germans realized this and did as much as they could to prevent human errors. Among other protective actions, the Germans divided their communications system into more and more networks, each with its own Enigma setups and procedures. As a result, Germany's enemies had to tackle not one but dozens of different systems each day. Also, the Germans frequently changed the books that informed all the members of a network which wheels and plugboard settings to use during a calendar period. The Germans were particularly sensitive to a weakness in all encryption systems, the vulnerability of internal indicators. They took many steps to hide them from their enemies. Indicators were the brief instructions in each transmission that told a recipient how to set the remaining components of his Enigma, the ones not specified in a network's instruction books. Unlike the keys specified for all users in a network, indicators were selected by operators and changed with each message. Unfortunately for the Germans, they found no way to prevent their enemies from using those indicators to penetrate some of the "E" networks. The indicators were what allowed Poland's cryptanalysts to enter the Enigma systems in the early 1930s.

Only a Few Were Able and Willing to Tackle "E"

Given the sophistication of the German systems, it hardly seems fair that Enigma had to be tackled by a new, small, and endangered nation. In the 1930s, Poland was an artificial creation of the peace of World War I. It had a very tenuous hold on its future because of ethnic conflicts and because Germany and the Soviet Union were waiting for any opportunity to reclaim chunks of what they asserted were their historic lands. Poland's leaders were especially fearful of Germany and its intentions. Knowing it would never be able to match the power of a modernized German army, they decided that intelligence gathering was a necessity. As a result, they spent a significant portion of their budgets on cryptanalysis. Poland created what Stanford Hooper yearned to have at OP-20-G, an office devoted to pure cryptanalysis. Its codebreaking bureau was able to recruit several bright young mathematicians who, as early as 1930, began to apply group theory and other advanced mathematical and statistical techniques to the German Enigma system. With the help of stolen documents provided by the

French, the Poles began to understand and then penetrate the Enigma. They were reading many German systems by the mid-1930s. By supplementing their mathematical analyses with the weaknesses of some of the operational uses of the Enigma, such as repeating the indicators for a message or picking keys in a nonrandom way, the Poles were able to avoid using brute force searches that tested every possible "E" setting. They even learned how to avoid using data heavy statistical analysis. A significant and fundamental discovery by the Poles was that the forbidding and seemingly impregnable plugboard was irrelevant in some cryptologic contexts. The discovery about the plugboard reduced the number of tests needed to identify an Enigma's setup by millions.

The Poles Automate Cryptanalysis in Their Special Way

The Polish group also called upon automation in the early 1930s. Much work and genius went into the invention of an electromechanical machine, the Cyclometer, which automatically generated all the patterns produced by various Enigma settings. The Cyclometer was not a statistical machine nor a device that could lead to a modern computer, however. It was an electromechanical rig that produced a card catalog so that analysts, in just a few minutes, could go from the indicators in a message to the Enigma setup. The Poles went further. To counter modifications to the "E" systems, they invented techniques using punched overlay sheets and a light source. It was much like the system later used by the British and American cryptanalysts and was similar to what postwar information scientists called the Peek-A-Boo system.[7] The most famous of the Poles' brilliant devices was too specialized to be transferred to peacetime work, however.

In 1938, to meet a change in the way the Enigma's settings were communicated, the Poles invented their version of an electromechanical automaton, the Bomba.[8] It was a means of compensating for the impossibility of applying pure cryptanalysis to the "E" problem. Rapidly designed and built by a Warsaw electrical company, the Bomba was a set of linked Enigma machines that tested for the letter cycles produced by the setting indicators in Enigma messages. The special purpose Bomba was based upon a negative logic and used a special "crib" composed of the message indicators. The Bomba's goal was to eliminate the wheel orders and wheel positions that could not have produced the letter-to-letter cycles in an indicator. The machine spun its six sets of three wheels much faster than an analyst could reset an

Enigma and it reduced the search time for loops from days to less than two hours. A Bomba sped through more 17,500 wheel combinations, pointing only to the "E" setups that might have produced the cycle being tested. The Bomba did not flag the one correct set of wheel positions, it just filtered out all those that could not possibly have produced the letter cycles. It thus created a list of what came to be called "false drops" all of which had to be examined with hand methods.

The Poles had constructed six of the Bombas, one for each possible wheel order. That was adequate when the Enigmas came with only three encryption wheels to choose from. But, just as the first Bombas were put into operation, the Poles had to face an increase in the number of Enigma wheels, then, an alteration in the use of the "E" plugboard. Those changes demanded ten times the number of Bomba for a timely search. The Poles were too exhausted to produce so many additional machines.[9]

Meanwhile, the rich and powerful nations, including Britain and France, paid little or no attention to "E." Britain did make some breaks into the very simple Enigma systems used during the Spanish Civil War. Its small cryptanalytic group also did some cursory investigation of other major Enigma systems but they were hampered by the difficulties of intercepting German army messages and by the silence of its navy during the years of peace. Thus, in 1939, Britain did not have command of Enigma. Nor could its most powerful ally, France, penetrate any "E" systems. As a consequence, when Poland lost its power over the Enigma the allies became blind. On the eve of World War II, it was clear that Poland had waited too long to ask for help from its friends.[10]

Keeping the Bomba Secret for Too Long

For some good reasons, Poland had kept its success and techniques to itself. One of the most important reasons why it did not share its cryptanalytic treasures with Britain and France before 1939 was the threat of a security leak. The Polish "E" solutions were weak. Despite the brilliance of its young mathematicians, all of Poland's methods were sensitive to slight changes in either the Enigma machines or the procedures for their use. Even the Poles had not been able to achieve what Hooper and Wenger had hoped for, a robust and practical pure statistical cryptanalysis. The Poles needed cribs, repeated indicator settings and mistakes by "E" operators. Critical to their Bombas' success were "E" plugboards that changed only a few letters. Thus, any German suspicion of foreign penetration could and did lead to a sudden blackout. Just the addition of a wheel could cause havoc.[11]

Only when the invasion of Poland seemed imminent and when the Warsaw team could not sustain its automation efforts, did the Poles start to pass their secrets to their friends.[12] It was not until late summer 1939, when the Poles had to have help in producing more of their vital overlay sheets and Bombas, that Britain and France were informed of how the Polish men had been able to read Enigma messages. They were given copies of the Enigmas the Poles had reverse engineered and were told of the many ways to identify the various German Enigma radio networks. In return, the British began making the overlay Jeffry Sheets for the Poles. Then they attempted to conquer the latest round of changes in the German systems, the ones that had suddenly made the Polish Bombas ineffective.[13] Then, on the eve of the invasion of Poland, the Germans made several more shattering changes in their Enigma systems which made Britain's task near impossible. After France was overrun, Britain was left with the responsibility for making a new beginning against the Enigma.[14]

A Fresh Start Against "E"

Britain had begun to look at "E" and to pay increased attention to Japanese systems by the mid-1930s, but its codebreakers were not given the resources to launch a major cryptanalytic campaign until the invasion of Poland. Then, to exploit both her own previous work and the gifts of the Poles, Britain expanded its Government Code and Cypher School (GC&CS) and established the now famous Bletchley Park. Teams of brilliant men and women were recruited from the universities to work on the various Axis systems. Alan Turing was only one of the Bletchley wonders who were recognized experts in mathematics and logic.[15] Under intense pressure, by 1940 he and others at GC&CS began to create the many invaluable techniques and electrical devices that eventually gave birth to the Ultra Secret. For example, the first Bletchley version of its Bombe was in operation in early 1940. The next important configuration, with the ingenious diagonal board for the critically needed simultaneous testing of plugboard settings, was running by August.[16] That Turing-Welchman

Bombe of 1940 was a cousin, but a very distant one, of the Polish Bomba.

In 1939, when Britain's men learned of the Polish Bomba method, they decided that it would be foolish to build any more of the Warsaw machines. Alan Turing correctly predicted that the Bomba would become useless with a slight change in Enigma procedures because the Polish method was tied to the German's habit of repeating the indicator within each message--something they soon changed. Although actively seeking pure methods to attack the Enigma, such as his overlay sheet Banburismus attack, Turing had to recommend the use of a dependent and near brute force approach that was something like the Polish system.[17] Given the technology available to him, no other method seemed feasible. Thus, while he explored the application of statistical methods to the "E" problem, he sketched out a new Bombe that used some of the ideas of the Polish Bomba--but, the British Bombe and its logic were special.

Turing's Bombe was an electromechanical analog of the Enigma. It was based on identifying logical contradictions as represented by flows of electricity: Its banks of interconnected high-speed "E" wheels spun until they found a setting that might have produced the crib set up on the machine. Like the Bomba, it needed to search through all the wheel settings and it accepted the consequences of relying upon a special purpose machine. And, Turing's Bombe needed a great deal of prior information about German networks and their keys. His Bombe was premised on knowing the wiring and turnover pattern of each "E" wheel and it needed insights into the plugboard and other settings of each Enigma net. Turing knew his Bombe could have been made as useless as the Polish machine if the Germans significantly increased the number of letters changed by the "E's" plugboard, if they stopped using stereotyped phrases at the beginning of their messages or if they ended the practice of sending "E" messages on simpler cipher systems. However, Britain's decision to allocate scarce men and resources to Turing's approach was quite rational. The British had little choice but to accept making the heavy investment in a new set of Bombes to attack the three wheel Enigmas.

Turing made that more palatable by making his machine as universal as possible. Although it followed the logic of pointing to the wheel settings that could not be eliminated, it tested the settings against letter loops from within relatively long plain text phrases (cribs) in messages.

Relying upon words within messages rather than indicators guaranteed a longer life to his Bombes and promised fewer false drops. In fact, his machine was designed to vastly reduce the number of the false leads produced by the Polish Bomba. The British Bombe was much more discriminating because of its long crib and its increased number of interlocked wheels. A bit of luck made the Bombe even stronger. Before Turing had finished his design for a machine to attack the three wheel Enigmas, a young mathematician appeared at Bletchley Park whose insight multiplied the Bombe's abilities. Gordon Welchman's suggestion for the diagonal board allowed an instantaneous test for the influence of the plugboard setting and allowed the effective use of relatively "weak" cribs, ones without long letter loops.[18] Bletchley Park was also lucky to find Britain's version of the practical Joe Desch.

Analog and Parallel May Be Fast, But

When GC&CS thought of how to turn Turing's logic into hardware, it realized that it did not have time to experiment. Although electronics was tempting and although men like Turing knew that digital processing would become the basis for modern computers, a machine had to be put in operation in weeks, not years. Britain needed working machines immediately. If GC&CS had started its Bombe and automation projects years before,[19] it might have first sought the help of electronic and scientific wizards such as C. E. Wynn-Williams who would have explored new technological frontiers. But, in late 1939, GC&CS's managers had to turn to someone who could produce immediate and sure-fire technical results. They found the right man: "Doc" Harold Keen, the head engineer at Britain's version of IBM, the British Tabulating Machine Company.

Keen was asked to turn the Bombe design into hardware and do it quickly. Despite the very limited productive capacity at BTMC, he built a prototype in a few weeks and was able to begin sending operational Bombes to GC&CS in a few months. One reason for his fast work was the use of standard, tried-and-true parts and analog logic. He assembled the Bombe from the most reliable and available components on the shelves of BTMC.[20] Choosing electromechanical technology whenever possible did not make Keen's job easy, however. The cryptanalytical demands for absolute accuracy asked a great deal of the older technology. Keen did have to work some miracles. To fit Turing's logic, he designed new five inch drums that were hard rubber and metal-contact imitations of a double Enigma wheel.[21] Unfortunately, each drum had to have the wiring of one of the wheels available to an Enigma operator. The current technology did not allow the internal connections to be changed automatically. That meant the wheels had to be taken on and off the Bombe at each run. That was time consuming, labor intensive and error prone.

The drums were arranged in banks of three, each being a double analog of an Enigma scrambler unit. One wheel in each bank was run continuously, another moved after a full revolution of the first and the last stepped after the other two had completed their cycles. Some of the first Turing crypto-machines contained twelve banks of the double wheels making their cabinets the size of walk-in closets. As the Bombe's wheels spun over the commutator connections they created instantaneous multiple electrical pathways through the other banks. Then, the electrical charges went to the relays that matched the flows against the crib. At the same time, they surged through the Welchman diagonal board to test the assumptions about the setup of the "E" plugboard.

Keen did a marvelous job of coordinating the banks so they all moved in synchronization and one of his feats of magic was increasing their speed of operation. His machine was eight times faster than the Polish Bomba and was able to test the near 18,000 positions of the wheels in less than fifteen minutes. Even with the use of analog and parallel processing, that was pushing electromechanics to its edge. Keen overcame a great hurdle when he invented a new system to mark the wheel positions that could possibly have produced the crib. His Bombe had a relay network to monitor the spinning wheels, stop the machine's motor and shaft and allow the operator to note where the hit had occurred. Keen's task was made more difficult because he had to pass the output of the wheels through the diagonal board to test for another type of logical impossibility. The diagonal board was a twenty-six by twenty-six matrix of resistors that instantaneously sensed inconsistencies such as two different input letters being enciphered into the same output letter.

Keen's Bombes were amazing, but it took many of them to make a significant dent in any Enigma system. To test all possible wheel combinations against just one crib for a three wheel Enigma called for at least sixty machines. The Germans ran dozens of systems, and only hundreds of Bombes could have provided unaided coverage of them all.

And, the Bombes did not answer all the questions about a setup. They needed prior knowledge of wheel wiring and plugboard settings and their many drops called for a great deal of analysis after a run. Unfortunately, BTMC faced too many shortages of men and materials to keep up the early pace of production. Keen was able to send less than a machine a month to Turing during 1940 and 1941. In early 1942, the record was not much better.

To produce two of the Bombes a month stretched Britain's productive capacity. Bletchley Park was unable to build up enough of an inventory of them to seriously challenge any Enigma system until the end of 1942, and, in the first days of 1943, GC&CS still had less than fifty machines. That was hardly enough to tackle just one naval system, let alone the dozens of army and air force networks that demanded so much attention and which were as or more rewarding intelligence sources. The Bombes, however, were invaluable and they eventually became the means of entry into the many "E" systems. But it was not until mid-1942 that Britain's leaders ordered a shift in priorities and decided to commit massive resources to the Bombe program. Only when they seemed essential to victory in Africa and to the safety of the Middle Eastern oil supplies was "Doc" Keen given new factories and a large workforce. That allowed BTMC to produce some two hundred three wheel Bombes by the end of the war.[22]

Between the summer of 1939 and the attack on Pearl Harbor the British made progress against Enigma. But, GC&CS did not conquer it by 1942. And, what victories it had won did come not through pure mathematical methods or advanced machines. Even with the Bombes and the statistical Banburismus, the Enigma battle rested on a great deal of old-fashioned cryptanalytic insight and skulduggery. And, it was a war that was never fully won. All Enigma solutions were temporary.

"E" Remains Unconquered

The progress against "E" was slow. The first penetration of the vital German air force system came more than six months after receipt of the Polish secrets and its continued reading depended upon an insecure German indicator system. Then, the unravelling of the special German "E" system for the Norwegian campaign soon proved of little value for either military or cryptanalytic purposes. And, much of what was accomplished during the next year was the result of the use of cryptanalytic tricks, German mistakes and vital hints from captured documents and machines.[23]

To make the Bombes useful, the British had to spend much time struggling with the many German hand ciphers. They monitored other low level systems in order to find the vital cribs needed for the Turing machines. And, through much of 1940, after Germany made its indicator systems more secure, Britain's codebreakers had to rely on psychology more than mathematics. If German operators had stopped selecting Enigma indicators in very nonrandom ways or varied the form of their messages, GC&CS would have been unable to penetrate any of the army and air force systems. Pure cryptanalysis was for the future, not 1940 and 1941.[24]

Carefully used, "E" systems remained invulnerable, especially the German navy's. At the beginning of 1941, the U-boat systems could not be read and the temporary entry into them in mid-year came through captures of "E" wheels and documents as much as through advanced analysis. Despite all the skilled mathematicians, the dozens of tabulating machines, the captured Enigma wheels and the Bombes, Britain's hold on naval "E" was very limited and temporary.[25] GC&CS was so overwhelmed and its resources so stretched that in early 1941 it was unable to follow-up on the hints that the U-boat Enigma was to be altered[26]

As well, in 1941, Britain had yet to penetrate the high level Fish systems that would soon become vital to its intelligence estimates. The Fish system was used by the highest level German officials. Their messages contained much about long range plans, but Fish's automatic teletype-like encryption machines were too complex in their logic and its users too wary for a quick and easy entry.[27] The invulnerability of the Fish machines highlighted the dangers of relying upon special purpose devices such as the Bombe. The major Fish machine was, in essence, a binary additive device, piling layer upon layer of random additives to the original message. The Bombe had no power against it and traditional codebreaking methods were gaining little ground in 1941 and 1942. To crack Fish, Britain would have to focus much of its technical expertise on the creation of new special machines, such as the Robinsons and the Colossus, which moved GC&CS into electronics and tape processing.

Keeping Secrets, Secret, Again

Although Britain did not have much of an Ultra Secret in the critical months of 1940-41 she wanted to keep what she had to herself. Britain's codebreakers feared revealing their methods, even to the Americans whose military aid had become essential to Britain's survival.[28] They had good reasons for seeking a monopoly over Ultra. Among them was a not unwarranted fear that sharing with America would lead to breaches of security and the demise of Ultra.[29] Because the solutions to the Axis systems were not based on pure cryptanalysis, they were especially vulnerable to changes in codes, ciphers and procedures. A slip of the tongue or a too aggressive use of Ultra information by a military commander could lead to a devastating lock-out that might take months to overcome. The British crypto experts had to live by the rule that with each person who became aware of a secret, its value diminished exponentially.

There may have been promises of full cryptologic cooperation between Roosevelt and Churchill in mid-1940, but those agreements did not lead to Britain's cryptanalysts immediately telling all to the Americans.[30] Hints were dropped about the range of British powers during the fall of 1940 and Britain soon began to send the United States Navy information on the disposition of German forces,[31] but it was not until early spring 1941 that any details began to be revealed. Then, what Britain was able or willing to show the Americans was much less than expected. Some in the American cryptanalytic community became furious over the balance between what America gave to GC&CS and what it got in return.[32]

A delegation of American cryptanalysts from OP-20-G, the army's SIS and the FBI sailed for England in late January. They had some very precious cargo. They handed over two extremely valuable analogs of the Purple machine for the Japanese diplomatic ciphers, two copies of another Japanese enciphering machine and all the other keys to the top secret Magic system. In addition, all that the United States had on major Japanese attache, navy, and consular codes was surrendered. As with the Purple machines, giving those paper copies of the codes to Britain meant less was available to America's own codebreakers.[33] The American generosity did not end there, however. Britain was promised a continuous flow of cryptologic information, including the American Coast Guard's methods of tapping the German clandestine systems.[34]

In return, in early 1941, GC&CS opened its doors and made the American visitors feel quite welcome. But it could give them very little of real value, at least about "E." Britain shared its work on Japanese naval systems and the Americans were told something about the Bombe and its logic. The navy's men were given a paper outline of an Enigma and were handed a copy of a few days worth of very old keys. The army's representatives were given similar information and all were informed of the earlier successes against the German air force "E" and the system from the Norwegian campaign.[35] The Americans also received a stern warning: None of the information was to be revealed or to be used in any way that might endanger Ultra. What they did not get was what many had thought the trip across the Atlantic was really for, the keys to the naval Enigma. The Americans did not obtain an Enigma machine nor enough cryptanalytic information to allow the United States to break into the submarine "E" on its own.[36] How much the British told the Americans about the other "Es" and the many German minor code and cipher systems that had been conquered and the nature of the various radio nets is not known. Those other systems provided important military information and they aided entry into Enigma. Some released documentation on the state of American abilities in early 1942 suggests that OP-20-G and the army's SIS did not learn everything about the "other Ultras."[37]

A debate continues over how much Enigma information the British could have given the American visitors in the spring of 1941.[38] The consensus seems to be that the chain of raids and captures that allowed the British to enter the German naval system in mid-1941 came too late to be passed on to the American visitors. There simply was not very much to tell them about the naval "E." The British raids on the Lofoton Islands, captures of weather ships and the incredible seizure of the German U-boat U110, did not produce the information needed to sustain their attack on naval Enigma until May 1941.[39] That was well after the American cryptanalysts sailed home and, apparently, after Britain decided to more carefully guard her secrets. And, even after the seizure of the German documents, the British attack was not based on pure cryptanalysis. Penetration continued to depend on the capture of codes, setting instructions and a flow of cribs. Unlike the German army and air force "E" nets, the strict naval procedures precluded the use of such shortcuts as "cillies" and other methods based on operator errors.

Certainly, there was one very important thing the British were unable tell the Americans: Allied cryptological systems had been compromised. That was something as significant to the Atlantic war as breaking the Enigma. The British and Americans were about to pay a price as great as that for ignoring Enigma for so long. Just as the Americans sailed for GC&CS in February 1941, Germany's cryptanalysts broke into the Allied codes for the Atlantic convoys. The mastery of the convoy codes lasted for two years and accounted for a significant portion of the devastation in the Atlantic.[40]

Trust Builds Very Slowly

For a year after the American delegation left England there were few direct contacts between the two nations's cryptanalysts. There were some negotiating sessions about the range and degree of cooperation, but during the remainder of 1941 it seemed to many Americans that Britain became less, not more, willing to yield its growing pool of Enigma secrets.[41] Under some prodding from the United States, additional agreements were made in early and mid-1942, ones that began to move the two nations toward a level of unprecedented cooperation. Then, the sweeping October 1942 accords eased some tensions raised by an American navy threat to go its own way on Enigma. After that, the BRUSA pact of May 1943 was a major step toward openness with the army.[42] But, it was not until the UKUSA agreement of 1946 that the two nations forged that unique relationship of trust that was maintained throughout the Cold War.[43] For example, during World War II, OP-20-G hung back from agreements that would have forced it to be as open with the British as were the army and the FBI.[44]

The British were slow to reveal all about Ultra and there were more than a few frictions on the road to BRUSA and UKUSA, especially during 1942. The American cryptanalysts interpreted the agreements of 1941 to mean that Britain was to share all and that America was to become a full partner in Ultra. A copy of the British Bombe designed for the older three wheel machines was expected before the summer of 1942 and some Americans thought that all British information on new Bombes for the naval four wheel Enigma would be immediately sent across the Atlantic. The British did not seem to agree. And, there also was tension over the details of when and how Americans were to be allowed back into Bletchley Park. When a copy of the latest English

Bombe was not shipped to America on schedule, when it took six months of requests to obtain promised blueprints, and when Britain kept insisting that the United States work only on Japanese problems, some American codebreakers became skeptical of British intentions.[45] When the Germans changed their U-boat "E" system in early 1942 and locked out the British, the growing tension and worry at OP-20-G turned into suspicion and anger.[46]

America Without an Ultra

Whatever the British intentions concerning Ultra in 1941, and no matter how many Enigma-bashing tricks they passed on to the Americans, it is certain that the United States had no effective power over any major German cryptanalytic system at the end of 1941. OP-20-G had been unable to pay significant attention to Enigma. A small OP-20-G "E" group under Mrs. Driscoll had been set to work, but it produced few results.[47] At its entry into the war, OP-20-G had only the most rudimentary knowledge of the Enigma's logic and was not at all sure about the contours of the new U-boat system.[48] Some disgruntled American officers blamed Britain's unwillingness to share, but the reasons why American cryptanalysts were helpless lay in America, not Europe.[49]

Since the turn of the century, America's strategic planners had seen Japan as the enemy. It was viewed as the only major threat. Some in the American military did worry about Germany, but it seemed beyond imagination that France and Britain would be unable to contain her on the continent or would fail to block her navy and air force from making the Atlantic unsafe for America. Despite the experience in World War I, when German submarines crossed to American shores, few saw a need for a two ocean American navy or a two ocean cryptanalytic ability. The American war, it was thought, would be in the Pacific. Based on this assumption, there seemed no reason to target scarce intelligence resources on Europe. Even the Spanish Civil War did not lead to any valuable American inroads into the systems of the future Axis powers.[50] The anticipated enemy led to another dangerous assumption: No matter what the enemy did, the United States would have the time to prepare itself for war.

The most pessimistic American war plans, while allowing for initial conquests by the Orange (Japanese) forces in the Pacific, foresaw a decisive American victory. It was thought that much of the area in the

Pacific could be sacrificed to a Japanese assault without great cost to the United States. A secure American defensive perimeter would be established. Then, after American technology was awakened, the lost areas would be retaken while Japan was thrown out of China and forced back to its home islands. The worst case views of Germany's intentions had an even more optimistic tinge. If Germany did become aggressive, Britain and France would fight on for so long that America would have ample time to build a two front military capability.

Those assumptions were accompanied by ones about the nation's economy. Fundamental was that American industry would automatically provide any great technological advances needed by the military. Resistance to pleas for increased military research was the result of more than the isolationists' fears about "merchants of death." Deep down, American leaders thought that crash programs in technology and science would lead to timely and adequate solutions to the most dangerous threats to national security. It is no wonder that the calls by men such as Hooper and Bowen for ongoing research and Bush's drive to establish government sponsored science remained largely unanswered.[51]

Unfortunately for the American navy, the situation in Europe and Franklin Roosevelt's decisions in 1940 and 1941 suddenly made all those assumptions untenable. Europe, FDR ordered, was to take first priority, the navy was to wage a two ocean war, and, it was to do it immediately. The navy was not ready. Thus, despite a lack of resources, by spring 1941 American naval ships were involved in dangerous scrapes with German U-boats in the Atlantic. By autumn, the Americans were ordered to escort England-bound convoys.

OP-20-G was as unprepared as the rest of the navy. To fulfill its obligations in the Atlantic, it expanded its interception net. To please England, it put most of its men on tactical analysis rather than codebreaking. At the same time, the navy's cryptanalytic ally, the Coast Guard, launched an attack on German clandestine messages. But the spy messages and the bits and pieces from some cracks in the German diplomatic systems yielded little about the German navy. OP-20-G had no effective Atlantic cryptologic power and the navy had to rely upon British-supplied intelligence.[52] America's weakness is suggested by the following estimate of the use of OP-20-G's manpower in late 1941.[53]

Allocation of Navy COMINT Effort
For December 1941

	Japanese Diplomatic	Japanese Navy	German & Italian Navy
Intercept-D/F	30%	50%	20%
Decryption	12%	85%	0%
Translation	50%	50%	0%

Until early 1942 the consequences of the ignoring Europe's code systems were not apparent because Britain seemed to be making real progress against the U-boat Enigma. But, most important, Hitler refrained from attacking American shipping. However, when the U-boat command changed its Enigma and Hitler unleashed his American war, OP-20-G's cryptanalytic weakness became intolerable. When it was realized that Britain was closed out of the U-boats' new M4 Enigma Shark system and as Britain seemed more interested in the German army and air force systems, OP-20-G decided to find its own way to penetrate Enigma.

An American Ultra

Only a handful of people, but a handful that included President Roosevelt and his closest advisors, knew how much pressure there was for a change in American intelligence policy. There were demands that the United States break free of the dependency on Britain's intelligence services because even if Churchill convinced his codebreakers to focus on the Atlantic problem and to reveal all their technical secrets to the United States, America had to be sure of a continuing stream of information.[54] Americans did not want to left without power over "E." On top of the Atlantic shipping crisis, there was still worry that Britain might have to capitulate. If she did, at the very best, she would have to dismantle her GC&CS crew and reestablish what she could in North America. A more immediate threat was that bombing or sabotage might destroy England's cryptanalytic centers.[55] Thus, in spring 1942, the American navy was ordered to start forging its own "E" capability.

Despite the crisis in the Pacific and the old hopes of building general purpose computers, Howard's men and those in "M" were ordered to focus on the Atlantic Shark problem and to produce an immediate solution. OP-20-G even received some encouragement from the army's SIS. Breaking into the Atlantic submarine system and its new four wheel Enigma was important to the army as well as the navy. Both services feared that all the German services would turn to the new four wheel version.[56]

When the decision was made to create its own "E" solution, OP-20-G was very short handed and had to turn the work over to Engstrom's group of college men in the "M" section.[57] They began with few tools and the burden of Britain's fears of an independent American Ultra capability. Engstrom inherited the findings and methods of Mrs. Driscoll's earlier "E" group, the records of the Americans' 1941 visit to Bletchley Park, and the few chunks of information Britain had provided on its activities during 1941.[58] None of that was of great value. In fact, one reason for GC&CS's silence was its embarrassment over having neglected the hints about the introduction of the U-boat M4 machines. Little had been done during the year to design a new four wheel Bombe. A more basic reason was that Britain did not want to admit its failure to acquire the necessary copies of the new code books issued with the Shark M4. Until Britain could steal them or capture the German weather cipher and short signal codes, and thus gain a flow of cribs, even new Bombes would be of little value against Shark.[59]

Faster Than a Speeding Relay

Bletchley Park's very overworked men had let more than a year slip by without focusing significant resources on a Bombe for M4, the four wheel U-boat Enigma. The introduction of the fourth wheel had meant a twenty-six fold increase in the number of wheel orders that had to be examined. A set of new analytic machines was needed to run through the near one-half million positions in a reasonable time. The Germans' introduction of additional encryption wheels an operator could choose from presented as great a challenge. The expanded set of M4 wheels called for 360, not 60, Bombes for a simultaneous test of wheel combinations.[60] Changes in the related German codes, radio networks and procedures compounded those problems. The M4-Shark system was so difficult that many in GC&CS thought it would be more profitable to work on the tractable three wheel German systems and the spreading Fish networks. They could satisfy Britain's critical need for information on Africa and the Middle East. But, with prodding from men like Turing, Bletchley decided to commit some resources to conquering M4.[61]

GC&CS called on the famous Wynn-Williams and asked him to explore the use of electronics for a super-bombe. Williams had become famous because of his creation of the most advanced electronic radiation counters of the 1930s. Williams and electronics were natural choices because the speeds demanded by a four wheel Bombe seemed beyond the limits of "Doc" Keen's revolving commutators and the electrical relays that identified the position of a possible hit.

Williams spent many frustrating months trying to create an electronic Bombe. His efforts stretched into spring 1942, but with little more to show than a breadboard model of a primitive "E" wheel. It was not until then that "Doc" Keen's men at BTMC were contacted about the new Shark M4 problem. They were already stressed because of the sudden order to accelerate the production of the older three wheel Bombes, but they agreed to consider the four wheel Enigma problem. Immediately, the practical Keen rejected an electronic solution and began to give some thought to alternatives. He created the outlines of a new four wheel Bombe but advised GC&CS that it might take more than a year to design and build the first model.[62] His prediction proved correct. Britain would not have the first of its very few temperamental four wheel Bombes until early summer 1943.

Great American Expectations

Meanwhile, while Wynn-Williams continued to plod along with his ideas and constructed more breadboard circuits,[63] GC&CS learned of America's Ultra intentions. In spring 1942 it rushed a group of its leaders to the States hoping to reach an understanding that would protect its Ultra monopoly. March 1942 saw Britain strike the first of a series of new bargains. Desiring to keep control of Ultra, but faced with stubborn Americans who demanded an end to the U-boat threat, it assured OP-20-G that Shark was about to be beaten and it agreed to share more Enigma information. In exchange, it asked the Americans to concentrate on the Japanese problems and let Britain manage European intelligence. It promised the navy that it would soon create a new Bombe and assured the Americans they would not have to design their own. They pleaded with OP-20-G to refrain from doing anything that might lead the Germans to alter their systems.

The Americans desired cordial relations with the British but they would not abandon Enigma. They agreed to cooperate but stood by their commitment to an American program. The British had to yield to prevent a dangerous rupture. After some tugs of war, Alan Turing and other GC&CS experts arrived in America for conferences on a range of cryptanalytic and policy issues.[64] The Americans appreciated the increased flow of information and Britain's pledge that M4 would soon be conquered, but OP-20-G kept to its policy of independence and continued its own search. Unfortunately, the Americans began their project with a great deal of innocence and ignorance[65] as reflected by the late April 1942 memorandum that signaled the formal beginning of their technical research.

That historic OP-20-G directive gave a very incomplete view of Enigma, Shark, and the British Bombe. America's experts were able to outline only the workings of the older three wheel plugboard version of Enigma and they seemed uncertain about a key component, the reflector. Furthermore, OP-20-G's memorandum contained only the most general ideas about the British Bombe's logic.[66] But, the April memorandum asked a great deal of the OP-20-G engineers: It pointed them to the creation of a single machine that would outdo all of the British Bombes. They were given more than hints that they should design and build a new powerful American machine, an all-purpose crypto-computer. After reviewing all possible methods of attack against "E," OP-20-G admitted that it might have to turn to a crib-based approach. But, it continued on with its to fight to achieve Wenger's old dream of using pure techniques. Engstrom's men intensified their search for pure statistical and mathematical methods and machines.

Through the spring and early summer of 1942 the OP-20-G engineers explored the possibilities of such a high-speed electronic machine. They received some help from the British, gradually learning more about Britain's cryptanalytic methods, including those used to avoid testing all "E" wheel combinations. But, the Americans remained frustrated and very worried. They feared they would be unable to build their universal machine or even their own version of the English Bombe. Worse, OP-20-G's leaders deeply feared that even if they built such a Bombe, they would always remain dependent upon Britain for the necessary copies of captured "E" wheels, codebooks, and cribs. An electronic machine for statistical analysis seemed the only route to American independence. But the going was very difficult.

As spring 1942 became summer, "G" gave more weight to the possibility of having to turn to a crib dependent Bombe, but its men continued to hope they could devise pure statistical methods and machines. Critical to both the American Bombe and the search for a machine for pure analysis were breakthroughs in electronics and advice from the more experienced British cryptanalysts. Neither came easily.

Trying to Step Forward, Not Back

A few at OP-20-G were convinced that America would beat England's famed Wynn-Williams to a super high-speed electronic machine, but others in the OP-20-G group were less sure of an independent American success. They knew they needed British help, but they were becoming worried about England's abilities and intentions.[67] Despite the ongoing negotiations between the two sets of codebreakers, few Americans were satisfied. In 1942, GC&CS was becoming more open with the Americans and informed them of the Fish systems. But, Britain's men still seemed to hold back on the Bombe. Requesting blueprints of Britain's "latest" machines in May, the Americans hoped those details would prevent them from committing to an American Bombe that was inefficient or simply unworkable. Although offering GC&CS full information on all the other advanced high-speed cryptanalytic machines it was developing,[68] OP-20-G was made to wait for a reply to its specific requests and for a clear statement of British policy on cryptanalytic cooperation.[69] OP-20-G continued to get mixed responses from England.

In July, two OP-20-G men and others from the American army's cryptanalytic branch were welcomed at Bletchley Park and shown its wonders. But, at the same time, the navy had to formally request information on the English Bombe and the emerging new solutions to the Enigma systems. More fundamental, by the end of the summer, the Americans became worried that Britain would never devote enough resources to the Atlantic U-boat problem. OP-20-G's men tired of the constant assurances that a solution to the four wheel problem was imminent.[70] There was some foundation for the American concern.

Britain's Own Version of Bush's Electronic Dreams

By late spring 1942 Britain began to think that Shark might be too difficult to overcome without the capture of important documents, ones they might never obtain. As significant, GC&CS's policy makers and codebreaking gurus had begun to shift their focus to the Fish systems. The Bombes were special purpose machines and could not attack the devices used on Fish. Thus, as part of the reallocation of GC&CS resources, Wynn-Williams was asked to take on another job: devise a high-speed engine to crack the binary additive system of the Fish machines. He agreed and while continuing on with his electronic Bombe work, he designed the first of the Robinsons. Very soon, they were turned into hardware. One reason for the speedy move to production was that Williams went to the engineering teams at the research branch of British Post Office rather than to the overburdened men at BTMC. Unlike the group at BTMC, the telephone engineers had been involved in electronic work for several years and were quite willing to gamble on new technologies.

The first Robinson was delivered in early 1943, well before any of the newest models of Bush's Comparators reached OP-20-G's headquarters. Although Williams arrived at his Robinson designs independently and while several different types of Robinsons followed in the next two years, all shared a striking likeness to Bush's old ideas.[71] Robinson used high-speed punched tapes, photoelectric readers and some one hundred gas filled tubes to keep track of results.[72] The Robinsons shared something else with Bush's machines, the very serious problem of keeping the tapes in alignment. There were differences, however. The Robinson's target was a binary additive system. That called for a different use of the tapes. One tape was for a message, the other held the stream of binary additives that Fish's Tunny machine setting would produce. Fortunately for the British and the history of computers, that binary stream presented an opportunity to avoid the problem of aligning the tapes.

One of the British engineers called in to deal with the problems with the first Robinson had spent his career working on electronics for the phone system. He had a firm belief in and much skill in using tubes as switching devices. When he realized that the second Robinson tape was a stream of algorithm generated bits, he suggested that a machine be constructed that substituted tube circuits for the additive tape. Reckoning that the number of tubes needed for the generation of binary combination was reasonable, GC&CS gave the green light to construction of the Colossus.

The Colossus was something of a miracle of project management. It took less than a year to create what many consider the finest electronic pre-computer. Colossus kept twenty-five hundred tubes and a high-speed photoelectric paper tape reader in synchronization. It could even be coaxed into performing some primitive program steps and "if" statements. The first of more than ten versions was put into operation in January 1944.[73]

The Americans Almost Beat England to Electronics

While England was thinking about electronic machines the Shark-M4 problem continued to frustrate GC&CS's codebreakers and its machine designers. It was also creating more frictions between the British, OP-20-G, and the American army's SIS. The U-boat rampage in the Atlantic led to extreme criticisms of the American navy while the army was becoming worried that its men would go into battle in Africa and Europe without an "E" capability. As a result, OP-20-G put even more resources into its frantic effort to conquer the U-boat "E" and the army began to think of the machines it might need for what it called the "Yellow Problem."[74] The army's SIS had difficulties obtaining information and resources and did not launch a machine program until the fall, but at the beginning of summer 1942, OP-20-G hinted it had a solution to the M4. Within another two months it announced that its men had beaten Britain and the great Wynn-Williams to the creation of the heart of a fully electronic Bombe.[75]

It wasn't a universal machine, but no time was lost. OP-20-G was ordered to take the next steps. Wenger was given all the resources he desired and freedom from the Bureau of Ships's oversight. NCR was taken over by the navy to be a research center and possibly a production site. Joe Desch and his men were screened for a security rating and their laboratory was moved into a separate building. Marine guards with riot shotguns were sent to Dayton.[76] A call went to naval personnel to find the best electronic engineers whether or not they were in the navy and Joe Desch was ordered to expand his seventeen man civilian staff. John Howard's old group became an integral part of Howard Engstrom's "M" as it was reorganized to oversee the electronic Bombe work at NCR. Then, in early July, a contract was let that could accommodate, if needed, expenditures in the millions of dollars.[77]

Intense pressure was put on Howard and the others to complete the American electronic Bombe design. The war was not going well in the Atlantic, and, despite the American victory at Midway during the first days of June, the Pacific was still an American tragedy. In fact, the Midway victory was somewhat of an embarrassment to Wenger and those who had fought for so long to have naval cryptology centralized and equipped with very expensive machines. The turning back of the Japanese fleet in early June was in large part due to the long awaited reentry into the main Japanese naval code, JN-25. The navy's codebreakers learned of the Japanese plan to take Midway and Admiral Nimitz was able to lay a fatal trap for Yamamoto's most prized ships. But, it was a "mustang" officer, an ex-enlisted man, Joseph Rochefort in Hawaii, who stripped off the JN-25 additives and found meaning for the exposed code groups. His feat was accomplished with only a handful of tabulators and sorters run by bandsmen whose ship had been sunk during the December 7 attack on Pearl Harbor. He did not have the large staff deemed necessary in Washington and he used rather traditional methods to make his discoveries. When his analyses turned out to be correct and those done at the Washington center were proven wrong, the skepticism about the grand claims for scientific cryptanalysis increased. Wenger, Engstrom, and their like had to show some results.[78] The Bombe became important to M's survival as well as to the Battle of the Atlantic.

No Time for Electronics

The need for immediate results, the frustrations with the projects at Eastman-Kodak, Gray Electric, and IBM, and the imperative to regain control of the Atlantic, led the Bureau of Ships to grant more and more freedom to Engstrom and Wenger. With the help of Ralph Meader of the Radio Division's Special Applications Branch, OP-20-G's machine effort was becoming less and less befuddled by the Bureau's way of doing business. The very broad NCR "best efforts" contract of May 1942 had been a great step because it freed the "M" group from paperwork and bureaucratic domination. The old cordial relations between Desch and the young men from MIT also helped to create an open atmosphere in Dayton.[79] But, Wenger's goal of an independent "G" machine effort would not have been realized except for a very disappointing surprise at the end of the summer.

In late summer 1942, the engineers of the "M" group decided their work was far enough along to submit it to an experienced production engineer for examination. Of course, they turned to Joe Desch. He spent almost two months examining their bench model and their designs for an electronic Bombe.[80] At first, he was excited, but as he learned more about the architecture of the proposed machine and called on his experience with electronics he came to a devastating conclusion: An electronic Bombe was an impossibility![81]

There was not time, he said, to conquer the technical problems or to build the infrastructure needed by a machine that would have to go far beyond any existing electronic device. Desch pointed out that if the American electronic Bombe followed the architecture of Britain's, it would demand more than twenty thousand tubes run at speeds that challenged the technology of the era. A universal machine would need thousands more tubes and even higher speeds. The thousands of tubes would be difficult to acquire, would create too much heat and would demand more electrical power than could be supplied.[82] Desch was a highly respected man and his judgement could not be ignored.

Wenger, Engstrom, and Howard's MIT group were devastated. The entire Rapid Machine project was in danger. The promised electronic Bombe was a failure, the old Eastman and Gray projects were making little progress and, as a central cryptanalytic agency, "G" was unable to contribute much to the war effort.

Then, the practical shop floor trained Joe Desch came to the rescue.

A Crisis of Organization and Technology

Desch commanded so much respect that the responsibility for a new design was shifted to him. Necessarily, he was informed of one of America's and Britain's great secrets, Ultra. After some study of what was known about the Turing Bombe, he promised that he would be able to produce an electromechanical machine that could tackle the Shark M4. He declared he could create an original American Bombe--but a non-electronic one. Despite the inability of Britain to complete its new model, Desch was believed by the men at OP-20-G--he had to be.[83]

Immediately, a new effort, the second American Bombe project was begun. As a result, Wenger's dream of a Rapid Machine program was saved. He gained his workforce, his research group and his own factory, but at a price. All of that had to be devoted to creating a technological dinosaur. For most of the remaining war years, the electromechanical Bombes devoured the energies of "G's" engineers. To fulfill the commitment to Desch's necessary backwards technological leap, all the truly advanced projects and ideas were made stepchildren. They were given attention only when "G" was free of a major crisis or when there seemed to be no alternative but to explore advanced electronics.

The second American Bombe project almost faltered, but it eventually became a triumph for OP-20-G and the American intelligence community. The success of the Bombes and the allied work on machines for the Pacific war finally established the credibility Wenger needed to try to make research a permanent part of OP-20-G's peacetime operations. But the task of saving what had been created during the war was difficult. The Bombes proved very stubborn as did a postwar navy that favored a return to the Bureau's ways of doing things.

ERA Selector, circa 1950
(Hagley Museum & Library)

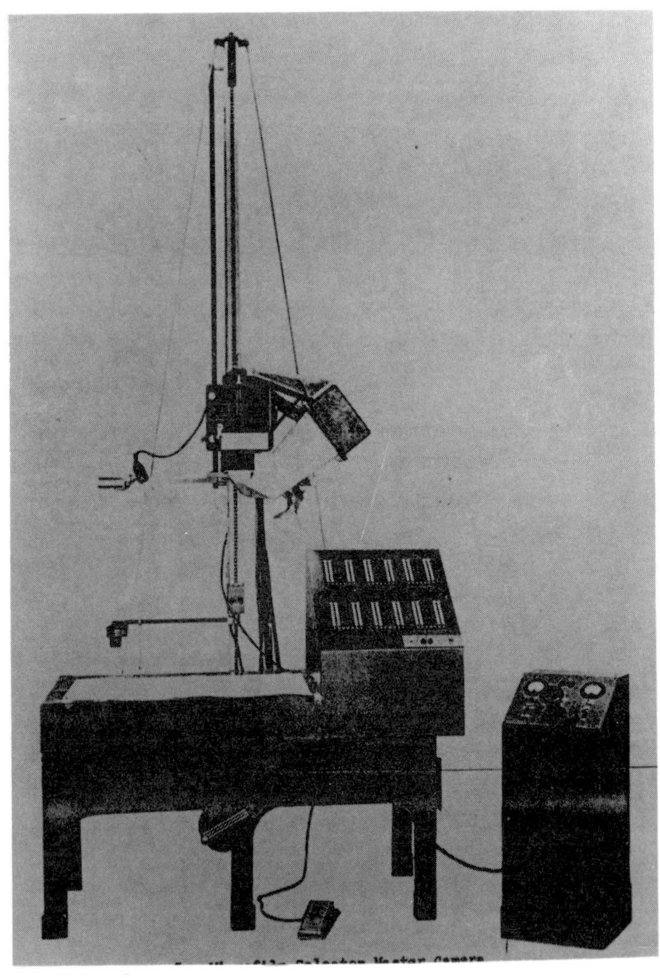

ERA Selector's Data Entry Device
(Hagley Museum & Library)

Chapter XII
Beyond the Bombe: Back to Hooper's Dream

More was at stake than Joseph Wenger's reputation when he accepted Joe Desch's professional judgement. In September 1942 new electromechanical machines seemed essential to ending the savagery in the Atlantic. Hundreds of Allied ships were being sunk and the life line to England was in jeopardy. And, the fulfillment of Desch's promise was vital to the future of advanced cryptanalysis in America. With the work at Gray and Eastman-Kodak stalled the failure to produce a machine to conquer the U-boat Enigma would have seriously threatened the Rapid Machine program. It would have ended any chance for OP-20-G to control its future. The damage would not have been limited to "G's" position in the American intelligence community.

Searching for a Place in Ultra

The second American Bombe project was part of an attempt to readjust the relationship between Britain's and America's codebreakers. Desch's Bombe was essential to OP-20-G gaining a greater role in the Ultra Secret and to becoming a producer of operational information. The Bombe was also entangled in the United States Army's struggles to play a larger role in European codebreaking. If Desch failed to create a machine at least many orders more powerful than the three wheel Turing Bombe, GC&CS would have been unlikely to take the American's threats to create their own Enigma capabilities seriously.[1] Without an American Bombe, the United States would have remained a consumer of British controlled Ultra information and OP-20-G would have continued under the old understanding: Both nations could pursue independent research but Britain would control all operational activities. The Americans had few bargaining chips. They did not have enough of a cryptanalytic advantage in the Pacific to use access to Japanese intelligence as a lever to open up Ultra. Although Britain had begun to ask for American help on the Atlantic problems, with the failure of the second Bombe project, it would have been very reluctant to make OP-20-G an equal partner.[2]

A Declaration of Independence

The friction with Britain over Ultra intensified soon after the approval of Desch's sketch of a modified British machine. With his outline in hand, OP-20-G decided to be very aggressive. Without having full knowledge of the workings of the old Bombes, without access to all of the anti-Enigma cryptanalytic techniques, without a detailed design for its Bombe and without any hardware for it in hand, OP-20-G more than hinted that it would build three hundred fifty of the Desch machines before spring 1943 when the U-boats were expected to launch a mass attack. America was notifying Britain that no matter what it took, the U-boat war would be won by the United States.

It was also giving GC&CS and its engineers a perhaps unintended slap in the face. The Americans must have seemed quite egotistical when they claimed that within a few weeks they could solve the technical problems that had stumped the great "Doc" Keen, then, immediately begin producing the advanced four wheel Bombes at a rate of more than two a day.[3] Desch and the "M" group were not consciously bluffing; they believed they could accomplish what seemed an impossibility to the British.[4] Like Vannevar Bush, they thought that American technology and mass production methods could work miracles.[5]

The British had no choice but to take "G" seriously and to make the best of the situation. They quickly dispatched another cryptologic delegation to the United States. Accepting what seemed to be the inevitable, GC&CS agreed to help the Americans although they continued to argue that European intelligence should be left to them. The British explained their methods of avoiding the need to run all the Bombe wheel combinations and orders to test a message. In response, the Americans tentatively agreed to build only one hundred Bombes.[6]

They also promised to share their Ultra information and technology with Britain and to coordinate all Ultra-based military and diplomatic actions. OP-20-G also made a firm pledge to do everything needed to make Ultra America's most guarded secret.[7]

Those October 1942 negotiations led to Britain giving "M" a somewhat greater operational role, or at least preparing them for one. GC&CS's representatives set "M's" men to using hand methods on various German systems and gave them more instructions on how to prepare menus (setups) for the Bombes.[8] During the next few months more and more technical details about Ultra flowed to the United States and more of Engstrom's bright young men in "M" travelled to England to work at GC&CS. But, the British retained the power to decide what information would and would not leave Bletchley Park. However, as Britain's own four wheel Bombe project dragged on without result, further agreements were signed allowing greater sharing.[9]

By early 1943, American cryptanalysts were applying British paper and tabulating machine techniques to crack some German messages intercepted by the British. Although GC&CS had begun to reenter the U-boat system in late 1942, the messages sent to America were usually those of the German air force.[10] However, the two nations prepared for a greater American role once the Desch Bombes were completed. A secret radio channel to the United States was established and the Americans learned enough to take increasing responsibility for a few more German systems. In late 1942, Alan Turing began a series of visits to America, telling "M" more about Ultra and the construction efforts on the latest British Bombe.[11] He and others from GC&CS even made trips to Dayton, Ohio to evaluate the work at National Cash Register. The cooperation continued. The two nations' intelligence services and the two Bombe projects became closer as 1942 ended. But, Desch's Bombe was an American product.

Although Desch based his first sketches on what he had been told of the British logic and hardware, and although GC&CS's codemen gave him essential information, Desch went his own way. Britain did not have any experts at NCR or OP-20-G and its comments on the American project, sometimes uncomplimentary, were not decisive. Desch and his NCR men and the young engineers in John Howard's "M" group took the very heavy responsibility of creating a unique machine and a pathbreaking production line to defeat the U-boats.

Desch Takes Charge

Desch was sure of success in the autumn of 1942. As soon as his general design was approved in September, he began to refine his ideas and looked forward to immediately building a prototype. Expecting to begin production within weeks, he expanded his research and development team. At the same time, the old engineering group from MIT was ordered to put the other OP-20-G machine projects on hold until the critical Bombes were ready. They soon moved to Dayton to help Desch. Signals from Deeds and the NCR administration indicated that the company and its employees would also give their all for the navy. Desch hired some ten more top civilian engineers and put them to work on a trial machine. In early October, Joseph Wenger was so confident that he began negotiations for the land and buildings to house the Bombes and their hundreds of operators, maintenance men, and armed guards.[12] Resources were not a problem. The second American Bombe project, which at one point would employ over a thousand manufacturing workers, received the highest possible priorities for personnel and material. It was so important that requests to the White House were processed within a day and cost overruns of incredible size were accepted without question. The jump from an estimate of two million dollars to one of four million dollars in a few months did not threaten the program.[13] And, the greatest efforts were made to keep the Bombe project secure. It had its own building in Dayton with armed Marines and special secret rooms to manufacture and use the Bombes. It was as or more secret than the atomic bomb program and it was more delicate. The Bombes could be rendered useless by changes in "E" and the greatest care had to be taken. To safeguard the machine OP-20-G refrained from using all of its powers. At times, "G" had to bow to the demands of other branches of the navy for personnel because to use its high priority rating too often might let the wrong people know of the American Bombe and the Ultra secret.[14]

Wenger Gets His Organization

The Bombe was so important that the Bureau of Ships had to grant all the wishes of Wenger, Engstrom, and Desch. The Bureau continued to be in charge of the purse strings and theoretically in charge of all technical details, but it yielded more and more autonomy to "G's" program. The freedom came in gradual steps but OP-20-G was able to convince the Bureau to create a new administrative organization for all the high-speed machine projects, the Naval Computing Machine Laboratory at Dayton, Ohio. In formal terms, the Bureau's NCML was the boss of the Dayton work, but by early 1943 it was a really a support organization for OP-20-G's group of engineers and scientists. Even the NCML's Ralph Meader became an integral part of Desch's operation. In practical terms, Wenger had finally achieved his goal of independence. His men from "M" determined what was needed and how the need was to be fulfilled. The NCML's role was to agree and expedite. There were no bureaucratic delays and "G" was able to determine its own technical future.

The "M" group was also gaining power. The country's best mathematicians, physicists, and engineers were brought into OP-20-GM. The new men were not the types who were willing to accept the military ways of performing their jobs. The "M" section had more than twenty percent Ph.D.s and all of its personnel had been screened for high intelligence, creativity and specific technical abilities. Its scientists and engineers were from the nation's top schools and companies. That allowed Engstrom to have a self-contained machine development group that easily challenged the Bureau's technical authority. Of importance to the nature of the postwar RAM program, the "M" engineers were integrated with the NCR workforce. That gave the machine designers the freedom to merge research and production and, combined with the virtual take over of NCR, it allowed Wenger a constant interaction with and power over the manufacturing process. That led OP-20-G to take its new Rapid Machine work away from the Bureau's old contractors and shift them to NCR. From mid-1942, when Colonel Deeds ordered NCR to accept the very broad "best efforts" contract, to the end of World War II, OP-20-G had its own development program at what was, in effect, its own factory.[15]

More Than Minor Delays

Such freedom and the massive resources the navy was willing to pour into Desch's project were not enough to sustain the hopes of September and October 1942, however. By November, questions were being raised about the progress at Dayton and by Christmas there was a growing chorus of complaints. At the opening of 1943 a prototype had not been assembled and there were serious questions about the practicality of the components that had been constructed.[16] Worse, Engstrom strongly objected to the design Desch put forward at the beginning of the year. He urged Desch to find some way to overcome the intense heat that would be generated by the machine's high-speed mechanical components and its electronics and asked him to keep the Bombe as close to an analog of the Enigma as possible.[17] Desch and his men found that a very difficult assignment.

The rejection of the plan for an electronic machine and the reversion to the electromechanical technology of the British Bombes had not led to the easy solutions "G" had expected. The Bombe and Rapid Machine project were in trouble again. At the beginning of 1943, the Bombe was tragically behind schedule and the Americans were yet to make a real contribution to Enigma problem. Worse, for a time, some in "M" worried that their opportunity had been lost because GC&CS was able to reenter the Atlantic U-boat system at the beginning of the year without the use of any four wheel Bombes. Old-fashioned cryptanalysis had again won the day. The reentry came through the capture of documents from a U-boat and the discovery of some very sloppy procedures on the Shark network. As a consequence, the British were able to crack the four wheel Enigma messages on their old Bombes.

If their reentry had not been based on the very weak foundation of easily changed German weather codes and what were known as "short signals," the British might have again complained about the waste of resources on the American Bombe project. But they and the Americans soon realized how temporary the new solution was. As the spring U-boat offensive opened, the Germans changed some of their codes and tightened up their procedures so that the Allies were again shut out of the submarine systems. They remained blind for a frightening ten days during what became the worst month in the history of the battle of the Atlantic. The destruction might have been greater, but another surge of the British codebreakers' intuitive insights allowed the three wheel British Bombes to be useful again.[18]

Saving the American Bombe

At least three months before that ghastly March U-boat foray, OP-20-G realized that Desch's machine was in serious trouble. Desch and his crew continued to face great technological hurdles. Wenger and Engstrom also sensed there were some organizational difficulties. They knew that OP-20-G's reputation was at stake and they went into action to try to save the project. The NCML's structure was formalized and higher priorities for parts were secured. Pressure was then put on the staff at NCR to work overtime. Joe Desch was told to drop his many other electronics projects for the NDRC, Aberdeen, and the army. And the navy went over the head of the new president of NCR and wrote directly to Colonel Deeds to make sure that NCR gave the Bombe project all it needed. Under prodding from the Chief of Naval Operations, Deeds quickly ordered Dayton to devote less time to its profitable war work and give the Bombe all of its attention.[19] There was some progress. The first design for the pilot model of the Bombe was submitted in January. By February, Desch and NCR ended their other jobs and were focusing on "G's" problems. The British, wondering whether or not to rely upon the behind schedule American effort, evaluated the latest NCR work and made several suggestions. Joe Desch and John Howard graciously responded to Alan Turing's recommendations and incorporated them in a second design even as they rushed to construct the first prototype.

There was increased effort at NCR as spring 1943 approached, but the men in Dayton were not keeping pace with the war.[20] OP-20-G, Desch and Howard had not been able to hold to the promise they had made in September. As the great Atlantic battle began in March, all that had emerged from some seven months of work were two wheezy prototype machines. No one was really sure that the two models, Adam and Eve, would prove themselves and serve as test beds for the vital production machines.

Despite all the problems in Dayton, OP-20-G could do nothing but continue to support the NCML-NCR work. OP-20-G bet more millions of dollars hoping that Desch's engineers could overcome the next set of technical problems. A note was sent to the White House and received an immediate response. FDR granted the American Bombe project the highest possible priority for materials and personnel and Wenger and Engstrom prayed that the American habit of throwing money at problems would again succeed. They instructed Desch to rush to the production stage and to stand ready to build as many as three hundred machines despite the earlier promise to GC&CS to build only one hundred. Living quarters for the WAVES who were to help wire and run the production machines were prepared. The construction of the special building for the Bombes in Washington was speeded and hundreds of subcontractors were ordered to stand ready to send thousands of intricate parts to Dayton. Desch then took the first steps in recruiting a huge civilian workforce and he began to plan how to divide the work for those unskilled employees from Ohio's small towns.[21]

There was progress at Dayton during April and May, but no machines! The pressures on OP-20-G and the NCML grew intense as the Atlantic became an American tragedy. The March 1943 convoy battles turned into the slaughter of May. Record numbers of Allied ships were sunk and there were real fears of the cord to Europe being cut. Still, no Americans Bombes appeared. The group at NCR could not even tempt the two Bombe prototypes to run for more than a few inadequate minutes. Fortunately for the Allies, the Atlantic quieted somewhat in late May as a combination of new fighting ships, tactics and signals intelligence finally made Admiral Doenitz's U-boat armada wary. Escort carriers, airborne radar, a central command center for subhunting (the Tenth Fleet) and changes in the once vulnerable Allied convoy codes began to bring the Atlantic under control. Enigma cracking played its part, but not through the promised American technological wonders, the Bombes.

A Bombe Too Late

Order was restored in the Atlantic before the first American Bombe was even put to its tests. The American's had not made their hoped for decisive contribution. That was evident in the round of negotiations between Britain and the United States in May 1943. The problems in the Atlantic and the coming European offensives called for another readjustment in the rules for cooperation in the intelligence field. The BRUSA agreement made the United States Army a partner in the Ultra Secret, but a junior one. More Americans were to go to England to work and study cryptanalytic methods and Britain agreed to establish teams to coordinate intelligence gathering and use. But, again, there was a price for the Americans. OP-20-G and the United States Army agreed to focus on the Japanese problems and to allow GC&CS to determine what the Americans would do or would not do against the Enigma and Fish systems. The Americans were given the chance to play an expanded role, but Britain kept command of the attack on M4 and the German army systems.[22]

As the mid-May negotiations came to a close, Joseph Wenger remained unsure of OP-20-G's future. Without the American Bombe there was no special OP-20-G European contribution and no way to prove the need for Rapid Machines. The "M" crew was using hand methods against Enigma, but with an embarrassing record of an average of six hundred hours needed to solve a key.[23] Fearful of seeing OP-20-G's men remain as apprentices, Wenger and Engstrom began to push Dayton. Even if "G" were too late to be the savior of the Atlantic, there was still much to do to counter the U-boats. Despite the period of calm after the spring debacle, no one was sure of the future of the convoys. New German technologies that could undermine the effectiveness of the Allies' subhunter groups were known to be under development. The German Army, Air Force, rocket development team, and police agencies showed signs of changing over to four wheel Enigmas. And, in the systems continuing to use the three wheel machines, anticipated alterations in procedures and in the use of their plugboards threatened another round of crises. If the American Bombes could be made to work, they still might play a significant role.

Wenger and Engstrom were convinced the NCML program should be continued. But if it were to survive, it had to produce machines and useful intelligence very soon. In late May, Wenger ordered Desch to allow the two temperamental prototypes to be used on messages sent from Washington. The results were to be forwarded to the British as examples of American abilities.[24] However, proving America's readiness to be a full Ultra partner was not easy given the state of the Dayton Bombes. Howard Engstrom, in charge of the new Enigma message work, felt defeated when Adam and Eve refused to run for more than a few hours without spurting oil or developing incurable cases of faulty electrical contacts.[25] As spring ended, the Bombe again seemed to be too much of a challenge, even for the talented Joe Desch.

A Program Based on Another Technological Bet

Despite the fears that the Bombe might never be ready for production, more of the navy's best engineers were sent to Dayton to establish the operational side of the NCML. They were to assist John Howard and John Coombs in testing the Bombes when they rolled off Desch's assembly line. While they waited, they were to help establish a temporary message analysis center at NCR.[26] Joe Eachus, the bright young OP-20-G mathematician who Engstrom had assigned to Bletchley Park in mid-1942, went to Dayton to advise on procedures.[27] NCR switched to twenty-four hour a day operations and the hundreds of new civilian employees went on double shifts. They began assembling the parts for the new Bombes before Desch and Meader were at all sure the American Bombe could be made operable.

To the great embarrassment of the Americans, there were more delays. Adam and Eve continued their tantrums as June approached[28] and the production model was yet to be assembled. Given the promises that had been made in September 1942, the American record seemed quite shabby. The tension mounted when it was learned that as Dayton again faltered, Britain completed its first four wheel Bombe, put its first tape and electronic Robinson to use and began the construction of the advanced electronic Colossus.[29] The men at NCR may have wondered if the NCML would become just a manufacturer of British designed machines.

Wenger's Rapid Machine program was losing credibility at home and in England at the same time that American naval leaders were undermining the trust that was essential to maintaining the pacts between Britain and America. The Americans decided, despite the danger of exposing Ultra, and thus making the Bombes on both sides of the Atlantic useless, to strike at all the German refuelling submarines in the Atlantic. Cutting off the U-boat fuel supplies was a brilliant tactical move but it made it difficult for the British to trust the Americans with more Ultra information. Any attack that was too successful, as had been the ones against the undersea tankers, could warn the Germans that Enigma had been penetrated. In Dayton, the first two weeks of June were difficult because of technical rather than diplomatic problems. Desch's engineers continued to struggle with the most fundamental elements of the machines, their commutators. Those large rotors seemed to be destined to overheat, loose their shape and create faulty electrical signals. The metal sensing brushes also seemed to have been meant only for slow and dependable tabulators. As quick-fixes were made to those parts, more oil leaks developed on the prototypes. Those problems raised such fears about the production model's design that assembly was halted. The situation was so grave that all message processing at Dayton was suspended.

Adam and Eve, the prototypes, were in too much trouble and too vital to working out critical technical problems to be used by the cryptanalysts in Washington. Desch's crew and Howard's NCML engineers put in longer hours using Adam and Eve to unravel the problems with the parts for the production machines. The commutators were reworked and the drive mechanisms altered.[30] By mid-June there were hopes that all the problems had been conquered.

However, the production crew had still not released the first two copies of the final model, Cain and Abel. Although Desch promised they would be ready for testing before mid-month, the delivery date slipped by. Everyone awaited them. They had to be made available for hardware and message testing before the final production designs could be approved. Desch pushed his people harder and the NCR factory began to assemble components at an even faster pace. They could only hope the parts would function when put together in the Bombe. Then, just as production was about to begin, Engstrom sent an urgent coded telegram to Joe Desch and Ralph Meader.[31]

The Wrong Bombe?

Howard Engstrom had learned of possible changes in the German Enigma's hardware and the procedures for its use. What had been mentioned as a possibility in September 1942 seemed to have become a frightening reality: the Enigma systems were to undergo changes that might make the Bombes ineffective. In response, on June 18, Engstrom requested what amounted to a new Bombe. He may not have realized how much he was asking of Joe Desch and the NCML. Engstrom wanted an automatic method of switching commutators and greater machine speeds. Yet, he said he did not want Bombe production delayed.[32] Desch, Meader, and Howard were stunned! They had already completed the production specifications for the subcontractors and had set their own assemblers to work. Joe Desch protested that the changes Engstrom desired were really calls for a new type of Bombe, one with features so advanced that it would be too complex to produce within a few months, let alone weeks.[33]

Desch was correct. Engstrom's functional requests could be satisfied only with a machine that approached the complexity of the modern general purpose electronic computer. That was impossible. There was no practical high-speed substitute for the many hard-wired rotor wheels that could be rearranged on the Bombe's drive spindles. Thousands of tubes in very dense circuits would be needed to imitate all possible rotor wiring on the more than sixty wheels on a Bombe. In addition, to reach the speeds Engstrom alluded to, the reliable gas-filled tubes would have to be replaced with unpredictable vacuum tubes. All that had been too much in the summer of 1942 when Desch originally rejected the idea of an electronic wheel, and, in the crisis months of 1943, Engstrom's request seemed beyond belief.

Ralph Meader, the Bureau's man in charge of the NCML, had usually acted as Wenger and Engstrom's right hand man. This time, he could not. He quickly supported Desch, sending Engstrom a quite direct rejection. He informed him that too much money had already been invested, too much precious material had been used and that the first model was too close to production to be thrown aside.[34] Engstrom had little choice but to accept the existing production model and hope that the proposed one hundred machines would be useful when they finally arrived in Washington.

July 26, a Day of Defeat

It took Joe Desch another month to send the first two production models to the test floor.[35] Then, he was able to have thirteen more of the new Bombes assembled by the last week of July--but none would work![36] July 26, 1943 was a critical day in the history of OP-20-G and the NCML. Desch and Howard's navy engineers feared the American Bombe might never be made operational. A year of work was almost declared a waste and the American Bombe came near to being abandoned. It was only Joe Desch's persistence and practical bent that saved the project. At the very last minute, he made a discovery that revived hope. Running the Bombe's bakelite code wheels at extreme speeds was again causing invisible distortions leading to false electrical contacts. Desch predicted that careful storage, handling, and refurbishing would solve the problem.[37] Again, his judgment was trusted. The wheels were reworked and production was resumed based on his hope that the last minute modifications would provide a permanent cure.

A Victory, a Bit Too Late

Desch had reason to demand faith in his machines and to be proud of what he had accomplished. Despite all the false starts, delays and problems he built one of the most complex machines in the world. The American Bombe contained thousands of high tolerance parts including some one thousand five hundred tubes arranged in what was very advanced circuitry. The 1943 Dayton Bombe was a seven foot high, eight foot long, two foot wide and five thousand pound marvel. It housed sixteen four wheel sets of enigma analogs and the Welchman diagonal board. It had all the circuits needed to link them together and test the hundreds of thousands of possible combinations of wheel positions against a text crib for inconsistency. Its sixty-four double enigma wheel commutators each contained one hundred and four contact points which had to be perfectly aligned when they touched the copper and silver sensing brushes. Such alignment and synchronization were difficult to achieve, especially for the fast wheel which rotated at close to two thousand rpm. Sensing brushes had to be kept free of oil and power had to be evenly delivered through a complex of motors, shafts and clutches. Running the Bombe's main shaft at two thousand rpm without creating the sparks and short circuits that ruined a test was also extremely difficult. Keeping the wheels in balance and in their original shape at such speeds was a triumph in itself, especially because the wheels had to be removed from the machine after each run.

Although Desch's model was based on the logic, parallel architecture and hardware of the British Bombe, his machine was an original. The truly distinctive part of Desch's machine was the its digital electronics. The sixty-four double commutators on the Bombes[38] could be driven at very high speeds by mechanical means, but motors and shafts and electromechanical counters were unable to track their position. The Desch Bombe's speed was so great that if a fast wheel dislodged from its spindle, it could disable an operator and fly through a wall. Few memory technologies could match such speeds.

The British had used a system of electrical relays within their Bombe to identify the positions of the wheels when a hit was encountered. The system had proven reliable, but in mid-1942, when Desch was informed that he was expected to create a machine some twenty-six times more powerful than the Turing Bombe, he knew that a relay system would be too slow. He turned to his experience with the NDRC counting circuits and the NCR electronic calculator and created a digital electronic tracking and control system that amazed the navy's engineers. His fifteen hundred tube system did more than record the position of a hit: It exercised control. It was able to track the wheel positions, signal the motor and the clutches, then reverse the machine's action until it had returned all the wheels to their hit positions. At that point, the wheel locations were printed and the operator could signal the machine to restart its search for consistencies.[39]

With the help of the electronic system, Desch came very close to achieving the original goals for the Bombe. His 1943 machine was two hundred times faster than the Polish Bomba, at least twenty times faster than the Turing Bombe and thirty percent faster than Britain's 1943 four wheel Bombe. His machine was able to run either three or four wheel tests and, with attachments that were added in later months, it could perform more than one test per run. Unfortunately, the goal of being able to run a four wheel Enigma test in the same number of minutes as a three wheel test on the older Bombes could not be fulfilled. Yet, taking only twice as long was impressive.[40] As important, Desch's Bombes proved to be very, very reliable. After their first shakedown runs they could be used twenty four hours a day.

The Bombes at Work, Perhaps

However, in September 1943 no one at Dayton was sure the Bombes would continue to function.[41] It was Desch's renewed optimism and a feared return of the U-boats that led Ralph Meader to begin to ship Bombes to OP-20-G's new Washington headquarters before testing had been completed. The machines began to arrive in the first week of September.[42] The Bombes were housed in the specially designed but not quite finished building Number 4 at the new Nebraska Avenue CSAW annex in Washington.

The Bombes under construction in Ohio were made more and more reliable, but some minor problems continued into the winter months. Most of the difficulties were procedural, not mechanical. The newly recruited Bombe operators had to be taught to avoid damaging the many delicate electrical connections when they attached the wheels to the drive shafts. Maintenance men had to learn to clean out all lint and dust on the wheels and the contacts and the cryptanalysts had to learn to build more effective menus for the machines. The supervisors of the machine rooms had to deal with the heat problem. The Bombes had their internal air conditioning, but not the building. The fifteen hundred tubes in each of the Bombes, combined with Washington's summer heat and humidity, called for a carefully regulated work regimen to avoid heat prostration.

By October 1943, most of the navy engineers had left Dayton and returned to Washington to supervise the Bombe operation. They planned to begin drawing up specifications for new Rapid Machines once the technical and procedural details for the Bombes were ironed out. The Dayton and Washington engineers could not devote much of their attention to new problems, however. The existing Bombes needed tending and there was mention of new versions of them to meet German challenges in late 1943. The immediate drag on the attempt to move back to more advanced machines was the Bombe production line. There were some problems with the suppliers and tie-ups at Dayton during fall 1943. NCR slipped beyond schedule. But, with the infusion of more manpower and the use of political pressure on the subcontractors, NCR was able to fulfill Desch's faith in the American mass production process.

Desch's manufacturing techniques gained the respect of the once skeptical British. By mid-November, Washington had over fifty bombes in operation and thirty more on-site.[43] The American navy finally began to be a truly productive Ultra member. By the end of the year, the first contract was completed[44] and Engstrom began to turn his crews to other technical and cryptanalytic problems. With the victory over the Atlantic submarines, an exhausted Joseph Wenger hoped the "M" group and the NCML could become self-directed and oriented to the future of Rapid Machines.

Although the second American Bombe project, from the first investigations to the last delivery, took almost a year longer than expected, Desch and OP-20-G received applause, not criticism in late 1943.[45] And when the Bureau's men looked at the overall cost of the project they found it difficult to complain. It cost more than two and one-half times more than originally planned, but the average investment in a Bombe was $45,000. That was a more than reasonable price for a machine that did the work of thousands of cryptanalytic clerks.[46] As a result of Dayton's achievement, the British found it impossible to continue on with a condescending attitude. In November, another important delegation arrived from England and began to entrust the Americans with more and more Enigma responsibilities. The Americans soon became the guardians of the U-boat work and Britain felt confident enough to concentrate on the Fish system and German army traffic.[47]

Once in Washington, the Bombes more than proved their worth. They had been needed. Without them, the American cryptanalysts had made little headway against Shark. The first time OP-20-G was able to tackle Enigma problems on any regular basis was in February 1943.[48] The results were disappointing. Then, better organization in Washington, more cryptanalytic clues from the British and the arrival of the Bombes radically changed the situation, as indicated by the average time OP-20-

G needed to break a U-boat Enigma message before and after the arrival of the Bombes.[49]

OP-20-G
Number of Hours Needed
to Decrypt an Enigma Message

Date	Average Hours
June 1943	600
July 1943	450
September 1943	72
December 1943 to end of war	18

More important than the speed of decryption was that the Allies' maintained control over the Atlantic Enigma. From mid-1943 to the end of the war, M4 was open to America and Britain. But, the American Bombes were born a bit too late.

By the time the Washington center received its machines the four wheel U-boat traffic was light. Other work had to be found for the near one hundred American machines. The navy's men soon began the analysis of other German Enigma systems. Though somewhat worried about breaching the agreement with Friedman's American army group, OP-20-G took on much German three wheel air force work.[50] To help with that and to speed all its Enigma processing, NCML built several attachments for the OP-20-G Bombes. Ones for three wheel Enigma tests, or for four wheel runs in which in was unnecessary to test all combinations of wheel positions, became known as Grenades."[51]

A Time of Triumph

By the fall of 1943, things were going much, much better for Wenger's dreams for a permanent RAM program. In addition to the Bombes, OP-20-G finally began to receive the Gray-NCR and the Eastman machines. The first of the several new Bush Comparators was put into operation in September. The new Comparator had a somewhat rocky career, however. When it arrived in Washington it had several flaws, including the incompatibility of its major components because of incorrect specifications sent to the contractors. It also proved to be much slower than desired. But the complaints about the machine's failings were turned to "M's" advantage. The critics were assured that placing the next developments in the hands of the OP-20-G-NCML group would prevent such mistakes.[52] The failings of Eastman-Kodak's devices were also used as arguments for an expansion of "G's" own research and development.[53] All in all, by January 1944, OP-20-G's RAM group seemed vindicated and ready to return to the extension of the microfilm and digital electronic technologies. Some hoped there would be time to search for a general purpose cryptanalytic machine, one that went beyond the Bush Comparator.

Meanwhile, the Army

While OP-20-G's cryptanalysts were establishing their place in European communications intelligence, the American army's codebreakers struggled to gain just a foothold. Unlike the navy, the American army was not involved in European related action until well after the outbreak of the war. It had a more difficult time than the navy in intercepting enemy messages and the British were much less in need of its cooperation.[54] Founded to replace Herbert Yardley's infamous Black Chamber in the late 1920s, the army's Signal Intelligence Service began with what Wenger yearned for, a core of young and talented civilian mathematicians. Under William F. Friedman they became renowned for their use of statistical methods.[55] Although separate from OP-20-G, the SIS had a gentlemen's agreement about cryptanalytic turf. Friedman's group agreed to focus on enemy army systems but to share a rather ill-defined zone of diplomatic and clandestine traffic with "G." The Coast Guard's cryptanalytic office, led by Friedman's wife, and the FBI's codebreaking group shared in tapping the diplomatic and clandestine traffic in the Americas. At times, those groups and the Federal Communication Commission's codebreakers irritated the army's SIS and were accused of poaching on army territory. But all the agencies had to live together in the 1930s and they arrived at a working balance that lasted until the outbreak of the war.[56]

The SIS may have wanted to be the predominant American cryptanalytic agency but it had to narrow its ambitions. It did not have the mandate or the resources to cover all systems or all the areas of the world. Like OP-20-G's crew during the 1930s, the SIS's men were directed to concentrate on Japan's secret systems. Only minimal attention was paid to Germany's communications because of the American war plans and the SIS's slim budgets. As significant to shaping SIS's history, it could not intercept adequate amounts of German army and air force traffic for analysis. The problems of intercepting enough military messages extended to the SIS's attack on Japan's army systems. Unlike the use of high powered radio by navies, the army and air forces of the world sent relatively few messages that could be intercepted from a distance. Even after the SIS constructed listening posts in the Pacific and the Canal Zone[57] it could not acquire military messages in enough "depth" for code or cipher breaking.[58]

Thus, Friedman's talented men and women spent much of their time on diplomatic communications. They could be intercepted and were valuable. By the late 1930s, SIS's young analysts were tapping the most precious diplomatic transmissions and in 1940 they laid the foundation for America's Magic by successfully attacking Japan's Purple enciphering machine system. It carried Japan's most important diplomatic messages to and from the world's capitals. With Magic, American leaders were informed of the highest level diplomatic if not military decisions by the Japanese government. Although Friedman's group received help from the navy in attacking Purple, Magic was seen as an SIS triumph by the nation's leadership.

Friedman's group had employed modern as well as traditional cryptanalytic techniques against Purple. A few years after OP-20-G began to use tabulating machines, the SIS established its first automation foothold.[59] Although it did not begin an OP-20-G-like Rapid Machine project before the war, the SIS hired a newly minted MIT electrical engineer at a critical stage in the Japanese diplomatic problem. That graduate of MIT's electrical engineering program, Leo Rosen, helped break the Japanese diplomatic machine and constructed its first analog.[60] The SIS was unable to exploit his talents to the fullest, however. Before the war it did not create a machine research group or go beyond building direct analogs of enemy machines. Even after Rosen returned from the Magic-Ultra exchange with GC&CS in the spring of 1941, the SIS did not launch a Rapid Machine development program.[61]

The Other American Ultra

When war broke out the SIS had little to do. It had no Enigma capability and it was unable to read the major Japanese or German military codes. "G," however, was overworked with naval systems so it turned all of the Japanese diplomatic work over to the SIS.[62] The Purple diplomatic challenge took much of the army's attention. That attention was well placed for much was learned about Germany as well as Japan from the messages. But when the SIS tried to establish an Enigma program and demanded to become a partner in Ultra, it found that it had little to negotiate with. Purple had been given away in early 1941.[63]

Throughout the war the SIS's men felt they had to fight much harder than the navy for British concessions on Ultra.[64] In early 1942, when Britain insisted that the SIS focus on the Pacific and trust GC&CS for adequate European and African intelligence, Friedman's codebreakers had to comply. Already having shared Purple and without the ability to intercept German messages, they had little leverage. They did win some points, however. SIS's leaders visited Bletchley Park and gradually learned about Enigma and the Fish systems. By the later years of the war, a large SIS team was in England running a section of the British Bombes and some of GC&CS's men worked in Washington. But, the army's codebreakers never developed an independent Enigma capability. Time after time, the SIS began "E" initiatives only to drop them because of the lack of intercepts and because of orders to yield to British demands.[65] And, the SIS was tormented by the Japanese army code problem. It was not until the spring of 1943 that the SIS centers in Washington and Australia were able to tap a major army system.[66] Perhaps it was the need to concentrate everything on breaking the Japanese codes that led the SIS to be somewhat behind the navy in establishing a group to develop rapid machines.

The Other RAM Program

But, some steps had been taken to begin an army machine program and to gain a share of Ultra. At the beginning of the war, the SIS's men learned of OP-20-G's Eastman and Gray contracts and agreed to at least support such efforts in spirit if not with funds. But, it placed its faith elsewhere during the first critical months of the war. The SIS made its own agreement with IBM and soon had scores of tabulating machines. Many IBM engineers were sent to Washington to make significant modifications to the tabs and sorters. By the end of war, the SIS had over four hundred IBM machines, was using a million IBM cards a day and was paying three-quarters of a million dollars a year in rental fees to Tom Watson.[67]

In the first months of the war the SIS focused on expanding its tabulator section and it was not until late 1942 that it decided to create a machine research group. The MIT man, Leo Rosen, was placed at its head.[68] He advised his superiors that the SIS should purchase almost two-hundred thousand dollars worth of copies of the OP-20-G sponsored machines from Eastman and Gray.[69] His major assignment, however, was to produce a machine to give SIS the kind of power the army thought OP-20-G was gaining over GC&CS through its emerging Bombe program. Rosen studied the navy's Bombe proposals in September 1942, reexamined what SIS had on the British Bombe, consulted with William Friedman, and recommended that the SIS create its own anti-Enigma machinery.

After some further study, in October 1942, the SIS decided to build its version of a Bombe and to do it independently of Britain and OP-20-G.[70] The next step was to decide which type of special machine. Friedman and Rosen explored several alternatives. Rosen's "F" team built an electronic Enigma wheel while Friedman made the rounds of the scientists associated with the NDRC's fire control computers.[71] Rosen's electronic option was rejected for the same reasons OP-20-G had dropped electronics during the summer. Then, one of the alternatives recommended by the NDRC experts was approved. Like "G," the SIS decided to take a backwards technological step in order to meet its Enigma crisis.

After consultations with the famous pre-computer builder George Stibitz (of Bell Laboratories and the NDRC fire control project) the SIS decided to spend one million dollars on a single huge relay Enigma analysis machine.[72] What became known as Madame X followed the general logic of the Turing attack on the Enigma, but it was significantly different from the British and the OP-20-G Bombes. Built with the help of the Western Electric engineer, Sam Williams, the SIS machine was in operation a year later, October 1943.[73]

Madame X (also known as 003) was huge. It contained enough advanced relay equipment for a telephone switching system for a medium size American city. It was so expensive and large because the

SIS had decided to be more elegant and innovative than the navy. It wanted one grand Enigma-fighting machine. The 003 contained some one hundred and forty-four enigma scrambler units as compared to the sixteen in the OP-20-G Bombe. The large number of "E" units were built into the machine for two reasons. First, the longer a crib and its chains, the fewer the false hits. Less precious time would be wasted hand testing the drops. Second, a large number of units linked through a central control system allowed several different menus to be run simultaneously.

The 003 was designed to be easy to use and to have a fast set up time. The army technicians flipped switches rather than having to place dozens of commutators on the machine as the navy's operators had to do. Very important and innovative was the automatic control of the stepping motion of the wheels. The relay circuits allowed the machine to use "non-metric" motion. Of course, 003's various control systems also made it much less labor intensive than the navy Bombes.[74]

Despite its great flexibility, 003 was not a perfect solution and it did not change the navy's mind about Bombe architecture. When OP-20-G decided to build a second set of some fifty machines, it found Desch's commutator design much faster and more efficient than a relay-based machine.[75] The navy evaluated 003 some three months after its birth and found serious deficiencies. The most startling was that the army's machine was a limited three wheel engine. It had been designed to challenge simpler Enigmas such as those used by the German army and air force. It could not be switched to a four wheel mode and twenty-six separate runs had to be made to test a four wheel message. That made the million dollar 003 equivalent to less than one forty-five thousand dollar navy Bombe for an M4 problem. The navy's engineers diplomatically pointed out that the Germans were beginning to change all the Enigma nets to four wheel systems.

As objectionable to the navy's engineers was 003's slow operating speed. Relays did not switch as fast as the spinning commutators. A single three wheel problem on the 003 took ten minutes of machine time or at least ten times what Desch's first production Bombs needed for a simple three wheel job. The automatic control system in Madame X did not fully compensate for the long running times. It took more time to set up a Desch Bombe because of the need to reset wheels and plug many wires, but that was done in parallel by a team for each of the Bombes. That decreased much of 003's advantage. The 003 had another feature that did not prove as powerful as hoped. The army machine had the circuits necessary for the "locator" task done separately by the navy's Hypo machine, but the navy's engineer-cryptanalysts did not find 003's automatic locator that attractive.

The navy also concluded that the 003 was not cost-effective nor efficient in terms of manpower utilization. Overall, the navy thought, the one million dollar army Madame X was worth only one navy Bombe and one Hypo machine. At the very least, the X cost twice as much per cryptanalytic output unit as the Bombes.[76] Similar army evaluations of the relay machine may have been part of the reason why the SIS did not build additional Madame Xs.[77]

The more important reason why only one 003 was built was the SIS's inability to convince the British to yield the messages and techniques needed to keep the machine busy. Friedman's men protested several times about lack of intercepts after 003 was constructed. They became very upset when, after attempting to use the 003 as a wedge to gain more from the British, they learned of how much OP-20-G had obtained from its announcement that it would build three hundred fifty Bombes. The army's relay Bombe did not win such victories. By the time of the BRUSA pact the SIS, much more than OP-20-G, had become a subsection of GC&CS, dependent upon its decisions about allocation of work and disclosure of techniques. Madame X did win some victories, however. As an engineering project and as an example of America's mass production capabilities, it captured the respect of the British engineers. As a result, Britain asked the SIS to help solve more complex engineering problems and gladly accepted some American machines within GC&CS.[78] By the end of the war, the SIS was busy creating very advanced electronic machines and, like OP-20-G, was hoping for a permanent in-house computer program.[79]

Finally, Some Forward Technological Steps

In late 1943, just as the first OP-20-G and SIS bombes were being completed, another stage in the development of cryptanalytic machines began. Both American engineering groups returned to a consideration of digital electronics. At the same time, they began to pay attention to the Japanese problems.

The war in the Pacific was an American show and the cryptanalytic work was not cluttered with the kind of difficulties that complicated the European relationships. OP-20-G and SIS had much more freedom and the British were more cooperative. Despite the greater freedom, the Pacific never received as much attention from OP-20-G's and SIS's machine builders as did the Atlantic. There was no crash program to develop expensive machines to conquer the Japanese code and cipher systems. However, the engineers in Washington and Dayton put a great deal of work into solving problems for the cryptanalysts assigned to the Asian traffic.

Lawrence Steinhardt had been left in Washington during 1942 and 1943 to design what became the Copperhead tape scanning systems and to start building very advanced analogs of several different Japanese encryption machines. Those analogs went far, far beyond the models of the Purple and the Red built during the 1930s. At first, however, the machines like the Viper and Python were just more advanced combinations of relays, plugboards, and stepping switches that mimicked particular Japanese encryption machines. But more and more electronics were added and the navy machines evolved from copies of the enemy's devices to become analytical engines. In fact, by the war's end, OP-20-G built its small version of an electronic Bombe to fight the Japanese, not the Germans.

The electronic Rattler was designed to attack a limited range of Japanese devices and used a modified crib approach. But, it was a true technical advance. However, it has never received the recognition it deserves--nor have some of the later machines for Japanese problems developed by the SIS.[80] The SIS digraph counter, Freak, was also an anti-Japanese machine, one which replaced the many electromechanical counters of NCR's old Mike with four huge bays of electrical condensers. It took the condenser storage technology beyond what had been accomplished by those who had explored it for the MIT computer and NDRC fire control projects.[81]

Although OP-20-G and the SIS turned to the Pacific after 1943, the Enigma continued to receive attention. The new work on it also contributed to the development of digital electronics. Several new advanced versions of the navy Bombes were built. They all continued to rely on some version of the spinning commutators and centered about analog processing, but each contained more and more electronic circuitry that made decisions on the basis of statistical cryptanalytic criteria. One machine even recognized letters. The SIS also built an electronic and digital Enigma-fighter at the end of the war, the Superscritcher. Like the navy's Duenna and Britain's Giant, it was designed to conquer the changes in the German's use of the Enigma's plugboard, ones that made the old Bombes ineffective.[82]

At Last, Electronics

The Americans also made some contributions to Britain's attack on the Fish system, again betting they could overcome problems with advanced electronics. Those and the other gambles paid off. By the time Japan surrendered, the Americans were building electronic machines using twice as many tubes as the British Colossus. The advances in electronics at the cryptanalytic centers were amazing. But, in several ways, the American's achievements were limited. The cryptanalytic problems they solved with digital electronics were not memory dependent and some of the new electronic machines they built were based on very clever ways to make analog technology imitate digital methods. And, the new machines were not true data processors. Although the navy had its Copperheads and Comparators, large files remained in the domain of the tabulators and sorters. However, the Rapid Machine efforts proved so valuable that in the last year of the war the army and navy engineers were allowed to begin relatively long-term projects. Their goal was to merge their new electronic expertise with the possibilities of Bush's tape and microfilm solutions to the memory problem.

Beyond the Comparator

By mid-1944, the Allies were sure of eventual victory and the cryptanalysts had a few moments to think of the postwar era. They did not have complete freedom to pursue the old dreams of mathematical methods and magical machines, however. There were recurrent crises during the remaining year that called Wenger's and Friedman's men away from any long-term development work and back to special purpose devices. OP-20-G's John Palmer, who before the war had lead IBM's electronic computer research, was pulled off of his investigations of magnetic data recording to build a huge six cabinet machine in three weeks of day and night work.[83] Then, just before the invasion of Japan, massive changes in its systems led "G" and the SIS to a frantic search to discover the nature of the new Japanese codes and ciphers and to change machines and procedures.[84] Such crises meant that while there was renewed interest in a general purpose rapid cryptanalytic machine, at the war's end there was no device that was a great advance on Bush's old Comparator. Worse, no one was sure there would ever be a general purpose RAM because the future of the advanced cryptanalytic and machine groups at OP-20-G and the SIS were in question.

As a result, both Wenger and William Friedman had to renew their crusades for machine programs. They created different solutions to the difficult problem of institutionalizing cryptanalytic research in the postwar years, but they faced similar challenges during the concluding months of the war.

The Chance to Begin an ERA

As the war was winding down, OP-20-G and the SIS knew they would be stripped of men and resources. Rosen's "F" branch was in jeopardy and Engstrom's "M" and the NCML faced extinction. The Bureau of Ships showed signs of tiring of the near autonomous NCML and "M" had its own special problems because of navy personnel rules. Holding onto its many exceptional scientists and engineers was an especially difficult and pressing problem. Without them, little progress could be made on methods or machines. There were no cryptanalytic think-tanks and all the private computing machine contractors made no effort to hide that they were tired of government work. As threatening, in 1945, there was no electronic computer industry and there was little indication that one would emerge. The simple answer to the problem, to keep all the key men in the army and navy, was never an alternative. Many of them were too old to remain in the regular military, others would not settle for the low military pay and neither service could create enough high paying civil service jobs to ensure a viable internal program. Friedman lobbied the army to maintain as many civilian slots as possible and he tried to create a joint machine development center with OP-20-G, but he had to settle for a small machine group in the SIS that could direct and oversee established contractors.[85] Wenger sought much more. Rejecting the suggestions for a joint army-navy program, he began an independent search for a practical solution.

At first, things fell into place. By the end of the war cryptanalysis and science had made some very good friends in the navy's hierarchy and in the White House. The critical victory at Midway and the Bombe program were just two of a long string of OP-20-G achievements that made the navy brass think "G" had more than made up for the Pearl Harbor fiasco. The Secretary of the Navy took great pride in OP-20-

G's achievements and the Chief of Naval Operations had become an ally.[86] That made Wenger's job much easier and his victories seemed to come one after the other in 1945. The Office of the Chief of Naval Operations helped overcome any objections from the Bureau and the NCML's life was extended, at least for a time. Continuous postwar funding seemed more than a possibility. In late summer 1945 a one-half million dollar, one year development contract was awarded to NCML-NCR. It included funds to work on a new general purpose Comparator. Wenger did not rest there, however. He presented a series of fact filled and passionate pleas for the money and organization needed to create an electronic machine to conquer the coming generations of enciphering devices. He pointed to the failures as well as the successes of "G" in World War II and warned of the unthinkable consequences of returning to the "unsponsored, ill-supported, meager organization of 1941," in the coming era of guided missiles and atomic bombs. He underlined that the United States could never again expect to have the time to make and correct fundamental mistakes as it did during World War II. He hammered at two other points: The traditional division between operational and Bureau powers would ill-serve a modern navy; and, that only a continuation of something like the cooperative relations between the "M" group, NCR and the NCML could save naval cryptanalysis.[87]

He was given assurances that OP-20-G would be allowed its own program and was told that navy money would be made available for continuous machine development. Then, Wenger received the wonderful news of the establishment of a long-term program to continue upgrading communications intelligence equipment and methods. More than money was promised. Project Monogram's funds and the other allocations of the immediate postwar years came with the pledge of autonomy for "G"; it would be allowed to direct its own work free from the Office of Naval Research, the Naval Research Laboratory, the naval electronics laboratories and, to a very great degree, the Bureau of Ships. The Rapid Machine program finally had a future.[88]

Well before Wenger worked out all the details of his agenda, he tackled the other side of the long-term research problem. Monogram and other navy contracts would supply the money, the remaining problem was: Who was to do the work? Wenger knew that he could not retain the full "M" group within the navy and that even Colonel

Deeds's company had tired of government contracts. He went to his old mentor Stanford Caldwell Hooper for advice. Then, in late 1944, he put Howard Engstrom, Ralph Meader, John Howard and another of the bright navy engineers, Bill Norris, to work on the suggestions.[89] They proposed what they thought was a way to permanently link science and innovation to the navy. It was a new version of Hooper's post World War I RCA. In 1945, Wenger's men recommended creating the private, for-profit, National Electronics Laboratory. The company was to be staffed by the talented young men from OP-20-G and the other advanced science agencies in the navy.[90] Wenger approved the idea, interpreting it as the chance to establish a new version of companies such as Sperry and Norden and SubSignal. He envisioned a firm that would devote itself to navy communications problems,[91] ranging from cryptanalysis to the physics of radio. He planned to retain a few technical men in the promised civilian scientific slots within OP-20-G, however. They would be needed to draw plans and to coordinate with the NCML and the new for-profit company.

As fast as possible, the plan was cleared with the hierarchy. Before Germany's defeat and despite the rumors that the army and navy cryptanalytic groups might be asked to merge,[92] the navy's legal experts gave the green light to "M's" officers, such as Engstrom and Norris, having an interest in the private company. Very clear signals were also given that OP-20-G contracts would automatically flow to the new firm. With those assurances, the word was spread within the navy and mathematicians, physicists and engineers from OP-20-G and other navy departments began to envision careers as civilian scientists working for the military. Most of the "M" engineering team, including Howard, Coombs and Steinhardt agreed to join, but those who had been IBM employees decided to return to their old company. Joe Desch and his men also opted to stay with their company, NCR.[93]

With the line-up of key men, the Engstrom-Norris group was ready to seek financing. Very important strings were pulled and Lewis Strauss, advisor to the presidents and future head of the atomic energy program, became interested in the project.[94] He almost convinced his investment company, the giant Kuhn-Loeb, to sponsor the new venture. He wanted Kuhn-Loeb to provide the Laboratory with a level of financial backing that would guarantee its future and its contribution to national defense.[95] Unfortunately for Wenger's dream, the firm's analysts determined that the National Electronics Laboratory's financial planning was not sound and that America had little need for another science organization. Kuhn-Loeb stepped out and the Engstrom-Norris group had to launch a hurried search for capital and a new name.

They faced more disappointments. America's old scientific organizations rejected them. The Rockefeller Foundation thought America had enough research institutions. A sponsor could not be found and the situation became critical. Wenger worried that the postwar "G" would be without its intellectual allies and without an integrated research and production team. At the end of 1945, he had his new research agenda and had promises of contracts, but he had no idea of where to find the men to build a full electronic Super Bombe, a new version of Mike, his grand universal Comparator, or even a viable punch for the old Comparators and the Copperheads.[96]

A savior finally appeared. But even the investment banker, entrepreneur and old friend of the navy, John Parker, could not piece together truly adequate funding. He could not even locate his new company near OP-20-G. Among Parker's many wartime enterprises was a military glider factory in St. Paul, Minnesota that was being phased out with the end of the war. He sought some use for the building and its equipment. Coming in contact with the Engstrom-Norris group through mutual friends in the military,[97] he was persuaded that a private version of the NCML-NCR could succeed. He agreed to gather minimal financing, to help with business matters and to set the new company up in his old factory.

The firm, now called Engineering Research Associates, immediately gained the navy's approval and it immediately won OP-20-G's big research contract.[98] Within a year of its early 1946 founding, ERA was a five million dollar a year business and seemed to be on the road to becoming a major force in the emerging American electronics industry. To continue the World War II relationship and to pay deference to the Bureau of Ships, the NCML moved into ERA's St. Paul factory. When Howard Engstrom, John Howard, Ralph Meader and the other major figures at "M" were finally released from military duty they immediately established an ERA office in Washington to solicit contracts for all types of mathematical and scientific work.[99] Soon, an old friend of "G" and naval science appeared; Stanford C. Hooper was made a paid consultant to ERA.[100]

A Bright Hope for Hooper's Dreams

By mid-1946, Wenger thought he had attained his goals. ERA was established and it contained most of the old "M" group. It had a broad contract with "G," one that gave it the freedom Bush had sought in the 1930s. ERA seemed stable and its men were happy with competitive salaries, stock in the company and the chance to do cutting edge work in computers, communications and operations analysis. The new Bureau contracting rules gave Wenger his independence and he began to feel confident that yearly research budgets of a million dollars or more would continue to be approved. He also had a small but effective cadre within OP-20-G to manage his technology program. Joseph Eachus, Howard Campaigne and James T. Pendergrass were top-flight young scientists who appreciated the role of mathematics and computers in cryptanalysis. Most importantly, ERA was launched on the mission of creating a general purpose cryptanalytic computer. It had the chance to turn the RAM effort into the most advanced computer development program in the world.[101]

But, ERA did not start its career with a leap into fully digital electronic computing. It had to begin with an attempt to build the next generation of Bush's machines. However, that assignment finally had the right context. In mid-1946, there was no great rush to produce a machine for a crisis. Although Joe Eachus had specific designs in mind, and although OP-20-G wanted a new piece of hardware, the project was as much a search for the perfect cryptanalytic machine with the most advanced features as it was a construction project.[102] All types of memory media, including microfilm, were explored as were new tubes and circuit designs. Quite naturally, John Howard was in charge of the operations side of the latest Comparator project, and, quite naturally, he relied upon his earlier experience and his MIT friends. He was assisted by John Coombs and Larry Steinhardt.[103] The project began under the name used by the British for their tape machines, Robinson, but soon gained a name with a similar American meaning, Goldberg. Both names pointed to ungainly and complex contraptions and both projects were designed to deal with the memory problem rather than to develop a programmable universal electronic computer.

Ideas and Ideals From the Outside

Goldberg's components, if not its architecture, shifted with the appearance of technological innovations. The machine became something of a test bed for each new technology and would have been the subject of even greater experimentation if ERA's and OP-20-G's attention had not been drawn to a new use of electronics.[104] Just as the Goldberg project was launched in St. Paul, and as Wenger's own research group was deciding whether or not to build an electronic Super Bombe, "G's" James T. Pendergrass enrolled in a summer institute on the programmable digital electronic computer. That seminar on a universal machine had evolved out of a relatively minor fire control related project at the University of Pennsylvania.[105]

The University of Pennsylvania's World War II contract with Army Ordnance came almost by chance. Just as the NDRC ended its computer program and as firms such as RCA rejected pleas to turn their hard-pressed engineers to low priority projects, Ordnance sought a way to speed the calculation of firing tables. With no other alternative, the army accepted the proposal of two young engineers at the Moore school. They promised to build an electronic version of Bush's great Differential Analyser. Fortunately for the history of computers, John Mauchly and Presper Eckert were given a great deal of freedom and time. Unlike the men at OP-20-G, they were not under intense pressures to immediately produce machines for crises. Their much delayed postwar delivery of the special purpose ENIAC was not treated as a sign of failure and their more advanced plan for a programmable universal electronic computer was quickly funded. With the help of the famous John von Neumann, they launched their EDVAC project and a series of seminars that attracted the pre and postwar generations of computer builders.[106] All those who had made contributions in the 1930s and during the war attended.

At the Moore School's summer program, OP-20-G's Pendergrass studied the designs of the ENIAC and those for the much more advanced EDVAC general purpose, programmable computer. He listened to the presentations of the other men who had begun to develop universal electronic machines. He was very impressed and immediately wrote a report which recommended the creation of a general, not special purpose, electronic machine for cryptanalysis. Through the use of "programs," Pendergrass insisted, one machine could perform all the major cryptanalytic tests. He described how the new universal computer went far, far beyond the Bush machines and their cousins such as Goldberg. His recommendation was well received and Wenger launched an investigation under a contract with ERA and the ONR. Very soon, ERA's men were thinking of going into the commercial computer business.[107]

In a short time, OP-20-G decided that a programmed computer was a necessity. It put aside the idea of building an electronic Super Bombe, sidestepped some serious objections from the Bureau about funding something it thought should be paid for by private companies, and ordered ERA to begin to build one of the world's first electronic binary programmable computers, the Atlas. Begun in mid-1947, it became a major project taking up much of ERA's energies for three years.[108] And, well before the original model was shipped to Washington, ERA laid plans to put similar machines on sale in the civilian market.[109] Fortunately for Goldberg, OP-20-G had more than enough money to continue exploring Bush's visions of special purpose photoelectronic machines as well as to investigate the potentials of the modern computer.

Crises Again: The Cold War

But, a leisurely research pace at ERA and "G" could not be maintained. In 1947, although Goldberg and Atlas continued as near blue sky projects, needs arose for more special purpose electronic cryptanalytic machines, ones to solve immediate cryptanalytic and intelligence problems. The Cold War began quite early for "G" and as a result ERA was put under great pressure to build a series of advanced yet crisis driven machines. Names like Omalley, Demon, Hecate, and Warlock became familiar as ERA was ordered to temporarily put aside the speculative Goldberg and money-starved Atlas and to use existing technologies to help solve critical intelligence problems.[110] Those machines incorporated much that was new, including magnetic drum memories (first operational in Germany) and advanced circuits, but they were in the tradition of World War II. They were built in response to specific problems; they were to be as simple as possible; and, they were to be finished in time to meet new cryptanalytic needs. All were rush jobs and caused strains at ERA.[111]

Unfortunately, the engineers at ERA, even with help from computer builders at MIT and other new centers, could not rush Atlas. Like all the other programmed computer projects in the nation, it dragged on well beyond original projections. New technical difficulties appeared each month and although OP-20-G's man Joe Eachus could understand the problems, the Bureau of Ships began to have additional misgivings about the navy, including the ONR, sponsoring such long-term development work.[112] The army's reviewers probably had similar feelings about what was happening with the SIS "F" section's projects.

The Army's Problems and Stratton's Dream Revived

The SIS also feared the loss of many of its engineers after the war. But, it was unable to create its own ERA. Its eventual solution was to do machine design in-house, go to contractors for components, then assemble the secret devices itself. That seemed quite efficient[113] but it was unable to follow that approach when it began its first general purpose computer, Abner. When the SIS decided it needed a modern computer, it contacted the National Bureau of Standards.

Standards had visions of becoming what Stratton had desired a generation before, the center for computer development in the nation. It was already helping several government agencies with their computer efforts by coordinating the work of different contractors and making suggestions about the logic and architecture of the new machines.[114] Thus, in late 1948, the SIS asked the National Bureau of Standards, not ERA, to build its Abner computer.[115] Then, it sat back and congratulated itself on taking the most cost-effective path to computer design and construction. But things simply did not work out. The NBS had too much to do and repeatedly pushed the SIS project aside. Finally, the "F" section's men decided to build their own machine and did so in rather makeshift quarters. Abner also turned into a four-year project.[116] Like OP-20-G's Atlas, Abner appeared much later than thought, cost more than thought and gave the appearance that the SIS's machine program was a bit too disorganized for continued self-direction.

Never a Microfilm Machine Will There Be, Perhaps

At ERA, the general purpose Comparator, Goldberg, was also allowed to just trickle toward completion. Many of its components were in advanced stages within the first two years, but Goldberg was not in operation until summer 1951. During its more than four years of development, almost every possible technology and architecture was explored, but Goldberg ended up being an elaboration on the early Comparators. Goldberg took photoelectric sensing and paper tape scanning to new technical heights. Very fast tape drives were completed by the end of 1947, allowing as many as four tapes to be run on top of each other. The drives ran the tapes at more than six times the speed of the older devices and were able to offset the tapes for IC testing without slowing the machine.[117] Goldberg was also an example of how much electronics had matured since 1945. A very complex and precise scanner was developed which included the photocells and circuits to sense each of the seven data and three control positions in each row on a tape. Goldberg's more than seven thousand tubes reflected the complexity of its digital circuits. It was able to perform many different cryptanalytic functions and its thirty-six decimal counting circuits allowed deep statistical analysis. Much was made automatic. It had banks of rectifiers and magnetic drums as well as special circuits to calculate the IC thresholds.

Although it was late in coming, Goldberg was the state of the art Comparator and contemporaries thought the more than one-quarter million dollars spent on it was a very wise investment. The engineers at ERA learned a great deal from its development and they transferred much of its technology to other machines. But one lesson they learned from Goldberg they did not seem to apply to other projects. Very early in Goldberg's history, it was decided that microfilm was not a wise choice for its memory.[118]

The Challenge of Turning Science into a Business

In 1947, while Howard and his men wrestled with Goldberg, ERA began to take shape as a military and private contractor. But its dual role quickly entangled it in a series of conflicts no one had foreseen in

1945. Joseph Wenger may have thought ERA would be OP-20-G's creature, but from its first days ERA's men had a somewhat different interpretation. As the early Cold War's demands began to pile up on ERA, "G's" assignments and the company's private work came into open conflict. As a result, the Bureau of Ships began to voice its old objections to ERA and to the way OP-20-G directed its work.

The conflicts were not the result of avarice or ineptitude. They came about because of lack of support for applied science before the Cold War created the science industry of the 1950s. Although John Parker had agreed to find important people to finance ERA, it began its life on a financial shoestring. It had little working capital and, for a time, survived only because the Bureau agreed to pay it as stages of projects were completed. ERA also began with a fear that the navy's work would be unable to sustain it. Each of the founding members was urged to search for other projects. That search developed its own dynamic and by the end of 1947 the navy's contracts accounted for less than one-half of ERA's business. Although that share varied from year to year, ERA soon had a life of its own and developed many outside ties and obligations. It joined with the National Bureau of Standards in the search for a commercially viable electronic computer; it gained a prestige contract from the ONR to survey all computer logic and technology; it had contracts with the atomic energy agencies; it was developing civil air control systems; and, one of its divisions was designing sanitary trucks for airports. ERA even signed a contract to develop a magnetic drum computer for IBM.[119]

All that activity did not lead to financial security nor to harmony within the company. But, it did lead to protests by OP-20-G, and, in September 1947, John Parker had to sternly remind all the ERA men that the "G" work was and would remain the company's first priority. He informed the St. Paul and Washington branches that he understood the need for civilian contracts, but he emphasized they were endangering ERA's standing with the navy.[120] ERA's expanding activities also led to another round of protests by the Bureau of Ships.

Within a year of ERA's founding, the Bureau was complaining about "G's" awarding so few contracts to the navy's laboratories, the use of a private plane to shuttle ERA's executives around the country and the separate Washington ERA office that seemed to have nothing to do with the NCML. By mid-1947, the Bureau was insisting on the maintenance of project schedules and it began to exert much more power over the OP-20-G-ERA work. Those actions did not settle matters, however. Throughout 1948 and 1949 the Bureau kept up the demands for an end to the special relationship between OP-20-G and ERA. The Bureau was ready to take further steps.[121]

The pressures compounded the problems ERA faced as its managers tried to turn a group of ex-academics and very creative engineers into businessmen. There were internal disagreements about ERA's place in science and arguments also developed over which projects to support. ERA's founders began to drift apart. By late 1949, key engineers were leaving to find positions in the emerging commercial electronic computer industry. One of the first men to leave was John Howard and one of the reasons for his departure was ERA's attempt to revive Bush's Rapid Selector.

The grand hopes of 1946 had turned into frustration for the bright engineers like Howard, as well as for the managers of ERA. The young and innovative firm had been founded on the premise that civilian and military work were compatible. The engineers expected to find that innovations in one realm would immediately transfer to the other. The cross-seeding, they thought, would guarantee technological progress within the firm. The money-men in the company, such as Meader and Parker, thought that the special relationship with the navy would provide a level of economic security the company needed while it created a niche for itself in the new science and high-technology markets they saw emerging in the civilian economy. They never imagined that defense and civilian work would come into conflict.

But ERA's attempt to build a new Rapid Selector proved that many of the assumptions of ERA's technical men and managers were incorrect. The project became a technical, financial, and managerial nightmare. The engineers could not make military technology work in a practical civilian setting, they could not please their defense and academic customers at the same time, and the Selector project became a financial sink-hole for the company.

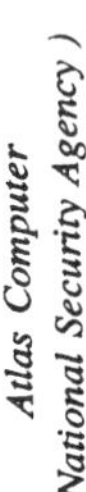

Atlas Computer
(National Security Agency)

Chapter XIII
The Postwar Trauma:
The Reappearance of the Other Memex

Engineering Research Associates had such a turbulent history because it was an expedient rather than a permanent solution to the problem of establishing a balanced relationship between science and the military. Its productive but short life began as a compromise between Wenger's and Hooper's earlier dreams of independence and the realities of postwar demobilization. ERA was a means of compensating for the institutional vacuum that existed during the brief but important period between the end of World War II and the early 1950s when the Cold War turned science into a business.[1]

Big Science Emerges

In the half decade between the surrender of Japan and the outbreak of the Korean War, the United States became the center of the struggle against the Soviets. But, the nation's foreign policies and military strategies were not always clear or predictable. Defense spending remained low, no one was sure of the outcome of the debates over the unification of the nation's armed services and arguments continued over the relationship between academia, industry and the military. ERA's splintering and then its purchase by the giant Remington-Rand Corporation in the early 1950s was ironic, but perhaps inevitable. ERA had been founded with the hope of avoiding the problems associated with large-scale government contractors, but with the long awaited fixing of American policy and the development of a computer industry, ERA had to become part of the bureaucratic system Hooper and Bush had so disliked. The stress of acting as OP-20-G's handmaiden and trying to compete in the wider market became too great. The sudden rise of competitors for its military work was the final blow for ERA.

The maturation of the new Cold War defense industry, the nation's commitment to unifying and expanding its communications intelligence services and the new relationship between academia and the military made ERA's ill-defined attempt to become a combination of secret workshop, think-tank and traditional contractor untenable.

In the Interim, Before Big Science, 1945-1950

In 1945, military demobilization meant the end of much of big wartime science. The NDRC/OSRD was abruptly ended as were many corporate and military-academic research programs. At the same time, America's businesses turned to the production of consumer goods. Companies without a large consumer base, such as Vannevar Bush's friend, Raytheon, searched for new products and markets to avoid paring back to their prewar size. More established firms, such as IBM, RCA and NCR, declined further government contracts to avoid loosing their place in the private markets. At the universities it seemed that very important links between science and application would be forever severed. The vast radar program at MIT's "Rad Lab," electronics at the Applied Physics Laboratory at Johns Hopkins, and Cal Tech's missile program were in jeopardy. Academics who had tasted the thrill of wartime work feared having to return to their rather boring and certainly ill-paid academic careers.[2] More than symbolic, many of the atomic bomb projects and related institutions faced extinction.

As threatening to the cause of American research was the absence of a civilian science policy. Despite the pleas of men like Bush to recreate the NDRC as a large permanent federal program for elite civilian science, the government seemed to be moving back to its prewar pattern. The fight to establish the National Science Foundation bogged down in the same arguments over elitism and congressional control that had threatened the NDRC during the war.[3] The prospect of the federal government's role in science being determined by congressmen, or worse, by decisions within well intentioned but budget starved federal agencies, frightened all those who had shared in the bounty and power of the NDRC's war programs.

The nation faced the possibility of returning to the thin and weak scientific structure of the 1930s. The old federal science organizations, such as the National Research Council, ended the war as powerless as they were in the 1930s. The National Bureau of Standards's desire to revive Samuel Stratton's grand visions was applauded, but it rested on very shaky financial and political foundations. Standards did not have the resources to become the nation's center for computer development and applied mathematics. The Office of Naval Research's policy of supporting abstract academic work was appreciated, but it too had limited budgets and survived by keeping a low political profile.[4] Although the military bureaus had learned that science could produce results, and while they were embarking on high technology programs such as jet propulsion and missile development, their ability to fund abstract investigations was very limited. The bureaus were able to support some development programs immediately after the war, such as the computer projects at the Institute for Advanced Study, the University of Pennsylvania, and even MIT, but the scale of financing was far, far below that of the war years.

The institutions of old American science could not cope. The private philanthropies were revived but even the mighty Carnegie and Rockefeller foundations could not match the federal accomplishments of World War II. As before, professional organizations had little to spend. They could encourage their members and they could lobby government, but they had no financial muscle. American higher education was growing, but more in terms of student population than financial independence. As in the 1930s, American universities and their faculties had to go begging to the outside world to finance research. The war years had, in fact, compounded the problems of academics. As their research became more relevant and tied to technology, it became more expensive. The days when the University of California's E.O. Lawrence could make fundamental contributions to his field using parts from an abandoned naval radio transmission system were gone.[5]

Little Libraries, Again

Documentalists were among those who did not wish to see an end to the generosity and advances of the war years. The flood of programmatic military research had led to thousands of new reports and a recognition of the need for advances in data retrieval. The creation of massive data bases and recovery systems in organizations like the OSS had demonstrated the potentials of new tools such as the microfilm aperture card.[6] The huge microfilming projects at the military engineering bureaus created visions of revolutionary changes in the library.[7]

Many hoped that such massive projects would be continued and would inspire similar civilian projects. However, money for the support of visionary information programs was difficult to find. Few sponsors appeared for the Documentation cause although the military continued to underwrite a handful of efforts. At the air force's new Wright Field center there was a pathbreaking attempt to devise methods of indexing and retrieval for masses of scientific documents. The inheritors of the Manhattan Project also tackled the problem of the new scientific library.[8] But the projects were few and they did not offer research funding to outsiders. Some professional organizations rekindled their interest in indexing and abstracting, but even the mighty Chemical Foundation and the American Medical Association had limited powers.

Documentalists like Ralph Shaw and Vernon Tate had to scurry for any support to continue their 1930s crusade to modernize the library and those who had made advances at the military medical libraries feared they would have to cut programs and research.[9] Even the great and powerful Vannevar Bush found it difficult to find his way during the first years of peace. Although he remained in Washington at the Carnegie Institution he was unsuccessful in his attempt to establish a peacetime version of his elite science NDRC. Especially frustrating was his struggle to automate the library. The Rapid Selector was important to Bush's postwar ambitions, but its history during and after the war was as troubled as in the 1930s.

The Selector, Again

By 1944, the programs and projects at the NDRC/OSRD settled down and Bush had time to return to his own interests. He decided to remain in Washington to head the Carnegie Institution rather than return to MIT. But, the Institute was central to all his plans. Bush had kept in close contact with his colleagues and the school's administrative officers. Many of them had become important in the NDRC in Washington, but others had stayed in Cambridge to supervise MIT's immense military programs and to define the Institute's postwar policies. Predictably, Bush gave them many suggestions about MIT's future. Among them were proposals to have the Institute bring the Rapid Selector back to life and to energize his Center of Analysis.

While Bush explored new funding opportunities for his computing and machine center at MIT, he developed rather detailed plans for the Selector. In January 1944, he wrote to Harold Hazen and declared that it was time to establish MIT as a leader in the emerging field of information technology.[10] Bush had dropped the idea of making the Selector a statistical machine and had returned to his old faith in bibliographic mechanization. For unexplained reasons, he had not badgered the NDRC to create a Selector project. Rather, he suggested that MIT itself finance the next phase of the Selector's life.

Bush convinced Harold Hazen to act as the Selector's godfather and provided him with arguments to present to those who controlled MIT's purse strings. Bush admitted to Hazen that John Howard had been correct in 1940. A Selector, he wrote, could not compete with other retrieval methods if information was hierarchically organized. He also confessed that the earlier Selector project had suffered because of inattention to coding schemes. But, Bush was sure that the Selector was the best possible machine for materials that were indexed by multiple subjects and that any coding problems could be overcome. There would, he said, be a vast market for Selectors. The key was to persuade MIT to finance a demonstration project that would prove the Selector's worth and that would show that scientists, not old-fashioned librarians and abstractors, should be in charge of scientific information systems.

In early 1944, Bush wanted to demonstrate the Selector's potential by having MIT's electrical engineering department create a large patent file, with each patent coded by experts in specialized fields. Relying on such specialists, he promised, would not lead to semantic chaos because they would need a list of less than two thousand terms. Bush was sure that MIT's investment would inspire the United States Patent Office to finance a major project for data retrieval systems. Once the Patent Office began to move, Bush thought, other sponsors would appear and would call on MIT to modernize the American library. Unfortunately, he did not recognize how much the war and the NDRC projects had changed MIT.

Big Science and a New MIT

Harold Hazen immediately took Bush's proposal to the Institute's governing board. In January 1944 his expectations were high because of Bush's declaration that the Selector was as great a step for science as the Differential Analyser.[11] But, within days, Hazen and Bush received the first of many shocks. Despite Bush's national stature and despite the rumblings about binding the patent project with another to redo the MIT libraries, his proposal was rejected.[12]

Although being assured that the Selector's technology had matured and that scientific information retrieval had a commercial future, the MIT board decided that such a project was an inappropriate target for university funding. It was not the only one of Bush's old contacts to turn away from his bibliographic ideas. Bush was finding that postwar America had little to offer researchers.

Of special concern to Bush was the end of the understandings with the Research Corporation, NCR, and Eastman. The Research Corporation, which had the responsibility for handling the business aspects of the old Selector, washed its hands of the machine. The war had stripped it of its leading men, such as Carroll Wilson, and there was no one available to push the Corporation to overcome the patent examiner's final rejection of the 1940 Selector claims.[13] NCR and Eastman, already tired of government and academic work, also signaled their unwillingness to rejoin Bush's information crusade or his attempt to breath life into the Center.[14] Hazen and Bush were discouraged, but neither abandoned the Selector or the MIT Center.

Other matters took up much of his time, but in mid-1945 Bush returned to his crusade to conquer the information problem. Hazen, responding to Bush's prompting, located John Howard who was still at OP-20-G's Washington center. Then, Hazen, Howard, and Bush began to discuss the future of microfilm retrieval devices.[15] Neither Bush nor Howard dwelled on the failure of the 1938-40 project. Howard wrote that the old Selector was but a skeleton stripped of its parts and recommended starting any new construction from the very beginning. He alluded to great advances in photoelectronic technology and said he looked forward to working on a Selector-like device in the future. Optimistic, Bush and Howard agreed that an article on the Selector and its successes would be appropriate and might bring some sponsors. While both thought it would be a fitting end to the first phase of the Selector's history, they let the opportunity slide.[16] Howard became immersed in the formation of ERA and Bush again put the Selector on hold. He finished an article on Memex, not the Selector.

The Memex article he had written in the 1930s was finally prepared for publication in 1945. Bush hoped that it would generate interest in practical applications of his favored technologies of photoelectricity and microfilm.[17] Although later generations have viewed Memex as Bush's greatest contribution to information science, he had a different view. Soon after the Memex article was published, Bush revealed that he did not have Memex at the top of his agenda. When asked by the head of the MIT library system to speak to a national assembly of librarians, Bush responded:[18]

> I am now weary and the thought of trying to present this subject to a group of librarians appals (sic) me. It was all right to stir them up with the article on Memex, for they could not possibly tell whether I was being serious or not and besides it was an arm's length affair anyway. To appear directly on the same subject before a group of librarians would be quite an undertaking.

While he was preparing Memex for publication, Bush became involved in a number of more immediate problems. He tied himself to the attempts of Ralph Shaw and others to create a national publications board to deal with the mountains of American wartime scientific materials.[19] Bush also returned to his study of microfilm technology and investigated attempts to create science information systems in Europe.[20] In addition, he turned back to his old interest in advanced computation. By the time of Germany's surrender, Bush began a campaign to rescue the Center of Analysis at MIT.

During the war, the Center had become a contract computation site for the military and had halted its machine development work. With the senior faculty busy with NDRC projects, the Center lost much of it momentum. As a result, by 1945 it was in trouble. The termination of the military contracts threatened lay offs and the competition from other computer development centers, such as those under Howard Aiken and John Von Neumann, put the Center at risk. Bush recognized the threats and decided to help. Joining with Sam Caldwell, who had returned to MIT from his NDRC assignments, he searched for a way to save his Center.[21] Bush wrote to the heads of the nation's leading corporations, such as Boss Kettering, asking for support and promising a new national computing facility for industry. Little came from the corporations in response to the mid-1945 pleas, however. Even the news from MIT was unpleasant.

Bush had spent much time attempting to stir interest within MIT. He was not successful because the Institute had changed. Like other major universities, it and its faculty had entered a new era of expectations during the war. After the experiences with such huge projects as the Rad Lab, the old Center of Analysis was not attractive to the younger men at the Institute nor to its financial officers. In fact, the Rad Lab men were creating something of a competitor to the old Center. They were starting a new group for electronics to serve as a replacement for the vast NDRC project. Unlike Bush, they had found working with the military rewarding and wanted to gain a large share of whatever the armed services had to offer in the postwar era.[22]

Turning Away from the Center

Because of the different orientation to the future of MIT, Bush had a difficult time finding any allies at the Institute. The men at the new electronics center did not wish to participate in the Bush-Caldwell plans and Bush's Center became something barely tolerated by MIT's administration. The Center, the administration emphasized, was not, as promised, self-supporting.[23] Its end seemed near, but Bush was able to call on the aid of an old friend of his, Warren Weaver of the Rockefeller Foundation.

Weaver returned from his NDRC duties with an intense desire to serve the cause of applied mathematics. His experiences during the war had convinced him of the value of computers to mathematicians. In 1945, when Bush and Sam Caldwell approached him about supporting the MIT projects, Weaver was at the center of mathematical and computer development in the nation and he knew of the plans of other respected academics to establish computer programs in America and Europe. In addition, he joined with Claude Shannon to write a theoretical volume that became a foundation for early postwar information science, *The Mathematical Theory of Communications*.[24]

It took some forceful arguments by Bush and Caldwell to convince Weaver that it would take too long for others who sought money from him, such as John Von Neumann and Howard Aiken, to produce useful machines. To win Weaver's favor, Caldwell promised to construct a new and valuable computer for science and to do it quickly. He was able to gain a six figure grant to begin the design of a fully electronic new Rockefeller computer.[25] Caldwell also asked for additional funds to immediately build a huge relay computer, one to be used while the electronic machine was being designed and constructed. The request for the relay machine was turned down, but the 1946 grant for the electronic device was an impressive one for the time.

Bush was delighted, but within a few months he became disappointed and embarrassed. Caldwell found it impossible to build a machine or to save the Center! Although having the high status grant in hand, he could not gain the support and cooperation of other MIT groups. He could not even energize his own project's staff. Especially troubling was an MIT project that had begun as a graduate student's wartime effort to create a universal flight trainer for the navy. By 1946, it became one of MIT's first Big Science projects. The military tolerated almost constant and fundamental changes in Jay Forrester's work. It had evolved into one for the design and construction of an advanced digital electronic computer.[26] In what would become a classic of grantsmanship, his Whirlwind project triumphed over cost overruns and delays and received levels of financial support that made the 1946 Rockefeller grant seem inconsequential.

A First, a Grant Is Returned

Unfortunately for the old Center's future, Forrester and his supporters wanted to maintain a separate existence. During the first months of the new Rockefeller grant, that did not seem to be too much of a problem. But, in early 1947, when the Rockefeller work was making little if any progress, having both of the computer projects at MIT became an embarrassment to Weaver and to the Institute's administration. Weaver called on the two groups to cooperate and urged the Center's people, such as Norbert Wiener, to concentrate on designing and constructing the Rockefeller computer. Despite the very direct urging, the situation became almost chaotic; certainly, by spring 1947, it was unproductive. Conditions were so grave that in June the president of MIT concluded that the Bush-Caldwell work should be ended and the money returned to the Rockefeller Foundation. Whirlwind became the computer project at MIT. Bush's Center of Analysis soon withered because of faculty and administration disinterest while the Institute became one of the first universities tied to new bounty of the Cold War.[27]

While the sad history of the new Rockefeller machine was unfolding and while MIT began to entangle itself in the type of university-military connections that Bush had tried to avoid in the 1930s, Bush was attempting to revive the Selector and to modernize the library.

Back to the Library and Aids to Learning

In 1945, frustrated by the disinterest of librarians, Bush asked his contacts to explore the possibilities of renewing some old Selector friendships. The FBI fingerprint problem was mentioned as was the possibility of convincing *Life* magazine to use the Selector for indexing its thousands of pictures. One colleague suggested linking up with the naval engineers who were becoming deeply involved in a massive project to microfilm manuals and blueprints.[28] Bush also toyed with the idea of joining with the MIT chemist, James Perry, who was busy working on chemical information systems. But, Bush soon became convinced that Perry was too attached to tabulators to be a true advocate of film and photoelectricity.[29] Bush contacted the Patent Office again with hopes that if its men did launch a retrieval project they would buy a Selector.[30] Then, he turned to another prewar connection.

Bush put the men at the MIT Library to work on a grant proposal that, he hoped, would convince his colleagues at the Carnegie foundations to restart the Scientific Aids to Learning program. John Burchard and Vernon Tate soon laid out plans for the scientific library of the future. But, as they were developing their proposal, chance again played a role in the history of the Rapid Selector. An unexpected sponsor appeared.

The Selector Finds a Documentalist Friend

After almost three years of frustration, prospects suddenly were bright. This time the sponsor was not interested in business systems but with what had been Bush's major concern in the 1930s, scientific bibliography. But, again, Bush's projects rushed to failure. Stubborn technologies, poor management and a lack of interest in the needs of the library seemed to doom all of Bush's attempts to solve the information problem. It seemed as if Bush and his fellows learned no lessons from the experiences with the Comparator and the Selector during the 1930s. However, in the first months of 1947, there was no sign the mistakes of the past would be repeated. Bush's project appeared to be starting off on the right foot and he was even cooperating with librarians and Documentalists.

In late 1946, Ralph Shaw of the Department of Agriculture Library wrote to Bush asking to borrow the old Selector.[31] Shaw, one of the first American Documentalists, had returned to the Department of

Agriculture Library after spending the war participating in exciting military information projects.[32] That work inspired him to do more to modernize the Agricultural Library and to exploit microfilm. His letter to Bush outlined his plans to coordinate all the agricultural research literature. His hope was to use the Selector to go beyond the expensive printed bibliographies of agricultural science that became outdated as soon as they were compiled. The Selector, Shaw said, would allow researchers to be informed of all the current research projects in the world. Shaw's letter piqued Bush's interest and he began to consider the possibilities of government sponsorship. Except for the ideas concerning the Patent Office and the FBI, Bush had given little thought to tying the fate of the Selector to government agencies. Although he was on important military review boards and remained a major figure in Washington, Bush continued to fear government entanglements.[33] That fear was intensified just before Shaw reawakened hopes for the Selector.

The Comparator Threatens the Selector

In October 1946, the navy informed Bush that it was going to patent the secret Comparator. It expected him to review the application and complete the related paper work. Bush's reaction was explosive. His dislike of the bureaucracy escalated because the Selector's future was put in jeopardy.[34] The machine seemed threatened by some of the claims for the Comparator. His reaction might have been a bit less negative if his Selector had not been dealt a severe blow just a few months before. The last patent application for it had been turned down and all of the MIT-Eastman-NCR work of the late 1930s was left unprotected.[35]

At first, Bush did not voice concerns about the navy's patent threat to the Selector but he did send a protest about the breach of security. Just mentioning the secret machine in a letter, Bush said, was dangerous. He also complained that the navy was imposing on him. Then, without mentioning the Selector, he protested what he saw as much too broad patent claims in the draft application. He consented to sign over the patent rights to the navy, but he insisted that it do all the work on the patent application and he demanded that the claims be made narrower.[36] Unless restricted, Bush feared, the navy's claims might foreclose any possibility of the kind of patent protection needed to entice a manufacturer to produce a Selector.[37]

Bush did not inform Ralph Shaw of such worries. In response to Shaw's 1946 inquiry Bush told him that the first Selector had been cannibalized during the war but that Shaw would be free to use a Selector if one was ever built. He then said something startling. He told Shaw that the Selector carried no patent complications and that it could be considered in the public domain. Hoping that Ralph Shaw's great library would be able to find the money to subsidize the construction of a new machine, Bush told Shaw to contact John Howard at ERA. Howard, Bush pointed out, was writing a major article on the Selector and would be interested in Shaw's offer. Bush did not reveal his and Howard's desperate search for funding and the many leads they had chased since the end of the war.[38]

The late 1946 opportunity for the Selector almost died. After Shaw contacted Howard he realized that his ambitions for the Agricultural Library and the Selector lacked a very important resource, money. The Department of Agriculture was not able to subsidize the machine or the project. Then, Shaw called on John Green, a man who had also been exploring new bibliographic methods, including microfilm selectors.[39] Green headed an organization that had an immediate need for new information technologies and it had some funds.

John Green's background was in engineering but he became important to information management in America when he was asked to head the new Office of Technical Services within the Department of Commerce. The OTS was an organization Bush and Ralph Shaw helped to establish during the last months of the war. Its mission was to aid American technology and science by distributing declassified American and foreign technical reports. Of special importance were the tons of captured German scientific documents that were being indexed and microfilmed. Green had good reason to expect that the new Selector might be funded by the Department of Commerce because the OTS and document distribution fit into the Department's hope to play a major role in democratizing the American economy. Bush was pleased to hear of Green's interest and thought the OTS bibliographic mission a better showcase for the Selector than Shaw's or the Patent Office's projects. Shaw also realized the importance of the OTS to the future of information processing and was willing to set aside Agriculture's immediate needs and cooperate with Green.

Shaw and his Documentalist associates began to play a very important role in shaping the information policies of OTS. Shaw's experience with microfilm and his background in technical indexing proved central to Green's drive to turn the war into a scientific windfall for American industry.[40] John Howard and ERA soon became as important as Shaw to Green's OTS.

The ERA Arises

While Shaw and Green were shaping OTS's policies, John Howard, Lawrence Steinhardt and John Coombs were exploring the possibility of manufacturing Selectors for the general market. Their surveys of market potential indicated that insurance companies, intelligence agencies and engineering contractors were awaiting a Selector. Steinhardt looked forward to selling at least one hundred reasonably priced machines.[41] Bush's ex-students thought a new Selector would not be a technical challenge because of all the development work that had been done on similar devices since the 1930s.

A great deal had been invested in harnessing Bush's technologies in the previous decade and Howard and his men had been involved in most of the projects. By the end of 1941, almost one-hundred thousand dollars had been spent on the Selector and its cousin, the Comparator. Multiples of that amount must have been spent by OP-20-G on its tape scanning and microfilm machines during the war. In fact, perhaps as much money was spent on the development of optical tape and microfilm scanning equipment at MIT and OP-20-G before the war's end as on the development of the impressive Rockefeller Analyser or the great pre-computer, the ENIAC. Those levels of investment and the work that was about to begin on OP-20-G's Goldberg made it easy to imagine that any remaining technical problems would just be minor irritants.[42]

During 1945, Howard had frequent discussions with Bush about the future of the Selector. Then, in late 1946, he asked Bush for help for ERA's Selector cause. He proposed they finally write a definitive article on the Selector for a major journal[43] and he asked Bush's advice about describing the Selector at the American Chemical Society's convention. The Society was one of the established leaders in the indexing of scientific literature and a presentation at its convention would be a fine way to gain some publicity for a Selector, especially one built by ERA. Despite his earlier statement to Shaw about the Selector being in the public domain, Bush advised Howard to be a bit cautious because of the danger of publicity to any future patent claims.[44] In response, John Howard backed away. Later, Shaw and Green took over the responsibility for publicity. Shaw, for example, found the temptation of the Chemical Society's 1949 meeting too great and made a short presentation on the Selector's past and future.[45] He proudly announced that two years of work by OTS and ERA had led to a major breakthrough in information technology.

A Question of Logic, Again

In early 1947, on the basis of a gentleman's agreement, ERA began to invest its engineers' time in designing a machine for OTS. No money or contract was in hand although Green promised fifty-six thousand dollars to ERA for construction. In return, Green and Shaw looked forward to having a Selector within six months. An important part of the OTS package was that Ralph Shaw was promised twenty thousand dollars to devise a coding scheme and to prepare enough data to allow a test of the Selector in a systems context. Shaw, an experienced Documentalist, was also to deal with the economics of filming and abstracting and all the logistics of the Selector system. With such indications that the old mistakes would not be repeated, Bush declared the project was off to a wonderful start and offered to provide all the help he could to his "boys" at ERA. He sent them his Selector files and obtained relevant documents from the Research Corporation to speed patent applications.[46]

Everyone was enthusiastic. With the country's most experienced engineers and one of the nation's most respected Documentalists in charge, the project seemed foolproof. Word of it was spread to the library and microfilm community and a spirited interchange about optimal coding for such machines began. The arguments lasted for several years, with articles and notes by information retrieval experts appearing in the leading journals.[47] Two of those who joined in the coding debate, Calvin Mooers and James Perry, were of importance to Vannevar Bush's hopes for his Selector. Both men were based at MIT and both were influential in the Documentation and microfilm circles. Bush did not ask them to participate in the 1947 project, but he needed their approval of the Selector.

Another Generation of Documentalists

Calvin Mooers was an unusual mathematics graduate student at MIT. During the war he worked at the Naval Ordnance Laboratory and became involved in its amply funded project to build an electronic computer under the direction of John V. Atanasoff. Atanasoff had developed an electronic special purpose computer at Iowa State University during the 1930s and had played a peripheral role in the NDRC fire control work. At the outbreak of the war he moved to the NOL and dropped his interest in computers until the Laboratory started its postwar project. But, Atanasoff again found more important work and left the young Calvin Mooers with most of the responsibility for the NOL computer. He did his best, but the spreading disinterest in the work and harmful evaluations by outside consultants led to a demeaning end to the project.[48] Mooers left the NOL in frustration and decided to complete his education at MIT.

More than his computer experience made Mooers important to Bush. Mooers had married into the family of the leading Documentalist, Watson Davis. Partially because of the family ties and because there were signs that information retrieval might become an industry, Mooers became involved in the field and developed his own coding and indexing ideas. Later, he began his own information management company. His Zator system became well known and he became an influential figure in the early information science community. In 1947, although still a graduate student, Mooers's opinions were important to the success of the Selector. As critical were those of a more senior man at MIT, James Perry.[49]

An MIT graduate, James W. Perry started his career as a chemist but during the 1930s he began to devote himself to the problems of scientific bibliography and information retrieval. After the war, he became one of the most aggressive advocates for the mechanization of literature searching and a driving force behind the American Chemical Society's committees which were exploring the use of punch card machines for automatic indexing and information retrieval. His work included the development of sophisticated coding schemes for chemical and other literature. Perry went on to become a member of the famous Western Reserve University's Center for Documentation and Communications Research in the mid-1950s. Housed within the WRU library school and under the direction of another Documentalist, Jesse H. Shera, the Center devoted itself to defining the new information science and serving the needs of Cold War research. WRU later built its own huge experimental special purpose electronic bibliographic computer.[50]

But, in 1947, Perry was still at MIT and was hard at work for the Chemical Society. He was also irritating Vannevar Bush. Among the reasons for Bush's alienation was that just as Shaw and ERA were beginning their Selector project, Perry began to establish strong ties with IBM and its information guru, H. P. Luhn. In the spring of 1947, Perry helped to conduct a survey of all library machines. That led to a visit to the venerable Tom Watson. Watson agreed to devote IBM's resources to the creation of information machines and assigned Luhn to the project. Luhn invented special tabulating and sorting machines in the following years, including his impressive Luhn Scanner, which used photoelectric card sensing to augment the power of relays and traditional IBM electromechanical equipment. By the 1950s, Luhn became known as an information expert in his own right although he remained a faithful IBM employee and an effective defender of its technologies.[51] Perry, at least in Bush's view, had become an advocate for punch card solutions to the scientific information problem. While Bush was attempting to establish his Selector, Perry criticized its architecture and allied coding schemes and then brought IBM's machines and ideas onto the MIT campus.[52]

A Machine Begins to Emerge

Of course, Ralph Shaw and the ERA engineers did not wait for a conclusion of the debates over coding schemes for the Selector. In early 1947, John Howard and John Coombs assumed the role of consulting engineers while Larry Steinhardt, who had worked so hard on the Copperheads, took on the immediate design responsibilities. He met with Shaw and drew up a plan for the new version of the Selector. Steinhardt was so pleased with his first designs he predicted that ERA could begin to mass produce basic Selectors at prices attractive to a wide range of customers. Spurred by the promised developmental funds from OTS, Steinhardt began to make inquiries about sales to Prudential and OP-20-G.[53] While ERA explored the commercial market, Shaw informed the library world that a wonderful machine that would be one hundred and eighty times faster than the IBM sorter would soon be available and that it held the potential to revolutionize indexing and retrieval.[54]

Architecturally, the 1947 Selector was not revolutionary. Although altered, it was little different from the failed 1940 machine. The Selector that ERA developed for Shaw and Green had the same general profile and logic as the first device. The physical layout of codes and abstracts was also the same. Modifications were determined by the desire to make the machine a commercial product rather than by special library related goals. Like its parent, the 1947 Selector was to scan a high-speed microfilm tape, select abstracts on the basis of a code mask and, with a super-fast flash, reproduce desired abstracts on another reel of film. Although high speed was a central goal, technical problems soon led the ERA engineers to seek a maximum of three hundred feet per minute for the data tape. That was the speed of the early machine.[55] Despite the 1940 criticisms of the Selector's inflexibility and despite an attempt by Shaw and Steinhardt to solve any logical problems before devising hardware, the 1947 Selector was not designed to handle multiple classifications or "and-or" search logic. It was to have only one scanner and it to be was a much simpler one.

There was a very important alteration in the new design. To minimize construction and maintenance cost it was decided to use the blackout system for selection. Although it was later claimed that Shaw suggested this feature,[56] it probably was chosen as a result of the ERA men's wartime experience with machines such as ICKY. It was hoped that the blackout feature and Shaw's coding scheme would allow the machine to use only one photocell, not the thirteen of the 1930s version. This was a very important change and one with significant consequences for the usefulness of the new Selector.[57] The problem of the cost of data entry was also addressed, if not solved, in 1947.

To speed data entry, the light target system of World War II's microfilm analysers was used to implant codes on the microfilm. The light bank was integrated into a new document camera system, however. The code lights would be set with a complex keyboard built to fit Shaw's demand for room for six, seven-digit identification codes. Shaw felt that the new keyboard would allow an operator to efficiently enter the six different subject codes for an abstract. In addition, there was to be an improved data entry camera and World War II's V-mail microfilm machines were to be used to provide quick and cheap paper copies of the selected abstracts. Trying to allow for the accumulation of a backlog of search requests, the inquiries were to be in the form of reusable punch cards.

The complementary, blackout coding of selection mask and index areas simplified the engineering problems but led to other types of difficulties. No one at ERA seems to have checked on the originality of their blackout system or to have thought to immediately file a patent application.[58] The blackout feature also brought logical constraints. Shaw's investigations and the 1940 traumas over the Selector should have warned that the blackout system multiplied the dangers of relying upon raw speed and a single scanner. The 1947 blackout system could only respond to exact matches and the new Selector proved even less useful for generic searches than the first Bush bibliographic machine.[59] The 1940 model at least had the potential for logical flexibility because it had one cell for each code area. Those cells might be wired to a plugboard for "short circuiting."

In addition to the blackout test, there was one other major change to the original Selector design, but it came later and was not foreseen in early 1947. During the development cycle of the ERA Selector, an attempt was made to surmount the old problem caused by the flash camera systems inability to keep up with the speed of the master film. In the postwar version, a special clutch was added to the master tape drive which, in combination with look-ahead sensing of the abstracts, slowed the master film when closely spaced selected items were encountered.[60]

The Project Unravels

In the spring of 1947, Steinhardt was pleased with his design and felt confident enough to turn details over to younger engineers in St. Paul. But, just as he did, problem after problem arose. Patents, the complexities of government contracting, an overburdened staff and technical quirks played the same roles as in the 1930s. Even Bush's old nemesis, the Bureau of Ships, took shots at ERA and, then, the Selector.

Business difficulties hit first. Perhaps because of Bush's assurances, neither Green nor Howard conducted a fresh patent search before starting the project. The business managers at ERA, already worried about beginning work before there was a contract with OTS, demanded a clarification of the patent situation. Some of the managers had been at the Bureau of Ships and knew of the many patent complications involved in government work. On the one hand, and despite Bush's statements, they were fearful that ERA would endanger itself by stepping on established patents. On the other hand, the contract Green and the Department of Commerce proposed seemed to contain provisions that might block ERA from taking any new patents. Without patent protection the Selector, they thought, could not be a profitable commercial product. They advised dropping the OTS work, if not the Selector itself! When Green and Shaw criticized Steinhardt's first design, the managers' suggestion received immediate and very serious consideration.[61] The Selector was about to be aborted.

ERA's managers demanded that if work was to continue, Commerce had to take full responsibility for any patent infringements. Green did not have the power to guarantee that. A stand-off developed. It was only Bush's intervention that prevented ERA from withdrawing from the project in the spring of 1947.[62] Bush's last minute assurances that the new machine could be built without infringing on any patents saved the Selector.[63] Bush may also have played a key role in solving a more immediate problem: Green's inability to secure the promised money for the Selector project.

The postwar American government was very budget conscious. The Department of Commerce suffered along with the military services and many of the ambitious projects it had drafted had to be curtailed.[64] John Green was one of those who was told to back away from risky projects. The Department could not find the some seventy-five thousand dollars he needed. Thus, in early summer, after perhaps six months of design efforts, ERA's managers ordered still another halt to Commerce's Selector project. They had waited too long, they said, for the promised funds and an acceptable contract.

Many of the documents that could establish the details of the story of the 1947 contract problem are lost, but its general outlines can be sketched. It is clear that John Green had been too confident of the Department of Commerce's willingness and ability to fund the data retrieval project. He was also unaware of some of the hidden requirements in Commerce's contracts. Unable to gain the expected straightforward grant from the Department, he had pieced together promises of funding from its various branches. That took a few months. One of those pieces, the small amount from the new division that was mandated to stimulate invention in the private sector, the IRD, carried some unexpected burdens. Besides requiring that all patents resulting from the work it financed be placed in the public domain, it held that its contribution was a loan, not a grant, to a contractor. It demanded that contractors repay all of the "loan." When a new contract was at last signed in May 1947, Green and ERA's managers may have thought Commerce had agreed to waive those IRD requirements.[65]

But, things went wrong, again! For unspecified reasons, Commerce refused to make any payments to ERA although the company had already spent several months working for OTS. ERA stopped all work in June. Then, yet another round of negotiations began.[66]

Bush again played a major role. He forged what then seemed a fair agreement about the patent issue. To ease ERA's continuing patent anxieties, he exerted pressures to prevent outsiders from publishing articles on the Selector.[67] He also calmed the nerves of the ERA men by assuring them that the demands imposed because of the use of the IRD funds would not be burdensome.[68] With everyone satisifed, ERA agreed to resume work while it waited for another formal contract. When it was finally signed in August 1947, Commerce and ERA accepted the fact that a Selector could not be finished in time. They agreed upon a new and distant delivery date. All expected to have a finished machine and successful system by June 1948. The new contract did not solve all the old problems or prevent new ones, however. Despite Bush's help, and good-faith on everyone's part, the agreement contained some ambiguities that again threatened the relationship between the Shaw-Green-Bush circle and the crew at ERA. But, there were more reasons for the harmful frictions than differing interpretations of the mid-1947 contract.

Too Much Success, and Too Much Bureau, Again

As with Bush's timing for beginning the Comparator in the 1930s, ERA's work started when the company suffered from too much success. In mid-1947, ERA was a very busy place, although a financially shaky one. Its important engineers were overburdened with entrepreneurial as well as technical responsibilities. By the time the Selector project was restarted in mid-1947, ERA had gained several important and critical navy contracts and was about to launch into the development of one of the first modern electronic computers. And, in addition to the Rapid Selector, there were several other commercial projects being considered.[69]

The workload and the emerging Cold War were leading to problems with the navy. Just as the Selector contract was signed in August, ERA came under great pressure from the Bureau of Ships. BuShips demanded that schedules be drawn and met and it made some ominous noises about the way OP-20-G's secret contracts were awarded and administered.[70] The special treatment ERA was receiving did not sit well with a Bureau that had to deal with congressional inquiries as to compliance with general contract regulations. The need to meet deadlines and to fend off the BuShips's threat to its major source of income, OP-20-G's work, made it difficult for ERA to concentrate on the new Selector.

The navy's complaints were not the only cause of difficulties. Immediately after the signing of the formal contract in August 1947, more disagreements with the OTS arose. When Green and Shaw saw the detailed ERA design they again protested and demanded it be reworked and approved by them before ERA rushed into full development. The managers at ERA, working under a June 1948 contract termination date, reacted with their own protests and blamed the delays and cost over-runs on Commerce's slow response to its proposals. In turn, Shaw and Green became very concerned about the possibility that ERA might abandon them and the Selector. By fall 1947, they were more than worried about the project and their reputations. Some of their growing anxieties were due to the complaints about Commerce's intrusions into the private economy. The IRD program was becoming a special target for those upset about government inefficiency and creeping socialism.[71] It was not just politics that was causing problems, however. The Selector project was, in fact, far behind schedule and in trouble; so much so that Howard and Steinhardt had to be called away from other work in late 1947. They took some immediate action and tried to get the project back on schedule, but they faced a difficult challenge.

They found that some serious technical mistakes had been made and they learned of a major oversight. In the last months of 1947, it was discovered that the fast-flash mechanism which was so vital to the machine was unavailable. Lawrence Steinhardt had to write Harold Edgerton at MIT for help.[72] That was only one of many delays. The project did not run smoothly after the acquisition of Edgerton's lamp system. In fact, it was not until June 1948, when the Selector was supposed to be in operation in Washington, that the blackout scanning system received its first successful bench test.[73]

The Selector was not only behind schedule, but over-budget and a threat to ERA's financial survival. ERA was too new and too small to carry development costs on its own and the OTS had no more money to give.[74] That magnified the other problems. At the end of 1947, ERA again complained about the messy patent situation and demanded that Commerce take full responsibility--or, allow ERA out of its remaining obligation. ERA did not wish to spend any more time or money on what might become an unmarketable product or one that would tangle it in litigation with such giants as IBM.[75] The tensions grew and there was another confrontation.

When ERA discovered that the pay-back and public domain provisions that went along with IRD contributions had not been fully waived, it consulted its attorneys seeking ways around the OTS contract and its deadlines. ERA's top managers also dropped some subtle hints that additional money would be needed to complete Shaw's machine. More frightening, they hinted that all they had promised was a design, not a functioning machine.[76]

Green and Shaw were appalled. They rushed to Vannevar Bush's offices in Washington with a long list of complaints about his "boys" at ERA. What Bush heard made him furious.[77] Green told Bush that ERA was so far behind schedule that the entire document retrieval project was endangered. Worse, they said, ERA had declared that all their contract called for was a paper design, not a machine.[78] Bush's anger was evident when he agreed with Green and Shaw that extreme pressures had to be applied, including a threat to immediately terminate the ERA contract and to give it to a company that would build a machine within the budget and time limitations.[79]

A Letter and Warning from Bush

Bush did much more. He contacted some of the higher-ups at ERA and then wrote a letter that would have destroyed most young men. His letter to John Howard on March 16, 1948 contained a very severe scolding and a demand, call it an order, to ERA to produce a working machine for Shaw on time and within the financial guidelines. In very direct words, Bush told his ex-student that his problem was one of pretention: that he and his co-workers were doing too much managing and too little of what Bush had always told his young men to do, keep their hands on a project and "get the job done."

And, said Bush, there were too many unjustified excuses for the delay in the program. He wrote off the patent difficulties as minor and told Howard that any existing claims could be circumvented through creative engineering. Bush concluded with a none too subtle hint that if the machine was not delivered he would do very little to help ERA or Howard in future.[80]

Bush's letter had its intended effect. Howard immediately wrote to Green stating the project was on schedule and that promises would be kept despite the design-only threats by ERA's management.[81] Attempting to mend fences, Howard wrote to Bush explaining that the navy's highly secret and important work had taken first priority.[82] But Howard did not cite what may well have been a significant reason for the delays at ERA and its desire to submit only a paper design. He may have been afraid of insulting Bush. Because of its most secret work, ERA's men knew how quickly technology was changing and they may have feared that producing a machine based on prewar options would become an instant and embarrassing dinosaur. In fact, in 1949, just after the long awaited delivery of Shaw's Selector, Steinhardt developed an outline and business plan for a Selector that was in tune with current technology. It centered about the use of magnetic recording and the high-speed printing of abstracts originally recorded in binary code on microfilm.[83]

Despite the fast changing technical options, in mid-1948, ERA followed Bush's maxim of "getting the job done." Under great pressure, ERA began to pour money into the OTS Selector project although important navy work such as Goldberg was far behind schedule. But, ERA again missed deadline after deadline. June 1948 and the end of the Commerce contract came without a machine being anywhere near ready. Despite the desire to please Bush, ERA's managers soon realized the company would be unable to meet even its extended schedules. In a critical mid-1948 meeting, ERA's most prestigious members, including Howard Engstrom, conferred with Bush and Green and convinced them to allow ERA, using its own funds, to continue with the project and to produce a device. They pleaded for another extension--of almost a year.[84] Bush thought an additional twelve months at ERA's expense was, in the context, reasonable, but Green was under a great deal of pressure from the Commerce Department. He and Shaw needed a machine and publicity for their work as soon as possible. They could not admit to a seventy-five thousand dollar project that had no results and they were worried about the possible ramifications of public knowledge of the now unusual agreements with ERA.

The resulting tension was intolerable to many at ERA. John Howard, the Selector's big brother, decided to leave ERA in the summer of 1948. His role in what had become a chaotic and perhaps hopelessly over-budget project made it difficult for him to stay. Others soon found the conflicts at ERA unbearable. It seemed impossible for the young company to please its military and its civilian masters, especially when OP-20-G was itself caught in a struggle for survival.[85]

However, ERA did go on to assign men and resources to the Selector and tens of thousands more was spent on the machine. ERA finally turned a Selector over to Shaw and Green in January 1949, a bit ahead of their last dooms-day deadline.[86] Shaw also increased his efforts during 1948. He published a major article in the *Journal of Documentation*, announcing the Selector and its virtues to his information science colleagues. He used the article to advertise the machine and to heal many bruised egos.[87] He paid deference to Bush and explained his goals of flexible and creative indexing for scientific material. Shaw hailed Bush's idea of "associations" and more than hinted that his Selector and his coding scheme came close to the ideals of a Memex.

John Green also hurried into print. He contributed a major piece[88] which emphasized the coming contributions to science. But he made a mistake that again strained the relationship with ERA. In good-faith, and because he was so committed to the scientific ethic, Green informed his readers that the Selector was in the public domain. Soon, again to the disbelief of ERA's men, another author stated that anyone could come to the Department of Commerce and copy the diagrams for the device.[89] ERA's managers and engineers were very upset with Green's assertion concerning the patent status of the Selector, especially because the company had begun another battle with Commerce over patents. At the same time, it was engaging in negotiations for possible sales of its next version of a Selector to, among others, the Central Intelligence Agency.[90] As a result, yet another standoff developed.

Trying to protect its market position, ERA refused to cooperate in filing patent claims with the Department. Soon, it made another startling declaration. ERA's leaders decided to do much more than refuse to put the machine in the public domain. They announced that all the significant innovations in the machine had been invented after the termination of the Commerce contract. ERA, they said, would file independently and would not give the government the usual free-use license--despite all the previous contributions and compromises by the government. Vannevar Bush's reaction to Norris's proclamation is not documented but it is easy to imagine what he thought.[91]

The Selector Dies, Again

Shaw and Green were angered but they had more to be unhappy about than the jumbled patent situation. After some six months of testing and adjustments in Washington, they unveiled the Selector to much publicity and with many promises.[92] Then, almost immediately after the opening ceremonies, Shaw and Green found themselves with a cause, but without a machine. The Selector did not work!

By the time the ERA Selector was delivered to Shaw in early 1949, hundreds of thousands of dollars had been invested in the development of the Bush selectors, with few results. Shaw's model alone cost over one-hundred thousand dollars and it had been nurtured by the best engineers in the nation. But the machine would not function, at least effectively.[93] More than hardware was at fault. Within a few months it was also realized that Shaw's twenty thousand dollar coding scheme, with its long randomly assigned code numbers and cumbersome code book, was not the promised panacea.[94] Shaw and Green did not give up, however. Too much time and money had been invested and too many reputations were at stake. Shaw, for example, was establishing himself as an international expert in mechanized scientific bibliography and he was one of the joint authors of a major declaration of the coming of the information age.

As the Selector was undergoing its birth pangs in Washington, he joined with the noted and very influential physicists, Louis N. Ridenour and Albert G. Hill, to publish the powerful statement for the support of automated libraries for scientists, *Bibliography in the Age of Science*.[95] It linked the mechanization of the library with the future of the nation. At the same time, Shaw wrote many articles for those within the library and document fields extolling the virtues of the Selector. It was, he claimed, better than the world's first commercial computer, the UNIVAC, for information processing and much better than all other existing mechanical aids. And, as before, he saluted microfilm as the best of all memory mediums.[96] Thus, in 1950, there was too much at risk for him to allow an end to Bush's machine. Shaw and Green decided to rescue the Selector. Unfortunately, there were few to help them. The Department of Commerce had no funds to give, and, after all the previous conflicts, Shaw was unable and probably unwilling to turn to ERA.

Life and Death Yet Another Time

ERA was busy with its own new Selector projects, such as a confidential one for Bell and Howell. Bell and Howell had decided to enter the expanding microfilm market and asked ERA to build a small selector to attach to its new readers. ERA produced a photoelectric device centered on a simplified binary coding scheme with a limit of one thousand twenty four possible codes. The system was economic and followed the logic of many of OP-20-G's World War II machines: when a hit was detected the motor driving the microfilm real was cut-off and a hand search was made to locate the correct frame.[97] In addition to its new tie to Bell and Howell, ERA was caught in a major patent battle over the Selector's blackout principle. The patent office rediscovered Goldberg's claim and one by an employee of the company that was soon to take over ERA, Remington-Rand. Shaw seems to have added to the patent confusion by claiming to be the originator of several related ideas.[98]

Without prospects of more funds from the Department of Commerce and left adrift by ERA, Shaw and Green again sought out Vannevar Bush.[99] In early 1950, they told him of the major weakness of the machine. The mechanism needed to slow the tape was unreliable and when it did work it caused the Selector to be too slow to be effective. Something, they said, had to be done to allow closely spaced selected items to be photographed without bringing the machine to a halt. They also described what had turned out to be an overly complex data entry system. Bush was still vitally interested in the Selector and he probably felt guilty because he had encouraged Shaw to seek out ERA. So, he devoted much time to the problem, both as an engineer and as an administrator. He suggested the use of a new high-speed camera that would eliminate the need to slow the master film and he seems to have arranged for his old colleague from the Research Corporation, Carroll Wilson, to have his new agency, the Atomic Energy Commission, donate tens of thousands of dollars to finance a rebuilding of the Selector.[100] Bush may also have been the one who arranged for the Carnegie Foundation to give Shaw a rather handsome grant to pursue his more general microfilm interests.[101]

Shaw and Green decided to stay within the government for the machine's repair. They turned to the National Bureau of Standards and its multi-talented Jack Rabinow. John Green convinced the NBS to use the money Bush had acquired to redo the ERA Selector. After Rabinow and his associates reworked the scanning, reproduction, and data entry systems, Shaw regained hope. That was very short-lived, however. Both the machine and the coding system again proved to be impractical. By 1952, Shaw abandoned the machine, giving his blessing to the idea of donating its parts to the NBS![102]

It took longer, but Ralph Shaw also abandoned his almost messianic general crusade for mechanized bibliography. He remained an advocate and an important figure in the library and emerging information science communities[103] but the second failure of his Selector began to temper his faith. As late as 1956 he announced that a mere fifty thousand additional dollars invested in research and development could produce Selectors that held entire articles and that could be mass produced for less than twenty thousand dollars each.[104] But his writings contained increasing numbers of warnings about blind faith in library automation and about believing those with promises involving technological marvels that were, at best, decades in the future.[105]

Questioning Library Automation

By the end of the 1950s, Shaw went beyond cautions concerning the false economics of automation. Increasingly, he stressed the need to consider all the steps involved in any process. He began to make public the failures of the 1950 Selector and admitted that faulty technology was not the true culprit. He confessed that he had made mistakes when estimating the efficiency of the Selector. Because of the time needed to load and unload tapes, he said, the expensive machine could do only forty-eight runs in a working day. In addition, the cost of indexing and data entry proved to be far greater than expected. Worse, were the logical mistakes. He admitted that he had not been able to establish a balance between the categories needed for universal library service and the type of expert coding that Bush so favored. The code system he was once so proud of was, he admitted, unsuited to both the librarian and the specialist. He said, "The basic error was the assumption that we could run fast enough to avoid pre-classification; yet, in terms of the total amount of material in the research library, this experiment showed the futility of running rather than thinking."[106]

Shaw's writings became even more critical of the Selector and other automation projects. In a 1958 article he presented a long list of errors and shortcomings that was a repeat of John Howard's in 1940. Shaw pointed out that the best of foreseeable new systems, such as magnetic wire, took from ten to one hundred times longer to locate a fact than hand examination of books and card files. And, he said, they were all much, much more costly than the "old-fashioned" methods. Like John Howard, he found it impossible to cite a truly effective use for high-speed bibliographic machines.[107] Still, Shaw could not let go of his commitment to automation, microfilm and the idea of the Selector. At times, he called for more Selector projects, including one to create an inexpensive version without the automatic reproduction feature. He continued to be an advocate for microfilm and even suggested creating a microfilm library of the best one hundred thousand books from Harvard. He hoped it would be sold to other colleges. And, Shaw never gave up trying to find ways to conquer the problem of indexing scientific articles. He continued to believe that the growth of scientific publications called for an innovative approach to the library and the bibliographic problem.[108]

Vannevar Bush also kept his faith and interest despite setbacks worse than those Shaw had experienced. Bush had to contend with the failure of two more heroic attempts to rescue his ideas and his Selector. Then, he had to stand by while those who had blocked or ignored his work took over the burden and glory of automating information retrieval.

Chapter XIV
A Machine for the Cold War and Big Science: Not for the Library

Vannevar Bush had not surrendered his bibliographic dreams to the precariously funded Office of Technical Services nor had he been defeated by the MIT Board's refusal to see the potential of automated information retrieval. In 1945, after the Board rejected his patent proposal, Bush made an end run and began to use the Institute's libraries as a platform for his ideas. Initially, he hoped to combine efforts at the library with the advances he planned for his old Center of Analysis. The decline of the Center did not lead Bush to abandon his bibliographic cause, however. Bush persevered and convinced the head of the MIT libraries, John Burchard, to launch a major information project at the Institute. While the Shaw-ERA saga was unfolding, Bush guided Burchard in drafting a plan and aided him in the search for funds needed to create the science library of the future.

Another Man for the Library

Bush had great confidence in Burchard. Although he was not a professional librarian or a Documentalist, his background seemed perfect for the task of creating the library for science. Burchard was a 1920s MIT graduate in architectural engineering who became a manager of research and patents for a large New England industrial firm. While there, he wrote several architectural histories and became a recognized expert on the evolution of the house. His continued academic interests led Burchard to return to MIT in the late 1930s to fill a series of administrative posts. He was appointed as director of the MIT libraries in mid-1944. Extremely important to his relationship with

Bush, Burchard also served as an NDRC administrator. That led to many stimulating contacts with Bush who came to admire Burchard so much that he asked him to write the history of the Institute's wartime activities. Burchard did that and much more. In recognition, in 1948, he was asked to become the Institute's Dean of Humanities. Besides fulfilling his many postwar administrative duties at MIT, he became a national figure in library design and a consultant on matters of civil defense.[1]

Bush and Burchard had discovered their mutual interests in information management during the war. They discussed the problem of scientific bibliography, the potentials of microfilm and the coming library crisis. They shared a belief in the dire forecasts of Fremont Rider in his very gloomy book, *The Scholar and the Future of the Research Library*.[2] Rider charted the exponential growth of publications and predicted a disaster in library financing and space allocation. Rider declared that America's libraries would soon run out of room. While he explored many space saving methods of housing books and articles he remained convinced that only radical changes would save the library.

Burchard was concerned about more than the management of library space. He was deeply interested in information management and became an admirer of microfilm and the Rapid Selector. Hoping to find an answer to the information problem, Burchard studied the most advanced scientific bibliographic systems, including the one at the central scientific agency in France. In 1945, he was ready to modernize MIT's libraries. He scouted the country for allies and although he did not have the funds to sponsor a new Selector, he kept in contact with John Howard to monitor the progress of his work on information machines.[3] He also taught himself much about Documentalism and sought out its leaders.

Because Bush had lost much of his fear of the Documentalists during the early 1940s and began to see them as possible colleagues, Burchard attempted to bring engineers and Documentalists together at the Institute. Especially important was that Burchard convinced Vernon Tate to leave the National Archives and come to MIT.

Microfilm and Scientific Aids, Again

Vernon Tate was one of the nation's leading microfilm experts and had been a major figure in the Documentalist movement since the

1930s. He had the added distinction of being important in the traditional association for librarians.[4] During the war Tate had become deeply involved in microfilming and retrieval projects for various military and intelligence agencies. He wanted to transfer what he had learned to the problem of scientific bibliography. Once at MIT, his ideas impressed Burchard and he arranged for Tate to replace him as head of the Institute's libraries.[5] As soon as Tate was settled in, he and Burchard sketched their ideas for new information systems for science. With the cooperation of Vannevar Bush, they began to devise a strategy to raise the funds they needed to fulfill their grand ambitions. It was quite natural for them to turn to the old philanthropic organizations and to tailor grant requests to match their interests. So, Burchard decided that a proposal to give the Scientific Aids to Learning Project a second life provided the best chance of financing his new library. He knew he had an attractive package to offer to the foundations, including the correct mix of people. Vernon Tate had acted as the microfilm expert for the 1930s Learning project;[6] Bush had always had a hand in Learning and he remained a major force within foundation circles; and, the original project had not had a formal conclusion, just a halt because of the war. In addition to promising to complete the first Learning project's work, Burchard and Bush spiced their proposal with some tantalizing new visions for the organization of information.

Bush also had some new ideas. He was sure they would attract the interest of the scholarly community. For example, he pushed for the creation of a lap-top reader to make microfilm acceptable to scholars. The proposed device, Bush claimed, could make microfilm have the look and feel of a book. Bush and the inventor of the instant camera wanted Burchard to solve all the proposed reader's technical problems, then turn the plans over to Eastman-Kodak for mass production.[7] Bush also wanted to save researchers from having to make trips to the library and thought that microfilm libraries on a desk might be possible. Of course, Bush wanted Burchard to pursue all the other earlier Aids to Learning interests.

It did not take long for Burchard and Tate to draft a general but very attractive proposal. They did not have much of a wait for a response. A handsome grant in excess of one-hundred thousand dollars came from the Carnegie Corporation.[8] The new three-year Aids to Learning project at MIT was to focus on the futures of printing, microfilm, moving pictures, sound recording, and automated bibliographies. The funding seemed generous and all were positive about the project, especially Vannevar Bush. In early 1948 he was sure that Burchard would develop his lap-top microfilm reader and his microfilm library on a desk and that Burchard would incorporate the Selector in his long-term plans for the scientific library. Also, Bush thought the project would explore his Memex and, perhaps, go beyond it.

Beyond Memex

Bush put even more of his hopes in the new Aids to Learning project when he learned of the problems with the OTS-ERA Selector. In the spring of 1948 he became distraught over the ERA-Shaw effort. He thought Shaw's work was doomed and feared that he might never be able to convince another sponsor to fund a Selector. The major stumbling bloc, Bush reasoned, was the cost of the data base needed to demonstrate the value of a Selector. He was very depressed. Then, typically, Bush regained his energy and proposed a new technological solution, one that went beyond both the Selector and the Memex. To avoid the difficulty of financing the creation of a data base, he proposed a revolutionary new system. It would spread the cost of building and maintaining a file over many researchers and would eliminate the need for the expensive mechanical "desk" for each Memex user.

Bush's new creature was radically different from his microfilm machines. Bush quite seriously proposed that a fully automated central Selector-Memex be built of relays and spinning data drums. A researcher was to pick up his phone, dial the machine's number then dial the code for the information he desired. The computer's logic would search the files until the correct information was located. Then, the data would be read from the magnetic or film drums which were to hold sound tracks. A voice synthesizer, like the one used for stock exchange quotations, would read the requested data to the researcher.[9] Bush thought all the basic technology was in place and that only the coding scheme for the information presented a major challenge. He informed John Burchard of his idea and hoped the Learning group would flesh out the details of the phone Selector-Memex. Bush told his scientist-entrepreneur friends, such as Louis Ridenour, of his new technical plan and of his other hopes for the renewed Learning project.

Burchard and Tate shared Bush's expectations about the Learning work. They published articles in major journals that contained exuberant claims. After establishing the need for a library revolution by declaring the book an outdated form of communication, and underlining the coming "Waterloo of Science" because of the difficulty of accessing scientific literature, they proclaimed the Learning project to be the cure for all the library problems. But, almost as soon as the new Scientific Aids to Learning Project began, Burchard, Tate and Bush had to face great disappointments. The project slowed to a crawl within a few months. It appeared to be in worse trouble than the OTS-ERA Selector![10]

Another Project That Wouldn't

In the spring of 1949 Bush felt betrayed. He wrote heated letters to his old friend John Burchard demanding that something be done to rescue the Learning project. In response to Bush's criticism, Burchard created a supervisory board and appointed a new project chief. Burchard did not select a librarian or a Documentalist to head the project, however. His choice was Albert G. Hill, a noted physicist who had been involved with atomic energy development and who was currently the head of MIT's Laboratory of Electronics. That was the department that had evolved out of World War II's Radiation Laboratory. Its men were the ones who had refused to cooperate in saving Bush's old Center of Analysis in 1945.

Albert G. Hill was an excellent administrator and a fine scientific spokesman, but he found it impossible to turn the Aids to Learning project around.[11] Bush continued to complain and threaten.[12] Burchard pleaded with Bush and explained that little could be done to construct machines or systems until the coding problem was solved. He promised to make more changes in personnel, including dropping James Perry if he did not obtain his own funding.[13] Bush remained dissatisfied and concluded that Burchard was not using the grant for library goals but was just subsidizing the research of favored MIT men. That research, Bush wrote, had little to do with any of the purposes of the grant, the Selector, the Memex or the lap-top microfilm reader.

Bush did not mince words and was as direct as he had been with John Howard. He told Burchard that unless the project was put back on track the money should either be returned to the Carnegie Foundation or be used to hire people from outside MIT, people who were willing and able to help the cause of the library.[14] Burchard did neither, but he was able to calm Bush. The project continued on and Burchard came from that attempt to create a microfilm library for a researcher's desk and the second Scientific Aids to Learning project continued to drift. At the project's end, Bush, Tate and Burchard had very little to show for the one-hundred thousand dollars of the Carnegie Foundation's money. To add to Bush's disappointments, the Learning project ended just as Ralph Shaw had to admit that his Selector project was a failure.[16]

There Wasn't a Library Problem After All

There was something more depressing than the death of the two projects in the early 1950s. For Bush, the most disappointing part of the history of Scientific Aids project was what John Burchard told him and the world's scientific community. In personal letters to Bush and in a major address to an international gathering of scientific bibliographers, Burchard explained that the Learning project and all the other attempts to automate scientific bibliographies failed because scientists did not care!

He informed Bush that the "best men" at MIT did not want to participate in the Aids to Learning project because they saw little value in it. Then, in his speech to the important group at the UNESCO conference on scientific abstracting, he made it clear that very few scientists in the world wanted or needed advanced library automation. Burchard claimed that most working academics did not think there was an information crisis and that the push for automation was the result of the clamor of only a very few engineers and scientists. Later in his life, Burchard went even further in questioning the very premises of Bush's library projects. When MIT became involved in the 1960s INTREX information project, Burchard voiced the opinion that humanists needed automated systems even less than scientists and that library funds were better spent buying books than indexing them.[17]

Patents and Failure, Again

Despite such a devastating message from a close associate, Vannevar Bush did not give up on the Selector or his ideas for the new scientific library. He had one more chance to see his two decades of work rescued from defeat. The opportunity came in the mid-1950s when Bush was asked to help the Patent Office.

At the end of the war, after MIT had refused to fund his proposal, Bush stepped back from his plan to redo the patent system. But, he could not stay away for long. Just before Ralph Shaw contacted him about adopting the Selector and while he was advising John Burchard on how to approach the foundations for support, Bush resumed his attack on the Patent Office. By late 1946, he was coaching its men on the inadequacy of their indexing and retrieval systems and marshalling the resources of the old scientific community to support at least a pilot program to revamp the patent files. Bush tried to gain the help of the National Research Council, hoping it would provide the Office with the money it needed to review its systems and, perhaps, to finance a Selector.[18] Bush was unable to muster all the political and financial resources he needed in 1947, but he did not abandon his interest in patents.

After a wait of five years he became deeply involved with another round of Patent Office work. In the early 1950s, for the first time, there was some true hope of success. The Patent Office was forced to act because congress had ordered it to mechanize its searching procedures.[19] Bush was put in charge of forming committees to explore a revision of the office's methods. Expectedly, the project drew the attention of all the Documentalists and those who were beginning to call themselves information scientists. During 1954, Bush was besieged with outlines of new techniques and machinery for information retrieval.

The Patent Office work had the potential to be the most important civilian information retrieval experiment in history. Bush thought it would lead to a knowledge revolution in every science and professional field, including law and medicine.[20] The great names in postwar information services, such as Taube and Perry,[21] became important to the project, but Bush relied upon his old academic contacts, especially men from MIT.[22] He even called upon John Green to arrange to have the failed Shaw Selector formally transferred to the National Bureau of Standards so that its men could judge its potential for the Patent Office project. Bush also had his friends contact all the companies making information products, from Ridenour's Telemeter Magnetics to Joe Desch's National Cash Register, in hopes of finding executives willing to invest corporate funds in developing new technologies.[23] Bush and his colleagues studied the Patent Office procedures, then examined all the current ideas for indexing and all the available and proposed retrieval machines. Bush put together the final report.

It was a very difficult one for him to write. He had to admit that after some twenty years of work on the Selector, scientific coding, and indexing, no machines and no classification systems were ready.[24] The best he could do was recommend that groups be established within the National Bureau of Standards and the Patent Office to constantly survey information retrieval technology. Bush must have known that the Department of Commerce would never have the funds to launch a major initiative.[25]

For the Cold War, Not the Library

The National Bureau of Standards established a small program and cooperated with a new group within the Patent Office, but Standards had neither the money nor the political mandate needed to create an information revolution.[26] And, just as the Standards group began its work, the power and initiative in information retrieval and technology passed from those who were concerned with the scientific library to those responsible for winning the Cold War.

By the mid-1950s, a new era in Documentalism had begun, one in which Bush played, at most, a minor role. Bush did not want to accept it, but the older American scientific community showed little interest in the Selector and the Memex. For example, Bush's own creation, the National Science Foundation, did not step forward to subsidize a Selector. It and the Memex ideas were handed to others with interests different from those of the men of Bush's generation. Although the dialogue of the mid-1950s was still couched in terms of the library and scientific bibliography, Documentalism and information technology came to have new goals and sponsors.[27] No one came forward to attempt to build Bush's creativity machine, the Memex, but the needs of the military and the American intelligence agencies led to massive projects to rescue the Selector--or at least the idea of using coded microfilm and photoelectricity for information machines.

The next round of selectors and their new technical cousins never appeared in a library; they were not used for scientific bibliography; they were not used for creative "association"; and, Vannevar Bush had little to do with them. The largest and most technically ambitious of the film projects of the 1950s and 1960s were for the military bureaucracies and intelligence agencies. Some were machines for secrecy, ones built for the Central Intelligence Agency and the National Security Agency, while others were for the massive bureaucratic technical data centers of the military and its contractors.[28] But, even with unlimited resources, the Cold War agencies could not make Bush's dreams of the 1930s come true. Huge projects in the 1950s were unable to produce microfilm retrieval machines that matched his technological and economic promises. Despite all the research into his technologies, the Selector-like machines of the 1950s and 1960s were too expensive for libraries to purchase and maintain. Of course, Memex remained just a technological fantasy.

In fact, little mechanization of any type appeared within the traditional domains of librarians, catalogers, and indexers after World War II. What there was centered around the less expensive and more reliable electromechanical tabulators. And, among those tabulator users, few had a need for or were able to afford the more advanced IBM equipment such as that designed by H. P. Luhn. Even the research librarians at the nation's most wealthy chemical companies, who had been some of the leading advocates of bibliographic mechanization, remained dependent upon IBM's stock equipment.[29] The decisions to stay with older technologies were not the result of ignorance or conservatism. After two decades of attention, microfilm retrieval machines remained far from being reliable and affordable library fixtures.

During the 1950s and early 1960s many of the technical problems that had frustrated Bush, Howard and Shaw were overcome. But each advance underscored how much Bush's 1930s promises had demanded of his three favorite technologies. Some relatively simple and affordable versions of microfilm search machines appeared in the late 1960s, but just as significant cost reductions seemed possible, new technologies overwhelmed microfilm. The electronic computer was maturing and its huge and fast magnetic memory became the hope of those who wanted to mechanize bibliographic searching. For those whose concern was with reproduction, the appearance of the xerox machine provided a convenient solution. By the 1970s, microfilm was an answer to only one of the library problems. It became an archive medium used to reduce storage costs and it freed the library from the burden of shelving rarely used materials.[30]

Trying Again and Again and ...

However, in the 1950s, few could envision the ungainly electronic computer as an information machine. Memory remained the stumbling block and microfilm continued to be seen as the medium with the most potential. With the Haloid Company yet to rename itself "Xerox" microfilm also seemed the most efficient way to reproduce and store documents. Thus, despite the failure of Shaw's Selector, Bush and the Documentalists continued to have faith in microfilm devices as saviors of the library. They had little idea of how the Cold War would change the Selector's career.

To understand how the Selector and its relatives became creatures of America's international responsibilities means stepping back to the immediate postwar years at the Eastman-Kodak company and then to the third wave of attempts to rescue Bush's Selector during the mid-1950s.

Back to Microfilm and Rochester

At the end of the war Eastman-Kodak did not renew its 1930s relationship with Vannevar Bush and his Selector, but the groups that had worked on Eastman's World War II microfilm machines and its fire control computers continued their explorations. There were very good business reasons for the attention to microfilm. The postwar years were the Golden Age of microfilm.[31] It was the technology for copying and storing information. By the 1960s microphotography became a major industry grossing a half-billion dollars a year.[32] There were many independent firms, but Eastman-Kodak was central because of its chemical expertise and its long experience in microphotography. Eastman was a supplier of the raw materials of microfilming and its Recordak Company set the economic boundaries of the copying industry. Of course, Eastman wanted to maintain its share of the business and bureaucratic markets. The company improved all its microfilm related offerings and continued some research into machines for information retrieval. It even invested in systems for the new electronic digital computer.

At the end of the war, microfilm seemed to be an answer to the computer's memory and input and output needs. The best magnetic drums, such as those on OP-20-G's Goldberg or Waldron MacDonald's Magnefile, were able to hold only one hundred and fifty thousand characters. Magnetic tape remained slow and unreliable and card readers were only slightly faster than in the 1930s. Thus, microfilm, although nonerasable, was the technology of hope for computer designers who wanted machines that were more than mathematical "number crunchers."[33] While the chemists and optical experts at Eastman worked to improve the quality of film and microfilm cameras, A. W. Tyler and his men cooperated with the first computer builders, such as John von Neumann and Jay Forrester. One goal was to develop very dense binary coded microfilm for ultra high-speed input and output. Some experts calculated that microfilm input systems would be three times more effective than magnetic tapes and at least one hundred and twenty times faster than IBM's most sophisticated card readers.[34] The Eastman group invested a great deal in a reader-recorder system for Forrester's Whirlwind mathematical computer but it also investigated the possibilities of their own Selector-like machines.[35]

Tyler's work on the high-speed light systems to record computer output improved the old light-box systems of OP-20-G's machines. He and his men also did yeoman work on the photocell scanning systems needed for selection. As they improved the computer related components, they began to think of creating their own retrieval device. At one time, Tyler's men wanted to use Morse's method of track-like coding for a selector because it allowed much higher data density than a dot system. But they found that even the best emulsions would not support what was discovered to be a very demanding technology. As a result, they made a commitment to perfect microfilm binary coding and they explored new tape drives and scanning systems. With the help of other groups at Eastman they tried to make the quantum technical leap necessary for instant development of output film.[36] That last goal proved illusive, but Tyler and his men continued to struggle to find a way to offer Eastman's customers a retrieval machine. The going was not easy and Eastman worried about Tyler's expenditures. Then, the Cold War and its information needs redirected much of the effort at Eastman's Rochester center.

Machines for Secrecy, Again

The air force's intelligence and logistics services needed an advanced information machine and in the early 1950s they began a long-term arrangement with Eastman that led to millions of dollars in subsidies to create the fantastic Eastman Minicard system.[37] Minicard was a major research and development program. By the time the huge microchip Minicard was completed and some five installations were in operation, almost as much had been spent on Minicard as on all of OP-20-G's RAM machines of World War II.[38] The initial Minicard took longer to develop and cost more than OP-20-G's path breaking Atlas electronic computer.[39]

The Minicard project was not a boondoggle. The incredibly high cost of the system and its long development cycle were the result of the many difficult problems involved in automating intelligence tasks. Information processing was and is a much greater technical and logical challenge than calculation. For example, compared to Minicard, OP-20-

G's Atlas had an easy job. It was designed to speed mathematical and statistical calculation. The cryptanalytic problems it attacked called for relatively little high-speed memory and it used fixed algorithms. Its function was to crunch numbers within its electronic calculating unit and infrequently print some results. In contrast, the intelligence and secrecy problems the Minicard system was expected to conquer demanded little calculation and a great deal of memory manipulation and output. There was no off-the-shelf technology or logic for such tasks.

Minicard's sponsors had, in fact, asked Eastman to accomplish the near impossible. The air force wanted instant access to graphics (pictures and diagrams) of potential targets, routes and equipment. Computers could not do that because of the memory problem and their reliance upon binary coding. In the 1950s and early 1960s, digitizing the alphabet was a challenge; digitizing and storing drawings and maps was an impossibility. And, there were no rapid graphic printers. Printers of the time were slow and were most were restricted to numbers and letters.[40] Only microfilm seemed to have any chance to store and deliver densely packed digital and analog information. But, microfilm continued to have many, many problems, as Bush's young men at ERA had discovered.

Tyler's Eastman-Kodak engineers identified the problems that had led to the defeat of the 1940 Selector and Shaw's 1950 device. That led to Minicard being very different from Bush's Selector. To overcome the limitations of serial data organization and the near impossibility of adding and deleting items from Selector files, the Eastman group decided to abandon one of the central features of the Bush Selectors, rolls of microfilm. While continuing to rely upon photoelectric sensing and comparator-like logic, they shifted to the use of microfilm chips. Those chips became the center of Minicard's technology. They were tiny, about one inch by one-half inch, but they held more than three times the amount of information of typical microfilm. But, more than the possibilities of increased density had led to the commitment to the chips; chips could be sorted. The separate Minicard chips, which held a set of identification codes and as much as twelve pages of text and graphics, allowed random access, sorting and easier updating of files. Tyler hoped that would allow the creation of a retrieval system that went beyond the best of the IBM card equipment as well as the old Bush Selectors. In particular, he hoped that in the long run his men would create a system that would be more than competitive with the IBM-related aperture card.[41]

The aperture card had its origins in the world of secrecy rather then in the many IBM microfilm activities of the 1930s. During World War II, the man in charge of the pictorial division of the OSS sliced rectangles out of IBM cards and inserted small bits of microfilm in the holes. The remainder of the card was used for codes for indexing the information on the film. Sorting machines were used for data retrieval. The inventor, John Langon, found that the cards and the microfilms survived passing through the sensing and sorting mechanisms and he convinced IBM that his cards would not harm its machines. Tom Watson decided to help Langon improve his system. By the end of the war many in the information field had become dependent on aperture cards. The system appeared so useful that a private company, Filmsort, was established and prospered.[42] Filmsort did not become a giant, but its machines, and those of such microfilm-chip companies as that of Professor Samain of France, were handy and inexpensive. They attracted many users and in the 1950s they were the competitors that Eastman would have to beat in the civilian market.

Although Eastman had hopes of a competitive selector, the air force's requirements led to the development of a complex and very expensive system. Tyler's group was able to speed data entry and found it easy to rig the electronics needed for complex "and/or" and greater-than/less-than selection. But, as Bush had discovered in the 1930s, mechanical problems were much harder to conquer. The use of the chips trapped Eastman in a host of very difficult mechanical challenges. Tyler's men endured years of frustration trying to perfect the transport devices needed to make the chips move fast enough.

After weighing hardware costs against processing needs, Tyler's group arrived at a complex design. They placed their microfilm chips on metal sticks, two thousand to a stick. Once the subfile or "stick" was inserted into a sorter or selector, the chips were drawn at high speeds past photosensing stations. Perfect alignment was needed because the code area was so tiny. After being scanned, the chips were routed to sorting pockets, or to reproduction stations, or placed back onto the file-stick. Selected chips were duplicated at a rate of two per second, then the originals were automatically returned to their proper subfiles. All that ultra high-speed movement had to be done without bending or scratching the chips.

After weighing hardware costs against processing needs, Tyler's group arrived at a complex design. They placed their microfilm chips on metal sticks, two thousand to a stick. Once the subfile or "stick" was inserted into a sorter or selector, the chips were drawn at high speeds past photosensing stations. Perfect alignment was needed because the code area was so tiny. After being scanned, the chips were routed to sorting pockets, or to reproduction stations, or placed back onto the file-stick. Selected chips were duplicated at a rate of two per second, then the originals were automatically returned to their proper subfiles. All that ultra high-speed movement had to be done without bending or scratching the chips.

It took many years, but in 1958, Eastman's men presented the world with what seemed to be a technical miracle, the first Minicard. Tyler could not meet all of his early goals, but the transport mechanisms worked at what was at least twice the raw speed of an IBM sorter and no human intervention was needed for multiple column sorting. In addition, Minicard was able to select items through much more complex search criteria than the most advanced Luhn-type IBM equipment. It did not reproduce selected items on-the-fly, as Bush's 1930s machines promised to, but the chips allowed searches impossible with film roll machines or tabulator equipment.[43] Minicard was impressive, received magnificent reviews and seemed to have easily triumphed over the aperture card systems. Within a few years, at least four more Minicards were constructed for government agencies.

There was a drawback to the Minicard, however. It was incredibly expensive. A complete system called for rooms full of equipment and a highly trained staff of operators and maintenance men. The initial cost of the equipment was staggering. A single early Minicard installation would have paid for one-third of OP-20-G's World War II Bombes, sixty of Samain's machines or a dozen or so devices for the aperture card systems. The price for the Minicard systems that were installed around the nation came close to exceeding all the grants by the private Council on Library Resources in its first decade of life.[44] Some of the later Minicard systems cost as much as two million dollars. Few but the military could afford Eastman's prestigious offering. With such price tags and a final output rate of one hundred twenty selected items per minute, criticism of Minicard would have been expected. Yet, in the context of the needs of the Cold War, the

Minicard seemed as great a contribution as the machines that fought the Battle of the Atlantic.[45]

Minicard was not the only microform project that resulted from the bounty of the Cold War. The million dollar machine that IBM built for the Central Intelligence Agency during the late 1950s received the same awe-struck reception. IBM's Walnut was a room size combination of photographic, electronic and mechanical machines to upgrade older aperture card systems. Like Minicard, Walnut appeared to be much faster than the Rapid Selector because it divided its files into smaller units and because it relied upon an IBM 1410 computer with a large random access magnetic drum. The indexes to its data files and short abstracts were kept on the drum. Using a flexible search logic, Walnut read the drum then punched out cards containing the abstracts and data file addresses of the selected items. After a user reviewed the selected cards, he submitted the addresses for the desired information. Walnut would then automatically search its micro-strip files.

Those microfilm chips and the files were unique. Text and graphics were photographed onto thin strips of microfilm. The strips were placed in small canisters which were held in Walnut's mechanized bins. The canisters were automatically plucked and presented to the Walnut reproduction device. Then, the desired strip was selected and scanned to locate the information with the requested address. Once located, the desired page was reproduced on an aperture card.[46] Later IBM microchip efforts were more technically refined, but they also remained too costly for anything but the Cold War.[47]

Fortunately, some microchip machines were simpler and less expensive. But systems such as those produced by Magnavox performed fewer functions than Walnut or Minicard and continued to cost tens of thousands of dollars. Eastman's Miracode machines of the late 1960s (some of which returned to the use of reels) allowed searching with relatively complex requests but they were slow and demanded a great deal of support. They also remained too expensive and unhandy for the library and, like Minicard and Walnut, were usually found in institutions for defense.[48]

The Bureau Gets the Final Word

The more direct technical and institutional descendants of Vannevar Bush's Selector were also brought to life by America's military. The history of Bush's thirty years of devoted attempts to put microfilm and photoelectricity together reached an ironic end because of the Cold War. The only Bush-type Selector ever put into useful operation was not built for scientists or research libraries or even the new academic-military think-tanks. It was financed and used by the organization that caused Bush and Stanford C. Hooper so much agony in the 1930s and that had so much to do with the death of Engineering Research Associates, the navy's Bureau of Ships. The Bureau of Ships was not the first of the Cold War organizations to attempt to rescue the Bush Selector, however. Bush's machine had to go through another set of agonies before it became a creature of the naval bureaucracy. Just after the OTS Selector was abandoned, secrecy again shaped the Selector's history.

The first attempt to revive the Selector after the failure of Ralph Shaw's 1950 project was directed by the ultimate Cold War organization, the Central Intelligence Agency. Formed in 1946, the Central Intelligence Agency had inherited the vast data collections of its World War II precursor, the Office of Strategic Services. The very wealthy CIA was, of course, building its own enormous files on the economics, politics, and cultures of all foreign nations. By the early 1950s it had millions if not billions of records and its manual and electromechanical indexing and retrieval systems were overwhelmed. Its indexing methods were advanced but cumbersome. In some of its systems it took several tabulator cards just to hold the index entries for a document. As the Cold War deepened, it became clear that old methods and mechanisms would not be able to cope with the agency's expansion. The CIA was in an information crisis and it was willing to spend whatever was necessary. It had the funds to try every possible alternative, including a new version of Bush's Selector.

Perhaps because of the previous sales pitch by ERA and Bush's ties to the CIA,[49] in the early 1950s, the agency decided to invest in a Selector. Unfortunately, it made its decision just as ERA was falling apart; just as Shaw was abandoning the OTS machine; and, just as the National Bureau of Standards was suffering through its own financial and political traumas. With no established company available, the agency gave the project to a Yale economist who had served the OSS and who continued on was as one of the CIA's intellectuals. The agency felt confident in him and Yale because they were old friends of American intelligence.[50] The CIA had no objections when the project director chose the electrical engineering department of his school to develop the new Selector's hardware. The young engineers at Yale immediately began what became a three year project to create the perfect information machine. They received much advice from the men at the National Bureau of Standards. The college students needed help because the information problem they were trying to solve was too complex for the simple architecture and hardware of the Shaw-ERA version of the Selector.

The Yale team set out to build a microfilm (not chip) machine. Its film was to hold records that contained almost five thousand indexing bits for each of its millions of documents. The microfilm had to have room for four thousand eight hundred code positions in addition to the full text and graphics of the associated documents. To exploit the index system, the simple four photocell scanner of the revised ERA machine had to be replaced with a very complex one housing tens of individually addressed cells. The perfect-match logic and circuitry of the ERA machine was also insufficient and the Yale group began to develop what should have been incorporated in the 1940 Selector, the ability to test for "and/or" and less-than/greater-than conditions. They also created an improved version of the light-box data input mechanism. Then, they began work on a system that would allow on the fly reproduction of selected items without slowing their Selector.[51] The Yale team accomplished a great deal. They built shop models of their input camera system and the complex electronic comparator for their machine. They were ready to build the remaining components. But, the Selector suffered another defeat. For unexplained reasons, the Yale project was halted just as Vannevar Bush began his final Patent Office project.[52] Thus, in the mid-1950s, the Selector bounced back to Washington and into another struggle for its life.

For a few months it appeared that two of Bush's life long dreams were about to merge and be fulfilled. Reform of the patent system and the Selector became tied to each other. As part of the National Bureau of Standards's responsibilities in the patent project, it was asked to investigate the potentials of a new Selector. The work got off to a slow start, but in 1956 the CIA sent the remnants of its Selector to Washington. With great expectations, the NBS examined the Yale components with an eye toward building a Patent Office Selector. But little came of the investigation because the entire Patent Office project began to drift. The Office was not pushing for a solution and the NBS did not have the funds to do much by itself.[53] The Selector was about to be put aside once again. Then, it was suddenly rescued a final time. The situation was filled with irony, however. The hero was Bush's and Hooper's old nemesis, the Bureau of Ships.[54]

The Bureau of Ships was in desperate need. The navy had launched a major microfilming initiative during World War II and used millions of feet of film for manuals, drawings and correspondence. Learning of the work in 1945, Bush gave some thought of approaching the navy about sponsoring a Rapid Selector. Nothing came of the idea,[55] but navy microfilming continued after the war with the Bureau of Ships playing a central role. By the mid-1950s, the Bureau's data collections had grown so large that it began a major information management program. It refined several systems, such as its cardotype, and then decided its system needed full automation.[56]

BuShips went to the National Bureau of Standards in 1956 for advice, just as the Yale-Patent Office Selector was being evaluated. The men at Standards, who were exploring many different information retrieval systems, recommended a Selector for the Bureau of Ships's problems. The Bureau agreed to support a development program and the Standards's group immediately began work, hoping that the navy's money would speed the development of the microfilm computer input system they were beginning to explore for the Census Bureau.[57] It took NBS's engineers five years, but in 1961 the Bureau of Ships had the world's first operational Selector.

The men at Standards had started by assembling a rather jury-rigged machine from the Yale remainders. Their patched together model was used for experimentation as early as 1959.[58] Pleased with the first results, NBS began work on a more advanced design that in many ways went beyond Bush's early specification.[59] The 1961 Selector had sensors and electronics allowing as many or more selection options than the Yale machine and it was able to copy the selected documents without slowing the master film. Most important, the machine worked. It was put to use at the Bureau of Ships as was a commercially produced version.[60] And the work on the Selector did help the NBS develop its later and very original series of FOSDIC machines. Built for the Census and the Weather Bureau, the FOSDICs were initially designed for speeding computer input, but some models included selection systems as sophisticated as those on the Bureau's Selector. However, they were not reproducing document machines.

The Machine for Bureaucracy

With the delivery of the Selector to the Bureau of Ships, Bush seemed to have been vindicated. The success of Bush's Selector was more apparent than real, however. In fact, the Bureau of Ships's machine underlined the failure of many of Bush's implicit technical promises. The new Selector was not a machine for abstracts, or the library, or association. It was not a bibliographic machine and it did nothing to prove that Memex was a physical possibility. It was a machine for bureaucracy, in fact, just one bureaucracy. No record has been found of a Selector being used outside of the Bureau of Ships. More importantly, despite more than two decades of progress in microfilm and electronics, and despite the some twenty five years of work on Selector-like devices, the 1961 Selector could not keep many of Bush's promises.

The NBS's BuShips Selector was expensive, huge, and relatively slow. It cost more than one-hundred thousand dollars, took up a sizeable portion of a room and was not as cost-effective as hoped.[61] The expense of preparing and retrieving items remained significant[62] and fundamental physical limitations remained. Although there had been much work on photoelectric and microfilm systems since Bush first specified his machine, the NBS engineers were unable to pack codes or data as densely as Bush promised in the mid-1930s.[63] The low density meant relative inefficiency. The code area required by the photoelectric sensors was much larger than in the 1940 version and the NBS designers decided that the documents had to be recorded at less than one-half the density of the 1940 Selector. The raw speed of the machine was also very limited. The 1961 Selector was not as fast as Bush had promised for his Selector two decades before. The microfilm tape on the NBS machine worked at three hundred and sixty feet per minute, not five hundred. As a result, the 1961 model searched some sixteen thousand items a minute, far less than the promised sixty thousand. When one compensates for the 1961 version's use of entire documents, not short abstracts, the comparison is less depressing. But the NBS machine was unable to meet many of Bush's goals of the 1930s.[64]

There was more bad news. By the time the NBS Selector began operating and when the mainstream librarians began to think of bibliographic automation through microfilm,[65] the incredible pace of change in electronic computers was making the Selector appear as a hangover from another era. It was less than five years between the appearance of Bureau of Ships's Selector and the emergence of the mass produced computer, the IBM 360. By the mid-1960s, erasable magnetic recording devices, high-speed printers, the lowered cost of computers, and even xeroxing made the microfilm selection machines less and less attractive.[66] Because of the technological progress of the computer in the 1960s, few of the many special purpose microfilm machines, including the Selector, survived through the decade. The maturation of the electronic general purpose computer also changed the nature and vocabulary of Documentalism. It became "information science" and its new professionals talked of electronics and bytes rather than microfilm and diameters of photographic reduction.

Not a Happy Ending

Microfilm retrieval and some of Bush's greatest dreams seemed to have reached a sad end in the 1960s. Bush retired to his Belmont, Massachusetts home in 1958 where he reflected on his life, wrote a great deal, and stayed at least peripherally involved with the information problem. Bush also kept in touch with the advances in engineering and electronics.[67] He must have known of the Bureau of Ships project and its results and he must have sensed that it was really the last gasp for his bibliographic and secrecy machines. In early 1959, he was informed that OP-20-G had used his Comparators for a decade but, by 1952, they had been superseded by new equipment using new technologies.[68] From his contacts with MIT's INTREX information project of the 1960s, he learned that microfilm retrieval systems seemed old and worn to the new generation of engineers.[69] Bush must also have been discouraged to learn that so little attention was being paid to his Memex despite all the advances in computers and electronics.[70] Bush was disappointed, but he did not give up on the Selector or Memex. He never lost his technological optimism and, although he was in his mid-seventies and was more introspective, he continued to lobby for his bibliographic and intellectual ideas if not hardware.

There were a few times when he confessed that his proposed Memex machine of 1945 was a true fantasy[71] and he did turn to modern computer technology when he discussed the next version of a Memex. But, his later writings treated the Selector as a success and he continued to refer to microfilm as a near wonder technology. Bush also continued to believe that association and bibliographic control by experts could solve the information problem. As late as the mid-1960s, he implied that personal indexing would automatically fulfill the needs of the library. He continued to define the library problem from a specialist's perspective and he continued to place ultimate faith in the ability of the new physical scientists and engineers to bring the information age to life.

The Saddest Thing of All

The other man for technology, Stanford C. Hooper, had a much less pleasant retirement. At the end of his life Hooper was disappointed about what had happened to his fight for science and innovation. In particular, his relationship with Engineering Research Associates did not end happily. Because of his views on how the navy should organize research for the Cold War and his ties to ERA, the navy's bureaucracy turned on the man who had done so much to modernize naval communications and cryptanalysis.

In 1943, Hooper had consented to stay in the navy, but his wartime service as an advisor on electronics was limited by a serious illness. Long stays in hospitals and the need to escape the cold winters in Washington restricted his contributions during the remainder of his life. However, Hooper remained active. Although retired, he continued to serve on many science related military boards and his previous contributions to electronics led to more civilian accolades. In 1945, for example, he received a high honor from the Franklin Institute for his "pioneering leadership and practical realization of discovery in the field of radio for the U. S. Navy." At the same time, he began to act as a consultant to several small but important electronics firms.[72]

Like Bush, Hooper became more reflective during his semi-retirement. But, unlike Bush, he changed his views on how to best integrate science and the military.[73] During the later years of the war he began to question his earlier faith in the ability of universities and large corporations to solve the navy's problems. Hooper was turning into a technological populist.[74] Hooper's populism had been emerging since the 1930s when he began to feel that the major electronics companies were stifling innovation through patent control. He became suspicious of their commitment to advancing technology and the nation. His fears were confirmed when the largest corporations refused to follow the lead of the smaller companies and let the government have free use of their patents during the war. Then, he became very worried about America's future in electronics when the major corporations would not create the postwar open patent pool the smaller and more innovative companies needed to survive.[75] An even greater threat to the navy and the nation, in Hooper's opinion, was the drive by the corporations to create a single huge international communications company.[76]

Hooper became frightened of big business and discouraged by its attitude toward the needs of the military. He felt betrayed by those he and the navy and the nation had done so much for. He was especially hurt by the actions of the company that he had helped to establish at the end of World War I, RCA. His frustrations grew and in late 1947 he wrote his old friend the chief executive of RCA, David Sarnoff:[77]

> We have not had that talk yet. Meanwhile I worry about you more and more. Arch conspirator Joseph Stalin says our system of Democracy cannot succeed because our heads of monopolies become so powerful that they influence public officials more and more to make the monopolies more powerful, so in time we will be worse than state owned, -owned by a few people instead. The point is are you a big enough man to show Joe that he is wrong, in so far as the Communications-Electronic field is concerned. So far your record is straight for monopoly... I see every move you make here in Congress, in the government departments and Commissions, and there is always your guiding hand in the background. You must take personal stock, and choose now whether to keep your company's temporary interests ahead of the future interests of the nation. Certainly in the end you will be better off with the latter interest uppermost. You sought my advice for many years. Listen now. I am one of the half dozen persons but for anyone of whom you would not have been where you are, so listen.

Hooper also worried about the attempts of academics to stake claims to a major share of military research funding and their demands for a vast and centralized postwar federal agency to mimic the NDRC. He feared that a continued involvement of the nation's universities in development projects would lead to a stifling of creativity. Academics, he wrote, should confine themselves to the most abstract research. Allowing them to move into development during the war had set a dangerous precedent. He thought a huge permanent civilian version of Bush's expansive wartime program would become politicized and noncreative.

Hooper even distanced himself from the Office of Naval Research because of what he saw as its overly academic orientation. Uppermost in his mind was the fear that university research would kill off innovative small businesses. With universities yielding patents to the government, he argued, small businesses would be without necessary patent protection. He stated that only the corporations, with their great financial reserves, could survive in a patent free environment. With politicized university programs and the monopolistic tendencies of the corporations, Hooper argued, the nation's military research would become expensive and nonproductive.[78] He continued to distrust in-house military research and all types of bureaucracy. He lobbied for a top level board of scientific military men like himself to oversee whatever research the bureaus were allowed to pursue, but he had a much more comprehensive formula for the troubled relationship between science and the military. Hooper arrived at his new solution to the problem of innovation well before Engineering Research Associates faced its times of trouble in the late 1940s.

The End of Several ERAs

Hooper made his position very clear and, as he had done in the mid-1930s, he alienated many of those who would have the final word in shaping America's institutions. Hooper's prescription was to force the large, monopolistic corporations to share their patents and research findings with smaller firms; to shift government research subsidization to companies like ERA; and, to revise the patent system so that smaller firms had incentives to be innovative.[79] He saluted Henry Wallace's attempts to turn the Department of Commerce and the National Bureau of Standards into engines for small business as well as Wallace's policy of favoring new start-up companies like ERA. Of course, Hooper stepped on many corporate and bureaucratic toes. That was unfortunate because by the late 1940s his client, ERA, needed all the help it could get. It was in financial as well as political trouble. Despite it ties to the NBS, the ONR and even IBM, it faced hard economic times. Partially because of its link to Hooper and because of the unpredictable course of unification of the military intelligence agencies, it was also becoming mired in political problems.[80]

The conflict over the Shaw-Green Selector had not been the only source of trouble at Engineering Research during the late 1940s. It became increasingly difficult for the ex-academics and scientists to keep their small company solvent as more firms began to compete in the expanding military and science related computer markets.[81] On top of the financial woes was an increasing number of attacks by the navy bureaus.[82] The drive for efficiency that came with the integration of the communications intelligence agencies also took its toll. Soon, the army and navy cryptanalytic groups had only a very small technical contingent whose job was to draw up functional specifications to be submitted for open bid by established contractors, contractors who knew how to follow bureaucratic procedures and who could survive on low margin government contracts.[83]

The technological politics of the Cold War also played a role. In 1950, just as ERA's leaders were searching for a financial sponsor to rescue them, they received a body blow from Drew Pearson. In his Washington Merry-Go-Round column[84] his men exposed the special relationship between ERA and the navy. The criticism led the navy to take a harder look at the company and to tell the intelligence agencies to return to the bureaucratic way of doing business. The navy's auditors, angered over the special open end contracts with ERA, paid such meticulous attention to ERA's internal accounts that bad feelings developed on both sides. The navy threatened to terminate much of the vital secret work at ERA while its president, John Parker, let loose some verbal blasts that further eroded the necessary trust between the navy and the company.[85] Relations with the navy bureaus had soured so much by the late 1940s that Joseph Wenger was unable to arrange for either a ceremony for or a letter of special thanks to the ERA engineers who had designed and built the astounding Atlas computer. IBM's men did receive formal thanks for their new work, however.[86]

More than heated emotions and battles over protocol were at work to endanger ERA and Hooper. The military bureaucracy, busy trying to define and control the massive Cold War technological industry, managed a direct slap at Stanford C. Hooper. In the early 1950s, near the end of his life, he had to undergo a demeaning questioning of his integrity because of his relationship with ERA.[87]

During World War II, Hooper had stood in the background, but in 1944 and 1945 he gave advice on how to structure ERA as well as general encouragement to those who established the company. Perhaps he contributed some very badly needed money at the critical moment when even John Parker could not find backing for a science company. Then, in 1947, his ties to ERA's operations became direct when he was asked to provide the kind of guidance he was giving to several other small electronics companies. His arms-length role in ERA was formalized in 1949 when the company agreed to pay him three thousand dollars a year (only fifty-seven dollars a week) to act as a "technical" consultant. The job did not lead to luxury for him as he was allowed no more than twenty-five dollars a week for travel and entertainment expenses. He was permitted to buy into ERA's group insurance plan[88] but that was certainly not a handsome perk.[89]

The relationship pleased everyone until ERA was purchased by the giant Remington-Rand. Unfortunately, Hooper had opposed the purchase because he wanted ERA to remain flexible and focused on the needs of the intelligence community. He thought that Remington would not devote itself to the navy's work despite having its research being directed by the famed head of the Manhattan Project, General Leslie Groves.[90] Eventually, Hooper accepted the Remington purchase because there seemed no other financial alternative and because he thought that the link to Remington might have another important bonus. Being tied to Remington, he wrote, would ease the navy auditors' pressures on ERA. Sadly, with the take over, the navy intensified its reviews of ERA, and, it began to question Hooper's connection.

Remington was asked to justify all its military related expenditures. In particular, the company was ordered to show that Hooper had played a "technical" role. At the same time, Hooper was asked to explain and defend employing a chauffeur-houseman and charging part of the expense to his ERA account. The sum was less than one thousand dollars a year.[91] Hooper, disabled and almost seventy years old, did not try to evoke sympathy by mentioning his illness. He just described the business need for a driver and for someone to help with chores around the house, such as serving table at business dinners. He satisfied the executives at Remington, but not the navy. Although it was commonplace for active Rear Admirals and the executives of the firms Hooper dealt with to have a car and driver, his explanation did not please the navy.

Worse was to come for the old man who had done so much for the American navy. Remington could not muster the evidence necessary to show that Hooper had played a technical role. As a result, in 1954, Remington was notified that Hooper had not been and was not a legitimate employee of ERA. Therefore, declared the navy's attorneys, none of the payments to him could be charged to government contracts.[92]

That decision came just a year before Hooper passed away. And it was just the last in a series of rather disheartening encounters between Hooper and ERA and the navy. Reflecting on his long-term relationship with Engineering Research Associates, Hooper wrote to the head of the ERA division of Remington-Rand:

> Then there is the little matter of over $20,000.00 which Johnny [Parker] really promised me, but I can't bring that up to R. R. [Remington-Rand]. His failure on that made me sell my lot in Miami Beach and give up our years of hope and planning for a house on La Gorce (?) Island (and a new car!) but that can't be helped. It was pretty hard on my wife.[93]

Notes

Explanation of Citation Formats

The research for this book travelled through several disciplines and more than five decades of bibliographic styles. The result was that I encountered many different formats for the citation of books, articles and unpublished materials. From all those, I had to select one for each type of material. For the published documents I decided to risk all and use a single and hopefully reasonable format. I chose a middle-of-the-road style that will probably make everyone somewhat unhappy. I hope that the form of citations for unpublished materials, many of which were truly "primary," is also reasonable. Because the majority of government documents from the intelligence agencies were not formally registered, and because there were so many documents in each of the files from the major court cases, I decided to add, when appropriate, short titles in the citations. To aid future researchers, including myself, I have enclosed a short summary of a document's contents or a paraphrase of the initial sentences of a memorandum to aid recovery. Such researcher-created titles are indicated by the use of ' marks while the titles created by the historical actors are enclosed in traditional quote marks. Thus, 'Wenger Memo on Bombe' was created by me, while, "Memorandum on Bombe," indicates a title found on a document.

Hopefully, another decision about citations was reasonable. I tried to strike a balance between length and usefulness. I attempted to minimize abbreviations while avoiding a too lengthy note section. For example, I avoided such unsightly things as HML for the Hagley Museum and Library, or LC for the Library of Congress. But, I decided to take a few shortcuts. Among the more frequent abbreviations are: NARA for the National Archives and Records Service; NSA for the National Security Agency; and ONR for the Office of Naval Research. Other abbreviations are explained in the Terms and Abbreviations section of this book's front matter.

Many of the most important documents in this study were acquired through FOIA requests. I was fortunate to be the first outsider to see detailed information about the work at NCR-NCML. Much of the FOIA material has never been formally archived and I have had to be somewhat creative in citing it. However, the terms I have used, such as NSA RAM File, will lead future researchers to the same evidence.

CHAPTER I

1. James R. Beniger, *The Control Revolution* (Cambridge, Mass.: Harvard University Press, 1986). Joanne Yates, *Control Through Communication* (Baltimore: Johns Hopkins University Press, 1989). William Aspray (ed), *Computers Before Computing* (Ames, Iowa: Iowa State University Press, 1990). Michael Rogers Rubin, and Mary Taylor Huber, *The Knowledge Industry in the United States* (Princeton: Princeton University Press, 1986). These provide a useful summary of much of the previous work on the information "industries."
2. James R. Beniger, *The Control Revolution* (Cambridge, Mass.: Harvard

University Press, 1986). Francis L. Miksa (ed), *Charles Ammi Cutter: Library Systematizer* (Littleton, Colo.: Libraries Unlimited, 1977).

3. Jack Rubin, *A History of Micrographics: In the First Person* (Silver Spring, Md.: National Micrographics Association, 1980). Marc Steven Kolopsky, "Remington Rand Workers in the Towandas of New York, 1927-1956," (Ph.D. Thesis, State University of New York, Buffalo, 1986).
4. W. Boyd Rayward, "The case of Paul Otlet, pioneer of information science, internationalist, visionary: reflections on biography," *Journal of Librarianship and Information Science* 23(1991): 135-144. Dorothy B. Lilly, and Ronald W. Trice, *A History of Information Science 1945-1985* (New York: Academic Press, 1989). Irene S. Farkas-Conn, *From Documentation to Information Science* (New York: Greenwood Press, 1990).
5. The history of Europe's new information systems movement is just emerging. See, John Metcalfe, *Information Retrieval, British and American, 1876-1976* (Metuchen, N. J.: Scarecrow Press, 1976). R. A. Fairthorne, *Towards Information Retrieval* (New York: Archon Books, 1968). Phyllis Dain, and John Y. Cole (ed), *Libraries and Scholarly Communication in the United States* (New York: Greenwood Press, 1990), 1-12.
6. Dorothy B. Lilly, and Ronald W. Trice, *A History of Information Science 1945-1985* (New York: Academic Press, 1989), 1.
7. The story of the impact of the massive funding of abstract as well as applied science as a result of the Cold War has been the subject of many histories but a full account awaits a new generation of historians. Helpful works are, Peter Galison, and Bruce Hevly (ed), *Big Science: The Growth of Large Scale Research* (Stanford: Stanford University Press, 1993). Derek J. DeSola Price, *Little-Science Big-Science--and Beyond* (New York: Columbia University Press, 1986). Daniel J. Kevles, *The Physicists: The History of the Scientific Community in Modern America* (New York: Knopf, 1978). A book that arrived after the completion of this manuscript is a brilliant example of what is to come. See, Stuart W. Leslie, *The Cold War and American Science: The Military-Industrial-Academic Complex at MIT and Stanford* (New York: Columbia University Press, 1993).
8. Dorothy B. Lilly, and Ronald W. Trice, *A History of Information Science 1945-1985* (New York: Academic Press, 1989), 3-4.
9. James M. Nyce, and Paul Kahn, "Innovation, Pragmaticism and Technological Continuity: Vannevar Bush's Memex," *Journal of the American Society for Information Science* 40(1989): 214. James M. Nyce, and Paul Kahn (ed), *From Memex to Hypertext: Vannevar Bush and the Mind's Machine* (Boston: Academic Press, 1991).
10. The 1947-50 Selector was tested in a government library but never used operationally. All the spin-offs of the Selector were for government bureaucracies or military agencies.
11. The National Science Foundation sponsored research in and programs for scientific data retrieval and the Johnson administration did pass some sweeping library legislation. The NSF contributions were significant but the general subsidy program came to little.

CHAPTER II

1. Karl L. Wildes, and Nilo A. Lindgren, *A Century of Electrical Engineering and Computer Science at MIT, 1882-1982* (Cambridge: MIT Press, 1985), 7. Samuel C. Prescott, *When MIT Was "Boston Tech," 1861-1916* (Cambridge: Technology Press of MIT, 1954). The name, "Comparator," was probably selected for Bush's 1930s cryptanalytic machine because of the earlier MIT device created by the Institute's founders.
2. Peggy Aldrich Kidwell, "American Scientists and Calculating Machines--From Novelty to Commonplace," *Annals of the History of Computing* 12(1990): 1-40. William Aspray, and Michael Gunderloy, "Early Computing and Numerical Analysis at the National Bureau of Standards," *Annals of the History of Computing* 11(1989): 3-11. Rexmond Cochrane, *Measures for Progress: A History of the National Bureau of Standards* (Washington: G. P. O., 1966).
3. James S. Small, "On The Relation between Science, Technology and Engineering in the Context of the post-Second World War Development of Electronic Analogue

Computers," in *Workshop: Technohistory of Electrical Information Technology* (Muchen: Deutches Museum, 1991).

4. There is as yet no full history of Powers and Remington-Rand. For an insight into Powers's career and problems see the forthcoming, 'Before the Univac' by this author. Arthur Norberg,"High Technology Calculation in the Early 20th Century: Punched Card Machinery in Business and Government," *Technology and Culture* 31(1990): 753. C. E. Forbes (ed), *America's Foremost Business Leaders* (New York: np, 1948), 371-9. Important are: Thomas O'Keefe, "Chronological History of Tabulating Machines" April, 1956 and, J. T. Ferry, 'History of the Punched Card, 1965' in the collection of primary documents from the Sperry-Univac archives (Accession 2015 Remington-Rand/ERA Materials) now held at the Hagley Museum and Library. Also informative is the just published, James Cortada, *Before the Computer* (Princeton: Princeton University Press, 1993).
5. Geoffrey Austrian, *Herman Hollerith, Forgotten Giant of Information* (New York: Columbia University Press, 1982). David F. Noble, *America By Design: Science, Technology and the Rise of Corporate Capitalism* (New York: Oxford University Press, 1979). Daniel J. Kevles, *The Physicists: The History of the Scientific Community in Modern America* (New York: Knopf, 1978).
6. James M. Nyce, and Paul Kahn (ed), *From Memex to Hypertext: Vannevar Bush and the Mind's Machine* (Boston: Academic Press, 1991), 113-144.
7. Larry Owens, "Straight Thinking: Vannevar Bush and the Culture of American Engineering," (Ph.D. Thesis, Princeton University, 1987). Larry Owens, "Vannevar Bush and the Differential Analyser: The Text and Context of an Early Computer," *Technology and Culture* 27(1986): 63-95. Montgomery B. Meigs, "Managing Uncertainty: Vannevar Bush, James B. Conant and the Development of the Atomic Bomb, 1940-45," (Ph.D. Thesis, University of Wisconsin, Madison, 1982). Stanley Goldberg, "Inventing a Climate of Opinion: Vannevar Bush and the Decision to Build the Bomb," *ISIS* 83(1992): 429. G. Pascal Zachary, "Vannevar Bush Backs the Bomb," *Bulletin of the Atomic Scientists* 48(1992): 24.
8. James M. Nyce, and Paul Kahn (ed), *From Memex to Hypertext: Vannevar Bush and the Mind's Machine* (Boston: Academic Press, 1991), 235-353, especially, Linda C. Smith, "Memex as an Image of Potentiality Revisited," 261-286. Adele Goldberg (ed), *A History of Personal Workstations* (Reading, Mass.: ACM Press, 1988). On Bush's science policies in the post WWII era, Daniel J. Kevles's preface to, Vannevar Bush, *Science- The Endless Frontier* (Washington: NSF, circa 1992), ix-xxxiii.
9. Colin Burke, "A Practical View of Memex: The Rapid Selector," in James M. Nyce, and Paul Kahn (ed), *From Memex to Hypertext: Vannevar Bush and the Mind's Machine* (Boston: Academic Press, 1991), 145-164.
10. Bush's patent history was traced through the historical files at the U. S. Patent Office's Crystal City, Virginia facility.
11. Bernard Williams, "Computing With Electricity, 1935-1945," (Ph.D. Thesis, University of Kansas, 1984), 48.
12. Library of Congress, Papers of Stanford C. Hooper, Box 16, 'Binaural Sons of the C', June 1, 1934.
13. Otto J. Scott, *The Creative Ordeal: The Story of Raytheon* (New York: Atheneum Press, 1974).
14. Bernard Williams, "Computing With Electricity, 1935-1945," (Ph.D. Thesis, University of Kansas, 1984). Larry Owens, "Straight Thinking: Vannevar Bush and the Culture of American Engineering," (Ph.D. Thesis, Princeton University, 1987). Bush successfully courted the leaders of almost every high-tech related corporation in America. General Electric, Eastman, NCR, General Motors, and many other large corporations were familiar Bush stomping grounds. Significant yet unexplained, Bush did not develop cordial and profitable connections with the two major manufacturers of calculating equipment, IBM and Remington Rand. History would have been different if IBM had chosen MIT over Columbia and Harvard universities for its attention and if Remington's leader had made a commitment to academic research.
15. Vannevar Bush, *Pieces of the Action* (New York: Morrow, 1970). Larry Owens, "Straight Thinking: Vannevar Bush and the Culture of American Engineering," (Ph.D. Thesis, Princeton University, 1987).
16. Vannevar Bush, *Pieces of the Action* (New York: Morrow, 1970). NDRC and its successor, the OSRD, were very elitist and Big Science oriented. James Phinney

Baxter, *Scientists Against Time* (Cambridge, Mass.: MIT Press, 1968), and Irvin Stewart, *Organizing Scientific Research for War: The Administrative History of the Office of Scientific Research and Development* (Boston: Little-Brown, 1948).
17. Vannevar Bush, *Pieces of the Action* (New York: Morrow, 1970).
18. Vannevar Bush, "The Differential Analyser," *Journal of the Franklin Institute*, vol. 212 No.1270-32 (October, 1931): 452. Larry Owens, "Straight Thinking: Vannevar Bush and the Culture of American Engineering," (Ph.D. Thesis, Princeton University, 1987), 255.
19. Larry Owens, "Straight-Thinking: Vannevar Bush and the Culture of American Engineering," (Ph.D. Thesis, Princeton University, 1987), 289-90.
20. Frank Cameron, *Cottrell: Samaritan of Science* (New York: Doubleday, 1952).
21. Unfortunately, there are no in-depth works on Edgerton and his company. Karl L. Wildes, and Nilo A. Lindgren, *A Century of Electrical Engineering and Computer Science at MIT, 1882-1982* (Cambridge: MIT Press, 1985) contains a chapter on Edgerton and his group. A collection of his work is in, Harold E. Edgerton, *Stopping Time* (New York: H.R. Abrams, 1987). On General Radio, Donald B. Sinclair, *The General Radio Company, 1915-1965* (New York: Newcomen Society, 1965).
22. For example, Bush asked the Rockefeller Foundation for help as soon as the first large analyser was completed, but he had to wait close to six years for their aid. See, Rockefeller Archive, RG12.1, Diaries of Warren Weaver.
23. Search of U. S. Patent Office Historical files, Crystal City, Virginia 1989.
24. An overview of the results of his attempts, from the 1930s to the post-war era, is found in, MIT Archives, AC4 Boxes 30 and 36, 'Center of Analysis'.
25. Vannevar Bush, "Instrumental Analysis," *Bulletin of the American Mathematical Society* 42 (October, 1936): 649. Karl L.Wildes, and Nilo A. Lindgren, *A Century of Electrical Engineering and Computer Science at MIT, 1882-1982* (Cambridge: MIT Press, 1985), 230-3.
26. Smithsonian History of Computers Interviews, "Gordon S. Brown," January 27, 1970, provides a fascinating overview of many of the efforts at the Institute in the 1920s and 1930s.
27. Charles S. Bashe, et al, *IBM's Early Computers* (Cambridge, Mass.: MIT Press, 1985). Michael R. Williams, *A History of Computing Technology* (Englewood Cliffs, N. J.: Prentice-Hall, 1985). G. W. Baehne (ed), *Practical Applications of the Punched Card Methods in Colleges and Universities* (New York: Columbia University Press, 1935) all provide overviews of 1930s digital technology and attempts to create computing centers. On Harvard's efforts, in addition to Aiken's machine, Rockefeller Archives, RG12.1, Diaries of Warren Weaver: October 5-24, 1939.
28. There were several companies that made similar devices for gun control systems for the military, however. See the Barber-Coleman and Hannibal Ford companies. Note that Ford was interested in building a version of an analyser and, perhaps, donating it to Cornell University. See, press releases by the Sperry Corporation, "Hannibal Ford," "Ford Instrument Company." On Ford and Bush, Rockefeller Archives, RG12.1 Diaries of Warren Weaver, March 3, 1935.
29. We have yet to have a technical history of the "tab" era that shows how they were used, but general overviews of needs and demand are found in: James R. Beniger, *The Control Revolution* (Cambridge, Mass.: Harvard University Press, 1986), and in the brilliant, Martin Campbell-Kelley, "Industrial Assurance and Large-scale Data-Processing," *Technohistory of Electrical Information Technology* (Munchen: Deutsches Museum, 1991).
30. Irene S. Farkas-Conn, *From Documentation to Information Science* (New York: Greenwood Press, 1990).
31. Frederick Luther, *Microfilm: A History 1939-1900* (Annapolis: National Microfilm Association, 1959). William White, *Subminature Photography* (Boston: Focal Press, 1991). Joel Stebbins, "The Electric Eye in Astronomy," *Cooperation in Research* (Washington, D.C.: The Carnegie Institution of Washington, 1938), 75.
32. C. E. Wynn-Williams, "The Use of Thyratrons for High Speed Automatic Counting of Physical Phenomena," *Proc. Royal Soc.* Ser. A., v. 132 (July, 1931): 295. H. J. Reich, *Theory and Application of Electron Tubes* (New York: McGraw-Hill, 1939). Keith Henney, *Electron Tubes in Industry* (New York: McGraw-Hill, 1937).

33. One of the puzzles in the history of the Comparator and the Selector is how frequently Bush either missed or failed to mention the many existing applications and patents related to photoelectric data processing. Of great import was his belief that IBM did not have a significant foothold and that, if it gained one, it would use patents to protect its electromechanical devices. Hagley Museum and Library, Accession 1825, *Honeywell v Sperry-Rand* Trial Records, October 25, 1937, Research Corporation to Deeds of NCR, 'Patents'.
34. Bernard Williams, "Computing With Electricity, 1935-1945," (Ph.D. Thesis, University of Kansas, 1984), and Karl L. Wildes, and Nilo A. Lindgren, *A Century of Electrical Engineering and Computer Science at MIT, 1882-1982* (Cambridge: MIT Press, 1985) give descriptions of the developments.
35. Karl L. Wildes, and Nilo A. Lindgren, *A Century of Electrical Engineering and Computer Science at MIT, 1882-1982* (Cambridge: MIT Press, 1985), Chpt. 4. H. L. Hazen, and G. S. Brown, "The Cinema Integraph," *Journal of the Franklin Institute* (July/August, 1940): 34. On the amazing Wavelength machine, MIT Archives, AC4 Boxes 30 and 36, "Center of Analysis," and, Box 36 Folder 1, "The MIT Wavelength Project."
36. Hagley Museum and Library Accession 1825, *Honeywell v Sperry-Rand* Trial Records, NCR Depositions, Bush to Deeds 'Analyzing Equipment', May 19, 1938. Deeds to Bush, August, 1937, 'Rapid Selector'. Bush to Deeds, October 14, 1937 'Edgerton'.
37. Larry Owens, "Straight Thinking: Vannevar Bush and the Culture of American Engineering," (Ph.D. Thesis, Princeton University, 1987), 78. A valuable insight into the new Analyzer project is, Charles Babbage Institute, Interview by William Aspray with Dr. Frank M. Verzuh, February 20 and 24, 1984.
38. Bush's acceptance of digital calculation, as evidenced by the plans for the electronic calculator, the Selector, and the Comparator, calls into the question the thesis that he was wedded to analog models and calculation. See Larry Owens, "Vannevar Bush and the Differential Analyser: The Text and Context of an Early Computer," *Technology and Culture* 27(1986): 63-95.
39. On the genesis of Memex, James M. Nyce, and Paul Kahn, "Innovation, Pragmaticism and Technological Continuity: Vannevar Bush's Memex," *Journal of the American Society for Information Science* 40(1989): 214. E. Goldberg, U. S. Patent 1,838,389, Statistical Machine, December 29, 1931, Filed April 5, 1928.
40. Hagley Museum and Library, Accession 1825 *Honeywell v Sperry-Rand* Trial Records, August 13, 1937, Bush to Deeds, 'Rapid Selector'.
41. Rockefeller Archives, RG12.1, Diaries of Warren Weaver: Bush Visit March 12, 1937, 'FBI Machine'; Bush visit October 28, 1938, 'Carnegie Plans'. RG1.1, 224D 2 23, April 14, 1937, Bush Letter to Weaver, "A Reference Selector." RG12.1, Box 68, Diaries of Warren Weaver, Bush to Weaver, November 29, 1937.
42. Rockefeller Archives, RG1.1 224D 2 23, April 14, 1937, Bush letter to Weaver, "A Reference Selector." A technical description is found in, Thomas C. Bagg, and Mary Elizabeth Stevens, *Information Selection Systems: Retrieving Replica Copies: A State of the Art Report* (Washington, D.C.: National Bureau of Standards, Technical Note 157, December 31, 1961), 20. On the FBI problems, Library of Congress, Papers of Vannevar Bush, John Howard File, Bush to C. Wilson, April 15, 1940, 'Rapid Selector'.
43. Vannevar Bush, "Instrumental Analysis," *Bulletin of the American Mathematical Society* 42(1936): 649. This paper had been given as a major address on January 2, 1936. Larry Owens, "Straight Thinking: Vannevar Bush and the Culture of American Engineering," (Ph.D. Thesis, Princeton University, 1987), 79. William H. Radford, "Notes on Arithmetical Machine Memoranda," Unpublished typescript, MIT, Dec. 7, 1938, as cited by Brain Randell, *The Origins of Digital Computers* (Berlin: Springer-Verlag, 1982), 502. Exactly when Bush began the design of the Rapid Arithmetical Machine is unclear but he must have begun thinking of it by 1936. The first memo on it seems to have been written in January, 1937. Hagley Museum and Library, Accession 1825 *Honeywell v Sperry-Rand* Trial Records, Box 67, William Radford, "Report on An Investigation of the Practicality of Developing a Rapid Computing Machine," October 15, 1939. On analog computers, Gramino A. Korn, and Theresa M. Korn, *Electronic Computers (DC Analog Computers)* 2nd ed. (New York: McGraw-Hill, 1952).

CHAPTER III

1. David K. Van Keuren, "Science Progressivism, and Military Preparedness: The Case of the Naval Research Laboratory, 1915-1923," *Technology and Culture* 33(1992): 710-736.
2. The best source of information on Hooper is the collection of his papers at the Library of Congress. It is more than well indexed in, Library of Congress, "Silas Casey, Stanford Caldwell Hooper: A Register of Their Papers in the Library of Congress," Naval Historical Foundations Collection. It also contains an excellent sketch of his career. A useful chronology is in the biography compiled by the Naval Historical Center, Washington, D.C.. On the evolution of Hooper's important views of the role of patents, Library of Congress, Hooper Papers, Box 21, August 17, 1945, 'There are now four bills'. Very useful on Hooper and technical radio matters is the collection of his papers at the Smithsonian Institution.
3. NSA RAM File, Hooper to OP-20-G, 'Cryptanalytic Machines', September 26, 1930, and Library of Congress, Papers of Stanford Caldwell Hooper, Box 18, Hooper to Secret Naval Board, 'Staff Corps Personnel', February 7, 1936.
4. Useful on inventors and invention in the era of World War I are, Thomas Parke Hughes, *Elmer Sperry: Inventor and Engineer* (Baltimore: Johns Hopkins University Press, 1971), and Daniel J. Kevles, *The Physicists: The History of the Scientific Community in Modern America* (New York: Knopf, 1978).
5. Linwood S. Howeth, *History of Communications Electronics in the United States Navy: With an Introduction by Chester W. Nimitz* Bureau of Ships, Office of Naval History (Washington: GPO, 1963), 412-414. On different post-WWI approaches to integrating science with the navy, see, *US Naval Administration in World War II: SECNAV Administrative History: Office of Research and Inventions 1 July-31 December 1945*. Note that Hooper is not mentioned in this or other works related to naval science policy although he was of great importance. Perhaps his later problems with the bureaucracy and isolationism account for his invisibility. On his isolationist connections: Burton K. Wheeler with Paul F. Healy, *Yankee From the West* (New York: Doubleday, 1962), 18-20, 386, and Ladislas Farago, *The Game of the Foxes* (New York: David McKay, 1971), 477-8.
6. Library of Congress, Papers of Stanford Caldwell Hooper: Jewett to Hooper, March 24, 1933, Box 15; 'Binaural Sons of the C', March 26, 1933, Box 16; and, Hooper to Redman, 'Scientific Visits' May 3, 1934, Box 16.
7. Library of Congress, Papers of Stanford Caldwell Hooper, 'Memorandum on Johns Hopkins Group Visit', November 3, 1937, Box 17.
8. Rockefeller Archives RG12.1, Diaries of Warren Weaver, 'Visit of Hooper and Lemmon', June 10, 1938.
9. Library of Congress, Papers of Stanford Caldwell Hooper, 'To CNO: NRC', January 31, 1935, Box 17, and on the 1930s National Research Council program for the military, Box 21, August 17, 1945, 'Rough Draft of Comment by S. C. Hooper', 3. The National Academy of Science formed a special Navy Department Scientific Advisory Committee before World War II. *US Naval Administration in World War II: SECNAV Administrative History: Office of Research and Inventions 1 July-31 December 1945*.
10. Library of Congress, Papers of Stanford Caldwell Hooper, 'To CNO OP14', September 2, 1937.
11. Library of Congress, Papers of Stanford Caldwell Hooper, 'To CNO OP14', September 2, 1937.
12. Burton K. Wheeler with Paul F. Healy, *Yankee From the West* (New York: Doubleday, 1962), 18-20, 386, and Ladislas Farago, *The Game of the Foxes* (New York: David McKay, 1971), 477-8.
13. The ONR became a blessing to the universities after World War II when it replaced the NDRC to subsidize research until the National Science Foundation was created. Harvey M. Sapolsky, *Science and the Navy: The History of the Office of Naval Research* (Princeton: Princeton University Press, 1990). The ONR is put into perspective in, Thomas A. Guniston, and Roger L. Geiger (ed), *Research and Higher Education: The United Kingdom and the United States* (Buckingham: Open University Press, 1989), 3-17.
14. Paolo E. Coletta (ed), *The American Secretaries of the Navy*, vol. III, 1913-72 (Annapolis: Naval Institute Press, 1980), 663, dates the height of the conflict in 1933-34. But Harvey M. Sapolsky, "Academic Science and the Military: The

Years Since World War II," in Nathan Reingold (ed), *The Sciences in the American Context* (Washington: Smithsonian Institution Press, 1979), 379-399, describes a longer battle.

15. Harold G. Bowen, *Ships Machinery and Mossbacks: The Autobiography of a Naval Engineer* (Princeton: Princeton University Press, 1954), 119-20.
16. Harold G. Bowen, *Ships Machinery and Mossbacks: The Autobiography of a Naval Engineer* (Princeton: Princeton University Press, 1954), 45. Bowen's role in the evolution of the ONR is traced in Harvey M. Sapolsky, *Science and the Navy: The History of the Office of Naval Research* (Princeton: Princeton University Press, 1990).
17. Informative overviews of the impact of radio on national policies and the military are found in, Daniel R. Headrick, *The Invisible Weapon: Telecommunications and International Politics* (New York: Oxford University Press, 1991), and Arthur R. Hezlet, *The Electron and Sea Power* (London: 1973).
18. NARA RG457: SRH-150 "Birthday of the Naval Security Group"; SRH-305, "The Undeclared War: History of R. I." by Laurance Safford; SRMN-084 "Evolution of the Navy's Cryptologic Organization"; and SRH-152 "Historical Review of OP-20-G, 17 February, 1944."
19. NARA RG457, SRH-355 "Naval Security Group History to WWII." To confuse historians even more, the Bureau of Engineering became the Bureau of Ships just before the war. OP-20-G was also in charge of the codes and ciphers the navy used.
20. Harold G. Bowen, *Ships Machinery and Mossbacks: The Autobiography of a Naval Engineer* (Princeton: Princeton University Press, 1954). Linwood S. Howeth, *History of Communications Electronics in the United States Navy: With An Introduction by Chester W. Nimitz* Bureau of Ships, Office of Naval History (Washington: GPO, 1963), 433.
21. Robert William Love (ed), *The Chiefs of Naval Operations* (Annapolis: Naval Institute Press, 1980), viii, 92.
22. David Kahn, "Pearl Harbor and the Inadequacy of Cryptanalysis," *Cryptologia* 15(1991): 274.
23. Louis Kruh, "Tales of Yardley: Some Sidelights to His Career," *Cryptologia* 13(1989): 327-356. NARA RG457, SRMD-018 "Mexican Intercept Messages 1912-1924, MI-8."
24. Much to Hooper's dismay the remainder of the secret fund may have been returned just as he took over "G".
25. NARA RG457, SRH-355, "Naval Security Group History to World War II," 85.
26. The navy's cryptanalysts were not entirely isolated from other American cryptologic centers. During World War I Agnes Meyer went to Riverbank and later worked for some time in Yardley's Black Chamber. That little known connection helps fill the gap concerning the breaking of Japanese codes during the 1920s. The navy must have known of Yardley's success through Meyer. Her stay with Hebern must have helped the OP-20-G group understand much about the new enciphering machines. Later, Mr. Bogel went to OP-20-G after the Black Chamber was closed down. In addition, it is now known that the navy turned over their work on Japanese diplomatic codes and ciphers to William Friedman's group in the early 1930s when the army's Signal Corps took over the Black Chamber. NARA RG457, SRH-355, "Naval Security Group History to World War II," 20-35.
27. NARA RG457, SRH-305, "The Undeclared War: The History of RI," 15 November,1943," by Laurance F. Safford, Captain, U. S. Navy, 001-3, and SRH-355, "Naval Security Group History to World War II," 28.
28. NARA RG457, SRH-355, "Naval Security Group History to World War II," 82.
29. Interviews and correspondence with Waldron S. MacDonald, 1987-91. MacDonald stated that Bush was the one that convinced the navy to investigate high-speed devices. It is more than likely that Bush was in touch with Hooper before 1930 about such matters. See also, Library of Congress, Papers of Stanford Caldwell Hooper, Box 21, August 17, 1945, 'Rough Draft of Comment', 3.
30. A useful history of the introduction of these machines is, NARA RG457, SRH-004, "The Friedman Lectures on Cryptology."
31. On the emergence of the cipher machines, Cipher A. Deavours, and Louis Kruh, *Machine Cryptography and Modern Cryptanalysis* (Dedham, Mass.: Artech House, 1985), Chpt. II.

32. Cipher A. Deavours, and Louis Kruh, *Machine Cryptography and Modern Cryptanalysis* (Dedham, Mass.: Artech House, 1985), 212, 218. NARA RG457, SRH-305, "The Undeclared War: The History of RI," 15 November,1943," by Laurance F. Safford, Captain, U. S. Navy, and SRH-355, "Naval Security Group History to World War II," 161. *A History of Communications Intelligence in the United States With Emphasis on the United States Navy* (NCVA), 12. A wonderful insight in OP-20-G's methods is in, Lt. L. F. Safford, "The Functions and Duties of the Cryptologic Section, Naval Communications," *Cryptologia*, 16(1992): 265-281.
33. NSA RAM File, Hooper to OP-20-G, 'Cryptanalytic Machines', September 26, 1930.
34. NARA RG457, SRH-151, "Military Study: Communications Intelligence Research Activities, 30, June 1937, by J. N. Wenger," 16.
35. He was correct. Although part of his and Safford's plan included establishing cryptanalytic training courses to recruit and maintain a cadre of skilled technicians, very few stayed in the program during the 1930s. Only two or three men, after nearly a decade of effort, were ranked as skilled cryptanalysts--and they were mathematicians in academic institutions. NARA RG457, SRH-355, "Naval Security Group History to World War II," 330.
36. Louis Kruh, "Why Was Safford Pessimistic About Breaking the German Enigma Cipher Machine in 1942?" *Cryptologia* 14(1990): 253-257.
37. NSA Release, Ray Schmidt, "The First Lady of Naval Cryptology," 44. David Kahn, *Codebreakers: The Story of Secret Writing* (New York: Macmillan, 1967), 417. Library of Congress, Papers of Stanford Caldwell Hooper, Box 17, Inspector of Machinery, U. S. Navy to Miss Agnes M. Driscoll, Navy Dept., 22 October, 1935. Susan M. Lujan, "Agnes Meyer Driscoll," *Cryptologia* 15(1991): 47.
38. Useful on the history of America's encrypting machines are NARA RG457, SRH-004, "The Friedman Lectures on Cryptology," and, Cipher A. Deavours, and Louis Kruh, *Machine Cryptography and Modern Cryptanalysis* (Dedham, Mass.: Artech House, 1985), 69. On mathematical and statistical approaches, Abraham Sinkov, *Elementary Cryptanalysis* (Washington: AMA, 1966), and the series of military lessons by Friedman now being published by Artech house. See, William F. Friedman, and Lambros D. Callimahos, *Military Cryptanalytics*, Parts 1 & 2 (Laguna Hill, Calif.: 1985). Perhaps because his work was so advanced the contributions of the mathematician Lester Hill to military cryptanalysis remain guarded.
39. A book that overstates the case against the historical importance of formal analysis but which is still useful is, Nigel West, *The SIGINT SECRETS: The Signals Intelligence War, 1900 to Today, Including the Persecution of Gordon Welchman* (New York: 1986). A very revealing and important document for the history of OP-20-G and American cryptanalysis is found in Louis Kruh, "Why Was Safford Pessimistic About Breaking the German Enigma Cipher Machine in 1942?" *Cryptologia* 14(1990): 253.
40. NARA RG457, SRH-355, "Naval Security Group History to World War II," 80. C. A. Deavours, "The Black Chamber: A Column: La Methode Des Baton," *Cryptologia* 4(1980): 240-247.
41. NARA RG457, SRH-305, "The Undeclared War: The History of RI, 15 November,1943," by Laurance F. Safford, Captain, U. S. Navy."
42. Hooper's power to do this may have been based on the connections he established earlier in his career when he was the head of the Bureau of Engineering's new radio-sound division.
43. NARA RG457, SRH-355, "Naval Security Group History to World War II," 80. U. S. Navy - Office of Information, Biographies Branch, 13 February, 1958, " R. Adm. J. N Wenger, USN, Ret."
44. NSA RAM File, OP-20-G to Chief of Naval Operations, 'Cryptanalytic Machines--Photocells', November 11, 1931.
45. Photoelectric sensing for "sorting" has a long and complex history. See, for example, the patents of Michael Maul of Berlin dating from at least 1927 which were assigned to IBM. See U. S. patents 2000403-4. A Westinghouse engineer created an optical card sorter that caught Hooper's interest. *Electronics* 3(October, 1931), 157. The 1930s work of the German, Emanuel Goldberg, who also invented the microdot, became of great significance to Bush's plans after World

War II. Michael K. Buckland, "Emanuel Goldberg, Electronic Document Retrieval, and Vannevar Bush's Memex," *JASIS* 43(1992): 284.

46. Library of Congress, Papers of Stanford Caldwell Hooper, Box 17, Lemmon to Hooper, 'Radio Typewriter', April 3, 1935. Walter Lemmon may have been the liaison who helped OP-20-G convince IBM's electromatic division to devise the pseudo teletype-tape system "G" had in operation by 1942 to, hopefully, replace the difficult to handle IBM cards. There is little documentation on the planning for the Letterwriter equipment but its nature suggests that OP-20-G was looking forward to doing away with tabulator cards as soon as possible. Walter Lemmon also seems to have unwittingly sponsored British propaganda efforts when his international radio station WRUL was "used" by the BSC, *Washington Post*, Sept. 17, 1989, C2, "Britain's War in the U. S."

47. Among Hooper's and Wenger's recommendations was the exploration of the new statistical-mathematical techniques being used in the advanced sciences. Although professional mathematicians were not brought into OP-20-G until the onset of World War II (such as Howard Engstrom, Andy Gleason, and Marshall Hall) at least the younger men at OP-20-G were sent back to school for classes in statistics in the mid-1930s. NARA RG457, SRH-355, "Naval Security Group History to World War II," 268. The influence of Lester Hill during the prewar years remains to be traced.

48. By the early 1930s, some scientists were using tabulating machines for advanced calculating. G. W. Baehne (ed), *Practical Applications of the Punched Card Methods in Colleges and Universities* (New York: Columbia University Press, 1935) gives an insight to some of the uses and some of the special devices attached to the tabulators. Also useful for an understanding of pre-computer calculation are: William Aspray (ed), *Computing Before Computers* (Ames, Iowa: Iowa State University Press, 1990), and Arthur Norberg, "High Technology Calculation in the Early 20th Century: Punched Card Machinery in Business and Government," *Technology and Culture* 31(1990): 753.

49. NSA RAM File, 'McClaran to Director of Naval Communications', January 7, 1932. NARA RG457, SRH-355, "Naval Security Group History to World War II," 75. The code was put into operation in December of 1930 and, luckily for the Americans, used until late 1938.

50. The pressures on OP-20-G multiplied because of a bizarre occurrence in 1930-1. The former head of the State Department's and Signal Corps' cryptanalytic agency, Herbert Yardley, published his infamous book, *The American Black Chamber*. It revealed the United States' ability to read various Japanese code and, perhaps, cipher systems. NARA RG457, SRH-151, "Military Study: Communication Intelligence Research Activities," 9.

51. NSA RAM File, 'McClaran to Director of Naval Communications', January 7, 1932.

52. NSA RAM File, Huckins to Bureau of Engineering, 'IBM Rental', May 15, 1933.

53. On the ordering of the IBM equipment, NSA, Lou Holland, "Development of Machine Processing in the Naval Security Group," 12. NARA RG457, SRH-355, "Naval Security Group History to World War II," 79, 65. NSA RAM File, 'McClaran to Director of Naval Communications', January 7, 1932. The approval of the rental came in late January, 1932 and the first machines were on-site in February which suggests how urgently they were needed. OP-20-G had to beg for a continuation of funds for the machines and it took adroit manipulation of budgets to find the funds for even 1933 and 1934. NSA RAM File: Hooper to CNO 'IBM Budget Cut', April 5, 1933; Huckins to CNO, 'Rent IBM Time', June 16, 1933; and Bureau of Engineering to OP-20-G, 'IBM' July 25, 1933. The history of the financing of the navy tab machines illustrates how a cost conscious and perhaps isolationist Congress fought the development of a modernized intelligence system.

54. Hans P. Luhn, *Review of Information Retrieval Methods* (Yorktown Heights: IBM, October 1958). Hans P. Luhn, *The IBM Electronic Information Searching System* (Poughkepsie, N.Y.: IBM, 1952). NARA RG457: SRH-361, "History of the Signal Security Agency"; SRH-274, "Military Cryptanalysis, Part II," 401-412; and, SRH-004, "The Friedman Lectures on Cryptology."

55. Claire K. Schultz (ed), *H. P. Luhn, Pioneer of Information Science: Selected Works* (New York: Spartan Books, 1968).

56. Cipher A. Deavours, and Louis Kruh, *Machine Cryptography and Modern Cryptanalysis* (Dedham, Mass.: Artech House, 1985), 212. Hooper was especially worried about Britain's new shipboard cipher machines in the early 1930s. NSA RAM File, Hooper to OP-20-G, 'Cryptanalytic Machines', September 26, 1930.
57. The IBM corporation certainly would not approve of such a comment but even though academics were using the machines for statistical analysis and IBM was beginning to sponsor research centers such as the one at Columbia University, their electromechanical devices were not mathematical machines. By the late 1930s add-ons to the devices did allow greater flexibility but the relay banks for false addition and subtraction and the selection of messages with certain codes were amendments, not fundamental changes to the OP-20-G equipment. G. W. Baehne (ed), *Practical Applications of the Punched Card Methods in Colleges and Universities* (New York: Columbia University Press, 1935). Note that IBM did build full relay computers for Army Ordnance during World War II and that, beginning in the late 1930s, it had pilot projects for the development of electronic calculation. In the late 1930s, it may have sponsored the giant Aiken electromechanical computer project at Harvard University because it realized that "tabs" were not powerful enough for the new scientific problems. On tabs for cryptanalysis, NARA RG457, SRH-274, "Military Cryptanalytics, Part II," 401-412.
58. J. W. Bryce, U. S. Patent "Statistical Machine," Filed February 19, 1936, awarded July 26, 1938, #2,124,906. J. W. Bryce, U. S. Patent, "Film Data Selecting and Viewing Machine," July 6, 1943, 2,323,372. The navy may have had some difference table relay banks on their tabulators to help tackle superencryptions, see David Kahn, "Pearl Harbor and the Inadequacy of Cryptanalysis," *Cryptologia* 15(1991): 287.
59. NSA, Lou Holland, "Development of Machine Processing in the Naval Security Group." The Germans and the British were also heavy users of tabulating equipment for cryptanalytic purposes during World War II. But exactly when they began using such machinery remains unknown. See, W. Jensen, "Hilfsgerate der Kryptographic," (1952) as held in the files of Professor Brian Randell, and H. Rohrbach, "Mathematische und maschinnelle Methoden beim chiffrieren und dechiffrieren: *FIAT Review of German Science 1939-1945: Applied Mathematics Field Information Agencies: Technical, Office of Military Government for Germany*, 1948. These and, David Kahn, *Codebreakers: The Story of Secret Writing* (New York: Macmillan, 1967), 440, indicate the Germans went beyond mere additions to tabulators and also used equipment based upon teletype tape. Despite the many volumes on Ultra, the British experience with tabulating machines remains an untold story. Only passing mention is made of their use by GC&CS. See the hint that Remington-Rand had told Germany about the possible uses of such machinery for its cryptological work during the early 1930s as in, NSA Ram File, Wenger to Director, 'Remington Rand', December 5, 1932. Britain must have experimented with tabulators in the mid-1930s and in 1939 it gave some thought to a film machine to replace its "sheets," F. H. Hinsley, *British Intelligence in the Second World War*, vol. III (London: Her Majesty's Stationery Office, 1985), 951.
60. NARA RG457, SRH-355, "Naval Security Group History to World War II," 161.
61. Within a few months of the introduction of the first Japanese enciphering devices, OP-20-G made inroads into the system and the machinery. How the navy was able to find the ever changing settings for the machines and how it was able to understand the inner mechanism of devices such as the Red machine have not yet been fully explained. But it seems that the success of its approach led its operational staff away from explorations of advanced digital devices. There are mentions of "indicator" systems which suggest that Driscoll and her crew used them rather than pure analysis to crack the early machines. Thus, the focus was put on the construction of direct analogs of the Japanese machines. The main function of the analog was to decipher messages after hand methods were used to find settings. Ronald Lewin *The American Magic* (New York: Farrar-Strauss, 1982), and his, *The Other Ultra* (London: Hutchinson, 1982). Richard J. Aldrich, "Conspiracy or Confusion? Churchill, Roosevelt and Pearl Harbor," *Intelligence and National Security* 7(1992): 335-346.
62. "R. Adm. J. N. Wenger, USN, Ret.," NAVY-Office of Information, Biographical Branch, 13 February 1958. The navy was not as supportive of signal intelligence

as this description of Wenger's European junket might suggest. Wenger travelled to his new Asian assignment by way of Europe at his own expense because the navy would only pay for the most direct route. Wenger and Hooper were so committed they were willing to use their own funds to keep abreast of cryptologic developments. Interviews with Jeff Wenger.

63. NARA RG457, SRMN-084, "The Evolution of the Navy's Cryptologic Organization," and, SRH-264, "A Lecture on Communications Intelligence, by Capt. J. N. Wenger, USN, August 14, 1946."
64. NARA RG457, SRH-151, "Military Study: Communication Intelligence Research Activities," 008.
65. NARA RG457, SRMN-083, "Military Study of Secret Radio Calls, January 1938."
66. Linwood S. Howeth, *History of Communications Electronics in the United States Navy: With an Introduction by Chester W. Nimitz* Bureau of Ships, Office of Naval History (Washington: GPO, 1963), 538.
67. NSA RAM File, Hooper to Secret Naval Board, "Communications Plan', February 7, 1936.
68. John C. Walter, "William Harrison Standley," in Robert William Love, Jr. (ed), *The Chiefs of Naval Operations* (Annapolis: Naval Institute Press, 1980), 93.
69. NARA RG457, SRH-355, "Naval Security Group History to World War II," 99.
70. Library of Congress, Papers of Stanford C. Hooper, Box 18, 'Johns Hopkins-Atomic Energy', November 3, 1937.
71. Vannevar Bush, *Pieces of the Action* (New York: Morrow, 1970), 71, and Library of Congress, Papers of Stanford Caldwell Hooper, Box 16, 'Binaural Sons of the C', June 1, 1934. One of Hooper's most valuable connections with the scientific elite was the "alumni" club for those who had worked at the two major sonar development sites during World War I. He quite possibly met with Bush in its informal context. He certainly had later contacts with Bush when they were both associated with the NACA. MIT was a major training resource of the navy during WWI and it had the Pratt School of Naval Architecture. Karl L. Wildes, and Nilo A. Lindgren, *A Century of Electrical Engineering and Computer Science at MIT, 1882-1982* (Cambridge: MIT Press, 1985), 393.
72. NARA RG457, SRH-355, "Naval Security Group History to World War II," 269, 'Hooper to Wenger' November, 1935, and 270, January 2, 1936, 'Bush Report'. Many of Bush's remembrances of the OP-20-G project, as stated in, Vannevar Bush, *Pieces of the Action* (New York: Murrow, 1970), 192-5, are not fully supported by the documentation.
73. NSA was unable to provide copies of the four Bush reports. As will be discussed, the later four general reports were for the design of the machine that became known as the Comparator. Bush's initial report to Hooper and Wenger was probably much more general and was most likely concerned with very broad issues of communications technology. Bush's oral history version of the negotiations does not quite fit with other evidence, MIT Archives MC143 111a to 116.
74. A useful long-term view of academic-military relations is, Henry Etzkowitz, "The Making of An Entrepreneurial University: The Traffic Among MIT, Industry, and the Military, 1860-1960," E. Mendelsohn, et al, (ed), *Science, Technology, and the Military*, 12(1988): 524.
75. NARA RG457, SRH-355, "Naval Security Group History to World War II," 270.
76. NSA RAM File, Hooper to Secret Naval Board, 'Communications Plan', February 7, 1936.

CHAPTER IV

1. *Historical Statistics of the United States: From Colonial Times to 1957* (Washington, G. P. O., 1960), W 79-94, 693.
2. Alfred Charles True, *A History of Agricultural Experimentation and Research in the United States, 1607-1925* (Washington: GPO, 1932). Stow Persons, *The University of Iowa in the Twentieth Century: an Institutional History* (Iowa City: University of Iowa Press, 1990). Alan I. Marcus, *Agricultural Science and the Quest for Legitimacy: Farmers, Agricultural Colleges, and Experiment Stations,*

1870-1890 (Ames: Iowa State University Press, 1985). Clark R. Mollenhoff, *Atanasoff: Forgotten Pioneer of the Computer* (Cambridge: MIT Press, 1984).

3. William Aspray, and Michael Gunderloy, "Early Computing and Numerical Analysis at the National Bureau of Standards," *Annals of the History of Computing*, 11(1989): 3-11. Stephen G. Nash, *A History of Scientific Computing* (New York: ACM Press, 1990), espec. John Todd, "The Prehistory and Early History of Computation at the National Bureau of Standards," 251-268. Nancy Stern, *From ENIAC to UNIVAC: An Appraisal of the Eckert-Mauchly Computers* (Bedford, Mass.: Digital Press, 1981).
4. Robert F. Kohler, *Partners in Science: Foundations and the Natural Sciences, 1900-1945* (Chicago: University of Chicago Press, 1991). Robert F. Kohler, "The Ph.D. Machine: Building on the Collegiate Base," ISIS 81(1990): 638-662.
5. On the growth of the American university and college in the nineteenth century, see my article in Konrad Jarausch (ed), *The Transformation of Higher Learning, 1860-1930* (Chicago: University of Chicago Press, 1983). On the many fragile compromises built into the American higher system during its formative stage of modernization, Laurence R. Veysey, *The Emergence of the American University* (Chicago: University of Chicago Press, 1965). For the attempts to integrate the higher education system and foundation-giving, Hugh Hawkins, *Banding Together: The Rise of National Associations in American Higher Education, 1887-1950* (Baltimore: The Johns Hopkins University Press, 1992).
6. See Robert E. Kohler's argument concerning the evolution of university research in his, "The Ph.D. Machine: Building on the Collegiate Base," *ISIS* 81(1990): 641-2.
7. Marilyn Tobias, *Old Dartmouth on Trial: The Transformation of the Academic Community in Nineteenth-Century America* (New York: New York University Press, 1982).
8. Karl L. Wildes, and Nilo A. Lindgren, *A Century of Electrical Engineering and Computer Science at MIT, 1882-1982* (Cambridge: MIT Press, 1985), 161.
9. One of the most underrated collections of articles in American history, is, Nathan Reingold (ed), *The Sciences in the American Context: New Perspectives* (Washington, D.C.: Smithsonian Institution Press, 1979). Although more than a decade old, it contains articles with themes that have set the tone for the history of science and education in America. Of special import for the history of science and the foundations is the chapter by Stanley Coben, "American Foundations as Patrons of Science," 229-249.
10. Robert F. Kohler, *Foundations and the Natural Scientists, 1900-1945* (Chicago: University of Chicago Press, 1991). Roger L. Geiger, *To Advance Knowledge: The Growth of American Research Universities, 1900-1940* (New York: Oxford University Press, 1986).
11. Robert E. Kohler Jr., "Warren Weaver and the Rockefeller Foundation Program in Molecular Biology: A Case Study in the Management of Science," in Nathan Reingold (ed), *The Sciences in the American Context: New Perspectives* (Washington, D.C.: Smithsonian Institution Press, 1979), 249.
12. Warren Weaver, *Scene of Change: A Lifetime in American Science* (New York: Charles Scribner and Sons, 1970), 58.
13. Rockefeller Archives, RG12.1, Diaries of Warren Weaver: November 8, 1932 'Visits to Centers'; March 29, 1935 'Bush Differential Analyser'; May, 1935, 'Hannibal Ford' Box 68; and January 1939 to May 1939, 'Visits of Caldwell, Fry, Wiener'. Larry Owens, "Straight Thinking: Vannevar Bush and the Culture of American Engineering," (Ph.D. Thesis, Princeton University, 1987), 68.
14. Larry Owens, "Straight Thinking:Vannevar Bush and the Culture of American Engineering," (Ph.D. Thesis, Princeton University, 1987), 78-79.
15. Rockefeller Archives, RG12.1, Diaries of Warren Weaver, October 28, 1938, 'Bush on Carnegie plans'.
16. Larry Owens, "Straight Thinking:Vannevar Bush and the Culture of American Engineering," (Ph.D. Thesis, Princeton University, 1987), 87.
17. Rockefeller Archives, RG12.1, Diaries of Warren Weaver: May 1, 1940 'Atanasoff Visit'; October 24, 1939, 'Tour of Computing Centers'; 'Visit to Boston', October 29, 1939; October 5, 1939, 'Howard Aiken Visit'; May 24, 1939, 'Visits of Harrison and Caldwell';and January 1, 1939, 'Visit to MIT'.

18. Weaver also surveyed the activities at the Department of Agriculture. Rockefeller Archives, RG12.1, Diaries of Warren Weaver, December 13, 1938, 'Microfilm, visits to Dept. of Agriculture, Library of Congress and other U. S. sites '.
19. Claude E. Shannon, and Warren Weaver, *The Mathematical Theory of Communication* (Urbana. Ill.: University of Illinois Press, 1949).
20. Robert F. Kohler, *Partners in Science: Foundations and the Natural Sciences, 1900-1945* (Chicago: University of Chicago Press, 1991), 82-89
21. Rockefeller Archives, RG12.1, Diaries of Warren Weaver, July 28, 1938 'Microphotography', 'Center of Analysis'; and March 24, 1938 'Bush Selector'; Box 68, May 24, 1939, 'Visits of Harrison and Caldwell'.
22. John Y. Cole, " The Library of Congress and American Scholarship, 1865-1939," in Phyllis Dain, and John Y. Cole (ed), *Libraries and Scholarly Communication in the United States* (New York: Greeenwood Press, 1990), 53, describes the enormous project which grew after Rockefeller gave almost one-half million dollars in 1927.
23. *National Cyclopedia of American Biography*, Edwin Emery Slosson, vol. 32, 373-4. Jack Rubin, *A History of Micrographics: In the First Person* (Silver Spring: National Micrographics Association, 1980), 58. Claire K. Schultz, and Paul L. Garwig, "History of the American Documentation Institute," *American Documentation* 20(1969): 152-60. Library of Congress, Papers of Vannevar Bush, Ralph R. Shaw, "Machines and the Bibliographic Problems of the Twentieth Century." Michael K. Buckland, "Emanuel Goldberg, Electronic Document Retrieval, and Vannevar Bush's Memex," *JASIS* 43(1992): 284.
24. Michael K. Buckland, "Emanuel Goldberg, Electronic Document Retrieval, and Vannevar Bush's Memex," *JASIS* 43(1992): 284. Rockefeller Archives, RG12.1, Diaries of Warren Weaver, July 28, 1938, 'Bennett's Micro-plates'.
25. Ralph R. Shaw, "Management, Machines, and the Bibliographic Problems of the Twentieth Century," in Jesse H. Shera, and Margaret E. Egan (ed), *Bibliographic Organization* (Chicago: University of Chicago Press, 1951): 200-225. Claire K. Schultz, and Paul L. Garwig, "History of the American Documentation Institute," *American Documentation* 20(1969): 152-60.
26. Rockefeller Archives, RG12.1, Diaries of Warren Weaver: Bush Visit April 12, 1937, 'FBI Machine'; Bush visit, March 24, 1938, 'Rapid Selector'; Bush visit, October 28, 1938, 'Carnegie Plans'; and Bush visit, March 24, 1938, 'Rapid Selector'. Rockefeller Archives, RG1.1 224D 2 23, April 14, 1937, Bush Letter to Weaver, "A Reference Selector." Hagley Museum and Library, Accession 1825, *Honeywell v Sperry-Rand* Trial Records, Bush to NCR, March 1, 1938.
27. Rockefeller Archives, RG12.1, Diaries of Warren Weaver, July 20, 1938, ' I. Stewart -SAL, Caldwell Grant'.
28. Rockefeller Archives, RG12.1, Diaries of Warren Weaver, October 28, 1938, 'Bush on Carnegie plans'. Larry Owens, "Straight Thinking: Vannevar Bush and the Culture of American Engineering," (Ph.D. Thesis, Princeton University, 1987), 8, 65.
29. Rockefeller Archives, RG12.1, Diaries of Warren Weaver, October 28, 1938, 'Bush on Carnegie plans'. NSA RAM File, December 10, 1938, Safford to Bush, 'Machine running well, take a year off'.
30. Ronald Clark, *Tizard* (Cambridge: MIT Press, 1965), 128.
31. Daniel J. Kevles, *The Physicists: The History of the Scientific Community in Modern America* (New York: Knopf, 1978), 296.
32. Ronald W. Clark, *Tizard* (Cambridge: MIT Press, 1965).
33. Ralph B. Baldwin, *The Deadly Fuze: The Secret Weapon of World War II* (San Rafael: Presidio Press, 1980).
34. An important article on the history of both mechanical and electric-electronic fire control devices is, A. Ben Clymer's, "The Mechanical Analog Computers of Hannibal Ford and William Newell," *Annals of the History of Computing* 15(1993): 19-34.
35. Carroll Pursell, "Science Agencies in World War II: The OSRD and Its Challengers," in Nathan Reingold (ed), *The Sciences in the American Context: New Perspectives* (Washington, D.C.: Smithsonian Institution Press, 1979), 359.
36. Vannevar Bush, *Pieces of the Action* (New York: Morrow, 1970), 31-52. Harvey M. Sapolsky, *Science and the Navy: The History of the Office of Naval Research* (Princeton: Princeton University Press, 1990). Carroll Purcell, "Science Agencies

in World War II: The OSRD and Its Challengers," in Nathan Reingold (ed), *The Sciences in the American Context: New Perspectives* (Washington: Smithsonian Institution Press, 1979), 359-378.

37. Bernard Williams, "Computing With Electricity, 1935-1945," (Ph.D. Thesis, University of Kansas, 1984), 56.

38. Kendell Birr, "Industrial Research Laboratories," in Nathan Reingold (ed), *The Science in the American Context: New Perspectives* (Washington: Smithsonian Institution Press, 1979), 199-205.

39. Leonard S. Reich, *The Making of American Industrial Research: Science and Research at GE and Bell, 1876-1926* (New York: Cambridge University Press, 1985). A fascinating article with much to say about both research and computing programs at Westinghouse is, William Aspray, "Edwin L. Harder and the Anacom: Analog Computing at Westinghouse," *Annals of the History of Computing* 15(1993): 35-49.

40. Rockefeller Archives, RG12.1, Diaries of Warren Weaver, January 3, 1936, 'Thorton Fry Visit, Applied Mathematics'. Bernard Williams, "Computing With Electricity, 1935-1945," (Ph.D. Thesis, University of Kansas, 1984), 106.

41. John C. Schmidt, *Win-Place-Show: A Biography of Harry Straus* (Baltimore: The John C. Whiting School of Engineering, The Johns Hopkins University, 1989). Strauss financed the Eckert-Mauchly endeavor until his sudden death. Nancy Stern, *From ENIAC to UNIVAC: An Appraisal of the Eckert-Mauchly Computers* (Bedford, Mass.: Digital Press, 1981).

42. Michael R. Williams, *A History of Computing Technology* (Englewood Cliffs, N.J.: Prentice-Hall, 1985), 226-240. NARA RG227, OSRD Div. 7 Section 7.1 Box 42, Joseph Desch to George Stibitz, NDRC d7, 1942, 'Report of NCR Electronic Calculator'. Letter to author from George R. Stibitz, June 7, 1987.

43. Hagley Museum and Library, Accession 1825, *Honeywell v Sperry-Rand* Trial Records, March 1942, Eastman Kodak 'Fire control contract dd-24926'; February, 1942, S. B. Williams to NDRC, ' Fire control proposal'; Reports on Electronic Computer Designs by S. B. Williams, November 1941, January 1942, March 13, 1942; and August 5, 1942, Hibbard to ATT re NDRC Fire-control project. Bernard Williams, "Computing With Electricity, 1935-1945," (Ph.D. Thesis, University of Kansas, 1984), 296.

44. Library of Congress, Papers of Vannevar Bush, Hazen File, January 21, 1944, Bush to Hazen, 'Get MIT to support patent selector project'. For an insight into the patent question in the 1930s, Larry Owens, "Patents, the "Frontiers" of American Invention and the Monopoly Committee of 1939: Anatomy of a Discourse," *Technology and Culture* 32(1991), 1076-1093.

45. Reese V. Jenkins, "Technology and the Mass Market," *Technology and Culture* 16(1975). Carl W. Ackerman, *George Eastman* (New York: Houghton-Mifflin, 1930). Karl L. Wildes, and Nilo A. Lindgren, *A Century of Electrical Engineering and Computer Science at MIT, 1882-1982* (Cambridge: MIT Press, 1985), 49. It may be that Eastman-Kodak's interest in "digital" calculation began with its own project for a device somewhat like Bush's projected rapid selector. Hagley Museum and Library, Accession 1825 *Honeywell v Sperry-Rand*, Chronological File, Sulzer to Bush, 'Morse Patent', February 6, 1939; Bush to Deeds 'Rapid Selector.' March 1, 1938.

46. Michael K. Buckland, "Emanuel Goldberg, Electronic Document Retrieval, and Vannevar Bush's Memex," *JASIS* 43(1992): 284.

47. Michael K. Buckland (ed), Emanuel Goldberg, "The Retrieval Problem in Photography (1932)." Hagley Museum and Library, Accession 1825, *Honeywell v Sperry-Rand* Trial Records, August 5, 1942, Hibbard to ATT re NDRC Fire-control project. NARA RG227, OSRD Div. 7, Records of the Administrative Office, Contract Reports, Box 762, November 16, 1942, Eastman Kodak Report on Fire-control computer. NARA RG227, OSRD Div. 7, Records of the Administrative Office, Contract Reports, Box 763, October 19, 1942, Fordyce Tuttle, Eastman Kodak Report of Fire Control Computer. C. E. Kenneth Mees, *Theory of Photographic Processes* (New York: Macmillan, 1944).

48. C. E. Kenneth Mees, *The Theory of Photographic Processes* (New York: Macmillan, 1944).

49. Hagley Museum and Library, Accession 1825, *Honeywell v Sperry-Rand* Trial Records: Bush to NCR, March 1, 1938; Eastman-Bush, December 2, 1938; and Sulzer to Bush, 'Morse Patent', February 6, 1939. As Buckland, above, states,

"Eastman had knowledge of the work of Emanuel Goldberg and it hired his son to work in its laboratory in the mid-1930s." Morse filed his patent on June 23, 1938, and received it on September 8, 1942, #2,295,000.

50. On Deeds, Isaac F. Marcossen, *Wherever Men Trade* (New York: Dodd-Meade, 1948), and *Colonel Deeds: Industrial Builder* (New York: 1947).
51. Stuart W. Leslie, *Boss Kettering* (New York: Columbia University Press, 1983).
52. Library of Congress, "Silas Casey: Stanford Caldwell Hooper: A Register of their Papers in the Library of Congress," Naval Historical Foundations Collection, 'Chronology and Biographical Sketch'. Vannevar Bush, *Pieces of the Action* (New York: Morrow, 1970), 30.
53. On the financial situation of NCR in the early 1930s, NCR, *1923-1951: The Accounting Machine Era* (NCR, circa 1985), 19.
54. Martin Campbell-Kelley, *I C L: A Business and Technical History* (New York: Oxford University Press, 1989) is invaluable and is probably the best work to date on the history of computers. Arthur Norberg, "High Technology Calculation in the Early 20th Century: Punched Card Machinery in Business and Government," *Technology and Culture* 31(1990): 753, adds some business and technical details.
55. NSA RAM File, Memorandum December 13, 1933, 'Breakdown of IBM Machines', and, Report of Meeting, IBM-OP-20-G, May 23, 1934.
56. Hagley Museum and Library, Accession 1825, *Honeywell v Sperry-Rand* Trial Records, NCR Deposition, May 24, 1923, patent application of Justin A. Compton for NCR.
57. Hagley Museum and Library, Accession 1825, *Honeywell v Sperry-Rand* Trial Records, Chronological File, Letters to Singer, Kettering, etc. for support for Center of Analysis, 1945. On Kettering's influence see, Hagley Museum and Library, *Honeywell v Sperry-Rand* Trial Records, Deposition of Joseph Desch and, Smithsonian Institutions, History of Computers Project, Interview with Joseph Desch.
58. Copies of his patents were located in Bush's files at the Library of Congress.
59. Hofgaard is little remembered despite the advanced nature of the machine and, surprisingly, little had been done on the NCR project. Patent history is the basis for most of the generalizations concerning Hofgaard. Rolph Hofgaard, U. S. Patent 2,262,235, November 11, 1941. NCR may have acquired the Hofgaard machine when it purchased the Remington Cash Register Company in 1931 NCR, *The Accounting Machine ERA*, 24. One great irony was when the army's cryptanalysts decided to build a relay "bombe" they did not turn to the contractor working for the navy, NCR, but to Bell for the relay-based "Madame X." Hagley Museum and Library, Accession 1825, *Honeywell v Sperry-Rand* Trial Records, Deposition of Joseph Desch.
60. On the late 1930s computers and their builders: Michael R. Williams, *A History of Computing Technology* (Englewood Cliffs, N. J.: Prentice-Hall, 1985), and, Paul Ceruzzi, *Reckoners: The Pre-history of the Digital Computer* (Westport, Conn.: Greenwood Press, 1983).
61. Remington-Rand / Powers was also building a version of a centralized system for the retail market and Caldwell was working on a magnetic disk version for NCR by the outbreak of the war. Brian Randell (ed), *The Origins of Digital Computers: Selected Papers* (New York: Springer-Verlag, 1982), 130. Hagley Museum and Library, Accession 1825, *Honeywell v Sperry-Rand* Trial Records, Chronological file, January 17, 1940, Caldwell to NCR, and February 7, 1940, Caldwell to NCR, report, 'A Multi-total Electronic Analysis Machine'.
62. Hagley Museum and Library, Accession 1825, *Honeywell v Sperry-Rand* Trial Records, Deposition of Joseph Desch. Smithsonian Interview with Desch and Mumma. See the Hofgaard patents, 2,262,235 of November 11, 1941, and 2,019,704, November 5, 1935. The relationship between the Hofgaard work and the postwar posting-payroll machines of NCR in unknown.
63. Library of Congress, Papers of Vannevar Bush, Bush had copies of various Hofgaard patents in his papers.
64. Keith Henney, *Electron Tubes in Industry* (New York: McGraw-Hill, 1937).
65. On the early work on electronics, microfilm and magnetics at IBM, including the post WWI explorations by Bryce, Charles S. Bashe, et al, *IBM's Early Computers* (Cambridge, Mass.: MIT Press, 1985). "The Light He Left Behind," (James Bryce), *Think* April, 1949: 5-31.

66. Hagley Museum and Library, Accession 1825, *Honeywell v Sperry-Rand* Trial Records, Chronological File, March, 1937, letters re visit by Green and Sullivan of NCR to MIT to view electronic work.
67. The Rapid Selector was already designed, including the decision to use 35mm film, microphotography, coding, and possibly, complex recognition circuits. Rockefeller Archives RG1.1 224D 2 23, April 14, 1937, Bush Letter to Weaver, "A Reference Selector."
68. Bush would not have revealed any secret work to the NCR men but the navy counting rings and other circuits were, by themselves, not classified. Bush did state to men like Deeds that the Rapid Arithmetic machine ideas came from earlier "government" work. Hagley Museum and Library, Accession 1825, *Honeywell v Sperry-Rand* Trial Records, NCR Depositions, Bush to Deeds 'Analyzing Equipment', May 19, 1938. Rockefeller Archives RG12.1, Diaries of Warren Weaver, Bush visit October 28, 1938, 'Carnegie Plans'.
69. There is no evidence on whether or not Bush and Deeds knew that IBM was beginning to explore electronic calculation but they must of been aware, because of patent claims, of IBM's growing interest in microfilm and allied devices, including a "statistical" machine. Hagley Museum and Library, Accession 1825, *Honeywell v Sperry-Rand* Trial Records, Chronological File, March, 1937, letters re visit of Green and Sullivan to MIT to view electronic work.
70. Hagley Museum and Library, Accession 1925 *Honeywell v Sperry-Rand* Trial Records, July 1, 1937, NCR to Caldwell, '$10,000 Fee', and August 13, 1937, Bush to Deeds 'Photoelectric Selector'.
71. For example, it was not until a year later that Deeds decided to establish an independent electronics laboratory at NCR under Joseph Desch. Desch, however, was left with the impression that the relationship with MIT was established after his lab was founded. Hagley Museum and Library, Accession 1825, *Honeywell v Sperry-Rand* Trial Records, Desch Deposition. Eugene Kniess, "First Electronics Research Lab Rediscovered," *NCR Dayton* 6(1973): 1-3.
72. It seems that negotiations led NCR to ask only for licensing rights on the Selector by late 1938. Rockefeller Archives RG12.1, Diaries of Warren Weaver, Bush visit October 28, 1938, 'Carnegie Plans'. Hagley Museum and Library, Accession 1825, *Honeywell v Sperry-Rand* Trial Records, October, 1938, Caldwell to NCR 'Rapid Project," and, November 11, 1938 'NCR to Send $2,000 for Rapid Project."
73. Hagley Museum and Library, Accession 1825, *Honeywell v Sperry-Rand* Trial Records, May 19, 1938, Bush to Deeds 'Center of Analysis'. A general overview of the machine and project is in, Brian Randell (ed), *The Origins of Digital Computers: Selected Papers* 3rd ed., 294, and Bernard Williams,"Computing With Electricity, 1935-1945," (Ph.D. Thesis, University of Kansas, 1984), 137-170.
74. Hagley Museum and Library, Accession 1825, *Honeywell v Sperry-Rand* Trial Records, October, 1938, Caldwell to NCR memoranda re Rapid projects. On a second machine, Rockefeller Archives RG12.1, Diaries of Warren Weaver, Bush visit October 28, 1938, 'Carnegie Plans'.
75. Hagley Museum and Library, Accession 1825, *Honeywell v Sperry-Rand* trial records, November 11, 1938 'NCR to Send $2,000 for Rapid Project'. Caldwell's Rapid Arithmetic work also led to his design of a magnetic disk based electronic sales-inventory computer for NCR as cited above.
76. Rockefeller Archives, RG12.1, Diaries of Warren Weaver, March 24, 1938, 'Bush visit'. Rockefeller Archives RG1.1 224D 2 23 April 14, 1937, Bush to Weaver, "A Reference Selector." Rockefeller Archives, RG12.1, Diaries of Warren Weaver, October 28, 1938, 'Bush on Carnegie plans'.
77. Hagley Museum and Library, Accession 1825, *Honeywell v Sperry-Rand* Trial Records, November 11, 1938 'NCR to Send $2,000 for Rapid Project'.
78. Hagley Museum and Library, Accession 1825, *Honeywell v Sperry-Rand* Trial Records, Caldwell to NCR, September 28, 1939, 'Overbeck to Replace Radford'. Bernard Williams, "Computing With Electricity, 1935-1945," (Ph.D. Thesis, Princeton University, 1984), 172. On the magnetic recording work and patents, Hagley Museum and Library, Accession 1825, *Honeywell v Sperry-Rand* Trial Records, Caldwell to NCR January 17, 1940, February 7, 1940, April 14, 1940, July 22, 1940, and July 23, 1940.

79. Hagley Museum and Library, Accession 1825, *Honeywell v Sperry-Rand* Trial Records, July 23, 1940, Caldwell to H. N. Williams of NCR, 'Magnetic Recording Patents and Taylor to NCR', and August 27, 1940, 'Magnetic Recording Research Contract'.
80. Hagley Museum and Library, Accession 1825, *Honeywell v Sperry-Rand* Trial Records, October 31, 1940, Caldwell to NCR, 'Patent Policy'.
81. Hagley Museum and Library, Accession 1825, *Honeywell v Sperry-Rand* Trial Records, February 7, 1940, S. H. Caldwell, "NCR: A Multi-total Analysis Machine Using Magnetic Storage."
82. Hagley Museum and Library, Accession 1825, *Honeywell v Sperry-Rand* Trial Records, November 4, 1939, Caldwell to Deeds, 'Mahony Associates Totalizator'.
83. Hagley Museum and Library, Accession 1825, *Honeywell v Sperry-Rand* Trial Records, Deposition of Joseph Desch; 'Report of Joseph Desch on Electronics Laboratory to H. N. Williams' August 16, 1938. Eugene Kniess, "First Electronics Research Lab Rediscovered," *NCR Dayton* 6(1973): 1-3.
84. Interview with W. S. MacDonald. He stated that Bush asked if he wanted a job at NCR.
85. Hagley Museum and Library, Accession 1825, *Honeywell v Sperry-Rand* Trial Records, 'Report of Joseph Desch on Electronics Laboratory to H. N. Williams', August 16, 1938.
86. Hagley Museum and Library, Accession 1825, Honeywell v Sperry-Rand Trial Records, Desch Deposition, 'Report of Joseph Desch on Electronics Laboratory to H. N. Williams' August 16, 1938.
87. The formal agreement for the calculators came in October, 1938. Hagley Museum and Library, Accession 1825, Honeywell v Sperry-Rand Trial Records, October, 1938, Caldwell to NCR, 'Rapid Project', and November 11, 1938, 'NCR to Send $2,000 for Rapid Project'. Rockefeller Archives RG12.1, Diaries of Warren Weaver, Bush visit October 28, 1938, 'Carnegie Plans'. Larry Owens, "Straight Thinking: Vannevar Bush and the Culture of American Engineering," (Ph.D. Thesis, Princeton University, 1987), 81.
88. Hagley Museum and Library, Accession 1825, *Honeywell v Sperry-Rand* Trial Records, Desch Deposition, and Reports of April 28, 1939 and March 25, 1940. Smithsonian Interviews with Desch and Mumma.
89. Hagley Museum and Library, Accession 1825, *Honeywell v Sperry-Rand* Trial Records, Desch Deposition, 'Report of Joseph Desch on Electronics Laboratory to H. N. Williams', August 16, 1938; Desch to Williams August 20, 1939; and Report to Williams, March 25, 1940.
90. Desch became central to electronic fire control work, to atomic measurement, to ballistics measurement, and to the Bombe and other electronic cryptanalytic machines. As an example of some of his advanced tube work, NARA RG227, OSRD Div. 17 Contractors' Reports, OSRD Rpt. #492, Electronic Accumulator Research, National Cash Register Company, March 17, 1942, NDCrc-63.

CHAPTER V

1. W. Boyd Rayward, "The case of Paul Otlet, pioneer of information science, internationalist, visionary: reflections on biography," *Journal of Librarianship and Information Science* 23(1991): 135-144. James M. Nyce, and Paul Kahn (ed), *From Memex to Hypertext: Vannevar Bush and the Mind's Machine* (Boston: Academic Press, 1991).
2. W. Boyd Rayward, "The case of Paul Otlet," *Journal of Librarianship and Information Science* 23(1991): 135. Jack Rubin, *A History of Micrographics: In the First Person* (Silver Spring: National Micrographics Association, 1980). Irene S. Farkas-Conn, *From Documentation to Information Science* (New York: Greenwood Press, 1990), 4. John B. Blake (ed), *Centenary of Index Medicus: 1879-1979* (Bethesda, Md.: U. S. Dept. of Health and Human Services, 1980). Dorothy B. Lilley, and Ronald W. Trice, *A History of Information Science, 1945-1985* (New York: Academic Press, 1989).
3. Claire K. Schultz, and Paul Garwig, "History of the American Documentation Institute: A Sketch," *American Documentation* 20(1969): 156-7.
4. Carl F. Kaestle, et al, *Literacy in the United States: Readers and Reading Since 1880* (New Haven: Yale University Press, 1991), 54-5, 65.

5. Allen Kent, and Harold Lancour (ed), *Encyclopedia of Library and Information Science* (New York: M. Dekker, 1968) vol. 1, 267, "American Library Association."
6. Carl M. White, *The Origins of the American Library School* (New York: The Scarecrow Press, 1961), 65.
7. There were specialized library organizations such as the Association for Medical Librarians founded in the late nineteenth century. Later, associations for "special," usually corporate librarians, and for leaders of the major academic research libraries, were formed. But the membership of these elite organizations remained small and they could not dictate curricula or shape ALA policy. Pamela Spence Richards, "Professional Transformation in Early Twentieth Century Europe: A Review Essay," *Journal of Library History* 20(1985): 81-5.
8. James R. Beniger, *The Control Revolution* (Cambridge, Mass.: Harvard University Press, 1986). Wayne A. Wiegand, *The Politics of an Emerging Profession: The American Library Association, 1876-1917* (New York: Greenwood Press, 1986). Fremont Rider, *Melvil Dewey* (Chicago: American Library Association, 1944). William Landram Williamson, *William Frederick Poole and the Modern Library Movement* (New York: Columbia University Press, 1963). Sidney Ditzion, *Arsenals of a Democratic Culture: A History of the American Public Library Movement in New England and the Middle States from 1850 to 1900* (Chicago: American Library Association, 1947). The early work of the Library Bureau reflects the original intention of the library founders to be information managers.
9. William G. Rothstein, *American Physicians in the Nineteenth Century: From Sects to Science* (Baltimore: Johns Hopkins University Press, 1972). Donald G. Davis, Jr., and Phyllis Dain, "History of Library and Information Science Education," *Library Trends* 34(1986): 357. Phyllis Dain, and John Y. Cole (ed), *Libraries and Scholarly Communication in the United States* (New York: Greenwood Press, 1990).
10. Arthur T. Hamlin, *The University Library in the United States: Its Origins and Development* (Philadelphia: University of Pennsylvania Press, 1981), 183, 206. John Y. Cole, "The Library of Congress and American Scholarship, 1865-1939," Phyllis Dain, and John Y. Cole (ed), *Libraries and Scholarly Communication in the United States* (New York: Greenwood Press, 1990), 45. Rutherford D. Rogers, and David C. Weber, *University Library Administration* (New York: H. W. Wilson Company, 1971), 183.
11. Frank B. Rogers, "Index Medicus in the Twentieth Century," in John B. Blake (ed), *Centenary of Index Medicus: 1879-1979* (Bethesda, Md.: National Library of Medicine, 1980), 53. Wyndham Davies Miles, *A History of the National Library of Medicine* (Bethesda: National Library of Medicine, 1982), 111.
12. Frank B. Rogers, "Index Medicus in the Twentieth Century," in John B. Blake (ed), *Centenary of Index Medicus: 1879-1979* (Bethesda, Md: National Library of Medicine, 1980). Wyndham Davis Miles, *A History of the National Library of Medicine: The Nation's Treasury of Medical Knowledge* (Bethesda, Md.: U. S. Dept. of Health and Human Services, G.P.O., 1982). John Y. Cole, " The Library of Congress and American Scholarship, 1865-1939," in Phyllis Dain, and John Y. Cole (ed), *Libraries and Scholarly Communication in the United States* (New York: Greenwood Press, 1990). Margaret C. Schindler, "The Preparation of the Bibliography of Agriculture," in Jesse H. Shera, and Margaret E. Egan (ed), *Bibliographic Organization* (Chicago: University of Chicago Press, 1951), 226-235. On the Documents Expediting Project, Arthur T. Hamlin, *The University Library in the United States: Its Origins and Development* (Philadelphia: University of Pennsylvania Press, 1981), 195.
13. John B. Blake (ed), *Centenary of Index Medicus: 1879-1979* (Bethesda, Md.: U. S. Dept. of Health and Human Services, 1980), 53, contains a survey of indexing services in various academic fields. On some of the first professional indexing services, Allen Kent, and Harold Lancour (ed), "American Chemical Society Information Program," *Encyclopedia of Library and Information Science* (New York: M. Dekker, 1968) vol. 1, 247. William Campbell Steers, *Biological Abstracts/BIOSIS : The First Fifty Years, the Evolution of a Major Science Information Service* (New York: Plenum Press, 1976).
14. Accompanying other institutional changes in America in the 1890s, the emerging professional organizations began to sponsor indexing and bibliographic

projects. Prominent at the turn of the century were projects such as the American Historical Association's bibliographies and the *Engineering Index* and *Chemical Abstracts*.

15. Alexandra Oleson, and John Voss (ed), *The Organization of Knowledge in Modern America, 1860-1920* (Baltimore: Johns Hopkins University Press, 1979). Arthur T. Hamlin, *The University Library in the United States: Its Origins and Development* (Philadelphia: University of Pennsylvania Press, 1981), 182, 187.
16. Laurence R. Veysey, *The Emergence of the American University* (Chicago: University of Chicago Press, 1965). Ralph R. Shaw (ed), *The State of the Library Art* Vol. 12 Part 2 (New Brunswick, N.J.: Rutgers University Press, 1960), 2-21. D. R. Jamison, "Mechanized Bibliographic Aid," *The Library Association Record* 53(July 1951): 216. One of the reasons for the lack of participation by the mainstream librarians may have been that the growth rate of non-scientific literature had begun to level off after World War I while scientific publication multiplied exponentially. See, *Historical Abstracts of the United States*, on copyrights, journals, and publication of new books, 1870-1930.
17. William Landram Williamson, *William Frederick Poole and the Modern Library Movement* (New York: Columbia University Press, 1963). Wyndham Davis Miles, *A History of the National Library of Medicine: the Nation's Treasury of Medical Knowledge* (Bethesda, Md.: U. S. Dept. of Health and Human Services, G.P.O., 1982). Very useful for the library leaders is, G. S. Bobinski, et al, *Dictionary of American Library Biography* (Littleton, Colo.: Libraries Unlimited, 1978).
18. Several important recent historians of the American library have focused on the evolution of the major research libraries in the nation and interpreted their travails as the "problem." See, Phyllis Dain, and John Y. Cole, (ed. *Libraries and Scholarly Communication in the United States*, New York, Greenwood Press, 1990), espec. 6-43.
19. Sidney Ditzion, *Arsenals of a Democratic Culture: A History of the American Public Library Movement in New England and the Middle States from 1850 to 1900* (Chicago: ALA, 1947).
20. Wayne A. Wiegand, *The Politics of an Emerging Profession: The American Library Association, 1876-1917* (New York: Greenwood Press, 1986), 12, 230. Fremont Rider, *Melvil Dewey* (Chicago: American Library Association, 1944).
21. Even in the postwar era, the library related reform movements were not oriented to the majority of libraries or run by typical librarians. See the cant of the fabled Council on Library Resources. Allen Kent (ed), *Encyclopedia of Library and Information Science* (New York: M. Derkin, 1968), "Council on Library Resources, Inc." vol. 6, 219.
22. George Sylvan Bobinski, *Carnegie Libraries: Their History and Impact on American Public Library Development* (Chicago: ALA, 1969). John B. Blake (ed), *Centenary of Index Medicus: 1879-1979* (Bethesda, Md.: U. S. Dept. of Health and Human Services, 1980). Carl F. Kaestle, et al, *Literacy in the United States: Readers and Reading Since 1880* (New Haven: Yale University Press, 1991). Sarah K. Vann, *Training for Librarianship Before 1923* (Chicago: American Library Association, 1961), 169.
23. *Historical Abstract of the United States*, 1921, 885.
24. Francis L. Miksa, "Melvil Dewey: The Professional Educator and His Heirs," *Library Trends*, 34(1986): 359.
25. Carl M. White, *The Origins of the American Library School* (New York: The Scarecrow Press, 1961), 85.
26. Sarah K. Vann, *Training for Librarianship Before 1923* (Chicago: American Library Association, 1961). The citations in H. G. T. Cannon's, *Bibliography of Library Economy... 1876-1920* (Chicago: American Library Association, 1927), reflect the orientation of the mainstream librarians.
27. Even in the 1930s, when support from foundations allowed higher salaries and more advanced library training, eighty percent of the library school students with college education had taken degrees in the social sciences and humanities. William Landram Williamson, "A Century of Students," *Library Trends* 34(1986): 433.
28. Allen Kent (ed), *Encyclopedia of Library and Information Science* (New York: M. Derkin, 1968) vol. 1, "American Library Association," 269.
29. Mary Niles Maack, "Women in Library Education: Down the Up Staircase," *Library Trends*, 34(1986): 401.

30. Useful on the Chicago experiment is, John V. Richardson, *The Spirit of Inquiry: The Graduate Library School at Chicago, 1932-51* (Chicago: ALA, 1982). The work by L. Houser, and Alvin M. Schrader, *The Search for A Scientific Profession: Library Education in the U. S. and Canada* (Metuchen, N. J.: The Scarecrow Press, 1978) is more general, but the authors show the struggles of Chicago's original social science approach and then the more practical curricula under Wilson.
31. William Landram Williamson, "A Century of Students," *Library Trends*, 34(1986): 439. Philip A. Metzger, "An Overview of the History of Library Science Teaching Materials," *Library Trends*, 34(1986): 469. Pamela Spence Richards, "Professional Transformations in Early Twentieth Century Europe: A Review Essay," *Journal of Library History* 20(1985): 81, points out that Europe, with its more centralized government and economy, was able to establish schools for different types of library training, including documentalist schools for those intending to work with corporate and scientific information. The American condition would not allow such specialization.
32. Laurel A. Grotzinger, "Curriculum and Teaching Styles: Evolution of Pedagogical Patterns," *Library Trends*, 34(1986): 451. Carl M. White, *The Origins of the American Library School* (New York: The Scarecrow Press, 1961), 147, 181.
33. John Metcalfe, *Information Retrieval, British and American: 1876-1976* (Metuchen, N. J.: The Scarecrow Press, 1976), 43. Francis L. Miksa (ed), *Charles Ammi Cutter: Library Systematizer* (Littleton, Colorado: Libraries Unlimited, Inc. 1977), 58. Allen Kent, and Harold Lancour (ed), *Encyclopedia of Library and Information Science*, (New York: M. Dekker, 1968). vol. 11, "Index, indexer, indexing," 288.
34. Arthur T. Hamlin, *The University Library in the United States: Its Origins and Development* (Philadelphia: University of Pennsylvania Press, 1981), 206.
35. For example, Frederick Keppel of the Carnegie Corporation became an advocate of microfilm and the use of tabulating machines for bibliographic work. James W. Perry, Allen Kent, and Madeline M. Berry, *Machine Literature Searching*, (Cleveland: Western Reserve University Press, 1956). The first decade of the American Documentation movement saw important librarians from traditional libraries in leading positions in the ADI. But their influence quickly diminished in the early 1950s. Claire K. Schultz, and Paul L. Garwig, "History of the American Documentation Institute -- A Sketch," *American Documentation*, 20(1969): 157. On separation continuing into the 1960s, Irene S. Farkas-Conn, *From Documentation to Information Science* (New York: Greenwood Press, 1990), 143.
36. Wyndham Davis Miles, *A History of the National Library of Medicine: The Nation's Treasury of Medical Knowledge* (Bethesda, Md.: U. S. Dept. of Health and Human Services, G.P.O., 1982), 127.
37. W. Boyd Rayward, "The case of Paul Otlet, pioneer of information science, internationalist, visionary: reflections on biography," *Journal of Librarianship and Information Science* 23(1991): 135-144. Ralph R. Shaw, "Management, Machines, and the Bibliographic Problems of the Twentieth Century," in Jesse H. Shera, and Margaret E. Egan (ed), *Bibliographic Organization* (Chicago: University of Chicago Press, 1951), 200-225.
38. Irene S. Farkas-Conn, *From Documentation to Information Science* (New York: Greenwood Press, 1990), is the best single work on the early years of Documentalist movement.
39. *National Cyclopedia of American Biography*, vol. 32, 373. Hugh Hawkins, *Banding Together: The Rise of National Associations in American Higher Education, 1887-1950* (Baltimore: The Johns Hopkins University Press, 1992).
40. Roger Geiger, "After The Emergence: Voluntary Support and the Building of American Research Universities," *History of Education Quarterly*, 25(1985): 369.
41. Frank Cameron, *Cottrell: Samaritan of Science* (New York: Doubleday, 1952), 343. Claire K. Schultz, and Paul L. Garwig, "History of the American Documentation Institute," *American Documentation* 20(1969): 154.
42. Vernon Tate (ed), *Proceedings of the Tenth Annual Meeting and Convention* (The National Microfilm Association, Annapolis, Md., 1961), 303.

43. Irene S. Farkas-Conn, *From Documentation to Information Science* (New York: Greenwood Press, 1990), 12.
44. Irene S. Farkas-Conn, *From Documentation to Information Science* (New York: Greenwood Press, 1990). Claire K. Schultz, and Paul L. Garwig, "History of the American Documentation Institute," *American Documentation* 20(1969): 152-60.
45. Irene S. Farkas-Conn, *From Documentation to Information Science* (New York: Greenwood Press, 1990), 7.
46. Claire K. Schultz, and Paul L. Garwig, "History of the American Documentation Institute--A Sketch," *American Documentation* 20(1969), 153.
47. Irene S. Farkas-Conn, *From Documentation to Information Science* (New York: Greenwood Press, 1990), 18.
48. Watson Davis, "Microphotographic Duplication in the Service of Science," *Science*, 83:2157 May 1, 1932, 402. Frank Cameron, *Cottrell: Samaritan of Science* (New York: Doubleday, 1952), 360. Irene S. Farkas-Conn, *From Documentation to Information Science* (New York: Greenwood Press, 1990), 17-20.
49. Fremont Rider, *The Scholar and the Future of the Research Library* (New York: Hadham Press, 1945). Vernon Tate (ed), *Proceedings of the Tenth Annual Meeting and Convention* (Annapolis: National Microfilm Association, 1961, 299). Fremont Rider, *Compact Book Storage* (New York: Hadham Press, 1949). Steven Leach, "The Growth Rates of Major Academic Libraries," *College and Research Libraries*, 37(1976): 222-45.
50. Jack Rubin, *A History of Micrographics: In the First Person* (Silver Spring: National Micrographics Association, 1980), 39. For a short time, the ALA sponsored the *Journal of Documentary Reproduction*. It dealt with many of the issues of concern to those building photo reproduction centers in their institutions.
51. Wyndham Davis Miles, *A History of the National Library of Medicine: The Nation's Treasury of Medical Knowledge* (Bethesda, Md.: U. S. Dept. of Health and Human Services, G.P.O., 1982), 279. Watson Davis, "Microphotographic Duplication in the Service of Science," *Science*, 83: 2157 May 1, 1932, 403. Frank Cameron, *Cottrell: Samaritan of Science* (New York: Doubleday & Co., 1952), 361. Claire K. Schultz, and Paul L. Garwig, "History of the American Documentation Institute," *American Documentation* 20(1969): 152-60.
52. Emanuel Goldberg, U. S. Patent 1,838,389, Statistical Machine, December 29, 1931, Filed April 5, 1928. Michael K. Buckland, "Emanuel Goldberg, Electronic Document Retrieval, and Vannevar Bush's Memex," *JASIS* 43(1992): 284. Frederick Luther, *Microfilm: A History 1839-1900* (Annapolis: National Microfilm Association, 1959). William White, *Subminiature Photography* (Boston: Focal Press, 1991). William White, "The Microdot: Then and Now," *Intelligence and Counterintelligence*, 3: 249-269. Ralph R. Shaw (ed), *The State of the Library Art* (New Brunswick, N.J.: Graduate School of Library Service, 1961), 173. Ralph R. Shaw, "The Rapid Selector," *Journal of Documentation* 5(1949): 164-71.
53. Vernon D. Tate, "Photography in Research-PostWar," *Review of Documentation*, 14(1947): 778. William White, "The Microdot: Then and Now," *Journal of Intelligence and Counterintelligence*, 3: 249. William White, *Subminiature Photography*, (Boston: Focal Press, 1990).
54. Frederick Luther, *Microfilm: A History 1839-1900* (Annapolis: National Microfilm Association, 1959). Jack Rubin, *A History of Micrographics: In the First Person* (National Micrographics Association, 1980), 43.
55. Carl W. Ackerman, *George Eastman* (New York: Houghton-Mifflin, 1930). Frank L. Hilton, Jr., "Microfilm Systems--The First 40 Kodak Years," *Journal of Micrographics* 1(1968): 117-125. John K. Boeing, "Recordak," *Journal of Documentary Reproduction* 3(1940): 153-168.
56. Thomas C. Bagg, and Mary Elizabeth Stevens, *Information Selection Systems: Retrieving Replica Copies: A State of the Art Report* (Washington, D.C.: National Bureau of Standards, Technical Note 157, December 31, 1961), 18. Irene S. Farkas-Conn, *From Documentation to Information Science* (New York: Greenwood Press, 1990), 18-19. Watson Davis, "Memorandum of Visit with Dr. Vannevar Bush, November 15, 1932," Washington, D.C., Documentation Institute of Science Service, Document # 11, November 20, 1932. Rockefeller Archives RG12.1, Diaries of Warren Weaver, November 11, 1937, 'Davis Visit'.

57. Ross C. Cibella, *Directory of Microfilm Sources: Including Photostat Service* (New York: Special Libraries Association, 1941).
58. Jack Rubin, *A History of Micrographics: In the First Person* (Silver Spring: National Micrographics Association, 1980), 56. Davis helped finance the development of a special camera system by R. H. Draeger of the Naval Medical School and several attempts at building inexpensive microfilm readers. Claire K. Schultz, and Paul Garwig, "History of the American Documentation Institute: A Sketch," *American Documentation* 29(1969): 153.
59. Claire K. Schultz, and Paul L. Garwig, "History of the American Documentation Institute," *American Documentation* 20(1969): 153.
60. Claire K. Schultz, and Paul L. Garwig, "History of the American Documentation Institute," *American Documentation* 20(1969): 153.
61. For biographies of the second generation Documentalists, Bohdan S. Wynar (ed), *Dictionary of American Library Biography* (Littleton, Colo.: Libraries Unlimited, 1978), 476-80, 512-3. Wayne A. Wiegand (ed), *Supplement to the Dictionary of American Library Biography* (Englewood, Colo.: Libraries Unlimited, 1990), 119-23.
62. Irene S. Farkas-Conn, *From Documentation to Information Science* (New York: Greenwood Press, 1990). Claire K. Schultz, and Paul L. Garwig, "History of the American Documentation Institute," *American Documentation* 20(1969): 152-60.
63. Vannevar Bush, "As We May Think," *Atlantic Monthly*, 176(1): 101-8.
64. Bush rarely mentioned the work of any others, no matter what the topic. This seems to be part of his style. However, that makes it difficult to know if he truly was ignorant of such things as Otlet's work on hypertext-like ideas or the many microfilm machines of the 1930s. W. Boyd Rayward, "The case of Paul Otlet, pioneer of information science, internationalist, visionary: reflections on biography," *Journal of Librarianship and Information Science* 23(1991): 135-144.
65. Linda Smith, "Memex as an Image of Potentiality Revisited," in James M. Nyce, and Paul Kahn (ed), *From Memex to Hypertext: Vannevar Bush and the Mind's Machine* (Boston: Academic Press, 1991), 261.
66. James M. Nyce, and Paul Kahn (ed), *From Memex to Hypertext: Vannevar Bush and the Mind's Machine* (Boston: Academic Press, 1991).
67. James M. Nyce, and Paul Kahn (ed), *From Memex to Hypertext: Vannevar Bush and the Mind's Machine* (Boston: Academic Press, 1991), 101.
68. James M. Nyce, and Paul Kahn (ed), *From Memex to Hypertext: Vannevar Bush and the Mind's Machine* (Boston: Academic Press, 1991), 69.
69. Allen Kent, and Harold Lancour (ed), *Encyclopedia of Library and Information Science* (New York: M. Dekker, 1968) vol. 6, "Council on Library Resources," 223. Carl F. J. Overhage, and J. Francis Reintjes, "Project Intrex: A General Review," *Information Storage and Retrieval* 10(1974): 157-188. Carl F. J. Overhage, and R. Joyce Harman, *INTREX: Report of A Planning Conference on Information Transfer Experiments, September 3, 1965* (Cambridge: The MIT Press, 1965). J. C. R. Licklider, *Libraries of the Future* (Cambridge: MIT Press, 1965).

CHAPTER VI

1. A recent study of the messages intercepted by the Americans in 1941 concludes that if there had been the manpower to decode all the messages it would have been clear that Pearl Harbor was a target. Frederick D. Parker, "The Unsolved Messages of Pearl Harbor," *Cryptologia* 13(1991): 295.
2. Library of Congress, Papers of Stanford Caldwell Hooper: March 3,1933 to January 1, 1935, Correspondence with Redman and Jewett: 'Contact scientists'; June 1 1934, 'Binaural Sons of C'; October 20, 1935 'Travel to Laboratories'; Box 18, Hooper to Secret Naval Board, "Communications Plan', February 7, 1936; June 10, 1935, 'McDowell, Contact scientists'; and November 20, 1935, 'Travel to Boston'. Navy Biographies Section OI-140, 27 April 1945, "Rear Admiral Stanford C. Hooper, U. S. Navy, Deceased." NARA RG457, SRH-355, "Naval Security Group History to World War II," 269.
3. Note that Hooper's plan came almost a decade before the British began their now famous project at Bletchley Park to develop automata for cryptanalysis. For an example of the results of his efforts to modernize OP-20-G, NARA RG457,

SRMN-083, "Military Study of Secret Radio Calls," January 8, 1938, by Joseph N. Wenger.

4. Harold G. Bowen, *Ships Machinery and Mossbacks: The Autobiography of a Naval Engineer* (Princeton: Princeton University Press, 1954). Jack Sweetman, *American Naval History: An Illustrated Chronology of the U. S., Navy and Marine Corps 1775-Present* (Annapolis: Naval Institute Press, 1984), 154, and Robert William Love (ed), *The Chiefs of Naval Operations*, (Annapolis: Naval Institute Press, 1980), 89-99.
5. The navy did not include signals-intelligence into its formal war plans until 1937. NARA RG457, SRMN-084, "The Evolution of the Navy's Cryptologic Organization," 3. On the attacks against military and diplomatic codes in the early 1930s, NARA RG457, SRH-159, "Preliminary Historical Report of the Solution of the 'B' Machine," 12. RG457, SRH-355, "Naval Security Group History to World War II," 82. NARA RG457, SRH-305, "The Undeclared War: The History of RI," 15 November, 1943," by Laurance F Safford, Captain, U. S. Navy.
6. See, Harold G. Bowen, *Ships Machinery and Mossbacks: The Autobiography of a Naval Engineer* (Princeton: Princeton University Press, 1954), on the battle over high-pressure steam and formation of combined bureau in 1939. NARA RG457, SRMN-084, "The Evolution of the Navy's Cryptologic Organization," 3. A very useful survey is, David Kahn, "Roosevelt, Magic and Ultra," *Cryptologia* 16(1992): 289-319.
7. Library of Congress, Papers of Stanford Caldwell Hooper: March 3,1933 to January 1, 1935, Correspondence with Redman and Jewett; 'Contact scientists'; June 1, 1934, 'Binaural Sons of C'; October 20, 1935 'Travel to Laboratories'; Box 18, Hooper to Secret Naval Board, 'Communications Plan', February 7, 1936; June 10, 1935, 'McDowell, Contact scientists'; and November 20, 1935, 'Travel to Boston'. RG457, SRH-355, "Naval Security Group History to World War II," 269. Navy Biographies Section OI-140, 27 April 1945, "Rear Admiral Stanford C. Hooper, U. S. Navy, Deceased.
8. Library of Congress, Papers of Stanford Caldwell Hooper: June 10, 1935, 'McDowell, Contact scientists'; November 20, 1935, 'Travel to Boston'; Box 18, 'Johns Hopkins-Atomic Energy', November 3, 1937; and March 3, 1933 to January 1, 1935, Correspondence with Redman, Jewett, 'Contact scientists'. NARA RG457, SRH-355, "Naval Security Group History to World War II," 268-269.
9. NARA RG457, SRH-355, "Naval Security Group History to World War II," 269, 'Hooper to Wenger' November, 1935, 270, January 2, 1936, 'Bush Report'. Office of Naval Research, Bush Comparator Patent file, #2,873,912.
10. A thorough search of the OP-20-G archives and the holdings of the NRL and, by implication that of the Bureau of Ships, did not lead to the recovery of a copy of the original outline or Bush's first sketches of the Comparator.
11. NSA RAM File, January 28, 1936, DNC to Bureau of Ships, 'Support Bush proposals'. Library of Congress, Papers of Stanford Caldwell Hooper, Box 18, Hooper to Secret Naval Board, 'Communications Plan', February 7, 1936.
12. Rear Admiral Edwin T. Layton, *And I Was There: Pearl Harbor and Midway--Breaking the Secrets* (New York: William Morrow, 1985), 97, 102. NARA RG457, SRH-355, "Naval Security Group History to World War II," 161, 178. Cipher A. Deavours, and Louis Kruh, *Machine Cryptography and Modern Cryptanalysis* (Dedham, Mass.: Artech House, 1985), 218. Jurgen Rowher, *The Critical Convoy Battles of March 1943* (London: Ian Allan, 1977), 232.
13. NSA RAM File, January 28, 1936, DNC to Bureau of Ships, 'Support Bush proposals,' and July 21, 1936, Bureau of Engineering to OP-20-G 'BuEng refuses Bush'. NARA RG457, SRH-355, "Naval Security Group History to World War II," 269.
14. NSA RAM File, December 20, 1937, Safford Memorandum 'History of Comparator'. NARA RG457, SRH-355, "Naval Security Group History to World War II," 269, 270, 404.
15. Linwood S. Howeth, *History of Communications Electronics in the United States Navy: With an Introduction by Chester W. Nimitz* Bureau of Ships, Office of Naval History (Washington: GPO, 1963), contains summaries of contract regulations.

16. The generalization concerning patent rights is not based upon a specific document but upon "context." This author does not believe, however, that Bush would have demanded rights to parts that should have been kept secret.
17. Office of Naval Research, patent application file for Bush's Comparator, October, 1946, Patent #2,873,912 issued August 28, 1959. On Bush's view of the relationship with the navy, MIT Archives, MC143 Reel 2-a, 111.
18. Interviews with Waldron S. MacDonald.
19. NSA RAM File, McClaran to Bureau of Engineering, 'Recommend Bush', January 28, 1936, and NARA RG457, SRH-355, "Naval Security Group History to World War II," 269.
20. NARA RG457, SRH-355, "Naval Security Group History to World War II," 69, July 21, 1936 Bureau of Engineering to OP-20-G, 'Did not Promise'.
21. There is some indication the Bureau's men eventually outlined their solution but no documents have been released. In the absence of any specifics one can only guess at their alternative. Wenger remarked that the Bureau never really understood what he wanted. NARA RG457, SRH-355, "Naval Security Group History to World War II," 269.
22. NARA RG457, SRH-355, "Naval Security Group History to World War II," 161,177,208, 210, 261. On the power of the modified tabulating equipment, NSA Lou Holland, "Development of Machine Processing in the Naval Security Group," and NARA RG457, SRH-274, "Military Cryptanalytics, Part II," 401-412.
23. NARA RG457, SRH-355, "Naval Security Group History to World War II," 177. On use of relays and "class selectors" which allowed subgroup tallies useful for all types of analysis, not just code work: NSA RAM File, OP-20-G to Bureau of Engineering, March 22, 1938, and June 24, 1938, 'IBM Purchases'.
24. Harvey M. Sapolsky, "Academic Science and the Military: The Years Since the Second World War," in Nathan Reingold (ed), *The Sciences in the American Context: New Perspectives* (Washington: D.C.: Smithsonian Institution Press, 1979), 379.
25. Susan M. Lujan, "Agnes Meyer Driscoll," *Cryptologia* 15(1991): 47. James Rusbridger, and Eric Nave, *Betrayal at Pearl Harbor* (New York: Summit Books, 1991). Cipher A. Deavours, and Louis Kruh, *Machine Cryptography and Modern Cryptanalysis* (Dedham, Mass.: Artech House, 1985), 218. NARA RG457, SRH-355, "Naval Security Group History to World War II," 161, 247. The Holtwick M-1 machine was in operation by mid-1937, perhaps earlier.
26. NARA RG457, SRH-355, "Naval Security Group History to World War II," 270. On the role of the new head of the Office of Naval Intelligence, Jeffery M. Dorwart, *Conflict of Duty: The United States Navy's Intelligence Dilemma 1919-1945* (Annapolis: Naval Institute Press, 1983). NSA RAM File, L. F. Safford to OP-20--A, 20 December, 1937. On Bush's first plans, NARA RG457, SRH-355, "Naval Security Group History to World War II," 223.
27. NSA RAM File, September 12, 1936 'New Bush plan,' and September 18, 1936, Hooper to Bush, 'Research group approves your plans'.
28. NSA RAM File, September 18, 1936, Hooper to Bush, 'Research group approves your plans'.
29. NSA RAM File, December, 1936, 'DNC orders cooperation'.
30. Interview with W. S. MacDonald. Hooper may have kept in touch with the project through casual visits to the machine when it was being installed in Washington in 1938. And, when the project was finally rescued by Bush in 1941, Hooper was sent a courteous letter by the OP-20-G men informing him that the project was again in high-gear. NSA RAM File, Safford to Hooper, 'Comparator' November 19, 1940.
31. Jeff Wenger interview with W. S. MacDonald, March, 1991.
32. In 1939, Joseph Mumma, the second ranked electronics engineer at NCR, had a salary of $2,700 a year. Hagley Museum and Library, Accession 1825, *Honeywell v Sperry-Rand* Trial records, Deposition of Joseph Mumma. On the amount of Bush's fee, NSA RAM File, Wenger to OP-20-G, 'Comparator Project', March 25, 1938.
33. According to one participant, W. S. MacDonald, Bush, under great pressure, took advantage of that provision and sent in reports that were merely quick rewrites of the specifications that he had sent to the men building the prototype of his device at MIT. Interview with Jeff Wenger, March, 1991.

34. Interviews with Waldron S. MacDonald. NARA RG457, SRH-355, "Naval Security Group History to World War II," 404.
35. NSA RAM File, Safford memorandum, December 20, 1937, 'Bush Project'. NARA RG457, SRH-355, "Naval Security Group History to World War II," 270, 357. W. S. MacDonald interview with Jeff Wenger March, 1991.
36. On the 1937 and 1940 patents and their history, Hagley Museum and Library, Accession 2015, Unprocessed ERA materials from Sperry Archives, November 1, 1949, Memo to File, Selector Infringement Search. Accession 1825, *Honeywell v Sperry-Rand* Trial Records, August 13, 1937, Bush to Deeds; and October 25, 1937, Research Corporation to Deeds. Library of Congress, Papers of Vannevar Bush, October 22, 1937, 'Selector patent claims'. By this date the men on the navy project had begun to turn in their components and final reports. The Cinema Integraph project began in 1934 and ran for several years. Smithsonian Interview with Gordon S. Brown, 35. George R. Harrison, "The M. I. T. Wavelength Project," *Physical Society Progress Reports* 8: 212-230. Bush told his men the Selector benefitted from it. Rockefeller Archives RG12.1, Weaver Diaries April 4, 1937, 'Bush visit'.
37. On the idea of a larger project developing: Library of Congress, Papers of Vannevar Bush, Box 67, MacDonald File, Bush to MacDonald, 'Excellent Lead', October 18, 1938, and NSA RAM File, Wenger Report, 'Bush Visit' April 25, 1938. Engineering Research Associates was a realization of the attempt to use the work to found a new business for his "boys." Ironically, the first engineer was not part of ERA, nor was Bush. NARA RG457, SRH-267, "The Birth of ERA."
38. Interviews with W. S. MacDonald.
39. NSA RAM File, Wenger Report, 'Bush Visit' April 25, 1938, and December 12, 1937, Bush to DNC, 'Wenger's Duty' in which Bush states his personal role had been completed.
40. Rockefeller Archives RG12.1, Diaries of Warren Weaver, March 29, 1935, 'Bush Visit'.
41. The award came in June, 1935. Larry Owens, "Straight Thinking: Vannevar Bush and the Culture of American Engineering," (Ph.D. Thesis, Princeton University, 1987), 78. Rockefeller Archives RG12.1, Diaries of Warren Weaver, March 29, 1935, 'Bush visit'. Rockefeller Archives, RG12.1, Diaries of Warren Weaver, Bush Visit April 12, 1937, 'FBI Machine'.
42. Larry Owens, "Straight Thinking: Vannevar Bush and the Culture of American Engineering, (Ph.D. Thesis, Princeton University, 1987), 79. The $85,000 grant was awarded in early March 1936, and Bush promised to deliver what was obviously a pathbreaking device (because of its use of tubes and circuits) within three years. The machine, however, took almost seven years to develop to an operational stage and even then some components were not working. Engineers' salaries were assumed to be $2,500.
43. Rockefeller Archives RG12.1, Diaries of Warren Weaver, Box 68, May 24, 1939, Visits of Harrison and Caldwell. The machine was partially completed in 1942. Larry Owens, "Straight Thinking: Vannevar Bush and the Culture of American Engineering," (Ph.D. Thesis, Princeton University, 1987), 163, claims the machine was only one-half complete in 1942.
44. V. Bush and S. H. Caldwell, " A New Type of Differential Analyser," *Journal of the Franklin Institute*, 240(1945): 255-325.
45. Hagley Museum and Library, Accession 1825, *Honeywell v Sperry-Rand* Trial Records, NCR Deposition Records, May, 1938, NCR to MIT 'Caldwell Function Device'.
46. Rockefeller Archives, RG12.1, Diaries of Warren Weaver, January 1, 1939, 'Visit to MIT'. Rockefeller Archives, RG12.1, Diaries of Warren Weaver, Box 68, May 24, 1939, Visits of Harrison and Caldwell.
47. On IBM, Wallace J. Eckert, and the Columbia University center, Bashe, *IBM's Early Computers*, 22-3. On the little known move by Harvard University's mathematics department to establish a computation center with the Aiken machine as a "draw," Rockefeller Archives, RG12.1, Diaries of Warren Weaver, 'Visit to Boston', October 29, 1939. The Analyser project was also very over budget as early as 1939. Weaver offered more funding, but Bush had to transfer money from the Carnegie grant to MIT's Center of Analysis to Caldwell. Rockefeller Archives RG12.1, Diaries of Warren Weaver, Box 68, May 24, 1939, Visits of Harrison and Caldwell.

48. Although Larry Owens, "Straight Thinking: Vannevar Bush and the Culture of American Engineering," (Ph.D. Thesis, Princeton University, 1987), 80, claims that the Rapid Arithmetical machine took first place, other evidence indicates the Rockefeller machine remained the priority. Charles Babbage Institute, Interview by William Aspray With Dr. Frank M. Verzuh, February 20 and 24, 1984. Hagley Museum and Library, Accession 1825, *Honeywell v Sperry-Rand* trial records, October,1938, 'Caldwell to NCR', Caldwell suggested that all Rapid work be shifted to NCR because of the Analyser backlog. In late 1938, Bush stated that he didn't know how long the project could survive. At the end of 1939, in response to complaints, Caldwell promised NCR, which was sponsoring several MIT projects, that all resources would be shifted to the NCR work. But the demands of the Analyser prevented that. Hagley Museum and Library, Accession 1825, *Honeywell v Sperry-Rand* Trial Records, Caldwell to H. N. Williams of NCR, July 17, 1939. Library of Congress, Papers of Vannevar Bush, Box 67, Bush to MacDonald, December 2, 1938 'Job-Rapid Project'.

49. V. Bush, and S. H. Caldwell, " A New Type of Differential Analyser," *Journal of the Franklin Institute*, 240(1945): 256. The men who took over the calculation projects at MIT did not stop seeking funds although they were swamped with work. In late 1939, they asked if NCR would be interested in sharing work on an electronic race track totalizator to be sponsored by a private company. Hagley Museum and Library, Accession 1825, *Honeywell v Sperry-Rand* Trial Records, November 4, 1939, Caldwell to Deeds, 'Mahony Associates Totalizator'.

50. Hagley Museum and Library, Accession 1825, *Honeywell v Sperry-Rand* Trial Records, Carton 67, William Radford "Report on An Investigation of the Practicality of Developing a Rapid Computing Machine," October 15, 1939, Appendix III, List of Numbered References. Hagley Museum and Library, Accession 1825, *Honeywell v Sperry-Rand* Trial Records, NCR Depositions, Bush to Deeds 'Analyzing Equipment', May 19, 1938. Radford had been one of the "boys" at MIT who survived on the 1930s version of "soft-money" being a research assistant there from 1932 to 1939. Caldwell put him to work on the Rapid Arithmetical problem in early 1937 and he produced his report on "The Practicality of Developing a Rapid Calculating Machine," October 15, 1939. Rockefeller Archives, Papers of Warren Weaver, January 16, 1946, letter, S. H. Caldwell to Weaver, 'Center of Analysis', 4.

51. Rockefeller Archives RG12.1, Diaries of Warren Weaver, December 13, 1938, 'Microfilm'. Hagley Museum and Library, Accession 1825, *Honeywell v Sperry-Rand* Trial Records, Bush to Deeds; September 1937 and October 14, 1937, 'Edgerton-Microfilm'. Caldwell's conclusions were made known to the scientific community by mid-1938. Rockefeller Archives, RG12.1, Diaries of Warren Weaver, July 28, 1938, Visit of Irvin Stewart. Caldwell had analyzed the survey of calculation needs of American science done by the Scientific Aids to Learning Project. Larry Owens, "Straight Thinking: Vannevar Bush and the Culture of American Engineering," (Ph.D. Thesis, Princeton University, 1987), 65, 80. Hagley Museum and Library, Accession 1825, *Honeywell v Sperry-Rand* Trial Records, November 4, 1939, Caldwell to Deeds, 'Mahony Associates Totalizator'.

52. Interview with W. S. MacDonald.

53. The machine did not have a name until some years later. Who borrowed the name, Comparator, from the nineteenth century MIT device remains unknown.

54. NARA RG457, SRH-355, "Naval Security Group History to World War II," 208, 247.

55. NSA RAM File, OP-20-G to Bureau of Engineering, 'Plugboards for Reproducing Punch', July 7, 1936. NSA, Lou Holland, "Development of Machine Processing in the Naval Security Group," 9. Holtwick had created several small mechanical machines that cost less than $300 each for Japanese problems. The Bureau helped build them. NARA RG457, SRH-355, "Naval Security Group History to World War II," 210, 257, 261.

56. On the role of thefts and the use of 'tricks' to limit the amount of needed analysis, Louis Kruh, "Why Was Safford Pessimistic About Breaking the German Enigma Cipher Machine in 1942?" *Cryptologia* 14(1990): 253, and F. H. Hinsley, et al, *British Intelligence in the Second World War* (New York: Cambridge University Press, 1979-), passim. Note that in the 1920s and 1930s OP-20-G and the SIS also used such tricks as analyzing Japanese cipher system indicators to understand the wiring and settings and thus avoided attempting the impossible "pure

analysis." NARA RG457, SRH-361, "History of the Signal Security Agency, Vol. 2, The General Cryptanalytic Problem." NCVA, "A History of Communications Intelligence in the United States With Emphasis on the United Sates Navy," 12.

57. Cipher A. Deavours, and Louis Kruh, *Machine Cryptography and Modern Cryptanalysis* (Dedham, Mass.: Artech House, 1985). David Kahn, *Codebreakers: The Story of Secret Writing* (New York: Macmillan, 1967). William F. Friedman, and Lambros D. Callimahos, *Military Cryptanalytics* Parts 1 & 2 (Laguna Hills, CA: Aegean Park Press, 1985).

58. D. H. Lehmer, " A History of the Sieve Process," in N. Metropolis, et al, (ed), *A History of Computing in the Twentieth Century* (New York: Academic Press, 1980), 445.

59. Office of Military Government for Germany, Field Information, Hans Rohrbach, "Matematische und Maschinelle Methoden Beim Chiffrieren und Dechiffieren," 233. W. Jensen, "Hilfsgerate der Kryptographie" (1952) as supplied by Professor Brian Randell. NSA RAM File, "M.A.C. Outlines #17, 70mm Comparator," 2, for indications of German optical systems. Note the Germans seemed to have rejected Zuse's machine in 1942, Brian Randell (ed), *The Origins of Digital Computers: Selected Papers* (New York: Springer-Verlag, 1982), 296. Poland introduced its cyclometer to produce a catalog of the output of various Enigma wheel settings in 1937. The Polish work has been well summarized in F. H. Hinsley, et al, *British Intelligence in the Second World War* Vol. III Part II, Appendix 30, 945-959.

60. The patent claim was filed on April 22, 1937. William F. Friedman, and Vernon E. Whitman, Electric Control System for Tabulating Cards, Documents and the Like, U. S Patent 2,224,646, December 10, 1940.

61. Gordon Welchman, *The Hut Six Story* (New York: McGraw-Hill, 1982), 295-309.

62. NARA RG457, SRH-274, "Military Cryptanalysis." NARA SRH-004, "The Friedman Lectures on Cryptology."

63. David Kahn, *Seizing the Enigma* (Boston: Houghton-Mifflin, 1991), 87, and Cipher A. Deavours, "The Black Chamber: A Column: La Methode Des Baton," *Cryptologia* 4(1980): 240-247. There are reports that the Americans, including the Coast Guard group charged with attacking the ciphers of the rum-runners, were able to break into the simple commercial version of the Enigma during the 1920s. Malcolm F. Willoughby, *Rum War at Sea* (Washington: GPO, 1964).

64. David Kahn, *Seizing the Enigma* (Boston: Houghton-Mifflin, 1991), 141.

65. David Kahn, *Seizing the Enigma* (Boston: Houghton-Mifflin, 1991), 141.

66. W. S. MacDonald Interviews.

67. The history of the Comparator project is drawn from the scattered navy documents and from interviews with the man who supervised its construction, Waldron S. MacDonald.

68. Karl L. Wildes, and Nilo A. Lindgren, *A Century of Electrical Engineering and Computer Science at MIT, 1882-1982* (Cambridge: MIT Press, 1985), 147-153.

69. Interview with W. S. MacDonald by Jeff Wenger, 1991.

70. MacDonald's statements about his career and education are verified by patent office records and MIT student history records.

71. Letter to author from MIT registrars's office. In his first interview, MacDonald stated that he went to MIT in June, 1937. But in his second interview he cited September as the day he began his duties. I have accepted the second date because it makes more sense in light of the previous pace of the work and MacDonald's desire to also enroll in the graduate program in the department.

72. See for example, #2,504,996, filed February 1, 1943.

73. Baird began his optical and spectrochemical instrument firm in 1936. The war and then the very important help of ARD turned his innovations into a major business. American Research and Development Corporation, "Sixth Annual Report, 1951," and, "Seventh Annual Report, 1952."

74. Interviews with W. S. MacDonald. Patents: magnetic memory #2,852,76 and Magnefile, #2,879,000.

CHAPTER VII

1. Paul F. Ceruzzi, *Reckoners: The Prehistory of the Digital Computer* (Westport, Conn.: Greenwood Press, 1983).
2. Michael R. Williams, *A History of Computing Technology* (Englewood Cliffs, N. J.: Prentice-Hall, 1985). Nancy Stern, *From ENIAC to UNIVAC: An Appraisal of The Eckert-Mauchly Computers* (Bedford, Mass.: Digital Press, 1981).
3. Interviews with W. S. MacDonald.
4. MacDonald filed a significant patent for a recording and measuring instrument in late July, 1937 which was assigned to Foxboro. The patent number was 2,184,620. Bush filed Selector patents on October 22, 1937 and was very busy soliciting support for the Selector. Library of Congress, Papers of Vannevar Bush, Selector Patent Application files, October, 1937 to 1949. Hagley Museum and Library, Accession 1825, *Honeywell v Sperry-Rand* Trial Records, August 13, 1937, Bush to Deeds, 'Rapid Selector'.
5. NARA RG457, SRH-355, "Naval Security Group History to World War II" 257. NSA RAM File, Bush to Courtney, December 11, 1937 'Wenger's duty', November 2, 1937, 'Wenger to Holtwick'.
6. NSA RAM File, Safford to Bush, 'Comparator works better than expected', December 10, 1938. My estimate is that the Comparator never ran, at more than 20,000 comparisons a minute. The estimate is based on the card reading speed of typical tab machines of the era, 120 cards per minute.
7. NARA RG457, SRH-355, "Naval Security Group History to World War II," 222. Library of Congress, Papers of Vannevar Bush, Box 49, July 13, 1940, John Howard, "Progress Report on the Rapid Selector Research."
8. On Wenger's hope for a 20,000 per minute rate, NARA RG457, SRH-355, "Naval Security Group History to World War II," 223. NSA RAM File, OP-20-G to OP-20-A, 'Meeting with Dr. Howard' November 5, 1941. At a late 1941 meeting on improved machines, Howard gave an estimate of 5,400 letter counts a minute with the counters being able to work at 120,000 counts a minute.
9. NARA RG457, SRH-355, "Naval Security Group History to World War II," 429,
10. Because the Comparator read ten data columns at a time, more sophisticated IC tests could be done at the same rate as single letter tallying. Bush and Wenger may not have realized the potentials of the modified tabulators. The Comparator had five counters as did tabulators. Thus, several fields could be processed in parallel. The navy may not have analyzed all the (n*(n-1)) combinations, but have been satisfied with only a portion of the possible offsets of the messages.
11. In some systems, messages were much, much longer. Thinking their Fish system was beyond attack, the Germans sent very lengthy reports on it. F. H. Hinsley et al, *British Intelligence in the Second World War* vol. III, 1 (London: Her Majesty's Stationery Office, 1984), Appendix 2, 477.
12. Bush gave about one second for each line of printing. This time was estimated via the description in the NSA RAM File, "M.A.C. Outlines #17, 70mm Comparator," and my knowledge of the 1938 Comparator.
13. Table 7.1 shows the power of various devices, including the Comparator (run at various projected speeds) relative to tabulators operating at their typical one hundred twenty comparisons a minute. A cell entry in the table gives the worth of the alternative machine in terms of the hypothetical raw power of the number of tabulators. Thus, a sorter running at full speed was worth three tabulators while the speed of a typical teletype system of the era was five times greater than the tabulators'.

Table 7.1
Efficiency of Various Devices
Relative to Tabulator
-Rate of Comparison-
(entry = Alternative's rate / tab rate)
Tabulator Speed 120 Comparisons
per Minute

Sorters	3

Teletype readers	5
Bush Comparator at 5,000 per minute	42
Bush Comparator at 10,000 per minute	83
Bush Comparator at 20,000 per minute	165
Bush Comparator at 40,000 per minute	340
Bush Comparator at 80,000 per minute	680

14. Even in the late 1940s, the most sophisticated high-speed transmission 'baud rates' were in the range of 1800 characters a minute--or more than ten times slower than Bush needed in order make the navy machine an attractive alternative. There were special high-speed drives for sending bulk messages and during World War II 'flash' systems were developed. Those devices, however, were not proven in the mid-1930s. The talking picture industry did not provide much help. In the 1930s, moving picture film was moved at less than 300 feet per hour. On tape speeds and densities, Hagley Museum and Library, Accession 2015, Remington-Rand, ERA materials, S. Ruebens, "Investigation of Solid Acoustic Delay Lines," Contract Nobs-28476, August 1, 1947, 1. The Colossus read at 5,000 characters a second, Brian Randell (ed), *The Origins of Digital Computers: Selected Papers* (New York: Springer-Verlag, 1982), 349. It is not certain that this means that 5,000 serial characters passed the reading head of its tape scanner. The Robinsons, the British versions of the tape-optical machines (but ones for binary comparisons) read at 2,000 a second. Tape readers used by the navy in WWII ran at about 10 characters a second. The 1948 figure is in Samuel S. Snyder, "Abner: The ASA Computer, Part I: Design," *NSA Technical Journal* 25(1980), 59.
15. NARA RG457, SRH-355, "Naval Security Group History to World War II," 222.
16. The second version of the Bush Comparator is known to have had five separate counters. In 1941 there was some thought of only three. The specifications for the 1938 machine seem to have been lost, but the sketch of it by Mr. MacDonald suggests that it might have had as many as five counters and it certainly had a plugboard with the ability to select the "and" conditions.
17. NSA RAM File, OP-20-G to CNO, January 1, 1932, 'Tabulators'. Unfortunately, neither man left a record of exactly what speed demands were established, but some of the hints that have survived and some reasonable assumptions allow an idea of the tests they used and the requirements they established.
18. A very important spinoff of the navy Comparator was a 1938 project at NCR. Desch used 35mm film with punched holes on an optical comparing device for a utilities billing machine. Hagley Museum and Library, Accession 1825, *Honeywell v Sperry-Rand* Trial Records, August 16, 1938, Desch to Williams, 'Laboratory work', and August 30, 1939, Desch to Williams 'Work at Laboratory'.
19. Bernard Williams, "Computing With Electricity, 1935-1945," (Ph.D. Thesis, University of Kansas, 1984). Final OSRD Report, Div. 17, George E. Beggs Jr. and F. L. Yust, *Development and Application of Electronic Counting Circuits*, 1946, espec. Chpt. 9.
20. Several late 1930s projects at MIT explored magnetic memory and many variations of storage based on electrical charges. See, Hagley Museum and Library, Accession 1825, *Honeywell v Sperry-Rand* Trial Records, Carton 67, William Radford "Report on An Investigation of the Practicality of Developing a Rapid Computing Machine," October 15, 1939."
21. William Aspray (ed), *Computers Before Computing* (Ames, Ia.: Iowa State University Press, 1990).
22. By 1940, both were achieved by an MIT group--but on another experimental machine, the Rapid Selector. However, the Selector did not require the matching of two tapes and had a larger code area.
23. The planned Rapid Selector was to contain about 120 lines per inch and ran at approximately 300 feet per minute. Rockefeller Archives RG1.1 224D 2 23, April 14, 1937, Bush Letter to Weaver, "A Reference Selector." Russell C.

Coile, "Libraries for Engineers and Scientists: Scientific Aids to Documentation," University of Kentucky Libraries, Occasional Contributions No. 61, February, 1954, 5, shows that in 1940 the Selector had a lower density but a higher speed of some 500 feet per minute.

24. Michael K. Buckland, "Emanuel Goldberg, Electronic Document Retrieval, and Vannevar Bush's Memex," *JASIS* 43(1992): 284. On the 1937 and 1940 patents and their history, Hagley Museum and Library, Accession 2015, unprocessed ERA materials from Sperry Archive, November 1, 1949, Memo to File, Selector Infringement Search, and Accession 1825, *Honeywell v Sperry-Rand* Trial Records, August 13, 1937, Bush to Deeds, and October 25, 1937, Research Corporation to Deeds. For the Rapid Selector. the engineers were able to create sensing heads for densities of about 60-100 per inch. In 1940, the Selector contained some 10 "frames" per inch which apparently were 6 lines long given a line density of 60 per inch.
25. I assumed that one-half the tape was blank tape which yielded an average of sixty characters a foot.
26. The search was well informed. Bush had begun exploration of such media in the early 1930s and his Analyser group was also searching for the right optical-tape combination.
27. Some of Bush's colleagues were exploring the use of sheets, plates and optical disks for their scientific measuring devices and for the MIT computer projects. Rockefeller Archives, RG12.1, Diaries of Warren Weaver, July 28, 1938, 'SAL Project and Bennett's microsheets and plates', and Hagley Museum and Library, Accession 1825, *Honeywell v Sperry-Rand* Trial Records, William Radford, October 15, 1938, "Report on an Investigation of the Practicality of Developing a Rapid Computing Machine."
28. NSA RAM File, OP-20-G to Bureau of Engineering, 'Rapid Equipment', March 29, 1938.
29. A density of ten or eleven per inch was assumed as indicated by the description of the later army version of 1944 which reached twelve and one-half per inch with an average over the entire tape of six and one-quarter per inch. On the cost of the Eastman tape, NARA RG457, SRH-355, "Naval Security Group History to World War II," 276, and NSA RAM File, CNO to Bureau of Engineering, April 29, 1938.
30. In later models of the Comparator the stepping could be from one to ten characters after each pass. NSA RAM File, "M.A.C. Outlines #17, 70mm Comparator," April, 1947.
31. Later machines that Bush's team helped to build had the same general architecture as the Comparator but used reels with rather complex control mechanisms. NSA RAM File, Communications Intelligence Technical Paper-42, "Copperhead I Theory and Copperhead I Equipment." One contemporary remembered stepping done through different length tapes, but MacDonald mentioned stepping switches.
32. Howard Aiken's early computer, the ASCC, used a tape rig similar to the one chosen for the Comparator. During World War II the Americans and the British also used a pulley and loop system for the follow-ons to the Comparators indicating that it was a sound method. Michael R. Williams, *A History of Computing Technology* (Englewood Cliffs, N. J.: Prentice-Hall, 1985), 245. Brian Randell, "Colossus: Grandfather of the Computer," in B. Randell (ed), *The Origins of Digital Computers* (New York: Springer-Verlag, 1982), 350.
33. Interviews with W. S. MacDonald.
34. The less than four mile per hour estimates is based on MacDonald's statement that the tubes could switch at a rate of 5,000 a second but that speed was not utilized for counting because of the tape limitations. Based upon that and other evidence cited in the text, I estimate that the tape transport ran at about 2.5 miles an hour. Based on the later estimates of some 5400 tests per minute, the tape probably ran at approximately 100-150 feet per minute after the rebuilding at MIT in 1941. On tape readers, Anthony Ralston (ed), *Encyclopedia of Computer Science* (New York: 1976), 1033-70. Brian Randell, "Colossus: Grandfather of the Computer," in B. Randell (ed), *The Origins of Digital Computers* (New York: Springer-Verlag, 1982), 350. By the 1960s, photoelectric readers had become commonplace but the speed of commercial versions seems to have remained relatively low, much less than the speed of the war time British devices.

35. Joel Stebbins, "The Electric Eye in Astronomy," in *Cooperation in Research*, (Washington: the Carnegie Institution, 1938), 75-90.
36. Hagley Museum and Library, Accession 1825, *Honeywell v Sperry-Rand* Trial Records, Carton 67, William Radford "Report on An Investigation of the Practicality of Developing a Rapid Computing Machine," October 15, 1939.
37. Richard Taylor worked on many of the early MIT computing projects, then took charge of the Center of Analysis during the war. Hagley Museum and Library, Accession 1825, *Honeywell v Sperry-Rand* Trial Records, July 23, 1940, Caldwell to Williams of NCR. 'Richard Taylor on your work'. MIT Archives AC4, Box 45, September 5, 1946, Killian to Taylor. 'Center not self-supporting'.
38. This estimate is based upon: thirty tubes in a ring, 333 coincidences a second calling for a binary switching rate of 9999 per second. In late 1941, after a major reworking of the first model of the Comparator, the MIT group claimed its counters could handle 2,000 letter per second which implies a 60,000 per second switching rate. They looked forward to using new tube and circuit designs to increase the count to 100,000 per second. NSA Ram File, OP-20-G to OP-20--A, November 5, 1941. The binary switching rate, it should be noted, is not equal to the testing of coincidences rate. Note that MacDonald claimed his 1938 tubes switched at 5,000 p.s. when on good behavior.
39. In fact, for another of its projects, MIT put a young man to full time work to explore and refine vacuum tubes for computers. That work would come to play a significant part in the American atomic bomb program. Hagley Museum and Library, Accession 1825, *Honeywell v Sperry-Rand* Trial Records, January 26, 1940, Caldwell to NCR, 'Overbeck multifunction tube, Digitron', and March 27, 1942, MIT to Desch, 'Overbeck going to Fermi Laboratory'.
40. Paul F. Ceruzzi, *Reckoners: The Prehistory of the Digital Computer* (Westport, Conn.: Greenwood Press, 1983). Charles S. Bashe, et al, *IBM's Early Computers* (Cambridge, Mass.: MIT Press, 1985), 36-39.
41. Bruno Rossi, "Method of Registering Multiple Simultaneous Impulses of Several Geiger's Counters," *Nature* vol. 124 # 3156 (April 26, 1930): 636. The production version of the Bush Comparator certainly had such circuits and some participants claimed with certainty that the 1937-8 device also had them. See, Smithsonian Interview with Howard Campaigne and letter from Campaigne to Brian Randell.
42. Waldron MacDonald claimed he had to rework all the circuits and that binary switching speeds did not exceed 5,000 per second. MacDonald interviews, 1987-1991.
43. The navy's later Letterwriters and its Copperheads used a modified baudot coding. NSA RAM File: 'Machine Comparisons', June 1946; Communications Intelligence Technical Paper-42, "Copperhead I Theory and Copperhead I Equipment"; and Communications Intelligence Paper-41, "Copperhead I Punch and Copperhead I Scanner."
44. NSA RAM File, July 18, 1938, Safford to Bush, 'Machinery Arrived'.
45. In 1940-41 it seems it was decided to use a new navy teletype on the planned microfilm Comparator and one was shipped to the group at MIT. NARA Suitland Archives, Bureau of Ships General Correspondence, November 10, 1941, 'Teletype to MIT'.
46. Library of Congress, Papers of Vannevar Bush, Box 67, Bush to Moreland, 'MacDonald's Graduate Work', October 18, 1937.
47. NSA RAM File, Wenger Report, 'Bush Visit' April 25, 1938. Waldron S. MacDonald interviews. NARA RG457, SRH-355, "Naval Security Group History to World War II," 299.
48. Interviews with Waldron S. MacDonald, 1987-1991.
49. Wenger to Holtwick, et al, November 2, 1937. On December 30, 1937, Safford also wrote a complementary report. NARA RG457, SRH-355, "Naval Security Group History to World War II," 257, 270.
50. NSA RAM File, December 12, 1937, Bush to DNC, 'Wenger's Duty' states that the project was nearly completed and Bush's role is about over.
51. Waldron S. MacDonald Interviews. MacDonald wanted to expand the plugboard's powers to make the machine perform even more functions but was told to follow the original specifications.
52. W. S. MacDonald Interviews, 1987-1991.

53. Library of Congress, Papers of Vannevar Bush, Box 67, Bush to Moreland, 'MacDonald's Graduate Work' October 18, 1937.
54. Library of Congress, Papers of Vannevar Bush, Box 67, MacDonald to Bush, July 25, 1939. And, interviews with MacDonald.
55. Exactly when MacDonald was hurt or how long he was away from the project remains unspecified. The injury was serious and long lasting, however. MacDonald complained about what was at least energy loss for more than a year. Library of Congress, Papers of Vannevar Bush, Box 67, MacDonald to Bush, July 25, 1939, 'Ticking on all six again'.
56. NARA RG457, SRH-355, "Naval Security Group History to World War II," 268. NSA RAM File, December 11, 1937, Bush to Courtney, 'Wenger's Duty'.
57. NARA RG457, SRH-355, "Naval Security Group History to World War II," 268.
58. NARA RG457, SRMN-001, "Military Study of Facsimile, By Lt. J. N. Wenger, USN."
59. NAVY-Office of Information Biographical Branch 13 February 1952, "R. Adm. J. N. Wenger, USN, Ret." NSA RAM File, March 17, 1938, OP-20-G to Bureau of Engineering, 'Comparator Equipment'.
60. NARA RG457, SRH-355, "Naval Security Group History to World War II," 270, December 20, 1937 Safford to OP-20-G 'Bush Project', and NSA RAM File, McClaran to Bureau of Engineering, 'Recommend Bush', January 28, 1936.
61. Office of Research and Inventions patent application sheet of 10-29-46 lists April, 1938 as the time of the first successful witnessed run. ONR, patent file for Bush Comparator, #2,873,912.
62. Interviews with Waldron S. MacDonald. NARA RG457, SRH-355, "Naval Security Group History to World War II," 299, and NSA RAM File, Wenger Report, 'Bush Visit' April 25, 1938.
63. NSA RAM File, May 2, 1938, Safford to OP-20-G 'Request to Hire MacDonald'.
64. NARA RG457, SRH-355, "Naval Security Group History to World War II," 272, 276. NSA RAM File, OP-20-G to Bureau of Engineering. 'Rapid Equipment', April 29, 1938, and May 17, 1938, 'Comparator Equipment.'
65. NARA RG457, SRH-151, "Military Study: Communication Intelligence Research Activities," 022, indicates that the first Bush machine was paid for out of a special fiscal 1938 allocation. The proposed budget for 1939 contained a request for a similar amount but it may have been for a "payback" for the first expenditure.
66. NRA RAM File, September 16, 1938, OP-20-G-Bureau of Ships, 'Budget Request'.
67. The exact amounts spent on and budgeted for the Comparator in 1938 and 1939 remain unknown. NARA RG457, SRH-355, "Naval Security Group History to World War II," 276, 240. The budget request for fiscal 1939 included items for building new machines and new components such as a rapid "locator." This may have been a means of locating code groups, a function later embodied in the machines designed by Larry Steinhardt, or, it may have been an automation of the methods of overlay sheets to determine code-wheel orders and setting as used by Mrs. Driscoll. RAM File, CNO to Bureau of Engineering, September 16, 1938, 'Development of Special Communications Devices'.
68. NSA RAM File, Wenger Report, 'Bush Visit' April 25, 1938, and Wenger to Bush, December 1, 1936, 'Young Men Needed'.
69. Library of Congress, Papers of Vannevar Bush, Box 67, MacDonald File, Bush to MacDonald, 'Excellent Lead', October 18, 1938.
70. NARA RG457, SRH-355, "Naval Security Group History to World War II," 440.
71. The machine arrived at the Navy Yard on June 24. It had been badly jostled on the trip and refused to run. NSA RAM File, July 18, 1938, OP-20-G to Bush 'Machine Has Arrived'. It took Dulong some three weeks to tease the machine into its first non-MIT test run. NRL, Bush Comparator patent application file, October 29, 1946, 1.
72. NSA RAM File, July 18, 1938, Safford to Bush, 'Machinery Arrived'.
73. NSA RAM File, July 18, 1938, Safford to Bush, 'Machinery Arrived'. NRL patent application file, October 29,1946, 1.

74. NSA RAM File, May 17, 1938, 'Comparator Equipment', and July 18, 1938, Safford to Bush, 'Machinery Arrived'.
75. This estimate is based upon data found in NSA RAM File, Safford to OP-20-A, November 5, 1941. It reported on the results of more than a year's additional work on the first Comparator and gave a figure of 5,400 letters per minute. Thus, the first version must have performed at a slower rate. Note that in the November estimate, a very high letter rate was cited but because much improved versions of the Comparator built during the war operated at half that speed, Safford must have made his estimate using the rate of ten cells operating in parallel. The 5,000 binary switch estimate is from the MacDonald interviews.
76. Navy Biographies Section OI-140, "Rear Admiral Stanford C. Hooper, U. S. Navy, Deceased."
77. Jack Sweetman, *American Naval History* (Annapolis: Naval Institute Press, 1984), 156.
78. Jeffery M. Dorwart, *Conflict of Duty: The United States Navy's Intelligence Dilemma 1919-1945* (Annapolis: Naval Institute Press, 1983), 93, 99. NSA RAM File, OP-20-G to Bureau of Engineering, March 22, 1938 and June 24, 1938, 'IBM Purchases'. Cipher A. Deavours, and Louis Kruh, *Machine Cryptography and Modern Cryptanalysis* (Dedham, Mass.: Artech House, 1985), 212. NSA, Theodore M. Hannah, "Frank B. Rowlett: A Personal Profile," 116. Rear Admiral Edwin T. Layton, *And I Was There: Pearl Harbor and Midway--Breaking the Secrets* (New York: William Morrow, 1985). NARA RG457, SRMD-019, "The Panay Incident."
79. Library of Congress, Papers of Vannevar Bush, Box 67, MacDonald to Bush, July 25, 1939, 'Ticking on all six again'.
80. NSA RAM File, May 17, 1938, 'Comparator Equipment', and CNO to Bureau of Engineering, September 16, 1938, 'Development of Special Communications Devices'.
81. This is based on MacDonald's $20.00 per diem at six days a week for four months. NSA RAM File, April 25, 1938 Wenger to DNC, 'Report on Comparator', and May 2, 1938, OP-20-G, "Request for funds for Comparator'. NARA RG457, SRH-355, "Naval Security Group History to World War II," 299. Library of Congress, Papers of Vannevar Bush, Box 67, MacDonald file, October 14, 1938, Bush to MacDonald, 'New job for MacDonald'.
82. Library of Congress, "Silas Casey: Stanford Caldwell Hooper: A Register of their Papers in the Library of Congress," Naval Historical Foundations Collection, Chronology. Interview with Waldron S. MacDonald.
83. Interviews with W. S. MacDonald.
84. Library of Congress, Papers of Vannevar Bush, Box 67, MacDonald File, Bush to MacDonald, 'Excellent Lead', October 18, 1938.
85. Library of Congress, Papers of Vannevar Bush, Box 67, MacDonald to Bush, July 25, 1939, 'Ticking on all six again'. Interviews with W. S. MacDonald.
86. NSA Lou Holland, "Development of Machine Processing in the Naval Security Group," 10.
87. NSA RAM File, OP-20-G, 'List of statistical machinery', December 1, 1939.
88. Ironically, MIT would soon provide the army's cryptanalytic group with an electrical engineer, Leo Rosen, who quickly became the leader of the group that constructed a model of Purple and that became the electronics research group in the SIS. NSA, Theodore M. Hannah, "Frank B. Rowlett: A Personal Profile," 18.
89. NSA RAM File, Safford to Bush, December 10, 1938, 'Fine Job on Comparator'.
90. NSA RAM File, Bush to Safford, December 13, 1938, 'Naval Reserve'.
91. RAM File, CNO to Bureau of Engineering, September 16, 1938, 'Development of Special Communications Devices'.
92. NARA RG457, SRH-355. "Naval Security Group History to World War II," 300.
93. NSA RAM File, OP-20-G, 'List of statistical machinery', December 1, 1939.
94. NSA RAM File, August 22, 1939, Safford to Radio Division, Bureau of Engineering, '$10,000 for Analytical Research'.
95. Library of Congress, Papers of Vannevar Bush, Box 67, MacDonald File, Bush to MacDonald 'OP-20-G Project' August 31, 1940. NARA RG457, SRH-355, "Naval Security Group History to World War II," 270, 405.
96. NSA RAM File, Safford to Hooper, 'Comparator' November 19, 1940.

97. NSA RAM File, Safford, July 18, 1940, 'Emergency plans'. NSA RAM File, OP-20-G June 14, 1940 'Readiness plans'.
98. Library of Congress, Papers of Vannevar Bush, Box 67, MacDonald File, Bush to MacDonald 'OP-20-G Project' August 31, 1940.

CHAPTER VIII

1. Karl Wildes, and Nilo A. Lindgren, *A Century of Electrical Engineering and Computer Science at MIT, 1882-1982* (Cambridge: MIT Press, 1985). Larry Owens, "Vannevar Bush and the Differential Analyser: The Text and Context of an Early Computer," *Technology and Culture* 27(1986): 63-95.
2. A book with much insight into both Bush and Wiener is Steve J. Heims, *John Von Neumann and Norbert Wiener: From Mathematics to the Technology of Life and Death* (Cambridge, Mass. : MIT Press, 1980).
3. Karl Wilde, and Nilo A. Lindgren, *A Century of Electrical Engineering and Computer Science at MIT, 1882-1982* (Cambridge: MIT Press, 1985), Chpt. 4. H. L. Hazen, and G. S. Brown, "The Cinema Integraph," *Journal of the Franklin Institute* (July/August, 1940), 19. George R. Harrison, "The M. I. T. Wavelength Project," *Physical Society Progress Reports* 8: 212-230.
4. Smithsonian Interview with Gordon S. Brown, conducted by Richard R. Mertz, January 27, 1970, 5, and Bernard Williams, "Computing by Electricity, 1935-45," (Ph.D. Diss. University of Kansas, August, 1985), 55. The Integraph work may have had a very direct link to the Selector. It may have been the source of the reduction to practice needed for the Selector patent applications of October, 1937. Joel Stebbins, "The Electric Eye in Astronomy," in *Cooperation in Research* (Washington: The Carnegie Institution, 1938), 75-90. W. J. Eckert, "Electronic and Electromagnetic Measuring, Computing and Recording Devices," in *Centennial Symposia, Harvard Observatory Monographs Symposia Dec. 1946* (Cambridge: The Observatory, 1948), 169-178.
5. Jack Rubin, *A History of Micrographics: In the First Person* (Silver Spring: National Micrographics Association, 1980). John K. Boeing, "Recordak," *Journal of Documentary Reproduction* 3(1940): 153-168. Frank L. Hilton, Jr., "Microfilm Systems--The First 40 Kodak Years," *Journal of Micrographics* 1(1968): 117-125.
6. Hagley Museum and Library, Accession 1825, *Honeywell v Sperry-Rand*, Trial Records, Chronological File, Sulzer to Bush, 'Morse Patent', February 6, 1939.
7. J. W. Bryce, U. S. Patent 'Statistical Machine', Filed February 19, 1936, awarded July 26, 1938, #2,124,906. J. W. Bryce, U. S. Patent, "Film Data Selecting and Viewing Machine," July 6, 1943, 2,323,372. "The Light He Left Behind," (James Bryce), *Think* (April, 1949): 5-31. Bryce was IBM's top inventor-researcher. Jack Rubin, *A History of Micrographics: In the First Person* (Silver Spring: National Micrographics Association, 1980).
8. Thomas C. Bagg, and Mary Elizabeth Stevens, *Information Selection Systems: Retrieving Replica Copies: A State of the Art Report* (Washington, D.C.: National Bureau of Standards, Technical Note 157, December 31, 1961), 18.
9. Claire K. Schultz, and Paul L. Garwig, "History of the American Documentation Institute," *American Documentation* 20(1969): 154.
10. Rockefeller Archives, RG12.1, Diaries of Warren Weaver, November 29, 1937, 'Visit of Watson Davis'. Library of Congress, Papers of Vannevar Bush, Box 31, Bush-Davis Correspondence, 1938-9.
11. Rockefeller Archives, RG12.1, Box 68, Diaries of Warren Weaver, Bush to Weaver, November 29, 1937.
12. Library of Congress, Papers of Vannevar Bush, Box 31, Bush-Davis Correspondence, 1938-9. Rockefeller Archives, RG12.1, Diaries of Warren Weaver, November 29, 1937, 'Visit of Watson Davis'.
13. James L. Pike, and Thomas C. Bagg, "The Rapid Selector and Other NBS Document Retrieval Systems," in Vernon Tate (ed), *Proceedings of the Eleventh Annual Meeting and Convention* (Annapolis: The National Microfilm Association, 1962), 227. Claire K. Schultz, and Paul L. Garwig, "History of the American Documentation Institute," *American Documentation* 20(1969): 154.
14. Rockefeller Archives RG1.1 224D 2 23 April 14, 1937, Bush to Weaver, "A Reference Selector."

15. Hagley Museum and Library, Accession 1825, *Honeywell v Sperry-Rand* Trial Records, August 13, 1937, Bush to Deeds, 'Rapid Selector'. Rockefeller Archives, RG12.1, Diaries of Warren Weaver, Bush Visit April 12, 1937, 'FBI Machine'. Library of Congress, Papers of Vannevar Bush, Howard File, April 15, 1940, Bush to Wilson 'Statistical Selector'.
16. Rockefeller Archives RG1.1 224D 2 23, April 14, 1937, Bush to Weaver, "A Reference Selector." As with all innovations, the use of optics and microfilm to store, locate and retrieve documents was shared by many inventors. A German film scientist, Emanuel Goldberg, designed a patented machine as early as 1931. About the same time, the Documentalists such as Watson Davis pushed ideas for similar devices and by the mid-1930s a host of inventors had filed claims. Thus, it is not clear that Bush was entirely original in his thinking on the Selector. At the same time, it is not clear that he used the ideas of others. A sampling of the many inventors is found in, Michael K. Buckland, "Emanuel Goldberg, Electronic Document Retrieval, and Vannevar Bush's Memex," *JASIS* 43(1992): 284.
17. L. G. Townsend, (1936), "Method of and Apparatus for the Indexing and Photo-transcription of Records," Patent 2,121,061, Filed July 6, 1936, awarded June 21, 1938. William F. Friedman, and Vernon E. Whitman, "Electric Control System for Tabulating Cards," Documents and the Like, U. S Patent 2,224,646, December 10, 1940. Hagley Museum and Library, Accession 1825, *Honeywell v Sperry-Rand* Trial Records: August 13, 1937, Bush to Deeds; October 25, 1937, 'Research Corporation to Deeds', and Chronological File, Sulzer to Bush, 'Morse Patent'" February 6, 1939. E. Goldberg, U. S. Patent 1,838,389, "Statistical Machine," December 29, 1931, Filed April 5, 1928. February 11, 1941, "Identifying Means," U. S. Patent 2,231,186.
18. On the 1937 and 1940 patents and their history, Hagley Museum and Library, Accession 2015, Unprocessed ERA materials Sperry Archives, November 1, 1949, Memo to File, 'Infringement Search', and ERA Box Project 1045 (E-45), November 1, 1949, 'Bell & Howell Microfilm selector and patents, including history of Bush patents'. Accession 1825, *Honeywell v Sperry-Rand* Trial Records, August 13, 1937, Bush to Deeds, and October 25, 1937, Research Corporation to Deeds. Rockefeller Archives RG1.1 224D 2 23 April 14, 1937, Bush to Weaver, "A Reference Selector," 4.
19. Rockefeller Archives RG12.1, Diaries of Warren Weaver, July 7, 1938, notes the role of Bush and his colleagues at MIT in trying to steer the Aids to Learning funds to MIT's proposed center. Michael K. Buckland, "Emanuel Goldberg, Electronic Document Retrieval, and Vannevar Bush's Memex," *JASIS* 43(1992): 284. Charles P. Bourne, "The Historical Development and Present State of the Art of Mechanized Information Retrieval Systems," *American Documentation* 12(1961): 108.
20. Rockefeller Archives, RG12.1, Diaries of Warren Weaver, October 28, 1938, 'Genetics Center'. Hagley Museum and Library, Accession 1825, *Honeywell v Sperry-Rand* Trial Records, October 14, 1937, Bush to Deeds, 'Carnegie SAL support'. Claire K. Schultz, and Paul L. Garwig, "History of the American Documentation Institute," *American Documentation* 20(1969): 155. James W. Perry, Allen Kent, and Madeline M. Berry, *Machine Literature Searching* (Cleveland: Western Reserve University Press, 1956).
21. Rockefeller Archives, RG1.1 224D 2 23, April 14, 1937, Bush Letter to Weaver, "A Reference Selector."
22. Rockefeller Archives, RG1.1 224D 2 23, April 14, 1937, Bush Letter to Weaver, "A Reference Selector," 7.
23. Rockefeller Archives, RG1.1 224D 2 23, April 14, 1937, Bush Letter to Weaver, "A Reference Selector," 16.
24. Rockefeller Archives, RG1.1 224D 2 23, April 14, 1937, Bush Letter to Weaver, "A Reference Selector."
25. Larry Owens, "Straight Thinking: Vannevar Bush and the Culture of American Engineering,"(Ph.D. Thesis, Princeton University, 1987), 65, 80.
26. Hagley Museum and Library, Accession 1825, *Honeywell v Sperry-Rand* Trial Records, August 8, 1937, Bush to Deeds, 'Selector', and Deeds to Bush', August 1937, 'Selector good idea'.
27. Bush was aware of the potential for business. Hagley Museum and Library, Accession 1825, *Honeywell v Sperry-Rand* Trial Records, Bush to Wilson, October 30, 1939, 'Townsend selector patent--microfilm v the punched card'.

28. After the 1920s and early 1930s work with NCR, Hofgaard continued with his projects, some of which included electronics. R. Hofgaard, Patent 2,337,553 filed April 5, 1940, awarded December 28, 1943, 'Device for Operating Machines from Control Tapes'. Charles S. Bashe et al, *IBM's Early Computers* (Cambridge, Mass.: MIT Press, 1985), Chpt. 2. Bush would not have revealed any secret work to NCR's men but the navy's counting rings and other circuits were, by themselves, not classified. Bush did state to men such as Deeds and Weaver that the Rapid Arithmetic machine ideas came from earlier "government" work. Hagley Museum and Library, Accession 1825, *Honeywell v Sperry-Rand* Trial Records, NCR Depositions, Bush to Deeds 'Analyzing Equipment', May 19, 1938. Rockefeller Archives RG12.1, Diaries of Warren Weaver, Bush visit October 28, 1938, 'Carnegie Plans'.
29. Hagley Museum and Library, Accession 1825, *Honeywell v Sperry-Rand* Trial Records, August 13, 1937, Bush to Deeds, 'Rapid Selector', and October 25, 1937 Deeds to Bush, 'NCR will support Edgerton'.
30. It seems that negotiations led NCR to ask only for licensing rights on the Selector by late 1938. Rockefeller Archives RG12.1, Diaries of Warren Weaver, Bush visit October 28, 1938, 'Carnegie Plans'. Hagley Museum and Library, Accession 1825, *Honeywell v Sperry-Rand* Trial Records, October, 1938, Caldwell to NCR 'Rapid Project," and November 11, 1938 'NCR to Send $2,000 for Rapid Project."
31. Michael K. Buckland, "Emanuel Goldberg, Electronic Document Retrieval, and Vannevar Bush's Memex," *JASIS* 43(1992): 284. John K. Boeing, "Recordak," *Journal of Documentary Reproduction* 3(1940): 153-168. Frank L. Hilton, Jr., "Microfilm Systems--The First 40 Kodak Years," *Journal of Micrographics* 1(1968): 117-125.
32. The gentlemen's agreement with NCR came in late 1937 and that with Eastman by spring 1938. The formal contracts were not signed until winter 1938, however. Hagley Museum and Library, Accession 1825, *Honeywell v Sperry-Rand* Trial Records: Bush to NCR, October 25, 1937 and March 1, 1938; and Eastman-Bush, December 2, 1938; February, 1938 to March 1, 1938, NCR-MIT-Eastman correspondence, 'Establish Rapid Selector project'.
33. Frank Cameron, *Cottrell: Samaritan of Science* (New York: Doubleday & Co., 1952). 162. MIT Archives AC4: Box 30, 'Center for Analysis, 1944'; Box 36, June 12, 1945, Office of the President, 'Center of Analysis'; and Box 246, Folder 17, 'Research Corporation and aggressive management'.
34. Hagley Museum and Library, Accession 1825, *Honeywell v Sperry-Rand* Trial Records, Bush to Deeds, September 1937 and October 14, 1937, 'Edgerton-Microfilm'.
35. Hagley Museum and Library, Accession 1825, *Honeywell v Sperry-Rand* Trial Records: October 25, 1937, Research Corporation to Deeds, 'Edgerton Patents'; April, 1937, NCR Engineers Green and Sullivan to Deeds on MIT visit'; and August 13, 1937, Bush to Deeds, 'Rapid Selector'.
36. On the 1937 and 1940 patents and their history, Hagley Museum and Library, Accession 2015, Unprocessed ERA materials from Sperry Archives, November 1, 1949, Memo to File, Selector Infringement Search. Accession 1825, *Honeywell v Sperry-Rand* Trial Records: August 13, 1937, Bush to Deeds; October 25, 1937, Research Corporation to Deeds; and October 30, 1939, Bush to Research Corporation, 'Townsend at Census Office'.
37. Thomas C. Bagg, and Mary Elizabeth Stevens, *Information Selection Systems: Retrieving Replica Copies: A State of the Art Report* (Washington, D.C.: National Bureau of Standards, Technical Note 157, December 31, 1961), 18. Hagley Museum and Library, Accession 1825, *Honeywell v Sperry-Rand* Trial Records, Bush to NCR, March 1, 1938.
38. MIT Archives, AC4 Boxes 30 and 36, "Center of Analysis," and, Hagley Museum and Library, Accession 1825, *Honeywell v Sperry-Rand* Trial Records, Bush to Deeds, March 1, 1938 and May 19, 1938.
39. Hagley Museum and Library, Accession 1825, *Honeywell v Sperry-Rand* Trial Records, Desch Deposition, 'Report of Joseph Desch on Electronics Laboratory to H. N. Williams' August 16, 1938, and February 21, 1942, Desch, 'Report to Management'. Library of Congress, Papers of Vannevar Bush, Box 95, Eastman-Kodak, May 24, 1940, Hazen to Bush 'Rapid Selector'.

40. Hagley Museum and Library, Accession 1825, *Honeywell v Sperry-Rand* Trial Records, 'Report of Joseph Desch on Electronics Laboratory to H. N. Williams' August 16, 1938. Rockefeller Archives, RG12.1, Diaries of Warren Weaver, October 28, 1938, 'Bush on Carnegie plans'.
41. Library of Congress, Papers of Vannevar Bush: Box 95, Howard to Sulzer, April 4, 1939; Box 52, Howard to Bush, November 11, 1939, 'Use of Selector'; and Box 52, Howard to Bush November 29, 1939, 'Use of Selector'.
42. Library of Congress, Papers of Vannevar Bush, Box 49, Folder 1184, July 13, 1940, John Howard, "Progress Report on the Rapid Selector Research." Hagley Museum and Library, Accession 1825, *Honeywell v Sperry-Rand* Trial Records, April 3, 1940, Wilson to Bush, 'Selector as a statistical machine'. Michael K. Buckland, "Emanuel Goldberg, Electronic Document Retrieval, and Vannevar Bush's Memex," *JASIS* 43(1992): 284.
43. Rockefeller Archives, RG12.1, Diaries of Warren Weaver, Bush visit October 28, 1938, 'Carnegie Plans',and Bush visit, March 24, 1938, 'Rapid Selector'. Rockefeller Archives RG1.1 224D 2 23 April 14, 1937, Bush to Weaver, "A Reference Selector," 2. Note that in 1939 he did court the men from the Census and the American Statistical Association and did so with a counting version of the Selector in mind. Library of Congress, Papers of Vannevar Bush, Hazen File, November 22, 1939, Bush to Hazen. Bush was also courting the Patent Office.
44. Rockefeller Archives, RG12.1, Diaries of Warren Weaver, October 28, 1938, Bush visit, 'Genetics Center'. Library of Congress, Papers of Vannevar Bush, Box 31, Bush-Davis Correspondence, 1938-9.
45. Library of Congress, Papers of Vannevar Bush, Box 95, May 24, 1940, Hazen to Bush, 'Rapid Selector'; Hazen to Eastman-Kodak, July 13, 1940, 'Add counters to Selector'.
46. On the 1937 and 1940 patents and their history, Hagley Museum and Library: Accession 2015, Unprocessed ERA materials from Sperry Archives, November 1, 1949, Memo to File, Selector Infringement Search; Accession 1825, *Honeywell v Sperry-Rand* Trial Records, August 13, 1937, Bush to Deeds; and October 25, 1937, Research Corporation to Deeds; October 25, 1937, Research Corporation to Deeds, 'Edgerton Patents'. Goldberg's work was cited by the patent examiner who examiner who dealt with the 1937 patent application.
47. Russell C. Coile, "Libraries for Engineers and Scientists: Scientific Aids to Documentation," University of Kentucky Libraries, Occasional Contributions No. 61, February, 1954.
48. Michael K. Buckland, "Emanuel Goldberg, Electronic Document Retrieval, and Vannevar Bush's Memex," *JASIS* 43(1992): 284.
49. Library of Congress, Papers of Vannevar Bush, Vita of Lawrence Steinhardt cir. 1950. Karl L. Wildes, and Nilo A. Lindgren, *A Century of Electrical Engineering and Computer Science at MIT, 1882-1982* (Cambridge: MIT Press, 1985), 68. L. Steinhardt " A New Method for Lighting Statuary," *The Technology Review*, July 9(1937): 404-5.
50. Rockefeller Archives, RG1.1 224D 2 23, April 14, 1937, Bush Letter to Weaver, "A Reference Selector." Rockefeller Archives, RG12.1, Diaries of Warren Weaver, October 28, 1938, 'Genetics Center'.
51. Hagley Museum and Library, Accession 1825, *Honeywell v Sperry-Rand* Trial Records, August 13, 1937, Bush to Deeds, 'Rapid Selector'. Rockefeller Archives RG1.1 224D 2 23, April 14, 1937, Bush Letter to Weaver, "A Reference Selector." Michael Buckland informed me that the films of the 1930s might not have been able to register images at the speeds Bush desired. Letter to author, May, 1993.
52. Rockefeller Archives, RG1.1 224D 2 23, April 14, 1937, Bush Letter to Weaver, "A Reference Selector." Later, the military and the MIT group found it more efficient to reverse the scanning and use the absence of light to select items as had Emanuel Goldberg. This change, while limiting the logic of the machines, did ease the optical-scanning problems.
53. Rockefeller Archives, RG1.1 224D 2 23, April 14, 1937, Bush Letter to Weaver, "A Reference Selector."
54. Rockefeller Archives, RG1.1 224D 2 23, April 14, 1937, Bush Letter to Weaver, "A Reference Selector," 13.
55. Library of Congress, Papers of Vannevar Bush, Box 49, Folder 1184, July 13, 1940, John Howard, "Progress Report on the Rapid Selector Research."

56. Rockefeller Archives, RG1.1 224D 2 23, April 14, 1937, Bush Letter to Weaver, "A Reference Selector," 12.
57. Library of Congress, Papers of Vannevar Bush, Box 95, March 12, 1940, Howard to C. Wilson of Research Corporation, 'Report on the Rapid Selector', 2.
58. Library of Congress, Papers of Vannevar Bush, Box 95, Bush to Carroll L. Wilson, April 15, 1940, 'Howard's Memorandum'.
59. Hagley Museum and Library, Accession 2015, Remington-Rand / ERA materials, 'Abstract of Morse Patent, December, 30, 1967', and Accession 1825, *Honeywell v Sperry-Rand* Trial Records, February 6, 1939, Sulzer to Bush, 'Morse Rapid Selector'. R. S. Morse, Patent 2,295,000, "Rapid Selector Calculator" Filed June 23, 1936.
60. Library of Congress, Papers of Vannevar Bush, Box 35, Eastman-Kodak, March 6, 1939, Bush to Sulzer, 'Morse Idea'.
61. Library of Congress, Papers of Vannevar Bush, Box 85, Howard to Sulzer, April 4, 1939, 'Rapid Selector'.
62. Library of Congress, Papers of Vannevar Bush, Box 85, Howard to Sulzer, April 4, 1939, 'Rapid Selector'.
63. Library of Congress, Papers of Vannevar Bush, Box 85, Howard to Sulzer, April 4, 1939, 'Rapid Selector'.
64. Library of Congress, Papers of Vannevar Bush, Box 95, May 24, 1940, Hazen to Bush, 'Rapid Selector'.
65. Library of Congress, Papers of Vannevar Bush, Box 95, March 12, 1940, Howard to C. Wilson of Research Corporation, Report on the Rapid Selector; Box 49, November 22, 1940, Hazen to Sulzer.
66. Library of Congress, Papers of Vannevar Bush, Box 95, March 12, 1940, Howard to C. Wilson of Research Corporation, "Report on the Rapid Selector."
67. Library of Congress, Papers of Vannevar Bush, Box 95, March 12, 1940, Howard to C. Wilson of Research Corporation, "Report on the Rapid Selector," 7.
68. On the 1937 and 1940 patents, Hagley Museum and Library, Accession 2015, Unprocessed ERA materials from Sperry Archives, November 1, 1949, Memo to File, Selector Infringement Search, and Accession 1825, *Honeywell v Sperry-Rand* Trial Records, August 13, 1937, Bush to Deeds, and October 25, 1937, Research Corporation to Deeds.
69. Hagley Museum and Library, Accession 1825, *Honeywell v Sperry-Rand* Trial Records, October 39, 1939, Bush to Research Corporation, 'Townsend patents'. L. G. Townsend, "Method of and Apparatus for the Indexing and Photo-transcription of Records," Patent 2,121,061, Filed July 6, 1936, awarded June 21, 1938. Townsend gave his home as Washington, D.C., and Bush claimed he was an employee of the Census Bureau, but a search through its directories yielded no information on him. As mentioned earlier, Friedman did not develop a machine for his IC method. William F. Friedman, and Vernon E. Whitman, "Electric Control System for Tabulating Cards, Documents and the Like," U. S. Patent 2,224,646, December 10, 1940.
70. Hagley Museum and Library, Accession 2015, Sperry Archive Materials, ERA Box, Project 1045 (E-45), November 1, 1949, 'Bell & Howell Microfilm selector and patents, including history of Bush patents'.
71. Library of Congress, Papers of Vannevar Bush, Box 49, November 22, 1940, Hazen to Sulzer.
72. Bush continued to lobby for support. A critical meeting was with the heads of the U. S. Census and the American Statistical Association in late 1939. Library of Congress, Papers of Vannevar Bush, Hazen File, Bush to Hazen, November 22, 1939 'Census and Statistical Use of Selector and Work for Center'.
73. Library of Congress, Papers of Vannevar Bush, Box 95, May 24, 1940, Hazen to Bush, 'Rapid Selector', 2. Hagley Museum and Library, Accession 1825, *Honeywell v Sperry-Rand* Trial Records, February 24, 1947, Caldwell to Bush, 'Wiener not at work on computer project'. Steve J. Heims, *John Von Neumann and Norbert Wiener: From Mathematics to the Technology of Life and Death* (Cambridge, Mass.: MIT Press, 1980).
74. Library of Congress, Papers of Vannevar Bush, Box 52, November 29, 1939, Howard to Bush, 'Use Selector for X-ray records at Mayo Clinic'.
75. Interview with Jeff Wenger, 1991.
76. Library of Congress, Papers of Vannevar Bush, Box 95, April 3, 1940, Carroll L. Wilson to Bush, and Howard to Wilson, 'Discussion of Possible Applications of the Rapid Selector'.

77. Library of Congress, Papers of Vannevar Bush, Box 95, April 3, 1940, Carroll L. Wilson to Bush, and Howard to Wilson, 'Discussion of Possible Applications of the Rapid Selector'.
78. Library of Congress, Papers of Vannevar Bush, Box 95, April 3, 1940, Carroll L. Wilson to Bush, and Howard to Wilson, 'Discussion of Possible Applications of the Rapid Selector', 4.
79. Library of Congress, Papers of Vannevar Bush, Box 52, August 14, 1940, Howard to Eastman-Kodak, 'Selector to locate archive business records'.
80. Library of Congress, Papers of Vannevar Bush, Box 95, April 3, 1940, Carroll L. Wilson to Bush, and Howard to Wilson, 'Discussion of Possible Applications of the Rapid Selector'.
81. Library of Congress, Papers of Vannevar Bush, Box 95, April 3, 1940, Carroll L. Wilson to Bush, and Howard to Wilson, 'Discussion of Possible Applications of the Rapid Selector', 10.
82. Library of Congress, Papers of Vannevar Bush, Box 95, April 3, 1940, Carroll L. Wilson to Bush; Howard to Wilson, 'Discussion of Possible Applications of the Rapid Selector', 1; and Bush to Wilson, May 15, 1940 'Selector only good for multiple index search'.
83. Library of Congress, Papers of Vannevar Bush, Bush to Wilson, May 15, 1940 'Selector only good for multiple index search'.
84. Library of Congress, Papers of Vannevar Bush, Box 52, Howard to Killian, March 21, 1946, 'Rapid Selector'. Laurance F. Safford, "Rhapsody in Purple," by Dundas P. Tucker, *Cryptologia* 6(1981): 196, 220.
85. Hagley Museum and Library, Accession 1825, *Honeywell v Sperry-Rand* Trial Records, December 2, 1941, NDRC to Desch 'Counter contract', and February 7, 1940, S. H. Caldwell, "NCR: A Multi-total Analysis Machine Using Magnetic Storage'. NSA RAM File, Report of R. I. Meader, Captain USNR to J. H. Wenger, Captain, USN, "14 Days Training Duty, Report of," January 21, 1949.

CHAPTER IX

1. Library of Congress, Papers of Vannevar Bush, Box 52, Howard to Killian, March 21, 1946, 'Rapid Selector'. Laurance F. Safford, "Rhapsody in Purple," by Dundas P. Tucker, *Cryptologia* 6(1981): 196-8, 220.
2. Library of Congress, Papers of Vannevar Bush, Box 52, Howard to Killian, March 21, 1946, 'Rapid Selector'.
3. Hagley Museum and Library, Accession 1825, *Honeywell v Sperry-Rand* Trial Records: NDRC Div. 13 to Desch of NCR, December 2, 1941, 'Howard counter project'; February 7, 1940, Caldwell to NCR, report, "A Multi-total Electronic Analysis Machine"; and April 18, 1941, S. H. Caldwell to NCR, 'Magnetic Recording Project'. NSA RAM File, Report of R. I. Meader, Captain USNR to J. N. Wenger, Captain, USN, "14 Days Training Duty, Report of," January 21, 1949.
4. What Howard developed in 1940 has to be inferred from the descriptions of the first new OP-20-G machines of 1942-3 and Howard's post 1945 ERA work on the Rapid Selector. See, for example, NSA RAM File, Communications Intelligence Technical Paper 1-a, "Technical Report: The Index of Coincidence Machine," March, 1945.
5. Daniel J. Kevles, *The Physicists: The History of the Scientific Community in Modern America* (New York : Knopf, 1978), 296.
6. Ronald W. Clark, *Tizard* (Cambridge: MIT Press, 1965).
7. On the American astronomers and electronic counting: H. Lifschutz, "New Vacuum Tube Scaling Circuit," *Physical Review* 57(1940): 243, and Charles Babbage Institute, Interview by William Aspray With Dr. Frank M. Verzuh, February 20 and 24, 1984.
8. N. Metropolis, et al, (ed), *A History of Computing in the Twentieth Century* (New York: Academic Press, 1980), 465.
9. Bernard Williams, "Computing With Electricity, 1935-1945," (Ph.D. Thesis, University of Kansas, 1984), 253.
10. Bernard Williams, "Computing With Electricity, 1935-1945," (Ph.D. Thesis, University of Kansas, 1984), 254.
11. Bernard Williams, "Computing With Electricity, 1935-1945," (Ph.D. Thesis, University of Kansas, 1984), 251. Desch received an impressive $112,000 under the first counter contract.

12. Charles Babbage Institute, Interview by William Aspray With Dr. Frank M. Verzuh, February 20 and 24, 1984.
13. Final OSRD Report, Div. 17, George E. Beggs Jr., and F. L. Yust, *Development and Application of Electronic Counting Circuits*, 1946, espec. Chpt. 9.
14. Hagley Museum and Library, Accession 1825, *Honeywell v Sperry-Rand* Trial Records, Desch Deposition. The NDRC '274' contract was signed on October 25, 1940.
15. These may have been used by the British during 1941 and 1942. Hagley Museum and Library, Accession 1825, *Honeywell v Sperry-Rand* Trial Records, Desch Deposition.
16. Ralph B. Baldwin, *The Deadly Fuze: The Secret Weapon of World War II* (San Rafael: Presidio Press, 1980).
17. Hagley Museum and Library, Accession 1825, *Honeywell v Sperry-Rand* Trial Records, March 27, 1942, MIT to Desch, 'Overbeck going to Fermi Laboratory', and Overbeck vitae.
18. Charles S. Bashe, et al, *IBM's Early Computers* (Cambridge, Mass.: MIT Press, 1985), Chpt. 2.
19. Hagley Museum and Library, Accession 1825, *Honeywell v Sperry-Rand* Trial Records, April 16, 1942, 'Conference on fire-control projects'. The ENIAC used a "memory" system from RCA that was quite like what was used on some OP-20-G and SIS machines and a counting circuit invented by one of RCA's men, Igor Grosdoff. N. Metropolis, et al, (ed), *A History of Computing in the Twentieth Century* (New York, 1980), 467. Hagley Museum and Library, Accession 1825, *Honeywell v Sperry-Rand* Trial Records, May 19, 1938, September 18, 1944. 'Army seizes Grosdoff patent'.
20. On the RCA machines, Bernard Williams, "Computing With Electricity, 1935-1945," (Ph.D. Thesis, University of Kansas, 1984), 256-266, and Hagley Museum and Library, Accession 1825, *Honeywell v Sperry-Rand* Trial Records, June 6, 1941, 'Caldwell visit to RCA'. NARA RG227, OSRD Div. 7, Records of the Administrative Office, Contract Reports, Box 762, November 16, 1942, Eastman Kodak Report on Fire-control computer. Perry Crawford, Jr., "Automatic Control By Arithmetical Operations," MS Thesis, MIT, 1942. Hagley Museum and Library, Accession 1825, *Honeywell v Sperry-Rand* Trial Records, NDRC, April 4, 1942, 'Conference on fire-control'.
21. Hagley Museum and Library, Accession 1825, *Honeywell v Sperry-Rand* Trial Records, August 5, 1942, Hibbard to ATT re NDRC Fire-control project. NARA RG227, OSRD Div. 7, Records of the Administrative Office, Contract Reports, Box 762, November 16, 1942, Eastman Kodak Report on Fire-control computer. NARA RG227, OSRD Div. 7, Records of the Administrative Office, Contract Reports, Box 763, October 19, 1942, Fordyce Tuttle, Eastman Kodak Report of Fire Control Computer.
22. Hagley Museum and Library, Accession 1825, *Honeywell v Sperry-Rand* Trial Records, August 5, 1942, Sigmund-Frederick of ATT re NDRC Fire-control project, and February, 1942, S. B. Williams to NDRC, 'Electronic fire control proposal'.
23. Bernard Williams, "Computing With Electricity, 1935-1945," (Ph.D. Thesis, University of Kansas, 1984), 293, 395.
24. Bernard Williams, "Computing With Electricity, 1935-1945," (Ph.D. Thesis, University of Kansas, 1984), 317. Hagley Museum and Library, Accession 1825, *Honeywell v Sperry-Rand* Trial Records, June 6, 1942, Weaver to participants 'Cancel fire-control work'.
25. NARA RG227, OSRD, Records of Office of Chairman, Box 1, October 1, 1940, Bush to Karl T. Compton, 'Request from the Navy'. NARA RG457, SRH-355, "Naval Security Group History to World War II," 405.
26. NARA RG457, SRH-355, "Naval Security Group History to World War II," 404, Safford to Hooper, November 19, 1940.
27. Laurance F. Safford, "Rhapsody in Purple," by Dundas P. Tucker, *Cryptologia* 6(1981): 221. Rear Admiral Edwin T. Layton, *And I Was There: Pearl Harbor and Midway--Breaking the Secrets* (New York: William Morrow, 1985).
28. The fear of defeat was quite real. Bletchley Park had scores of buses at the ready to race its staff to port cities where they were to board fast ocean liners for the United States and Canada.

29. Laurance F. Safford, "Rhapsody in Purple," by Dundas P. Tucker, *Cryptologia* 6(1981): 196, 220. NSA, Theodore M. Hannah, "Frank B. Rowlett: A Personal Profile," 18. NSA RAM File, Part II of Report to J. N. Wenger, Capt. USN, "Resume of the Dayton, Ohio Activity During World War II," (presumably a continuation of the Meader Report), 1. In contrast to Safford's interpretation and on America's first contact with British Enigma achievements, NARA RG457, SRH-361, "History of the Signal Security Agency, Volume Two, The General Cryptanalytic Problems," 019-021, 272. NARA RG457, SRH-145, 'Report of the Technical Mission to England' April 11, 1941, 002-004. But on how little Enigma ability OP-20-G had as late as the summer of 1943, NARA RG457, SRH-403, "Selections from the Cryptologic Papers of Rear Admiral J. N. Wenger, USN," 072-3.
30. NARA RG227, OSRD, Office of the Chairman, Box 1, Bush to Safford, October 28, 1940, 'Project Agreement'. NARA RG457, SRH-355, "Naval Security Group History to World War II," 404.
31. NSA RAM File, OP-20-A to OP-20-G, February 19, 1941, 'Supervise MIT Project'.
32. NARA RG227, OSRD General Correspondence, November 22, 1940, Hazen and Howard to NDRC 'Two Year Project'.
33. NARA RG227, OSRD General Correspondence, November 29, 1940, 'Bush Project'.
34. Hagley Museum and Library, Accession 1825, *Honeywell v Sperry-Rand* Trial Records, Hazen to Eastman-Kodak, November 22, 1940, 'Navy Project'.
35. Hagley Museum and Library, Accession 1825, *Honeywell v Sperry-Rand* Trial Records: January 3, 1940, Willis Overbeck, Arithmetic Machine Research Report; January 17, 1940, Overbeck and Caldwell to NCR 'Reports of tube work and magnetic recording work'; February 7, 1940, S. H. Caldwell, "NCR: A Multi-total Analysis Machine Using Magnetic Storage'; April 13, 1940, Caldwell to NCR, "Magnetic Recording Patents'; NDRC to Desch, NCR, December, 1941 - January, 1942, 'Fire control projects'; December 23, 1941, NCR to Caldwell, "Retainer restored'; August 27, 1940 'Magnetic Research, $5,000'; and May 27, 1941, NCR to Caldwell, '$4,000 for Magnetic Research'.
36. Hagley Museum and Library, Accession 1825, *Honeywell v Sperry-Rand* Trial Records, August 27, 1940 'Magnetic Research, $5,000', and May 27, 1941, NCR to Caldwell, '$4,000 for Magnetic Research'.
37. NSA RAM File, Safford to Radio Division, Bureau of Ships, November 2, 1940, 'Bush Project'.
38. Rear Admiral Edwin T. Layton, *And I Was There: Pearl Harbor and Midway--Breaking the Secrets* (New York: William Morrow, 1985), 78.
39. NARA RG227, OSRD, Office of the Chairman, Box 1, Bush to Safford, October 28, 1940, 'Project Agreement'. NSA RAM File, Safford to Radio Division, Bureau of Ships, November 2, 1940, 'Bush Project'. NARA RG457, SRH-355, "Naval Security Group History to World War II," 404.
40. NARA RG227, OSRD, Office of the Chairman, Box 1, Bush to Safford, October 28, 1940, 'Project Agreement'.
41. Library of Congress, Papers of Vannevar Bush, Box 67, MacDonald File, Bush to MacDonald 'OP-20-G Project' August 31, 1940, and April 17, 1941, NOL to Bush 'Re MacDonald'.
42. NARA RG457, SRH-355," Naval Security Group History to World War II," 405.
43. NARA RG227, OSRD Office of Chairman, General Records, Box 1, Bush to Compton October 1, 1940 'Navy Project'.
44. NSA RAM File, Safford to Radio Division, Bureau of Ships, November 2, 1940, 'Bush Project'.
45. NARA RG227, OSRD Office of the Chairman, Box 1, November 14, 1940, Bush to Compton, 'Howard Will Not Need Much Supervision'.
46. NARA RG227, OSRD Office of Chairman, General Records, Box 1, Bush to Howard November 27, 1940, and Howard to Bush December 14, 1940.
47. NARA RG227, OSRD Office of Chairman, General Records, Box 1: Bush to Howard November 27, 1940, and Howard to Bush December 14, 1940.
48. On who built the punch, NARA RG227, OSRD, Office of the Chairman, Box 1, Bureau of Ships to Bush, November 8, 1940, 'Howard Project Agreement'. The Yard technician, Don Seiler, who was so important to the Navy's ECM program and

to the building of the Purple analogs, may have been assigned to both the 1938 and 1940-41 punches.

49. NARA SRH-361, "History of the SSA," Vol. II, 027, and SRH-145 "Collection of Memoranda of Operations of SIS Intercept Activities and Dissemination, 1942-1945," 'Report of the Technical Mission to England' April 11, 1941, 002-013.

50. NARA Suitland, Bureau of Ships General Correspondence, June 2, 1941, Lybrand Smith of Bureau (later Research and Inventions) to Howard 'Doulong (sic) Going to MIT'.

51. NSA RAM File, January 2, 1942, Safford to Howard, 'Comparator Received 12-24', and January 6, 1942, BuShips to CNO, 'Manual for Comparator'.

52. The engineer was John F. Skinner, one of several IBM men who would participate in the navy program. NARA RG457, SRH-355, "Naval Security Group History to World War II," 440. Smithsonian History of Computer Project, Interview with Howard Campaigne.

53. Again, this may also have been a means of automating the use of the sheets used to attack wheel settings.

54. NARA Suitland, Bureau of Ships General Correspondence, June 2, 1941, Lybrand Smith of Bureau (later Research and Inventions) to Howard 'Doulong (sic) Going to MIT', and November 11, 1941, 'Doulong (sic) Visit'. Smithsonian History of Computer Project, Interview with Howard Campaigne.

55. The punches were redesigned and remanufactured several times during the war. After MIT made a try in 1940-41, the Gray manufacturing company made a version, then NCR redid them, then new designs were drawn for the postwar era. NSA RAM File, Communications Intelligence Technical Paper-42, "Copperhead I Theory and Copperhead I Equipment." NSA RAM File, OP-20-G to NCML-NCR, February, 1945.

56. NSA RAM File, Safford, OP-20-G to OP-20-A, 'Meeting with Professor Howard', November 5, 1941.

57. NARA RG457, SRH-355, "Naval Security Group History to World War II," 430. On Steinhardt visit, Smithsonian Institution, History of Computers Project, Interview with Howard Campaigne, 19.

58. Some $25,000 was promised to NCR in November, 1940. Some of it may have come from the original NDRC grant, but Bush apparently secured an additional grant for some thirty copies of the counters--although the NDRC was not to become involved in production. NARA Suitland, OSRD Contract Files, OEM-275 November 28, 1941, 'NCR-MIT counters'. Hagley Museum and Library, Accession 1825, *Honeywell v Sperry-Rand* Trial Records, December 2, 1941, NDRC D3 to Desch-NCR, '30 counter-printers'.

59. Hagley Museum and Library, Accession 1825, *Honeywell v Sperry-Rand* Trial Records, January 29, 1942, Desch to NCR ' Secret Work', and February 21, 1942, Desch, 'Report to Management'.

60. By this time, IBM was also working on a system to convert information on cards to other media using light registration. One of the men central to its early electronic work, Arthur H. Dickinson, submitted a patent application on a conversion device on June 16, 1939 and was granted a patent on May 21, 1940.

61. NARA RG457, SRH-355, "Naval Security Group History to World War II," 440.

62. Gordon Welchman, *The Hut Six Story: Breaking the Enigma Codes* (New York: McGraw-Hill, 1982). David Kahn, *Seizing the Enigma* (Boston:Houghton-Mifflin, 1991). The role of captures in the long awaited break into Japanese army systems is discussed in the very impressive, Edward J. Drea, *MacArthur's Ultra* (University of Kansas Press, 1992).

63. On the state of American readiness and some hints about the roles of Mrs. Driscoll and the team at SIS, compare, James Rusbridger, and Eric Nave, *Betrayal at Pearl Harbor* (New York: Summit Books, 1991), and the more scholarly, Edward J. Drea, *MacArthur's Ultra* (University of Kansas Press, 1992). NARA RG457, SRH-355, "Naval Security Group History to World War II," 440, 442. NSA RAM File, OP-20-G to OP-20-A, 'Meeting with Dr. Howard', November 5, 1941. However, Howard was told that the Driscoll problem was not of high priority. NSA RAM File, BuShips to Howard, November 11, 1941.

64. NSA RAM File, November 3 and 5, 1941, Howard-OP-20-G Reports on Meetings, and November 14, 1941, Bureau of Ships to Howard.

65. Photographic plates for data entry had been used on the Cinema Integraph and were being explored for use in the Analyser and the electronic computer at the Institute. NSA RAM File, January 5, 1942, Howard to OP-20-G, 'Report-Glass Plates'. Arnold Dumey letters to Brian Randell, 1975, 'deformation'.
66. NSA RAM File, January 5, 1942, Howard to OP-20-G, 'Report-Glass Plates'. NSA RAM File, OP-20-G to OP-20-A, 'Meeting with Dr. Howard' November 5, 1941.
67. For the man-year estimates a salary of $2,500 was used. The investment was $20,000 for the first Comparator, $25,000 for the Selector and $30,000 for the NDRC project to the beginning of 1942.
68. NARA RG457: SRH-279, "OP-20-G File Communications Intelligence Organization, 1942-46"; SRMN-084, "The Evolution of the Navy's Cryptologic Organization," 2; and SRH-306 "OP-20-G Exploits and Commendations World War II."
69. Interview with Jeff Wenger, 1991.
70. Safford became head of the communications security department which was at arms-length from OP-20-G after the reorganization of 1942. What remains unexplained is the failure of Safford and his men to spot the German's deep penetration of the Atlantic convoy codes during the first years of the war. On the importance of the German codebreaking in the Battle of the Atlantic, NARA RG457, SRH-403, "Selections from the Cryptologic Papers of Rear Admiral J. N. Wenger, USN," 70.
71. Burton K. Wheeler with Paul F. Healy, *Yankee From the West* (New York: Doubleday, 1962). Ladislas Farago, *The Game of the Foxes* (New York: David McKay, 1971). Hooper was called upon for many services, including advice on how to intercept German messages to and from South and Central America. Department of State, March 19,1942, 'Meeting with Mr. Burke', as in, John Mendelsohn (ed), *Covert Warfare: Intelligence, Counterintelligence & Military Deception During the World War II Era* (Garland, 1990).
72. NARA RG457, SRMN-083, "Military Study of Secret Radio Calls, January 1938."
73. Louis Kruh, "Why Was Safford Pessimistic About Breaking the German Enigma Cipher Machine in 1942?" *Cryptologia* 14(1990): 253-257.
74. All other major nations used the same techniques and had done so since World War I, but Wenger was America's advocate. NARA RG457, SRMN-083, "Military Study of Secret Radio Calls, January 1938."
75. NARA RG457, SRH-083, "Military Study of Secret Radio Calls, January 8, 1938 by J. N. Wenger."
76. On automatic direction finding equipment, NARA SRH-197, "US Navy Communications Intelligence, Organization, Liaison and Collaboration 1941-1945," 38.
77. Some reports indicate that in late 1941 the vast majority of the "G" workforce was busy with T/A rather than cryptanalysis. NARA RG457, SRH-403, "Selections from the Cryptologic Papers of Rear Admiral J. N. Wenger, USN."
78. NARA RG457, SRH-403, "Selections from the Cryptologic Papers of Rear Admiral J. N. Wenger, USN," 54.
79. NARA RG457, SRH-279 "OP-20-G, Communication Intelligence Organization 1942-1946."
80. NARA RG457, SRH-355, "Naval Security Group History to World War II," 265. Letter from Joseph Eachus to author. NARA RG457, SRH-153, "Liaison Activities in the U. K.," 41.
81. Figures come from NARA RG457: SRH-151, "Military Study: Communications Intelligence Research Activities, 30, June 1937, by J. N. Wenger" and SRH-150, "Birthday of the Naval Security Group"; and SRH-355 Part II, " Naval Security Group History to World War II." Unfortunately, some years had incompatible series. Thus, I have estimated the numbers for the beginning months of 1943 and 1945.
82. F. H. Hinsley, "British Intelligence in the Second World War: An Overview," *Cryptologia* 14(1990): 1-10. NARA RG457, SRH-152, "Historical Revue of OP-20-G." Apparently, the appointment of Redman as head of Communications created some friction at "G" and within the Navy in general. Ralph Erskine, and Frode Weierud,"Naval Enigma: M4 and Its Rotors," *Cryptologia* 11(1987): 235-244.
83. NARA RG457, SRH-152, "Historical Review of OP-20-G."
84. NARA RG457, SRH-355, "Naval Security Group History to World War II," 330.

85. NARA RG457, SRH-305, "The Undeclared War: The History of RI," 15 November,1943," by Laurance F. Safford, Captain, U. S. Navy.
86. Hagley Museum and Library, Accession 1825, *Honeywell v Sperry-Rand* Trial Records, November 4, 1941, Harrison to NCR, 'Counter project'. NSA RAM File, January 5, 1942, Howard to OP-20-G, 'Report-Glass Plates', and Part II of Report to J. N. Wenger, Capt. "Resume of the Dayton, Ohio Activity During World War II."
87. Hagley Museum and Library, Accession 1825, *Honeywell v Sperry-Rand* Trial Records, March 28, 1942, Harrison to NCR, 'Navy to take over NDRC counter contract'. NARA RG227, Papers of NDRC/OSRD, April 14, 1942, Harrison to Stewart, 'Navy take-Over of Comparator contract'. Hagley Museum and Library, Accession 1825, *Honeywell v Sperry-Rand* Trial Records, March 16, 1942, Stewart to Harrison, 'Bush angry over Navy take-over'. NARA RG227, March 18, 1942, 'Research Progress Report No. 7, The National Cash Register Company, Electrical Research Laboratory'. NARA Suitland, OSRD Contract Files, OEM-275 November 28, 1941, 'NCR-MIT counters'.
88. Library of Congress, Papers of Vannevar Bush, Box 52, October, 1942, Bush-Howard letters 'Re commission'.
89. Interview with Jeff Wenger, 1991. On Wright's role, NSA RAM File, "Conference With IBM," May 23, 1934. NSA. Lou Holland, "Development of Machine Processing in the Naval Security Group," 1.
90. NARA RG457, SRH-403, "Selections from the Cryptologic Papers of Rear Admiral J. N. Wenger, USN," 60. BuShips, NXs329 (945) 5-6-43, Pulse Spotter Equipment, Philco Corporation.
91. The Selector was hastily sent from Cambridge to Washington in the spring of 1942. It was stripped of many of its parts for an emergency, then sent to a closet for the remainder of the war. Library of Congress, Papers of Vannevar Bush, Box 52, Howard to Killian, March 21, 1946, 'rapid selector'.

CHAPTER X

1. NSA RAM File, Report of R. I. Meader, Captain USNR to J. H. Wenger, Captain, USN, "14 Days Training Duty, Report of," January 21, 1949.
2. Hagley Museum and Library, Accession 1825, *Honeywell v Sperry-Rand* Trial Records, April 2, 1942, 'Meader and Howard visit RCA'. NSA RAM File, Ralph Meader to J. N. Wenger, "Report of 14 Days Training Duty, 21 January, 1949", and Part II of Report to J. N. Wenger, Capt. USN, "Resume of the Dayton, Ohio Activity During World War II."
3. Engineering Research Associates, Inc., *High-Speed Computing Devices* (Los Angeles: Tomash Publishers, 1983), contains important biographies of the first men to work as engineers and managers at "M". NARA Suitland, NP43, US Bureau of Ships, NCML File, NCML Organizational Documents. NSA RAM File, April 28, 1942, 'OP-20-G to Meader at Eastman-Kodak'. Hagley Museum and Library, Accession 1825, *Honeywell v Sperry-Rand* Trial Records, July 10, 1942, Desch, 'NCR to John Coombs re work at Eastman Kodak', and Deposition of J. Desch. RAM File, History of OP-20-G /NCML/4e.
4. The estimate of when the IC machine was ready is based on very circumstantial evidence. But, is clear that it was in use well before any other Rapid device, including the American Bombe. NSA RAM File, Report of R. I. Meader, Captain USNR to J. H. Wenger, Captain, USN, "14 Days Training Duty, Report of," January 21, 1949, and Communications Intelligence Technical Paper 1-a, "Technical Report: The Index of Coincidence Machine" March, 1945.
5. Typically, there were other precursors of the IC machine, including patented devices intended for business applications. See. for example, H. Soper, U. S. Patent 1,351,692, August 31, 1920.
6. NSA RAM File, Communications Intelligence Technical Paper 1-a, "Technical Report: The Index of Coincidence Machine'" March, 1945. Correspondence of Arnold Dumey with Brain Randell, 1975.
7. NSA RAM File, OP-20-G to OP-20-A, 'Meeting with Prof. Howard' November 5, 1941, and Communications Intelligence Technical Paper 1-a, "Technical Report: The Index of Coincidence Machine'" March, 1945.
8. Four-character code groups were used in important German and Japanese systems. It is not known if Tessie was originally built for use against both of them. The Japanese high level fleet code used a four digit code. The very

important U-boat short signal code was used to flash location messages and was tapped by the allies for cribs. The short signals were also used as cribs into the four wheel Enigma systems. Tessie was modified later in the war specifically for the German short signals. RAM File, History of OP-20-G /NCML/4e, 106.

9. Letters from Joseph Eachus circa 1988.

10. Letters from Joseph Eachus circa 1988. Near the end of the war, counting circuits were added to the device making it a weak version of a microfilm Bush Comparator. NSA RAM File, History of OP-20-G /NCML/4e.

11. NSA RAM File, Report of R. I. Meader, Captain USNR to J. H. Wenger, Captain, USN, "14 Days Training Duty, Report of," January 21, 1949.

12. NSA RAM File, 'List of Equipment for Enigma Problems'. Note that high policy had led the navy to place little emphasis on Hypo during 1941. Howard was told that Mrs. Driscoll's problem was "not that important" and to place emphasis on other machines. NSA RAM File, November 14, 1941, Bureau of Ships to Howard, 'Driscoll's problem not that important'. Mrs. Driscoll's method may have been quite like Turing's Banburismus and thus amenable to mechanization. F. H. Hinsley, et al, *British Intelligence in the Second World War Vol. III Part II*, Appendix 30, "The Polish, French and British Contributions to the Breaking of the Enigma: A Revised Account," 959. Andrew Hodges, *Alan Turing: The Enigma* (New York: Simon and Schuster, 1983), 233.

13. Britain also had statistical methods, such as Banburismus, which brought forth some ideas about a film machine in England, perhaps as early as 1939. England may have built film devices that equaled or exceeded those built in the United States during the war. Andrew Hodges, *Alan Turing: The Enigma* (New York: Simon and Schuster, 1983), 178, 233.

14. The documentation for the OP-20-G machines that were ordered before Engstrom's group took effective charge seem to have been lost or misplaced. They were not found when a search was made by the navy under several different categories.

15. NSA RAM File, CNO, USNC, CITP TP-33 "Overhaul of Hypo #1," Washington, D.C., June, 1945. Letters to author from Joseph Eachus.

16. NSA RAM File, W. A. Wright to OP-20-G February 21, 1944, 'Comparison of Army and Navy Enigma Equipment'. NARA RG457, SRH-200, "Army-Navy Collaboration 1931-1945," 216-8. For later models and use against Japanese systems: NSA RAM File, June 16, 1947, OP-20-G Research Committee Meeting; January 5, 1945, 'Hypo Stepping Switch'; "History of OP-20-G /NCML/4e"; and CNO, U. S. Naval Communications, CITP TP-24 "JN-37 Problem on Hypo," Washington, D.C., May, 1945.

17. Hagley Museum and Library, Accession 1825, *Honeywell v Sperry-Rand* Trial Records, Deposition of Joseph Desch. NARA Suitland, OSRD Contract Files, OEM-275 November 28, 1941, 'NCR-MIT counters'. NSA RAM Files, Joseph Desch to OSRD, February 12, 1943, 'Only Navy work at NCR'.

18. NSA RAM File, CNO, U. S. Naval Communications, CITP "Machine Descriptions, Washington, D.C., circa 1945. 'Mike, Comparator; "M.A.C. Outlines #17, 70mm Comparator," April 1947. V. Bush, U. S. Patent, Feb, 17, 1959, "Electronic Comparator," 2,873,912.

19. The estimates of the number of Comparators built during the war vary from six to as many as twenty eight.

20. Office of Naval Research, Patent File on 'Electronic Comparator, Vannevar Bush'. V. Bush, U. S. Patent, Feb, 17, 1959, "Electronic Comparator," 2,873,912.

21. Hagley Museum and Library, Accession 1825, *Honeywell v Sperry-Rand* Trial Records, March 2, 1942, 'Howard and Meader visit RCA electronics laboratory', and July 10, 1942, Desch, 'NCR to John Coombs re work at Eastman Kodak'. NSA NCML-CSAW Message File, March 17, 1944 'Punch being modified at Gray'. NSA RAM File, History of OP-20-G /NCML/4e, June 4, 1945, 'Stop using Gray punches'.

22. NSA RAM File, Report of R. I. Meader, Captain USNR to J. N. Wenger, Captain, USN, "14 Days Training Duty, Report of," January 21, 1949. NSA RAM File, CNO, U. S. Naval Communications, CITP TS "Machine Descriptions, Washington, D.C., circa 1945. 'Mike, Comparator'. NCML-CSAW Message File, April 14, 1944, 'Punch being modified at Gray'. The American's were not the only ones to have problems with tape machines. Britain's attempts to create similar

machines, the Robinsons, faced even greater difficulties. As the new Bush Comparator was going into operation, Britain was still testing its first two tape systems and would soon turn away from such devices because coordinating the tapes was too difficult. Allen W. M. Coombs, "The Making of Colossus" *Annals of the History of Computing* 5(1983): 254. Brian Randell,"The Colossus," in N. Metropolis et al (ed), *A History of Computing in the Twentieth Century* (New York, 1980), 47-92.

23. NSA RAM File, "M.A.C. Outlines #17, 70mm Comparator," April 1947. The German inventor, Goldberg, had chosen the black-out methods. Emanuel Goldberg, U. S. Patent 1,838,389, Statistical Machine, December 29, 1931, Filed April 5, 1928.

24. RAM File, Communications Intelligence Paper 6, ICKY, Washington, D.C. April, 1945.

25. NSA NCML-CSAW Message File, messages to and from Dayton and Washington, November 1943 to March, 1945. NSA RAM File, "Final Report, Copperhead II," Communications Intelligence Paper-24, and Communications Intelligence Paper-41, "Copperhead I Punch and Copperhead I Scanner."

26. Later in the war Hypo was altered to perform some of the functions envisioned for Copperhead II. A Letterwriter relay box was put between the incoming tape and the analysis cards to produce new additives and apply them to message groups. The new message was then tested against a master film to locate groups and to test which page of the additive books produced the correct clear code groups. The modification was a lash-up and reflected that even late in the war OP-20-G was responding to crises. NSA RAM File, CNO, U. S. Naval Communications, CITP TP-24 "JN-37 Problem on Hypo," Washington, D.C., May, 1945.

27. Library of Congress, Papers of Vannevar Bush, Box 52, Howard to Killian, March 21, 1946, 'Rapid Selector'. Smithsonian History of Computer Project, Interview with Howard Campaigne.

28. NARA RG457, SRH-349, "Achievements of the SSA In World War II," 18. In January 1941 OP-20-G Washington had 16 IBM machines, in 1945, some 200. NARA RG457, SRH-197, "US Navy Communications Intelligence, Organization, Liaison and Collaboration 1941-1945." University of Pennsylvania, Van Pelt Library-Archives, Papers of John Mauchly, October 11, 1944, 'Mauchly notes on meeting with Kullback of ASA'.

29. David Kahn, *Codebreakers: The Story of Secret Writing* (New York: Macmillan, 1967), 443. Office of Military Government for Germany, Field Information, Hans Rohrbach, "Matematische und Maschinelle Methoden Beim Chiffrieren und Dechiffieren." W. Jensen, Hilfsgerate der Kryptographie (1952), as supplied by Professor Brian Randell.

30. NARA RG457, SRH-274, "Military Cryptanalytics, Part II," 406. On the "G" machines as of September, 1941, NSA RAM File, 'IBM Equipment', 10 September 1941. For a survey of IBM equipment, see, *Machine Methods of Accounting* (New York: IBM, 1937) and for insights into the post war equipment, Harry P. Hartkemeier, *Data Processing* (New York: John Wiley and Sons, 1966).

31. NARA RG457, SRH-274, "Military Cryptanalytics, Part II," 406-11.

32. David Kahn, *Codebreakers: The Story of Secret Writing* (New York: Macmillan, 1967), 441.

33. NSA, Tabulating Machine File, IBM Equipment OPNAV 10 Sept. 1941. The special equipments were: multiple column selector device (sorters); collator counting device; class selection devices for reproducers and tabulator; individual x distributors and digit selectors (tab); carry-over elimination devices (tab); alphabetical summary punching device (tab). See, for some explanation of the attachments, "Principle of Operation of the Alphabetical Accounting Machine: Type 405" (NY: Educational Dept. of the International Business Machines Corporation, circa 1942).

34. NSA, Tabulating Machine file, Safford to DNC, June 6, 1940 and July 18, 1940. NSA RAM File, DNC to Radio Division, Bureau of Ships, July 7, 1941, 'Double tab hours'. For a general description of the machines at OP-20-G, Lou Holland, "Development of Machine Processing in the Naval Security Group." On the Columbia University machines, J. F. Brennan, *The IBM Watson Laboratory at Columbia University* (Armonk, N.Y.: IBM, 1971). W. J. Eckert, "Electronic and Electromagnetic Measuring, Computing and Recording Devices," in *Centennial Symposia, Harvard Observatory Monographs Symposia*

Dec. 1946 (Cambridge: The Observatory, 1948), 169-178. On the cost of attachments supplied by IBM, "IBM Equipment, 10 September, 1941," and for those made at the Yard, NSA RAM File, December 10, 1940, OP-20-G to Bureau of Ships, 'Tabulator Equipment to Cavite'. NARA RG457, SRH-355, "Naval Security Group History to World War II," 404.

35. NSA RAM File, OP-20-G to Radio Sound Branch, September 5, 1941, January 16, 1942. NSA, Tabulating Machine File, July 24, 1941 and Dec 6, 1941 to Radio Sound Branch, Design Division, Bureau of Ships. On frictions with IBM, CNO to BuEng 1-3-24; 'Conference With IBM', May 23, 1934.

36. NSA, Tabulating Machine File, OP-20-G to BuShips, July 24, 1941.

37. Charles S. Bashe, et al, *IBM's Early Computers* (Cambridge, Mass.: MIT Press, 1985), 45.

38. NSA RAM File, 'Counting Devices'. Charles S. Bashe, et al, *IBM's Early Computers* (Cambridge, Mass.: MIT Press, 1985), 418. IBM sent many of its best managers and engineers into the cryptologic agencies during World War II. S. W. Dunwell, who was the head of the research branch for tabulators, future demands, headed the army cryptological tabulator department in Washington.

39. Jeff Wenger reported that in 1942 Joseph Wenger had to make a personal visit to Tom Watson to gain full cooperation. On Luhn, who went to work for IBM in 1941, James W. Perry (ed), *Symposium on Machine Techniques for Information Selection* (Cambridge: MIT, June 10, 1952). Hans P. Luhn, *Review of Information Retrieval Methods* (Yorktown Heights: IBM, October 1, 1958). On the parallel between his KWIC system and the searches for text in context by cryptanalysts, Claire K. Schultz (ed), H. P. Luhn, *Pioneer of Information Science: Selected Works* (New York: Spartan Books, 1968). His method of using all fields on a punch card were matched by the Camel systems of World War II.

40. Interview with Fred Parker and his award winning article, "The Unsolved Messages of Pearl Harbor," *Cryptologia* 13(1991): 295.

41. Library of Congress, Papers of Stanford Caldwell Hooper, Box 17, April 3, 1935, Lemmon to Hooper, 'radio teletype'. NSA RAM File, Report of R. I. Meader, Captain USNR to J. H. Wenger, Captain, USN, "14 Days Training Duty, Report of," January 21, 1949. Electromatic was purchased in 1933 and began its IBM life in 1934 with a very special electric typewriter that was engineered to produce the same mechanical action for every key no matter what a typist's stroke. IBM purchased more than one set of rights to advanced electric typewriters during the 1930s. Conversation with IBM archivist, October 28, 1991. IBM's control over the tabs may have been another reason for seeking its help because the navy did not want to be involved in patent battles.

42. IBM would offer similar equipment to commercial users after the war. For a list of Letterwriter CXCO equipment available from the newly named Justo-writer division of IBM in 1947, see Hagley Museum and Library, Accession 2015, ERA Materials, 'Seminar Meeting, Tuesday March 11, 1947'.

43. In October, 1991 the Library of Congress's holdings on IBM equipment were searched for reference to the Letterwriter equipment as were general guides to office equipment during the 1930s and 1940s. No references were found. On October 29, 1991 IBM archives agreed to search for information on both. No reply arrived. NSA RAM File, CNO, U. S. Naval Communications, CITP TS- "Machine Descriptions," Washington, D.C., circa 1945, 'Letterwriter'. NSA NCML-CSAW Message File, Desch to Meader, November 24, 1943, 'Electromatic typewriters', and July 1, 1944 'Design of Letterwriters'. Charles S. Bashe, et al, *IBM's Early Computers* (Cambridge, Mass.: MIT Press, 1985), 513-4, describes a somewhat different set of machines. He states that IBM had refused similar requests from businesses during the 1930s, not taking any action to create its teletype related equipment until early 1941 after being approached by the Army Air Force to link its communications systems more directly to tab processing. Charles Doty of IBM had the first test model of a tape to card converter ready in May 1941, but this was an Endicott built tape reader /code convertor attached to a traditional keypunch. The description given by Bashe makes this appear to be a different product line through a different segment of IBM.

44. Private Paper on NSA Machinery, 1985. NSA RAM File, CNO, U. S. Naval Communications, CITP TS- "Machine Descriptions, Washington, D.C., circa 1945. 'Letterwriter'. NSA RAM File, CNO, U. S. Naval Communications, CITP, "Machine Comparisons," June 1946.

45. Howard Campaigne, in his Smithsonian interviews, states that appreciable numbers of Letterwriters did not reach OP-20-G until 1943.
46. NSA RAM File, OP-20-G Research Committee meeting, May 26, 1949.
47. NSA RAM File, CNO, U. S. Naval Communications, CITP TS "Machine Descriptions, Washington, D.C., circa 1945. 'Mike, Comparator'.
48. NSA RAM File, CNO, U. S. Naval Communications, Tech paper TS-48, "Machine Comparisons," June, 1946.
49. 'Fruit Machine' USN#12 CXDGCNN-1-ADW. Smithsonian interview with Howard Campaigne, 27.
50. NSA RAM File, CNO to Bureau of Engineering, September 16, 1938, 'Development of Special Communications Devices'.

CHAPTER XI

1. NSA Bombe File, U.S. Navy Op-20-G/Op-20-2, Memo to Station X, "Decision regarding future E policy," app. May, 1942.
2. The Germans used other machines, such as the Khyra, in addition to the Enigma and those used on the Fish systems. But 'E' was the mainstay of the nation's cipher systems, at least until 1944. NARA RG457, SRH-361, "History of the Signal Security Agency." Ralph Erskine, "From the Archives: Tunny Decrypts," *Cryptologia* 12(1988): 59-61. Wolfgang Mache, "Geheimschreiber," *Cryptologia* 10(1986): 230-247.
3. Ralph Erskine, "From the Archives: Tunny Decrypts," *Cryptologia* 12(1988): 59-61. Wolfgang Mache, "Geheimschreiber," *Cryptologia* 10(1986): 230-247. On hand systems, Joseph S. Schick, "With the 849th SIS, 1942-5," *Cryptologia* 11(1987): 29-39.
4. Cipher A. Deavours, and Louis Kruh, *Machine Cryptography and Modern Cryptanalysis* (Dedham, Mass.: Artech House, 1985), 93.
5. Gordon Welchman, *The Hut Six Story* (New York: McGraw-Hill, 1982), 51.
6. David Kahn, *Seizing the Enigma* (Boston: Houghton-Mifflin, 1991), 71.
7. W. A. Wildhack, and Joshua Stern, "The Peek-A-Boo System in the Field of Instrumentation," in J. H. Shera, A. Kent, and J. W. Perry, *Information Systems in Documentation* (New York: Interscience Publishers, 1957), 213. For detail on the history of 'Boo' and the extensive attempts by the National Bureau of Standards to automate such systems in the 1950s, W. A. Wildhack, and Joshua Stern, "The Peek-A-Boo System--Optical Coincidence Subject Cards in Information Searching," in Robert S. Casey and James W. Perry, et al, (ed), *Punched Cards: Their Applications to Science and Industry* 2nd ed. (New York: Reinhold, 1958), 125-151.
8. Jean Stengers,"La guerre des messages codes, 1930-1945" *L'Histoire*, 31(1981): 19-31. Cipher A. Deavours, and Louis Kruh, *Machine Cryptography and Modern Cryptanalysis* (Dedham, Mass.: Artech House, 1985), 117.
9. Andrew Hodges, *Alan Turing: The Enigma* (New York: Simon and Schuster, 1983),175. Thomas Parrish, *The Ultra Americans: The United States' Role in Breaking the Nazi Code* (New York: Stein & Day, 1987),49. Cipher A. Deavours, and Louis Kruh, *Machine Cryptography and Modern Cryptanalysis* (Dedham, Mass.: Artech House, 1985), 117.
10. Cipher A. Deavours, and Louis Kruh, *Machine Cryptography and Modern Cryptanalysis* (Dedham, Mass.: Artech House, 1985), 118. Andrew Hodges, *Alan Turing: The Enigma* (New York: Simon and Schuster, 1983), 175, 184.
11. Cipher A. Deavours, and Louis Kruh, *Machine Cryptography and Modern Cryptanalysis* (Dedham, Mass.: Artech House, 1985), 98.
12. Wladyslaw Kozaczuk, *Enigma* (Frederick, Md.: University Publications of America, 1984). Jean Stengers,"Enigma, The French, the Poles and the British, 1931-1940," in Christopher Andrew, and David Dilks (ed), *The Missing Dimension* (London, 1984). Andrew Hodges, *Alan Turing: The Enigma* (New York: Simon and Schuster, 1983), 170-175.
13. Cipher A. Deavours, and Louis Kruh, *Machine Cryptography and Modern Cryptanalysis* (Dedham, Mass.: Artech House, 1985), 118. Andrew Hodges, *Alan Turing: The Enigma* (New York: Simon and Schuster, 1983), 175. C. A. Deavours, and James Reed, "The Enigma, Part I, Historical Perspectives," *Cryptologia* (October, 1977): 381-391.
14. Andrew Hodges, *Alan Turing: The Enigma* (New York: Simon and Schuster, 1983), 176. Some of the Scandinavian nations may have had sporadic successes

against Enigma and Fish, which they shared with Britain. But the true burden had to be carried by the British. *Cryptologia* 12(1988): 39, review of W. M. Carlgren, *Svensk Underrattelsetjanst 1939-45* (Stockholm, 1985).

15. Alan Hodges, *Alan Turing: The Enigma* (New York: Simon and Schuster, 1983). A. G. Denniston, "The Government Code and Cypher School Between the Wars," *Intelligence and National Security* I(1986): 48-69. Christopher Andrew, *Her Majesty's Secret Service: The Making of the British Intelligence Community* (New York: Penguin, 1987).

16. Martin Campbell-Kelly, *I C L : A Business and Technical History* (Oxford, Clarendon Press, 1989), 118. Gordon Welchman, *The Hut Six Story: Breaking the Enigma Codes* (New York: McGraw-Hill, 1982), 295. Cipher A. Deavours and Louis Kruh, *Machine Cryptography and Modern Cryptanalysis* (Dedham, Mass.: Artech House, 1985), 119, 124.

17. David Kahn, *Seizing the Enigma* (Boston:Houghton-Mifflin, 1991), 141. Andrew Hodges, *Alan Turing: The Enigma* (New York: Simon and Schuster, 1983), 233. The exact nature of the method remains a secret but hints suggest that it was much like IC. At one point, Turing may have considered building a film machine for the method rather than use punched overlay sheet because it would have speeded the search for 'coincidences' as did Bush's machine. But note that for Banburismus to be effective captures of tables of some of the Enigma settings were vital. In 1938, the British used another statistical test called SAGA. It also appears to be the kind of approach used by Mrs. Driscoll in America.

18. Andrew Hodges, *Alan Turing: The Enigma* (New York: Simon and Schuster, 1983), 176. Gordon Welchman, *The Hut Six Story: Breaking the Enigma Codes* (New York: McGraw-Hill, 1982), 295.

19. Thomas H. Flowers, "The Design of Colossus," *Annals of the History of Computing* 5(July 1983): 244.

20. Andrew Hodges, *Alan Turing: The Enigma* (New York: Simon and Schuster, 1983), 180. Martin Campbell-Kelly, *I C L : A Business and Technical History* (Oxford, Clarendon Press, 1989), 118.

21. Such commutator systems had been used in electrical timing instruments, but Keen did truly creative work.

22. Martin Campbell-Kelly, *I C L : A Business and Technical History* (Oxford, Clarendon Press, 1989), 119.

23. A. G. Denniston, "The Government Code and Cypher School Between the Wars," *Intelligence and National Security*, 1(1986): 49-69. F. H. Hinsley, "British Intelligence in the Second World War: An Overview," *Cryptologia* 14(1990): 1-10.

24. David Kahn, *Seizing the Enigma* (Boston:Houghton-Mifflin, 1991), 117, 122, 298.

25. Andrew Hodges, *Alan Turing: The Enigma* (New York: Simon and Schuster, 1983), 184. David Kahn, *Seizing the Enigma* (Boston: Houghton-Mifflin, 1991).

26. F. H. Hinsley, *British Intelligence in the Second World War*, Volume II (New York: Cambridge University Press, 1981), 747.

27. NSA, SRH391, "U. S. Cryptologic History: American Signal Intelligence in North West Africa and Western Europe," 116. Peter Calvocoressi," The Value of Enigma," *The Listener* 3(1977): 135-7. NSA RAM File, Memo to Station X, "Decision regarding future E policy," app. May, 1942. F. H. Hinsley, *British Intelligence in the Second World War*, Vol. I (New York: Cambridge University Press, 1981), 56. Ralph Erskine, "From the Archive: Tunny Decrypts," *Cryptologia* 12(1988): 59. Wolfgang Mache, "Geheimschreiber," *Cryptologia* 10(1986): 230-247. Nigel West, *GCHQ, The Secret Wireless War, 1900-86* (London: Weidenfeld and Nicolson, 1986), 191. D. W. Davies, "The Siemens and Haskle T 52 e Cipher Machine," *Cryptologia* 6(1982): 289-308. David Kahn, "The Geheimschreiber," *Cryptologia* 3(1979): 210-214.

28. This text was written before the appearance of Bradley F. Smith's, *The Codebreaker's War: The Ultra-Magic-Deals* (Novato: Presidio Press, 1993) which contains reference to British and American documents apparently not used in previous analysis of the British-American cryptologic agreements of World War II. Although Smith has some conclusions different from mine, I did not find it necessary to alter my text. Because of my evidence I remain convinced, for example, that the Americans took the lead in their Bombe program and that they intended to produce more than 300 machines. See Smith, 247.

29. Jurgen Rohwer, *The Critical Convoy Battles of March 1943* (London: Ian Allan, 1977), 240. Nigel West, *GCHQ, the Secret Wireless War, 1900-86* (London: Weidenfeld and Nicolson, 1986), 201, 210. F. H. Hinsley, *British Intelligence in the Second World War* vol. III, Part I, (1984), 52.
30. NARA RG457, SRH-361, "History of the Signal Security Agency, Volume Two, The General Cryptanalytic Problems," 017. Louis Kruh, "British-American Cryptanalytic Cooperation and an Unprecedented Admission by Winston Churchill," *Cryptologia* 13(1989): 123-134. Nigel West, *GCHQ*, 201. F. H. Hinsley, *British Intelligence in the Second World War* Vol. I (London: Her Majesty's Stationery Office, 1979) 155. NSA RG457, SRH-197, " U. S. Navy Communications Intelligence, Organization, Liaison and Collaboration, 1941-45." But both Britain and the Dutch provided the Americans with intelligence and cryptanalytic help on Japanese systems earlier than previously thought. See Rear Admiral Edwin T. Layton, *And I Was There: Pearl Harbor and Midway--Breaking the Secrets* (New York: William Morrow, 1985), 206. John W. M. Chapman, "Pearl Harbor: The Anglo-Australian Dimension," *Intelligence and National Security* I(1989): 451-481. James Rusbridger and Eric Nave, *Betrayal at Pearl Harbor* (New York: Summit Books, 1991).
31. NARA RG457, SRH-141, "Papers from the Personal Files of Alfred McCormick, Part 2, March 4, 1944," 'Memorandum for General Bissel, Army-Navy Agreement Regarding Ultra'. NARA RG457, SRH-152, "Historical Review of OP-20-G."
32. Laurance Safford, "Rhapsody in Purple," by Dundas P. Tucker, *Cryptologia*, 6(1981): 193-229, and 346-367. James Rusbridger and Eric Nave, *Betrayal at Pearl Harbor* (New York: Summit Books, 1991). NSA SRH-391, "U. S. Cryptologic History," 114, 117.
33. David Kahn, *Seizing the Enigma* (Boston:Houghton-Mifflin, 1991), 235-6. NARA RG457, SRH-145, "Collection of Memoranda on Operations of SIS Intercept Activities and Dissemination 1942-1945," 'Report of the Technical Mission to England' April 11, 1941, 002-013. Greg Mellen (ed), "Rhapsody in Purple: A New History of Pearl Harbor by Dundas P. Tucker," *Cryptologia*, 6 (1981): 193-228. More balanced views are in, Rear Admiral Edwin T. Layton, *And I Was There: Pearl Harbor and Midway--Breaking the Secrets* (New York: William Morrow, 1985) and, Edward J. Drea, *MacArthur's Ultra* (University of Kansas Press, 1992). The Americans did not give everything to the British, however. NARA RG298, Box 39, Memorandum of R. W. Sylvester to L. Terman, April 11, 1942, tells Terman not to disclose any cryptological work to the British. And the Americans also kept their very important SIGCUM enciphering machine from the British during much of the war. See, NARA RG457, RMA003, May 19,1944, Memorandum for Assistant Chief of Staff, G-2 from Office of the Chief Signal Officer.
34. NARA RG457, SRH-270, "Army Navy FBI COMINT Agreements of 1942" by Robert L. Benson, and the very useful, SRH-005, "Use of CX/MSS Ultra."
35. NARA RG457, SRH-361, "History of the Signal Security Agency, Volume Two, The General Cryptanalytic Problems," and SRH-145, "Collection of Memoranda on Operations of SIS Intercept Activities and Dissemination 1942-1945," 'Report of the Technical Mission to England' April 11, 1941, 002-013.
36. Laurance Safford, "Rhapsody in Purple," by Dundas P. Tucker, *Cryptologia* 6(1981), 193-229, and 346-367. NARA, RG457, SRH-361, "History of the Signal Security Agency," 259, 261. There is some reason to believe that Britain did pass on the ways to crack the simpler 1940 German air force systems. NSA RAM File, "Report to J. N. Wenger, Capt. USN, Resume of the Dayton, Ohio Activity During World War II," and, J. T. Pendergrass, "Cryptanalytic Use of High-Speed Digital Computing Machines," Top-Secret, 1946.
37. David Kahn, *Seizing the Enigma* (Boston: Houghton-Mifflin, 1991), 24, 111-32. NARA RG457, SRH-142, "Ultra and the Campaign Against the U-boat in World War II," by Commander Jerry C. Russell, 009. NARA RG457, SRH-349, "Achievements of the SSA In World War II." The army had little power over any Enigma systems well into 1944. NARA RG457, SRH-361, "History of the Signal Security Agency," Vol. II, 274.
38. The debate has now been extended to the question of how much Britain knew of Japanese systems. James Rusbridger and Eric Nave, *Betrayal at Pearl*

Harbor (New York: Summit Books, 1991). Rusbridger's assertions about Churchill's withholding of information in 1941 are unacceptable. It is known that before 1941 the British shared some work with the Americans and that while the American delegation was in England in 1941, the work of the Empire's Far East group was given to the Americans. A. G. Denniston, "The Government Code and Cypher School Between the Wars," *Intelligence and National Security*, 1(1986): 51. Rear Admiral Edwin T. Layton, *And I Was There: Pearl Harbor and Midway--Breaking the Secrets* (New York: William Morrow, 1985), 93.

39. Louis Kruh, "Why Was Safford Pessimistic About Breaking the German Enigma Machine in 1942?" *Cryptologia* 14(1990): 253-257. David Kahn, *Seizing the Enigma* (Boston: Houghton-Mifflin, 1991), 111, 137.

40. NARA RG457, SRH-403, "Selections from the Cryptologic Papers of Rear Admiral J. N. Wenger, USN."

41. David Kahn, *Seizing the Enigma* (Boston: Houghton-Mifflin, 1991), 237.

42. An invaluable document on British-U. S. Army relationships, NARA RG457, SRH-005, "Use of CX/MSS Ultra," and of equal value, "History of 3-US," as in John Mendelsohn (ed), *Covert Warfare: Intelligence, Counterintelligence & Military Deception During the World War II Era* (Garland, 1989).

43. For the complaints by the American army's SIS, see NARA RG457, SRH-361, "History of the Signal Security Agency" Vol. II. 249-275.

44. Nigel West, *GCHQ, The Secret Wireless War, 1900-86* (London: Weidenfeld and Nicolson, 1986), 200-224. Thomas Parrish, *Roosevelt and Marshall: Partners in Politics and War* (New York: W. Morrow, 1989), 442. James Bamford, *The Puzzle Palace* (Boston: Houghton-Mifflin, 1982), 314-317. NARA RG457, SRH-270, "Army Navy FBI COMINT Agreements of 1942" by Robert L. Benson.

45. Andrew Hodges, *Alan Turing: The Enigma* (New York: Simon and Schuster, 1983), 191. Laurance Safford, "Rhapsody in Purple," by Dundas P. Tucker, *Cryptologia*, 6(1982): 216-17. NSA RAM File: OP-20-G to GC&CS, July 7, 1942; OP-20-G to OP-20 September 3, 1942; J. N. Wenger to OP-20-GM, August 6, 1942 "We wish to construct..."; and Wenger to Ely, August 5, 1942; Engstrom to Meader re Turing visit, January 5, 1943. F. H. Hinsley, *British Intelligence in the Second World War* Vol. I, 56. Joseph Eachus, letter to the author, March 24, 1989.

46. "History of 3-US," in John Mendelshon (ed), *Covert Warfare* (Garland, 1989), 010-012.

47. The OP-20-G group may have been able to crack some low level weather codes by late 1941. The Coast Guard, under Mrs. Friedman, had tapped some clandestine systems. Those breaks were not significant, however. James Rusbridger, and Eric Nave, *Betrayal at Pearl Harbor* (New York: Summit Books, 1991). NARA RG457, SRH-270, "Army Navy FBI COMINT Agreements of 1942" by Robert L. Benson. David Kahn, *Kahn on Codes: Secrets of the New Cryptology* (New York: Macmillan, 1983), 161. The American army could not even intercept enough German messages to be able to apply what few tools it had in the first years of World War II. NARA RG457, SRH-361, "History of the Signal Security Agency," Vol. II, Chpt, XVI.

48. The new four wheel system was cracked by the group at Bletchley Park by December, 1942. But, the break was not a pure cryptanalytic one. It depended upon the capture of documents and the continued failure of the German system managers to follow basic security procedures. David Kahn, *Seizing the Enigma* (Boston: Houghton-Mifflin, 1991), 111.

49. Laurance Safford, "Rhapsody in Purple," by Dundas P. Tucker, *Cryptologia*, 6(1982), 193-229, and 346-367.

50. Some of OP-20-G's men were sent to college to take Spanish lessons during the period and, like Britain, the United States may have tried to employ the older Click and Rod methods against the simple Enigma machines used in the war. C. A. Deavours, "The Black Chamber: A Column: La Methode Des Baton," *Cryptologia* 4(1980): 240-247. NSA, Theodore M. Hannah, "Frank B. Rowlett: A Personal Profile."

51. Even Britain waited what now seems too long to organize its research. Ronald Clark, *Tizard*, (Cambridge: MIT Press, 1965).

52. The Coast Guard, which had been in charge of decrypting rum runner and other clandestine traffic for years, had as its chief cryptanalyst William

Friedman's wife. The clandestine system the Coast Guard attacked must have been very simple compared to the Enigma.

53. The official history of "G" gives the date of the first work on Enigma as the spring of 1941. A participant later recalled a group of some four people under Mrs. Driscoll in the summer of 1940, but the dates he gave for other events were also off by one year. See Louis Kruh, "Why Was Safford Pessimistic About Breaking the German Enigma Machine in 1942," *Cryptologia*, 14(1990): 256. The estimates of work are from, NARA RG457, SRH-152," Historical Revue of OP-20-G," 23. These figures conform to the dates on translations of German materials. American intercepts up to 1943 seem not to have been decrypted and translated until 1945 or later.

54. Andrew Hodges, *Alan Turing: The Enigma* (New York: Simon and Schuster, 1983), 235. F. H. Hinsley, *British Intelligence in the Second World War*, Vol. 3, Part I (London: Her Majesty's Stationery Office, 1984), 57. RG457, SRH-361, "History of the Signal Security Agency," 277.

55. NSA RAM File, 'To the President', March 17, 1943. On American independence, Andrew Hodges, *Alan Turing: The Enigma* (New York: Simon and Schuster, 1983), 235. RG457, SRH-361, "History of the Signal Security Agency: Vol. II, The General Cryptanalytic Problem," 260. Fears about GC&CS were not confined to the United States. For many months, buses stood by to take the codebreakers to ports where they could be evacuated to North America.

56. Thomas Parish, *The Ultra Americans* (New York: Stein and Day, 1986), 159. Ralph Erskine, and Frode Weierud, "Naval Enigma: M4 and Its Rotors," *Cryptologia* 11(October 1987): 235-247. F. H. Hinsley, et al, *British Intelligence in the Second World War* III part 2, (London: Her Majesty's Stationery Office, 1984), 778. On anti-submarine techniques, Edwin P. Hoyt, *The Death of the U-Boats* (New York: W. Morrow, 1988). On the fear that all services might shift to M4, NSA RAM File, Wesley A. Wright to OP-20-G, February 21, 1944.

57. NARA RG457, SRH-306, "OP-20-G Exploits and Commendations in World War II," 016. NSA RAM File, "Report to J. M. Wenger, Capt. USN, Resume of the Dayton, Ohio Activity During World War II," and J. T. Pendergrass, "Cryptanalytic Use of High-Speed Digital Computing Machines," Top-Secret, 1946.

58. F. H. Hinsley, et al, *British Intelligence in the Second World War*, Vol. III, Appendix 19, "The Breaking of the U-boat Enigma," 749.

59. F. H. Hinsley, et al, *British Intelligence in the Second World War*, Vol. III, Appendix 19, "The Breaking of the U-boat Enigma," 750. David Kahn, *Seizing the Enigma* (Boston: Houghton-Mifflin, 1991), 208.

60. F. H. Hinsley, *British Intelligence in the Second World War* Vol. I, (London: Her Majesty's Stationery Office, 1979), 55.

61. NSA RAM File, Wenger to OP-20-G, September 3, 1942, 'Cryptanalysis of the German (Enigma) Cipher Machine'.

62. Andrew Hodges, *Alan Turing: The Enigma* (New York: Simon and Schuster, 1983), 225-7.

63. Andrew Hodges, *Alan Turing: The Enigma* (New York: Simon and Schuster, 1983), 227.

64. NSA RAM File, Secret Memorandum of April 25, 1942, 'Construct a machine of the general type', and "Resume of the Dayton, Ohio Activity During World War II," 1. NSA SRH-391, "U. S. Cryptologic History," 117, 120-3.

65. NSA RAM File, Wenger to OP-20-GM, August 6, 1942, 'Recent Information on E'.

66. NSA Bombe File, "It is desired to construct..." April 25, 1942, and August 5, 1942, Wenger to Ely.

67. NSA RAM File, 'Decision Regarding Future E Policy', app May 1942, and 'For GC&CS', August 5, 1942.

68. NSA RAM File, app. May, 1942, OP-20-G to Station X, 'Latest Thoughts on Electronic Developments'.

69. Much of the information on GC&CS's actions and intentions remains in closed archives and some informed historical guesses have to be made. One of those is that GC&CS's failure to send requested documentation was as much the result of the slow pace of its four wheel Bombe program and a desire to keep-face as it was the result of a desire to monopolize all the "E" work.

70. NSA RAM File, OP-20-G to GC&CS, July 7, 1942, 'Eachus & Ely', and August 5, 1942, 'Send Wiring Diagram'. NARA RG457, SRH-306, "OP-20-G Exploits and

Commendations in World War II," 23, 'Shark was not all'. Andrew Hodges, *Alan Turing: The Enigma* (New York: Simon and Schuster, 1983), 236. F. H. Hinsley, *British Intelligence in the Second World War*, Volume II (New York: Cambridge University Press, 1981), 55-57.

71. Letters from Howard Campaigne to Brian Randell circa 1975. Thomas H. Flowers, "The Design of Colossus," *Annals of the History of Computing* 5(July 1983): 224. I. J. Good, "Early Work on Computers at Bletchley," *Cryptologia* 3(1979): 65-77.
72. The full details of the cryptanalytic techniques underlying the Robinsons remain as classified information. By the war's end, one of the Robinsons used four tapes.
73. Thomas H. Flowers, "The Design of Colossus," *Annals of the History of Computing* 5(July 1983): 240. Allen W. M. Coombs, "The Making of Colossus" *Annals of the History of Computing* 5(1983): 253-259. W. W. Chandler, " The Installation and Maintenance of Colossus," *Annals of the History of Computing* 5(1983): 260. Andrew Hodges, *Alan Turing: The Enigma* (New York: Simon and Schuster, 1983), 268. Although their documentation is still classified, there were additional electronic machines in GC&CS's arsenal by the end of the war. Apparently, they went beyond Colossus.
74. NARA RG457, SRH-349, "Achievements of the SSA In World War II," and SRH-361, "History of the Signal Security Agency."
75. NSA RAM File, OP-20-G to GC&CS, app. May, 1942, 'Future E Policy', and Wenger to Ely, August 5, 1942.
76. Hagley Museum and Library, Accession 1825, *Honeywell v Sperry-Rand* Trial Records, Deposition of Joseph Desch, and Chronological File, June 6, 1942, 'Armed Guards to Dayton'. NSA RAM File, Part II of Report to J. N. Wenger, Capt. USN, "Resume of the Dayton, Ohio Activity During World War II."
77. Contract NXs7892. NSA RAM File, Part II of Report to J. N. Wenger, Capt. USN, "Resume of the Dayton, Ohio Activity During World War II." RCA may have been the prime contractor, as indicated by, NARA, Suitland, Bureau of Ships General Correspondence N36-6 to C-N36-10, November 14, 1942. 'NCR Priority Rating'. It has proven impossible to trace the connection.
78. Ronald Lewin, *The American Magic* (New York: Farrar, Straus, Giroux, 1982), 85. Rear Admiral Edwin T. Layton, et al, *"And I Was There": Pearl Harbor and Midway--Breaking the Secrets* (William Morrow & Co., Inc., 1985), 95. W. J. Holmes, *Double-Edged Secrets* (Annapolis: Naval Institute Press, 1979). One story is that Washington found different additives from their JN-25 analyses and thought that Hawaii was far off-base regarding the recovered code groups.
79. NSA RAM File, Report of R. I. Meader, Captain USNR to J. H. Wenger, Captain, USN, "14 Days Training Duty, Report of," January 21, 1949.
80. NSA RAM File, August 5, 1942, Wenger to Ely. NSA RAM File, Part II of Report to J. N. Wenger, Capt. USN, "Resume of the Dayton, Ohio Activity During World War II." Hagley Museum and Library, Accession 1825, *Honeywell v Sperry-Rand* Trial Records, August 19, 1942, Desch to Engineering Department, 'Special Switch', and September 18, 1942, 'Change in Specifications'.
81. NSA RAM File, Part II of Report to J. N. Wenger, Capt. USN, "Resume of the Dayton, Ohio Activity During World War II."
82. The electronic American Bombe would have 64 double wheels calling for at least 7,000 tubes, probably twice that. Amplifiers and control electronic would probably have called for another ten thousand or so. Correspondence with Joseph Eachus. NSA RAM File, Wenger to GC&CS, September 4, 1942, 'Electronic Device'.
83. NSA RAM File, Part II of Report to J. N. Wenger, Capt. USN, "Resume of the Dayton, Ohio Activity During World War II."

CHAPTER XII

1. The four wheel Bombe should have been at least twenty-six times faster than the three wheel version to process ciphers at the same rate. Neither the British or Americans achieved that speed during World War II.

2. F. H. Hinsley, *British Intelligence in the Second World War*, Volume II (New York: Cambridge University Press, 1981), 56. For the independent research agreement, interview with Joseph Eachus. The situation with the American army may have been even more critical. It was a pure consumer of Ultra and much other intelligence during the North African invasion and as late as February 1943, it was dependent on GC&CS for German signals intelligence. NARA RG457, SRH-364, "History of the Signal Security Agency, Volume One Parts 1 and 2, 1939-1945."
3. NSA RAM File, September 3, 1942, Wenger to OP-20, 'Cryptanalysis of the German (Enigma) Machine'. F. H. Hinsley, *British Intelligence in the Second World War*, Volume II (New York: Cambridge University Press, 1981), 57. Hagley Museum and Library, Accession 1825, *Honeywell v Sperry-Rand* Trial Records, September 18, 1942, Desch to Engineering Department. Compare the Americans promised production rate with Keen's output. Martin Campbell-Kelly, *I C L : A Business and Technical History* (Oxford: Clarendon Press, 1989), 118-119. If the United States had built the 350 machines rather than the 100 in the first batch, the cost would have been a staggering $16,000,000 based on the $45,000 per machine for the production run.
4. While NARA SRH-391, "U. S. Cryptologic History," 119, states the Americans the navy planned to make the 100 machines at a production rate of one a day, RAM File, documents substantiate the 350 total and two per day estimates.
5. Evidence cited below indicates that in autumn 1942 the Americans did plan on more than 100 machines and production rate greater than Bradley F. Smith cites in his, *The Codebreakers War: The Ultra Magic Deals* (Novato: Presidio Press, 1993), 247.
6. Hagley Museum and Library, Accession 1825, *Honeywell v Sperry-Rand* Trial Records, September 18, 1942, Desch to Engineering Department. F. H. Hinsley, *British Intelligence in the Second World War*, Volume II (New York: Cambridge University Press, 1981), 56. NARA RG457, SRH-361, "History of the Signal Security Agency," 274. NSA RAM File: OP-20-G to GC&CS July 7, 1942; OP-20-G to OP-20- September 3,1942; J. N. Wenger to OP-20-GM, August 6, 1942; Wenger to Ely, August 5, 1942; and 'Engstrom to Meader re Turing visit', January 1, 1943.
7. Of course, the Americans did not suspect that Britain had its own Russian informant who was telling all to Stalin. Christopher Andrew, and Oleg Gordievsky, *KGB: The Inside Story of Its Foreign Operations from Lenin to Gorbachev* (New York: Harper Collins, 1990), 304.
8. NARA RG457, SRH-306, "OP-20-G Exploits and Commendations in World War II," 19. F. H. Hinsley, *British Intelligence in the Second World War*, Volume II (New York: Cambridge University Press, 1981), 57. Andrew Hodges, *Alan Turing: The Enigma* (New York: Simon and Schuster, 1983), 243.
9. Very useful on the question of the U. S. Army's Ultra struggle is, "Origins, Functions & Problems of the Special Branch, M. I. S.," in John Mendelshon (ed), *Covert Warfare: Intelligence, Counterintelligence and Military Deception During the World War II Era* (Garland, 1989).
10. Andrew Hodges, *Alan Turing: The Enigma* (New York: Simon and Schuster, 1983), 233, 240. NARA SRH-197, "US Navy Communications Intelligence, Organization, Liaison and Collaboration 1941-1945," British reports of OP-20-G contributions including Shark, 024-25, and February 5, 1943, 'GC&CS to OP-20-G, 'Thanks for Limpet work'.
11. Andrew Hodges, *Alan Turing: The Enigma* (New York: Simon and Schuster, 1983), 236. NSA RAM File, January 5, 1943, 'Report on Turing Visit to Dayton'.
12. Hagley Museum and Library, Accession 1825, *Honeywell v Sperry-Rand* Trial Records: July 22, 1942 Desch to Draft Board 'Coombs on secret project'; August 6, 1942, NCR to Signal Corps, 'Can not take new work'; and November 1942, Desch, 'List of men on secret project'. NSA RAM File, October 14, 1942, Memorandum for OP-20, 'Establishment of OP-20-G Activities at Dayton, Ohio'.
13. NSA RAM File: Director of Naval Communications to Vice Chief of Naval Operations, 'Navy Contract NXs7892', March 17,1943; 'From the President to Chairman of the War Production Board', March 17, 1943; and September 3, 1942, Wenger to OP-20-G, 'Two million for Bombes'.

14. NSA RAM File, Coded telex, 'Meader to Stone', June 15, 1943.
15. NSA RAM File, Report of R. I. Meader, Captain USNR to J. H. Wenger, Captain, USN, "14 Days Training Duty, Report of," January 21, 1949.
16. NSA RAM File: January 5, 1943, 'Report on Turing visit to Dayton'; January 20, 1943, Engstrom to Meader, 'Change Bombe Design'; and March 17, 1943 'Prototypes constructed'.
17. NSA RAM File, January 20, 1943, Engstrom to Meader, 'Change Bombe Design'.
18. F. H. Hinsley, et al, *British Intelligence in the Second World War* Vol. II, (New York: Cambridge University Press, 1981), Appendix 19, "The Breaking of the U-boat Enigma," 747-752. The best works on the fragility of the "E" solutions are: David Kahn, *Seizing the Enigma* (Boston:Houghton-Mifflin, 1991), and NARA RG457, SRH-403, "Selections from the Cryptologic Papers of Rear Admiral J. N. Wenger, USN."
19. NSA RAM File, December 11, 1942, Horn to Robinson, 'Procurement of Materials for 7892', and December 28, 1942, CNO to Deeds, 'Help needed on special project at NCR'.
20. NSA RAM File, January 5, 1943, Wenger to Meader, 'Turing Visit'. Andrew Hodges, *Alan Turing: The Enigma* (New York: Simon and Schuster, 1983), 236.
21. NSA Ram File: March 17, 1943, 'To the President, Bombe Project'; March 17, 1943, 'From the President, Bombe Project'; File Part II of Report to J. N. Wenger, Capt. USN, "Resume of the Dayton, Ohio Activity During World War II"; and January 12, 1943, NCR to NDRC, 'NCR will do only navy work'. Although the Bombe project ran well over its budget (100% or more) the average cost of the first 100 bombes was one-half the price of a single Mitchell bomber. *U.S. Airforce Museum*, Wright Patterson Airbase, 52.
22. NSA RAM File, May 19, 1943, 'Report of meeting with Travis-GC&CS will determine work'. F. H. Hinsley, *British Intelligence in the Second World War*, Volume II (New York: Cambridge University Press, 1981), 57.
23. NARA RG457, SRH-403, "Selections from the Cryptologic Papers of Rear Admiral J. N. Wenger, USN," 72.
24. NSA NCML-Message File, for example, June 4, 1943, 'Use most Adam-Eve time for real tests'.
25. NSA NCML-CSAW Message file, May 24, 1943, 'DC has sent test problems for prototypes', and May 29, 1943, 'Adam Eve have serious technical problems'. The first British four wheel Bombe was completed in June, 1943. F. H. Hinsley, *British Intelligence in the Second World War*, Volume II (New York: Cambridge University Press, 1981), 748.
26. Hagley Museum and Library, Accession 1825, *Honeywell v Sperry-Rand* Trial Records, May 15, 1943, Joseph Desch to W. G. Beyrer, 'Wages at the NCR Laboratory'. NSA NCML-CSAW Message File, May 31, 1943, Howard to Washington, 'Tell crew what plugboard is for'. NSA RAM File, History of OP-20-G /NCML/4e.
27. NSA NCML-CSAW Message File, May 28, 1943, 'Desch to Washington', and 'Eachus to Dayton'.
28. NSA NCML-CSAW Message File, May 29, 1943, 'Shorts and opens', and May 31, 1943, 'Can use part of machine only'.
29. NSA NCML-CSAW Message File, May 20, 1943, 'Redman Visit'. and May 29, 1943 'Adam and Eve problems'. F. H. Hinsley, *British Intelligence in the Second World War*, Volume II (New York: Cambridge University Press, 1981), 748. Andrew Hodges, *Alan Turing: The Enigma* (New York: Simon and Schuster, 1983), 267. W. W. Chandler, " The Installation and Maintenance of Colossus," *Annals of the History of Computing* 5(1983): 261.
30. NSA NCML-CSAW Message File, June 14, 1943, 'Cain and Abel'.
31. NSA NCML-CSAW Message File, June 18, 1943, 'Engstrom calls for major changes to Bombe, Meader refuses'.
32. NSA NCML-CSAW Message File, June 18, 1943, 'Engstrom calls for major changes to Bombe, Meader refuses'.
33. Engstrom had asked for a machine that did not need to have its rotors replaced for each run. He wanted an automatic system to change the rotor or wheel wiring and he wanted a machine that was much faster than the planned production model. He may not have realized it but he was asking for something close to an electronic computer--that could not built in a few months.

34. NSA NCML-CSAW Message File, June 18, 1943, 'Meader to Engstrom'.
35. The first "formal" production model was turned over to the navy at Dayton for testing on July 4, 1943 and its first test run was on July 23, 1943. Cain and Abel were off the line in the first week of July but were not ready for final testing until the last week of the month. Another complication was the delayed completion of the new building in Washington. Desch did make some minor changes after Engstrom's request. NSA NCML-CSAW Message File, July 6, 1943, July 26, 1943, and July 23, 1943, 'Status of Bombes'.
36. NSA NCML-CSAW Message File, July 26, 1943, Dayton to Washington 'Bombes may not work'.
37. NSA NCML-CSAW Message File, July 29, 1943, Desch to Engstrom, July 29, 1943, 'Fast wheel running too hot, bombe may not work'. Apparently, Desch had replaced the small fast wheel on the first prototypes with ones the same size as the others to please Engstrom.
38. NSA History and Publications Division, "The Bombe: Prelude to Modern Cryptanalysis." NSA RAM File, CNO, U. S. Naval Communications, CITP TS-3 "Drag Grenade," Washington, D.C., February, 1945. NSA RAM File, CNO, U. S. Naval Communications, CITP TS-11 "General Description of N-530, Bombe," Washington, D.C., circa 1945. Robert I. Atha, "Bombe! I Could Hardly Believe," *Cryptolog* 6(1985): 1-10.
39. NSA RAM File, CNO, U. S. Naval Communications, CITP TS-11 "General Description of N-530, Bombe," Washington, D.C., circa 1945.
40. For a three wheel run, the Polish Bomba took ninety minutes, the British version took an average of thirteen minutes. The American Bombe took less than one minute. For four wheel problems, the British four wheel Bombe took thirty minutes and the American twenty minutes. The Desch Bomb was also more than a competitor to the American SIS's huge advanced relay machine, Madame X, in terms of raw speed. Although Madame X cost one million dollars, it took ten times as long as a navy Bomb for a single three wheel run and thirteen times longer for a four wheel run. As noted below, the X was able to run more menus at one time. NSA RAM File, W. A. Wright to OP-20-G February 21, 1944, 'Comparison of Army and Navy Enigma Equipment'.
41. Robert I. Atha, "Bombe! I Could Hardly Believe," *Cryptolog* 6(1985): 1-10.
42. NSA NCML-CSAW Message File, September 3, 1943, 'Two bombes being set-up for tests in D.C.'.
43. NSA NCML-CSAW Message File, November 12, 1943, '85 Bombes in D.C.'
44. The first Bombe contract was terminated on December 1, 1943, but some of the first models continued to trickle into Washington as late as summer 1944. NSA RAM File, History of OP-20-G /NCML/4e, June, 1944, 'n530 bombes'.
45. NSA NCML-CSAW Message File, November 29, 1943, 'Bombe shipment from Dayton'.
46. NSA RAM File, Part II of Report to J. N. Wenger, Capt. USN, "Resume of the Dayton, Ohio Activity During World War II."
47. H. F. Hinsley, et al, *British Intelligence in the Second World War*, Volume II (New York: Cambridge University Press, 1981), 57-8 and 752. Andrew Hodges, *Alan Turing: The Enigma* (New York: Simon and Schuster, 1983), 262.
48. NARA RG457, SRH-403, "Selections from the Cryptologic Papers of Rear Admiral J. N. Wenger, USN," 71.
49. NARA RG457, SRH-403, "Selections from the Cryptologic Papers of Rear Admiral J. N. Wenger, USN," 72. These estimates were presented by a man who knew all the details, Joseph Wenger.
50. H. F. Hinsley, et al, *British Intelligence in the Second World War*, Volume II (New York: Cambridge University Press, 1981), 752. NARA RG457, SRH-141, "Papers from the Personal Files of Alfred McCormick, Part 2," March 4, 1944, 'Memorandum for General Bissel, Army-Navy Agreement Regarding Ultra'. Thomas Parrish, *The Ultra Americans: The United States' Role in Breaking the Nazi Code* (New York: Stein & Day, 1987), 79. NSA RAM File, February 21, 1944, W. A. Wright to OP-20-G, 'Comparison of Army and Navy Enigma Equipment'.
51. NSA NCML-CSAW Message File, July 20, 1943, 'New procedure, grenade', and August 14, 1943, 'Progress on grenade'. The grenades were also used on the 4 wheel problems when it was thought that one of the wheel settings was known.
52. NSA RAM File, CNO, U. S. Naval Communications, "Brief Descriptions of RAM Equipment," Washington, D.C., October, 1947. NSA RAM File, Report of

R. I. Meader, Captain USNR to J. H. Wenger, Captain, USN, "14 Days Training Duty, Report of," January 21, 1949.

53. NSA RAM File, CNO, U. S. Naval Communications, CITP TP-33 "Overhaul of Hypo #1," Washington, D.C., June, 1945.

54. Bradley F. Smith's, *The Codebreakers War* (Novato: Presidio Press, 1993), details the struggles of the army to gain entry into Ultra.

55. NSA Theodore M. Hannah, "Frank B. Rowlett: A Personal Profile," 5-22. NARA RG457, SRH-004, "The Friedman Lectures on Cryptology."

56. NARA RG457, SRH-403, "Selections from the Cryptologic Papers of Rear Admiral J. N. Wenger, USN," 05.

57. Thomas Parrish, *The Ultra Americans: The United States' Role in Breaking the Nazi Code* (New York: Stein & Day, 1987), 45.

58. NARA RG457, SRH-361, "History of the Signal Security Agency," Volume II, 82, and SRH-362 History of the SSA Vol. III, The Japanese Army Problems: Cryptanalysis, 1942-1945." Edward J. Drea, *MacArthur's Ultra* (University of Kansas Press, 1992), 10. NARA RG457, SRH-145,"Collection of Memoranda on Operations of SIS Intercept Activities and Dissemination 1942-1945," 01, and SRH-361, "History of the SSA, Vol. II, 250, 272." Ronald Lewin, *The American Magic* (New York: Farrar-Strauss, 1982).

59. NARA RG457, SRH-004, "The Friedman Lectures on Cryptology," 171.

60. Cipher A. Deavours and Louis Kruh, *Machine Cryptography and Modern Cryptanalysis* (Dedham, Mass.: Artech House, 1985), 238. NARA RG457, SRH-305, "The Undeclared War: The History of RI," 15 November,1943," by Laurance F. Safford, Captain, U. S. Navy, and SRH-159, "Preliminary Historical Report of the Solution of the B Machine."

61. NARA RG457, SRH-145, "Collection of Memoranda on Operations of SIS Intercept Activities and Dissemination 1942-1945," 'Report of the Technical Mission to England' April 11, 1941, 002-013.

62. Edward J. Drea, *MacArthur's Ultra* (Lawrence: University of Kansas Press, 1992), xii, 61-2.

63. Again, the documents found in the Garland *Covert Warfare* series are most rewarding. See, "History of 3-US," 010-026, and "Origins, Functions and Problems of the Special Branch, MIS." Useful background on army intelligence is in, Bruce W. Bidwell, *History of the Military Intelligence Division, Department of the Army General Staff: 1775-1941* (University Publications of America, nd).

64. NSA RAM File, June 23, 1943, OP-20-G to OP-20-, 'Army has agreed to tell England too much'. NARA RG457, SRH-349, "Achievements of the SSA In World War II," 31, and SRH-361, "History of the Signal Security Agency, Volume Two, The General Cryptanalytic Problems," 11-22, 250, 276-283.

65. NARA RG457, SRH-361, "History of the Signal Security Agency, Volume Two, The General Cryptanalytic Problems," 235-245.

66. Edward J. Drea, *MacArthur's Ultra* (Lawrence: University of Kansas Press, 1992), xii. Geoffrey St. Vincent, *On Ultra Active Service* (Richmond, Australia: Spectrum Publications, 1991), 194-231.

67. NARA RG457, SRH-349, "Achievements of the SSA In World War II," 18. University of Pennsylvania Van Pelt Library-Archives, Papers of John Mauchly, 2B-10:a 209.14, October 11, 1945 and April 14, 1945 'Visit to SIS and Cryptologic Problems'. NARA RG457, SRH-361, "History of the Signal Security Agency, Volume Two, The General Cryptanalytic Problems," 237.

68. NARA RG457, SRMA011, "Senior Staff Meeting Notes," August 18, 1942, Friedman memorandum 'Establish Section F'. David J. Crawford, The Autoscritcher and the Superscritcher, forthcoming, *The Annals of the History of Computing*, illustrates the advanced technical achievements of "F". In fact, "F" may have forged a bit ahead of OP-20-G in respect to the use of digital electronics. One reason may have been that "F" was under less pressure to solve immediate cryptologic crises. Again, NSA SRH-391, "U. S. Cryptologic History," contains dates somewhat different than those found in RAM file documents and other relevant SRH volumes.

69. NARA RG457, SRH-361, "History of the Signal Security Agency, Volume Two, The General Cryptanalytic Problems," 287.

70. NSA SRH-391, "U. S. Cryptologic History," 120, provides a hint that the SIS's relay machine may have first been explored by the British and shown to the

Americans under direct order from Churchill. Other sources, such as a letter from George Stibitz to the author, suggest the relay machine was an American idea.

71. NSA RAM File, J. N. Wenger to OP-20-G, September 3, 1942, "Part II of Report of J. N. Wenger, Capt. USN," 1. Letter to the author from George R. Stibitz, June 7, 1987. NSA RG457, SRH-361, "History of the Signal Security Agency," 250, 257, 272-3. At least one source claims that the American army's cryptologists were informed of and worked on the FISH traffic as early as August, 1942. That source also claims that some machines were built in America for the automated solution of that binary system. However, there is no claim that the army built anything like the Colossus for the problem. See, NARA RG457, SRH-349, "Achievements of the SSA In World War II," 18.

72. NARA RG227, Box 73, February 29, 1944, Stibitz to NDRC, 'Secrecy re NCR product'. Williams went on to build many huge relay computers for the military ordnance groups during World War II and he designed and patented an electronic computer. Michael R. Williams, *A History of Computing Technology* (Englewood Cliffs, N. J.: Prentice-Hall, 1985), 225-240. Hagley Museum and Library, Accession 1825, *Honeywell v Sperry-Rand* Trial Records, February, 1942, S. B. Williams to NDRC, 'Fire control proposal', and Reports on Electronic Computer Designs by S. B. Williams, November 1941, January 1942, March 13, 1942. NSA RAM File, September 3, 1942, 'Wenger to OP-20-G, bombe project'; September 9, 1942, 'Machine Research Section (F); "Part II of Report of J. N. Wenger, Capt. USN," 1; and October 10, 1942, 'Enigma Machine Contract'. Letter to the author from George R. Stibitz, June 7, 1987. The army's single machine cost over $1,000,000. NSA RG457, SRH-361, "History of the Signal Security Agency," 257, 272-3. NARA RG457, SRH-349, "Achievements of the SSA In World War II," 29.

73. NARA RG457, SRH-361, "History of the Signal Security Agency, Volume Two, The General Cryptanalytic Problems," 251.

74. NSA RAM File, February 21, 1944, W. A Wright to OP-20-G, 'Comparison of Army and Navy Enigma Equipment', and January 18, 1943, to OP-20-G/da, 'Report of Meeting on Army Bombe'.

75. NSA RAM File, Part II of Report to J. N. Wenger, Capt. USN, "Resume of the Dayton, Ohio Activity During World War II," and "History of NCML and OP-20-G-4E, June, 1944," 'n1530 bombes in operation'.

76. NSA RAM File, February, 21, 1944, W. A. Wright to OP-20-G. 'Comparison of Army and Navy Enigma Equipment'.

77. SIS did construct additions for 003. One was the Dudbuster which apparently eliminated more false hits. The only other SIS Enigma machine was the very complex Superscritcher of early 1945 which was designed to attack the latest modification to the Enigma. But it was not completed before the end of the war. David J. Crawford, The Autoscritcher and the Superscritcher, forthcoming, *The Annals of the History of Computing*. NSA RAM File, 'Cryptanalytic Equipment for Enigma Problems', 1945.

78. F. H. Hinsley, *British Intelligence in the Second World War*, Volume I (New York: Cambridge University Press, 1979), 58. NARA RG457, SRH-361, "History of the Signal Security Agency, Volume Two, The General Cryptanalytic Problems,"15, 243, 269, 277.

79. David J. Crawford, The Autoscritcher and the Superscritcher, forthcoming, *The Annals of the History of Computing*. NARA RG457, SRH-361, "History of the Signal Security Agency, Volume Two, The General Cryptanalytic Problems," 269-270.

80. NSA RAM File, CNO, U. S. Naval Communications, CITP TS-6 "Rattler," Washington, D.C., circa 1945. NSA NCML-CSAW Message File, October 22, 1943 Steinhardt to GM, 'Viper Design'; November 24, 1943, Ely to Desch 'Design of plugboard to automate Viper stecker analysis'; and August 14, 1943, 'Python to be shipped to Washington'.

81. On the Freak, private paper on cryptologic machines and, SSA, FOIA release, 'Freak'. Also useful on the army devices are the letters of Arnold Dumey to Brian Randell, circa 1975. The navy also worked on Rapid Machines to crack Hagelin ciphers. NSA NCML-CSAW Message File, December 6, 1944, Engstrom to Mumma, 'Satyr'. NSA RAM File, RICKY, 1945.

82. David J. Crawford, The Autoscritcher and the Superscritcher, forthcoming, *The Annals of the History of Computing*. NARA RG457, SRH-361. "History of the Signal Security Agency, Volume Two, The General Cryptanalytic Problems," 269-

270. NSA RAM File, CNO, U. S. Naval Communications, CITP-TS-39, "Duenna Operations Manual," March 1946, and TS-20 "Bulldozer Operating Manual."
83. NARA Suitland, NP43, US Bureau of Ships, NCML File, January 16, 1945, 'Commendation for John Palmer, et al'.
84. NARA RG457, SRH-361, "History of the Signal Security Agency, Volume Two, The General Cryptanalytic Problems," 292.
85. Friedman sought a joint army-navy program, but the navy never accepted the idea. NARA RG457, SRMA-011, "Senior Staff Meeting Notes," April 3, 1945, 'Friedman's joint work suggestion', 174, 231, 321. Samuel S. Snyder, "Abner: The ASA Computer, Part I: Design," *NSA Technical Journal* 25(1980): 49. On turf battles among the services, Louis Kruh, "Army-Navy Collaboration for Cryptanalysis of Enemy Systems," *Cryptologia* 16(1992): 145-164.
86. Robert William Love, Jr., *The Chiefs of Naval Operations*, (Annapolis: Naval Institute Press, 1980), 137-192.
87. NSA RAM File: August 21, 1945, 'Continuation and Development of Communication Intelligence'; Part II of Report to J. N. Wenger, Capt. USN, "Resume of the Dayton, Ohio Activity During World War II"; December 21, 1945, CNO to BUShips, 'Continue to fund NCML'; and March 21, 1946, OP-20-G 'History of Formation of ERA'.
88. NSA RAM File, December 20, 1945, 'ERA post war research plan', and July 20, 1946, Engstrom-BuShips, 'Use Naval laboratories, not ERA'.
89. NARA RG457, SRH-267, "History of Engineering Research Associates." NSA RAM File, September 12, 1947, 'Minutes of OP-20-2 Research Committee Meeting'.
90. NARA RG457, SRH-267, "History of Engineering Research Associates." NSA RAM File, January 2, 1945, Wenger OP-20-G to CNO, 'Plan for ERA', and August 21, 1945, 'Continuation and Development of Communication Intelligence [ERA]'.
91. NARA RG457, SRMN-084, "The Evolution of the Navy's Cryptologic Organization," 15.
92. NSA RAM File, August 21, 1945, 'Continuation and Development of Communication Intelligence [ERA]'.
93. Bright mathematicians and physicists also joined the new company. Hagley Museum and Library, Accession 2015, Unprocessed ERA Materials, ERA, Personnel Summaries, circa 1946, and Engstrom to Norris, September 11, 1946. The Staff of Engineering Research Associates, *High-Speed Computing Devices* (New York: McGraw-Hill, 1950). All departments of the navy were concerned about how to continue their advanced scientific work. U. S. Naval Administration in World War II, War History of the Naval Research Laboratory, Guide No. 134, and Harvey M. Sapolsky, *Science and the Navy: The History of the Office of Naval Research* (Princeton: Princeton University Press, 1990).
94. *Current Biography* (1947), 615-6.
95. NSA RAM File, February 12, 1945, Wenger OP-20-G to CNO, 'Plan for ERA'.
96. Hagley Museum and Library, Accession 2015, Unprocessed ERA Materials, Engstrom to Norris, September 11, 1946. NSA RAM File, December 20, 1945, 'ERA post war research plan', and December 21, 1945, CNO to BUShips, 'Continue to fund NCML'.
97. Important was Nelson Talbott, the powerful Dayton business executive
98. Charles Babbage Institute, "An Interview With James Henry Wakelin, Jr.," OH 104, Conducted by Arthur Norberg, February 27, 1986. Hagley Museum and Library, Accession 2015, Unprocessed Remington Rand / ERA materials, ERA Minute books 1946. NARA RG457, SRH-267, "History of Engineering Research Associates," 6-7. NSA RAM File: March 8, 1946, John Parker to Secretary of the Navy, 'Plan for ERA'; March 8, 1946, OP-20-G, 'List of research projects and secret ERA contract of 12-21-45'; and March 21, 1946, OP-20-G 'History of Formation of ERA'.
99. Hagley Museum and Library, Accession 2015, Unprocessed Remington Rand / ERA materials, ERA Minute books 1946-7.
100. Hagley Museum and Library, Accession 2015, Unprocessed Remington-Rand / ERA Materials, Letters and Memoranda Concerning Consulting Fees of Admiral Hooper, including, John E. Parker to Admiral S. C. Hooper, July 20, 1949. Library of Congress, Papers of Stanford Caldwell Hooper, Box 23, "Page #2" attached to letter to Rumbles of Remington-Rand, August 25, 1952.

101. NSA RAM File, December 20, 1945, 'ERA post war research plan'. Hagley Museum and Library, Accession 1901, Yuter Papers, June 6, 1946 to July 28,1946, ERA-NCML on 'Orion-Goldberg Project', and August 4-8, November 1-9, 1946, ERA reports 'Orion-Goldberg, binary and analog magnetic recording'. Hagley Museum and Library, Accession 2015, Unprocessed Remington Rand / ERA materials, August 17 1946, 'ERA salaries'. NSA RAM File: August 14, 1947, Bureau of Ships to ERA-NCML 'Task contracts causing problems'; June 3, 1946, NCML to ERA, have your work approved'; and July 22, 1946, CNO to Secretary of the Navy, 'Project Monogram'.
102. Hagley Museum and Library, Accession 1901, Yuter Papers, September, 1946 - November 1, 1946 reports 'Orion-Goldberg, binary and analog magnetic recording'.
103. Hagley Museum and Library, Accession 1901, Yuter Papers, June 6, 1946 to July 28,1946, ERA-NCML on 'Orion-Goldberg Project', and July 28, 1946 and August 4-8, November 1-9, 1946, ERA reports 'Orion-Goldberg, binary and analog magnetic recording'.
104. NSA, OP-20-G, J. T. Pendergrass, "Cryptanalytic Use of High-Speed Digital Computing Machines," 1946. NSA, Samuel S. Snyder "Influence of United States Cryptologic Organizations on the Digital Computer Industry," dates the beginning of Goldberg in 1947 perhaps on the basis of the contract for the machine rather than on the date of start of the explorations for a universal scanning machine.
105. Nancy Stern, *From ENIAC to UNIVAC: An Appraisal of the Eckert-Mauchly Computers* (Bedford, Mass.: Digital Press, 1981).
106. Martin Campbell-Kelly, and Michael R. Williams (ed), *The Moore School Lectures: Theory and Techniques for the Design of Electronic Digital Computers* (Cambridge, Mass.: MIT Press, 1985).
107. Erwin Tomash, "The Start of an ERA: Engineering Research Associates, Inc., 1946-1955," in N. Metropolis, et al, (ed), *A History of Computing in the Twentieth Century* (New York: Academic Press, 1980), 485-496.
108. Hagley Museum and Library, Accession 1901, Yuter Papers, May 20, 1947, ERA Tompkins Report on Atlas, 'shift Goldberg-Demon men to project'.
109. Samuel S. Snyder "Influence of United States Cryptologic Organizations on the Digital Computer Industry," *The Journal of Systems and Software* 1(1979): 90-91. Hagley Museum and Library, Accession 1901, Yuter Papers: Engineering Research Associates, October 9, 1946, Meeting on NBS computer plans, 'Summary of Computing Conferences'; Tompkins to Norris, October 19, 1946, 'Computing Business'; December 1946, 'Reports on OP-20-G Projects and Atlas Computer'; and Goldberg Report June 27, 1947.
110. Samuel S. Snyder "Influence of United States Cryptologic Organizations on the Digital Computer Industry," *Journal of Systems and Software* 1(1979): 89. Hagley Museum and Library, Accession 1825, *Honeywell v Sperry-Rand* Trial Records, November, 1947 and March 22, 1948, ERA, 'List of company projects', and June 1, 1948, ERA 'Emergency projects outrank Goldberg'. Hagley Museum and Library, Accession 1901, Yuter Papers, November 1, 1947, ERA , "List of Projects'.
111. NSA RAM File: May 15, 1949, 'Hecate'; March 28, 1949 'Hecate, Goldberg II'; and October 3, 1949, 'Demon, Atlas'.
112. Michael R. Williams, *A History of Computing Technology* (Englewood Cliffs, N.J.: Prentice-Hall, 1985), Chpt. 8. Smithsonian History of Computers Interviews with Albert Fenaughty, 1973 and with Emmett Quady, May 15, 1973, 'ERA'. NARA RG457, SRH-403, "Selections from the Cryptologic Papers of Rear Admiral J. N. Wenger, USN," February 15, 1951, 'BuShips refuses letter of commendation for Atlas', 38.
113. Samuel S. Snyder, "Abner: The ASA Computer, Part I: Design," *NSA Technical Journal* XXV No. 2 (Spring, 1980): 49. Samuel S. Snyder, "History of NSA General Purpose Electronic Digital Computers," DOD, 1964.
114. Mina Rees, "The Mathematical Sciences and World War II," *American Mathematical Monthly* 87(1980): 607-621. William Aspray and Michael Gunderloy, "Early Computing and Numerical Analysis at the National Bureau of Standards," *Annals of the History of Computing* 11(1989): 3-11. John Todd, "John Hamilton Curtiss, 1909-1977," *Annals of the History of Computing* 2(1980): 104-9. R. Cochrane, *Measures for Progress: A History of the National Bureau of Standards*

(Washington: G. P. O., 1966). Samuel S. Snyder, "Abner: The ASA Computer, Part I: Design," *NSA Technical Journal* 25(1980): 49.

115. Samuel S. Snyder, "Abner: The ASA Computer, Part I: Design," *NSA Technical Journal* 25(1980): 49. Samuel S. Snyder, "History of NSA General Purpose Electronic Digital Computers," DOD, 1964.

116. Samuel S. Snyder "Influence of United States Cryptologic Organizations on the Digital Computer Industry," *The Journal of Systems and Software* 1(1979): 92.

117. Hagley Museum and Library, Accession 1901, Yuter Papers: Goldberg Reports July-August, 1946; January 1, 1947; and September 22, 1947.

118. Hagley Museum and Library, Accession 1901, Yuter Papers, ERA, Goldberg Reports, July 1946, September 1946, and January 1, 1947.

119. Hagley Museum and Library, Accession 2015, Unprocessed Remington Rand / ERA materials, ERA Minute books 1946-50, and Accession 1825, September 26, 1950, 'Announcement of IBM Contract'.

120. NSA RAM File, September 26, 1947, John Parker to ERA Personnel, 'Navy work to get first priority'.

121. NSA RAM File: July 20, 1946, Engstrom-BuShips, 'Use Naval laboratories, not ERA'; August 12, 1946, BuShips-ERA 'DC Office not legal, no plane allowed'; and July 26, 1948, BuShips to ERA, 'All work to be done in St. Paul'.

CHAPTER XIII

1. *Historical Statistics of the United States: Colonial Times to 1957* (Washington: U. S. Dept. of Commerce, 1960), 719. James Pennick, *The Politics of American Science: 1939 to the Present* (Cambridge: MIT Press, 1972). Stuart W. Leslie, *The Cold War and American Science: The Military-Industrial-Academic Complex at MIT and Stanford*, (New York: Columbia University Press, 1993). Roger L. Geiger, "Science, Universities, and National Defense, 1945-1970," *OSIRIS* 2nd Series, 7(1992): 26-48.

2. Two very rewarding articles on the emergence of the postwar Cold War university are: Rebecca S. Lowen, "Transforming the University: Administrators, Physicists, and Industrial and Federal Patronage at Stanford, 1935-1949," *History of Education Quarterly* 31(1991): 365-388, and Stuart W. Leslie, "Playing the Education Game to Win: The Military and Interdisciplinary Research at Stanford," *Historical Studies in the Physical Sciences* 18(1987): 55-88.

3. Library of Congress, Papers of Vannevar Bush, Lybrand Smith Files, October 1942 - March 19, 1943, 'Comments on navy bureaucracy and Kilgore Bill'. Vannevar Bush, *Pieces of the Action* (New York: Murrow, 1970), 65. Very useful on Bush's philosophy and the struggle over the NSF is Daniel Kevles' introductory essay in the new edition of Bush's, *Science--The Endless Frontier* (Washington: NSF, 1990).

4. R. Cochrane, *Measures for Progress: A History of the National Bureau of Standards* (Washington: G. P. O., 1966). Harvey M. Sapolsky, *Science and the Navy: The History of the Office of Naval Research* (Princeton: Princeton University Press, 1990). Mina Rees, "The Mathematical Sciences and World War II," *American Mathematical Monthly* 87(1980): 607-621.

5. Linwood S. Howeth, *History of Communications Electronics in the United States Navy: With an Introduction by Chester W. Nimitz* Bureau of Ships, Office of Naval History (Washington: GPO, 1963).

6. Jack Rubin, *A History of Micrographics: In the First Person* (National Micrographics Association, 1980), 58, 74. Pamela Spence Richards, "Aslib at War: The Brief But Intrepid Career of a Library Organization as a Hub of Allied Scientific Intelligence 1942-1945," *Journal of Education for Library and Information Science*, 29(1989): 279-296. Irene S. Farkas-Conn, *From Documentation to Information Science* (New York: Greenwood Press, 1990). Wayne A Wiegand (ed), *Leaders in American Librarianship, 1925-1975* (Pittsburgh: Beta Phi Mu, 1988).

7. Library of Congress, Papers of Vannevar Bush, Box 95, September 24, 1945, 'Navy microfilming'. Frank Cameron, *Cottrell: Samaritan of Science* (New York: Doubleday & Co., 1952), 362.

8. Pamela Spence Richards, "Information Science in Wartime: Pioneer Documentation Activities in World War II," *Journal of the American Society for Information Science* 39(1988): 305. Library of Congress, Papers of Vannevar

Bush, Box 26, SAL File, Bush-Burchard, June 6, 1949, 'Wright Field project not satisfactory'.

9. Wyndham Davis Miles, *A History of the National Library of Medicine: The Nation's Treasury of Medical Knowledge* (Bethesda, Md.: U. S. Dept. of Health and Human Services, G.P.O., 1982), 289. Irene S. Farkas-Conn, *From Documentation to Information Science* (New York: Greenwood Press, 1990), 108.

10. Library of Congress, Papers of Vannevar Bush, Hazen File, January 21, 1944, Bush to Hazen, 'Get MIT to support patent selector project'.

11. Library of Congress, Papers of Vannevar Bush, June 6, 1946, Howard to Bush, 'Rapid Selector'.

12. Library of Congress, Papers of Vannevar Bush, January 31, 1944, Hazen to Bush, 'MIT rejects selector project', and May 19, 1945, Bush to Burchard, 'Louis Chereau's documentation center'.

13. The changed relationship between MIT and the Research Corporation may have been one of the motives for creating the American Research and Development Corporation which financed the work of bright young MIT men in the Cambridge area.

14. Library of Congress, Papers of Vannevar Bush, Box 52, Howard to Killian, March 21, 1946, 'rapid selector'. Library of Congress, Papers of Vannevar Bush, John Howard File, March 16, 1948, Bush to Howard, and June 6, 1946, Howard to Bush, 'Rapid Selector'.

15. Library of Congress, Papers of Vannevar Bush, Hazen to Bush, May 19, 1945, 'Rapid selector'.

16. Library of Congress, Papers of Vannevar Bush, Box 52, March 21, 1946, June 6, 1946, June 18, 1946, Bush-Howard letters, 'Rapid Selector'.

17. James M. Nyce, and Paul Kahn, "Innovation, Pragmaticism and Technological Continuity: Vannevar Bush's Memex," *Journal of the American Society for Information Science* 40(1989): 214. Vannevar Bush, "As We May Think," *Atlantic Monthly* 176(1945): 641-649.

18. Library of Congress, Papers of Vannevar Bush, Burchard File, June 19, 1947, Bush to Burchard, 'Selector speech to librarians'.

19. At the time, Bush and Burchard were also in contact with Louis Ridenour and were aware of Fremont Rider's work on the overcrowded library. Library of Congress, Papers of Vannevar Bush, Box 17, Bush-Burchard correspondence, 1945-6. Louis N. Ridenour, Ralph R. Shaw, and Albert G. Hill, *Bibliography in the Age of Science* (Urbana: University of Illinois Press, 1952), 3-29.

20. Library of Congress, Papers of Vannevar Bush: Box 52, Howard to Killian, March 21, 1946; May 19, 1945, Bush to Burchard, 'Louis Chereau's documentation center'; and September 24, 1945, 'BuShips microfilm project, Remington Rand'. Frank Cameron, *Cottrell: Samaritan of Science* (New York: Doubleday & Co., 1952)

21. MIT Archives AC4: Box 30, 1944, 'Center of Analysis'; Box 45, September 5, 1946, Killian to Taylor, 'Center not self-supporting'; and Box 204, June 1945-October 1945, 'Center of Analysis, Research Laboratory for Electronics'.

22. MIT Archives, AC4, April 17, 1946, Stratton to President, 'Will not merge with Center of Analysis', and Box 204, June 1945-October 1945, 'Center of Analysis, Research Laboratory for Electronics. Karl L. Wildes, and Nilo A. Lindgren, *A Century of Electrical Engineering and Computer Science at MIT, 1882-1982* (Cambridge: MIT Press, 1985). While Stuart W. Leslie's, *The Cold War and American Science* (New York: Columbia University Press, 1993), 25, emphasizes the role of the military in setting up MIT's substitute for the Rad Lab, other documents suggest the faculty were not passively responding to military demands.

23. Rockefeller Archives, RF RG1.1, records, April 4, 1946, November 8, 1946, Caldwell and Hazen to Weaver re Center of Analysis. MIT Archives, AC4: Box 36, "Center of Analysis, 1945; April 17, 1946, Stratton to President, 'Will not merge with Center of Analysis'; and Box 45, September 5, 1946, Killian to Taylor, 'Center not self-supporting'.

24. Claude E. Shannon, and Warren Weaver, *The Mathematical Theory of Communication* (Urbana. Ill.: University of Illinois Press, 1949). Herman H. Goldstine, *The Computer from Pascal to von Neumann* (Princeton: Princeton University Press, 1972), 215.

25. Rockefeller Archives, RG1.1, Papers of Warren Weaver, January 16, 1946, letter, S. H. Caldwell to Weaver, 'Center of Analysis', and records, April 4, 1946, November 8, 1946, Caldwell and Hazen to Weaver re Center of Analysis; Rockefeller Archives, RF RG1.1, MIT File, May 17, 1946 'Fund MIT project', and, June 6, 1947 Compton to Weaver, "Cancel Project and return funds'.
26. Kent C. Redmond, and Thomas M. Smith, *Project Whirlwind: The History of a Pioneer Computer* (Bedford, Mass.: Digital Press, 1980). Rockefeller Archives, RG1.1, Papers of Warren Weaver, March 4, 1947 letter, Weaver to Hazen, 'Center of Analysis, Cooperate With Forrester'.
27. Rockefeller Archives, RF RG1.1, MIT File, June 6, 1947 Compton to Weaver, "Cancel Project and return funds'. The demise of the second Rockefeller machine can not be explained by citing the possibility that it would have been an analog device. First, such machines were a very rational choice for engineering and other scientific calculation until the 1960s when digital computers became speed competitive. Second, it was not certain that the Rockefeller machine would have become an analog device. James S. Small, "On the Relations Between Science, Technology and Engineering in the Context of the post-Second World War Development of Electronic Analogue Computers," in *Workshop: Technohistory of Electrical Information Technology* (Munchen: Deutches Museum, February, 1991).
28. Library of Congress, Papers of Vannevar Bush, September 24, 1945, 'Buships Microfilm project'.
29. Library of Congress, Papers of Vannevar Bush, June 6, 1946, Howard to Bush, 'Rapid Selector'. In early 1947, IBM began its own information program by assigning H. P. Luhn to work on such problems. "The Light He Left Behind," (James Bryce), *Think* (April, 1949): 5-31. Claire K. Schultz (ed), *H. P. Luhn, Pioneer of Information Science: Selected Works*, (New York: Spartan Books, 1968). Ralph R. Shaw (ed), *The State of the Library Art* (New Brunswick, N.J.: Graduate School of Library Service, 1961). Robert S. Casey and James W. Perry (ed), *Punched Cards: Their Applications to Science and Industry* (New York: Reinhold, 1951), 3.
30. Library of Congress, Papers of Vannevar Bush, Box 90, Patent Project File, September 20, 1946 Bush-Patent Office Correspondence.
31. Library of Congress, Papers of Vannevar Bush, November 5, 1946, Ralph Shaw to Bush, 'Use of Selector in Dept. of Agriculture'.
32. Norman D. Stevens, *Essays for Ralph Shaw* (Metuchen, N.J.: Scarecrow Press, 1975), 5. Jack Rubin, *A History of Micrographics: In the First Person* (National Micrographics Association, 1980), 74. Irene S. Farkas-Conn, *From Documentation to Information Science* (New York: Greenwood Press, 1990). Bohdan S. Wynar (ed), *Dictionary of American Library Biography* (Littleton, Colo.: Libraries Unlimited, 1978), 476-481.
33. NSA RAM File, November 5, 1947, Wenger to Bush, 'Thank you for recent help'. Vannevar Bush, *Pieces of the Action* (New York: Morrow, 1970).
34. Library of Congress, Papers of Vannevar Bush, Box 81, Navy Dept. Files, October 9, 1946 to August 12, 1948, Bush to Conrad etc., 'Bush protests patent application'. Office of Naval Research, Patent File on 'Electronic Comparator, Vannevar Bush', examined 1991.
35. On the 1937 and 1940 patents and their history, Hagley Museum and Library, Accession 2015, Unprocessed ERA materials from Sperry Archives, November 1, 1949, Memo to File, Selector Infringement Search, and Accession 1825, *Honeywell v Sperry-Rand* Trial Records, August 13, 1937, Bush to Deeds, and October 25, 1937, Research Corporation to Deeds.
36. Library of Congress, Papers of Vannevar Bush, Box 81, October 9, 1946 to August 12, 1948, Bush to Conrad, etc., Office of Naval Research, Patent File on 'Electronic Comparator, Vannevar Bush', examined 1991, Bush protests patent application'. The navy's application had a long and tangled history with Bush refusing to contribute more than a signature. A patent was issued in 1959 after many claims were rejected because of previous work by Goldberg and a host of others who had built comparing machines during the 1930s and 1940s. The patent was drawn up by those who remained at OP-20-G's CSAW in Washington which helps account for some interesting anomalies, the most significant of which is that the patent description was of the Gray-NCR model, not the one claimed, the 1938 device built by MacDonald.

37. Library of Congress, Papers of Vannevar Bush, November 5, 1946, Bush to Ralph Shaw, 'Use of Selector in Dept. of Agriculture', and November 12, 1946, Fassett to Shaw, 'Selector in public domain'.
38. Library of Congress, Papers of Vannevar Bush, November 5, 1946, Ralph Shaw to Bush, 'Use of Selector in Dept. of Agriculture', and November 12, 1946, Bush to Shaw.
39. Claire K. Schultz, and Paul L. Garwig, "History of the American Documentation Institute," *American Documentation* 20(1969): 154. Tom Bower, *The Paperclip Conspiracy: The Hunt for the Nazi Scientists* (Boston: Little Brown & Co., 1987). Pamela Spence Richards, "Information Science in Wartime: Pioneer Documentation Activities in World War II," *Journal of the American Society for Information Science* 39(1988): 305. James M. Nyce, and Paul Kahn (ed), *From Memex to Hypertext: Vannevar Bush and the Mind's Machine* (Boston: Academic Press, 1991), 115. Thomas C. Bagg, and Mary Elizabeth Stevens, *Information Selection Systems: Retrieving Replica Copies: A State of the Art Report* (Washington, D.C.: National Bureau of Standards, Technical Note 157, December 31, 1961), 19.
40. Irene S. Farkas-Conn, *From Documentation to Information Science* (New York: Greenwood Press, 1990), 88, 111-3.
41. Hagley Museum and Library, Accession 2015, Unprocessed Remington-Rand / ERA materials, Project B-3005, January, 1947, 'Plan for new Selector', and February 25, 1947, Steinhardt to Engstrom, 'Market for Rapid Selector'.
42. Herman H. Goldstine, *The Computer from Pascal to von Neumann* (Princeton: Princeton University Press, 1972), Chpt. 4., and Nancy Stern, *From ENIAC to UNIVAC: An Appraisal of the Eckert-Mauchly Computers* (Bedford, Mass.: Digital Press, 1981).
43. Library of Congress, Papers of Vannevar Bush, March 3, 1946, Howard to Bush, and November 12, 1946, Bush to Shaw, 'Use of Selector in Dept. of Agriculture'.
44. Library of Congress, Papers of Vannevar Bush, June 6, 1946, Howard to Bush, 'Rapid Selector', and June 18, 1946, Bush to Howard and Bush to Burchard.
45. Library of Congress, Papers of Vannevar Bush, Box 92, March 3, 1947, Shaw presentation, 'Bush unable to come to meeting'. Engstrom gave a more detailed speech at the society in 1949. Hagley Museum and Library, Accession 2015, Unprocessed Remington-Rand / ERA materials, Project B-3005, September 20, 1949, Engstrom Speech on Rapid Selector at Chemical Society Meeting. Library of Congress, Papers of Vannevar Bush, John Howard File, March 16, 1948, Bush to Howard.
46. Hagley Museum and Library, Accession 2015, Unprocessed Remington-Rand / ERA materials, Project B-3005, March 16, 1947, 'Materials to be sent to ERA', and April 16, 1947, Howard to Bush.
47. Ralph R. Shaw (ed), *The State of the Library Art* (New Brunswick, N.J.: Graduate School of Library Service, 1961), 177. Library of Congress, Papers of Vannevar Bush, Box 92, Perry File, 'Shaw speech at Chemical Society', March, 1947.
48. Irene S. Farkas-Conn, *From Documentation to Information Science* (New York: Greenwood Press, 1990), 140. Library of Congress, Papers of Vannevar Bush, March 24, 1947, Burchard to Bush, 'Calvin Mooers'.
49. Louis N. Ridenour, Ralph R. Shaw, and Albert G. Hill, *Bibliography in the Age of Science*, (Urbana: University of Illinois Press, 1952), 4. Library of Congress, Papers of Vannevar Bush, May, 1955, Press release for new documentation program at Western Reserve University, 'Perry biography'.
50. Ralph R. Shaw (ed), *The State of the Library Art* (New Brunswick, N.J.: Graduate School of Library Service, 1961), 143, 166, 230. Library of Congress, Papers of Vannevar Bush, March 1947, May, 1954, James W. Perry correspondence.
51. Claire K. Schultz (ed), *H. P. Luhn, Pioneer of Information Science: Selected Works*, (New York: Spartan Books, 1968), 1. Hans P. Luhn, *Review of Information Retrieval Methods* (Yorktown Heights: IBM, 1958). H. P. Luhn, *The IBM Electronic Information Searching System* (Poughkepsie, N.Y.: IBM, 1952). Ralph R. Shaw (ed), *The State of the Library Art* (New Brunswick, N.J.: Graduate School of Library Service, 1961), 114. "The IBM 101 Electronic Statistical Machine," IBM, nd.

52. James W. Perry (ed), *Symposium on Machine Techniques for Information Selection* (Cambridge: MIT, June 10, 1952). H. P. Luhn, *The IBM Electronic Information Searching System* (Poughkepsie, N.Y.: IBM, 1952). Ralph R. Shaw (ed), *The State of the Library Art* (New Brunswick, N.J.: Graduate School of Library Service, 1961), 177. Library of Congress, Papers of Vannevar Bush, March 13, 1947, James W. Perry correspondence on selectors and indexing.
53. Hagley Museum and Library, Accession 2015, Unprocessed Remington-Rand / ERA materials, Project B-3005 September 20, 1949, Steinhardt to Engstrom, 2-25-47.
54. Ralph R. Shaw (ed), *The State of the Library Art* (New Brunswick, N.J.: Graduate School of Library Service, 1961), 175-7.
55. Russell C. Coile, "Libraries for Engineers and Scientists: Scientific Aids to Documentation," University of Kentucky Libraries, Occasional Contributions No. 61, February, 1954, 5.
56. John C. Green, "The Rapid Selector-An Automatic Library," *The Military Engineer* 41:283 (1949): 350.
57. John C. Green, " The Rapid Selector-An Automatic Library," *The Military Engineer* 41:283 (1949): 350. Shaw's demand for six codes next to the abstract called for very dense packing on the film, but it was thought that the new photographic techniques and the new scanning system would overcome the problem of light spilling from one area to another. Technical difficulties prevented reaching that goal, however. Eventually, four cells had to be used, one for each zone in the scanner's field. To deal with another unexpected difficulty with the camera system anticipatory scanners were added so that the master film could be slowed. Ralph R. Shaw (ed), *The State of the Library Art* (New Brunswick, N.J.: Graduate School of Library Service, 1961), 175. Thomas C. Bagg, and Mary Elizabeth Stevens, *Information Selection Systems: Retrieving Replica Copies: A State of the Art Report* (Washington, D.C.: National Bureau of Standards, Technical Note 157, December 31, 1961), 22.
58. The group at ERA should have known of Emanuel Goldberg's patents because they had been cited by the examiners who rejected the earlier Selector applications. However, Goldberg's exact system was different from the small binary codes used in the Selector. E. Goldberg, U. S. Patent 1,838,389, "Statistical Machine," December 29, 1931, Filed April 5, 1928. Hagley Museum and Library, Accession 2015, Unprocessed ERA materials from Sperry Archives, November 1, 1949, Memo to File, Selector Infringement Search, and Accession 1825, *Honeywell v Sperry-Rand* Trial Records, August 13, 1937, Bush to Deeds, and October 25, 1937, Research Corporation to Deeds. Hagley Museum and Library, Accession 2015, Unprocessed Remington-Rand / ERA materials, Project B-3005, May 7, 1951, 'Goldberg's Selector Patent'. NSA RAM File, "MAC Outlines #17, 70mm Comparator," April, 1947, claims that the first ideas for comparators were German.
59. Documents indicate that the general specifications of 1947 included the hope that the new Selector be able to make generic searches and to use cards as the selection masks. Hagley Museum and Library, Accession 2015, unprocessed ERA materials, 'Progress Report for the Microfilm Rapid Selector', Contract Cac-47-24 to 24 November 1947.
60. Hagley Museum and Library, Accession 2015, Unprocessed Remington-Rand / ERA materials, Project B-3005, January 1, 1949, 'Selector description'.
61. Hagley Museum and Library, August 12 - September 20, 1947, Selector correspondence and memoranda, Accession 2015, Unprocessed Remington-Rand / ERA materials, Project B-3005 File Boxes. Thomas C. Bagg, and Mary Elizabeth Stevens, *Information Selection Systems: Retrieving Replica Copies: A State of the Art Report* (Washington, D.C.: National Bureau of Standards, Technical Note 157, December 31, 1961), 19.
62. Library of Congress, Papers of Vannevar Bush, Box 37, April 9, 1947, Engstrom to Bush, 'Rapid Selector'.
63. Hagley Museum and Library, Accession 2015, Unprocessed Remington-Rand / ERA materials, Project B-3005, March 16, 1947, 'Materials to be sent to ERA'. Bush's prediction did not prove true and ERA gained only one minor patent on the Selector after years of work.
64. The NBS's ambitions to become the center for computer development and to maintain an advanced computing service also suffered. Its computer center had to

finance itself through contracts with other agencies that were seeking computers. John Todd, "John Hamilton Curtiss, 1909-1977," *Annals of the History of Computing*, 2(1980): 104-9. William Aspray, and Michael Gunderloy, "Early Computing and Numerical Analysis at the National Bureau of Standards," *Annals of the History of Computing*, 11(1989): 3-11. "Biography--Harry D. Huskey," *Annals of the History of Computing* 13(1991): 298. M. R. Hestenes, and John Todd, *NBS INA, The Institute for Numerical Analysis, UCLA, 1947-1954* (Washington: Mathematical Association of America, 1989). Herman H. Goldstine, *The Computer from Pascal to von Neumann* (Princeton: Princeton University Press, 1972), 246.

65. Hagley Museum and Library, Accession 1825, *Honeywell v Sperry-Rand* Trial Records, ERA Materials, March 19, 1947, 'Dept. of Agriculture Inquiries', May, 1947, Contract Cnc-47-24.

66. Thomas C. Bagg, and Mary Elizabeth Stevens, *Information Selection Systems: Retrieving Replica Copies: A State of the Art Report* (Washington, D.C.: National Bureau of Standards, Technical Note 157, December 31, 1961), 19.

67. Library of Congress, Papers of Vannevar Bush, John Howard File, July 28, 1947, 'To A. D. Little'.

68. Library of Congress, Papers of Vannevar Bush, Box 37, April 23, 1947. Engstrom to Bush, 'Selector Contract'.

69. Hagley Museum and Library, Accession 2015, Unprocessed Remington-Rand / ERA materials, Project B-3005, August 1947, 'Prudential possibilities'. Accession 1825, *Honeywell v Sperry-Rand* Trial Records, September 11, 1946, 'ERA projects'. Charles Babbage Institute, "An Interview With James Henry Wakelin, Jr.," OH 104, Conducted by Arthur Norberg, February 27, 1986. ERA sought and sometimes gained contracts for airline reservation systems, atomic energy, guided missiles and even airport equipment.

70. NSA RAM File, August 4, 1947, Bureau of Ships to NCML, 'Tighter supervision over ERA'.

71. Hagley Museum and Library, Accession 2015, Unprocessed Remington-Rand / ERA materials, Project B-3005, September 1948, American Patent Law Association materials, 'IRD'. Rexmond C. Cochrane, *Measures for Progress: A History of the National Bureau of Standards* (New York: Arno Press, 1976). Richard J. Walton, *Henry Wallace, Harry Truman, and the Cold War* (New York: Viking, 1976).

72. Hagley Museum and Library, Accession 2015, Unprocessed Remington-Rand / ERA materials, Project B-3005, September 15, 1947, Steinhardt to Edgerton, 'Selector parts'.

73. Hagley Museum and Library, Accession 2015, Unprocessed ERA materials, October 29, 1949, Sorenson to Steinhardt, 'First Test of scanner June 30, 1948', and Remington-Rand General Counsel to ERA, St. Paul, February 16, 1954.

74. Hagley Museum and Library, Accession 2015, Unprocessed Remington-Rand / ERA materials, Project B-3005, November, 1947, June, 1948.

75. Hagley Museum and Library, Accession 2015, Unprocessed Remington-Rand / ERA materials, Project B-3005, January 1948, ERA to Dept. of Commerce; March 4, 1948, 'Patent problems with Selector'.

76. Library of Congress, Papers of Vannevar Bush, March 8, 1948, Green to Bush, 'Arrested Progress of selector--design only'. Hagley Museum and Library, Accession 2015, Unprocessed Remington-Rand / ERA materials, Project B-3005: January - June, 1948, Selector correspondence; March 4, 1948, Cushman-Darby-Cushman' to Norris, 'Selector Patents'; and January 1, 1949, Norris to Dept. of Commerce, 'ERA Selector patents'.

77. Library of Congress, Papers of Vannevar Bush, Box 52, March 8, 1948, Green to Bush, 'Arrested Progress of selector--design only'; Box 52, March 16, 1948, Bush to Howard.

78. Library of Congress, Papers of Vannevar Bush, Box 52, March 8, 1948, Green to Bush, 'Arrested Progress of selector--design only', and Box 52, March 16, 1948, Bush to Howard.

79. Library of Congress, Papers of Vannevar Bush, Box 52, March 9, 1948, Green to Norris of ERA, 'Design only unacceptable'.

80. Library of Congress, Papers of Vannevar Bush, Box 52, March 16, 1948, Bush to Howard.

81. Library of Congress, Papers of Vannevar Bush, Box 52, March 18, 1948, Howard to Green 'Selector project on schedule'.

82. Library of Congress, Papers of Vannevar Bush, Box 52, April 13, 1948, Howard to Green 'Selector project on schedule despite priority navy work'.
83. Hagley Museum and Library, Accession 2015, Unprocessed Remington-Rand / ERA materials, Project B-3005, June 20, 1949, Steinhardt 'New Selector designs'.
84. Hagley Museum and Library, Accession 2015, Unprocessed Remington-Rand / ERA materials, Project B-3005, September 24 1948, ERA to Dept. of Commerce 'Request extension until April 1949'.
85. Library of Congress, Papers of Vannevar Bush, Box 52, Howard to Bush, July 25, 1948, 'Problems at ERA, resigning', and August 3, 1948, Bush to Howard, 'Job with Wenger'. Smithsonian History of Computers Interview with Albert Fenaughty, 1973. Howard continued on in the computer business and remained a major resource for the crypto community. On OP-20-G's struggle to survive in the late 1940s, Wayne G. Barker (ed), George A. Brownell, *The Origin and Development of the National Security Agency* (Agean Park Press: circa 1981), viii, 17, 84.
86. Hagley Museum and Library, Accession 2015, Unprocessed Remington-Rand / ERA materials, Project B-3005, January 31, 1949, Norris to Mally, 'Selector patents to ERA only'. Norris announced the selector would be shipped to Washington in early February.
87. Ralph R. Shaw, "The Rapid Selector," *Journal of Documentation* 5(1949): 164-71.
88. John C. Green, "The Rapid Selector-An Automatic Library," *The Military Engineer* 4:283(1949): 350-52.
89. Hagley Museum and Library, Accession 2015, Unprocessed Remington-Rand / ERA materials, Project B-3005, August 30, 1949, Sorensen to Steinhardt, 'Selector article says it is public domain'.
90. Hagley Museum and Library, Accession 2015, Unprocessed Remington-Rand / ERA materials, Project B-3005, March 31, 1950, Engstrom Notes on Meeting With Bush, 'Selector project'.
91. Hagley Museum and Library, Accession 2015, Unprocessed Remington-Rand / ERA materials, Project B-3005, January 31, 1949, Norris to Mally, 'Selector patents to ERA only'.
92. Hagley Museum and Library, Accession 2015, Unprocessed Remington-Rand / ERA materials, Project B-3005, June, 1949, 'Selector announcements'.
93. James L. Pike, and Thomas C. Bagg, "The Rapid Selector and Other New Document Retrieval Studies," *Proceedings of the National Microfilm Association Eleventh Annual Meeting and Convention*, Vernon D. Tate (ed), (Annapolis, Md.: 1962), 212-222.
94. Ralph R. Shaw, "Mechanical Storage, Handling, Retrieval and Supply of Information," *Libri* 8(1958): 1-46.
95. Both men had close ties to Vannevar Bush and MIT. Ridenour corresponded with Bush about the library problem and at the time of the publication of the book Hill had been put in charge of the new MIT Scientific Aids to Learning project. Louis N. Ridenour, Ralph R. Shaw, and Albert G. Hill, *Bibliography in the Age of Science*, (Urbana, Ill.: U. of Illinois Press, 1952).
96. Jesse H. Shera, and Margeret E. Egan (ed), *Bibliographic Organization* (Chicago: University of Chicago Press, 1951), 200-225.
97. The contract was concluded in 1949 and the selector was quickly built. Hagley Museum and Library, Unprocessed ERA materials, 'Description and Maintenance Manual, Model 2010A1 Microfilm Selector,' H. L. Daniels, F. W Kline, PX29384, October 5, 1950.
98. Hagley Museum and Library, Accession 2015, Unprocessed Remington-Rand / ERA materials, Project B-3005, October 28, 1949, Sorenson to Steinhardt, 'Brustman, Remington-Rand selector patent'. John C. Green, "The Rapid Selector-An Automatic Library," *The Military Engineer* 41:283 (1949): 350-2. Library of Congress, Papers of Vannevar Bush, Box 44, September 22, 1949, John C. Green to Bush, 'Goldberg Visit to Selector'.
99. James L. Pike, and Thomas C. Bagg, "The Rapid Selector and Other NBS Document Retrieval Systems," in Vernon Tate (ed), *Proceedings of the Eleventh Annual Meeting and Convention* (Annapolis: The National Microfilm Association, 1962): 214.
100. Ralph R. Shaw. "High Speed Intermittent Camera," *American Documentation* 1(1950): 194-6. There is some disagreement about how much the AEC

contributed. One source estimated some $50,000. Shaw's later statement of the cost of the modified Selector suggests that the AEC gave perhaps $30,000. Ralph R. Shaw, "Mechanical Storage, Handling, Retrieval and Supply of Information," *Libri* 8(1958): 31.

101. Claire K. Schultz, and Paul L. Garwig, "History of the American Documentation Institute," *American Documentation* 20(1969): 157.

102. James L. Pike, and Thomas C. Bagg, "The Rapid Selector and Other NBS Document Retrieval Systems," in Vernon Tate (ed), *Proceedings of the Eleventh Annual Meeting and Convention* (Annapolis: The National Microfilm Association, 1962), 215. Michael K. Buckland, "Emanuel Goldberg, Electronic Document Retrieval, and Vannevar Bush's Memex," *JASIS* 43(1992): 284.

103. Ralph R. Shaw, "Mechanical Storage, Handling, Retrieval and Supply of Information," *Libri* 8(1958): 4.

104. Ralph R. Shaw (ed), *The State of the Library Art* (New Brunswick, N.J.: Graduate School of Library Service, 1961), 180.

105. Norman D. Stevens, *Essays for Ralph Shaw* (Metuchen, N.J.: Scarecrow Press, 1975), 4. Ralph R. Shaw, "Mechanical Storage, Handling, Retrieval and Supply of Information," *Libri* 8(1958): 4. Library of Congress, Papers of Vannevar Bush, Box 90, Patent Project, September 24, 1954 to November 3, 1954, correspondence re Patent Office project, 'ADI Annual Report, Committee on Documentary Research, November 3, 1954'. Ralph R. Shaw (ed), *The State of the Library Art* (New Brunswick, N.J.: Graduate School of Library Service, 1961), 114, 180.

106. Ralph R. Shaw, "Mechanical Storage, Handling, Retrieval and Supply of Information," *Libri* 8(1958): 31.

107. Ralph R. Shaw, "Mechanical Storage, Handling, Retrieval and Supply of Information," *Libri* 8(1958): 1-46.

108. Ralph R. Shaw (ed), *The State of the Library Art* (New Brunswick, N.J.: Graduate School of Library Service, 1961), 180. Ralph R. Shaw, "Mechanical Storage, Handling, Retrieval and Supply of Information," *Libri* 8(1958): 31. Ralph R. Shaw (ed), *The State of the Library Art* Vol. 12 Part 2 (New Brunswick, N.J.: Rutgers University Press, 1960): 2-21.

CHAPTER XIV

1. Library of Congress, Papers of Vannevar Bush, Box 17, Bush-Burchard Correspondence. *Who's Who In America*, 1958-9, 392.

2. Fremont Rider, *The Scholar and the Future of the Research Library* (New York: Hadham Press, 1945). Library of Congress, Papers of Vannevar Bush, Hazen File, May 19, 1945, Hazen to Burchard, 'Louis Chereau's documentation center'.

3. Library of Congress, Papers of Vannevar Bush, Hazen File, May 19, 1945, Hazen to Burchard, 'Louis Chereau's documentation center', and Burchard File, June 18, 1946, Bush to Burchard, 'Rapid Selector speech'.

4. *Who's Who in America*, 1958-9, 1980. Library of Congress, Papers of Vannevar Bush, Ralph R. Shaw, "Machines and the Bibliographic Problems of the Twentieth Century," 55. Jack Rubin, *A History of Micrographics: In the First Person* (National Micrographics Association, 1980), 58. Pamela Spence Richards, "Information Science in Wartime: Pioneer Documentation Activities in World War II," *Journal of the American Society for Information Science* 39(1988): 302.

5. *Who's Who in America, 1968-9, 2155*. Library of Congress, Papers of Vannevar Bush, Box 17, February 17, February 25, and February 28, 1947 Burchard - Bush, 'Tate Aid to learning proposal and micro reader', and Burchard File, June 18, 1946, 'Rapid Selector article'.

6. Library of Congress, Papers of Vannevar Bush, Burchard File, February 17, February 25 and February 28, 1947 Burchard - Bush, 'Tate Aid to learning proposal and micro reader'. See, V. D. Tate, "The Present State of Equipment and Supplies for Microphotography," *Journal of Documentary Reproduction* 2(1938): 3-62. Vernon Tate, "From Binkley to Bush," *American Archivist* 10(1947): 249-57.

7. Library of Congress, Papers of Vannevar Bush, Burchard File, February 17, February 25, February 28, and April 2, 1947, Burchard - Bush, 'Tate Aid to

learning proposal and micro reader',and March 26, 1948, 'Telephone version of selector'.

8. Library of Congress, Papers of Vannevar Bush, Box 26, SAL File, "A Center for Scientific Aids to Learning at M.I.T.", and "The Library and the Technique of Research," *The M.I.T. Library Annual*, 1948. The grant was made in January, 1948. Library of Congress, Papers of Vannevar Bush, Burchard File, February 28, 1947, Burchard - Bush, 'Tate Aid to learning proposal and micro reader'.

9. Library of Congress, Papers of Vannevar Bush, Box 17, Burchard File, March 26, 1948, 'Telephone version of selector'.

10. Library of Congress, Papers of Vannevar Bush, Box 26, SAL File, May 4, 1949 - May 6, 1949, Bush to Burchard, 'SAL project a failure'.

11. Hill made a grand statement of the purposes of the center in Ridenour's famous, *Bibliography in the Age of Science* (Urbana: University of Illinois Press, 1952), 73, a book reflecting the late 1940's attempt to join Documentalists (Shaw) and applied scientist-engineers (Ridenour) and scientists (Hill).

12. Library of Congress, Papers of Vannevar Bush, Box 26, SAL File, May 4, 1949 - May 6, 1949, Bush to Burchard, 'SAL project a failure', and Bush-Burchard, June 6, 1949 - July 22, 1949, 'Faculty not interested in SAL'.

13. Library of Congress, Papers of Vannevar Bush, Box 26, SAL File, Bush-Burchard, May 6, June 6, and July 22, 1949, 'SAL failing but may be able to save it', and May 25, 1950, Burchard to Bush, 'Forrester to test desk library'. For an insight into Perry's long career and his contribution, Robert S. Casey and James W. Perry (ed), *Punched Cards: Their Applications to Science and Industry* (New York: Rheinhold, 1951), 3-4.

14. Library of Congress, Papers of Vannevar Bush, Box 26, SAL File, Bush-Burchard, June 8, 1949, 'Turn SAL funds over to others?'.

15. Library of Congress, Papers of Vannevar Bush, Box 26, SAL File, May 25, 1950, Burchard to Bush, 'Forrester to test desk library'.

16. Thomas C. Bagg, and Mary Elizabeth Stevens, *Information Selection Systems: Retrieving Replica Copies: A State of the Art Report* (Washington, D.C.: National Bureau of Standards, Technical Note 157, December 31, 1961), 23. Ralph R. Shaw, "Mechanical Storage, Handling, Retrieval and Supply of Information," *Libri* 8(1958): 1-46.

17. Library of Congress, Papers of Vannevar Bush, Box 26, SAL File, Bush-Burchard, June 6, 1949 - July 22, 1949, 'Faculty not interested in SAL'. J. E. Burchard, "The Waterloo of Science," *Rev. Doc.* 16(1949): 94-97. Carl F. J. Overhage, and R. Joyce Harman, *INTREX: Report of A Planning Conference on Information Transfer Experiments, September 3, 1965* (Cambridge: The MIT Press, 1965), 222.

18. Library of Congress, Papers of Vannevar Bush, Box 90, Patent Project File, September, 1946 - September 1954, Bush-Patent Office Correspondence, and Bush, September 20, 1946, January 9, 1947, 'Possible Patent Office project'.

19. Library of Congress, Papers of Vannevar Bush, Box 90, Patent Project, September 24, 1954 to November 3, 1954, correspondence re Patent Office project, September 24, November 1-2, 1954.

20. Library of Congress, Papers of Vannevar Bush, Box 90, Patent project Files, Bush Final Reports on Patent Office Project, July 22, 1954, December 20, 1954.

21. Library of Congress, Papers of Vannevar Bush, Box 90, Patent Project Files, Perry Correspondence, May, 1954,and November 1, 1954, Taube correspondence re Patent Office project. Mortimer Taube had left government service and had founded one of the first new information companies, Documentation Inc. In 1954, he claimed he had designed a machine for multiple (subject) coordinate searching which would also handle Bush's "associations." He asked Bush for a hearing and for support from the Patent Project.

22. Library of Congress, Papers of Vannevar Bush, Box 90, Patent Project Files, July 22, 1954 Bush 'List of possible members of project staff', and September 2, 1954 Green to lend Selector to patent project'.

23. Library of Congress, Papers of Vannevar Bush, Boxes 90 and 98, Patent Office Project, Bush letters to all major companies 'Automated retrieval systems', 1954.

24. Library of Congress, Papers of Vannevar Bush, Box 90, Patents Project File, October 13, 1954, Bush to Worthy, Report on Patent Project, and Patent project

Files, Bush Final Reports on Patent Office Project, November 1, December 1, 1945.

25. Library of Congress, Papers of Vannevar Bush, Box 90, Patent project Files, Bush Final Reports on Patent Office Project, November 1, December 20, 1954, 'Patent-NBS groups'. Bush did not remain pessimistic, however. See his, "Where Do We Go From Here," *Mechanical Engineer* (April, 1955): 302-4.

26. The NBS did explore logic and various machines and built pilot models of various devices such as its Integrated Logic Accumulating Scanner. J. H. Shera, A.Kent, and J. W. Perry, *Information Systems in Documentation* (New York: Interscience Publishers, 1957), 468.

27. For example, see the brief history of the ITEK Corporation of Waltham, Massachusetts, as in, Vernon D. Tate (ed), *Proceedings of the Tenth Annual Meeting and Convention* (Annapolis: The National Microfilm Association, 1961), 12.

28. Charles P. Bourne, "The Historical Development and Present State of the Art of Mechanized Information Retrieval Systems," *American Documentation* 12(1961): 108-110. Charles P. Bourne, *Methods of Information Handling* (New York: Wiley, 1963), 225.

29. For a bibliography on library use, Robert S, Casey and James W. Perry (ed), *Punched Cards* (New York: Reinhold, 1951), 460. Gilbert L. Peakes, "Report Indexing by Punched Cards," *Journal of Chemical Education* 26(1949): 139-146. Cloyd Dake Gull, "A Punched Card Method for the Bibliography, Abstracting and Indexing of Chemical Literature," *Journal of Chemical Education* 23(1946): 500-507. The Perry work at Battle Institute then Western Reserve University was somewhat of an exception in its attempt to build an electronic machine. Ralph R. Shaw (ed), *The State of the Library Art* (New Brunswick, N.J.: Graduate School of Library Service, 1961), 143. Integrated Logic Accumulating Scanner. J. H. Shera, A. Kent, and J. W. Perry, *Information Systems in Documentation* (New York: Interscience Publishers, 1957), 468. Library of Congress, Papers of Vannevar Bush, Box 90, May, 1955, James W. Perry correspondence on selectors and indexing, Press release for new documentation program at Western Reserve University'. James W. Perry, Allen Kent, and Madeline M. Berry, *Machine Literature Searching* (Cleveland: Western Reserve University Press, 1956).

30. Wyndham Davis Miles, *A History of the National Library of Medicine: The Nation's Treasury of Medical Knowledge* (Bethesda, Md.: U. S. Dept. of Health and Human Services, G.P.O., 1982), 368.

31. John K. Boeing, "Recordak," *Journal of Documentary Reproduction* 3(1940): 153-168. Frank L. Hilton, Jr., "Microfilm Systems--The First 40 Kodak Years," *Journal of Micrographics* 1(1968): 117-125.

32. Carl F. J. Overhage, and R. Joyce Harman, *INTREX: Report of A Planning Conference on Information Transfer Experiments, September 3, 1965* (Cambridge: MIT Press, 1965).

33. Magnetic recording remained very limited. The best drums of the time held only 150,000 characters at densities of 50 to 80 bits per inch. Hagley Museum and Library, Accession 1901, Yuter Papers, 'Goldberg Reports', 1947-1950. Hagley Museum and Library, Accession 2015, Unprocessed ERA Materials, Box 9, 'Goldberg Drum Capacity'. Charles S. Bashe, et al, *IBM's Early Computers* (Cambridge, Mass.: MIT Press, 1985), 125. Compare the drum densities with what was expected of microfilm during the late 1940s and early 1950s. Ralph R. Shaw (ed), *The State of the Library Art* (New Brunswick, N.J.: Graduate School of Library Service, 1961), 197. The Staff of Engineering Research Associates, *High-Speed Computing Devices* (New York: McGraw-Hill, 1950). A. W. Tyler "Optical and Photographic Techniques," *Annals of the Computation Laboratory of Harvard University* 16(1948): 146-150. R. D. O'Neal, "Photographic Methods of Handling Input and Output Data," *Annals of the Computation Laboratory of Harvard University* 16(1948): 260-266.

34. Hagley Museum and Library, Accession 1901, Yuter Papers, November 18, 1946, Goldstine of IAS to Crawford of ONR, 'Memory options'. A. W. Tyler "Optical and Photographic Techniques," *Annals of the Computation Laboratory of Harvard University* 16(1948): 146-150. R. D. O'Neal, "Photographic Methods of Handling Input and Output Data," *Annals of the Computation Laboratory of Harvard University* 16(1948): 260-266. Thomas C. Bagg, and Mary Elizabeth

Stevens, *Information Selection Systems: Retrieving Replica Copies: A State of the Art Report* (Washington, D.C.: National Bureau of Standards, Technical Note 157, December 31, 1961), 27. The Staff of Engineering Research Associates, *High-Speed Computing Devices* (New York: McGraw-Hill, 1950), espec. 439. Ralph R. Shaw (ed), *The State of the Library Art* (New Brunswick, N.J.: Graduate School of Library Service, 1961), 197.

35. Thomas C. Bagg, and Mary Elizabeth Stevens, *Information Selection Systems: Retrieving Replica Copies: A State of the Art Report* (Washington, D.C.: National Bureau of Standards, Technical Note 157, December 31, 1961), 27.

36. Morse filed his patent on his microfilm recovery machine on June 23, 1938, and received it on September 8, 1942, #2,295,000. A. W. Tyler "Optical and Photographic Techniques," *Annals of the Computation Laboratory of Harvard University* 16(1948): 146-150. The Staff of Engineering Research Associates, *High-Speed Computing Devices* (New York: McGraw-Hill, 1950), 321. Hagley Museum and Library, Accession 1901, Yuter Papers, November 18, 1946, Goldstine of IAS to Crawford of ONR, 'Memory options'.

37. Library of Congress, Papers of Vannevar Bush, Box 90, Patent project Files, Bush Final Reports on Patent Office Project, December 1, 1954. Ralph R. Shaw (ed), *The State of the Library Art* (New Brunswick, N.J.: Graduate School of Library Service, 1961), 188. Ralph R. Shaw, "Mechanical Storage, Handling, Retrieval and Supply of Information," *Libri* 8(1958): 32.

38. There was more than one and one-half million dollars in government subsidies and each installation cost at least that much. Thomas C. Bagg, and Mary Elizabeth Stevens, *Information Selection Systems: Retrieving Replica Copies: A State of the Art Report* (Washington, D.C.: National Bureau of Standards, Technical Note 157, December 31, 1961), 27. Charles P. Bourne, *Methods of Information Handling* (New York: Wiley, 1963), 223. Ralph R. Shaw (ed), *The State of the Library Art* (New Brunswick, N.J.: Graduate School of Library Service, 1961),188. Ralph R. Shaw, "Mechanical Storage, Handling, Retrieval and Supply of Information," *Libri* 8(1958): 32. Lauren B. Doyle, *Information Retrieval and Processing* (Los Angeles: Melville Publishing Co., 1975), 371. 94th U. S. Congress 2d Session, Senate, Report N0. 94-755, "Foreign and Military Intelligence, Book 1," (Washington: GPO, 1976): 263.

39. The best evidence suggests at least an eight year development period for the Minicard equipment, with some four years of intense government funding. The first Minicard was operational in 1958.

40. Irving L. Wieselman, and Erwin Tomash, "Marks on Paper," *Annals of the History of Computing* 13(1991), 63, 203.

41. Ralph R. Shaw (ed), *The State of the Library Art* (New Brunswick, N.J.: Graduate School of Library Service, 1961), 189.

42. Jack Rubin, *A History of Micrographics: In the First Person* (National Micrographics Association, 1980), 74. Lauren B. Doyle, *Information Retrieval and Processing* (Los Angeles: Melville Publishing Co., 1975), 271. F. Wilfred Lancaster, *Information Retrieval Systems: Characteristics, Testing and Evaluation* (New York: John Wiley, 1979). Pamela Spence Richards, "Gathering Enemy Scientific Information in Wartime: The OSS and the Periodical Republication Program," *Journal of Library History* 16(1981):253-264.

43. Thomas C. Bagg, and Elizabeth Stevens, *Information Selection Systems: Retrieving Replica Copies: A State of the Art Report* (Washington, D.C.: National Bureau of Standards, Technical Note 157, December 31, 1961). Charles P. Bourne, "The Historical Development and Present State of the Art of Mechanized Information Retrieval Systems," *American Documentation* 12(1961): 108-110. Ralph R. Shaw, "Mechanical Storage, Handling, Retrieval and Supply of Information," *Libri* 8(1958): 32.

44. *Encyclopedia of Library & Information Science* "Council on Library Resources, Inc.", 221.

45. Charles P. Bourne, *Methods of Information Handling* (New York: Wiley, 1963), 225.

46. Claire K. Schultz (ed), *H. P. Luhn, Pioneer of Information Science: Selected Works* (New York: Spartan Books, 1968). "IBM Demonstrates Walnut," *Computing News* 9, 201-9. Emerson W. Pugh, Lyle R. Johnson, and John H. Palmer, *IBM's 360 and Early 370 Systems* (Cambridge: MIT Press, 1991), 282, 533-538.

47. Emerson W. Pugh, Lyle R. Johnson, and John H. Palmer, *IBM's 360 and Early 370 Systems* (Cambridge: MIT Press, 1991), 282.
48. Frank L. Hilton, Jr., "Microfilm Systems--The First 40 Kodak Years," *Journal of Micrographics* 1(1968): 117-125. Charles P. Bourne, *Methods of Information Handling* (New York: Wiley, 1963). *Bibliography of Research Relating to the Communication of Science and Technical Information* (New Brunswick: Rutgers University Press, 1967). Lauren B. Doyle, *Information Retrieval and Processing* (Los Angeles: Melville Publishing Co., 1975).
49. Hagley Museum and Library, Accession 2015, Unprocessed Remington-Rand / ERA materials, Project B-3005, March 31, 1950, Engstrom Notes on Meeting With Bush, 'Selector project'. G. J. A. O'Toole, *The Encyclopedia of American Intelligence and Espionage: From the Revolutionary War to the Present* (New York: Facts on File, 1988), 97.
50. Robin Winks, *Cloak and Gown: Scholars in the Secret War, 1939-1961* (New York: Morrow, 1987). Thomas C. Bagg, and Mary Elizabeth Stevens, *Information Selection Systems: Retrieving Replica Copies: A State of the Art Report* (Washington, D.C.: National Bureau of Standards, Technical Note 157, December 31, 1961), 25.
51. James L. Pike, and Thomas C. Bagg, "The Rapid Selector and Other NBS Document Retrieval Systems," in Vernon Tate (ed), *Proceedings of the Eleventh Annual Meeting and Convention* (Annapolis: The National Microfilm Association, 1962), 215.
52. *Who's Who in America, 1960-61*, 2495. Richard Ruggles (Yale-Selector project) to Jacob Rabinow, Bureau of Standards, May - August 26, 1953, as supplied by James Nyce.
53. Don D. Andrews, "Application of High-Speed Computers to Information Retrieval," in Dr. Martha Boaz (ed), *Modern Trends in Documentation* (New York: Pergamon Press, 1959), 59.
54. James L. Pike, and Thomas C. Bagg, "The Rapid Selector and Other NBS Document Retrieval Systems," in Vernon Tate (ed), *Proceedings of the Eleventh Annual Meeting and Convention* (Annapolis: The National Microfilm Association, 1962), 215. Thomas C. Bagg, and Mary Elizabeth Stevens, *Information Selection Systems: Retrieving Replica Copies: A State of the Art Report* (Washington, D.C.: National Bureau of Standards, Technical Note 157, December 31, 1961), 40.
55. Vernon D. Tate, "Photography in Research--Postwar," *Rev. Doc.* 14(1947): 8-14. Frank Cameron, *Cottrell: Samaritan of Science* (New York: Doubleday & Co., 1952), 362. Library of Congress, Papers of Vannevar Bush, Box 52, March 16, 1948, Bush to Howard, and Box 95, 'Bennett and Navy blueprint microfilming'.
56. Howard R. Ball, "Bureau of Ships Rapid Selector," *Bureau of Ships Journal* 10(1961): 6-7.
57. James L. Pike, and Thomas C. Bagg, "The Rapid Selector and Other NBS Document Retrieval Systems," in Vernon Tate (ed), *Proceedings of the Eleventh Annual Meeting and Convention* (Annapolis: The National Microfilm Association, 1962). Thomas C. Bagg and Mary Elizabeth Stevens, *Information Selection Systems: Retrieving Replica Copies: A State of the Art Report* (Washington, D.C.: National Bureau of Standards, Technical Note 157, December 31, 1961), 48. Jack Rubin, *A History of Micrographics: In the First Person* (Silver Spring: National Micrographics Association, 1980).
58. Thomas C. Bagg and Mary Elizabeth Stevens, *Information Selection Systems: Retrieving Replica Copies: A State of the Art Report* (Washington, D.C.: National Bureau of Standards, Technical Note 157, December 31, 1961), 40. Howard Ball, "Information Retrieval System, Bureau of Ships," *Navy Management Review* 4(1959): 7-8.
59. Howard R. Ball, "Bureau of Ships Rapid Selector," *Bureau of Ships Journal* 10(1961): 6-7.
60. Charles P. Bourne, *Methods of Information Handling* (New York: Wiley, 1963).
61. Charles P. Bourne, *Methods of Information Handling* (New York: Wiley, 1963). Thomas C. Bagg, and Mary Elizabeth Stevens, *Information Selection Systems: Retrieving Replica Copies: A State of the Art Report* (Washington, D.C.: National Bureau of Standards, Technical Note 157, December 31, 1961).
62. James L. Pike, and Thomas C. Bagg, "The Rapid Selector and Other NBS Document Retrieval Systems," in Vernon Tate (ed), *Proceedings of the Eleventh Annual Meeting and Convention* (Annapolis: The National Microfilm Association,

1962). J. P McMurray, "The Bureau of Ships Rapid Selector System," *American Documentation* 13(1962): 66-8.
63. Rockefeller Archives RG1.1 224D 2 23 April 14, 1937, Bush to Weaver, "A Reference Selector."
64. The NBS model ran at approximately 350 feet a minute and used an 8 to 1 reduction, not 20 to 1. It held only one page of text in two inches of microfilm and thus had a data area twenty times the physical size (length) of the 1940 machine's film.
65. The most thorough survey of microfilm machines, by Bagg and Stevens, was partially sponsored by the CLR. Thomas C. Bagg, and Mary Elizabeth Stevens, *Information Selection Systems: Retrieving Replica Copies: A State of the Art Report* (Washington, D.C.: National Bureau of Standards, Technical Note 157, December 31, 1961).
66. Emerson W. Pugh, Lyle R. Johnson, and John H. Palmer, *IBM's 360 and Early 370 Systems* (Cambridge: MIT Press, 1991), 533-538. "IBM Demonstrates Walnut," *Computing News* 9(1961): 201-9.
67. James M. Nyce, and Paul Kahn (ed), *From Memex to Hypertext: Vannevar Bush and the Mind's Machine* (Boston: Academic Press, 1991), 113-145. Vannevar Bush, *Pieces of the Action* (New York: Murrow, 1970).
68. Office of Naval Research, Patent File on 'Electronic Comparator, Vannevar Bush', April 24, 1958, Bush to Kelly, 'Was my work of value to the navy?', and January 7, 1959, Kelly to Bush 'Used comparator for more than ten years'.
69. James M. Nyce, and Paul Kahn (ed), *From Memex to Hypertext: Vannevar Bush and the Mind's Machine* (Boston: Academic Press, 1991), 136. Carl F. J. Overhage, and J. Francis Reintjes, "Project Intrex: A General Review," *Information Storage and Retrieval* 10(1974): 157-188. Carl F. J. Overhage, and R. Joyce Harman, *INTREX: Report of A Planning Conference on Information Transfer Experiments, September 3, 1965* (Cambridge: MIT Press, 1965).
70. James M. Nyce, and Paul Kahn (ed), *From Memex to Hypertext: Vannevar Bush and the Mind's Machine* (Boston: Academic Press, 1991), 125.
71. James M. Nyce, and Paul Kahn (ed), *From Memex to Hypertext: Vannevar Bush and the Mind's Machine* (Boston: Academic Press, 1991), 166, 201.
72. Navy Biographies Section OI-140, "Rear Admiral Stanford C. Hooper, U. S. Navy, Deceased."
73. Library of Congress, Papers of Stanford C. Hooper, Box 21, Redmond to Hooper, March 1, 1944,and Hooper to Will Davis, May 14, 1945.
74. Library of Congress, Papers of Stanford Caldwell Hooper, Box 21, Hooper to Davis, May 14, 1945.
75. Library of Congress, Papers of Stanford Caldwell Hooper, Hooper to Davis May 14, 1945, and Box 21, E. F. MacDonald to Hooper, June 23, 1945.
76. Library of Congress, Papers of Stanford Caldwell Hooper, Box 22, Memo on Cable-Radio Merger Proposal, January 29, 1950, and Box 21, Memorandum for Honorable Will Davis, nd.
77. Library of Congress, Papers of Stanford Caldwell Hooper, Box 23, September 21, 1947, Hooper to "Dear David."
78. Library of Congress, Papers of Stanford Caldwell Hooper: Box 21 Ploser to Hooper, August 12, 1945; 'Memorandum To -' August 17, 1945; Box 22, Hooper to Steelman, September 19,1949; and Hooper to Mills, January 27, 1950.
79. Library of Congress, Papers of Stanford Caldwell Hooper: Box, 21, Memorandum for Honorable Will Davis, May 14, 1945; September 19, 1949, Memo. for Mr. Steelman; Box 22, January 27, 1950, 'Dear Mills'; and August 23, 1946, 'Joint Army Navy Research Board'.
80. Some insight into the problems of unification are found in, G. J. A. O'Toole, *Encyclopedia of American Intelligence and Espionage* (New York: Facts on File, 1988), 144, 315.
81. Hagley Museum and Library, Accession 2015, Unprocessed Remington-Rand materials, report of Peat, Marwick, Mitchell & Co., December 30, 1952.
82. NSA RAM File, July 26, 1948, BuShips to ERA, 'ERA work in St. Paul only'.
83. ERA supplied and consulted for the other computer companies of the time. OP-20-G and NSA gave a great deal of work to other companies such as IBM. The private firms may have protested ERA's special relationship, however, including the government's perhaps unintended sponsorship of patents. Hagley Museum and

Library, Accession 1825, *Honeywell v Sperry-Rand* Trial Records, ERA Minute Books, July 26, 1948, 'Engstrom report on IBM computer contract'.

84. *Washington Post*, August 16, 1950.

85. Library of Congress, Papers of Stanford Caldwell Hooper, Box 23, "Page #2" attached to letter to Rumbles of Remington-Rand, August 25, 1952.

86. That Atlas project, to build an OP-20-G electronic computer, was a near replay of the mid-1930s Bush episode. The Bureau of Ships tried to block its construction and Wenger and friends had to turn to the ONR and piece together their own funds to construct the machine. NARA RG457, SRH-403, "Selections from the Cryptologic Papers of Rear Admiral J. N. Wenger, USN," 38, 'Wenger to 03', February 15, 1951. Smithsonian Interview with Howard Campaigne. Hagley Museum and Library, Accession 1825, *Honeywell v Sperry-Rand* Trial Records, ERA, 'Summary of Computer Conferences Held October, 1946'.

87. The navy's sweep of ERA included another retired admiral who was tied to the company, Admiral McDonnell. Hagley Museum and Library, Accession 2015, Unprocessed Remington-Rand materials, H. S. Forrest to S. C. Hooper, July 27, 1953, 'Disallowance of Costs'.

88. Hagley Museum and Library, Accession 2015, Unprocessed Remington-Rand Materials, John E. Parker to Admiral S. C. Hooper, July 20, 1949.

89. An examination of the minute books of ERA indicates that Hooper was not a direct shareholder in the firm, but there is one hint (see below) that he may have helped establish the firm, perhaps with a financial investment. On the stockholders, Hagley Museum and Library, Accession 1901, Yuter Papers, Engineering Research Associates Minute Books, 1947-51.

90. Library of Congress, Papers of Stanford Caldwell Hooper, Box 23, Memorandum for John E. Parker, January 4, 1952, and Letter to A. R. Rumble, August 25, 1952.

91. Hagley Museum and Library, Accession 2015, Unprocessed Remington-Rand materials, Hooper to William Norris, May 12, 1953.

92. Hagley Museum and Library, Accession 2015, Unprocessed ERA materials, Remington-Rand General Counsel to ERA, St. Paul, February 16, 1954.

93. Hagley Museum and Library, Accession 2015, Unprocessed Remington-Rand materials, May 12, 1953, Hooper to Norris.

Index

About the Author

Colin Burke graduated from San Francisco State College. After spending almost twenty years as a professional musician he obtained his Ph.D. in history from Washington University, St. Louis. For the last two decades he has been a college professor at an East Coast university. He has published in the fields of American social and demographic history, the history of higher education, quantitative methods in history, the history of computers, and the history of information and cryptanalysis. He has received grants and awards from the Social Science Research Council, the Spencer Foundation, the National Endowment for the Humanities, and the National Science Foundation. In addition to teaching American history he worked as a systems analyst, taught systems classes, and taught courses in the history of computers and computing. He was lucky enough to be the senior Fulbright scholar in Poland during the year when Communism fell. He has served as a consultant to government departments and has been appointed as one of the very first Scholars in Residence at a significant government agency.